A Portrait in his Actions

THOMAS MOORE OF LIVERPOOL (1762–1840)

Part 1: Lesbury to Liverpool

PETER G. BOLT

Studies in Australian Colonial History No. 3

A Portrait in his Actions

THOMAS MOORE OF LIVERPOOL (1762–1840)

Part 1: Lesbury to Liverpool

PETER G. BOLT

Studies in Australian Colonial History No. 3

A Portrait in his Actions.
Thomas Moore of Liverpool (1762–1840)
Part 1: Lesbury to Liverpool

Studies in Australian Colonial History No. 3
© Peter G. Bolt 2010

Bolt Publishing Services Pty. Ltd.
ACN 123024920

www.boltpublishing.com.au

Cover photograph by Alice Bolt. Detail from
  Portrait of the Late Thomas Moore, Esq.
  Artist: William Griffith(s), 1840. Permission: Moore College.

ISBN   978-0-9803579-6-7 (Paperback)
        978-0-9803579-7-4 (e-version)

National Library of Australia Cataloguing-in-Publication entry

Author:	Bolt, Peter, 1958-
Title:	A portrait in his actions: Thomas Moore of Liverpool (1762-1840). Part 1: Lesbury to Liverpool / Peter G. Bolt.
Edition:	1st ed.
ISBN:	9780980357967 (pbk.)
Series:	Studies in Australian colonial history; 3
Notes:	Includes bibliographical references.
Subjects:	Moore, Thomas, 1762-1840.
	Moore, Thomas, 1762-1840—Childhood and youth.
	Moore, Thomas, 1762-1840—Travel.
	Pioneers—New South Wales—Biography.
Dewey Number:	994.02

Cover design and layout by Lankshear Design Pty Ltd
www.lanksheardesign.com | phone (02) 9868 7044

Printed by Ingram Spark

The first portraiture of Men is their own actions.

(Thomas Moore, 17th Memorandum. April 1822)[1]

Studies in Australian Colonial History

1. *Thomas Moore of Liverpool (1762–1840): One of Our Oldest Colonists. Essays & Addresses to Celebrate 150 Years of Moore College* (2007).

2. *William Cowper (1778–1858). The Indispensable Parson. The Life and Influence of Australia's First Parish Clergyman* (2009).
   —with a companion volume: a pictorial edition produced for *Cowper200*, the bicentennial celebrations of Cowper's arrival.

3. *A Portrait in his Actions. Thomas Moore of Liverpool (1762–1840).*
   Part 1: Lesbury to Liverpool (2010)
   Part 2: Liverpool to Legacy (forthcoming)

Table of Contents

	Preface	1
	Acknowledgements	3
	Abbreviations	5
	Introduction	7
1.	Lesbury: the Boy Becomes a Man (1762–1792)	13
2.	Adventuring (October 1792 to September 1796)	59
3.	Building the Dockyard (2 October 1796 to 7 May 1803)	123
4.	Timber & Trade (7 May 1803 to 13 August 1806)	195
5.	Sydney in Turmoil: Moore Amongst the Rebels (13 August 1806 to 31 July 1808)	257
6.	Speculator and Settler (31 July 1808 to 7 November 1810)	321
	Endnotes	381
	Bibliography	445
	Indexes	457
	Index of Names	460
	List of Plates	475
	List of Figures	477

Preface

2010 marks the Bicentenary of Macquarie's founding of Liverpool. On 7 November, Macquarie arrived at Moore Bank early in the morning. After a good breakfast, Thomas Moore joined the party to cross the river and watch the Governor select a suitable site. Moore heard the Governor (who would become his friend) pronounce the name of the new town (which he would then build). It is entirely appropriate therefore, that this volume is launched as part of Liverpool's Bicentennial celebrations, for it tells how Thomas Moore of Lesbury became Thomas Moore of Liverpool.

Acknowledgements

In researching the life of Thomas Moore, it has been a great delight to have so many deposits of historical material available under the care of thoroughly helpful people. At the top of my list is Dr Louise Trott, of the Sydney Diocesan Archives, whose respect for historical sources and commitment to historical inquiry is inspirational. I am grateful for her availability and helpfulness to me, a researcher at the historical end of things, despite her being the solitary archivist for a large working organization at the contemporary end. Thomas Moore's personal papers couldn't be in better hands.

I also acknowledge the valuable assistance afforded me by the librarians and archivists at The Mitchell Library—what a wonderful library!—and the State Library of NSW; the National Library of Australia; The National Archives (UK); the Museum of the Royal Engineers, Gillingham, Kent; The Guildhall, London; London Metropolitan Archives; Southwark Local History Library; and the Northumberland Records Office. In particular, thank you to Diane Clements, of the London Museum of Freemasonry; Chris Craven, Director, Museum of Freemasonry, Sydney Masonic Centre; and Dr Anthony Morton, Archivist, Royal Military Academy, Sandhurst, Camberley, Surrey. Richard Neville, of the Mitchell library, gave me assistance in gathering, and sometimes identifying, pictorial sources.

Amongst the many individuals who assisted in answering my queries or conducting research, I am grateful for Ann Coats for her search for Thomas Moore amongst the Naval Dockyards, and for Gilbert Provost, Jenny Fawcett, Andrea Corani, Nicholas Blake, Joan Druett, and Helen Oram for answering various maritime historical inquiries.

It was also a wonderful experience to accidentally come across Mr David Moor, a distant relative of Thomas, who generously shared with me the years of research that lie behind his family tree. I have fond memories of a day spent with David and his family when St Albans was deeply covered in snow in February 2009.

In Thomas's home territory, another chance encounter put me in touch with Mrs Lorna Gilroy, who offered and gave her assistance in tracking down records for Thomas's family history with an infectious enthusiasm. I count it a great privilege to have been in Lorna and George's hands in the same cold February, on a tour of discovery in the district where Thomas grew up. It was also a special honour to speak of Lesbury's lost son in the Lesbury village hall to about forty of the present day residents.

Thomas Moore saw the hand of God behind his life and behind the prosperity which enabled his generous benefaction to Moore College. Likewise I am thankful to God for the College that bears Moore's name and for being a part of the community of learning that finds its centre there. My colleagues on the faculty, the student body, the administrative and other staff, each make their unique contribution, providing a daily context of life-enhancing Christian fellowship and a positive and encouraging environment for research and learning. Alongside the concrete legacy of the City of Liverpool itself, including St Luke's, the positive and wholesome influence of the College graduates at the grass-roots level of Australian society (and that of elsewhere) across over 150 years, though less tangible, is a second major part of the legacy of Thomas Moore.

In particular, our librarians led by Julie Olston, do a wonderful job at managing a magnificent collection. The long-term interest of Kim Robinson in collecting Australiana benefits not only the Moore College community, but also other researchers, and, through their intellectual work, the wider Australian community.

I also owe a special debt of gratitude to the Librarians at Liverpool Public Library, especially Joanne Morris, and more generally Liverpool City Council, for their interest in the builder of their town, Thomas Moore and for the enthusiasm to host the launch of this book during the Bicentenary of its foundation.

It seems fitting at this time of celebration to once again bring Thomas Moore to Liverpool.

Peter Bolt
22 November 2010

Abbreviations

"	(with numerals) inch	LMS	London Missionary Society
"	(in a list) ditto, see above	LTO	Lands Title Office
£	pound	Mitchell	Mitchell Library, Macquarie St, Sydney
s	shilling	Moore	Moore College, 1 King St, Newtown.
d	pence	ML	Mitchell Library, Macquarie St, Sydney
ADB	*Australian Dictionary of Biography*		
BDM	Births, Deaths & Marriages	NA-UK	National Archives (UK), Kew
Col.Sec.	Colonial Secretary's Papers. Mitchell Library.	NBL RO	Northumberland Record Office
Cwt	hundredweight	NLA	National Library of Australia
Do	Ditto, see above	NSWSA	New South Wales State Archives
EIC	East India Company (British)	PRO	Public Records Office (UK). Now the National Archives, Kew.
HMS	His Majesty's Ship(s)		
HMAV	His Majesty's Armed Vessel	SDA	Sydney Diocesan Archives
HRA	*Historical Records of Australia* (F. Watson, ed.)	SG	*Sydney Gazette*
		SLNSW	State Library of New South Wales, Macquarie St, Sydney.
HRNSW	*Historical Records of New South Wales* (F.M. Bladen, ed.).	SRO	State Records Office (NSW)
HRNZ	*Historical Records of New Zealand* (R. McNab, ed.)	VOC	Vereenigde Ost-Indische Compagnie (Chartered East India Company, Dutch)
IJMH	*International Journal of Maritime History*	Vizt	namely; that is, precisely
IGI	International Genealogical Index		
JRAHS	*Journal of the Royal Australian Historical Society*		

Original spelling, grammar, mistakes and omissions are preserved in the citation of original sources.

Weights and Measures
Volume

Unit	Gallons	Litres
Gallon	1	4.55
Tierce	35	159
Hogshead	52.5	238
Firkin, puncheon, tertian	70	318
Pipe, butt	105	477
Bushel (Grain)	8	36

Weight

Unit	Equivalent	Metric
Ounces (oz)		
Pounds (lb)	16 oz	.453 kg
Stone (st)	14 lb	6.35 kg
Hundredweight (cwt)	8 stone	50.8 kg
Ton (t)	20 cwt	1,016 kg
Ton (capacity of ship)	100 cubic feet	

Length

Inch (in, ″)		2.54 cm
Foot (ft, ′)	12 inches	30cm
Yard (yd)	3 feet	90cm
Rod, pole, perch	16.5 feet	
Mile	1760 yards	1.6 km
1 League	3 mile	4.828 km
1 fathom	2 yards	1.85 m
1 nautical mile	6080 ft	1.853 km

Area

1 rood, rod (square measure)	1210 sq yds	.1012 ha
1 acre	4840 sq yds	.4047 ha

Introduction

We know what Thomas Moore looked like. Although in providing portraiture, some have occasionally mistaken him for his English poetical namesake, and still more have depicted him with a photographic fake, a very large portrait of him has indeed survived. Painted in 1840 just months before he died, William Griffith's 'Portrait of the Late Mr Thomas Moore, Esq.' enables later generations to know the man visually.[1] (Plates 1 and 2).

Present-day Sydney still bears silent witness to the first resident magistrate of Liverpool. A pioneer of the areas now known as the City of Sydney, Marrickville, Liverpool, and the Southern Highlands, his name is peppered amongst the street signs and place names, and even a whole suburb, Moorebank, takes its name from the property he built on the Georges River.[2] Moore College, training Christian ministers from 1856, although now in Newtown, opened in his old house in Liverpool under the provisions of his Will, bearing his name. The Anglican Church of Australia has benefitted from his substantial fortune in a number of ways, as have other denominations and a variety of societies established for the good of the colony, some of which have survived down to this day.

Despite this prominence, however, relatively little was known about the person behind the name until very recently. The first biographer to put pen to paper was F. B. Boyce, an Anglican Clergyman, who had trained at Moore College when it was still at Liverpool.[3] But even by 1914 when Boyce published his essay, much about Moore had already passed into obscurity.[4]

In his 1955 *Centenary History of Moore College*, Marcus Loane touched briefly on the College's founder. He followed this up in 1967 with an entry in the *Australian Dictionary of Biography*, from which several derivative dictionary articles have subsequently appeared.[5]

Although the first edition of the *Australian Encyclopaedia* (1926–1927) did not contain an entry on Moore, the second edition (1958) made up for the deficit with a brief entry, which drew heavily on Boyce. The third edition (1977) considerably abbreviated the entry, although adding Robinson's article (see below) to the bibliography, and the fourth and subsequent editions (1983[4], 1988[5], 1996[6]) removed the entry entirely—rather surprisingly given Moore's importance to the City of Sydney and the township of Liverpool, if nothing else![6]

The first more substantial examination of Mr Moore came in 1970, when Donald Robinson published 'Thomas Moore and the Early Life of Sydney', a careful study of Moore's 'dockyard years' (1796–1809). Five years later in an address to the Liverpool Historical Society ('Thomas Moore of Moore Bank 1762–1840: The Father of Liverpool, Benefactor of Mankind'), Robinson added further information to Moore's biography.[7] That same year, Eric Russell published *Thomas Moore & The King's Dock Yard 1796–1816*. Since it was produced in connection with the Gosford tourist attraction, *Old Sydney Town*, Russell's little booklet symbolically moves Moore from being someone of interest to ecclesiastical types (Boyce, Loane, Robinson), into the public domain of New South Wales history more generally, where he also properly belongs. Drawing upon and extending Robinson's 1970 article, Russell set Moore even more firmly in the context of the history of the King's Dockyard.[8]

When taken together, Robinson and Russell went a long way towards bringing Moore out of his obscurity. These two works substantially illuminated Moore's life from his arrival in the colony in 1792, through to his retirement as Master Boat Builder at the King's Dock Yard in 1809. The details of Moore's life both before and after that period, however, still remained clothed in mystery. As well as noting that 'no information of his earlier life has so far come to light',[9] Robinson also laid down a challenge for further examination of the latter years of Moore's life, and, indeed, beyond:[10]

> There is room for a further study of Moore's years at Liverpool, 1810–1840, his place in the life of the colony during those years, and of the history of his benefactions to the present day.

The issue with the latter years was simply that the relevant sources (of which there are many) had never been carefully examined in order to document what can be known of Moore's life.[11] The issue with Moore's earlier years was the obscurity of his origins and the apparent lack of source material by which it could be illuminated.

Although it was clear that Thomas Moore first arrived in Australia in 1792, already 30 years old, as for his early life he had long been like Melchizedek, 'without father or mother or genealogy' (Hebrews 7:3). Even when Boyce wrote in 1914, just two generations after Moore's death, he complained that very little was known about the man.[12] Subsequent writers were united in observing the deficiency of knowledge about the first thirty years of his life.[13] Even his country of origin was unclear, with one dictionary article claiming his roots in Ireland,[14] against all others who opted for England. Because of Bishop Broughton's reference to Archdeacon Scott at Whitfield and Rev. George Fielding at Bishop Auckland being in contact with Moore's family after he had died, Robinson looked in a more specific direction by hinting that Moore's origins lay in the Northeast of England.[15]

In 2005, the year before Moore College celebrated the sesquicentenary of its opening, I was granted a period of study leave from the College during which I planned to take up Robinson's challenge. I wanted to see what I could discover about Thomas Moore's early and latter years, planning to offer a couple of lectures on the man as part of the College's celebrations.[16] During the course of my research, I was delighted to come across several boxes of Mr Moore's personal papers. This discovery has taken my interest in Moore well beyond the College's year of celebration.[17] In working through this material across the last five years, it has become clear that the obscurity which once surrounded this man, a significant NSW pioneer and a prominent Anglican layman, has come to an end. The cache of letters, documents, business accounts and notebooks, provides detailed information about all stages of Moore's life in New South Wales. By further illuminating people, places and events associated with the colony's early political, military, trading, agricultural, economic, ecclesiastical, societal and residential communities (first those in Sydney and then those in Liverpool) across a fifty year period, Moore's papers also provide an important new 'slice-of-life' through a most significant period of our colonial history. Thomas Moore has stepped out of the shadows.

This new information, along with other sources in existence but hitherto unexamined, enables the first major biography of Thomas Moore of Liverpool to be written. Although a largely unsung hero, from the moment he became the Master Builder at the King's Dockyard in October 1796, Moore was a major figure in the early colony. As well as establishing a dockyard in the South Seas to serve the King's Ships, at a crucial period of British Naval and exploratory history, he increasingly took his place in the courts, the trading community, in banking, as a member of the Church, as a farmer and husbandman, and as a builder of bridges, roads, and, later, even a town.

As well as being part of the early residential community in Sydney, he was amongst the pioneers of the Marrickville district, owning a large amount of land between Petersham Hill and the Cook's River. After exerting his influence in Sydney Town for some thirteen years, and after being caught up in the famous 'Rum Rebellion' of 26 January 1808, Moore left Sydney to join the pioneers on the George's River. As the colony moved southwards his landholdings spread with it, from Liverpool to the surrounds of Campbelltown and on into the Southern Highlands. In his time, he was one of the major landholders in NSW, with interests in horse and cattle breeding, as well as leases, loans and mortgages.

As a Christian layperson, Moore also provides an important case study towards the project called for by Brian Fletcher:

> the religious beliefs and pursuits of free persons considered as a group have not received the attention they deserve. While the response of convicts to efforts to arouse their faith has been the subject of a major study, no attempt has been made systematically to examine the relationship between free persons and the churches.[18]

Thomas Moore grew extremely wealthy in these early days of NSW. While he was alive, he used his money for philanthropic and Christian causes, including the construction of Churches, both Anglican and non-Anglican, and to support various missionary causes. When he died, he left a substantial fortune to the Church of England for several specified purposes, including the endowment of the Bishop's See and the establishment of a College to train young men of the Protestant persuasion.

But we are jumping ahead of his story.

Moore had already moved to the George's River when Governor Macquarie decided to select a site in that district for one of his new regional towns. Moore subsequently played a significant role in the establishment of Liverpool and was a leading figure in that community until his death. As resident magistrate, the supervisor of public works, landlord, banker, churchman, and civic benefactor, from this promising new town in 'the interior' Thomas Moore contributed to a vast array of social and political causes that assisted this penal colony in its move towards becoming a free society.

The seventeenth aphorism Moore listed in a collection of 'memorandums and occurrences' reads: 'The first portraiture of Men is their own actions'.[19] Perhaps this expression alludes to the decision of Queen Elizabeth, who, to prevent unflattering depictions of herself, had a proclamation drawn up in regard to her commissioning a portrait of herself so that subsequent painters 'might at their pleasure follow the said pattern or first portraiture'.[20] Perhaps it ignores the technical sense of the expression and simply means that a person's actions are the first depiction of their life, long before paint hits the canvas. In any case, it shows that Moore put great stock on how actions display a person to others. We know what Thomas Moore looked like, not only through the Griffith portrait, but through the many actions he performed as he helped to build Australian society.

1

LESBURY: THE BOY BECOMES A MAN

(1762–1792)

On 16 November 1839, Thomas Moore, long-serving magistrate of Liverpool, New South Wales, stood in the new town Burial Ground. Having already arranged for a memorial tablet for his dear wife Rachel to be erected in St Luke's, this same month he paid Mr Clutter £252 for the work. It was a month for remembering the one he hoped to meet again in the Lord's Heavenly Kingdom, 'to praise the Lord to part no more forever'.[1]

Just over twelve months before, on October 18, Rachel had fallen down the stairs at home, hurting herself badly. At first she seemed to be recovering, but on 13 November she passed away. When she was interred three days later, Thomas wrote in his journal: 'a sorrowful day for me'. Ten days after the burial, he had the bricklayer open the vault to 'see if all was right' and 'found it all well', and paid the bricklayer £5 to close it all up again. With Rachel safely in the ground, on 28 November he went to Sydney to alter his Will to sign over his substantial fortune to the Church of England. On 1 December he paid Mr Hoskings the £130 for his 'dear wife's funeral expenses', adding in his journal: 'altho high I will paid it for her as the last tribute of affection'.[2] (Plates 3, 4 and 5).

Now, twelve months to the day after her burial, Thomas was again in Liverpool Burial Ground. Once again, he had the vault opened to 'see if all was right'.

> 1839, Nov. 16: Opened our Valt in the Burying Ground and found all dry and saw my Dear Wifes Coffin and it opened the same as when she was laid there 12 months ago and I made Room for myself to lay alongside of her when I am no more.[3]

Later generations more used to leaving death alone will no doubt find Moore's actions strange. But these are the actions of a man used to caring for one he loves. They are the actions of a man still in mourning. His full life and good memories combine to make him ready for his own imminent departure, when he will join his companion of over forty years.

The Burial Ground was a place of memory. (Figure 1). Perhaps he remembered back to when Governor Macquarie first ordered that such places for proper burial of the dead be set aside at an appropriate location in the five new towns marked out in 1810. Here at Liverpool, Moore contributed to the fund and supervised the enclosure of the old burial ground on Elizabeth and Castlereagh Streets which was used until 1821. And now Rachel was benefitting from the drier ground of the new burial ground on Macquarie and Campbell Streets. Clean and dry, just like the stonemason had reported ten days after her burial. Clean and dry.[4]

If a person looked Eastwards from the Burial Ground, it was towards the length of the George's River which swung to the right after coming past Liverpool township and then swept down towards Moore Bank. This was the riverbank home Thomas built for Rachel before they moved out here in 1809. It was a new beginning for the two of them. Not many others were here at that time. Not many at all.

A place of memories, along with all their happy sadnesses. Who would have thought Thomas Moore would marry a wife in this land so far from his home? Who would have thought he would live out his adult life here, and come to this point: standing next to her vault, waiting to join her in due course? Now that his adventure was coming to a close, Liverpool was a long way from Lesbury.

CHAPTER 1 ⚓ *Lesbury: the Boy Becomes a Man (1762–1792)* 15

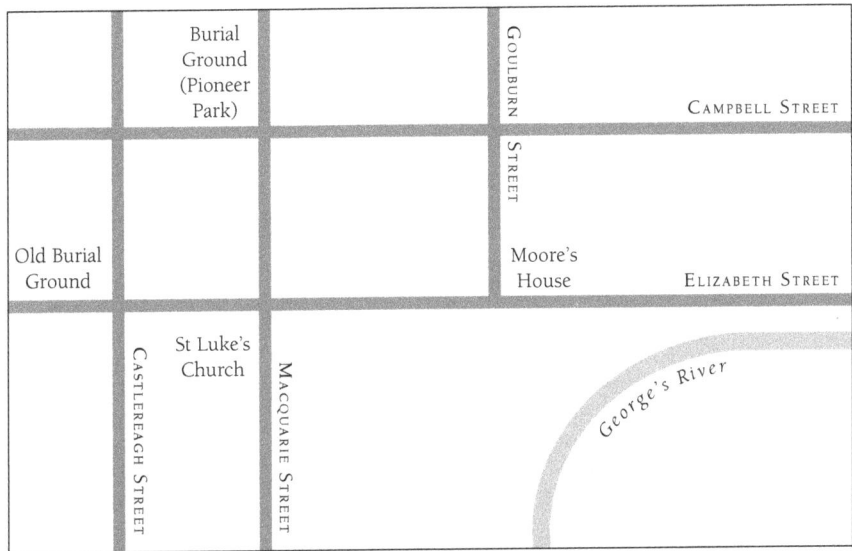

Figure 1. Liverpool Town plan showing Burial Grounds, Old and New.

LESBURY, NORTHUMBERLAND

It is only recently that Moore's origins have been uncovered. The discovery of his personal papers in 2005 brought to light some letters revealing the family connections. Amongst these papers there is a letter from his father, Joseph, written in 1806 from Lesbury, Northumberland, a little coastal village in the northeast of England.[5] The name 'Lesbury' is derived from the old English 'Laeces Byrig', meaning 'the fortified dwelling of a leech or physician'—but the significance of this for the founding of the village is unknown.[6]

Thomas Moore was born and raised in Lesbury. His father Joseph was a 'barn-man', or a husbandman[7]—someone who worked with animals. His mother's name was Mary. Joseph was christened at St Mary the Virgin, Holy Island (Lindisfarne) on 10 February 1723 and Mary, nee Hutson, was christened at Chillingham (c.28/1/1727), where the couple married on 8 December 1751.[8]

Although the year of Thomas Moore's birth is known to be 1762 from evidence at the other end of his life,[9] there is no firm evidence of the exact date he entered this world. But since he was christened on

18 June in Lesbury Parish Church, St Mary's, it must have been sometime in the first half of that year.[10]

The 2,624 acre Parish of Lesbury is bounded 'on the north by Long Houghton, on the west by Alnwick, on the south by High Buston and Shilbottle, and on the east by the German Ocean'.[11] (Figures 2 and 3). According to an 1828 Gazetteer, it consisted of the village of Lesbury-with-Hawkhill and the town of Alnmouth—at that stage, 128 houses total, with 84 of those in Alnmouth.[12] In 1801 its population was 874 persons.[13] Lesbury village is situated on the North bank of the River Aln, which is there crossed by a bridge, probably on the site of an old ford (since this is the tidal limit in the river), with the water mill so important to this agricultural village situated just near to it.[14] The very name of Alnmouth gives away the location of that larger borough, about a mile and a half downstream.

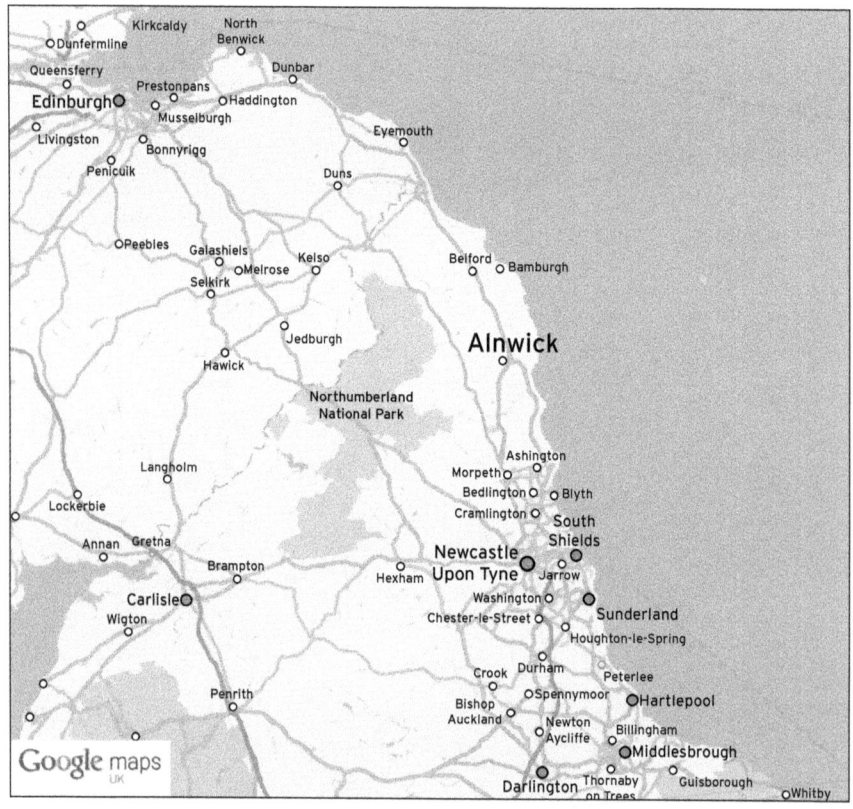

Figure 2. Map of the North East of England (2010).

CHAPTER 1 ⚓ *Lesbury: the Boy Becomes a Man (1762–1792)*

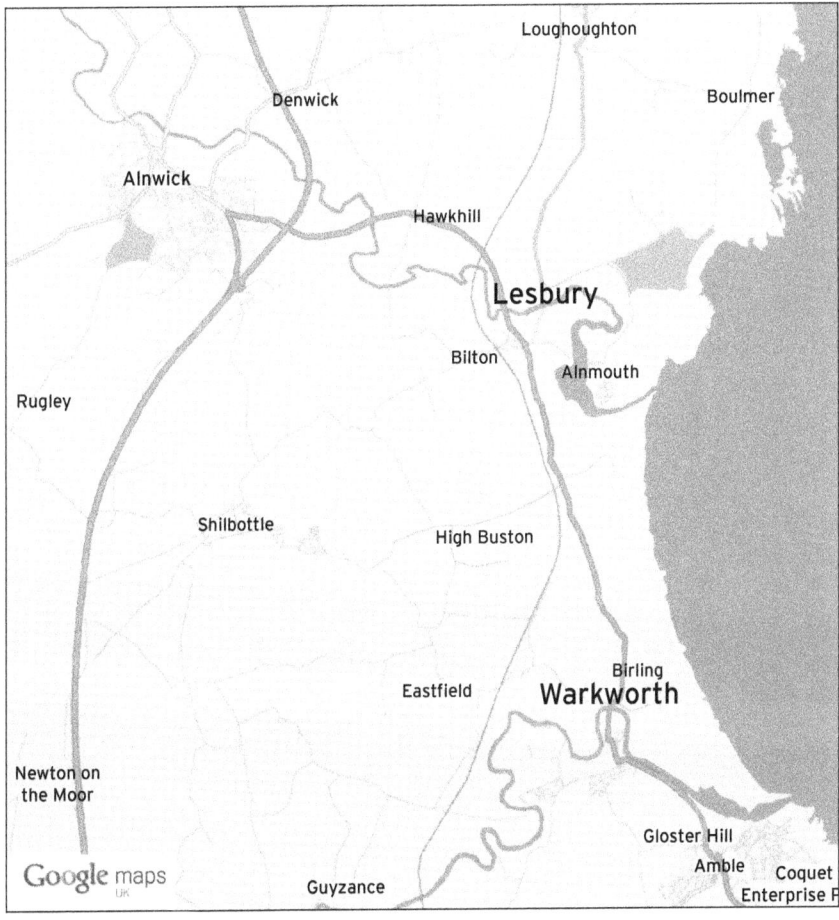

Figure 3. Lesbury district (2010).

On this part of the Northumberland coast, three major towns lie in close proximity. By Saxon times, the three towns had each developed their own characteristics:

> Alnmouth being a fishing community, Lesbury almost entirely agricultural, while Alnwick was probably more of an agricultural and marketing centre near the parting of the ways leading into the inland areas. Other than in their basic community occupations, however, the way of life in all three villages would have been much the same.[15]

For centuries Alnwick and Alnmouth had been boroughs, operating on 'a principle of an orderly and self-governing community'.[16] Between these two boroughs, Lesbury was left to carry on with the regular life of a rural village. Since the time Lesbury became an endowment of the Alnwick Abbey (established 1147), village life had centred around the church, to which everyone belonged and all paid their levied taxes and tithes.

In the early sixteenth century:

> Probably the absence of the commercial activity and incentive, which was so prevalent at that time in Alnmouth, made Lesbury appear to be a quieter and more sleepy place and thus more resistant to change and the Church was probably able to play a more positive and leading role there than was possible in Alnmouth.[17]

Then in 1536 dramatic change arrived with Henry VIII's dissolution of the monasteries. By taking over the Alnwick Abbey, the king also assumed the ownership of Lesbury and the chapelries of Alnwick, Alnmouth and Houghton.[18] With the tithes now going to the king, the parishes had to survive just on the tithes permitted the vicar. This hit Alnwick hardest, being formerly dependant upon the Abbey, but because Lesbury was a farming community, the vicarial tithes for the village would have remained quite steady, maintaining the church on a firmer footing and ensuring its continued influence in village life.[19]

Whereas alongside their resident church leader, the two neighbouring boroughs also had a civic authority (the borough council), at Lesbury there was really no other local authority but the representatives of the church.[20] This originally included the priest and churchwardens, but gradually evolved into a council known as 'the Four and Twenty' (as in Alnwick), and eventually (by 1858), as simply 'the Vestry'. While at Alnwick and Alnmouth, there was a three-fold division of responsibility between the local Gentry's bailiff, the town council and the church, the evolution at Lesbury went in the opposite direction, with the church council taking responsibility for virtually all matters conducted in the parish.[21]

Growing up in Lesbury, Moore would have experienced a farming community centred around the parish church, with local people influencing local matters. How much did this social arrangement shape his ideas as he later took his responsibilities for establishing the rural township of Liverpool, New South Wales?

THOMAS MOORE'S FAMILY

For many years Thomas Moore's origins were unknown—it was even disputed whether he came from England or Ireland.[22] The discovery of the family letters means that his family of origin can now be pieced together.[23] (Figure 4) Thomas's father, Joseph, wrote the letter already referred to in March 1806[24] to inform his distant children that their mother had died and been buried. In the course of doing so, he mentioned by name a number of his children and other people who are connected with the family. Further details of family members emerge from two letters from Thomas's brother, William, written to Thomas in 1839, and another to Bishop Broughton in 1842.[25] The information gleaned from these letters enables the Moor(e) family to be connected into a family tree, which had been constructed over many years by Mr David Moor—who has now learned of his distant Australian relative, and also of several relatives of whom he was previously unaware.[26] As a result, it is possible to put together a fairly good sketch of the inner connections and wider family friendships of the Moore clan.

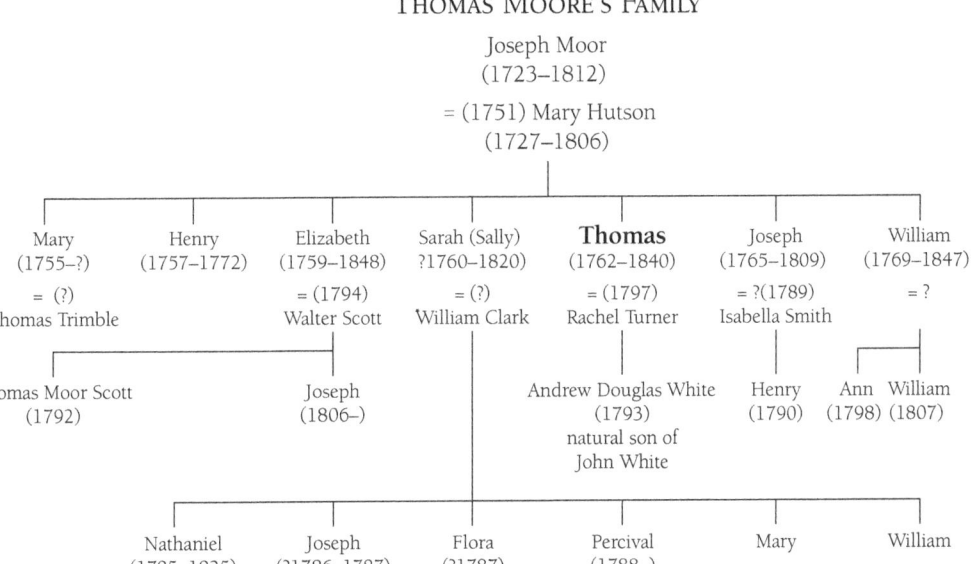

Figure 4. Thomas Moore's Family Tree.

Joseph, himself from a family of thirteen children, had seven children with Mary, six of whom can be properly sequenced. By the time Thomas was born in 1762, three of his siblings had already arrived Mary (1755), Henry (1757) and Elizabeth (1759). After Thomas was born, the Moors had two more sons, Joseph (1765) and William (1769). The family correspondence also shows one more sister, Sarah ('Sally')[27] whose exact birth date and position in the family still remains a mystery.

Mary

Joseph's March 1806 letter was written to a 'dutiful son and daughter' —evidently Sally (from an appended note from Rev. Percival Stockdale) and Thomas (from the fact that the letter eventually turns up amongst his personal papers). The letter briefly refers to their sister, Mary, when Joseph mentions that their mother's funeral was paid for by brother William and by 'thomas Trumble, your sister Mary['s] husband'.[28]

When Mary was christened at St Lawrence, Warkworth, on 11 May 1755, Joseph Moor was residing in Low Buston, a village to the south of Lesbury, half way to Warkworth.[29] A Thomas Trumble, son of Robert, was christened on 4 August 1751, although it is uncertain whether this was the Thomas who eventually married Mary. From her christening date, Mary was about seven years older than her brother Thomas.

Henry

Two years later, Joseph, Mary, and Mary junior, welcomed a son into the world. The family still lived at Low Buston, and Henry was christened at St Lawrence, Warkworth, on 25 September 1757.[30] Unfortunately, Henry died when he was about fifteen and Joseph buried him at St Mary's Lesbury, on the 28 June 1772.[31] When he died, his brother Thomas, about five years his junior, would have been old enough to feel his loss acutely.

Elizabeth

Elizabeth was born after Henry. The newly discovered letters reveal a great deal of information about Elizabeth, enabling the recovery of further records. When she was born—probably after June 17 and before July 7, 1759[32]—the family was still at Low Buston, and so, on 2 December 1759, she too was christened at Warkworth.[33] Elizabeth was therefore two and a half, or three years older than Thomas.

When she was thirty-three, and just after Thomas had arrived in New South Wales, Elizabeth bore a son out of wedlock to Walter Scott, a shepherd from Alnham. On 30 December 1792 at St Mary's Lesbury, she christened the boy, 'Thomas', perhaps indicating the affection between her and her brother.[34] Two years later Elizabeth and Walter married on 12 May 1794, at Eglingham where Walter was then residing, and Joseph Moor—either her father or her brother—stood as one of the witnesses.[35]

In December 1839 when William wrote to Thomas, he informed his distant brother that

> our Sister Elizabeth although a widow is still alive her Husband's name was Walter Scott a Shepherd he died last January, she resides with her Son Joseph who succeeded his Father, she has been blind for about two years and depends I believe entirely on her Son for Support. The rest of her family are married and dispersed with their families in various parts of the Country.[36]

Aged 80 Elizabeth was counted in the 1841 Census, when the records for the township of Beanley record her as living at Gallo Law with her son Joseph (age 35), his wife Isabella (age 30), their children James (9), Walter (5), Jane (3), Joseph (1) and Thomas (2 months). The household also included Susan Scott (40)—is this the widow of Thomas Moore Scott?—and ?her children Elizabeth (3) and Mary (15). Mary was listed as an agricultural labourer, as was John Churnyside (15), and the Household Servant was Mary Matthewson (15).[37] Elizabeth was still at Gallo Law when she died in 1848.

Joseph

After Thomas, Joseph was the next to be born, christened on 8 September 1765.[38] The Lesbury Register has a Joseph and Isabella from South Shields, baptising Henry, 27 June 1790, which is probably him, returning home for the baptism. He is probably also the Joseph Moore who married Isabella Smith on 10 May 1789, at St Hilda's

South Shields.[39] Joseph died in about 1809, and he had a son who died of cholera in about 1834—was this Henry, or another?[40]

William

The next son to be born after Joseph was William, who was christened at Lesbury on 25 June 1769.[41] It is thanks to William's later correspondence that we are able to establish many of the Moore family connections. When he wrote in 1839 and 1842, he was living in South Church, or Coundon, near Bishop's Auckland. He had a son William, and a daughter, Ann, and he died on 23 December 1847.[42]

Sally

The newly discovered letters reveal one further daughter, who went by the name 'Sally' (Sarah). Joseph wrote his March 1806 letter to Thomas and to Sally, at the same time enclosing a letter to Sally from Rev. Percival Stockdale.[43] Stockdale passes condolences to Sally on the death of her mother and he includes an epitaph he had written for Mary. He also passes on greetings to 'Mrs Clarke, and to you and your family', and hints that Sally is 'in the south of England'. As her father Joseph writes, he also tells Sally that he wants her to 'let William Clark know that I am desiris to have a line from him'.

With this cluster of names, it becomes clear that this is the family referred to in the Lesbury Registers on two occasions. Firstly, on 4 June 1786, two boys (probably not twins) were christened: 'Joseph and Nathanael, sons of William and Sarah Clarke were baptized by me, Percival Stockdale, vicar of Lesbury'.[44] Secondly, and sadly, just six months later on 16 January 1787, one of the boys was buried: 'Joseph, son of William and Sarah Clarke, of London'.[45] This latter reference confirms more precisely where 'in the south of England' the Clarks were residing, even if 'London' still begs further precision!

Almost forty years later, Nathaniel made inquiries with Lachlan Macquarie, ex-Governor of NSW and his uncle Thomas's friend, about coming to New South Wales as a settler.[46] In November 1824, he embarked for New South Wales, probably because of his health, which troubled him on the entire voyage. To while away the time, Nathaniel documented his voyage in a journal. After he arrived in Sydney, he enjoyed visiting his uncle Thomas at Liverpool,[47] whom he had almost certainly not seen since the earliest days of his childhood. Sadly, however, after just a few months to renew the relationship, in November 1825, Nathaniel died.[48] His journal, which remained in the possession of his uncle, provides further genealogical information for Sally's family, including Nathaniel's birthday (6/1/1785).[49]

A note in Thomas Moore's business notebook reveals that Sally died in January 1820.[50] From the fact that in 1806, Joseph wrote to Sally and Thomas together; from her son's attempt at re-connection with his uncle; and from Thomas's evident disappointment at hearing of her death, it can be surmised that there was a special relationship between these two siblings.

But when and where was she born? When and where did she marry? Where was she when she died? Although her family can be traced quite well, Sally herself remains shrouded in mystery.[51]

Having excluded her from being a twin of any of her siblings (for then she would have appeared alongside them in one of the christening registers), there are two options for Sally's place in the family. She could have been Joseph and Mary's first child, born somewhere between approximately, September 1752 (to allow for their December 1751 wedding) and, say, mid 1754 (to give room for Mary, christened in May 1755). Alternatively, she could be their fourth child, born in the window of opportunity between Elizabeth's birth in June 1759, and Thomas's in the first half of 1762. Perhaps the apparent closeness between the two suggests they were close in age, born in the gap between Elizabeth and Thomas, around 1760?

The Moore Cousins

Thomas's father Joseph (b. 1723) had several brothers and sisters, but perhaps only the youngest two lived locally in Lesbury.[52] Grace Moor, who married Joseph Ferrow on 22 June 1762, was probably Joseph's sister, but if she had any offspring, they are unknown.[53] James Moor, the Lesbury schoolmaster, was probably Joseph's brother.[54] Uncle James died just after Thomas had come to Australia (bur. 8/6/1794), but his wife Margaret (nee Linton, m. 4/7/1762)[55] survived until 1809.[56]

James and Margaret provided six cousins for Thomas. Robert (c. 5/4/1763) and Henry (c. 18/2/1765) were close enough in age to be his growing up companions;[57] followed by younger siblings Elizabeth (c. 6/10/1767), who died when she was nineteen (bur. 2/6/1786);[58] James (c. 24/6/1770) who died when he was twenty-three (c. 22/9/1793);[59] John (c. 26/6/1774);[60] and Joseph (c. 25/12/1778).[61]

Thomas Moore's Family Influence?

What did this family contribute to the shaping of Mr Moore of Liverpool? He had unpretentious beginnings, at home with his father's animals in a rural village, yet close to a busy port whose exports and imports daily spoke of a wider world of adventure, trade and commerce. The ever-imminent tragedies brought by sickness and death must have pressed home as the family coped with their various bereavements: his brother Henry, aged fifteen (1772) and his nephew Joseph, only nine (1787), taken in childhood; his cousins Elizabeth (1786) and James (1793) as they reached early adulthood. The moral failure of his sister Elizabeth may have given him feelings of sympathy for unmarried mothers and children born out of wedlock—feelings that perhaps revived when he met Rachel Turner and her son Andrew White, once he arrived in New South Wales.

THOMAS MOORE'S CHRISTIAN UPBRINGING

In his later life in Australia, Thomas Moore had a profound Christian faith and an active church involvement. Although little can be proved definitely about the Christian influences exerted upon him before he left his homeland, circumstantial evidence at least enables speculation about some possibilities.

To begin with what is clear, his family have proven and long-term associations with the Church of England. His father's roots go back to Holy Island, that is, Lindisfarne[62]—famous for the English saints, Aidan and Cuthbert. Arriving from the Irish monastery of Iona, Aidan founded a monastery here in AD 635, with the support of King Oswald, based at Bamburgh. From their island base, Aidan and his monks worked as missionaries amongst the people of Northumbria, setting up the first known school in the region, and introducing reading and writing, including Latin so that the Bible and other Christian works might be read. The boys they trained later spread the gospel across much of England. The community at the mouth of the Aln would have been amongst the earliest to receive the missionaries, who had some success in persuading them to forsake their old pagan ways and embrace Jesus Christ. The progress of their mission can perhaps be gauged by the fact that, according to Bede, in AD 684—only decades after Aidan came to Holy Island—a synod was held at Twyford—a place many identify as Alnmouth.[63]

Lindisfarne later established a reputation for its skill in Christian art—the beautiful illuminations of the Lindisfarne Gospels being the most famous surviving examples. The very popular St Cuthbert continued the ministry established by Aidan, before the island community was struck a devastating blow by the Viking attack of AD 739, during which many monks lost their lives. After the Norman Conquest (in 1066) the Benedictine monks of Durham, who had preserved the body of St Cuthbert, saw themselves as the inheritors of the Lindisfarne tradition and built another monastery on Holy Island, which lasted until the dissolution of the monasteries under Henry VIII (1536).[64]

It is impossible to know what influence this family connection to the earliest centre of Christian mission had upon the growing Thomas. But perhaps the memory of the gospel activity of these early monks played a role in inspiring the missionary vision that was clearly an important part of his own life after he settled in New South Wales.

Old Dissent: Outside and Inside the Church

Even though the lives of his family were closely entwined with the parish Church of St Mary's, Thomas would have grown up with some awareness of 'old dissent'—both outside and inside the Church.

In the former category, George Fox and the early Quaker 'Publishers of Truth' passed through Northumberland many times in the 1650s, and in the years that followed. Over time, Quaker meetings were established in Allendale, Coanwood, Winnowshill in Derwentside,

Newcastle upon Tyne—and also in Alnwick.[65] In Alnwick in the eighteenth century Mr John Doubleday, into whose hands the Abbey had then fallen, took active steps to propagate Quakerism. By 1728 there was a regular meeting in his house. This lasted until 1797 when Doubleday died and the Abbey was subsequently sold, at which point Quakerism in the region also apparently died. The time period of Quaker activity therefore overlaps with Moore's growing years, so it is something he could have been aware of, especially since, through its connection with the Abbey and the Castle, Lesbury tended to be oriented towards Alnwick, rather than Alnmouth.[66] Nevertheless the two are different towns and the likelihood of this meeting exerting a direct influence on the young Thomas is probably rather slim.

'Old Dissent' within the Church probably had more opportunity to influence him, for this was much more prevalent in Northumberland. Although Hickes reports no positive evidence that Lesbury or Alnmouth were affected by the spoliation of the 'extreme Puritans' during the period of the Civil War and the Commonwealth (1640–1660),[67] some in the Parish were fearful enough to take precautions. The medieval font in St Mary's Lesbury is one of the few in England to have escaped destruction at this time—rescued, according to local tradition, because it was buried for safekeeping.[68] Who were its protectors afraid of? It is also interesting that neither the vicar of Lesbury (Patrick Mackilwyan), nor the curate of Alnmouth (Robert Spence) were 'deprived of their livings in favour of visiting preachers' by the Puritans.[69] Was this for some accidental reason—perhaps the two towns were small enough to cause no real concern—or was it because they held Puritan convictions?

Although it is difficult to recover the exact situation in the parish of Lesbury, it is clear that Old Dissent was a significant part of Church life in Northumberland. So, for example, even in 1854 it could be reported that: 'in Northumberland, at the present day, many [Presbyterian] congregations date their existence from the Act of Uniformity'.[70] After the Commonwealth period, in the Great Ejection of 1662, thirty-eight Northumberland ministers were deprived of their livings as the Act of Uniformity was enforced—a number which is amongst the highest of all the Counties.[71] (Figure 5).

CHAPTER 1 ⚓ *Lesbury: the Boy Becomes a Man (1762–1792)*

Figure 5. Northumberland parishes with ministers evicted after 1662 Act of Uniformity.

When the Northumberland names on Thomas Coleman's list of the 'Two Thousand Confessors of Sixteen Sixty Two' are mapped, it becomes clear that the Parish of Lesbury was virtually surrounded by parishes, which had been in the hands of one of these 'Confessors'.

Lesbury Parish (along with neighbours Shilbottle and Guizance) floated on a sea of ten connected parishes whose Puritan ministers were ejected: beginning with those adjoining Lesbury, Long Houghton to the North (Samuel Lane), Alnwick to the West (Gilbert Rule), and Warkworth to the South (Archibald Moor),[72] and then spreading out through Felton, Edlingham, Whittingham, Alwinton (or Allerton), Eglingham, Chatton, Wooler and Ellingham.

Unlike that of Gilbert Rule, the curate at Alnwick, the names of Robert Spence (Alnmouth) and Patrick Mackilwyan (Lesbury) do not appear on Coleman's list. But what can be made of the fact that both of them were replaced (the former by Roger Spence; the latter by William Coxe) in the same year—1663? Although this date may be pure coincidence, with the Act of Uniformity passed in 1662, it is a suspicious year for a replacement to arrive.[73]

If the traditions of dissent, or otherwise, lived on in these places, it might also be worth noting that Thomas's father came from Holy Island and he married Mary in Chillingham. In 1662, neither place was deprived of their minister, perhaps a sign of being true to the High Church traditions against which dissent had been raised.[74] On the other hand, Joseph and Mary had their daughter Elizabeth baptised in Warkworth, where Archibald Moor had been ejected, and after Thomas's sister Elizabeth married Walter Scott in the parish of Eglingham, she dwelt the rest of her life in that parish, which was where a Puritan minister had been ejected in 1662 (John Pringle).[75]

Of course, no real conclusions can be drawn from this circumstantial evidence alone, but at least it shows that 'Old Dissent' within the Church was very much a part of the history of the Church of England in the county in which Thomas grew up.

Unitarianism

Before leaving 'old dissent' a word should be said about Unitarianism. If judged by the presence of its own chapels, Unitarianism could probably be dismissed as a fairly minor influence in Thomas's environment. A Unitarian Chapel was opened in Newcastle in Hanover Square, Newcastle, in 1727,[76] but the Chapel in Alnwick did not open until 1815.[77] On the other hand, there was a tendency for Dissenting congregations to become Unitarian, so the strong presence of Dissent in Northumberland, might therefore raise questions about the prevalence of Unitarian views.

When Thomas died he left a catalogue of the books on his bookshelf, which, at some 220 volumes, made up quite a substantial private library for these early colonial times.[78] Because Thomas's library contained a small number of books which could fall under suspicion of Unitarianism,[79] and one full-blown commendation of the Unitarian point of view, discussion of Thomas's English Christian influences should also include something about Unitarianism in the environment in which he originated. In his early days in New South Wales he had close connections with some more 'radical' thinkers, such as Surgeons John White and George Bass (and through family connections these continued), and this brought him into the circles of the 'Scottish Martyr', Rev. Thomas Fyshe Palmer. (Figure 6; Plates 16, 42).

Figure 6. Thomas Fyshe Palmer.

Because of his ministry before his transportation, Palmer has been classed amongst England and Scotland's 'eminent Unitarians'.[80] It is also interesting to notice that the book on Moore's shelf which directly promotes Unitarian views—Captain Thomas Ashe's *The Liberal Critic* (1812)—is a 'trashy novel' (the only book of this kind on the shelf), which purports to be, as the subtitle reveals, the *Memoirs of Henry Percy*.[81] Percy is, of course, the surname of the

Dukes of Northumberland, whose seat was at Alnwick Castle.

There are further circumstantial connections between Lesbury's Duke and Unitarianism through another 'eminent Unitarian', Rev. Theophilus Lindsey (1723–1808). Lindsey actively promoted the Unitarian cause from within the Church of England from his vicarage in Yorkshire from 1763 until 1773, but when Parliament finally refused to receive a petition he had helped to promote seeking clergy relief from subscription to the Thirty-Nine Articles, he resigned. He then moved to London, where he served in a Unitarian congregation in Essex Street, erecting a Chapel in 1778. As well as putting pen to paper about his need to leave the Church of England (*Apology*), in 1783 he wrote *An Historical View of the State of Unitarian Doctrine and Worship from the Reformation to our own Times*.

This man who became one of Unitarianism's leading figures had a sustained connection with Northumberland. When he was in his early thirties, for two years (1754–1756) he travelled extensively throughout Europe as tutor to Hugh Percy, the future Second Duke of Northumberland, then about twelve.[82] Following this tour of duty, the Earl of Northumberland (his charge's father, who became the First Duke in 1766) presented him to the rectory of Kirby-Wiske in the North Riding of Yorkshire. Here his scruples began to emerge, and they came to full flower after developing an intimate friendship with Joseph Priestley in 1769. During this period the same Earl invited him to become his chaplain in Ireland (1762). Although Lindsey declined, the invitation shows his continuing relationship with Northumberland. Once he had resigned from the Church of England and gone to Essex Street, a Mrs Rayner joined the congregation. Lindsey dedicated *An Historical View* to this woman, who was not only wealthy enough to be a liberal supporter of both Lindsay and Priestley, but she was also the aunt of the Duchess of Northumberland. With such connections, perhaps it is right to wonder what influence Lindsey's journey into Unitarianism had on his former pupil and his father, the Dukes under whose oversight lay the village of Lesbury?[83]

Once again, no direct influence on Thomas Moore can be proven from this circumstantial evidence, but it certainly alerts us to another interesting feature in the religious landscape of his village of origin.

New Dissent: Methodism and the Evangelical Revival

Even though its effects lived on, 'old dissent' was almost ancient history by the second half of the eighteenth century when Thomas Moore was growing up. Not so the 'new dissent' of Methodism and the Evangelical Revival. Later in his life, Thomas Moore displayed strong sympathies for the Methodists, and indeed was actively involved with their cause. He also associated with Evangelical Anglicans. Can any influences from the Methodist and Evangelical Revivals be identified upon his earlier life?

Perhaps Evangelical Anglicanism can be disposed of fairly quickly, by referring to G.R. Balleine's comment (1908):

> In Northumberland and Durham we have not been able to discover a single Evangelical in the eighteenth century. For some reason that is not altogether clear, the movement which gained so firm a footing in one corner of Yorkshire was very slow in finding its way into any of the neighbouring counties.[84]

Apparently, if Moore was going to be influenced by Evangelical Anglicanism, he would have to wait until he arrived in New South Wales, where he would run into the Yorkshire-influenced Chaplains Richard Johnson, Samuel Marsden, William Cowper and Robert Cartwright, as well as various lay persons with evangelical sympathies.[85]

As for Methodism, despite Hickes' comment that 'Methodists have been active in Alnmouth since the early days of the movement',[86] it is difficult to say exactly how early they began their activity along the Aln, and what the extent of their influence actually was. John Wesley, at the prompting of Selina, Countess of Huntingdon, began to preach to the miners of Newcastle in July 1743, where he received a good response.[87] Moving North, he visited Alnmouth in 1748, but he was not impressed with this 'small seaport town famous for all kinds of wickedness'.[88] Nevertheless, in 1749 the Newcastle Circuit was established, incorporating Northumberland, Cumberland, Westmoreland, part of Durham and a long way into Scotland. By 1766 only eleven chapels graced this vast amount of territory, and none was close to Lesbury.

But just like it is highly probable that Thomas Moore was well-aware of dissent of the old kind—it being such a strong feature of his part of Northumberland—it is also likely that he was at least aware of

Methodism, even if its influence along the Aln was probably not strong. There was, of course, no need to have a chapel to hear a Methodist preacher, but in Northumberland the major thrust of the Methodist preachers was in the mining communities in the southern districts, rather than in the more agricultural areas like Lesbury. Amongst the miners chapels were springing up as a sign, not of the start, but of the success of the movement: in 1759 at North Shields, Whitehaven and Teesdale, and in 1764 in Monkwearmouth and High-Street Sunderland. Perhaps Thomas would have picked up some second-hand knowledge of Methodism after his brother Joseph moved to South Shields, firmly a part of this area that was experiencing Methodist revival in increasing measure. If Thomas himself moved South to serve his apprenticeship (see below), this would have increased dramatically the likelihood of him coming across Methodist preaching.

The Church of England

But whatever the strength of these circumstantial speculations about the influence on Thomas from old and new dissent, it is clear that his family had a long association with the Church of England. The Parish church of St Mary's Lesbury was theirs. (Figure 7; Plate 6). It was here that most of the children were christened, as well as some of Joseph and Mary's grandchildren, visiting from other districts (no doubt for the occasion). Thomas's Uncle James was sexton at the church for a long time, and his father Joseph also held this role in 1806, perhaps taking it over after his brother died in 1794.[89]

When Thomas was born, Nathaniel Ellison MA was vicar of Lesbury (and also Kirkwhelpington) since 1750 until his death in 1775.[90] William Forster MA followed Ellison, holding the incumbency from 1775 until 1784. After the rather eccentric Rev. Percival Stockdale was presented to the parish in the Autumn of 1783,[91] this pastor with poetical pretensions had periods in which he did not reside in Lesbury, occasionally leaving a curate (such as J. Richardson, for example) in charge when he was forced to travel for the sake of his health. But, even if he may have dearly preferred to be amongst the literary society in London, he served as the vicar of Lesbury until his death in September 1811, the year before Joseph Moor died.[92] These were the men who held the charge of Thomas's home church. But little is known about the kind of ministry they exercised, and so it is difficult to assess their potential influence over the young Moore's Christian upbringing.

Figure 7. St Mary's Lesbury.

Because Thomas later supervised the building of St Luke's Liverpool, before leaving St Mary's Lesbury it might be worth noting that the two buildings bear some resemblance. Being built by the Normans and added to only slightly over the years, the Lesbury building is basically rectangular.[93] In contrast, from the sketch by Grose in 1771 we know that the church at Alnmouth was probably cruciform in shape,[94] so Thomas Moore would have also been familiar with this as an ecclesiastical possibility. Both churches were built about the same time, in the twelfth century, and by contrast with the elaborate structure at Alnmouth, the Lesbury church was basic, having a simple nave, a chancel, and a tower.[95] Thomas Moore may have had little input in the design of St Luke's, whose architect was Francis Greenway, but nevertheless its plain, rectangular features would have been strangely familiar from the church of his upbringing.[96]

THOMAS'S EDUCATION

Growing up in a farming community, with a father who reared and cared for farm animals, Thomas's practical training in animal husbandry would have begun at an early age. These lessons of his youth became important in New South Wales as he applied himself to his own animal husbandry, sometimes with sheep, but mostly cattle and horses.[97]

In his adult life, Moore was a keen supporter of more formal education. Not only did he build primary schools and support teachers, he also shared the vision for setting up higher-level education in the colony of New South Wales. He paid for his stepson's English education at Charterhouse and for his officer training for the Royal Engineers at Woolwich. Thomas also apparently encouraged his wife Rachel to receive some of the basic education of which she was deprived in her early life.[98] When he died, he left a large proportion of his substantial fortune to the founding of Australia's first tertiary educational institution. This high commitment to education probably came, however, not from having received positive benefits of schooling himself, but rather from having not received much at all. After his death, Bishop Broughton commended him—rather ironically, in a Latin oration—for his commitment to education, despite having none himself:

> One individual, a lowly man, and unlettered, [...] who (though himself destitute of literary accomplishments, yet being taught by some natural and innate power of discernment how great in the management of affairs is the use of them [...][99]

Once again, evidence about Thomas's education is entirely circumstantial and nothing can be proven. We know that he was a competent ship's carpenter. But even for those entering the Naval yards at this time, it was not normal for an apprentice shipwright to have any general education prior to his entry, and so practical was the training that it wasn't until 1806 that the Navy Board began recommending the boys be instructed in reading, writing and arithmetic.[100] There was a schoolhouse in Lesbury, endowed by a piece of land given by Mr Henry Strother in 1718. This endowment required the schoolmaster to charge lower than normal fees and to admit some poorer children *gratis*.[101] Presumably therefore, whatever the financial situation of his father, Thomas could have had an opportunity to attend. It may have also been an advantage that, for Thomas's entire life in Lesbury, the schoolmaster was his uncle, James Moor. Perhaps his uncle-cum-teacher gave him some basic instruction in reading and writing skills. From the standards of spelling and style of writing displayed in his personal papers, however, he does not appear to have achieved any high level skills in these areas. On the other hand, his accumulation of quite a substantial library (some 220 volumes), as well as his desire to keep abreast of the English newspapers, suggests that he certainly developed into a regular reader and at quite a high level. Good skills in mathematics, arithmetic, measurement and basic accounting are suggested by his evident ability as a ship's carpenter, his business acumen, and by his many accounts that have survived.

THOMAS MOORE LEARNS HIS TRADE

Despite the paucity of his early education, from all reports Thomas Moore was an excellent craftsman. When he arrived in Australia on 26 July 1792, he was the ship's carpenter on board William Raven's *Britannia*. During the time *Britannia* was in Australasian waters, Moore's reputation grew, as comments about the high standard of his work reached official ears.[102] In October 1793, when boasting to Lieut.-Governor King about a small vessel Moore had built in Dusky Bay, New Zealand, Captain William Raven noted that his carpenter showed discernment about the quality and usefulness of the native timbers, and that he cut the 'frame knees and crooked pieces' from timber 'growing to the mould'—that is, like traditional shipwrights he used various moulds to select timber where it grew, before the trees were felled and converted on the spot.[103] In a back-handed compliment, Raven, the Naval Officer, compared Moore's work with that of Naval shipwrights:

> The carpenter has great merit, and has built her with that strength and neatness which few shipwrights belonging to the merchant service are capable of performing.[104]

Perhaps Raven's comment can be taken somewhat prophetically, for as yet another high endorsement of Moore's workmanship, in September 1796, when Governor Hunter invited him to become the Master Boat Builder at the Government Dockyard, he replaced Daniel Paine—trained by the Navy at Deptford Yard. (Plate 11).

The high standard of his work and the manner in which he went about it makes it almost certain that Mr Moore served an apprenticeship under a skilful master craftsman. But, unfortunately, Robinson's remarks remain true that it is 'regrettable that we know nothing of where Moore may have received his earlier training'.[105] Raven's comment shows Moore was not trained in one of the dockyards of the Royal Navy, but which merchant yard gave him such high quality skills can only be guessed at.

An apprenticeship lasted for seven years, and, although for some apprenticeships a boy may have begun as early as twelve years old, if the Navy's example for shipwrights also carried over into the merchant yards, then he was more likely to have begun at fourteen.[106] Moore would have therefore served his apprenticeship from approximately 1776 through to 1783. Again, if the Naval regulations are anything to go on, although it was difficult to get a position, there was no examination required as long as a boy met the requirement of age and stature (he had to be taller than 4 ft. 10 inches).[107] As an apprentice at this time—again, according to Navy practice—he would have been required to hand over his entire wage to his master.[108] What would he have been paid? Presumably as an apprentice in a merchant yard, he would receive considerably less than time-served shipwrights and caulkers in the Naval dockyards, whose standard rate was consistent from 1660 until 1788, and even until 1809: 25 pence per day (2s 1d).[109] The masters also received an allowance for lodging and an allowance in 'chips'—that is, smaller lengths of timber for their own use.

As Thomas neared apprenticeship age, Lesbury was an ideal location for finding a master. At this time the Northeast of England was rapidly expanding as a shipbuilding region, affording him several good options for where he could learn his trade. Three places in particular can be canvassed, each with different pieces of circumstantial evidence suggesting potential for Moore's story.

CHAPTER 1 ↓ Lesbury: the Boy Becomes a Man (1762–1792)   37

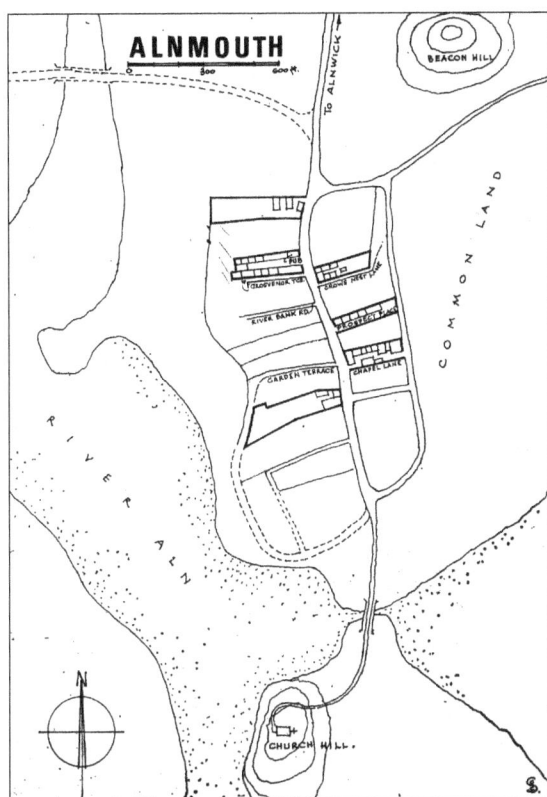

Figure 8. Map of Alnmouth.

Alnmouth

The easiest place for Thomas to find an apprenticeship was just a mile and a half down the river at Alnmouth—Lesbury's neighbouring 'large town'—even if this meant crossing over from the agricultural community in which he grew up, to join the fisher-folk and seafaring men who predominated in Alnmouth.[110] (Figure 8; Plate 7). This was the coastal end of the so-called 'Corn Road' that stretched from Hexham and passed through productive agricultural regions, bringing a flow of grain towards the waiting vessels in Alnmouth for export.[111] In the seventeenth and eighteenth centuries, the port of Alnmouth was not only important for exporting grain, but also for importing Baltic timber. Her significance began to decline in the early nineteenth century, especially after Christmas 1806, when a major storm broke through the spit of land from the coast to the river, seriously damaging the harbour.[112] But this was well after Thomas Moore's time. When the boy Thomas turned his heart towards a seafaring trade, Alnmouth was still a thriving port and a small-time ship-building town. The first vessel built there was one of 300 tons burthen, launched on 13 March 1763,[113] the year after Thomas was born. Just two years later, three more ships were launched: the *Brittania*, *Coquet Lass* and *Duchess of Northumberland*.[114]

Presumably this was big news for the district, and since the dates indicate that Thomas was growing along with the Alnmouth ship building industry, this could have been part of the inspiration behind him going into his trade. Alnmouth would be just a short walk down the river from Lesbury, so an apprenticeship there is certainly a possibility. Unfortunately, it is only the proximity that speaks loudly for this being the place of his training. No records have been recovered to confirm or deny this possibility.

If Thomas went further afield to take up his craft, the towns of South Shields and Sunderland were also live options. Both towns were advancing the industry at the time, helping to make the Northeast into one of England's leading ship-building regions.[115]

South Shields

The one thing that links Thomas Moore with South Shields is the fact that his brother Joseph was residing there in 1790.[116] There were at least five ship-building yards already established at South Shields by the beginning of Thomas's apprenticeship years,[117] and several others opened during the years of his servitude. Robert Wallis had been in business on Shadwell Street since 1729, and when he died in 1781 his three sons let his yard to John Wright, who was married to their sister Jane. In 1779 John had already opened his own yard on Shadwell Street, where William Forster (1773) and James Evans (1780) were also operating.[118] The year Thomas was born, Thomas Winship began building ships at the Low Dock on Wapping Street. His widow briefly took over when he died in 1768, before selling the yard the next year to the Broderick family. The Brodericks opened their own yard in 1773, and—in what seems to be a pattern for South Shields' ship builders—when Lockwood Broderick died in 1784, his widow took over, until 1787 when Lockwood Broderick III came of age. It is difficult to know what to make of widow Broderick's three-year 'rule', since in that time she had no less than thirty-one apprentices abscond![119] The Spring-Lane Dock was another possibility in the 1780s, under Simon Temple or James Evans.[120] Simon Temple also operated out of the Mill Dam, advertising a sale of a ship in 1780. Plenty of good training went on here, apparently, for when the elder Simon Temple went bankrupt in

1786 he advertised his yard for sale and 'fourteen apprentices, most of them as good as men'.¹²¹ The Middle Dock operated from the 1760s, under George Smith, then later by Hutchinson & Co (1777/78), then Banks and Liddle (1779), and then for many years Richard Bulmer, whose prosperity peaked in 1791 when he built or repaired five vessels.¹²² The High Dock run by Robert Wallis was first mentioned in 1778, and handed over to his sons when he died in 1781, only to be sold to Nicholson, Horn and Blenkinsop.¹²³ If Thomas served his apprenticeship somewhere in South Shields, there were plenty of good options for masters opening at various stages of his servitude. But if he stayed with the one firm for his entire time, beginning in 1776, then the possibilities narrow down to just four: Robert Wallis or William Forster on Shadwell Street, Winship-Broderick at the Low Dock on Wapping Street, or George Smith's operation at Middle Dock.

Sunderland

Sunderland is a third possibility for Thomas's apprenticeship, at the time fast becoming one of the perfect places for Thomas to learn his trade. A concrete connection between Thomas and Sunderland arises from the fact that this was where the *Britannia*, the ship that brought him to Australia, was built, completed in 1783 and repaired in 1785.¹²⁴

In the last quarter of the eighteenth century, rapid advances were occurring in the Northeastern shipbuilding industry around Sunderland.¹²⁵ By 1819, a contemporary source claimed that Sunderland's shipbuilding industry stood 'the highest of any in the United Kingdom, and gives employment to a great number of carpenters'.¹²⁶ In 1801, there were nine shipbuilding establishments in Sunderland. Even though there may have been slightly less to choose from twenty-five years earlier, this gives us some idea of the kind of options available to Moore as he served his apprenticeship.¹²⁷ Although Sunderland's output would not peak until 1840, when 251 vessels were built, it was still something of a record that 19 were completed in 1790.¹²⁸

Although some derogatory comments were cast from time to time, in general Sunderland ships were of a high standard and the Sunderland carpenters had a good reputation. There were numerous small firms, and small to medium vessels were the norm, and, as with other places in the Northeast, Sunderland carpenters were especially used to working with mixed woods, as a variety of timber was readily available in the port.[129]

Working with mixed woods was at the innovative end of the shipbuilding spectrum. English oak was regarded as the best—and, in some circles, the only—wood to use for this purpose. But the oak tree took one hundred years to mature, and, after one hundred years of seafaring warfare, oak was in short supply and a real crisis was looming.[130] Despite the dyed-in-the-wool approach of the southern Naval dockyards, in which wood other than English oak was regarded with suspicion, the merchant yards in the Northeast were already adept at utilising mixed and foreign timber. In view of the need for shipping if Britain was to retain to 'mastery of the seas', the oak shortage and alternative solutions must have been a frequent conversation amongst the sea chippies up and down the coastline.

In 1783 in Sunderland, the *Britannia* was just being completed. This was exactly the same time that Moore was emerging from his apprenticeship. If he was already in Sunderland, it is possible that he was even engaged in her building, before he joined her as her carpenter and she became his first vessel.

THE SOUTH SEAS IN THE PUBLIC IMAGINATION

The 1770s and 1780s were exciting times for a young apprenticeship heading for a career at sea. For some time the opening up of the South Seas ensured that adventure was in the air. Young boys like Matthew Flinders couldn't tear themselves away from Daniel Defoe's *Robinson Crusoe* (1719) and—when they could—they spent the time drawing maps of islands far away.[131]

When Captain Cook returned home in 1771 after mapping the East coast of Australia, this raised further interest in these southern waters, and a further mission for Cook. He left on his second voyage the following year, returning home in 1775 'famous not only for his discoveries, but also for the successful treatment of the health of his crew'.[132] Joseph Banks sailed as his botanist on the first voyage. It was his excitement at the new flora that gave Botany Bay its name. He almost sailed again on Cook's second voyage, but stayed home, where he gradually became a leading figure in scientific circles, and, in time, a leading advocate for things Australian. By the time Cook sailed away a third time, only to die on the Sandwich Islands, his voyages of discovery had already made their mark on the English imagination. But in 1784, the publication of the narrative of this final journey moved the public's excitement about the South Seas to even higher levels.[133] And of course, it was not just boyish adventure that seized the public mind—many already saw the commercial possibilities in these newly charted waters.

If Thomas Moore joined others reading Cook's narrative in 1784, he did so as someone just out of his apprenticeship with a lifetime of sea voyaging adventure pressing in upon his own imagination—along with its commercial gain. As a recently trained craftsman of shipyard timber, he would be well aware of the oak shortage in the country. Being from the Northeast he would already be familiar with working with mixed and alternative timbers. When this fresh, new, ship's carpenter turned his imagination to the new lands in the South Seas, surely his vision included the untapped potential of forests previously untouched by European tools.

Another use for the 'Great South Land' was also emerging as Moore entered the early days of practising his craft. After the American War of Independence, the transportation of felons to America ceased and the overcrowding in British gaols began to cause official alarm. In 1779, Sir Joseph Banks, Captain Cook's botanist on the *Endeavour*, suggested New South Wales as an alternative.[134] In August 1783, James Maria Matra, who had also travelled with Cook, wrote his 'Proposal for Establishing a Settlement in New South Wales', citing Sir Joseph Banks' high approbation of his scheme and listing the commercial gains that would accrue from this settlement 'designed to increase the wealth of the parent country, as well as for the emolument of the adventurers'.[135] He drew upon the intelligence gained from Captain Cook's voyage to New South Wales and New Zealand to speak of seal-skins that attracted high prices in China, as well as flax and timber suitable for naval purposes. In August 1786, the decision was made to establish a penal colony at Banks' Botany Bay.

Other commercial enterprises were also opening up. The Enderby family had been operating the 'oil and Russia' trade, which included New England. They owned the ships chartered for the cargoes of tea dumped into the Boston harbour in 1773. That same year they began the Southern Fishery for sperm whales, operating out of London. By 1785 they had seventeen ships and by 1790 sixty-eight. From 1786, as spokesmen for the Southern Fishery, principal owner Samuel Enderby, along with Alexander Champion and John St Barbe, appeared frequently before the Committee of the Privy Council for Trade and Plantations, urging 'an unlimited right of fishing in all seas', that is, the breaking of the stranglehold on commercial seafaring granted to the East India Company. Gradually under Government pressure the Company assented to modify geographical limits, to issue licenses, and to relax other restrictions. By 1801, with the exception that the China waters were still closed to them, the Southern Fishery had gained virtually total freedom.[136]

After sending *Emilia* whaling into the Pacific around Cape Horn in 1789, the Southern Fishery gained a three-year fishing license from the East India Company for the Sunderland-built *Britannia*, co-owned by John St Barbe and her Captain, William Raven R.N.[137] On the way out to the waters around New South Wales and New Zealand, Raven was also contracted to deliver much-needed stores to the newly founded penal colony at Port Jackson.

THOMAS MOORE—MILITIAMAN?

After Thomas Moore settled in Sydney he became a Lieutenant, and then a Captain, in the Loyal Sydney Volunteer Association—the New South Wales militia. This may indicate that he had military experience before he left England, and certainly the times in which he grew up gave him the opportunity to gain it.

In 1757, Parliament passed the Militia Act (30 George II 25), directing that, after a period of dormancy, militia regiments be re-established in the counties of England and Wales. In the awareness that a voluntary system would not adequately fill the ranks, from the beginning this entailed a form of conscription. Under the direction of

CHAPTER 1 ↯ *Lesbury: the Boy Becomes a Man (1762–1792)*

constables, parishes were required annually to make lists of adult males, aged eighteen to fifty, and to hold ballots to choose some of them for compulsory service. If those so chosen—known as 'principals' or 'drawn men'—were unwilling, they had to find someone to serve as their substitute.[138] By the 1760s most counties were holding annual ballots.

The list of men nominated for the Militia from Lesbury in 1762, the year Thomas was born, does not include his father Joseph, and his uncle James the schoolmaster appears, only to be struck off as 'unfit'.[139] Under the 1757 Act, this could have been because he was a teacher, a group explicitly excluded—along with peers, clergy, peace officers and apprentices. However, under the 1758 Act (31 George II 26), no names were to be excluded—a stipulation that prevailed until 1831. From 1762 the upper age was lowered to 45, but at only twenty-eight this made Thomas's uncle James still eligible, meaning that he was declared unfit because of some physical or other health issue. The absence of Joseph, Thomas's father, thirty-nine in 1762, is more of a mystery. Perhaps the family was still residing in Warkworth parish, where Elizabeth was christened in December 1759, with the militia list compiled before they moved in time to have Thomas christened at St Mary's in June 1762. Or perhaps the list is simply inaccurate: despite what ought to have been the case, it is unlikely that these lists were always complete.

As Thomas reached military age (he turned 18 in 1780), England suffered from rising anxiety about hostile forces from outside. It seemed to come from all sides: the American War of Independence (1775–1783), the increasing number of privateers raiding English ships, and the radical political ideas that were festering their way towards the French revolution (1789–1799) and yet another war with France (1793). The militia units began to be reassembled.

Although there may have been others who shared his name, it is interesting to note that a Thomas Moore appears on the Northumberland Militia lists, precisely in the period our Thomas would be available.[140] He enrolled in Lieut-Col. Matthew Bell's Company, on 24 November 1781—when Thomas from Lesbury would be nineteen-turning-twenty. He is listed in the company examined from

25th December to 24th June and at Chatham camp, 2 September 1782, but for the examination at Morpeth on 25 February 1783, he was registered as sick. In May of that year, there was a reduction of the Northumberland Militia at Alnwick.[141] Almost ten years later in the examination held June to December 1792, Thomas Moore no longer appears. Is the absence explained by the fact that, by that time, Mr Moore from Lesbury had already departed for New South Wales?

Exact identification of this militia-man with the young man from Lesbury may not be possible. Since the 1758 Act, Thomas would not be excluded even if serving an apprenticeship. But, perhaps his trade may speak against the identification, since his craft oriented him towards the sea. As the national anxiety was increasing, he may have been a candidate less for the militia, than for impress into the Navy.

Whatever the case, 1792 was certainly a good time for Thomas Moore, ship's carpenter, to leave England's troubled shores. This was the year that 'the volcano of the French Revolution burst forth in all its terrific grandeur, and fixed the attention of every civilized country'.[142] By 10 December, the Northumberland Militia had been ordered to assemble in Alnwick. After several months of effigies of Thomas Paine burning throughout the country, on 13th 'the common council of Newcastle passed resolutions expressive of their determination to support the constitution, to repress the dangerous spirit of disaffection, and to promote a veneration for the laws'. On the 17th another meeting of 'the gentlemen, clergy, freeholders, burgesses, and inhabitants of the town was held in the Guildhall, when resolutions were adopted to support the magistracy in preserving the peace, and in bringing to legal punishment all persons concerned in seditious publications'. By February the following year, 'the seamen belonging to the port of Newcastle associated to defend themselves against the threatened impress', and a subscription was opened to encourage volunteers for the Navy.[143] By 1793, the war with France had begun.

THOMAS MOORE IN LONDON

Moore's exact movements after his apprenticeship are not known, but if we presume he joined the *Britannia* in 1783 as he came out of

CHAPTER 1 ⚓ Lesbury: the Boy Becomes a Man (1762–1792)

his apprenticeship and she out of the Sunderland dockyard, then his destiny at that point became tied up with hers.

After two years of voyaging, she was back in Sunderland for repairs in 1785, at which point she was also sheathed with copper over boards.[144] If Moore had not joined her in 1783, this was a second occasion when he could have picked her up in the Northeast.

Once on board, the *Britannia* would have taken Thomas to London, for this was where the Southern Whale Fishery based its operations. When he was in port, he no doubt used the opportunity to visit his sister Sally, her husband William Clark, and their family. It is possible that William himself worked for the Southern Fishery. In Joseph Moore's 1806 letter to Sally, he speaks of William Raven as if he is William Clark's master. Was the Captain William Clark who sailed the Southern Fishery's *Sparrow* out of Yarmouth on 6 November 1789, Sally's husband?[145] If there was some connection through his sister, then this may have assisted young Thomas gaining the position on the *Britannia*. Or, alternatively, perhaps it was Thomas getting the position that somehow landed Sally her husband.

The first piece of extant evidence about Moore's adult life dates to after Thomas arrived in London. On 6 July 1790, John McCormick, Grand Secretary of the freemasons 1785–1790, issued a travelling certificate for Thomas Moore. It attested that 'Brother Thomas Moore is a regular Registered Freemason in the Lodge No 3 in the Kingdom of England and has during his Stay amongst them behaved himself as became an honest and worthy Brother'.[146] This Lodge also went by the name the 'Antients Lodge No 3B', or the 'Friendship' Lodge, and it met at the George and Vulture Tavern, Lower Shadwell. The 'Antients' Lodge was opposed to those affiliated with the Premier Grand Lodge of England. It was formed in 1751, by a group of mainly Irish masons, who were not happy with the English Lodge.

There is no evidence that Moore continued to be a member of a lodge after he arrived in Sydney, although several of his friends were masons, including Governor Macquarie, John Harris, and Robert Campbell. According to Masonic records, Thomas became a mason in 1790, there is no record of him belonging to another lodge in England, and his membership had ceased by 1791. Travelling certificates such as this one were issued to enable a member of one lodge, if on a journey, to be accepted into another.[147] In other words, in July 1790 Thomas was getting ready to sail.

If Moore was already aboard the *Britannia* by 1790, after the ship was surveyed in August, he sailed under W.Warng and/ or D. Young from London to 'the Straits'.[148] This could simply be a way of referring to the waters at the other side of the world, which might mean that the *Britannia* followed the example of the *Emilia*, sent by Enderby around Cape Horn in 1789 into the Pacific in search of whales. But it could also be used more precisely, which means that Moore would have sailed to the Straits of Malacca, the corridor to the lucrative trade of places like Batavia and Bengal and, for those permitted, even China. With that voyage over, in 1791 Young commanded her on a voyage to Antigua in the Caribbean.[149] Then in 1792, *Lloyds Register* again listed her as sailing to this location, but plans must have changed. For from mid-February 1792, the *Britannia* was sailing for New South Wales,[150] with Thomas Moore as her ship's carpenter, and Captain William Raven in command.[151]

WILLIAM RAVEN

Moore and his family would be entwined with Captain William Raven (1756–1814) for the next two decades. Raven was a larger than life character—as Daniel Paine would say when he met him in May 1796, he was a *Great Commander* (truly so for he was almost as big as three common sized men)![152]

When he joined the Navy in the West Indies, although he was only twenty-two he entered as master of the sloop *Tobago*—an indication of him having already acquired considerable ability, possibly in merchant ships. Despite being wounded twice in 1780 while master of the *Albion*, he survived 'a dozen sea battles against French and Spanish privateers in the West Indies'.[153] In July 1783 Trinity House examiners declared him fit to be master of any of His Majesty's ships of the third-rate, and he took charge of the *Grampus* for three years.[154] In May 1786, he received a certificate for first-rates, but his next naval service would not be until 1791, with a brief stint on the *Duke*.[155] At

CHAPTER 1 ⚓ *Lesbury: the Boy Becomes a Man (1762–1792)* 47

an even later stage, in 1798 he would also take HMS *Buffalo* to New South Wales to replace the *Supply*.[156] But in 1786, now fully rated, he left the Navy for another sort of adventuring—just in time to avoid the outbreak of war in 1793.[157]

On 18 August of that year, the British Government announced the Royal decision to establish a penal colony at Botany Bay.[158] The subsequent need for convict transportation, as well as the possibility of new avenues of trade and commercial ventures afforded by Britain moving into the South Seas, created interest amongst entrepreneurially minded consortia such as the Enderby's Southern Whale Fishery.

In 1786, William Raven was in command of *Saucy Ben*, owned by Hall and Co, London, but by 1788 he was on the *Jackall*, owned by St Barbe and Co, London.[159] He was still in charge of the *Jackall* in 1789, which had evidently been engaged in sealing, for the remaining seal skins of her cargo were advertised at the end of July.[160] According to a list of ships from the Southern Whale Fishery cleared 1 Jan to 1 November 1789, just two weeks after the sale Raven and the *Jackall* embarked on her next voyage.[161]

This list of the shipping associated with the Southern Whale Fishery was published 'as the importance of this Fishery, and its increasing trade, do not seem to be fully known to the public, nor its apparent beneficial consequences clearly apprehended'. When the House of Commons had discussed the Fishery in 1786, it had agreed to a sliding scale of bounties to be paid to encourage not only tonnage of oil, but speed of delivery.[162] After the Spanish had seized some of the cargo of English ships in Nootka Sound, out of a claim for Spain's prior sovereignty in this part of the world, the House of Lords discussed the matter, during which it was requested that information be laid before the House about the state of the trade to the Northwest coast of America and of the Southern Whale Fishery. When it was pointed out that there was no trade to the North West—to which the opposition rightly suggested that if this were so then no ships could have been seized in Nootka Sound—the motion was amended to request information only about the Southern Fishery.[163] This request had come from the Lords in May of 1790, just 3 months before the advertisement appeared.[164]

While Raven was still on the *Saucy Ben*, the Government began acting on the planned Botany Bay settlement. On 12 October 1786, Arthur Phillip R.N. received his commission as Governor and on 25 April 1787 he received his instructions.[165] (Plate 8). On 13 May 1787, the two naval escorts, six convict transports, and three storeships for food and supplies that made up the First Fleet sailed from Portsmouth.[166]

Rachel Turner on the Lady Juliana

At the end of that same year, as the First Fleet was still sailing towards its destination, a young woman of about twenty-seven was tried at the Old Bailey on 12 December, for 'feloniously stealing, on the 29th day of October last' a pair of metal butter boats and various items of cloth from the household of Cleophas Comber, where she had served for about six months.[167] The total value of the items stolen came to £2.5s. While her mistress was 'lying in the straw' (waiting to give birth), Rachel Turner was accused of the theft and the items were discovered in her box. At the trial it came out that the nurse had been saying some things which implied a relationship between Comber and Rachel, and the defence suggested that this had caused problems with his wife, which Comber denied. Rachel had put her mark on a confession at the time, but the court was not impressed with it, since it was 'a confession of the law and the fact too'. Although Comber had denied that there was any promise or threat made before the confession, Rachel told the court that he had told her that if she confessed, he would forgive her. Despite Comber himself admitting she was previously of good character, and two witnesses swearing to the same, Rachel was found guilty. The court then rebuked her for instructing her Counsel 'to throw out such insinuations, the object of which was to destroy the domestic peace of your master and mistress; therefore it will be considered in your punishment'. She was sentenced to transportation for seven years.

Just over eighteen months later, Rachel Turner was amongst the 226 female convicts placed upon the *Lady Juliana*, which sailed for Sydney on 29 July 1789—well ahead of the rest of the Second Fleet which did not leave until January 1790. Most of the women on board were in Rachel's age bracket, although there were still plenty younger than she was.[168] (Figure 9).

CHAPTER 1 ⚓ Lesbury: the Boy Becomes a Man (1762–1792)

Age	Number
over 50	8
40–49	15
30–39	40
20–29	116
10–19	51
14	6
13	1
11 (Youngest)	1

Figure 9: Ages of female convicts on Lady Juliana.

It took a horrendous 309 days before the *Lady Juliana* reached Sydney on June 1790. When Collins later recounted the October 1792 arrival of her surgeon in the colony for his second visit, he used the occasion to once again shudder at the memory of this voyage:

> [Oct 1792] There arrived in the *Royal Admiral* as a superintendant charged with the care of the convicts, Mr. Richard Alley, who formerly belonged to the *Lady Juliana* transport, in quality of surgeon, in the memorable voyage of that ship to this colony; a voyage that could never be thought on by an inhabitant of it without exciting a most painful sensation.[169]

In terms of the health of the women on their arrival, however, the situation was surprisingly good. Chaplain Richard Johnson (Plate 14) reported that: 'The *Lady Juliana* brought out from England two hundred and twenty six women convicts, out of which she had only buried five, though they had been on board for about fifteen months'.[170] As the other ships in the Second Fleet arrived, it was discovered that they were not so fortunate—even though their sailing time was half that of *Lady Juliana*.[171] As well as commiserating and praying with these later arrivals, and handing out books to those who could read, Johnson helped the sick out of his own stores, gaining the prisoners' respect. One of them reported that if it were not for his assistance, few would have recovered.[172] (Figure 10 compared with 11).

Ship	Number	Died on board	Landed sick
Neptune	520	163	269
Scarborough	252	68	96
Surprise	211	42	121

Figure 10: R. Johnson's Estimates of mortality and morbidity on Second Fleet ships.

	Convict	Marines
Male	36	1
Female	4	1
Children	5	1

Figure 11: John White's statement of mortality and morbidity on First Fleet ships.

Overall Deaths: 48 (out of 1014).
Mortality rate amongst convicts: 3 per cent.

On the first Sunday after *Lady Juliana* arrived, Chaplain Johnson provided divine service for her female convicts. According to David Collins, 'Mr Johnson, with much propriety, in his discourse, touched upon their situation, and described it so forcibly as to draw tears from many who were the least hardened among them'. Robinson assumed that Rachel would have been amongst those women whom Governor King later (in 1806) described as 'well-behaved'. Unlike 'the worst description of females who come to the colony', that is, those who follow their convict husbands who become receivers of stolen goods or display dissolute lives, these others are 'amongst the comparative few who came from the English counties [...] who soon after their arrival are selected and applied for by the industrious part of the settlers, with whom they either marry or cohabit; nor does a separation often occur, several making themselves very useful not only in domestic concerns and rearing stock, but also in agriculture, &c'. If this assumption is correct, then perhaps Rachel was also at the lower end of the spectrum of hardness, and it would be interesting to know how she responded to the evangelical preaching of Richard Johnson that day.[173]

Rachel was assigned as servant to Surgeon-General John White—who had arrived on the First Fleet, but was still living under canvas at this stage. John White led a very busy existence in these early days of the colony, giving himself not only to his medical work, but also to exploration and the collection of specimens of fauna and flora.[174] Not previously a natural historian, he was prompted into this by a friend, but soon he devoted almost every spare daylight hour to collecting, rightly earning him the pride of place as 'Australia's first resident naturalist of any public significance'.[175] He published a *Journal* that was well received and widely read, but it stops in November 1788 and the notes he made of his next six years in Sydney are now lost.[176] (Plate 16).

He was about 30 years of age when he arrived with the First Fleet in January 1788. In the following August, perhaps exacerbated by 'celebratory alcohol' after the celebrations of the Prince of Wales' birthday, Chief Surgeon White fired shots at his assistant, William Balmain, in Australia's first duel—either expressing or creating a rift between the two that would never heal.[177]

Early in 1789 he dealt with an outbreak he thought was smallpox, which reduced the aboriginal population by half. White brought four of the local people in for treatment. Two died, but a boy of about eight, Nanbaree, and a girl of about thirteen, Abaroo, survived. Abaroo went to live with Richard and Mary Johnson, and White adopted the boy, renaming him Andrew Snape Hamond Douglas White—the first three names after White's patron—although he was still better known by his own name. He later acted as White's gamekeeper and hunter, served as a seaman on the *Reliance* from 1795, and for a time with Flinders on the *Investigator* in 1803. He died on 12 July 1821 aged about 40, at James Squires' home in Kissing Point, and was buried in the same grave as Bennelong—the aboriginal man captured and brought to the settlement in 1789 and who returned to England with Arthur Phillip in 1792 to be presented to George III.[178] (Plate 17).

By 1790 White had become rather depressed at the state of his surroundings. Throughout 1789 the health of the colony had improved, but the food supplies were diminishing. The *Sirius* was wrecked at Norfolk Island in March 1790, and Governor Phillip was forced to send his only remaining vessel, the *Supply*, to Batavia to stave off the colony's starvation.[179] Amongst the dispatches for England on board, White wrote a desperate letter to a friend, which was later published in the *Public Advertiser*.[180] He reported that the colony's supplies would be gone in seven months, and that past efforts at growing grain did not hold much hope for the future. His only solution was to immediately withdraw everyone from the settlement. White and his assistants began fishing every second night to supplement the food supply. Then on 3 June 1790, the *Lady Juliana*, sailed through the heads, bringing some much needed food, along with a cargo of female convicts.[181]

Presumably because of his position, Surgeon White accompanied Captain Tench to be among the first to board the *Lady Juliana* when she arrived in heavy seas at the Harbour's mouth.[182] Rienits comments that 'for White, it was to mean an end to the hunger of the soul that gnaws at men too long apart from women', for among the convicts was Rachel Turner, who 'became White's housekeeper and afterwards his mistress, and then [...] the mother of his child'.[183]

As the three remaining vessels from the Second Fleet (the *Guardian* having been wrecked) arrived, the medical team was stretched to the limit. 'Neglect, brutality and deliberate starvation had killed on the voyage more than 250 men and 11 women of a total of a few over one thousand embarked'.[184] Even as the ships sailed into the harbour those who had lately died were thrown overboard to be later cast upon the shore. Of about 750 convicts to land, about two-thirds required hospitalisation, thus adding further strain to the overstretched food supplies, without giving any return in the form of labour or any other positive contribution.[185] In October 1790, the *Supply* returned without much food itself, but reporting that a Dutch ship was on its way with more. When the *Waaksamheyd* arrived on 17 December full rations could at last be restored, and so 'the most critical [year] in the colony's history' ended on a much better note.[186]

Since his arrival, John White had been accommodated in a tent. Now assigned Rachel as his housekeeper, presumably she needed a house to keep. So, by the end of 1790 plans were in place to build him a house near the hospital, by April 1791 work had begun, and by June, the Surgeon-General and Rachel Turner finally had a roof over their head.[187]

This was just in time for the next onslaught. On 9 July 1791, the *Mary Ann* arrived as the first of the ten convict-laden vessels of the Third Fleet, the rest of which dribbled in from August to September.[188] With conditions improved from the notorious Second Fleet, fewer of the 2000 convicts embarked had died at sea, and relatively few required hospital care because of the voyage. John White was no doubt relieved, that is, until severe dysentery began to break out and the number of sick and the death-rate increased rapidly.[189] As 1792 opened, the situation was no better and by March most of the recently arrived convicts were still unfit for work.[190] By April famine was once again a serious concern.[191] With the colony again on the brink of disaster, relief began to arrive with a cargo of grain from Calcutta, brought by the *Atlantic* on 20 June. Five weeks later more relief arrived from England. Bringing clothing, flour and salt meat, and news that two more ships were on their way, into Port Jackson sailed William Raven's *Britannia*. (Plate 20)

THOMAS MOORE SAILS FOR NEW SOUTH WALES

When John White's depressed letter from New South Wales was published in the *National Advertiser* on 31 December 1790, no doubt its rather public complaint prompted people in many circles—Government and otherwise—to take some action on behalf of the colony to ensure its survival. It is not hard to imagine the commercially minded men of the Southern Fishery seeing this as a potential opportunity. Enderby, Champion and St Barbe were pressing for the southern waters to be opened up, thus breaking the East India Company monopoly. Now with a starving colony to feed, they managed to secure the contract for transporting stores—as well as a license from the Company to permit their fishing in those waters for a further three years.

On 23 Jan 1792 *Britannia*, Captain Raven, was cleared for Botany Bay,[192] and on 16 February she sailed from Greenwich,[193] laden with the much-needed supplies. After touching at Falmouth, she arrived in Port

Jackson just twenty-three weeks later.[194] The *Britannia*'s voyages to New South Wales and beyond were recorded in some detail by her fourth officer, Robert Murray, from the time of sailing through until he joined Brampton's *Endeavour* in August 1795.[195] Murray's journal has survived.

Figure 12. Sailor's day symbols used by Murray in his journal and Moore in his business note books.

By 2 March 1792, the ship reached Teneriffe, in the Canary Islands, crossed the Tropic of Cancer on the 7th, the equator on 7 April and the Tropic of Capricorn on 25th. On 2 June the ship received injury after being struck a heavy blow by a sperm whale. As ship's carpenter, Thomas Moore would have had some work to do to repair the damage. A week later strong gales caused the wheel ropes to jam in the lading block, causing the ship to breach and the whole of the decks to be underwater—more work for the carpenter. On 27 June, Murray specifically notes that, in the midst of strong breezes and squally conditions, 'carpenter stocking anchors'. On 24 July part of New South Wales was spotted, then Pigeon House Mountain on 25th, and at 7pm on the 26th they reached the entrance to Port Jackson, making sail for the heads at dawn the next day (27th). The Colonial Office had calculated that the colony at Sydney Cove would run out of beef and pork rations on 29 July 1792, and the *Britannia*, carrying 101,664 pounds of beef, 203,520 pounds of pork, and 48,809 pounds of flour, arrived on the 26th.[196] No doubt this impeccable timing was the first event to enhance William Raven's reputation. Just on a decade later David Collins would look back on Raven's initial period in New South Wales and say that his 'services to the colony in the private ship *Britannia* cannot easily be forgotten'.[197]

CHAPTER 1 ⚓ *Lesbury: the Boy Becomes a Man (1762–1792)*

THOMAS MOORE'S FIRST TASTE OF SYDNEY (JULY–OCTOBER 1792)

By 8pm on 27 July, the *Britannia* was safely moored in Sydney Cove and Thomas Moore could begin to take a good, long look at the town that would one day be his home. (Plate 22)

For the next month, one of the main activities in Sydney Cove was the discharge of the *Britannia*. This had already begun for the *Atlantic*, since her arrival in 20 June. Major Grose was very unimpressed with the quality of stores supplied by the *Atlantic*, claiming that 'not a single article was received by the *Atlantic* which in any other part of the world would have been served as a ration', and exclaiming, 'to what cause the colony was indebted for the trash brought by the *Atlantic* I never could discover'.[198] Unfortunately, Raven's cargo was also found deficient, both in amount and quality, and only what was deemed merchantable was paid for, and the rest was immediately sold at public auction for stock feed.[199] Nevertheless, with the arrival of the stores from both vessels, the colonists felt that their fortunes had now changed:

> In the consequence of the arrival of the *Britannia*, the commissary was on the following day directed to issue, *until further orders*, the following weekly ration, viz to each man 4 pounds of maize, 3 pounds of soujee, 7 pounds of beef, or in lieu thereof 4 lbs. of pork, 3 pints of peas or dholl, and ½ a pound of rice.
>
> Two thirds of the man's ration was directed to be issued to each woman and to every child above ten years of age; one half of the man's ration to each child above two, and under ten years of age; and one fourth of the man's ration to each child under two years of age.
>
> Thus happily was the colony once more put upon something like a full ration of provisions; a change in our situation that gave universal satisfaction, as at the hour of the arrival of the *Britannia* there were in the public store only twenty-four days salt provisions for the settlement at the ration then issued.[200]

Presumably, during this period, Moore was engaged in the usual duties of a ship's carpenter while not at sea—checking the ship for damage or wear, repairing any damage, securing on shore any supplies specific for his role, including plank and other timbers that may be required on the next voyage. Since carpenters cut such timber from the forests themselves, this would have given Moore his first taste of Australian timber in the Australian bush. Little did he know how many more times he would go on such expeditions.

Over the next few years, Robert Murray used each opportunity afforded by the *Britannia*'s presence in Sydney Cove to reflect upon the state of the colony. His first impressions were very positive. Trade was well regulated—still enabling a moderate profit of 200 per cent; criminal justice was meted out by Governor, Judge-Advocate and the Criminal Court; every provision was given to those who wish to cultivate a farm; and, in general,

> it is universally acknowledged that the present Governor [Phillip] has done wonders. The great quantity of land leased, and in cultivation, is a proof sufficient of the abilities of its Governor.[201]

Overall, things were proceeding well under Governor Phillip. Just four and a half years after the First Fleet arrived, Thomas Moore was able to see the infant colony struggling to get on its feet. A fair system of commerce permitting a moderate profit had been established; processes for criminal justice were in place; and a group of pioneering farmers had enthusiastically begun to cultivate the soil, such as it was. Commerce, justice, and the land: three things that would occupy Moore for the rest of his days in New South Wales. As he became acquainted with Sydney from July to October 1792, the colony's promising beginnings under Governor Phillip surely struck a chord with his own pioneering spirit.

Through his friendship with Raven, perhaps this was also the occasion that Thomas Moore became acquainted with John White, who later became one of his friends.

White's recently built brick dwelling near to the Cove when finished would have been a perfect place to entertain the visitors from England who brought relief to the colony—and to his own anxieties—with such providential timing. And if Thomas Moore was amongst the Surgeon's new friends, then he would have met Rachel Turner for the first time, as she served the guests in her new home.[202]

On the surface of things, it probably looked like Surgeon White was prepared to settle in Sydney for some time. But, in fact, he was

CHAPTER 1 ⚓ *Lesbury: the Boy Becomes a Man (1762–1792)*

increasingly thinking about going home. The strain on Surgeon White since the arrival of the Third Fleet must have been enormous, with only four medical men to assist him with the mounting crisis.[203] When, due to declining health, Governor Phillip decided to return to England on the *Atlantic* in October 1792,[204] White also began to think of returning home. In December 1792, he informed his patron Hamond, now a Commissioner of the Navy, that he had applied for leave of absence or permission to return to England on half pay.[205]

Perhaps even in these early days Thomas Moore was beginning to catch a vision of other possible futures for his life—now such a long way from Lesbury.

2
ADVENTURING
(OCTOBER 1792 to SEPTEMBER 1796)

On 28 July 1792, Raven's crew began preparing to discharge the cargo. When the task was completed, by 19 August the *Britannia* was no longer in the service of Government.[1] Despite Raven's aim to profit from sealing and whaling, things turned out a little differently from what he had planned. From 1792 to 1796 the *Britannia*'s 'real business […] was feeding and fostering the colony of New South Wales, bringing cargoes from the Cape of Good Hope, Brazil, Batavia and India'.[2]

THE BRITANNIA'S VOYAGE TO THE CAPE, VIA DUSKY BAY

While the rest of the crew were unloading, as carpenter Thomas Moore would begin to prepare the *Britannia* for sea. Repairs had to be done. Fresh timber cut from the bush and brought on board. If he had heard the rumours of Port Jackson's magnificent harbour with timber reaching down to the water's edge, now was Moore's chance to see it with his own eyes and to begin to gain experience with the native timbers of New South Wales. (Plate 22).

On 8 September the ship was hauled out of the cove and on the 10th they worked her down to Bradley's Head, where they anchored, wind bound. (Plate 20, detail). While waiting there, Murray reports that:

> We were chartered by 10 officers of the Civil and Military, to proceed to the Cape of Good Hope, by way of Cape Horn and Sta Catherina, leave being granted us to stop on our way at Dusky Bay in New Zealand, to leave a number of hands to collect Seal skins for the China market while we performed our voyage.[3] (Plates 20 and 36).

The Officers of the NSW Corps were beginning to make their move. They recognised advantage in their position, and opportunity in these troubled early times of the colony. Major Francis Grose had arrived on 14 February 1792, and a letter home in April showed that he had already noticed some possibilities. (Plate 9). He described the colony in Edenic terms:[4]

> to my great comfort and astonishment, I find there is neither the scarcity that was represented to me, nor the barren sands I was taught to imagine I should see; the whole place is a garden, on which fruit and vegetables of every description grow in the greatest luxuriance. […]
>
> I live in as good a house as I desire; and the farm of my predecessor, which has been given to me, produces a sufficiency of every thing for my family.

Things were so good, in fact—as he added in a postscript: 'You may rest assured, that hunger and misery attack none here, but those who are too idle to help themselves'.

But there was also something missing in Grose's new Eden:

> Nothing is wanting here but oxen and black cattle; within five Miles of my habitation there is food in abundance for many thousand head of cattle; and we have not 20 Cows in the Colony. Could we once be supplied with Cattle, I do not believe we should have occasion to trouble Old England again.

CHAPTER 2 ↓ *Adventuring (October 1792–September 1796)* 61

Grose was certainly not someone who was 'too idle to help himself'. Hainsworth has pointed out that a 'substantial body of legend' has sprung up around the exploits of Grose and his companions. However,

> whatever their shortcomings as officers and gentlemen, the trading officers of the New South Wales Corps were the founders of Australian commerce.[5]

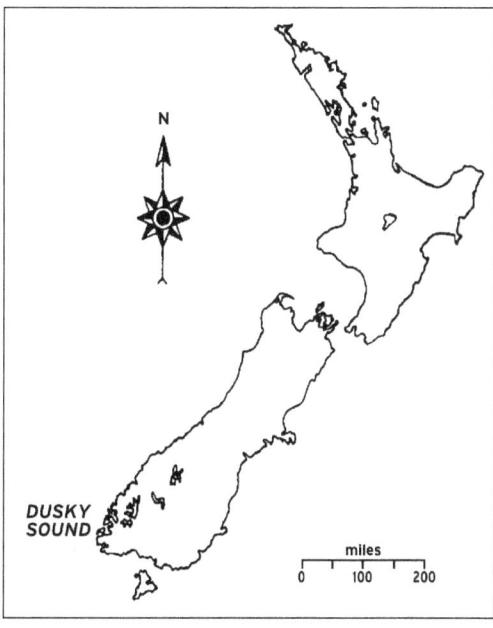

Figure 13. Map of New Zealand showing Dusky Bay.

On 2 April 1792, precisely the same day Grose was writing home from his newfound garden of God in the South Seas, his fellow officers launched Australia's first trading venture, when they paid Captain Manning of the *Pitt* £1440 in Paymaster's bills, just before his departure for Bengal.[6] At least eight of the officers of the Corps had pooled their resources, presumably to buy goods from India for on-sale in the colony. (Figure 14). Although Hainsworth does not list Major Grose as a participant in the 2 April transaction, the opportunity it presented to shape a new future for himself surely must lie behind the excitement he expressed in his letter to his unknown correspondent.

Their means of payment is significant for their success. When the British Government sent the First Fleet to Botany Bay to establish a penal colony there were no plans to provide it with its own legal tender. With everyone either being a convict or a Government employee sent to look after them, the entire population initially was victualled from the Government stores, so perhaps the means of purchasing goods did not even seem necessary. But anyone who gave it much thought surely would have seen that this situation could not last too long. For the first decades, the lack of currency introduced many problems into New South Wales, left to find its own ways of payment for goods and services.

> Throughout the period to 1821, New South Wales had no Treasury and no local, officially-issued money, minted or printed. The long years during which this situation rendered the development of commerce difficult and its practice hazardous demonstrate how slight was the home Government's active interest in commercial development. Meanwhile the currency situation together with the difficulty of finding staples to export or accessible markets in which to sell such staples as they [were] found, combined to make the prison half of the colony of enormous importance to the traders, and indeed to all settlers of whatever origin. Of all the prison's institutions the Commissariat Store was the most important and influential.[7]

In order to feed the convicts, and the civil and military establishment, and other free settlers, the Commissariat had to make purchases from local farmers or traders, and from ship's captains bringing goods from elsewhere. The Commissariat paid in bills on the British Treasury, making it the biggest source of sterling in the colony.

Officer	Amount (£)
Captain Nepean	337
Captain Hill	308
Adjutant Rowley	295
Lieutenant Beckwith	66
Lieutenant Laycock	60
Lieutenant Laing	30
Ensign McKellar	22
Ensign Piper	20

Figure 14. Officers of the New South Wales Corps who paid Captain Manning, *Pitt*, in Paymaster's Bills, April 1792.[8]

Because the paymaster of the New South Wales Corps (who, for many years, was John Macarthur) 'could draw upon the regiment's London banker-agents so far as its funds or credit would stretch',[9] he was the second biggest source of sterling. Apart from whatever amount of gold or silver that came into the colony with convicts, free settlers, soldiers, or passing ship's captains, that was basically it for sterling. It is understandable, therefore, that a complicated barter system grew up, with payments being made in goods, or crops, through Store receipts later consolidated into Treasury notes by the Governor, and, in time, promissory notes which themselves became 'currency' for the colony. Although the soldiers of the Corps were also paid in 'property' (goods), or in copper coin, right up until the time of Governor Bligh (August 1806 onwards),[10] their officers received Paymaster's bills. Because this gave them a source of funds that were welcomed by the ship's captains, this also gave them an advantage over all others when it came to purchasing goods from beyond the colony and is probably the reason they gained a monopoly in the 1790s. In 1792 to 1798, just seven years, the officers invested £36,844 in Paymasters bills.[11] Because their Paymaster's bills gave them a direct supply of sterling, which was not available to the other settlers and civil officers, this automatically gave them 'the lion's share' of the other Treasury bills. By dint of circumstance, therefore, rather than contrivance, they were set up to become the colony's middle-men, the 'funnel through which imported goods flowed out to the settler, and through which in return grain and meat then flowed back from the settler to the Commissariat'.[12] (See Figure 15).

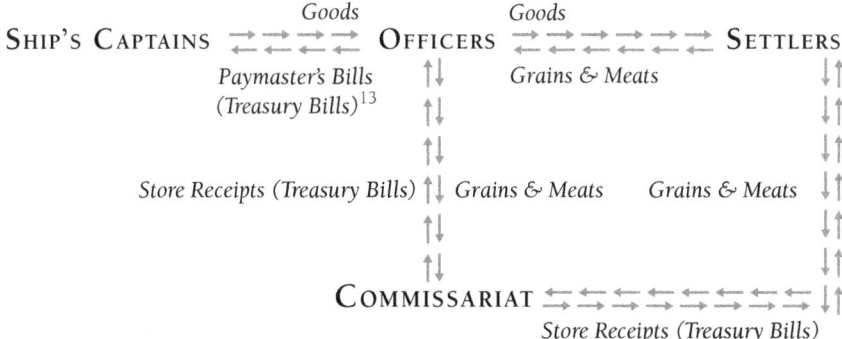

Figure 15. Role of the Officers in Commercial Transactions in 1790s.

When the *Royal Admiral*, Captain Bond, arrived in October 1792, shops were opened in Parramatta and Sydney to retail her cargo. The officers bought a great deal of her cargo, their Paymaster's bills being readily acceptable to Bond. Presumably their purchases were for on-selling to other settlers at something of a profit. It was also an historic moment when licenses were issued to some now unknown persons to retail the spirits in Bond's cargo, with unfortunate consequences prescient of future problems in the colony. Governor Phillip, about to leave the colony, was disappointed to see the opportunity of this influx of bounty squandered away:

> Several of the settlers [...] conducted themselves with the greatest impropriety, beating heir wives, destroying their crops in the grounds and destroying each others property. [...] The indulgence which [...] the Governor intended for their benefit was most shamefully abused, and what he suffered them to purchase with a view to their future comfort, was retailed among themselves at a scandalous profit.[14]

October presented another trading opportunity in that the *Britannia* was preparing to sail—and Grose seized it with both hands. Murray's somewhat confused comment on the Bradley's Head transaction appears to have been written with the wisdom of some later hindsight:

> It may not be improper to remark that we were to purchase at the Cape of Good Hope articles of trade, exclusive of the Cattle, such as Brandy, Wine, Sugar, Tobacco, Price Goods &c &c, for the use of the New South Wales Corps, it being a custom to pay them in one article or other of this sort, at only 200 per cent, which was at this time a moderate [price], and the greatest profit suggested to be gained as I shall hereafter have occasion to mention this in a most explicit manner.[15]

Grose had initially gone to Governor Phillip on 2 October with the suggestion of hiring the *Britannia*, but had met with a cool reception. Phillip questioned the propriety of hiring a private vessel, already granted a fishing licence by the East India Company, not wishing to open up 'a door to contraband trade'. He also questioned the necessity of such a measure, since, as Raven had reported, two further shiploads

CHAPTER 2 ⚓ *Adventuring (October 1792–September 1796)* 65

of stores were on their way. If it was necessary, then it would best be done by sending a vessel already in 'public employ', such as the *Atlantic*, already lying in the harbour, or one of the two vessels reported to be on their way.[16] After initially arriving on 20 August 1791, the *Atlantic* had had permission to proceed to Calcutta before returning home, but she had been hired by Grose to bring further supplies from Calcutta back to Sydney, sailing on 25 October. This also meant that 'every officer had had the opportunity to order goods by her'.[17] (Figure 16).

Major Grose wrote to Governor Phillip two days after their conversation to report that, after gathering his captains together and pooling their funds, the *Britannia* had, in fact, been chartered. Raven had agreed to 'let his ship for the sum of £2,000; and eleven shares of £200 each were subscribed to purchase the stock and other articles'.[18] From 10 to 22 October, fourteen Paymaster's bills were written to Raven, totalling £1,922.[19] In explaining why this had been necessary, Grose's description of the state of affairs is somewhat jaded compared to the Edenic terms he used just six months earlier:[20]

> The situation of the soldiers under my command, who at this time have scarcely shoes to their feet, and who have no other comforts than the reduced and unwholesome rations served out from the stores, has induced me to assemble the captains of my corps for the purpose of consulting what could be done for their relief and accommodation.

The captains had agreed, pooled their funds, and hired the *Britannia*, settling matters with Raven, 'who is also an owner'. Grose therefore requested Phillip that he might:

> by representing the necessities of my soldiers, protect this ship from interruption as much as you can, and that you will assist us to escape the miseries of that precarious existence we have hitherto been so constantly exposed to.

Phillip was not pleased. The same day, he wrote a reply to Grose, remonstrating with this decision and repeating the arguments he had put to him two days previously. He then wrote a letter to his superior in England, Henry Dundas, explaining the situation and enclosing

Grose's letter and his own reply. Here he protests that he had informed Grose that he had a very different opinion about the propriety and necessity of this action, but admits that he could not prevent it. Nevertheless, he agrees that he does not think his Majesty's service will suffer, given the terms expressed in Grose's letter. He concludes by requesting copies of the Acts governing the Southern Fishery. Presumably Phillip had realised that, now that *Britannia* had arrived representing that consortium, he and future Governors will need to know the law respecting their operations. Phillip also hints that his health is not good, and hopes that 'after the arrival of the first ships', he will be at liberty to return to England, from where he feels he can render 'greatest service' to the colony by showing 'what may, and what may not, be expected from it'.

POSITION	PERSON	ESTIMATED SHARE
Paymaster	John Macarthur	Very profitable share
Company Commanders:	Paterson, Johnston, Foveaux, Hill, Rowley, Nepean	The lion's share
Junior Officers:	Beckwith, Clephan, Prentice, Piper, McKellar, Laing, Surgeon Harris, Chaplain Blain	A more modest share (they had no company funds with which to speculate)

Figure 16. Estimated share of profits from Officer Trading.[21]

The charter of the *Britannia* was a done deal. In November the officers paid a further £500 to purchase goods, including rum, gin, wine and tobacco, from the American ship *Philadelphia*, but *Britannia* transaction demonstrates that 'the officers were not content simply to make casual purchases from chance callers for re-sale at highly inflated prices. They were now fully-fledged importers ordering specific merchandise'.[22] Nevertheless, they did this fairly infrequently over the next decade:

CHAPTER 2 ⚓ *Adventuring (October 1792–September 1796)*   67

> The chartering of the *Britannia* in 1792 and 1794 and of the *Thynne* in 1799 appears to have been the only instances of ships chartered by officers to procure cargoes. Otherwise they seem to have purchased cargoes brought speculatively, persuaded captains to return with specified merchandise, or perhaps to have ordered through their Calcutta agent, Augustus Beyer.[23]

As Raven accepted the deal with the Officers off Bradley's Head in October 1792, he saw his profits multiplying, with this new deal adding further cash to his original scheme, which remained unimpeded. But the new destination required 'a new set of operations', including cutting hay for 40 head of cattle they were to bring from the Cape.

> The ship was well calculated for bringing cattle, having a very good between-decks; and artificers from the corps were immediately employed to fit her with stalls proper for the reception and accommodation of cows, horses, etc. A quantity of hay was put on board sufficient to lessen considerably the expense of that article at the Cape; and she was ready for sea by the middle of the month.[24]

While they were refitting, Raven had another drama to keep him occupied. About midnight on 10 October, while Raven was asleep in a hut on shore, a man entered his hut and took his watch and a pair of knee-buckles. Raven woke up as he was leaving the room, in time to rescue a box containing a valuable time-piece and some money. A couple of days later a settler, Charles Williams informed on convict Richard Sutton, who had apparently attempted to sell the goods to him. The matter was heard in court, but Sutton had a good enough alibi to be acquitted, even though those who sat on the court were convinced that he had committed the crime.[25]

By October 22, they were ready for sea and worked out on 23rd, Raven carrying Governor Phillip's despatches for England containing a request for twelve months' provisions for the colony.[26] Murray's log begins again as the *Britannia* left Port Jackson on 25 October 1792, that night noting that they had spotted a school of sperm whales, given chase, and managed to kill one of them, which yielded ten barrels of oil.[27] At 2am on 3 November the snow-capped peaks of New Zealand were sighted. Heavy seas made it difficult to enter Dusky Bay, but on Tuesday 6th, they had anchored in Facile Harbour, and two days later they made Pickersgill Harbour.[28] (See Figure 17; Plates 20, 36).

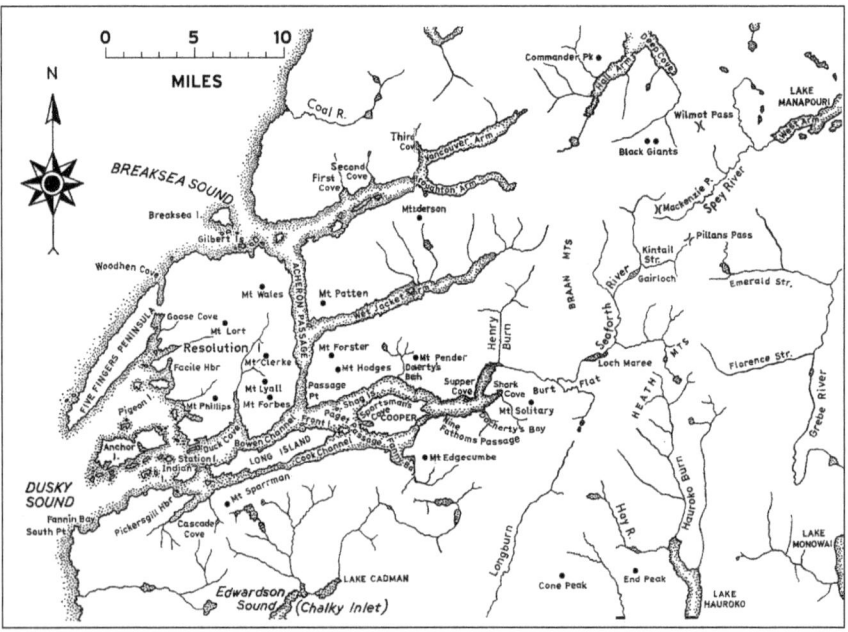

Figure 17. Dusky Bay, New Zealand.

THOMAS MOORE AT DUSKY BAY (6 NOVEMBER 1792 TO 19 OCTOBER 1793)

The dreadful weather of their first two days prevented much exploration, but on 8 November on arrival at Pickersgill, a party went on shore for two hours, to explore the point of land on which Cook's astronomer, Mr Wales, had made an observatory.[29] Murray's comments included some on the felled timber that had lain around since 1773, whose part preservation was taken as 'proof that the wood is of great durability'.[30] Given that these observations are the kind a ship's carpenter would make and that Murray elsewhere draws upon his carpenter's advice about timber, it seems highly probable that Thomas Moore was also amongst this group.[31] Such an immediate shore excursion would have been the normal routine for ship's carpenters, for, when not at sea, their tasks included gathering timber for present and future repairs—especially the 'crooked timber' that was so essential for the vessel, but, because it had to be just the right shape for its intended placement in the ship, so often difficult to find. (Figure 18).

Figure 18. Crooked Timber. Trees of the right shape for ship's timbers had to be found.

Moore must have seen what he required, for the next day (9 November), while the Chief Mate went to the seal island, 'the Carpenter was well emp^d in falling trees for spars and plank for the Ships use'.[32] In the following days, despite heavy rain, the reports from the seal islands were so good that by Saturday 10th, Raven 'determined to leave a party here to collect skins for the China Market'.

The repeated specification of seal skins 'for the China market' no doubt goes back to a report from Captain James Cook's experience at Dusky Bay in 1773. Cook had procured some seal skins, which 'then sold in China at 400 hard dollars each, though for the few they brought home, of the same quality, they only received about ten pounds each'.[33] For those suggesting the founding of a colony at Botany Bay, such as J.M. Matra, this raised hopes of a much more favourable trade with China. If a locally based seal industry could gain such prices, then the necessity of sending great quantities of silver to cover Chinese imports (mainly of tea) would be diminished. Raven and his business partners, John St Barbe[34] and the Southern Fishery, on the other hand, would have had in mind, not only their country's profit, but their own.

During further exploration, on Tuesday 13th, they sighted some people in a hut. When they fled, Raven's party landed and the captain left two knives in the hut. All this time, Thomas Moore was busy, for the carpenter's job when on shore was as clear as it was urgent:

> At daybreak on Wednesday 14th the party departed and got back to the ship at 7am, 'it was fair weather all this forenoon and we were emp^d cutting wood, spars & plank for the Ship.

Raven's plans to leave a sealing party gave Moore an additional task.

> The afternoon continued fair and the people were emp^d as before ment^d at 6AM the Captn & party set off for Luncheon Cove to build an house for the Sealing party.

> From this time until ~~Monday~~ Saturday Dec 1st, we were employed building the dwelling and another House and getting the Ship ready for Sea.

This would be the first dwelling built by Europeans in New Zealand.[35] (Plate 21). On 1 December, the *Britannia* worked her way out and made sail. After speaking of the decision to leave a party in Dusky Bay and making mention of the dwelling built for them, Murray makes no mention of the eleven men left behind, apart from saying that those on the ship felt the shock of an earthquake, which 'was felt in a more violent manner by the people at the House'. The second officer, William Leith, was left in charge,[36] and the Carpenter, Mr Thomas Moore, was also amongst the little number.

Since Murray remained on the *Britannia*, Moore's time at Dusky Bay remains without record. At the end of February 1793, the group almost had a visit from the two Spanish ships, *Descuvierta* and *Atrevida*, commanded by Don Alexandro Malaspina and Don Josè Bustamante, which were sailing on a scientific expedition. Sailing from Manila, Philippines, and following 'the exact details which Capt. Cook, with his usual accuracy, has given' they were able to make it to Dusky Bay on 25th. Alarmed at the rugged entrance to the Bay, they despatched the armed boat of the *Descubierta* to take some exploratory

CHAPTER 2 ⚓ *Adventuring (October 1792–September 1796)* 71

soundings and to ascertain the possibilities for 'watering and wooding'. The boat returned at 9pm, with good reports about the depth of water, and the abundance of wood and water, also reporting that they saw a few birds, not a single seal, no shellfish, and 'not a sign, however remote, of inhabitants'.[37] Leith's party must have cut a rather low profile—and hidden their seals!

As the weather turned worse, with North winds and heavy fog, and with the poor Filipino crew suffering from the extraordinary cold, after making a few failed attempts to make the entrance to the Bay, the Spaniards decided to leave their gravitational experiments to another future opportunity they would have in crossing the same parallel. They sailed for Port Jackson to repair their ships and rest the crew. Upon arrival, they found that Governor Phillip had left the colony in December 1792, and so they were warmly received by Major Grose, now Acting Governor for the time being.[38]

The *Britannia* sailed to Cape of Good Hope, via Santa Catherina on the Brazil coast, arriving on 25 March. This afforded Raven the opportunity to hear from some other captains 'of the agitated state of Europe; of the naval and military preparations which were making in our own country', causing him to wonder if any ships would be spared for New South Wales.[39] After transacting her business, she was back at anchor in Sydney Cove on 26 June 1793.[40] Collins noted that,

> about nine o'clock at night the *Britannia* was safe within the Heads, having to a day completed eight months since she sailed hence. The length of time she had been absent gave birth to some anxiety upon her account, and her arrival was welcomed with proportionate satisfaction.[41]

Murray's observations on the state of the colony under Major Grose show that he had already detected a marked change since the previous visit: 'the very great difference between the present state of this, and its former one, is beyond conception; the meanness practiced by the Officers of the NSW Corps exceeds all I could possibly suppose Usurers capable of'.[42] He illustrates by calculating the profits made by the Officers on the trade goods brought from the Cape by the *Britannia*. Sugar bought for 6d /lb was sold for 2 or 3 shillings. Spirits bought for 2 s/ gallon, sold at 30s; and wine costing 2s/ gallon, sold for 24s. The prophets on spirits and wine are even greater, because they are watered down prior to sale, enabling a gallon to make 37/6, and selling it by the bottle rather than the gallon enables a further 6s in the gallon, increasing the price to 43/6.

Murray also explained how the military had instituted new methods of making money through buying corn and selling it to the Government (thereby gaining Treasury Bills and the advantage this brought). His example is of a small farmer induced with grog until he signs over his farm and crop for ¼ of its real value to his creditor, an Officer of the NSW Corps.[43] They also established a scheme of cutting Spanish Dollars in pieces in such a way as to dishonestly increase their profit.[44] Because the Officers of the NSW Corps have already found ways of adulterating sugar, flour and Indian meal, Murray lays down the challenge for some convict to study chemistry, in order to find ways of adulterating other sale items, such as soap, candles, tea, coffee, and butter.[45]

Murray's account provides evidence in support of the stereotype of the officers constructed by the pioneers of Australian history writing:

> Historians have criticized the officers because, it is alleged, by their profiteering, their tempting the settlers with rum and their monopolizing of the Commissariat Store, great numbers of the farmers were involved in financial ruin and their farms passed to their officer-creditors by foreclosure.[46]

Although the profit made by the sale of sugar imported on this voyage was more moderate (300%), the profits on the alcohol were enormous, at 1,400% for spirits and 1,100% for the wine. Hainsworth cautions against generalising these kind of figures across the officers' trading years, as if they were common:

> If the officers had realized 1,000 per cent on only five per cent of their outlay in Paymaster's bills alone, this would have represented a return of more than £200,000 on just that small portion! Where was such a sum to be found in a miserable prison settlement in only eight years' trading, and that sum only a small fraction of the total return?[47]

CHAPTER 2 ↕ *Adventuring (October 1792–September 1796)* 73

The profits made on spirits (and other forms of alcohol) continued to incite the concern of various Governors, rather than profit-making as such. Hunter himself apparently questioned some of the rumours in the colony suggesting that enormous profits could be made in such a short time ('How is it possible?'), and expressed his only concern to be the spirits.[48] The officers were not the only ones in quest of large profits. Reports of soldiers disposing of the tobacco and sugar their officers served them from the *Britannia* too quickly, and a bottle of spirits being bartered for up to six times its value led Grose to give an order that no convict should exchange spirits with soldiers for any article served them by their officers, and if any person attempted to sell spirits without a license, the goods would be seized and their house pulled down.[49]

Care should also be taken in generalising Murray's example of the farmer who sold his farm at ¼ of its value to pay his officer-creditors. 'Although some officers did buy out small settlers the surviving evidence does not confirm the traditional picture of foreclosing officers with a mortgage in one hand and a bottle in the other'.[50] Hainsworth's analysis of the Settlers' Muster Book from 1800, shows that of the land holdings of the 29 military and civil officers' 51% were grants, 11.7% acquired from fellow officers, 4% bought from soldiers, and only 6 per cent were purchases of 30 acre grants and these were not always purchased from the original grantees. Brian Fletcher's study of the small farmers in Governor Hunter's period also found little evidence for the stereotype. Fletcher noted that thirty-five per cent of those granted land in 1795 still retained it in 1800, and there were a variety of reasons other than officer exploitation for the Hawkesbury farmers' troubles in 1800: economic depression, floods, unsuitable soil, the unsuitability of many of the ex-convicts to agriculture.[51]

While in Sydney, the *Britannia* had some necessary repairs done, which, even without her carpenter's supervision, Raven 'declared had been as well executed by the artificers of the colony as if the ship had been in England'.[52] After delivering her cargo and refitting the ship, on 24 July the *Britannia* assisted in the launch of the *Francis*— the first vessel constructed in the colony, which had come out in frame in the *Pitt*—now with a mast cut by Moore at Dusky Bay and in the command of William House, the late boatswain of *Discovery*, Captain Vancouver.[53] It was named after Grose's son, whose birthday was launch day. Raven was then ordered to superintend her fitting for sea and to take her in company to Dusky Bay. The plan was for the *Francis* to return to Sydney bringing news of the New Zealand venture, while Raven's *Britannia* would sail for Calcutta for a cargo of salt provisions for the colony.[54] When Grose wrote about the plan to his superiors, he said he was following intimations that the Bengal market ought to be tried. Despite his difference of opinion with Phillip about the previous charter of the vessel, Grose now states sweetly that he would have preferred to use the *Boddingtons*, currently in the harbour and already working for the Navy, but, unlike the *Britannia*, she would not be ready for sea for six weeks, and was a shilling per ton more expensive.[55] Collins also observed that the *Britannia* was the better vessel, for she 'had moreover the advantage of being a coppered ship'.[56] So Raven received his second charter, being required to purchase 'an equal quantity of Irish Beef and Pork [that is, Salt meat], if to be procured', or Pork if there is no Beef; or, if no meat at all, 37 tons of sugar, and the remainder of the stowage in rice and dholl. For hire and freight Raven would receive 14/6 per ton each month for 300 tons.[57]

Having turned some profitable business from their first charter of the *Britannia*, some of the officers of the Corps parted with their Paymaster's bills to Raven, so that he might secure a cargo for them on this next voyage. On 3 September Raven received three bills totalling £1,995, one of which was for £320, consisting of contributions from Johnston (£65); Foveaux, Paterson and Harris (£60); Macarthur (£35); and McKellar and Piper (£20). Paterson's total contribution to Raven's second voyage was £500—nearly twice his annual salary.[58] (See Plates 10, 38, 39, 40).

Thankfully for those waiting in the cold at Dusky Bay, the Charter specifically permitted their recovery:

> The said Ship or Vessel may, on her sailing from hence, proceed to Dusky Bay, in New Zealand, for the purpose of receiving on board, the Officers, and Seamen of the said Ship, who were left there, to prosecute the design of the Voyage, on which the said Ship sailed from England; The said Willm. Raven, covenanting

and agreeing not to remain in the said Bay longer than seven Days, for the purpose above mentioned; but should it be necessary for the said Willm. Raven to remain in the said Bay, longer than the Time above limited, then and in that Case the Number of Days which the said Ship may exceed the Time above limited, in her Stay in the Place aforesaid, are to be Deducted from the Monthly Pay of the said Ship.

Grose also directed Raven to send back to Sydney, by way of the *Francis*, 'all such information respecting that extensive bay, and the seal-fishery in its vicinity, as he should be of opinion might in anywise tend to the present or future benefit of his Majesty's service as connected with these settlements'.[59]

Amongst the letters for England carried by the *Britannia*, Rev. Richard Johnson included a request for reimbursement of expenses for the building of a church—£67 12s. 11½d. (Plate 14). Not a friend of the Chaplain, Grose took the opportunity to include his own covering letter, in which he observed that 'Mr Johnston [sic], who is one of the people called Methodists, is a very troublesome, discontented character' and that 'his charge for this church is infinitely more than it ought to have cost, and his attempt to make a charge of it at all surprises me exceedingly'—because Johnson had said he was building it at his own expense.[60] Even though Johnson was an ordained minister of the Church of England, the slur 'methodist' was used for those whose sympathies and practices showed they were influenced by the eighteenth century Evangelical Revival. Once Thomas Moore settled in the colony, he, too, would join cause with the 'methodists'. It is left to speculation whether Moore had visited Johnson's congregation during his first visit to Sydney Cove, but if he had, the next time he sat under Johnson's preaching, it would be in a building that the Chaplain had erected himself—and to Grose's chagrin, then sought reimbursement.

In December 1792, when Governor Phillip left Major Francis Grose in charge, he immediately replaced the civil magistrates with his officers, and soon gave them generous grants of land. On 12 February 1793 Surgeon John White received 100 acres in the 'Kangaroo grounds', near George Johnston's Annandale Farm, which he called 'Hamond Hill Farm', after his patron Andrew Snape Hamond.[61] On

15 May 1793 the Surgeon-General was also granted a 14 year lease in town, 'on the road leading to the hospital, and adjacent to the wharf on the west side of Sydney Cove' for the purpose of building a residence.[62] (Plates 34 and 35, Figure 29). By the time of Raven's visit in June, if he was entertained by John White during this stay, he would have found Rachel heavily pregnant. The convict servant had become the mistress, and was about to become the mother. From all appearances, it looked like John White was settling down.

About the same time as White received his town leasehold, Hamond received notification of White's leave request, sent with Governor Phillip on the *Atlantic* in December 1792.[63] On 31 May he wrote to Nepean in favour of White's return to England. At the end of June, Dundas, Nepean's replacement, wrote to Grose, leaving it to him to decide if the surgeon's absence would be detrimental to the colony. As John White was pining for home, on 23 September 1793, just a few weeks after the *Britannia* sailed out of the heads to pick up Thomas Moore and his friends from Dusky Bay, Rachel Turner bore him a son.[64]

THE *BRITANNIA*'S ABORTIVE VOYAGE TO CALCUTTA, VIA DUSKY BAY (7 SEPTEMBER 1793 TO 1 JUNE 1794).

According to Murray's journal, the two vessels sailed on 7 September 1793, and entered Dusky Bay on 27th.[65] They fired six guns, near Anchor Island,

> and we kept impatiently looking out for the boat which at [...?] we saw pulling round the So pt of Anchor Is, at noon brot up in Anchor Isl Harbour. Mr Leith and five others came on board, who informed us that all the rest were well, which gave us no small satisfaction.

That night everyone dined on board the ship, and the last of their livestock, a goat, was killed to help celebrate the reunion. The eleven men had been on what was, to them, 'a desolate and uninhabited Island, without any communication of any sort, and without any kind of refreshment than what we left them'.[66] (Figures 19 and 20; Plate 21).

Thomas Moore had been busy during the days of their isolation.

They had built a Vessell of Sixty or Seventy Tons and had proceeded so far in this as to have been able to have left the place in 3 months from the time of our arrival.[67]

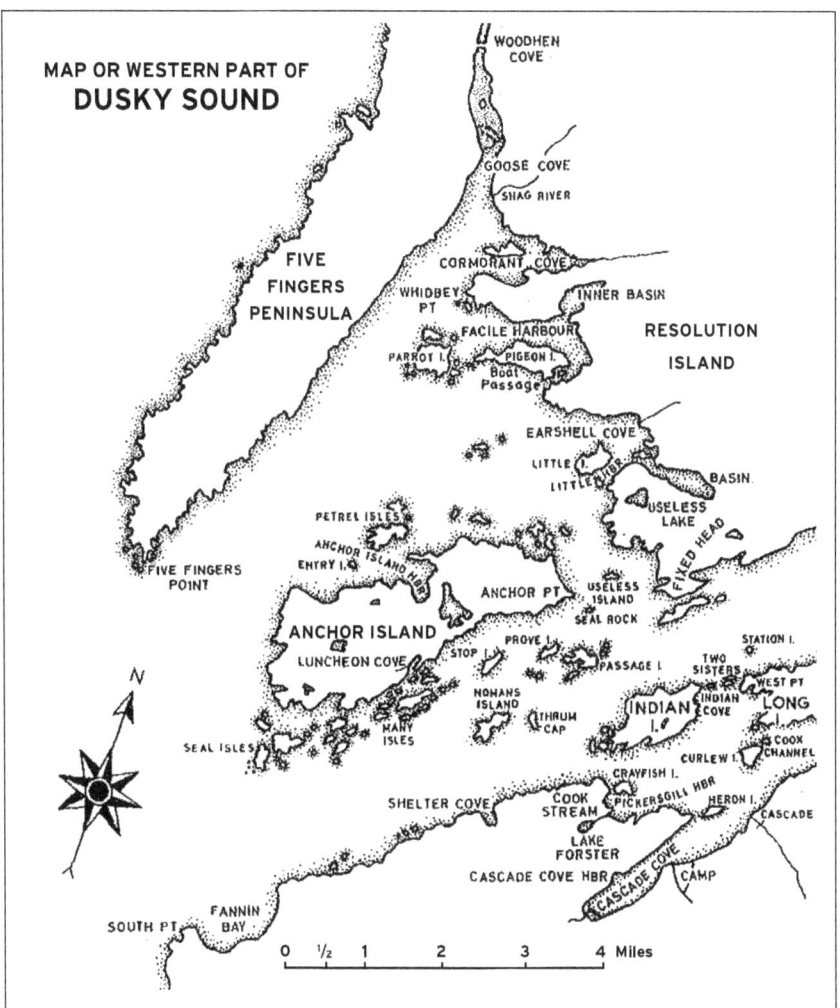

Figure 19. Anchor Island, Dusky Bay.

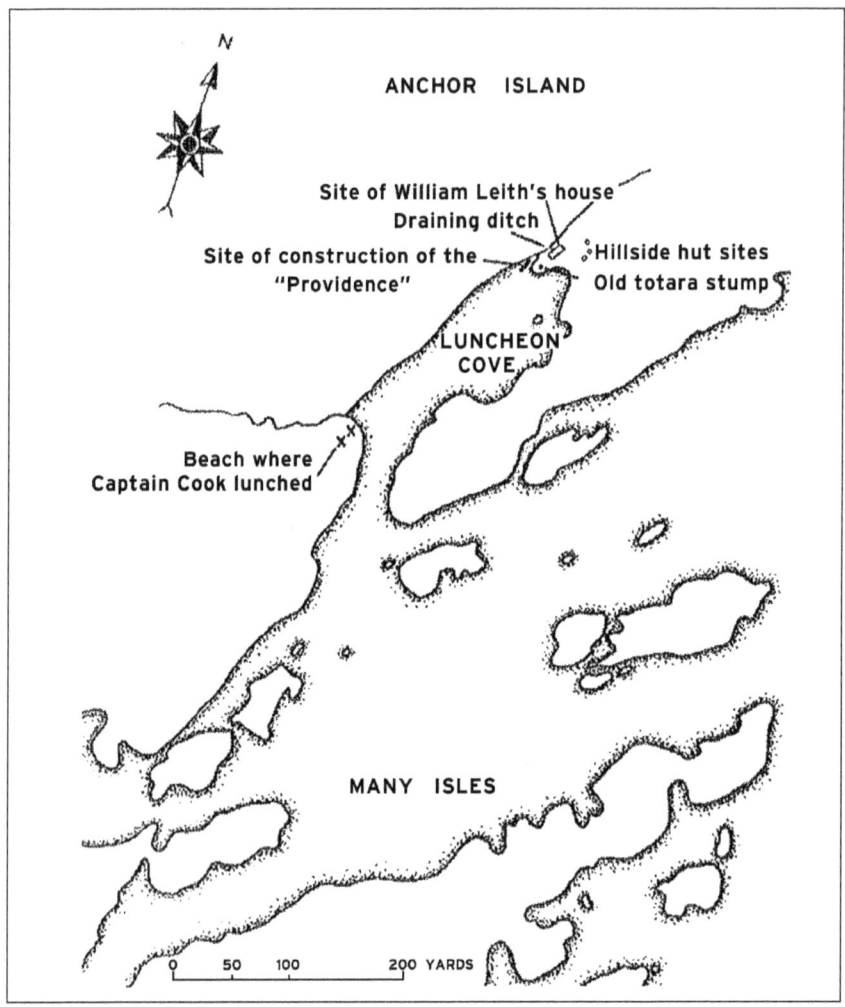

Figure 20. Luncheon Cove, Anchor Island, Dusky Bay

Although he wouldn't have realised it at the time, building this schooner would bring a change of direction to Thomas Moore's life. Not only had he built the first European dwelling in New Zealand to house the sealing party, but he had also all but completed the first European ship out of native New Zealand timbers. Just two years later, in October 1795, Murray would return to Dusky Bay with Captain Bampton's *Endeavour*, which was in such very bad shape that they launched Moore's schooner, christened her the *Providence* and sailed away.[68] Although Moore's renown for building her was already

CHAPTER 2 ↓ *Adventuring (October 1792–September 1796)* 79

established by that stage, the launch of the *Providence* certainly did it no extra harm.

The master craftsman in Moore must have felt the frustration of being unable to complete her in September 1793, but time was against them, as Murray explained:

> Circumstances however prevented us from carrying this into execution, the time limited by our Charter to stay at Duskey Bay was 14 Days beyond that time we were not to be considered in the service of Government nor should we receive Pay until the time of our departure if we exceeded it. It therefore became necessary to prepare for an early departure.[69]

After ten months of patiently working on his own vessel, Moore was suddenly back to the routine of the ship's carpenter that he knew so well. The *Britannia* was badly in need of repair:

> 28th September. The Following morning was accordingly spent in getting a part of the Stores &c which we had left, with a quantity of Plank intended for the Ships Decks they being in a wretched condition. We found the weather in general unfavourable for our purpose, blowing chiefly very hard from the NE and being attended with very heavy rains.
>
> Every opportunity was made use of for getting on board the above mentioned articles, which was done, the Rigging repaired and every necessary completed on Wednesday October 9th, and on [Thursday] we unmoored and warped out of the Harbour into the Inlet between one of the Parrot Islands and the Pt of Anchor Island we found the swell setting very heavy into the Bay and so little wind that attempting to get [out] was impossible. We got 3 or 4 Boats loads of wood and spent the remainder of the day which was a fine one, in pleasant exercise [?].[70]

When the *Fancy* arrived on 11 October, Thomas Moore was soon getting her ready for the return voyage.

> She now wanted every assistance, they had not been able to make her Stay. She wanted repairs which they were unable to give her, and without which it would have been impossible to have ventured to P[ort] J[ackson] again. We returned onboard in the

evening and 2 Boats were dispatched to bring her to Facile Harbour where she arrived the day after. We were now all hands emp^d in making a Bowsprit and repairing her rudder & Sawyers were cutting plank for her. On Sunday 20th of October we had completely fitted her to proceed on her Voyage we got underway and made sail out of the Sound with the *Francis* in Company.[71]

The two vessels parted company immediately, with the *Francis* arriving back in Sydney on the 7 November. At the beginning of the voyage, with Raven's concurrence, she had been rigged as a schooner, not as the sloop she was built to be. The voyage to New Zealand proved this to be a mistake, especially in the heavy winds and seas she had encountered, for, as Collins reports: 'for a schooner she was too short, and, for want of proper sail, she did not work well. Four times she was blown off the coast of New Zealand, the *Britannia* having anchored in Dusky Bay sixteen days before the *Francis*'.[72] As well as reporting on the performance of the vessel itself, those on the *Francis* brought news to Sydney about another vessel recently built:

> Mr. Raven found in health and safety all the people whom he had left there. They had procured him only four thousand five hundred seal-skins, having been principally occupied in constructing a vessel to serve them in the event of any accident happening to the *Britannia*. This they had nearly completed when Mr. Raven arrived. She was calculated to measure about sixty-five tons, and was chiefly built of the spruce fir, which Mr. Raven stated to be the fittest wood he had observed there for ship-building, and which might be procured in any quantity or of any size. The carpenter of the *Britannia*, an ingenious man, and master of his profession, compared it to English oak for durability and strength.[73]

This comparison with the oak shows more than Moore's northeastern training in working a variety of woods. He was well aware of the rising desperate shortage of English oak for building ships of war, and also of the official naval prejudice against anything but oak for that purpose. As he felled and worked the New Zealand timber, he was gathering intelligence which he hoped might prove useful for His Majesty's fleet at home. However, apart from the interesting news of Moore's shipbuilding brilliance at Dusky Bay, the report from New

Zealand held no great promise to the colonists across the Tasman:

> Nothing appeared by this information from Dusky Bay, that held out encouragement to us to make any use of that part of New Zealand. So little was said of the soil, or face of the country, that no judgment could be formed of any advantages which might be expected from attempting to cultivate it; a seal fishery there was not an object with us at present, and, beside, it did not seem to promise much.[74]

They were relieved, however, to learn that the twelve people left for ten months on an island 'the inhabitants whereof were known to be savages, fierce and warlike' had survived hale and hearty. The only conclusion to be drawn was that the locals must have not known that they were there![75]

When she parted with the *Francis*, the *Britannia* sailed towards Norfolk Island, since Raven already had a case or two of scurvy on board and—in this post-Captain Cook era of English seafaring history—he wanted to secure some fresh fruit and vegetables. On her arrival on 31 October, Governor King sent an order for Raven to take two New Zealanders, Tooky and H/Woodoo, back to the Bay of Islands. Under Vancouver's instructions these two young men had been captured by Lieut. Hanson in the *Daedalus*, taken to Port Jackson, and then on 24 April 1793 to Norfolk Island on the *Shah Hormuzear*. The plan was to have them instruct the people in the manufacture of the flax plant, but they managed to impart them all they knew in just one hour![76] Since then they had keenly wanted to go home, but every vessel to arrive at Norfolk Island was usually going the other way. This time, King decided to take decisive steps to get them home—despite the trouble it landed him in with his superior officer.[77]

On 2 November 1793, Raven wrote to comply with King's requisition order. This gave him the opportunity to report on what had gone on in Dusky Bay, while it was still fresh in his mind.[78] He told of his first plan, that after discharging his cargo at Port Jackson he was to go to Dusky Bay to procure 'seals' skins for the China Market'; of accepting the Officers of the New South Wales Corps' charter; and how he asked second mate Mr Leith 'to remain behind at

Dusky Bay with a party of men and the carpenter'. Raven adds that Leith assented 'in the most unequivocal and manly manner you can conceive'. The reasons for the special mention of Moore (although not by name) become obvious as the letter proceeds.

Raven was well aware of the risks—and how this may look to others—so he was careful to articulate the provisions he had made for their minimisation:

> The prospect of procuring skins and leaving my people in safety I thought might justify my conduct, and acquit me of any reproach for hazarding the event of so singular a speculation. By the latter part of November we had completed a dwelling-house, 40 feet long, 18 broad, and 15 high, and had landed provisions and stores for twelve months. I also left ironwork, cordage, and sails, &c, for the building and rigging of a small vessel, which I had directed them to construct for their conveyance to some friendly port, as an unforeseen accident might prevent the return of the ship. On 1 December 1792 we sailed, and left our shipmates perfectly satisfied with their situation and the attention I had paid to their comfort and protection.

Raven passed over telling King about the circumnavigation of the globe, because nothing occurred 'which can afford you either information or amusement', passing quickly to their return to Port Jackson on 26 June 1793. He then tells of Grose's Charter of 26 August, to fetch provisions from India for the colony, granting leave to pick up his people from New Zealand, and requesting Raven to send 'every information respecting them and the nature of the place, &c', and mentions that the *Francis* came along for this purpose. On arrival at Dusky Bay, Leith immediately met the ship, and they found all but one (the seaman Thomas Wilson) in good health. They had collected 4,500 seal skins, with which Raven was satisfied, even though not up to his expectations. But it was the work of Thomas Moore that provided the real interest for Captain Raven:

> What excited my admiration was the progress they had made in constructing a vessel of the following dimensions:—40 ft. 6 in. keel, 53 ft. length upon deck, 16ft. 10 in. breadth, and 12 feet hold. She is skinned, ceiled, and decked, and with the work of three or

CHAPTER 2 ⚓ *Adventuring (October 1792–September 1796)* 83

four men for one day would be ready for caulking. Her frame knees and crooked pieces are cut from timber growing to the mould. She is planked, decked, and ceiled with the spruce fir, which in the opinion of the carpenter is very little inferior to English oak.

While on timber, Raven paused for a further comment about its usefulness:

There are various kinds of timber in Dusky Bay, but that which is principally fit for shipbuilding is the spruce fir, which may be cut along the shore in any quantity or size for the construction of vessels from a first-rate to a small wherry.

These comments on timber are laden with meaning for those—like Raven and King—familiar with things Naval. As the English oak supplies to the Naval yards dwindled further every day, the eyes of some, at least, began to turn to more distant parts of the globe for replacement timber.[79]

In summing up his description of the Dusky Bay vessel, Raven—the Naval officer!—has high praise for Thomas Moore's workmanship:

Her construction is such that she will carry more by one-half than she measures, and I am confident will sail well. The carpenter has great merit, and has built her with that strength and neatness which few shipwrights belonging to the merchant service are capable of performing.

The letter concludes by telling of the late arrival of the *Francis* and again, how Raven had cared for the greater good:

We had then been waiting several days for a wind, and now found it necessary, as well for the good of his Majestie's service as for the safety of the schooner, to remain and assist her with our carpenter to repair several defects, and to furnish boats to procure ballast, &c &c.

They sailed on 21 October and the *Francis* parted company the same day, heading for Port Jackson as planned. Raven concludes his comments by noting that they had seen 'three natives' the first time they had visited, but they had run off, and Mr Leith did not see any inhabitants during the whole of his time, apart from once finding a fire.

Having accepted Lieut.-Governor King's commission, and filled him in on the latest news from the South Island of New Zealand, Raven and the *Britannia* turned back towards the North Island—to the Bay of Islands. Starting off on 9 November, this little excursion occupied the ship for nine days. Governor King would have had the opportunity on this voyage to meet the carpenter who had been praised so highly by his Captain. Other passengers on the trip included Rev. James Bain, Mr Thomas Jamison, Mr W.N. Chapman, two non-commissioned officers, twelve privates, and one convict.[80] It seems that amongst the passengers Moore's New Zealand-built ship was the talk of the voyage.

Thomas Jamison had come out with the First Fleet as surgeon's mate on the *Sirius*, and, since March 1788 had been the surgeon on Norfolk Island.[81] He was also so impressed with what he learned about Moore's ship-building prowess, that he mentioned it in the opening paragraph of a letter to a friend at Lincoln, reporting on what he had learned of New Zealand on the voyage. When this was subsequently published in *Saunder's News-Letter* in July 1794, the fame of Moore's vessel (even if its builder remained anonymous) gained an even wider audience:[82]

> During their stay at this bay they built a small vessel of 150 tons burden, entirely out of the wood of the country, which, they say, is equal to the English oak, and grows in great abundance.

This brief voyage from Norfolk Island gave Moore his first experience of the Bay of Islands. Here he met many people from the two friends' tribes—some of whom came on board to sleep the night. Since carpenters were also involved in the firing of the guns, Moore probably lent a hand as the cannon made their salute to satisfy the request of the Chief.[83] The talk of the mess, he also had the opportunity to meet the Governor and his passengers, amongst whom he would later take his place in Sydney society.

Major Grose was not pleased with King purloining the *Britannia* for this little jaunt to New Zealand, nor with him leaving Nicholas Nepean in charge of Norfolk Island in the meantime. This disagreement occasioned a series of letters between the two men and their English

CHAPTER 2 ⚓ *Adventuring (October 1792–September 1796)* 85

superiors, with Portland eventually finding nothing in King 'which calls for serious reprehension'.[84] One of the reasons for Grose's ire was that the *Britannia* was 'charged with a business of such importance to the colony'. In his own defence, King pleaded that he was sure that, given Raven's planned route and the prevailing seasonal factors, the delay would have made no difference. Collins reports his perspective:

> It was not imagined that this delay in the *Britannia*'s voyage would be of any consequence, as Mr. Raven purposed making what is called the Eastern Passage; that is, between the south end of Mindanao and Borneo; and it was known that the eastern monsoon did not set well in, nor was attended with good weather in those seas before December or January.[85]

They were back at Norfolk on 18th November, and, after collecting Governor King's dispatches for England, they sailed at noon on the 22nd.[86]

BOUND FOR BENGAL

Leaving Norfolk Island for Bengal through the Eastern Passage, it was time for the *Britannia* to receive some much-needed repairs, now that she had recovered her carpenter. Having cut and loaded the plank at Dusky Bay, Thomas Moore began to install the new deck as the normal shipboard activity was going on around him. On 29 November 1793 Murray noted, 'Carpenter employed laying a new Main Deck', and on 11 December he was still hard at it, 'Carpenters & all hands empl^d Shifting Starb^d side of the Main Deck'.[87]

They arrived at Zamboangan [southern Philippines] on 18 January 1794, but when they attempted to leave they found that the anchor was stuck. On the 24th, after heaving at the purchase, the anchor and 20 fathoms of cable were lost.[88] Presumably Moore would have subsequently been engaged in making a replacement—another duty of the ship's carpenter.

On 2 February 1794 the ship passed Point Romania, at the end of the Malaysian peninsula. From here the plan would have been to continue below the island of Temasek (Singapore), swing around into the Straits of Malacca and then sail through their 900 km-long (550 miles) waters in a North Westerly direction and on to Calcutta, the capital of British India. The Straits held two dangers to avoid, the local pirate and the international privateer. Each was a form of piracy and each—rather strangely for being on the other side of the world—a complication of European politics. (Plates 18 and 19).

Local piracy in East and Southeast Asia is as old as seaborne trade. In its oldest form it operated on a simple premise: the pirate was the predator and the merchant ship the prey.[89] After the Portuguese took Malacca in 1511 and opened the floodgates to other European plunderers, traders and colonists—in Spanish, Dutch and British forms—this 'international' influence complicated the relationship between local piracy and trade 'since piracy was used by European colonisers as means to control seaborne trade and to expand their influence and domains'.[90]

The actors involved in this conflict fought out by so many vessels in these waters were the large 'states'—the European nations and China—and the local people of the area.

Already by the colonial period, trading ports had become established at locations most advantaged by the monsoon season.[91] Trade routes through South East Asia to India can be documented some three centuries before Christ, and, in time, even to the Roman Empire. In 1368 China banned private trading and began to revive and establish official trade routes. In July 1402 Admiral Zheng was sent for this purpose to Malacca with an armada of 62 treasure ships and 225 smaller vessels, with a total of 28,000 persons on board, and seven further voyages took place between 1405–1433. China operated on the 'tributary' system of trade, that is, those nations which wished to trade with her had to pay a tribute to China for the privilege, which also entailed taking on Chinese customs and calendar, thus effectively legitimising her suzerainty.[92]

Records as far back as the first-century show the sea-trade in this area was accompanied by piracy, but as the seaborne trade increased the Straits of Malacca became a piracy-prone area, especially around the island of Temasek (which Raffles named 'Singapore' in 1819). Even by 1349 it was said that in these waters 'the inhabitants are addicted to piracy', and as the 14th century opened this was where the Chinese pirate Chen Zuyi, who had fled to Sarawak, was operating, robbing ships as they passed through the Straits. Admiral Zheng, with his great armada courting Malacca to come into China's tributary system, was sent to suppress Chen's pirates.[93]

The arrival of the Europeans in the area introduced other factors encouraging piracy. After 1498 when Vasco de Gama successfully found a sea-route to the spice islands, around the Turkish-held land-based trade routes the Portuguese captured Malacca in 1511, thus bringing the Europeans into South East Asia, where they would not only rival China, but also each other. By taking Malacca, 'the lynchpin of seaborne trade', the Portuguese sought to establish their monopoly over the spice trade. In 1521 Magellan reached the Philippines, bringing the Spaniards into the region, and beginning the 'galleon trade', trading silk and cotton and other wares from China to the Acapulco merchants who paid in silver—a trade which peaked in 1597, and only ceased in 1815. When the Netherlands declared their independence from Spain in the late sixteenth century they vigorously entered international trade and politics. The VOC (Dutch East Indies Company) was formed in 1602, and within a decade they had taken the Portuguese out of the trade. In 1619 they seized Jakarta, renamed it Batavia, and there established VOC headquarters. (Plates 18 and 19). In 1624 they took Taiwan from China, and in 1641 Malacca from the Portuguese.[94]

The British East India Company (EIC) was established in 1600, two years before its Dutch counter-part, by which time the British had already been importing spices from this region for some sixty years. The EIC soon realised that a variety of South East Asian goods were vital for trade to China, and in 1615 founded factories in Eastern Indonesia, where they could access cloves, nutmeg and mace, thus threatening the monopoly of VOC. In 1622 the Dutch killed the factors and workers at the EIC factory at Ambon, ending a century of British involvement in the spice islands.[95]

But by the time the *Britannia* was sailing towards the Straits of Malacca, this was all ancient history. In 1786 the English had leased Penang Island in Malaya from the local Sultan. With the VOC on the decline, and England moving towards having mastery of the seas—

now even possessing a nearby outpost in New South Wales—His Britannic Majesty was getting back in business in South East Asia.[96]

One of Britain's increasingly popular products at this time was opium, grown in India, transported along the Straits of Malacca, and on to a burgeoning market in China. The opium trade was related to England's own drug of choice. In 1664, 'when Charles II received two pounds of black, strange-smelling leaves from China', England began a love affair with tea that soon threatened to ruin her economy.[97] Not really interested in British goods, China insisted on being paid in Spanish silver dollars, which was something of an international currency at the time. This led to a staggering imbalance of trade during the years 1710 to 1759, and to correct it British traders were desperately in search of something China wanted as much as the British wanted tea.[98] Britain's troubles increased when the American war of independence (1775–83) dried up her supplies of Spanish silver, and she was left with no alternative coinage.[99]

Others had sold opium to China before, but in 1781 Britain began to sell the drug in large amounts into the country, not through official channels—for opium was illegal—but by selling the Bengal-grown product to British traders for distribution. In August 1793—one month before the *Britannia* began her voyage from Sydney to Bengal—the British sent Lord George Macartney, one-time Governor of Madras (1780–1786), to gain permission for British ships at Canton, with an offer to end the opium trade if permission was granted. Even though the emperor was not at all impressed with the 600 or so gifts Macartney brought with him, in keeping with the Chinese 'tributary' mentality, he received them as tribute from a vassal. At dawn on 14 September 1793, Macartney was granted an audience with the emperor, but refused to 'kowtow' (do obeisance) to the emperor unless the Chinese court officials did the same to a portrait of George III. Nobody ended up bowing, and the Chinese emperor wrote a curt letter to the English king, saying that he 'set no value on strange objects and [had] no use for your country's manufactures'.[100]

So the opium trade continued—and with a vengeance. Whereas in 1773, opium earned the EIC £39,000, in 1793 the company sold to China alone £250,000 worth of the drug to an increasingly addicted

CHAPTER 2 ⚓ *Adventuring (October 1792–September 1796)* 89

market, and England's imbalance of trade began to be reversed. Despite China's 1799 condemnation of the trade with an official decree, between 1806–1809 China paid £7 million Spanish dollars for opium, and in the early decades of the nineteenth century, the EIC kept the price artificially high to target the upper classes, and to neatly balance the trade account without bankrupting the Chinese treasury.[101]

When she sailed past St John's Island, to the south of Temasek (Singapore) (Figure 20), heading for the Straits of Malacca, in a recapitulation of hundreds of years history the *Britannia* was attacked by pirates[102]—although in the days of Chen Zuyi's pirates at least they had the sense to let the vessels go through safely in this direction, and attack them when they were laden with goods coming back through![103] The pirates that engaged Raven and his crew for some six hours were most probably a squadron of local pirates from either the Iranun or the Balangingi peoples.

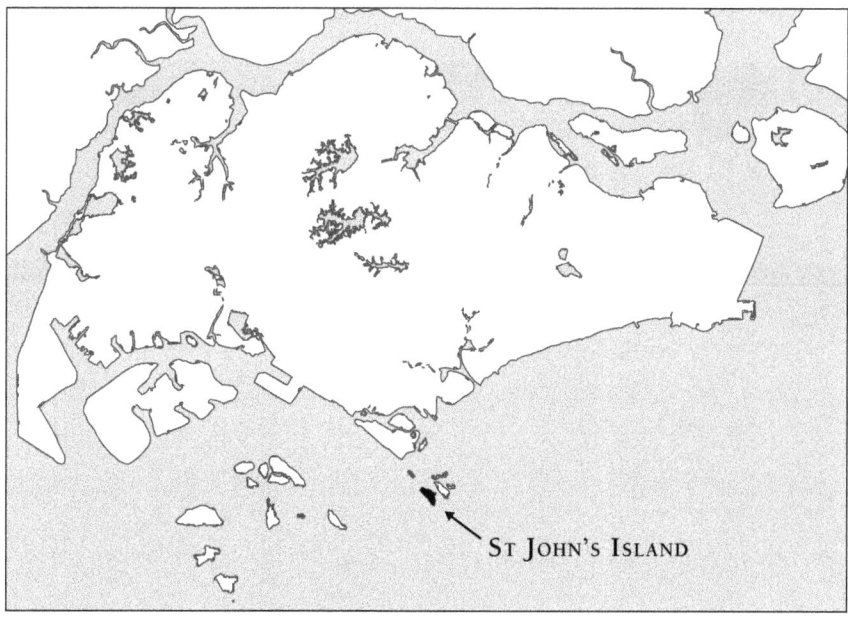

Figure 21. St John's Island, Temasek (Singapore).

Piracy in South East Asia reached its golden age in the nineteenth century. But it was strongly on the rise at the end of the eighteenth, and the factors allowing it to flourish were well-embedded. As a consequence of the Europeans seizing the various trading ports the local sultans lost control of the trade networks and so they were deprived of their previous revenues from trade. As the indigenous people had to therefore fend for themselves, piracy increased.[104] The Iranun and Balangingi were based in the south of the Philippines, where they were sponsored by the local sultans,[105] but their swiftly moving proas under oar and sail took them from Jolo to Singapore to Makassar giving them a more extensive territorial reach than any other raiding group in Southeast Asia.[106] Despite the best efforts of the Spanish (the colonial power in the Philippines) from 1778 to 1793, these groups, 'the most feared of all pirates',[107] continued to swarm over the islands in the 1790s, making mockery of the efforts to eradicate them and establishing a reputation that justifies the closing period of the eighteenth century being called 'the Age of the Iranun'.[108]

> By the 1780s maritime raiding or "piracy" in Southeast Asian waters—although common in the past—began to occur far more frequently than colonial authorities cared to admit. The regularity of the Iranun sweeps led the authorities in Singapore and other straits settlements to refer to the months of August, September and October as the *musim lanun* ['Iranun season'].[109]

The geography of this region favoured the pirates. The Iranun operated from 'the mangrove-lined inlets, bays and reef strewn islets', and with so many places to retreat that the Europeans despaired of ever being able to annihilate them.[110]

> They preyed on the increasingly rich shipping trade of the Spanish, Dutch and English, and Bugis and Chinese, and seized their cargoes of tin, opium, spices, munitions and slaves as the merchants headed to and from the trading centres of Manila, Makassar, Batavia, and Penang.[111]

Even though February was not *musim lanun*, as the *Britannia* rounded Point Romania, with Temasak in sight, her crew beheld the terrifying sight of these fearsome raiders bearing down upon them, 'the "nemesis"

CHAPTER 2 ⚓ *Adventuring (October 1792–September 1796)* 91

of virtually everybody in late eighteenth [...] Southeast Asia'.[112] Soon they would be fighting for their lives.

At first it was just one vessel, about twenty oars per side, which fired on them with round and grape shot. About 11am, nine other proas joined the fray. The *Britannia* was disadvantaged against these oared vessels by nearly calm conditions, but managed to score well with her guns. As ship's carpenter, Thomas Moore had a most important role during battle: below decks patching the ship from any cannon damage; above decks ensuring any valuable spars and masts broken off were fished out of the sea. Although Murray's account does not report any major damage on this occasion, Moore and his assistants would have been ready to swing into action.

With the fleet of proas 'about two gun shots' distance from them, Murray reported that,

> with great reluctance we gave up the passage thro the Straits of Mallacca having only a few pounds of gunpowder left with this scarcity of ammunition & but 30 hands to oppose 12 large proas each carrying upwards of one hundred men and mounted with a nine or 12 pounder besides swivels.[113]

Murray's memory would be vivid of this incident, because he himself was in command of the vessel at this stage. Noticing a 'fine breeze' had just begun to blow from the West, he took advantage of it and ran. The pirates gave up chasing them about 3pm, and they sailed on. When the wind dropped about 7pm, Murray gave the order to drop anchor. Having been chased away from the Straits of Malacca (their route to Calcutta), by 11 February they reached a safe haven in Batavia Road (Jakarta Harbour). (Plate 18). Here they discovered the second kind of piracy they needed to avoid: the privateer.

Arriving at Jakarta, the *Britannia* crew 'received unpleasing intelligence [of] a war with France'.[114] After their months of sailing in remote waters, this was their first opportunity to catch up with the news that the French Revolutionary forces had executed Louis XVI on 21 January, and declared war upon Britain and her Dutch allies on 1 February, 1793.[115] In the harbour they sat with a fleet of Dutch ships, as well as two French Privateers taken as prizes to 'a Company of British Ships fitted out at Bengall as Letters of Marque'—the *William Pitt, Houghton, Britannia* [not Raven's], *Nonsuch* and *Nauthilus*. In other words, these English vessels were now privateers for the East India Company, and they had successfully captured two vessels operating for the French—the European war had reached as far as the Straits!

They learned how the French had been making preparations to attack Batavia. The *Pigot* and *Princess Royale* had already been captured by the French and taken to Mauritius, and the *Benivolen* [?] taken and ransomed. In return, the *Resolve* and *Vengeance*—presumably the two French Privateers in Batavia Road—had been taken by the *Britannia* and *Nonsuch*. The news learned in Jakarta caused Murray and others to wax theological:

> at the same time, we were, by all persons, congratulated on our good fortune in escaping the numerous Privateers which infested the Straits of Malacca, Banea and the Java Sea; Our encounter with the Malay Proa, now appeared as an interposition of Providence, to prevent our falling into the hands of the French and our safe arrival at Batavia was looked upon, by every person, as a prodigy.[116]

Since the encounter with the pirates had prevented the completion of the voyage to Calcutta, Captain Raven applied to the Governor and Council whether he could procure his supplies from the Company's Stores here in Batavia—that is, the British East India Company.[117] When Cook visited Batavia in 1770, the VOC monopoly was still in place in the South East Asian region. But by the time Raven was seeking stores for Sydney, the Dutch company had been in trouble for some time, due to a combination of 'bad business practices, corruption among company employees and a profitless war'. The final blow had fallen in 1780, when the Netherlands declared support for the American Revolutionaries. At that point,

> England sank more Dutch ships than it could replace, and in the treaty ending the war in 1783, the Dutch were forced to give up all monopoly trading claims. Indonesian ports were open to foreign shipping, and the VOC found it could no longer compete with other traders. The Company declared bankruptcy in 1791; seven years later its holdings were taken over by the Dutch Government.[118]

CHAPTER 2 ↓ Adventuring (October 1792–September 1796) 93

Thus the East India Company was on the scene to receive Raven's request. At first he was offered stores at prices far above what he was authorised to pay. But then, Ambassador Y.H.S. Vincent informed him of a more congenial price, to which Raven agreed and so the stores were loaded.[119]

The visit to Batavia also ensured that the news of Britannia's voyage made it into the shipping intelligence reaching England.[120] Explaining why he had bought stores from the EIC at Batavia, rather than proceeding as contracted to Bengal, Raven later submitted his own report of the dramatic events in which his ship had been caught up:

> I had proceeded on my passage to Bengal so far [as] the eastern entrance of the Straits of Malacca, and was there engaged for six hours by a fleet of proas armed and full of men, when, after having nearly expended all our powder, the pirate obliged me to relinquish that passage. I arrived at Batavia on the eleventh of February, and there received information that French privateers were so numerous that a passage to Calcutta could not be effected without the greatest hazard of falling into their hands.[121]

Captain W. Bampton had been slightly ahead of the Britannia, and, he too, told a similar story when he wrote to Paterson on 1 June 1795 just after arriving in the Endeavour in Port Jackson:

> On my arrival at Batavia I was informed of the French war, and that the Straits of Sunda and Banca were infested by a number of French privateers, which obliged me to remain near a month after the ship was ready for sea until I could get the Dutch frigate, the Amazon, to convey me through the straits, which was late in December, and it was the 1st of February [1794] before I arrived at Bombay.[122]

While at Batavia Road in 1770, the crew of Captain Cook's Endeavour had fallen sick with malaria and dysentery.[123] Now in February 1794, the crew of Raven's Britannia also began to fall to what Collins called, 'the well-known insalubrity of the climate'.[124] Mr Gloucester died after a week of illness. As the ship's Caulker, he would have been one of Thomas Moore's closest working companions on board. His wife and two children were also part of the ship's company, and the 'innocent prattle' of his infant daughter Mary had endeared her to everyone. Mrs Gloucester, who was a drunk and neglectful of her children, took Mary on shore where the little girl also caught the fever and subsequently died. Murray reported that a Gentleman, whose name he had forgotten took the remaining child, 'ridding the unhappy woman of what she thought an incumbrance'.

Captain Nicholas Nepean, the officer whom Lieut.-Gov. King had left in charge of Norfolk Island during the brief voyage to New Zealand to return Tooke and Woodoo, already sick enough to be sent home from Sydney in the first place, became very ill at Batavia. As the *Britannia* sailed he was left behind, but within a matter of days (17 February) he took passage on the *Prince William Henry*, bound directly for England.[125]

The *Britannia* was stricken severely by the crew's illness. Murray was sure that the water they had loaded at Bantam was 'what affected every person in ship':

> We had beside the Captain, 1st and 2nd Officers, 11 persons sick, and unable to do duty[.] out of 19 of which Officers &c the ships company consisted, we had 4 in a watch with the Officers and these more like Phantoms than Men.[126]

This number was too few to furl the topsails, and to do other such duties. A fortnight later, all but three were better, with Murray being the last to recover.

Murray's illness meant that his log was not well kept during this period. To switch to our shore-based commentator, Collins reported that at 7am on 1 June 1794,[127] the ship entered Port Jackson and was moored by noon—with a story to tell!

> June] The signal for a sail was made in the morning of the first of June, and was conjectured to be for one of the ships expected to arrive from England; but in a few hours word was brought that the *Britannia* was safe within the harbour. This arrival gave general satisfaction, as many doubts about her return had been created by some accounts which the master of the *Indispensable* had heard at the Cape of Good Hope, of the Bay of Bengal being full of French privateers.
>
> On Mr. Raven's arrival at the settlement, we learned that he

had been forced to go to Batavia instead of Bengal, having been attacked in the Straits of Malacca by a fleet of piratical Proas, which engaged him for six hours, and from whom he might have found some difficulty to escape, had he not fortunately killed the captain of the one which was nearest to the *Britannia* when in the act of making preparations for boarding him. At Batavia he was informed that his passage to Bengal was very precarious, from the number of French privateers which infested the bay, as well as the west coast of Sumatra, several vessels having arrived at Batavia which had been chased by them. Mr. Raven, therefore, determined to load the *Britannia* at Batavia, and, after some necessary arrangements with the governor-general and council, purchased the following cargo [...][128]

THOMAS MOORE'S SECOND SOJOURN IN SYDNEY (1 JUNE TO 31 AUGUST 1794)

Moore had been absent from Sydney for 20 months, from 8 September 1793 to 1 June 1794. He now had three months to get better acquainted with the colony (from 1 June to 31 August 1794). He found the colony in some distress about the European war, and other matters.

The colony was anxiously awaiting news of Captain Bampton, suspecting the worst.[129] They were, at this stage, unaware of him successfully arriving in Bengal and Raven's news from Batavia flamed other rumours of him having met with disaster:

> At Batavia Mr. Raven learned that the *Shah Hormuzear* sailed from thence for Bombay three months before he arrived there; and the report we had heard of the disaster, which befell the boat and people from that ship, in the passage through the Straits between this country and New Guinea, was confirmed at Batavia. As, however, Mr. Bampton had not since been heard of, it was more than probable he had fallen a prize to some of the privateers which were to be met with in those seas.[130]

Murray did not have much to say about the state of the colony during this three month visit. In part, this was because he was severely ill for much of it. After the *Britannia*'s arrival in Port Jackson, Murray noted that he had been sick since April and had only maintained a journal for this period by copying Raven's. He was ill for ten weeks of the three months *Britannia* was in Sydney. He was still sick enough when she was about to sail again for Raven 'with his usual generosity' to suggest he stay behind. But Murray decided to sail—very much against the advice of Surgeon John White 'who with great assiduity & tenderness had attended me in my illness'. He was pleased to learn that two Naval Surgeons, Kent and Bell, were joining them for the next voyage to the Cape, and he hoped he would recover by the time he reached there.[131]

But it was not simply his illness that thwarted his comments on the colony. In his opinion, his previous observations still applied—the only difference being that the situation was even worse: 'I now thought (whatever might have been my opinion before) that Tyranny Oppression and Fraud had arrived at their Meridian in Port Jackson under the Auspices of the Officers of the New South Wales Corps'.[132]

Presumably Thomas Moore also participated in the deck-board chatter of prices and rorts and dodgy dealing encountered by the crew when on shore. All of this would be forming impressions on his mind that would colour his own commercial dealings in the years to come when he stepped permanently onto that same shore and took his place amongst the emergent new traders.

In August 1794, once again the officers of the Corps put their money in Raven's hands for further future profits—to the tune of £3,263 in Paymaster's bills. The principal traders were Paterson, Johnston, Foveaux, Rowley, Macarthur, who all had company funds to draw upon. Surgeon Harris was also involved to a lesser extent, and Laycock, perhaps accumulating funds to his advantage from his position as Quartermaster, was also a substantial investor. (Figure 16 and 22). The junior officers had no access to funds to the same extent, but they were catered for by splitting a cargo up into smaller parcels. On this voyage, the officers were trying their hand at purchases from the Cape of Good Hope, and they insured the *Britannia* on the return journey when it would be carrying their cargo, with their London agent, Messrs Cox & Greenwood.[133] As already noted, the officers'

CHAPTER 2 ⚓ *Adventuring (October 1792–September 1796)* 97

ready access to sterling through their Paymaster's bills and the consequential larger share of the Treasury bills enabled them to gain a monopoly on wholesale importing, thus avoiding the extravagant mark-ups from ship's captains.

OFFICER	AMOUNT (£.S.D)
Capt. Paterson sent to the Cape	250.0.0
Note	45.9.7
Capt. Foveaux sent to the Cape	250.0.0
By Bill	29.18.0
Capt. Johnston sent to the Cape	250.0.0
By Bill	29.18.0
Lieut. Rowley sent to the Cape	250.0.0
By Bill	87.0.0
Note to Mr Laing	40.0.0
Mr. Harris sent to the Cape	100.0.0
By Bill	28.0.0
Mr Palmer's Account	1028.6.6 ½
Lieut. Macarthur	756.4.0 ½
Mr Piper	4.0.0
Mr Laycock's order Lowe	64.0.0
Making in all	£3,212.16.2

Figure 22: Officers' Payments to W. Raven, August 1794.[134]

Unquestionably, by their initiative the officers launched Australian commerce, and if they had not done so there might very well have been little wholesale importing, indeed little commerce above the level of the crudest barter, for some years. Significantly this monopoly of wholesale trade lasted only as long as there were no other colonists with access to substantial sterling resources in cash or credit.[135]

The civil officers did not enjoy the same access to funds as the military, but they certainly shared similar advantages, such as receiving a Government salary. Thomas Moore would one day be amongst that group, taking his place amongst the group of new traders who arose after 1800, but for the present, like his companion Robert Murray, he was one of those on board the *Britannia* able to observe the officers' enterprise, and to talk about how it was being done.

Moore's visit to Sydney enabled him to join in the birthday celebrations for King George III, reported by Collins: 'His Majesty's birthday did not pass without that distinction which we all, as Englishmen devoted to our sovereign, had infinite pleasure in showing it'.[136] Thomas had not been in Sydney with the *Britannia* on her previous visit, so this was his first experience of His Majesty's colony under Major Francis Grose.

No doubt Moore would have learned of Grose's change of practice in regard to land grants.[137] Apparently without specific instructions from his superiors, Grose issued about 25 acres (10 ha) of land to serving members of the Corps who requested them. The Home Office permitted land to the officers, but Grose exceeded this permission by also providing ten convicts to work their farms, provisioned from the Government stores. The civil officers were also treated with similar indulgence. By now some convicts were completing their sentences and Grose also provided small holdings to these emancipists and the small number of free settlers who had come to the colony.

Grose must be credited for opening up the richly endowed soil of the Hawkesbury region to farming, where a large number of these small holders settled. His new practices arose out of the conviction that 'the community stood to benefit far more from the exertions of private individuals than from government enterprise'.[138] The public farms had not performed well enough to feed the settlement and Grose pinned his hopes on private farming, especially that of his fellow officers. Despite having other detrimental effects on the colony, his regime certainly gave a boost to its primary production.

Murray was not the only contemporary to criticize some of the abuses introduced at this time. When Governor Hunter arrived and asked them their opinion of this period, the chaplain Richard Johnson

CHAPTER 2 ⚓ *Adventuring (October 1792–September 1796)* 99

and his new assistant Samuel Marsden, who had arrived on the *William* on 10 March 1794 (Plate 15), as well as Thomas Arndell, raised their voices against a variety of moral abuses, no doubt with some exaggeration.[139] In 1794, however, the small holders were situated pretty well, even if they were subject to greater exploitation by the officers as time went on. Nevertheless,

> by encouraging the officers' farming pursuits and allowing them to engage in trade, Grose enabled them to secure a hold over the colony which they were soon to exploit in their own interests. Unwittingly he helped to create problems that none of his immediate successors was able to surmount.[140]

In the months before *Britannia* brought Moore back to Sydney, land began to be granted in the district of Bulanaming. Here, between the area known as Petersham Hill and the Cook's River, Robert Abell, John Jefferies, Thomas Hughes, Thomas Alford, and James Young, who had all originally come to the colony as convicts, each received 30 acres of land early in 1794, and Nicholas Divine, Supervisor of convicts, received 120, and Thomas Smyth, storekeeper, 30 acres. In October, Edward Laing, Surgeon's mate in the Corps, and in November, one Thomas Wood also received grants in this area (100 and 30 acres).[141] In time, Moore himself would pursue his own farming interests in this district, and perhaps even now as it was opening up, he began to imagine himself as one of its pioneers.

This visit also gave Thomas Moore the opportunity to make his re-acquaintance with Surgeon John White, whether through a visit to his home, or when the surgeon was giving medical attention to Robert Murray in his illness. Circumstances had changed for White and Rachel Turner. White had already applied for leave, even before Rachel bore him a son (23 September 1793).[142] Just over a month after the birth, the *Surprize* arrived (25 October), bringing James Thompson to take over from Arndell at Parramatta and news that another surgeon, Samuel Leeds, was soon to be on his way. It also carried a letter informing White that his application for leave had been approved.[143] As a tug in the opposite direction, about this time he received another 30 acres of land and, on 30 November, the new baby was christened at St Phillip's, Andrew Douglas(s) White.[144] Now with property, a child, and the woman who had given him that child, White had considerable pressure to stay within the colony. But the call from home proved too strong for him.

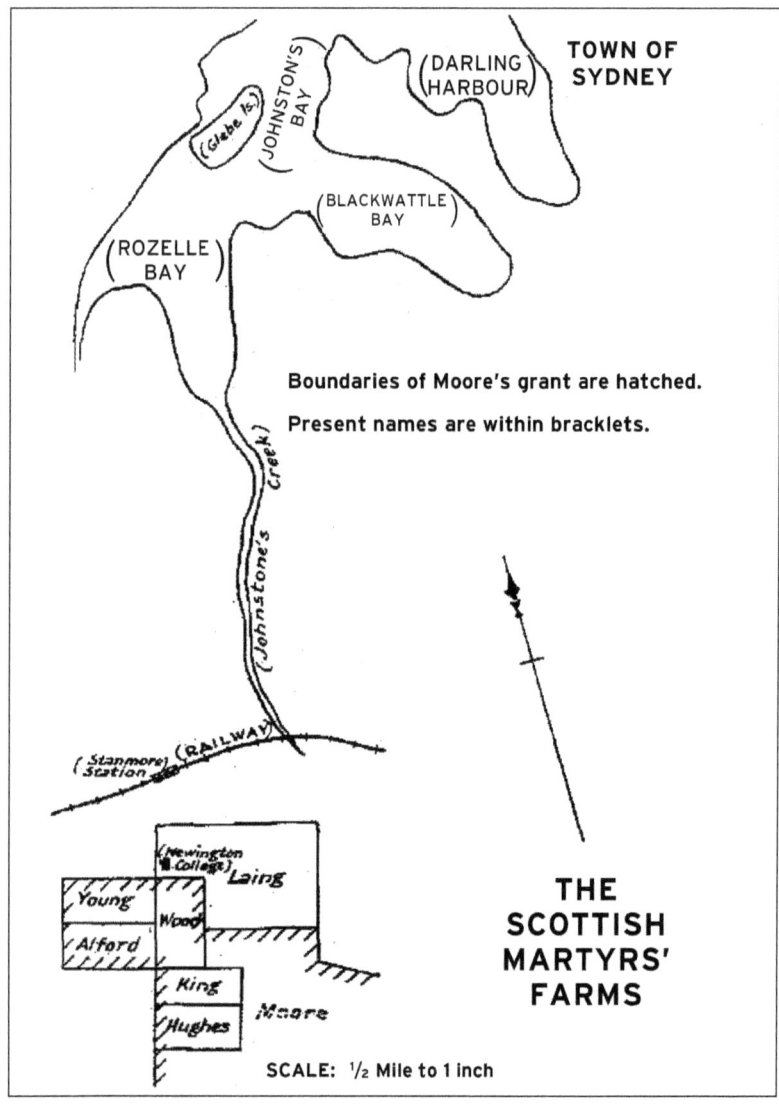

Figure 23. The Northern Corner of Moore's Bulanaming Property in relation to earlier land grants.

SYDNEY TO THE CAPE AND BACK (1 SEPTEMBER 1794 TO 3 MARCH 1795)

The *Britannia* weighed anchor for the Cape on 1 September 1794, with *Speedy* in company until the 19th. Once they had arrived,[145] Murray made some remarks on Table Bay on 16 November 1794, noting that:

> The distance we have sailed by Log since leaving Pt Jackson has been 10264 miles 2 fms, which in ten weeks and 5 days I consider to be very good going for a Merchant Ship.[146]

The various supplies destined for the Officers of the NSW Corps were loaded: brandy, wine, preserved fruits, butter, beef, mutton, and other items. Murray found the supplier, Mr Conrad John Gie, 'punctually an honest man'. Although Murray had been led to believe that at the Cape, 'the Ladies were not overscrupulous in the distribution of their favours', he was able to report things differently:

> I cannot say, but, that, I found Virtue as highly and generally revered among the Fat Dutch Dames and young maides at the Cape as among the most virtuous women I have known in Engd[147]

—apart from showing a certain 'freedom of speech' in the epithets used to abuse a wayward servant, for example.

After making sail at 5am on 12 January 1795, just six weeks later a part of New South Wales was sighted from the mast head on 26 February, and at noon on 2 March they entered the heads of Port Jackson to anchor and then work up to the Cove at 3am the following day.[148] Murray rounds off the voyage by noting:

> Since leaving Pt Jackson we have been 125 days at Sea and have a second time circumnavigated the Globe. Our distc sailed per log has been 16977,7 miles nearly that is, on an average 136 m 6 fms per day, or 5.5 an hour, the whole voyage.[149]

THOMAS MOORE'S THIRD VISIT TO SYDNEY (4 MARCH TO 17 JUNE 1795)

Thomas Moore and his shipmates had been absent from Sydney for six months and three days. When the cargo was unloaded, it included 33 new horses to be introduced to the colony—of the 40 that were loaded, one stallion, 29 mares, and 3 fillies had survived the voyage.[150] When Paterson gave a tally of the livestock on 15 June 1795, this brought the total number of horses in the colony to 49.[151] The arrival of the horses was big enough news to receive mention in a letter from Chaplain Richard Johnson, who also notes the asking price of one of them was £100.[152] At a later date, Thomas Moore became a breeder of horses, and horses of some note. Travelling with these mares from the Cape gave plenty of time for conversation and thought about their advantages to the new colony. The prices they fetched upon their arrival would have alerted him to their value as a profit-fetching commodity.

Captain William Paterson also wrote home about the horses. (Plate 10). He had been administrator of the colony since Major Grose left in December 1794—a post he would hold until Governor Hunter arrived in September 1795. He also reported the news from the *Experiment*, which also arrived in December 1794 from Bengal, that a large ship, the *Neptune*, had sailed with supplies from Bombay in July under the contract entered into with Captain Bampton, but she had been lost in the monsoon.[153] The *Experiment* had taken a cargo of 'the mahogany and cedar of this country, in the hope that if it should prove valuable in India it may be of advantage to his Majesty's interest in any future intercourse with that country which may be directed by Government'.[154]

Although not Irish himself, this visit to Sydney gave Thomas Moore a taste of Irish celebration:

> on the 17th [March] St Patrick found many votaries in the settlement. Some Cape brandy lately imported in the *Britannia* appeared to have arrived very seasonably; and libations to the saint were so plentifully poured, that at night the cells were full of prisoners.[155]

After disgorging her cargo, the *Britannia* was hauled into the stream.

The long-awaited Captain William Wright Bampton sailed up the harbour on Sunday 31 May, anchoring in the cove about 5 pm. His new ship was the 800 ton *Endeavour*, Bombay built, and laden with

132 head of cattle, rice and other articles.[156] For about two weeks prior to the departure of the *Britannia*, the *Endeavour* was at anchor alongside, enabling conversation between the two Captains. It appears that they made two arrangements with each other.

The first involved Robert Murray. Raven suggested to Robert Murray that he leave his employ to become Bampton's fourth officer. Although sad to leave the *Britannia*, Murray saw the sense in making this change for the sake of his advancement. His departure, however, means that we lose our commentator on the *Britannia* before her final trading voyage.

The second arrangement that was made between the two Captains concerned the vessel that Thomas Moore had built in Dusky Bay. When the *Endeavour* arrived in Sydney, she was already in a bad state. Just after the new Governor, John Hunter, arrived in September 1795, Bampton sailed for Dusky Bay. By the time the *Endeavour* reached New Zealand she was leaking so badly that Bampton scuttled her in Luncheon Cove. On the basis of later letters from Bampton, Collins reports that:

> By good fortune the vessel which had been built by the carpenter of the *Britannia* (when left there with Mr John [sic, his name was William] Leith the mate, and others, in that ship's first voyage hence to the Cape of Good Hope) being found in the same state as she had been left by them, they completed and launched her, according to a previous agreement between the two commanders. [...] He accordingly, after fitting as a schooner the vessel which he had launched, and naming her the *Providence*, sailed with her and the *Fancy* for Norfolk Island.[157]

'By previous agreement between the two commanders', suggests that, while the *Britannia* and the *Endeavour* were sitting next to each other in Sydney, Bampton had learned from Raven about Moore's vessel, and an agreement was reached that Bampton should take it as a replacement for his badly leaking ship. The two arrangements between Raven and Bampton may well be related. Did Bampton hire Robert Murray to ensure that he could find Moore's Dusky Bay vessel once again?[158]

After sailing to Dusky Bay in company with the *Fancy*, Captain

Dell, the ship was in even worse repair. On Saturday 12 October 1795, Murray took Bampton to find what he had come for:

> On the morning of this day I attended Captains Bampton and Dell to Luncheon Cove with an intent of seeing the vessel which Capt Ravens People had built and left there; we arrived at about 9 o'clock and landed at the Wharf, which was still standing, but was knocked off the posts which supported it, by the carelessness of the boats crew; we caught a few fish in the entrance of the cove, which we fried, and ate in the house; we afterwards looked at the vessel and I was a little vexed to hear them express a dislike to almost every part of her. We found in the House which had, thro' violence of the weather lost a part of its thatch, a number of casks [... of salt] The Try Pot and steam were as they were left. The plank which had covered the vessel and drying House, had a part blown off, but was sound, and well seasoned. Some of the planks of the vessel had shrunk and a plank or two on the bows at the wooden ends had rent. We set off for the Seal Islands at 11 am [...].[159]

Evidently, according to these dispassionate observers at least, Thomas Moore's vessel was not as highly regarded as it was in the initial reports from others. Murray's vexation at these comments, however, shows that his regard for Moore does not seem to have diminished at all. As he saw all the Dusky Bay timber once again, he recalled Moore's opinion of it in his journal:

> The timber which grows here, would answer very well for plank, for the Ship Builder, Joiner, or Cabinet Maker. This is the opinion of our Carpenter in the *Britannia*, he being as well acquainted with its properties as any man of his profession; and the Joiner preferred it to the wood of Port Jackson or the Brazil Wood. But I think it would be a task of some trouble, to get a Cargo of spars, sufficiently long for the masts of ships.[160]

At about 65 or 150 tons (depending on the report), the *Providence* was a dramatic 'downsize' from the *Endeavour* (800 tons), and not enough for Bampton to accommodate his crew and the forty-some stowaways he had discovered after leaving Sydney. After most were placed on the *Providence* and the *Fancy*, Bampton had to leave 'the

CHAPTER 2 ⚓ *Adventuring (October 1792–September 1796)* 105

remainder to proceed in a vessel which one Hatherleigh (formerly a carpenter's mate of the *Sirius*, who happened to be with him) undertook to construct out of the *Endeavour*'s long-boat'.[161] Even though, as even Murray himself later complained, she was a 'bad sailer',[162] the schooner built by Thomas Moore from native New Zealand timbers just two years before, finally took to the open sea.

Jno Hunter Esqr	Governor General
Capt W Paterson	Lt Governor for the time
Dd Collins Esqr	Judge Advocate
Jno Palmer Esqr	Commissary
Augustus Alt Esqr	Surveyor General
Mr Wm Grimes	Asst to do
Mr T Laycock	Deputy Commissary
Mr Williamson	Do do
Mr Wm Balmain	Senior Surgeon
Mr T Arndell	2d do
Mr Jas Tomson	3d do
Mr R Atkins	Judge at Parramatta
Mr Thos Smith	Store Keeper
Mr Wm Broughton	do
Mr Wm Baker	Superintendent
Nichs Devine	Do
Mr Tho Brewer	Provost Marshall
Revd R Johnson	Chaplain to the settlement
Revd S Marsden	Assist do

Figure 24: Robert Murray's list of 'The establishment at New South Wales', August 1795.

After being away from Port Jackson for six months, the *Britannia*'s carpenter now had half that time again available to enjoy Sydney. On

4 June 1795 he again found himself in town for the celebrations of His Majesty's birthday. The commissary gave out some extra rations to soldiers and those victualled from the stores. At noon the regiment fired three volleys and at 1 p.m. the *Fancy* and the *Britannia* gave a twenty-one gun salute.[163] (Figure 24).

If Moore went to visit the Whites, it was too late for him to catch up with John. The Surgeon had already left the colony on 17 December 1794, sailing with Major Grose on the *Daedalus*, with fellow passengers the Rev. Bain, Chaplain to the Corps, and Assistant Surgeon Mr Laing.[164]

In the last few weeks he was in the colony, John White had fallen in amongst the company of 'radicals', such as Rev. Thomas Fyshe Palmer, to whom Laing sold his Bulanaming farm. Palmer had been an eminent Unitarian in England and Scotland[165] before he was transported to New South as one of the 'Scottish Martyrs'—five political reformers sentenced in Scotland for sedition in 1793. (Figure 6 and 23). Palmer arrived in Sydney in October 1794 and 'soon became friendly with White, largely because both men were humanists and were actively interested in natural philosophy, and also, perhaps, because White realized that the reformer had been badly treated'.[166] Although their friendship lasted less than two months, White gave Palmer a house and four acres of land, and when he left Sydney in December 1794, he took documents in which Palmer described what had happened on his voyage. These were published in 1797.[167]

When John White returned to England, he left Rachel Turner behind in the penal colony to which she had been transported. But what happened to her infant son? In 1962, in his 'Biographical Introduction' to White's *Journal*, Rienits wrote that White 'apparently took his infant son, then aged 15 months'. Recognising no doubt the grief that this would have caused Andrew White's mother, Rienits found pleasing compensation in that

> two years later (11 January 1797), Rachel Turner married at St Phillip's Church, by special permission of Governor Hunter, a free settler, Thomas Moore, who became one of the colony's wealthy inhabitants and founder of the Moore Theological College.[168]

Rienits therefore supposed that after White reached Cork on 28 June

1795, and soon afterwards London:

> His first task was to find someone to care for his infant son. The responsibility seems to have been accepted by Elizabeth Waterhouse, sister of White's First Fleet companion, Lieutenant Henry Waterhouse, who was to become the wife of George Bass; for later in his life, Andrew Douglas spoke of her affectionately as "the earliest friend of my infancy" and named her as first beneficiary in his will.[169]

When Robinson wrote his 1970 article, he followed Rienits' suggestion that John White took Andrew home with him to England.[170] However, when further evidence surfaced in letters from Henry Waterhouse to Thomas Moore, Robinson appended a 'Postscript' revising this opinion. The Waterhouse correspondence strongly suggests that Andrew stayed in the colony when his father left in 1794, that Thomas Moore assumed responsibility for the boy when he married Rachel in 1797, and that Thomas and Rachel sent Andrew to England in the care of Henry Waterhouse in 1800.[171] In other words, when John White left the colony in December 1794, he not only left Rachel in New South Wales, but also his infant son Andrew.

Perhaps Rachel was better off without him. This would probably be the opinion of Thomas Watling, the first professional artist to arrive in the colony. (See Plates 16, 17, 22, 24). After arriving in the colony on the *Royal Admiral* on 7 October 1792, Watling was immediately assigned to White to assist him with sketching the flora and fauna. His sketches later bedecked White's published *Journal of a Voyage to New South Wales* (1790). Watling was not impressed with White's treatment of him, referring to himself as 'genius in bondage to a very mercenary, sordid person', and, additionally alluding to White as 'some haughty despot'.[172] Although there were certainly those who spoke well of Surgeon White, there were others who may have concurred with Watling's opinion. Lieutenant Ralph Clark, for example, who was teased mercilessly by White on the voyage out to New South Wales, or Lieutenant John Long with whom White quarrelled and almost fought a duel, or his assistant William Balmain, with whom he did fight a duel and against whom he apparently sustained a great deal of ill-feeling.[173]

On the other hand, although he left Rachel in the colony, White continued to be involved with Thomas, Rachel and Andrew over the years to come. On 30 October 1795, Under-Secretary King sent copies of the sentences of Rachel Turner and Margaret Dawson with his despatches. Margaret was the housekeeper and de facto of Surgeon Balmain, and the two women, placed in such similar circumstances, and living close to each other on High St (Plates 34 and 35), had become good friends. Under-Secretary King's covering letter drew attention to the fact that, 'the term of years for which those women were sentenced to be transported has been for some time concluded'.[174] In 1970, Robinson asked:

> Was the despatch regarding just these two women coincidental? Was it perhaps prompted by some representation on White's part, designed to put Rachel's freedom beyond dispute? He had arrived in London in July that year, and would have had access to the Under-Secretary in the ordinary course of his duty.[175]

Robinson's suspicions are confirmed by an incidental comment from Dan Byrne some time later:

> Shelton's Account No. 12 dated 17 October, 1795, was taken with Daniel Bennett for the *Indispensable*, Capt Wilkinson, 351 tons. Again, Shelton is mysterious. He made a copy certificate of the conviction of Rachel Turner "by Mr Pollocks desire and delivered same to Mr White, Surgeon-General of NSW to take out with him [...] The like of Margaret Dawson".[176]

Thus, when the *Indispensable* arrived in Sydney on 30 April 1796 bringing news of Rachel's emancipation, this was courtesy of John White and a sign of some kind of continuing care for her, even if he had left her behind.

Rachel reaching the end of her servitude was one of two circumstances Robinson speculated may have influenced White in his decision not to return to NSW; the other being the presence of Thomas Moore.[177] Thomas had three opportunities to become acquainted with Rachel, when he was with the *Britannia* in Sydney Cove between voyages, whether 1792, 1794, or 1795.[178] In August 1792, John White had been part of the team which conducted the survey of the

Britannia's damaged stores, which certainly gave him acquaintance with Captain Raven, and the opportunity to meet his carpenter.[179] White received his town lease from Grose on 15 May 1793, and Raven received a lease on the adjacent block in the Paterson months on 14 March 1795—after John White had already left the colony. (Plate 10).[180] According to Robinson:[181]

> The most natural place for Moore to have lodged onshore would have been the vicinity of these houses, perhaps even in the house of either Raven or White. There is every likelihood that he was well acquainted with both White and his housekeeper during his first visits to Sydney. Later, White allowed Moore the virtual ownership of his house, and entrusted him with the agency of his other properties.

Rachel received the news of her emancipist status soon after the Under-Secretary's letter was delivered to Hunter on 1 May. Moore arrived back in Sydney on 11 May, presumably lodging nearby once again, perhaps even next door in Raven's newly acquired leasehold. By September, Hunter had appointed him to build the dockyard, just down the street. Now that John White was no longer in the colony, perhaps Thomas showed her and Andrew a little more attention, and gradually she became one of the reasons he eventually decided to leave the adventuring life on the *Britannia* and to settle in Sydney.[182] However, to jump ahead in the story a little, the news that John White was definitely not going to return was not posted in Sydney until 17 May 1797,[183] by which time Thomas and Rachel had been married for four months. Robinson quite sensibly surmises that:[184]

> Considering Moore's reputation for probity, it seems likely that he would have acted with White's knowledge and approval in making an honest woman of Rachel, and this means that the whole matter must have been in White's calculations during 1795 and 1796 as he considered whether or not to return to the colony.

Was prior knowledge of White's non-return also part of any calculations Rachel and Thomas may have been discussing?

TO INDIA (18 JUNE 1795 TO 11 MAY 1796)

On the 18 June 1795 the *Britannia* sailed again from Port Jackson, this time for India.

> As the state of the settlement at the time of her departure required every exertion to be made in procuring an immediate supply of provisions, Mr. Raven was directed to repair to Batavia, to procure there if possible a cargo of European salted meat. The necessity of his immediate return was so urgent, that if he found on his arrival that only half a cargo could be got, he was to fill up the remainder of the stowage with rice and sugar, and make the best of his way back. If salted provisions were not to be got at Batavia, he was to proceed to Calcutta. Should circumstances run so much against us, as to cause his failure at both these ports, Mr. Raven was at liberty to return by way of the Cape of Good Hope, as provisions were at any rate to be procured, if possible.[185]

We no longer have Murray on board the *Britannia* to provide the details of the voyage. However, after Raven had returned to the colony, he gave advice about the best way to make the voyage, and from Collins' comments ('This passage the *Britannia* performed in sixty-five days from Port Jackson to Batavia'), it is clear that his advice described the voyage that he actually made. Since the route to India depends wholly on the season, firstly, he describes the route to be taken between October to the beginning of March:

> [...] which ought to be the latest period that any ship should attempt a northern passage, he recommended making Norfolk Island; and thence, passing between the Loyalty islands[186] and New Caledonia, to keep as nearly as circumstances would allow in the longitude of 165 degrees East; until the ship should reach the latitude of 8 degrees South; and then shape a course to cross the equator in 160 degrees East; after which the master should steer to the NW by N or NNW until in the latitude of 5 degrees 20 minutes or 5 degrees 30 minutes North; in which latitude Mr. Raven would run down his longitude, and pass the south end of Mindanao, and between that island and Bascelan; and thence through the straits of Banguey into the China Sea. In running this passage, it would be necessary to pay attention to Mr. Dalrymple's charts of those islands, etc. which Mr. Raven found very accurate.[187]

CHAPTER 2 ⚓ *Adventuring (October 1792–September 1796)*   111

This most recent voyage, however, beginning as it did on the 18 June, required a different route:

> If leaving Port Jackson any time between the beginning of March and the 1st of September, Mr. Raven would prefer passing through a strait in the longitude of 156 degrees 10 minutes E or thereabout; and from the latitude of 7 degrees 06 minutes E to 6 degrees 42 minutes S which divides some part of the islands of the New Georgia of Captain Shortland; thence through St. George's Channel to the northward of New Guinea, through Dampier's Strait, down Pitt's Passage, to the southward of Boutton, and through the Straits of Salayer, into the Banda or Amboyna Sea. This passage the *Britannia* performed in sixty-five days from Port Jackson to Batavia; which, had it not been for calms she met with off the coast of New Guinea, would in all probability have been performed in six weeks, or thereabout.[188]

According to Collins, she had 'anchored in Gower's Harbour, New Ireland (on the 16th of July), where she completed her wood and water', and sailed on the 23rd, which provides rough dates for the three weeks of calms.[189] This was not an easy time for Raven and his crew—as came out in a trial some years later.

When the *Britannia* sailed from Port Jackson, an unplanned passenger had crept on board. John Chilton had come to the colony as a convict after being sentenced to death for highway robbery in October 1791, but then receiving a commutation of his sentence to transportation to NSW for life. In 1805, when he was tried again for having escaped from 'Botany Bay' and returned to England, Captain Raven gave evidence in his favour from the time he was on board the *Britannia*.[190]

Chilton had not left New South Wales with the Governor's permission, but had escaped 'in the ship *Britannia*, for Bengal, where the prisoner entered into the pilot's service; he shipped himself on the 6th of October, 1795, on board the ship *Minerva*'. Raven testified that Chilton was a stowaway, discovered about three days after leaving Port Jackson, and staying with Raven for about three months, until they arrived at Calcutta, Bengal. Raven was impressed with his conduct, and his testimony probably saved the 62 year old Chilton's life. After being sentenced to death (the second time in his life!), the jury recommended mercy due to his good conduct since leaving Botany Bay. In the course of giving his character reference, Raven revealed further details about the voyage:

> I never saw a man behave better in my life, and the circumstance that caused me to mark his conduct above the rest of the people was, we were without provisions almost, for about three weeks, on the north coast of New Guinea, when the rest of the crew were murmuring, and seemingly inclined to mutiny, I never heard a syllable of discontent from this man all the time.[191]

Thus, after sailing from a colony rather desperate for supplies, the *Britannia* had had her own food crisis. Being 'without provisions almost, for about three weeks' on the North coast of New Guinea, with many of the crew on the brink of mutiny. If the fact that Raven remembers that Chilton was not among those murmuring means that he stood out from the crowd, then this indicates that Raven had trouble with the majority of the 30-man crew. Presumably Thomas Moore's rank on the ship not only prevented him from murmuring against the Captain, but involved him in assisting Raven to pacify the men in these this hungry couple of weeks.

Raven also took another extra passenger from Sydney on this voyage, an aboriginal youth who had received the name 'Tom Rowley', after Captain Thomas Rowley of the regiment. Two years later, when back in the colony, he was killed by two men who were acquitted at trial, the court having found Tom was shot accidentally. In reporting the case in October 1797, Collins noted that the lad had accompanied Raven to Bengal in 1795.[192] During the voyage, Moore had the opportunity to get to know young Tom, as he had already gotten to know Nanbaree, in John White and Rachel Turner's household. These conversations no doubt prepared him for the days to come when the settlers around Liverpool had trouble with the original custodians of the land. At that time it was noted how well Moore got on with 'the natives'.

The ship arrived at Batavia on 2 September. Raven quickly decided that he would be too long detained by the government if he waited for them to make a determination about supplying provisions, so he sailed

CHAPTER 2 ⚓ *Adventuring (October 1792–September 1796)* 113

on the 7th for Bengal. This took them past the scene of their conflict with the pirates, but this time they made it into the Straits of Malacca and arrived in the Ganges on 12 October.[193]

When the *Britannia* sailed through the Straits, a new political situation prevailed, having been established rather dramatically with the arrival of British Fleet in these waters with some force only weeks before.

After the French Revolutionary armies had taken the Netherlands, Malacca was handed over to the British to avoid it being taken by the French. The British fleet arrived at Malacca Road in August, and the commanders delivered a letter written in February requiring the Governor, Abraham Couperus, to admit them as friends and allies, and to hand over all authority over defence and military operations. Although willing to receive the British as allies, Couperus felt it was against his sense of honour to hand over command of the fort. Negotiations across 15 to 17 August 1795 failed to get him to surrender the command, and so by 9 p.m. on the 17th, the British troops were landed on the beach. Reports of what actually happened next are not straightforward, but it appears that a 'purely nominal skirmish' ensued, with no casualties on either side. By 10pm, in fact, not only had Couperus' surrender document been received by Captain Brown on his ship, but Brown had signed off on receiving it and arrangements were being made to negotiate British possession of the town. With the rapidity with which events occurred, it is understandable that rumours of treason have attached to Couperus' name. However, it seems that when faced with the initial refusal of the British to compromise their demands for surrender of command, he came up with his own solution.

> Couperus' decision to resist was a reluctant one and it may well be that he resolved privately to restrict actual hostilities to a minimum, while preserving his honour by making an outward show of resistance.[194]

Sailing when she did, the *Britannia* would have been one of the first ships to go through the Straits after the British had assumed power in Malacca.[195] Last time it was pirates and privateers, but this time, she made it through safely to Calcutta.[196] (Plate 19).

News of *Britannia*'s arrival at Bengal reached Sydney via McClellan of the *Experiment*, who arrived back again on 24 January 1796.[197] The version of events that came to Sydney by this means suggested that, after arriving at Batavia, Raven had quickly learned that it was unsafe, so he left the port after about four or five days, managed to escape being captured and arrived at Bengal, from whence he had planned to sail in December 1795.

In fact, the shoe appears to have been placed firmly on Raven's other foot. While in India filling the vessel with stores, Raven also entered into negotiations with the honourable East India Company, which made the *Britannia* an active participant in the war. Whereas previously she had feared the French Privateers, now she herself became a privateer, receiving the Letters of Marque that enabled her to legitimately engage enemy vessels on behalf of the East India Company in order to take them as prizes of war.

As a consequence of this new capacity, on 18/12/95 Thomas Moore also received a commission from the East India Company.[198]

> WHEREAS open Hostilities have taken place between His Most Sacred Majesty the King of Great Britain and the French Nation, **AND WHEREAS WE THE SAID UNITED COMPANY** are duly authorized and empowered, [...] to raise and maintain Forces and Armies both by Sea and Land, and to appoint such and so many Generals, Commanders, and other Officers, as we shall think fit for the purpose of encountering and resisting by Force of Arms, all and every the Enemy and Enemies of our said Sovereign Lord the King [...] and the said Enemies and every of them, their Ships, Armour, Ammunition, and other Goods, to invade and destroy in such manner as in and by the said Charter [...]
>
> do by these presents and under and by Virtue of the Royal Charter aforesaid, constitute and appoint you T. Moore to be a Lieutenant in our Naval and Marine Service for and under our Presidency of Fort William in Bengal, and to be Second Lieutenant of the *Britannia* Ship of War employed in our said Naval and Marine Service against the said French Nation, during the Hostilities aforesaid [...] but without any Pay, Subsistence, Charge, Allowance, or other Compensation whatsoever [...]

CHAPTER 2 ⚓ *Adventuring (October 1792–September 1796)* 115

> AND we do by these presents authorize and empower you the said T. Moore by force of arms or otherwise to apprehend, seize and take the Ships and Goods belonging to the French Nation, [...] and, to bring the same to such Port as shall be most convenient in order to have the same legally adjudged and condemned as Prizes [...] AND for the better and further encouragement of you the said T. Moore and of the Owners, Commissioned and Warrant Officers, Seamen and others, of and belonging to the said Ship *Britannia* and in lieu of Pay, Subsistence, and other Charges and Allowances WE THE SAID UNITED COMPANY do hereby relinquish and quit claim to all and every Part or Parts, Share and Shares of and in all each and every Ship or Vessel, and of and in all Stores, Goods, Arms, Ammunition, and other Articles whatsoever, taken or found in or on board of all each and every Ship or Vessel, which shall be captured and finally condemned as lawful Prize, by the set Ship *Britannia*.

This is the second oldest document we have from Moore, after the 1790 travelling certificate from the Freemasons Lodge. Even though he had escaped Militia service as English tensions were escalating in the shadow of the French political situation on her doorstep, he now found himself caught up in the war with the French after all—on the other side of the world.

Ever alert for a business deal, Captain Raven also got the ship involved in a potential new scheme for enlisting troops into the Bengal Army from amongst the convicts in New South Wales. As Collins reported after the *Britannia* had returned to Sydney:

> On board of this ship arrived two officers of the Bengal army, Lieutenant Campbell and Mr. Phillips, a surgeon of the military establishment for the purpose of raising two hundred recruits from among those people who had served their respective terms of transportation. They were to be regularly enlisted and attested, and were to receive bounty-money; and a provisional engagement was made with Mr. Raven, to convey them to India, if no other service should offer for his ship.[199]

Raven would, of course, profit from this arrangement, as the Bengal Military Department explained to Hunter:

> On consulting with Captain Raven, we find that if your concurrence be obtained, and provided you have no immediate service on which his ship can be more usefully employed, he is willing, after receiving his discharge from the service of Government, to proceed with 200 recruits to Bengal, where we have agreed to allow him £2 a man for the passage and subsistence of each recruit he may land at Fort William.[200]

The *Britannia* shipped cargo at Calcutta for some months, but, even so, they were not able to secure the required stores. On 1 February 1796, Raven therefore sailed for Madras, where he anchored on the 15th. (Plate 19).

> Not being able to procure at Calcutta the full quantity of provisions that his ship could contain, he sailed for Madras on the 1st of February, where he anchored on the 15th. There he completed his cargo, and sailed, with five homeward-bound [ie to England] Indiamen, on the 27th of the same month.[201]

Light and contrary winds made the voyage to Sydney long and tedious. On Wednesday 11 May 1796, she sailed into the harbour, 'to the great satisfaction of the settlement at large', 'entering this port for the fifth time with a valuable cargo on board'.[202] Collins speaks of Sydney's joy at receiving Raven's bounty:

> we were all well pleased to be in possession of the comforts he brought us from that part of the world, and to congratulate him on his personal escape from the sickly and now inimical port of Batavia, as well as from the cruisers of the enemy, with which he had reason to suppose he might fall in on the Indian coast.[203]
>
> [...] She was now freighted with salted provisions, and a small quantity of rice on account of government, procured by order of the presidencies of Calcutta and Madras. On private account, the different officers of the civil and military departments received the various commissions which they had been allowed to put into the ship; and one young mare, five cows, and one cow-calf, of the Bengal breed, were brought for sale.[204]

THOMAS MOORE'S FOURTH VISIT TO SYDNEY

If this was the *Britannia*'s fifth visit to Sydney, it was Thomas Moore's fourth. This time, however, he was here to stay. While Moore had been away, a new Governor had arrived in New South Wales. On 7 September 1795, Governor John Hunter had arrived on board the *Reliance*, Henry Waterhouse, in company with the *Supply*, William Kent. In the future Captain Henry Waterhouse and his Surgeon on the *Reliance*, George Bass, would become entwined closely with Thomas Moore and his family. Arriving in the same party were two more officers of the New South Wales Corps, as well as Mr S. Leeds, assistant-Surgeon, and Mr Daniel Paine, Master Boat Builder.[205]

When the EIC recruitment officers, Lieutenant Campbell and Mr Phillips, disembarked to explain their enlistment scheme, it initially appeared plausible to the colonists, for, as Collins explained, 'we imagined that the execution of it would be attended with much good to the settlement, by ridding it of many of those wretches whom we had too much reason to deem our greatest nuisances'. But then they discovered the recruiting officer had been instructed to enlist no-one of 'known bad morals', so the perceived benefit to the settlement suddenly plummeted. Not only would the bad characters they would want to go stay, but it was also feared that good settlers might be induced to enlist, leaving their farms, and their families a burden on the stores. The Governor therefore decided to await further communication from his superiors on the subject, and suggested that there may be many good recruits amongst 'that class of our people who, being no longer prisoners, declined labouring for government, and, without any visible means of subsisting, lived where and how they chose'.[206]

Since the arrival of the new Governor, the Johnsons, at least, detected changes for the better. Mary wrote just before Christmas in 1795,

> since that time the Lord's Day has Been Better observed we have a tolerable Congregation not quite so good as yours—the Governor and his family always attending on Sunday morning I wish the other officers would take example By him—I still hope to see a reformation among these poor unhappy people.[207]

By July 1796, the *Britannia* had been discharged of her cargo and was refitting for sea. Even though he had not done much fishing to speak of, Raven's three-year licence issued by the East India Company was coming to an end, and he was in search of further profits to be made from his voyage home. While Carpenter Moore and his team made the necessary repairs and improvements for the forthcoming long voyage, Raven therefore

> proffered her to the Governor for the purpose of going direct to England, if his excellency should have any occasion to employ her in such a voyage. There were at this time several soldiers in the New South Wales Corps wholly unfit for service; the governor had for some time intended to send home Mr. Clark, a superintendant of convicts, whose engagement with the crown had expired; and James Thorp, a person who had been sent out with a salary of £105 per annum, as a master millwright, but who was at this time unemployed in the settlement. To ease government at once of these expences, the Governor thought it advisable to charter the *Britannia*, for the purpose of taking home such invalids and passengers as might be ordered, at the rate of fifteen shillings per ton per month; the charter to be in force on the first day of the ensuing month.[208]

Thus, by Raven's initiative some little income was achieved and a date of sailing was now set. Hunter, on the other hand, by this arrangement was able to not only ship those invalided out of the military, but also to '[exonerate] the colony of a number of useless people whose contracts with Government have terminated'.[209] He elaborated further in another letter a week later, saying that one of the pressing reasons he engaged the *Britannia* was in order to remove

> the continual expence as well as burthen to this colony occasioned by persons sent here upon salaries who have not yet been of any use, and who having served the time contracted or agreed for by Government are by that contract to be sent home at the expence of the Crown.[210]

On 21 September, 'the invalids and passengers who were returning to England in the *Britannia* being embarked, that ship, the *Reliance*, and the *Francis* schooner, hauled out of the cove preparatory to their

CHAPTER 2 ↓ *Adventuring (October 1792–September 1796)* 119

departure'.²¹¹ Collins himself was on board, with commissary Palmer on the *Reliance*, both of whom had been in the colony from its inception and both were gratified at the changes that had come about. When they left the stores were full, and the houses of the inhabitants not only contained 'most of the comforts', but also 'not a few of the luxuries of life', due to the trade that had occurred with India and other parts of the world—directed by the Officer-Trader monopoly notwithstanding. Collins concluded, therefore, that 'the former years of famine, toil, and difficulty, were now exchanged for years of plenty, ease, and pleasure'.²¹²

The *Britannia* sailed on 29 September in company with the *Reliance* and the *Francis* to Norfolk Island, at which point the *Francis* was to return to Sydney, leaving the other two vessels to proceed to the Cape of Good Hope. As passengers on the *Britannia* sailed Captain Paterson, Lieutenants Abbot and Clephan, one sergeant and seventeen privates of the Corps with their wives and children, Judge-Advocate Collins, Assistant-Surgeon Leeds, Thomas Clark, former superintendent of convicts, James Thorp the master millwright, and several other persons. At Norfolk Island, Lieut.-Gov. King was taken on board, departing for England on a period of leave after 'a long state of ill-health'.²¹³ After leaving Port Jackson on 29 September 1796, the *Britannia* was at Norfolk Island between 16 and 23 October, rounded Cape Horn on 16 December and at the Cape one month later. Here almost all the ship's company were either pressed into, or volunteered for, the king's service and repairs were difficult to get done, so they remained about eight weeks. With the threat of enemy craft, they unsuccessfully waited at St Helena for a few weeks for a convoy, and finally, avoiding the enemy in the Channel, arrived at Liverpool on 27 June 1797.²¹⁴ One month later the *Britannia* was able to sail to Gravesend, and her five and a half years of adventuring were over.²¹⁵

THOMAS MOORE SETTLES IN NEW SOUTH WALES

But when the *Britannia* sailed for home, she left Thomas Moore in Sydney. Governor Hunter had come to New South Wales with a dream to build a Naval Yard, and with a promising young man to be devoted to the task. But less than twelve months after their arrival, Daniel Paine had proven insufficient for Hunter's hopes and had fallen amongst those the Governor was reluctant to pay.

According to his account books, Thomas Moore's first activities as a trader come from this period, immediately after the *Britannia* arrived back in Sydney in May 1796, and these activities were of two kinds.[216]

Firstly, as a wholesaler Moore sold some goods, which he had evidently purchased in Bengal for his own onsale. On 18 May he sold John Stogdell, the First Fleet convict who became a prominent settler along the Hawkesbury himself, and who helped to develop Commissary Palmer's farm in that district as well: 7 Cases of Brandy @ £7 ea, £49; 1 Qumr Chest of Tea 300 Rupees, for £37-10; and a dozen cups and saucers, for £1. Tea and chinaware, along with silks, were classic Chinese merchandise, and in Sydney spirits were the only thing more valued.[217] No doubt Moore made a bit of money in this transaction and presumably so did Stockdell when he retailed the merchandise for a profit along the River.

As well as making some sales from his own imported exotics, when the *Britannia* sailed away, Moore acted as dealer or agent for the sale of goods belonging to two other members of the *Britannia* crew. His account book shows that on behalf of Captain William Raven, he sold chests of Tea (£30 each), sugar and pieces of fancy cloth to Mr Smith—probably Thomas Smyth—and to Sergeant Akin. At the same time, an account was opened for a Mr John Leith, who seemed to specialize in various kinds of whips, which he sold to Simeon Lord for a total of £18-19-2. Once again, this looks like a wholesaler's transaction—given the number of whips sold—and Lord would have then acted as retailer.

John Leith was probably also one of Moore's shipmates on the *Britannia*. Although this cannot be definitively proven, it is suggested by the fact that Leith's accounts are contiguous with Raven's and that he was selling such exotic items at this time. He turns up again in Moore's accounts in 1802 as 'Captain' Leith, which indicates he was certainly a seafarer. In addition, when Collins narrated the story of the sealing party from the ship being left at Dusky Bay, he mistakenly called second mate William Leith, John.[218] Did he do so because he was aware from his own experience of the crew when in Sydney that there was also a Leith by that name on board?

Thomas Moore's account books show little evidence that he continued as a wholesaler in the next several years after his initial trade in 1796. Two years later he sold 81 bushels of wheat to John Stogdell @ 10s, total cost £40-10-0, as well as advancing him £12 cash and selling him two yards of broad cloth @30s (£3) and a new tea kettle (£1-5-0). The same year he also sold two watches to James Hanks (£5-5-0 and £4-15) and paid £1 on Hanks' behalf to William Roberts. But these seem to be the only possible wholesale trades recorded in this period. However, if wholesaling only lasted for a moment, once Moore started acting on behalf of others, his taste for being an agent or dealer—especially for seafarers—seemed to last for years.

It is impossible to know how much the presence of Rachel influenced Thomas in deciding to stay in New South Wales. Comments from his pen from much later in life show a deep affection for his wife, but when did that affection first strike him?

When they first met, she was the housekeeper-mistress of Surgeon John White, but White had left her and her infant son behind when he returned home in December 1794. Since that time, it remained uncertain in Sydney whether he was going to return to New South Wales or not. It seems clear, however, from White's perspective in England, that he had no intention of returning. On 5 September 1795 White 'was restored to half pay, and sixteen days later he was appointed surgeon of the hospital ship *Spanker*, a position he held until the following July'. It was about the same time that White made arrangements for a copy of Rachel's sentence to be sent to NSW to prove her emancipation.[219]

Meanwhile in Sydney, because Balmain had petitioned for extra staff, the new Governor, John Hunter, wrote to Portland, who responded by writing to White on 10 August 1796 demanding that the Surgeon return to the colony immediately on the *Ganges*, sailing within the week, or on the *Britannia* (not Raven's) sailing within three weeks, at pain of losing his appointment. Once the demand had been made, White immediately declared that he would not return, for Portland wrote the next day (11 August 1796) informing Hunter that

William Balmain had been appointed 'chief surgeon, in the room of Mr White, who declines returning to the settlement'.[220]

On the eve of the *Britannia*'s departure, the Governor announced several appointments to various positions in the establishment of the colony. Captain George Johnston was appointed aide-de-camp to the Governor; Rev. Richard Johnson and William Balmain magistrates in the town of Sydney; James Williamson was to do the duty of commissary while Palmer was absent on leave; Thomas Smyth was provost-marshal; William Stephenson, a store-keeper; George Barrington, superintendent of convicts. It was also time for a change for Mr Moore, 'second mate' on the *Britannia*, for the same Government Order announced:

> Mr Thos. Moore is appointed to the place of master boat-builder, in the room of Mr Daniel Paine, commencing on the 2nd instant.[221]

This would be a post he held for the next 13 years. If Collins' prophecy proved true, then Moore was about to enter the colony's 'years of plenty, ease, and pleasure'![222]

3
BUILDING THE DOCKYARD
(2 OCTOBER 1796 to 7 MAY 1803)

Thomas Moore took over duties as Master Boat Builder of the colony on 2 October 1796. His first task was to build a proper dockyard. John Hunter had big plans for this dockyard. Whereas Hunter's first appointment to this position was a disappointment, Thomas Moore combined his skill and energy to make Hunter's vision a reality.

MOORE'S PREDECESSOR: DANIEL PAINE

When the First Fleet arrived in January 1788, it came with specific orders preventing the building in the colony of boats with a keel of more than twenty feet, in order to protect the trade monopoly of the East India Company.[1] In December 1788 Mr Reid, carpenter of the *Supply*, erected a boatshed on the eastern shore of Sydney Cove (Plates 22, 24 cf. 29), and as early as 1792 Arthur Phillip drew attention to Sydney's need for 'one or two good shipwrights' to keep the local marine craft in good repair.[2] But it was the mounting crisis of the shortage of England's shipbuilding timber that led to John Hunter being instructed to find someone 'to fill the office of boatbuilder &c at Port Jackson'. Out of curiosity and a desire to see foreign climes, one Daniel Paine from the Deptford Naval Dockyard applied and was accepted. Paine had served his apprenticeship under William Hunt (1784–1791),[3] and he presented to Hunter as 'a Clever young man [...] well recommended to me both for his Theoretical and practical knowledge'.[4] Travelling with John Hunter on Captain Henry Waterhouse's *Reliance*, in company with George Bass, Matthew Flinders, and the Australian Aboriginal, Bennelong (who had gone with Governor Phillip in December 1792, met George III, and was now on his homeward journey),[5] Daniel Paine arrived in Sydney on 7 September 1795 to begin his duty as the colony's first Master Boat Builder.[6]

Although Paine left a journal, it does not reveal much about his role. According to his editors Knight and Frost:

> Paine is curiously and disappointingly silent where we might have almost wished him to be eloquent. Apart from describing the qualities of some fifteen varieties of New South Wales timber, he offers few details of his work, which must have constituted the substantial beginning of Australian boat-building.[7]

In fact it is rather unclear whether Paine made any real 'beginning' to Australian boat-building at all.[8] Presumably his duties centred around Mr Reid's boat-shed, for construction of the dockyard proper only commenced in Moore's time, June 1797.[9] It is certainly possible that he 'clearly performed his official duties diligently',[10] but there is little evidence to prove that he did.

His own relative silence about his activities is matched by a similar silence in the official record. He is listed on the Return of Civil Officers in October 1795, and he is still on the Return of 20 September 1796—despite the order replacing him with Thomas Moore being issued on the 13th.[11] The only duty explicitly connected with Paine's name is the registration of the boats of the colony. Hunter's orders directed owners to present their vessels to Paine for marking. However, this order was given on 18 July 1796,[12] at which time the series of events leading to

CHAPTER 3 ⚓ Building The Dockyard (2 October 1796 to 7 May 1803)

Paine's dismissal had already begun and perhaps his personal involvement, even with this task, may have therefore been rather minimal. Even so, painting numbers on boats is a far cry from building them!

In December 1795, Hunter was concerned about the urgent need to rebuild or repair the boats of the colony, being convinced that 'no time must therefore be lost in putting them in such a state as to render them safe and useful'.[13] From Paine's journal,[14] however, it seems that the new Master Boat Builder was otherwise occupied at this time. As his only entry for December 1795, he states that he 'was busily employed in getting a House fitted up in the Town'. He had been staying out of town on Nicholas Divine's farm at Bulanaming, but this had proved too inconvenient. To be fair, his move was apparently motivated by his work, for he comments that his workmen required close supervision. But nevertheless, his own lodgings seemed to take his entire attention in December—if his journal entry is anything to go by. This continued into January, when he was 'fully employed in fitting up my Premises with Stock Yard and other conveniences and preparing the Garden for the production of Roots and Vegetables &c'. There is not much evidence that Hunter's Master Boat Builder shared the Governor's urgency for boat repairs.

The record does, however, contain several items of work, which would naturally fall under the purview of his position. In January 1796, the American vessel, *Otter*, called in for repairs, departing 18 February.[15] Since Hunter reported that his locals assisted in these repairs, no doubt Paine was also involved.[16]

1796

When the *Otter* left Sydney, it was discovered that Thomas Muir, who—with Thomas Fyshe Palmer, Maurice Margarot, William Skirving, and Joseph Gerrald—was one of the famous 'Scottish Martyrs', had escaped upon her; one of the first facts noted by Paine in his newly begun journal not related to his domestic activities.[17] The group was rapidly and further depleted one month later, when Gerrald died on 14 (or 16) March and Skirving within the same week.[18] This was the end of this group, for Margarot had already been excluded by the others for his attempt to implicate Palmer in a mutiny on the voyage out, and even after the other three had gone, Palmer presumably continued with the decision to place him 'in Coventry'.[19]

While the alienated Margarot lived separately with his wife who had accompanied him to New South Wales, the other Martyrs lived in close proximity to each other. In town, Palmer and Muir lived together and Skirving and Gerrald in houses alongside, and the three men also had neighbouring farms 'in the country'. This much is clear from a letter Palmer wrote to the famous Unitarian minister, Rev. Theophilus Lindsey, in September 1795: 'Mr Muir lives with me and [...] he, Skirving, and I live in great cordiality; our houses at Sydney are contiguous, as also our farms in the country'.[20] However, the exact location of the Scottish Martyrs' farms has been obscured. On 13 December 1794 Muir informed a friend, 'I have a neat little house here, and another two miles distant, at a farm across the water, which I purchased'.[21] When narrating Muir's escape, Collins referred to this farm, noting that whilst in New South Wales Muir 'chiefly passed his time in literary ease and retirement, living out of the town in a little spot of ground which he had purchased for the purpose of seclusion'.[22] A later French account (after his escape, Muir reached France, where he died in 1798) reported that he had 'stayed about two years on this remote shore, where he sometimes applied himself to the cultivation of a small piece of land with the help of two servants who had followed him', often reading or fishing.[23] Because of Muir's reference to 'two miles distant, [...] across the water' J.H. Watson identified his farm with the 30 acres granted to Samuel Lightfoot in February 1794, opposite Sydney Cove in what is now known as Milson's Point.[24] As James Scott has shown, however, there are several reasons why this identification does not fit, and, in any case, there are positive indications that Muir's farm was actually in Bulanaming.[25]

This is proven by the location of Thomas Fyshe Palmer's farm, which, according to his letter to Lindsey, was right next to Muir's. On 11 December 1794, just two days prior to Muir writing to his friend, Palmer purchased Edward Laing's farm for £84.[26] This farm suits Muir's own description, because it was roughly two miles by road out of town (probably more like three) and with the small boat he was permitted to keep it was easily accessible by water from Sydney, after a further walk up Johnston's Creek. (Figure 23).

CHAPTER 3 ⚓ *Building The Dockyard (2 October 1796 to 7 May 1803)* 127

The farms of the Scottish Martyrs hold further interest for the life of Thomas Moore. The paper-work connected to land grants during this period of colonial history is not as good as it could be. There was no special office for registering sales of land and, Scott explains, 'it appears to have been the custom when farms were sold to hand over the deed of grant together with a receipt for the purchase money. In some cases an endorsement was made on the deed, giving particulars of the sale'.[27] Although we know that Palmer purchased Laing's farm, it is difficult to say which grants were sold to Muir and Skirving. Scott felt 'impelled towards the conclusion' that Muir bought one, and Skirving three or four of the five grants to Hughes, Alford, Young, Wood, and King.[28] Scott then observes that 'the whole of these five grants was consolidated into a grant of 470 acres, dated October 5, 1799, to Thomas Moore, the master boat-builder'.

When Moore later sold these farms as part of a larger package of land to Robert Wardell on 21 July 1830, he apparently had to explain his lack of genuine legal title to the five cancelled grants that had been bundled into his 470 acres. The conveyance insisted that Moore was 'justly lawfully and rightfully possessed of them and seized in his demesne as of fee'. Presuming that this was to confirm 'that he became possessed of them in a way that was perfectly above board, but that he was unable to obtain the signatures of the rightful owners', Scott further speculates:

> after the escape of Muir and the death of Skirving, Palmer, as their best friend, exercised a verbal power of attorney, took charge of their deeds and in all good faith sold them to Moore with the intention of handing over the proceeds to the representatives of Muir and Skirving when he returned to his native land.[29]

From a 'radical' family himself,[30] Daniel Paine can be linked with these men during his brief time in Sydney, perhaps also mixing with the wider circle in their company, such as Captain Henry Moore, James Ellis and the three surgeons John White, John Boston, and George Bass.[31] Since he initially resided at Nicholas Divine's farm in Bulanaming, this puts him in the neighbourhood of the Martyrs' farms, where they spent much of their time, for the seclusion—which, of course, meant out from under the close scrutiny of government eyes. Paine also spent time with Margarot, the Martyr out of favour with the others. When Paine fell foul of the authorities at the end of his time, his association with these political radicals proved detrimental to his reputation. Although unsubstantiated, rumours circulated that George Washington had sent the *Otter* to extract Muir and any of the other Martyrs who wished to leave.[32] Paine's access to the *Otter* during her repairs raises the interesting possibility that he may have helped prepare for Muir's escape.

On 26 Oct 1795, Bass and Flinders had sailed on one important voyage of discovery, and on 24 March 1796, Paine's fellow-passengers on the *Reliance*, departed on their second. Paine may have supervised the building of the second *Tom Thumb*, which conveyed them on their journey.[33] If so, he did engage in some little boat-building during these early months—and with a significant vessel.

If there is only a little information about Paine's boat building and ship repairs, there is not much more for his timber-gathering. However, this is probably not the kind of 'event' that would often make it into the record and it is, in fact, likely that this was one of Paine's major interests. The need for naval supplies lay behind his original appointment. His *Journal* shows that he had become familiar with the native timbers, for he was able to describe some fifteen varieties in the midst of his remarks on New South Wales.[34] When the *Journal* abruptly ends, he is in the Philippines with clear plans to set up a sawmill to harvest the country's native timber.[35] Being a child of Deptford raised during the looming timber crisis, the need for naval timber would have been deeply ingrained in him and this may well have been where he spent his energies in New South Wales.

When the *Britannia* arrived back in Port Jackson, Daniel Paine added his own subtle criticism of the Officer-Traders and their enterprises.

> May 10. Arrived the *Britannia*, Captn Raven from Madras with some Provisions of the Colony but the greater part of her Cargo belonging to the Gentlemen Monopolisers she having been taken up for about half her Burthen on Account of Government by the former temporary Governor whereby the Officers were accommodated with

CHAPTER 3 ⚓ *Building The Dockyard (2 October 1796 to 7 May 1803)* 129

> proportionable ventures on very advantageous terms by Captn Raven & Co on board the said Ship but on which some doubts were entertained respecting the General Interest of the Colony being benefited of Individuals interested there was none.[36]

Despite his convoluted and sarcastic evaluation of the benefits to the colony of the *Britannia*'s partnerships, Paine provides a fulsome description of the larger-than-life William Raven's reception in the colony:

> So great was the anxiety with which the *Britannia* and Captn Raven had been expected and the many Doubts and fears under which some People laboured for their Safety so high that my Concern mingled with Curiosity had been excited for a Sight of this Ship and her *Great Commander* (truly so for he was almost as big as three common sized Men).
>
> *Great* and *tumultuous* was the *Joy* and *ludicrously extravagant* was the *Exhibition* of it on the Arrival and Landing of this *Great Man*. He was met and attended by the Principal Officers of the Colony, the Military Band playing and a Chaise belonging to Colonel Paterson the Military Commandant was brought by the Soldiers to the landing place in which his Ponderous Body was placed and dragged by a Circuitous Route to the Barracks amidst the noisy Huzza's of the Soldiers the Town in an uproar and the Music at one Time even struck up the *Military* Air *He Comes the Hero comes*.
>
> Having with some difficulty alighted at one of the Officer's Houses orders were then given that the Soldiers should drink Captn R.'s Health in some Bengal rum and towards the close of the Day its Effects were visible in a number of his Welcomers.
>
> Such were the *Honours* paid to this *Great Man* much greater than those paid to Governor Hunter on his Arrival although his Character and Virtues were well known in the Colony. But he brought no Supply of Rum with him![37]

Paine was eventually dismissed as Master Boat Builder as a result of a series of events arising from the robbery of his house on 5 July 1796.[38] While Paine spent the evening with Maurice Margarot, one of his servants, David Lloyd, used Paine's gun to kill the intruder and was convicted of manslaughter and sentenced to 600 lashes. Paine forcibly expressed his disagreement and was found guilty of contempt of court. When he would not agree to make an appropriate concession to the court, he was dismissed from his position and, on 2 October 1796, Thomas Moore commenced work 'in his room'.

During David Lloyd's trial (8 July 1796), a deponent mentioned in passing 'a black man that had been up with Mr Paine's people cutting timber'.[39] The editors of his *Journal* comment that 'this remark suggests that Paine drew on Aboriginal knowledge to identify suitable timbers and locate stands of them'.[40] Soon after Hunter arrived, he had issued orders to prevent indiscriminate cutting of timber on crown land:

> in order to preserve as much as possible such timber as may be of use either for building or for naval purposes, the King's mark will be forthwith put on all such timber, after which any person or persons offending against this Order will be prosecuted. This Order extends only to grounds not granted to individuals, there being a clause in all grants from the Crown expressly reserving for the use thereof such timber as may be growing, or to grow hereafter, upon the said land which may be deemed fit for naval purposes.[41]

Presumably it would have been Paine's responsibility to seek out these trees and to mark them with the King's mark—probably the broad arrow traditionally used for this purpose.[42] (Figure 33). This, in itself, would have been a time-consuming exercise. The comment at the deposition, however, also indicates that some cutting of the timber had probably begun. Normally timber was stored and seasoned for a matter of years before being used in shipbuilding, but with only Reid's boat shed to work from and a proper dockyard still in the future, it is difficult to imagine Paine having the advantage of a seasoning shed for cut timber. When combined with the small amount of evidence of actual ship-work, this may indicate that in the short couple of months Paine was Master Boat Builder, he spent much of his time marking naval timber, without necessarily cutting much of it down.

Given his experience with Paine, we are left wondering if Hunter's thoughts included his Deptford-trained Master Boat Builder when in August he complained that 'in many of those people recommended to

Govern't at home to fill little offices here much imposition has been practis'd'. Given the rumours he had already heard about Paine's successor, we can also wonder if he numbered Thomas Moore amongst 'some of the ingenious people who are sometimes to be found here', whose appointment would not only be cheaper (there being no need to ship them out), but better.[43]

Whatever his reasoning about the two men, Hunter let Paine go, and hired Thomas Moore to start work on 2 October 1796. From that moment, Moore was in New South Wales to stay.

MOORE BEGINS THE KING'S DOCKYARD

This was the era in which the English Naval Yards were under the supervision of 'Carpenter Master Shipwrights'. In the Royal Dockyards since the mid-seventeenth century, 'the Master Shipwrights were recruited from the Assistant Master Shipwrights, who in turn were advanced from the Master Boatbuilders, Master Mastmakers and Master Caulkers', who were recruited from shipwrights and carpenters of H.M. ships. The Master Shipwrights for foreign yards were usually selected from naval ship's carpenters, or from Assistant Master Shipwrights of the home yards. After the School of Naval Architecture was established in 1811, this led to the extinction of the 'Carpenter' Master Shipwright.[44]

When Paine was appointed and when Moore succeeded him, both men bore the official title 'Master Boat Builder'. Given the prohibition on building ships that was imposed upon the colony to protect the EIC interests, it was probably not appropriate to suggest that Sydney had 'shipwrights'. It is interesting to notice, however, especially in the light of Hunter's desire to build a Naval Yard, that Thomas Moore gradually acquired the latter title as well. Probably also because of the 'no ship-building' policy, the Sydney dockyard was apparently not listed as one of the overseas naval yards. (Figure 25). This is an injustice, however, since for many years the King's Dockyard in Sydney Cove kept His Majesty's Ships afloat, providing much-needed repairs and refits for the vessels that sailed into the South Seas—and at a crucial period of British seafaring history.

Name	Carpenter of H.M.S.	Where Master S/wright	When Appointed
Elias Marshall	*Britannia*	Halifax	3/2/1793
James Smith	*Magnificent*	Jamaica	4/2/1793
William Hill	*Invincible*	Antigua	3/3/1794
Francis Adams	*Queen*	Gibraltar	15/2/1794
William Burnett	*San Josef*	Martinique Gibraltar	30/1/1796 10/8/1804
Thomas Moore	**Merchant Ship *Britannia***	Sydney	13/9/1796
Edward Carey	*Victory*	Gibraltar	21/3/1803
William Lemon	*Impregnable*	Antigua	26/11/1804
William Bunce	*St Vincent*	Bermuda	28/11/1806
John Clark	*Ville de Paris*	Cape of Good Hope	27/12/1810

Figure 25: Carpenter Master Shipwrights in Foreign Yards from 1790 to 1810.[45]

Hunter may have had the vision, but it was Thomas Moore who brought this dockyard into existence. It was the opportunity of a lifetime to be invited to fill this position. Even if Moore had been a carpenter on one of the King's ships, the chances of him rising through the ranks of the Royal Dockyards in England to Master Shipwright would have been slim indeed.[46] When Thomas was doing his apprenticeship, even entry to the yards was difficult. Even when this problem was solved by the outbreak of the war with France (1793), every shipwright had to work his way up from the floor, and the selection process was haphazard, favouring those who were actually apprenticed to already serving officers. That it was impossible for an apprentice of an ordinary shipwright to gain such a position is demonstrated by the fact that 'all of the Master Shipwrights in the last quarter of the eighteenth century had been apprenticed to former Master Shipwrights'.[47] Given the length of time it took to rise through the ranks, the average age of attaining the rank of Master Shipwright was thirty-five, of attaining the first post as Master Shipwright, forty-five, and that of the last posting, sixty.[48] But all of this is rather moot, for, as a carpenter from a merchant yard, Thomas Moore would not be in the running at all. And yet, at the other side of the world this thirty-four year old ship's carpenter apprenticed in a merchant yard in the Northeast of England and freshly off a merchant ship, now found himself appointed to realise Hunter's vision for a Naval Yard in Sydney Cove.

Hunter almost certainly heard of Moore's prowess in ship-building after the vessel he built in New Zealand became a matter of public renown. Hunter's first tour of duty in New South Wales was commanding the *Sirius*, part of the First Fleet. By the time Raven first arrived in the *Britannia*, Hunter had already returned home,[49] and so his first meeting with Raven would have been in May 1796, soon after Raven's rather extravagant welcome back to Sydney of a scale even beyond that given to the Governor. Just like Hunter would have already heard of Raven before he left England, no doubt he had already heard of the ship built at Dusky Bay as the news filtered back through P.G. King and other official channels to those at home. With the arrival of Raven and the *Britannia* in May 1796, Hunter now had his chance to hear the story first-hand, and even to meet the much-renowned carpenter who had performed such an amazing feat almost single-handedly in the world's most distant backwater. Captain Raven had noticed the skill with which his ship's carpenter worked exceeded that usually found in those trained in merchant yards. Just four months after he first had the opportunity to meet Mr Moore, Hunter, disappointed with his Deptford trained Daniel Paine, took a risk with one of the 'ingenious persons' who was already on the spot in Sydney.

Having done his apprenticeship somewhere in the Northeast of England, Moore was already at the leading edge of shipbuilding, especially with his openness to building with timbers other than oak. Given the increasing difficulty of procuring the various pieces of 'crooked timber' necessary to build the wooden ships, innovative designs had begun to appear which minimised the need of some of these pieces. The ship that Moore commenced in 1797, but which was only completed long after his time at the King's Yard (she was launched in 1816 as the *Elizabeth Henrietta*), appears to have been an innovative design. The 1804 painting of Edward Dayes shows it on the stocks in Moore's dockyard, with the straight uppers of 'modern' shipbuilding practice, rather than the curved timber required by those building ships in a previous era. (Plates 27, cf. 26 and 28, and Figure 28). Apparently the Scottish Martyr and Unitarian minister, Thomas Fyshe Palmer, in partnership with John Boston and James Ellis, managed to build a ship from the information he found in an encyclopaedia he brought with him.[50] Presumably Palmer's information would be a little more dated than that in front of the trained Thomas Moore.

CAT. NO	BOOK TITLE
1.13	L Euler, *A Compleat Theory of the Construction and Properties of Vessels with Practical Conclusions for the Management of Ships made Easy to Navigators* (1776; new edition 1790).
1.14	Peate's *Lectures*. Possibly the syllabus for *A Short Account of a Course of Mechanical and Experimental Philosophy and Astronomy* (1744)
2.8	J. Ozanam, *Recreations in Mathematics* (1696, 1708, 1803)[51]
3.1	P. Kelly, *A Practical Introduction to Spherics and Nautical Astronomy; being an attempt to simplify those Sciences* (1796).
3.15	? M. Sibly, *Astronomy and Elementary Philosophy* (1789).
5.10	D. Steel, *The Elements and Practice of Rigging and Seamanship* (1794).
5.11	A. & J. Churchill, *A Collection of Voyages and Travels* (1704, 1732, 1752).
6.12	*Sea Sermons*. ? Perhaps H. Valentine (1635), or J. Ramsay (1781).
7.5	W. Falconer, *An Universal Dictionary of the Marine* (1769, 1771, 1780, 1784).
8.11	J. Seller, *Practical Navigation. An Introduction to that whole art* (1669).
9.2	Anonymous, *The Shipbuilder's Repository; or A Treatise on Marine Architecture* (1788).
9.7	Lots of Maps
	Almanacs and Calendars

Figure 26: Books of interest to the Seafarer on Thomas Moore's bookshelf.[52]

CHAPTER 3 ↓ *Building The Dockyard (2 October 1796 to 7 May 1803)* 135

By the end of his life Moore had accumulated a substantial library, which included several important works relating to his work as a ship's carpenter. (Figure 26). Moore had none of the older works of interest to the seafaring trades in 1635,[53] but he possessed several of the volumes circulating in the eighteenth century.[54] The older volumes, A. & J. Churchill, *A Collection of Voyages and Travels*, originally published in 1704, but more recently in 1752, not only contained accounts of various voyages, which would naturally be of interest to the seafarer,[55] but it also published material on navigation, and, for the first time, Book 3 of W. Monson's *Naval Tracts* which dealt with shipbuilding.[56] It was probably in common use by the time Moore was under instruction. In a similar category, Moore's bookshelf included one of the two classics on shipbuilding, Falconer's *Universal Dictionary of the Marine*, first published in 1769, but running into many editions with at least six editions in the time from when he started his apprenticeship until he sailed for Australia (1776, 1779, 1780, 1784, 1787).[57] Presumably it was during this period, that he acquired this, 'the standard work'.

Several volumes on Moore's shelf, especially when taken together, suggest that he was keenly interested in keeping up with the leading-edge thinking of his trade. Euler's *Théorie complete de la Construction & de la Manoeuvre des Vaisseaux* (1773) appeared in English in 1776,[58] that is, just as Thomas Moore was beginning his apprenticeship. If he acquired this as it was published, he would be learning with the most recent textbook in his hand. The same can be said for the anonymous *The Shipbuilder's Repository*, which, although undated, can be securely ascribed to 1788.[59] This volume is both theoretical and practical, but the practical side dominates. As Moore commenced as ship's carpenter on the *Britannia*, did he purchase this volume, another 'latest'— the most recent book on Naval Architecture—to equip him in his various tasks? David Steele's two-volume work, *The Elements and Practice of Rigging and Seamanship*, became a standard work amongst shipwrights, with detailed instructions and diagrams relating to rigging, masts and re-masting, and a glossary of all relevant terms.[60] It was only published in 1794, well after Moore had left England, but it is tempting to speculate that he acquired a copy soon after its publication, shipped to Australia, just as he was beginning his work at the Dockyard. Its many topics would be of vital interest to him in his new role: Mast-making, Rope-making, Anchor-making, Sail-making, Block-making, Rigging, Seamanship, Naval Tactics, etc, and after the initial quarto edition the many reprints in octavo would make it a handy pocket-book for any master boat-builder or master shipwright. Before leaving Moore's professional library, it might also be worth noting that he did not have any of the high-level books on Naval Architecture that were starting to come out. In the early years of the nineteenth century the new mood for a more theoretical training for shipbuilders would clash with the older, practical emphasis.[61] Like other 'Carpenter' Master Shipwrights, Thomas Moore had a very practical training. His library clearly reveals him to be a ship-builder at the practical end, but at the same time, it suggests that he liked to keep up to date with the various advances in thinking that governed that practical task.[62] His Northeast training gave him facility in working with other timbers and the Dusky Bay vessel had already whet his appetite for what could be done with the timber of these new climes. And now, Hunter's offer opened up even more opportunities. In a new dockyard in the colonies, far from the conservatism of the English yards, his creative juices should be able to really flow.

But the job opportunity of a lifetime was probably not the only factor that took Moore from the sea to the land. For by October 1796, he was probably already well-acquainted with Rachel Turner.

THE WEDDING

When Donald Robinson assured his 1970 readers of the probity of Rachel marrying Thomas Moore in January 1797, some months before the news of White's non-return to Sydney was officially proclaimed, he hinted that she must have had a previous arrangement with her ex-lover.[63] Whereas Robinson had only Rienits' 'Biographical Introduction' to assist him, the fuller biography of E.C. Nelson now enables a further piece of the puzzle to fall into place.

John White was almost forty when he returned to England after his stint in New South Wales. He lived in London for a few months when he first returned, enjoying some fame because of his published journal and the botanical samples he had sent home which had been drawn and published by others.[64] After being restored to half-pay in September 1795, he was nominated as a Fellow of the Linnean Society on 17 November. After resuming his career as a naval surgeon on the hospital ship *Spanker* in December, on 19 January 1796 his nomination to the Linnean Society was successful and he became a Fellow. In August 1796, when he received the ultimatum to return to New South Wales and declined, Surgeon John White joined the yacht *Princess Augusta*, but by the end of the year he had transferred to HMS *Royal William*. On 12 December 1799, he was transferred to Sheerness Yard where he stayed until 24 September 1803, when he moved to Chatham Yard to serve out the rest of his time before being superannuated on 15 January 1820.[65]

But to back track to the time he initially returned, residing in the Parish of St Mary le Bone proved advantageous for him, and on the leap year date of 29 February 1796, White married one of the daughters of the parish, Elizabeth Priscilla Losack, aged 35.[66] Over the next several years, John White pursued the medical qualifications he never had when he came to New South Wales,[67] and Elizabeth bore him several children: Richard Hamond, Clara Christiana, and Augusta Catherine Anne (who went by the name 'Anne').[68]

There was therefore plenty of time for the news of White's wedding to reach New South Wales, even if he had not chosen to tell Rachel beforehand. In other words, everything was totally above board when, on 11 January 1797, Rachel married Thomas Moore, with Richard Johnson officiating:[69]

> The solemnization of the Matrimony By special Permission of his Excellency John Hunter Esq' Governor &c Between Thomas Moore & Rachel Turner married the 11 day of January in the year of our Lord one thousand seven Hundred & ninety seven By me Richard Johnson. This marriage was solemnized between us [T. Moore signed; Rachel Turner signed] in the presence of. [Thos. Smyth; Margt Dawson].

Margaret Dawson was the housekeeper-de facto of John White's Assistant Surgeon, William Balmain. When she attended the wedding, she was heavily pregnant, for the birth of her first child to Balmain was just ten weeks away.[70] Thomas Smyth had come to New South

Wales as a sergeant in the marines and had been appointed Superintendent of Stores by Governor Phillip about the same time that Moore had first arrived in Sydney in 1792. He was well reputed among Moore's shipmates on the *Britannia*. When Robert Murray stayed at his store in 1795, he wrote:

> Having no accommodation, I slept on shore at Mr Smiths, the Store Keeper, the character of that Gentleman is so well known by persons who visit Port Jackson, that any tribute I could pay would be superfluous.[71]

Presumably Moore also got to know Smyth when still carpenter on the *Britannia*. Smyth received a lease in High Street in November 1794,[72] so lived in Rachel's neighbourhood. In October 1799, Smyth and Moore would also become neighbours through gaining adjoining farms at Bulanaming.[73] In January 1797, Smyth stood with Margaret Dawson to witness Thomas and Rachel coming together in holy matrimony. The knot tied, Thomas was devoted to Rachel for the next forty years—and to her son Andrew.[74]

As Thomas and Rachel were exchanging vows in Sydney, Henry Waterhouse was on an historic voyage to the Cape of Good Hope. At the end of September, his *Reliance* had sailed in company with the *Supply* on the same mission and with Raven's *Britannia* returning to England.[75] Others had made this voyage before, of course, but in 1797 Waterhouse brought back from the Cape a number of sheep of the Spanish breed—later more commonly called merino. This cargo therefore held promise for the future of Australian primary industry.[76]

Although Australia began as a penal colony, it was only a matter of time before questions began to be asked about its future as a nation. Growth towards maturity would require breaking free from an economy basically reliant upon the government stores (and so on convicts)[77] and the development of its own economy and industry. It was in this context that a number of people began to look for potential Australian products that could be exported in order to return a profit. The search for a 'staple' would take the early entrepreneurs into seal skins, whale oil, and timber, but, in time wool was one of the products, which, at least in the eyes of some, held enormous potential.

CHAPTER 3 ⚓ *Building The Dockyard (2 October 1796 to 7 May 1803)* 139

When the First Fleet arrived in Australia in January 1788, it brought a small handful of sheep from England.[78] Exactly one hundred years later, Australia was proclaimed to be 'the first among the nations in the production of wool'.[79] A key factor leading to this position of prominence was the development of Australia's distinctive fine wool through the introduction and selective breeding of the merino.

One of the long-running debates of Australian history concerns the question: who really deserves the credit for introducing the merino into Australia?[80] Is it the colourful Captain of the NSW Corps, John Macarthur?[81] Or is it the famous chaplain, Samuel Marsden,[82] whom Governor King called 'the best practical farmer in the colony'?[83] (Plates 12, 15, 39). Both men (and in the case of Macarthur, his wife Elizabeth) played a significant role in the development of the NSW wool industry through selective breeding of merino, along with a few others, such as Alexander Riley and his family.[84] The potential value of wool to Australia began to be more widely appreciated in 1812 when, for various reasons, some of Marsden's fleeces fetched enormous prices in the English market, as did fleeces from Marsden, Macarthur and Riley in the following year.[85] This continued to happen, until this first boom peaked about 1825, before the harder times of the second quarter of the century.[86] Without a doubt, in these early days the two significant names were those of Marsden and Macarthur.[87]

Macarthur has been called 'Australia's first major entrepreneur',[88] and his skills were honed to perfection as Paymaster of the Officer-Traders in the heady days of the 1790s monopoly. His motives were undoubtedly connected to his 'ruthless pursuit of wealth',[89] whereas Marsden's agricultural pursuits in large part arose from his view of Christian mission as a civilizing force in the world.[90] But, despite their different motivations, both these men had a far-sighted vision of the place of wool as a future export for the colony. While other farmers were largely killing their sheep for mutton,[91] these men were carefully breeding theirs to produce better wool. And the key to this programme in these early days was the introduction of the merino to the colony. However, neither men can take the credit for the merino's introduction. That honour belongs to Captain Waterhouse.

This is the report that Sir Joseph Banks had already heard by

1803:⁹² 'They were originally procured from Spain by C'l Gordon, who imported them into the Cape of Good Hope, and purchas'd of his widow, I think, by Capt. Waterhouse, of H.M. Navy, who carried them from thence to Port Jackson'. Three years later, he confirmed the report by writing to Waterhouse, who then gave his own account of the historic 1796–1797 voyage:⁹³

> In <u>1797</u> I arriv'd in the <u>Reliance</u> at the Cape of Good Hope, together with the <u>Supply Capⁿ Kent</u>, and Brittania Transport, on board the Reliance was the Commissary for the purpose of purchasing Cattle for the Settlement on board the Brittania Govʳ King & Colonel Paterson on their way to England. Both which Gentlemen had been acquainted with Colonel Gordon who lost his life there—<u>Colⁿ Gordon</u> had imported a few Spanish sheep to the Cape which had increas'd to <u>thirty two</u>. <u>Mʳˢ Gordon</u> was then going to Europe & for some reason did not chuse to leave any thing that had belong'd to her late Husband at the Cape, she gave <u>three</u> Spanish sheep to <u>Govʳ King</u> and <u>three</u> to <u>Colⁿ Paterson</u>, the remainder I understood were offerd to the <u>Commissary</u>, but he <u>declin'd to purchase them</u> on the part of Government. They were then offer'd to <u>me</u>, as I could not afford to purchase the whole, Captⁿ Kent (that they might not be lost to the Colony) offer'd to <u>take half, a[nd he] receiv'd thirteen</u>, and I took Govʳ Kings on [board] the Reliance, <u>Colⁿ Paterson</u> took his to <u>England</u> to present to Sir <u>I Sinclair</u>, we paid Mʳˢ Gordon <u>four pounds</u>⁹⁴ apiece for them, the expences on delivery, was about <u>one pound ahead</u> more, the expence for food &c for the passage was very considerable, unfortunately Govʳ Kings sheep had been brought to the Cape Town some time before ours, & put with some others, by which they became <u>diseas'd</u> & communicated it to ours, his <u>three died</u> soon after they came onboard, I do not recollect the numbers I had alive when I arrived at Port Jackson,⁹⁵ but think more <u>than half</u>, Capⁿ Kent who I understood shared his with Lieuᵗ <u>Braithwait</u>, I believe lost all, from the circumstance of his applying to me for one immediately on my arrival, I do not recollect if Lieuᵗ Braithwaite had one or two alive.

In 1797, Waterhouse had written a version to his father, which itemized the menagerie the *Reliance* shipped back to the colony:⁹⁶

I left the Cape [...] the 11th of April, and with a ship most completely full, having on board forty-nine head of black cattle, three mares, and one hundred and seven sheep. I believe no ship ever went to sea so much lumber'd.

The passage to Port Jackson normally took from 35 to 40 days, but on this occasion the *Reliance* took 78. Waterhouse had purchased much of the stock for himself—three cows, two mares, and 24 sheep, according to his own report. After reaching Sydney, this entailed a change of life for him:

In consequence of having so much stock, I thought it necessary to get a farm, and found the cheapest way was to purchase one. I have therefore given one hundred and forty pounds for one, with a good house, &c, on it. I am at present so well pleased with it that I do not mean ever to part with it.[97]

The property causing Waterhouse such delight was that known as 'The Vineyard' at Parramatta.[98] This was one of the first four land grants in NSW, issued on 22 February 1792 by Arthur Phillip to James Ruse, Robert Webb, William Reid, and to Phillip Schäffer,[99] who received 'the Vineyard. He was a German brought to the colony for his expertise in farming, but who did not really perform as well as expected. When Captain Henry Waterhouse required a farm, Schäffer therefore sold it to him in August 1797.[100] Two months later, Waterhouse was also granted a further 4.5 acres of land abutting 'The Vineyard'.[101] In 1812 Waterhouse gave Thomas Moore the job of managing his NSW property, which soon devolved into selling it all up, after Henry died in July of that year.[102]

	No	Balance
Widow Gordon	32	32
King & Paterson	6	26
Kent & Braithwaite's half	13	13
Waterhouse's half	13	
Waterhouse's loss	6 or 7	7 or 6

Figure 27: Waterhouse Sheep available for distribution.

In his 1806 letter to Banks, Waterhouse also spoke of what happened to the Spanish sheep when they arrived in the colony.[103] If widow Gordon had 32, gave 6 to King and Paterson, Kent & Braithwaite took half, and then all of Kent's, some of Braithwaite's and half of Waterhouse's died on the voyage, Waterhouse must have only had about 6 or 7 merino left by the time he arrived in Port Jackson. Since some of the ewes had lambed, this was as something of a bonus to be added back into the equation. Waterhouse did not keep them all, but he expressly desired to distribute them amongst the other colonists.

> I offer'd all mine to the Governor
> but I suppose he was satisfy'd as they were in the Colony, as he declin'd purchasing them.
>   Cap^n McArthur then offerd fifteen Guineas a head provided I would let him have the whole this I declined wishing to distribute them
>   I supply'd Cap^n Kent, Cap^n McArthur, Cap^n Rowley, & Mr Marsden. As the Spanish Ewes had Lambs (none but Spanish Rams running with them) I supplyd Mr Williamson, Mr Moore, Government and in fact any person who wish'd to have them.[104]

Mere arithmetic suggests that it would be difficult for the persons listed here to have received much more than one ewe apiece, perhaps with her lamb to boot. (Figure 27). However many survived from amongst Braithwaite's six or seven also enriched the NSW flocks in some small way. It is interesting to notice that Waterhouse, who did not see himself amongst the factions of New South Wales, deliberately refused to supply Macarthur with his entire number. He nevertheless supplied sheep to Macarthur and his fellow Officer-Trader Rowley, and to Williamson who was also connected to that circle. But perhaps as his own small protest against the monopoly—and as a sign it might be breaking down—he also gave sheep to those outside these circles: to his fellow Naval officer Kent, to Chaplain Marsden, and to Mr Moore.

Although the identity of the 'Mr Moore' who received a share of the Spanish sheep from Waterhouse has sometimes been left open,[105]

CHAPTER 3 ⚓ *Building The Dockyard (2 October 1796 to 7 May 1803)* 143

some have mistaken him for William Moore of the NSW Corps,[106] and others have anachronistically misidentified him as solicitor W.H. Moore—who only arrived in Sydney in 1814.[107]

The 'Mr Moore' was, in fact, Thomas the recently married Master Boat Builder. This identification is proven by a letter from Henry Waterhouse, written on 20 October 1804, evidently in response to Thomas Moore sending him a report of the bad state of his farm. After asking Thomas to assist Captain Rowley in doing anything that may improve the situation, Waterhouse then ventures an opinion on the future of Australian wool. He says,

> The spanish wool, & some of the woods of N.S. Wales, I believe will shortly be an object of attention to Government, from which I think you may profit, by keeping your wool & & c.[108]

Although we could wish that he had spelled out what he meant by '& & c', this tantalisingly brief comment is most illuminating for the purposes of our puzzle. By the time of this letter, Moore had been the official 'Purveyor of Timber' for the colony for over one year.[109] In view of England's urgent need of timber for shipbuilding, the Australian timber was being touted as another potential export for the colony. Indeed, the letter from Moore to which Waterhouse was responding had been conveyed by the *Calcutta*, which, as we shall see below, had returned to England laden with samples of Australian timber for this purpose—loaded by Moore's endeavours.[110] In this letter, Waterhouse encourages Moore by informing him that 'some of the woods of N.S. Wales, I believe will shortly be an object of attention to Government'. But, for the purposes of the 1797 sale of sheep, his mention of the other potential Australian export is noteworthy. In Waterhouse's opinion, the Government will soon turn its attention to Australia's 'Spanish wool'. This being so, if the market is about to begin its boom, then those holding Spanish sheep will, of course, begin to make a profit. Waterhouse therefore counsels his old friend that he also may soon begin to make some money, 'by keeping your wool & &c'.[111] Waterhouse evidently knew that Thomas Moore had some Spanish sheep because he had been the one to sell them to him in 1797. What he did not realise, however, is that by the time he wrote in 1804, Thomas Moore's husbandry had already moved in a different direction.

The purchase of the sheep, however, shows that even in 1797, having made a little money already from his Government salary, Moore was beginning to expand his interests into farming. But it raises the question, where did Thomas Moore keep the sheep he purchased from Waterhouse? The first recorded land granted him was a parcel of 470 acres given by Governor Hunter in October 1799,[112] that is, two years after the sheep arrived. If this date represents the first time he actually received land, since he probably only purchased a couple of sheep at the most, presumably he could have housed them on someone else's property.[113] But since he was acquiring sheep (and perhaps at least by 1799, horses),[114] it is probably more likely that he already owned—or occupied—some land. If he had designs on settling in Sydney even while he was still on the *Britannia*, he may have received a grant of land prior to actually settling in the colony, during the period when Major Grose or Colonel Paterson was in charge, when records were not well kept.[115] Captain Raven had acquired some land during this time, for example, and perhaps Moore did as well—or perhaps he put his stock on Raven's land in the Eastern Farms?[116] Or, alternatively, he may have purchased someone else's land grant prior to 1799. Such a purchase would not appear in the records, just like Waterhouse's purchase of Phillip Schäffer's property 'The Vineyard' does not appear in the official records, yet the extant deed proves that it actually occurred. It is also interesting to notice that the records of Thomas Moore's first land grant in 1799 are annotated in such a way as to allow for the possibility that he may have already held the land for some time. When Hunter submitted his return of 6 February 1800, which reported on lands granted since 1 August 1796, it is clear that Moore received this land earlier than Hunter's period of Government, for his 470 acre grant is listed as being given 'by different Governors, but renewed in one grant by Governor Hunter'.[117]

Later Governor King complained, 'Unfortunately, it is individuals who possess the Spanish rams; and I believe they do keep the breed as pure as possible'.[118] But not everyone was assiduous in their care of their flocks. For some, the sheep became a ready source of mutton. For

CHAPTER 3 ↭ *Building The Dockyard (2 October 1796 to 7 May 1803)* 145

others, perhaps proper breeding was just too difficult, especially given the limited numbers of sheep they may have had in their possession. Although his reasons remain unknown, despite buying some of the first merinos in Australia in 1797, Thomas Moore was amongst those who did not maintain a long-term interest in sheep. Although his flocks numbered 40 head in 1800, by 1801 he had dispensed with his flocks, as he gradually moved more into horses and cattle.[119] In the search for staples, other more immediate opportunities for trade were emerging.

Even by 1797, the colony was not a happy place. In August when Henry Waterhouse wrote to his father about the voyage from Cape Town, he added a word that sounded strangely prophetic of events to come some ten years later. He asked father William to be quiet about what he has said about the colony, for 'Something serious will happen here shortly. Luckily for me, I am out of all partys and scrapes, […]'.[120] The early 1790s was the period of NSW history when the Officers of the NSW Corps had acquired a monopoly of wholesale trade, and had done quite well for themselves. There were signs, however, that this was beginning to break down, opening the way for a new trading class to emerge. Even the manner in which Waterhouse distributed his merino can be seen not simply as a little protest against the former regime, but an indicator that new possibilities were opening up.

In October, after some convicts seized a boat and escaped, Hunter issued an order forbidding boats to be built for private purposes and ordering the registration of all boats already built. Registered boats were to have a number painted on their stern.[121] Since Hunter had already ordered the registration and marking of boats in July of the year before,[122] this must indicate either that it was not done properly—perhaps due to Paine being distracted with the events leading to his dismissal—or that other boats had been built in the meantime.

While forbidding private boat building, Governor Hunter was concerned to be able to properly service the public shipping. In November 1797, he wrote home to Secretary Nepean, concerned about the state of His Majesty's ships in the colony. He had already written about the 'very decay'd state' of the *Supply*, and 'her consequent condemnation', but now he writes with the additional concern about the *Reliance*. Waterhouse had struggled to get her back from the Cape in double the normal time. When she arrived, she was placed in Moore's hands to be hove down and surveyed. The results showed she was not much better off than the *Supply*. Hunter's report expressed his disappointment at this severe blow for the ocean-bound colony.

> She return'd from the Cape to this port, as the *Supply* had done, with her pumps going. I have, as well as our intire deficiency of every article of naval stores would admit, hove down the *Reliance*, and found that several of her butts in the guard-board streak were intirely destitute of oakham, and that there is much reason to believe from her weak condition that she will be frequently liable to spring leaks of this nature. I mean, however, to give her, by a complete set of riders fore and aft, as much strength as possible. My chief anxiety proceeds from the disappointment of her services for the present season, and the intire loss of those of the *Supply*, the fittest ship of the two for this service.[123]

Behind this report lies that of the survey conducted by Thomas Moore, John Coldwell, William Stevenson, and Robert Scott, which Hunter enclosed with his letter. Here Moore and his companions, with their more technical eye, provide further details as to what is required to refit the *Reliance*:[124] Figure 28.

> The hull being in a weak and feeble state it is necessary to have riders fore and aft, and standers between the riders to each deck, additional bolts to the brest-hooks and transoms where they can be got in, some hanging knees in the after part of the quarter-deck to support the stern.
>
> The topside waterways timber head stantions, &c, in want of caulking; one of the beams in the fore cockpit sprung and in want of securing. After the whole of the shipwright's work is completed to have her completely caulked.
>
> A leak close to the keel in the garboard streak on the larboard side, which will render it necessary to have the ship hove down.
>
> The plank sheer so much split and decayed, together with the quarter-deck stantions, that it is necessary the whole of the plank sheer and those stantions should be replaced with new ones.
>
> Until the plank sheer is taken off we are unable to assertain whether the waterways are fit to remain in the ship.

CHAPTER 3 ↓ *Building The Dockyard (2 October 1796 to 7 May 1803)* 147

The report sets the agenda for the work that Moore and his team would be engaged with during the next weeks and months. The repairs would involve the selection and cutting of timber in the Australian bush, of the right kind and the right shape. The crooked pieces and plank would then be fitted into the appropriate section of the ship and finally all would be recaulked. With the *Reliance* the only semi-serviceable ship in His Majesty's service, this was an important task, and so the King's Dockyard would be busily engaged in it as of highest priority. November-December, and even beyond, would be a busy time.

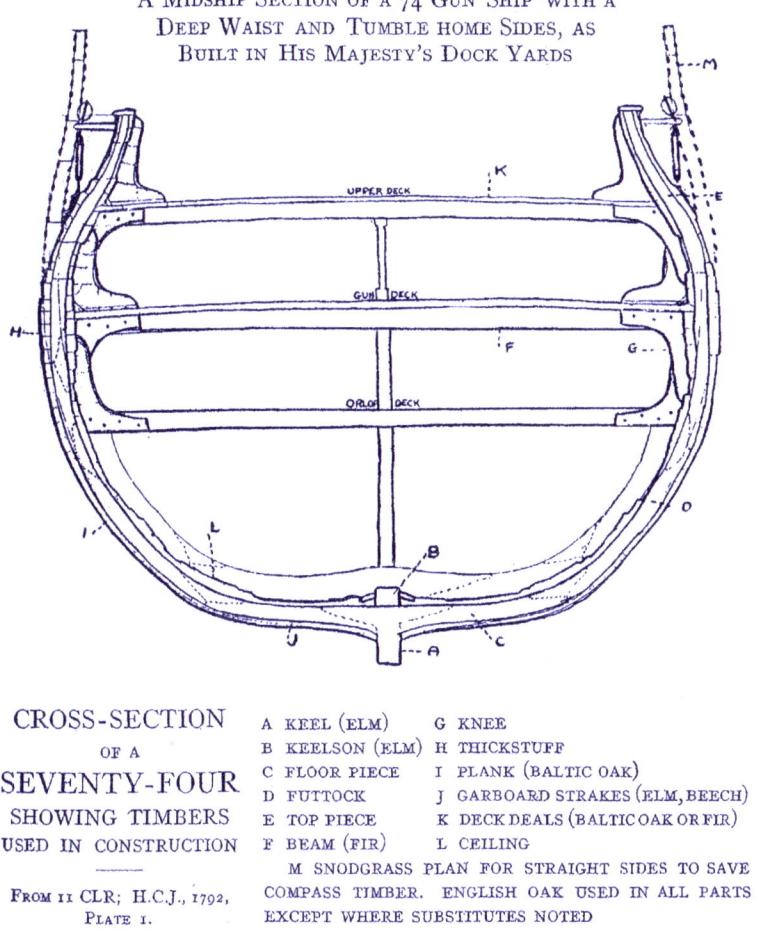

Figure 28: Midsection of 74 Gun Ship showing ship's timbers.

This busyness was apparently nothing new for Moore's programme across 1797. Despite being his first year of his marriage, he had enjoyed no biblical year of release from active service,[125] for 1797 had been a full year for Moore at the Dockyard. Under his direction a total of sixteen persons were employed—shipwrights, caulkers, boat-builders, labourers, and watchmen; as well as a team of two overseers and twelve men on two timber carriages to bring in timber for the dockyard, as well as the sawyers who cut it.[126] That year under Moore's direction, not only was *Reliance* repaired, but also the *Francis*, and the boats belonging to the hospital and the South Head service. Six new boats were also built: one for the *Reliance*; a longboat for the *Supply*; a new pinnace; a whaleboat for Parramatta; a new wood boat for the hospital; and 'a burthensome punt for discharging ships with the more expedition'.

Hunter's June 1797 report briefly itemized what Moore had achieved since October 1796, which consisted of rebuilding 'several of Govt's boats, which were become mere wrecks and useless'.[127] Presumably these were also the boats already mentioned above, as listed in the Return of Labour at Sydney, &c. This means that the work on the Dockyard itself must have been done since June 1797, and Hunter's final list for the year indicates that Moore and his fifteen companions had been rather active in providing their work place with the facilities it needed to properly perform its functions:

> Erected a steamer for seasoning of plank; pailed in the dockyard, hung gates, built sheds for boats and for the sawyers; lined the inside of the provision store; remounted upon new carriages the two brass field-pieces; made sheds, hacks, barrows, molds, &c for the brickmakers, the former ones having been suffered to go to decay.[128]

Evidently Moore had succeeded in achieving the first stage of Hunter's vision by abandoning Reid's boatshed on the Eastern side of the Cove (which remained the careening area. See Plate 29), and constructing a proper dockyard on the Western side. (Plates 26, 27, 28, 30, 31).

This second half of the year also saw Moore taking the initiative, presumably with Hunter's blessing, to move further ahead with the vision towards solving the shipping crisis of the colony. The *Supply* was cashiered, the *Reliance* in bad shape, but the *Francis* was still enabling regular traffic to Norfolk Island, even if unsuitable for anything else in the way of more distant voyages. The colony remained dependent upon supplies from elsewhere, and, without serviceable vessels of its own, the colony was completely reliant upon the initiative of others for supplies to be sent. Now that England was again at war with France, the freeing up of His Majesty's Ships to make the long voyage to Port Jackson with any kind of regularity was rather unlikely.

In November 1796, the Governor had hinted towards a solution, when he reported that the *Francis* was serving well enough, but 'if I had a sufficient strength of carpenters, I wou'd undertake to build one of 70 or 80 tons burthen, which I think would be highly serviceable between this and Norfolk Island'.[129] Hunter had already restricted the building of private vessels in New South Wales, and he repeated the same restriction for the residents of Norfolk Island, who were perhaps even more acutely aware of the need for shipping to ensure supplies.[130] But if there was to be no private shipbuilding, could the Government begin to step into the breach?

Since shipbuilding in New South Wales had been specifically forbidden, here we see Hunter gently 'pushing the envelope'. Now that he was actually in New South Wales, so far from home and surrounded by ocean, he no doubt realised the precarious situation this ruling had placed upon the colony. Not content with simple boatbuilding, or repairing HM ships, Moore and Hunter ensured that as the dockyard took shape, so did its first ship. It is no surprise that by the second half of 1797 Hunter's new Master Boat Builder had started work on the mooted vessel—only it was twice as large as that hinted at by Hunter in November 1796. It was not as if Hunter kept the vessel secret from his superiors, for buried at the end of the 'Report of Labour at Sydney &c', we read that Moore had 'layed the keel of a new brig of 150 tons burthen'.[131] After the *Providence*, he had started on his second vessel to be built of the native timbers of the southern hemisphere, and, with straight rather than curved top timbers which avoided the necessity of some of the 'crooked timbers' that were in such high demand. Moore was building a leading-edge craft with an innovative design.[132] (Plate 27).

While Moore was busy establishing the new dockyard, as part of their year's work the brick and stone layers had started on a house for Thomas and his new bride. From the time of their wedding, they had presumably been living in John White's house on Market Square, where Rachel had lived with Andrew since the Surgeon had left the colony (see Plates 22, 23, 24, 27, 30, 31, 34, 35). With Hunter's Dockyard rapidly taking shape, and the keel of its first major ship already laid down, it is interesting to note that Thomas Moore, commencing as the Master Boat Builder in October 1796, just over one year later also gained a new description: 'layed the foundation of a new house for the master-shipwright'.

This description 'Master Shipwright' puts Thomas Moore amongst a small group of people in the world at this time, and the number of those who looked after yards in the British colonies was even smaller. (Figure 25). As a Naval Captain himself, Hunter knew the importance of the dockyard for the continual servicing of His Majesty's Ships. This is clear from his report sent home in September 1800, when the 'naval yard' had taken fuller shape:

> Paled in a naval yard on the west side of the cove, and erected a joiner's and a blacksmith's shop; sheds for vessels repairing, and for the workmen; a steamer, a store-house, a warder's lodge, and an apartment for the clerk.[133]

Hunter had come with orders to erect a dockyard. The urgent needs of the colony had reinforced just how important this task really was —and he was thinking big. Here was Sydney's equivalent to England's Deptford, Woolwich, Chatham, Sheerness, Portsmouth, or Plymouth under construction. Here was another colonial dockyard to join those of Bermuda, Antigua, Gibraltar, Bombay, Calcutta, or the Cape of Good Hope.

What does this say about Moore? Hunter had specially selected Daniel Paine from Deptford for the duty, but Paine had failed dramatically to perform. Now, on the strength of Moore's reputation after building the *Providence* and his renown for an acute knowledge of native timber, Hunter at last had his man and the dream was taking shape before his eyes.

COLOUR PLATES ⚓ *A Portrait in his Actions. Thomas Moore of Liverpool (1762–1840)*

Plate 1. Portrait of the Late Mr Thomas Moore, Esq. 1840.
William Griffith. Photo: Alice Bolt (2010).

Plate 2. Frank Cash 'Portrait'. Photographic
manipulation
of Griffith portrait.
Loane, *Centenary History*, facing p.16

COLOUR PLATES ⚓ *A Portrait in his Actions. Thomas Moore of Liverpool (1762–1840)*

Plate 3. Portrait of Rachel Moore. Detail of Portrait of the Late Mr Thomas Moore, Esq. 1840, William Griffith. Photo: Alice Bolt (2010)

Plate 4. Memorial to Mrs Rachel Moore, St Luke's Liverpool. Photo: Peter Bolt (2006)

Plate 5. Headstones of Thomas & Rachel Moore, and Andrew Douglas White. Pioneer Park, Liverpool. Photo: Geoff Bolt (2006)

Colour Plates ⚓ *A Portrait in his Actions. Thomas Moore of Liverpool (1762–1840)*

Plate 6. St Mary's Lesbury and the author. Photo: Peter Bolt (2009)

Plate 7. Alnmouth, across the river from South. Church Hill is to the right of the river. Photo: Peter Bolt (2009)

COLOUR PLATES ↻ *A Portrait in his Actions. Thomas Moore of Liverpool (1762–1840)*

Plate 8. Captain Arthur Phillip, 1786. Artist: Francis Wheatley. State Library of NSW a928087.

Plate 9. Portrait of Captain Francis Grose.1790–1799. Artist: John Kay. National Library of Australia. nla.pic-an9597965

Plate 10. Colonel William Paterson, ca. 1800. Artist: William Owen. State Library of NSW a928495.

Plate 11. Vice-Admiral John Hunter, second Governor of NSW 1795-1800. Artist: William Mineard Bennett State Library of NSW a128403

COLOUR PLATES ⚓ *A Portrait in his Actions. Thomas Moore of Liverpool (1762–1840)*

Plate 12. Philip Gidley King, ca. 1800-1805.
State Library of NSW a830002

Plate 13. Admiral William Bligh, 1805. Artist: H.A. Barker.
State Library of NSW a1528244

Plate 14. Revd. Richard Johnson, B.A., chaplain to the
settlement in New South Wales, ca. 1787.
Artist: Garnet Terry. National Library of Australia.
nla.pic-an9594799

Plate 15. Reverend Samuel Marsden, formerly Senior Chaplain
of New South Wales and founder of the New Zealand mission.
Artist: Unknown. Richard Jones' Album.
State Library of NSW. a928171

COLOUR PLATES ⚓ *A Portrait in his Actions. Thomas Moore of Liverpool (1762–1840)*

Plate 16. Mr White, Harris and Laing with a party of Soldiers visiting Botany Bay. Artist: T. Watling.
© National History Museum, London. No. 38080. John White is the tall figure in the middle.

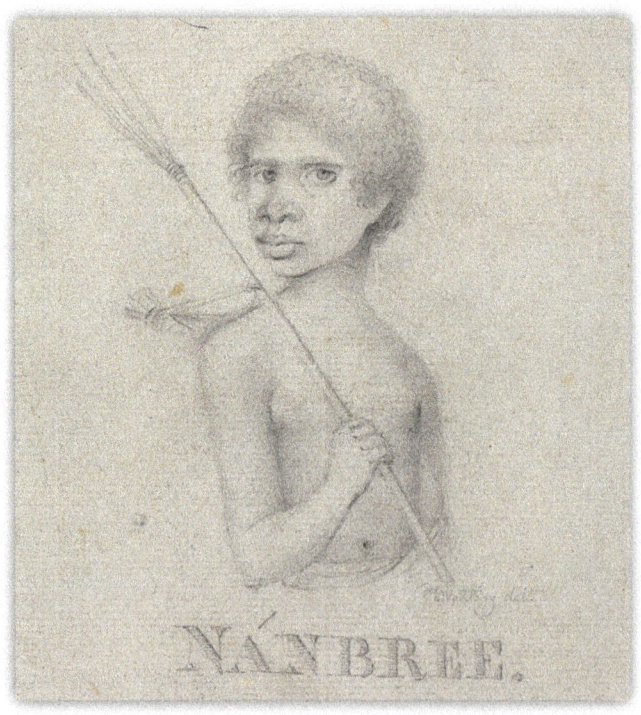

Plate 17. Portrait of an Aboriginal boy named Nanbree. Artist: T. Watling.
© National History Museum, London. No. 12034.

COLOUR PLATES ⚓ *A Portrait in his Actions. Thomas Moore of Liverpool (1762–1840)*

Plate 18. View of the City of Batavia from the Anchorage in the Roades, the church bearing S.S.W. off shore 1½ miles, 1791. Artist: George Raper. Raper Drawing – no. 31. © National History Museum, London. No. 15131.

Plate 19. Straits of Malacca.

COLOUR PLATES ↓ *A Portrait in his Actions. Thomas Moore of Liverpool (1762–1840)*

Plate 20. Kinkaid Map of Australia, 1790. Detail: Port Jackson. Published: Kinkaid, 1840.
National Library of Australia, MAP T 800

Plate 21. Luncheon Cove. Satellite photo showing: 1. Beach where Captain Cook lunched.
2. Site of the construction of the Providence. 3. Site of the sealing party's dwelling.

Alongside this new productivity at the Dockyard, Thomas Moore was putting down other kinds of roots in the colony which he now called home. Hunter's Returns for 31 December 1797, show that the colony now counted 26 Horses and 58 Mares; 132 Bulls and Oxen and 195 cows; as well as 4,247 hogs; 743 rams and 1,714 sheep; 781 goats and 1,495 she-goats; 3,361 ½ acres under wheat; 1,527 under maize; and 26 ½ under barley.[134] With the purchase of his Spanish sheep, Moore had begun his first steps in animal husbandry, which, over the years to come would grow into a major source of his income —even if this would not be through wool.

As the ships of His Majesty's Navy were increasingly occupied in the war, the men engaged in commerce were seeking ways to continue in business, despite it. On 26 December 1797 the Board of Trade discussed a petition from the Southern Whale Fishery, which sought to have the restriction imposed upon them by the 1795 Act (35 Geo III, c.92, An Act for further encouraging and regulating the Southern Whale Fisheries, passed 22 June 1795) removed. Thus far they were forbidden from proceeding north of the Equator and further east than 51 degrees E longitude, in order to protect the interests of the East India Company. The Board sent the memorial to the Company, hoping that the Directors 'will not be averse to a compliance with the prayer of the memorialists for the benefit of the southern whale fishery (which is become a very important branch of commerce)'.[135]

By January 1798, Hunter heard a report from Norfolk Island that the people left at Dusky Bay when Bampton wrecked the *Endeavour* in October 1796 had finally been rescued by an American vessel at Hunter's request, and taken to Norfolk Island.[136] As this news circulated in Sydney, it would have evoked in Moore memories of his own cold sojourn in that remote corner of God's earth.

His existence was becoming much more settled now the life of an adventurer was behind him. Against the politics of the empire at war, his duties at the Dockyard had a significance beyond the first impressions conveyed by its raw infancy on the edge of this remote cove. Increasingly, he took his part amongst the other civil officers assisting the Governor to keep law and order, and to build this developing society.

While Moore's team worked on the *Reliance*, doing the 'tedious repairs' to make her sea-worthy, Surgeon George Bass took the opportunity to explore. He sailed down the coast as far as it went, before turning Westwards for about 60 miles, thus establishing the existence of a strait between Van Diemen's Land and the mainland. This voyage of discovery was made possible by Governor Hunter having 'furnished him with an excellent whale boat, well-fitted, victualled and manned to his wish'.[137] This whale-boat—built from local banksia—was probably built by Mr Moore.[138]

On 18 June an agreement was signed between the military officers and other principle inhabitants of the colony, which effectively agreed to the officer-traders of the old monopoly acting as the agents for the other traders in regard to incoming merchandise from visiting shipping.[139] This then found expression in a Government and General Order issued on 25 June, advising all to keep their money to themselves 'until they are apprised by public notice that a cargo has been bought, the officers having undertaken the trouble of officiating as agents for the general benefit of the whole colony'.[140] Much has been made of this agreement, which appears to suggest that Hunter had sold out to the monopolists of the early 1790s. But the Officers had not been working alone. As Hainsworth argued, 'an underbrush of lesser dealers' grew up around them.

> Not wishing to soil their gentility by too blatant a descent into the market place, they permitted the retail trade to fall into the hands of ambitious and able (if uneducated) men with no gentility to lose. By doing so they made affluent those who would oust them from their position of privilege. The parasites slowly strangled the tree.

Rather than Hunter sanctioning the officers' monopoly through this agreement, and through the price-fixing agreement that soon followed,

> the pattern of commerce after 1798 suggests that it is reasonable to interpret this "monopolistic agreement" as a desperate attempt to shore up a crumbling dike. The officers had traded for six full years without such an agreement; within two years of signing it their day was over.[141]

As the dockyard duties continued and the trading patterns of his

CHAPTER 3 ⚓ Building The Dockyard (2 October 1796 to 7 May 1803)   153

friends and neighbours were changing, Moore's responsibilities as a civil officer in this early period meant that, on 20 August 1798, he sat on the Vice-Admiralty Court to try those involved in the mutiny on the *Barwell*.[142] The other members of the court were Captain Henry Waterhouse, R.N.; Lieutenants William Kent, Robert Braithwaite, John Shortland, and Matthew Flinders; Captains William Wilkinson and Charles Bishop; Augustus Alt, Esq.; Mr Thomas Arndell; Mr Andrew Gouldie, Gunner; and Richard Atkins as the Registrar. One of the first orders issued was for others who had been summoned to the Court, to show cause why they had not turned out for duty (Captain John Fearn; Robert Campbell; James Williamson; Roger Simpson). George Bond and some convicts appeared to plead not guilty, warrants were issued for several privates from the NSW Corps (John Murray, William Hallam, Gregory Bellow, James Nevil, James Owen—who when appearing proved his name to be John and so was discharged on the benefit of the misnomer). After several adjournments the court found insufficient evidence that Ensign Bond had incited a mutiny, but by this introduction to the court-room, Thomas Moore had been prepared a little for his thirty years as magistrate at Liverpool.

Dramatic news burst in upon the colony when, on 2 October the Church that Chaplain Richard Johnson built himself and at his own cost when Francis Grose was acting-Governor, was wilfully burned to the ground, possibly by convicts disaffected by having to attend.[143] By the end of year Hunter could report that the carpenters had 'fitted up a house for divine service, with a pulpit canopy, &c the former one being burnt'. His later explanation was more fulsome, explaining that this was a new storehouse with two wings 'converted into a temporary place for the performance of Divine worship, the former church, built by the clergyman, having been burnt down, certainly by design, but no reward (though one was offered by the General Orders of the 3rd October, 1798) could bring forth the offenders'.[144] The 1798 end of year report also noted that the brick and stone layers had laid the foundation for a new church, which would eventually emerge as the Church of St Phillip, Sydney.[145]

The same report noted that the blacksmiths had been serving the dockyard, for they had been involved with 'ironwork for the *Francis* and *Sydney*, schooners, and all the boats and buildings'. At the dockyard, Moore has gained extra workers, now employing 'twenty-one shipwrights, caulkers, boat-builders, labourers, and watchmen'. He had started building a small vessel 'of 28 tons burthen, instead of the *Cumberland*, which was stolen away'.

The allusion to this event helps to explain the name of this intended new schooner.[146] On 5 September 1797 a group of convicts had stolen the colonial vessel *Cumberland*, 'the largest and best in the colony belonging to Government' (Collins), when it was on its way to the Hawkesbury. Since Hunter had no other vessel to send, he despatched two row-boats. One went 40 miles along the coast southwards, and the other, under Captain Shortland, went 60 miles to the north, discovering Hunter's River on the way home. Collins description of the intended purpose of Moore's new boat, also suggests the link between this event and her name:

> A boat named the *Cumberland* was on the stocks, and nearly finished, of about 27 tons burden, intended to be schooner rigged and armed, for pursuing deserters; who were, at the time when her keel was laid, in the practice of carrying away the boats of the settlement.

In 1798, the dockyard had also 'made two new pumps for the *Francis*, schooner; repaired the *Sydney*, schooner, and all Government boats; roofed a workshop and storehouse for the joiners, watch-house, and an apartment for the clerk in the dockyard; repaired the *Norfolk*, sloop; made oars, pumps, spars, masts, and yards for her; built a skilling for Mr Balmain, the whole length of his house; repaired the longboat of H.M.S. *Supply*'.[147]

As well as laying the foundation of the new church, the brick and stone layers had been working in the dockyard, completing the walls of the joiner's shop, and building a smith's shop. They also 'stopt and whitewashed the house of the master shipwright', so Thomas and Rachel would soon be able to live in their new abode.[148]

Meanwhile in England, David Collins noted the ships that were about to sail for NSW.

> The king's ships on that station being ill calculated for the services

CHAPTER 3 ⚓ *Building The Dockyard (2 October 1796 to 7 May 1803)* 155

expected from them, having on board expensive complements of men and officers, and consequently but little room for cattle; and being beside so defective and impaired by time as to be unsafe to navigate much longer; two others have been provided, newer and more capable of rendering service to the colony. One of them, the *Buffalo*, commanded by Mr. William Raven, late master of the *Britannia*, is on the point of sailing, and is to take cattle to New South Wales from the Cape of Good Hope. The other is named the *Porpoise*, and has the same service to perform. A ship, called the *Minerva*, is also proceeding to Cork to take in a number of Irish convicts.[149]

The *Minerva's* convicts were those of the Irish uprising in 1798. Their presence in New South Wales would bring added consternation to her Governors, especially to Philip Gidley King.

Governor Hunter had his enemies in the colony, and in February Portland wrote to him of anonymous charges that had been made against his administration—a problem which would plague future Governors of New South Wales for many years.[150] King was already preparing to take his place. One-time Lieutenant Governor on Norfolk Island, King had been ordered back to take up the Governorship of NSW. In February 1799 he was busily making preparations to sail on the *Porpoise*. By December 1798, having heard that timber was in short supply at the Cape, Portland informed Governor Hunter that P.G. King planned to take the *Porpoise* into the Cape to see 'of the species and scantling of timber which is most wanted, for the purpose of enabling you to supply the Cape with that article, as well as coals'.[151] The search for staples for New South Wales' trade continued. Since it was part of his duties at the dockyard to supply timber suitable for naval purposes, this planned venture would entail an increased amount of work for Moore, if he had to also begin collecting for the Cape.

1799

Joseph Banks supplied King with a 3 to 4 ton garden. King struggled to accommodate this on board,[152] but Banks called 'a little conservatory of plants for New South Wales'.[153] The *Porpoise* would also bring to NSW three gardeners, one known as George Caley, who 'has more genius than both the others'.

In February 1799, while King stowed plants on the *Porpoise*, back in New South Wales Thomas Moore was again in the courtroom, but this time as a witness. In April 1809 Nichols would become the colony's first postmaster, but more importantly at this stage, he was one of Moore's neighbours. Nichols was charged with receiving stolen tobacco. The court consisted of Judge-Advocate Richard Dore, Naval men Captain Henry Waterhouse, Lieut. William Kent and Lieut. Matthew Flinders, and military officers Lieut. Neil McKellar, Lieut. James Hunt Lucas, and Ensign Nicholas Bayly.[154] Although having its own inherent fascinations, the trial is of interest for its incidental details revealing the Moore's living arrangements.

In his evidence, Moore testified to having known Nichols for a long time. As for his character, 'I have always found the prisoner in all dealings I have had with him punctual', and he has never known him to commit a dishonest act. The court asked Moore: 'Had the prisoner kept a disorderly house, must you not have known it, by being so near a neighbour to him?' Moore: 'I think I might; but I never saw it'.[155]

Moore and Nichols were near neighbours because Thomas and Rachel were still living in John White's house, next to that of William Raven, with both houses being on the Western side of the bulge in High Street known as market-place, just up from the Hospital wharf. (See Figure 29; Plates 34, 35, 27). In March 1804 the house was 'known by the name of Mr Moore's house [...] nearly opposite the hospital wharf'.[156] Isaac Nichols house was on the southern side of the approach to the wharf, and Daniel Cubitt's house was opposite that of Nichols', adjoining Mr Moore's Dockyard.

Nichols had other character witnesses, and a letter from Governor Hunter and George Johnston. Hunter testified to his good service as the principal overseer of the town gangs, performing his duty 'with unremitted assiduity'. Johnston testified similarly, having had Nichols under his direction for nearly two and a half years. Despite this array of witnesses to his good character, Nichols was sentenced to fourteen years' transportation to Norfolk Island, with labour in the gaol gang until the time of his embarkation.

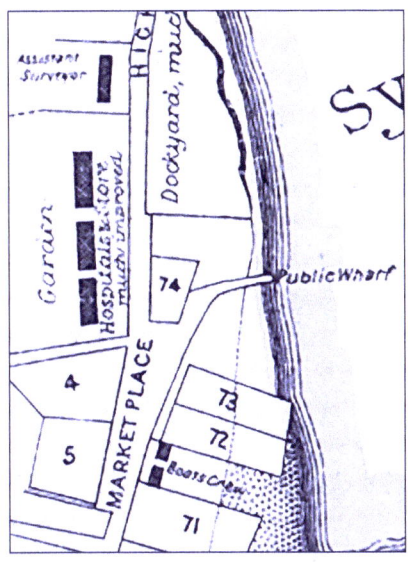

Figure 29. Detail from Meehan's 1807 Map (Plate 35) showing White (4), Raven (5), Nichols (73), and Cubitt (74) houses.

On hearing the court's verdict, Hunter immediately suspended the execution of the sentence and wrote to inform Judge-Advocate Dore of his decision.[157] With the three naval officers convinced of Nichols' innocence and the military officers keen on his prosecution, Hunter was convinced that things were not straightforward here. Nichols was one of the rising new class of emancipist traders and, as such, a threat to the old monopoly.

> The very success of men like Simeon Lord, Andrew Thompson, Henry Kable, James Underwood, Thomas and Mary Reiby, Isaac Nichols and Thomas Abbott suggests that officer dominance was being eroded before 1800.[158] (Plate 37)

By 1799 these emancipist traders must have been enjoying some success. In June 1799, just a few months after his trial, Isaac Nichols joined John Harris (emancipist publican), William Broughton, Henry Kable, James Underwood, James Larra, David Bevan, Daniel Cubitt, Michael Robinson, Robert Sidaway and Alexander MacDonald, in petitioning Hunter in support of Dore's writ system, which was an attempt to make it 'more difficult for debtors to frustrate their creditors'.[159] It is interesting to wonder about the conflict over trade that may lie in the background of Nichols' trial. Was there some reason the military officers wished him out of the way?

Believing that the witnesses had perjured themselves and Judge-Advocate Dore was himself not free from prejudice, Hunter referred the matter to England—a decision that was vindicated in January 1802 when Governor King was directed to grant Nichols a pardon.[160]

Captain Henry Waterhouse was a member of the Court. He wrote to give Hunter some observations on the trial, concluding that 'the smallest shadow of guilt cannot be attach'd to Isaac Nichols'.[161] Thomas Moore, William Miller (baker) and Daniel Cubitt, dealer, were near neighbours.[162] Like Waterhouse, Matthew Flinders also gave Hunter some later observations on the trial,[163] saying that he was sufficiently impressed with the testimony from Moore, Miller and Cubitt as to Nichols' good character, that it added to the other details of the trial to lead him to declare Nichols innocent.[164]

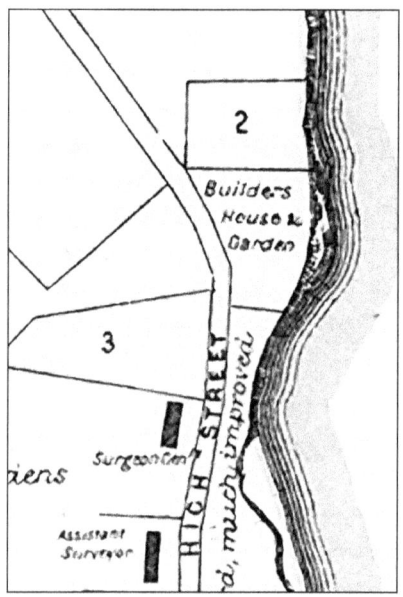

Figure 30. Detail from Meehan's 1807 Map showing Moore's house at the northern end of the dockyard, and that of William Balmain (3). Robert Campbell owned the land north of the triangular line, including the building (2).

The circumstances of the crime began on January 20, when Mrs Mullett was robbed of some tobacco, which had allegedly been taken to Nichols' house, and then hidden 'between two rocks near the new house building for Mr Moore'[165]—which indicates that the house being built for Thomas and Rachel at the end of High Street was not yet finished. (Figure 30). This also came out in James Mansfield's testimony: 'as he was going to the garden-house belonging to Capt'n Waterhouse, a man, well drest, passed him round the paling, near to the new house building for Mr Moore, and walked away very fast, having upon his shoulder a basket covered with a cloth, which he believed to be a basket of tobacco'.[166] More of the domestic arrangements of the houses came out in Lieutenant William Kent's observations on the trial, who had also found Nichols innocent:

> The dockyard is between the house of Isaac Nichols and Mr Moore's, and the fence of the dockyard runs into the water over the rocks on that side Sydney Cove, which rocks are steep to, so

CHAPTER 3 ↻ *Building The Dockyard (2 October 1796 to 7 May 1803)*   159

that there is no way of passing from Nichols's house to the two rocks where the tobacco was found, but on the main road, by the hospital and other public and private buildings, along which many people must have been passing and repassing.[167]

John White's market-square house can be seen in pictures of early Sydney. (Plates 22, 23, 24, 27, 30, 31). This is the house in which Rachel had lived since it was built, and in which Thomas joined her after they married in January 1797. The official residence for the master builder into which they moved once it was completed later in 1799, can also be clearly seen in depictions of the Western shore of Sydney Cove. (Plates 24, 26, 28, 30, 31). Robinson nicely described the house in its neighbourhood:

> The shore-line was precipitous at this point, and the large rocks at the water's edge, which formed an island at high tide, make it easy to identify Moore's house on early maps and drawings. It evidently had upper gable rooms, and stood back in its own garden, facing the Cove. Here, or hereabouts, had been the very first burial ground of the colony. Behind Moore's house, across the High Street, but a little further south, was the residence of Surgeon Balmain and the hospital buildings. To his north, where Captain Henry Waterhouse and John Baughan the master carpenter had originally resided, Moore's neighbour was merchant Robert Campbell, who purchased the Waterhouse and Baughan properties about June 1799, and so began his trading about the time of Moore's arrival at that end of High Street.[168]

As well as gaining a new official residence on the water, on 5 October 1799 Thomas Moore received his first officially recorded land grant. The 470 acres at Bulanaming was Hunter's consolidation of smaller amounts of land previously granted to others by different Governors. Moore's neighbours at Bulanaming by the end of 1799, according to Hunter's 1800 listing, were Provost-Marshall Thomas Smyth, who had acted as witness at Thomas and Rachel's wedding,[169] the convict superintendent Nicholas Divine, and a convict unnamed on this list. In the adjoining district of Petersham Hill were William Faithful, Rev. Richard Johnson, George Johnston, and three convicts.[170]

In 1799 Hunter also granted land to several members of the pioneer

Protestant mission, the London Missionary Society. These men had embarked from England in September 1796 on the *Duff*, arriving in Tahiti in March 1797. When the islanders became hostile eleven of the missionaries (four married men: James Fleet Cover, William Henry, Rowland Hassall, Peter Hodges; and seven single men: Samuel High Clode, John Cock, Edward Main, Francis Oakes, James Puckey, Wiliam Puckey and William Smith) sought refuge in Sydney, arriving on the *Nautilus* in 1798.[171] Of those that remained in the islands, more would find their way to Sydney in February 1800.[172] On 16 April 1799 Hunter granted 100 acres each to Francis Oakes, Rowland Hassall, James Cover and Edward Main, each described as 'Missionary from Otaheite'. Rowland Hassall received a one acre lease in Parramatta on 18 October 1799, when he is described as 'Missionary from Otaheite, and free settler', and William Smith, 'Missionary from Otaheite' received a grant of 100 acres at Prospect Hill on 12 October 1799.[173] Although some of the missionaries left the colony, those of their number who remained made a major contribution to building New South Wales. Over the years to come Thomas Moore would rub shoulders with some of them in a number of different capacities, sharing a common concern for the good of the society which they had adopted as home.

While Hunter was granting land in 1799, William Raven happened to be in town again to receive from his bounty. Raven sailed into Port Jackson on 3 May as Captain of the *Buffalo*, sent out to replace the *Supply*. Raven, 'whose services to the colony in the private ship *Britannia* cannot easily be forgotten',[174] true to his previous practice had picked up sixty-six head of cattle from the Cape of Good Hope to add to the herds in New South Wales. On arrival, he handed the command of the *Buffalo* over to Lieutenant William Kent with his officers and crew. When Raven was Captain of the *Britannia*, William Paterson had granted him 285 acres in the Eastern Farms and a lease in Sydney. In November 1799, while present in Sydney as 'Commander of the *Buffalo* to NSW', Governor Hunter confirmed these grants.[175]

Raven's presence in Sydney gave Thomas Moore the opportunity to catch up with his old Captain once again. It also enabled Rachel to acquaint herself with Mrs Raven, who had accompanied her husband on this voyage. Since Mrs Raven died in May 1801, perhaps the speculation is justified that she had taken the voyage for her health.[176] Presumably by this stage of the year the Moore's had moved into the new house built for them by government, but the Ravens house was still only a short walk down the High Street. It was probably a big surprise for Rachel, however, that entertaining Mrs Raven brought her into the court-room, when in November 1799 she was called before the Court of Civil Jurisdiction as a witness.

The *Buffalo* was also supposed to bring the artist John William Lewin to New South Wales (see Plates 28 and 29), but Lewin somehow missed the departure, even though his wife made it on board.[177] Raven and his wife befriended Anna Maria Lewin during the voyage. Once they arrived in New South Wales, presumably through the previous friendship between Thomas Moore and Captain Raven, Mrs Lewin was entertained by Rachel Moore,[178] and also made the acquaintance of Richard and Mary Johnson. (Plate 25)

When George Thompson spoke of Mrs Lewin engaging in sexual misconduct with the second mate of the *Buffalo*, Mr Michan and with Captain Callinder, she prosecuted him for defamation, in the name of her husband. Since John Lewin did not arrive until January 1800, Richard Johnson acted for her in prosecuting the charge. The court sat before Judge Advocate Gore on 4 and 30 November 1799, and then 3 February 1800.[179]

George Thompson called Rachel Moore as one of his witnesses, to speak of what had gone on in her house:

> Question. Have not Mr Michan and Mrs Lewin been at your house several times drinking tea
> Answer. Yes.
> Question. Did you ever see any familiarity between them at your house?
> Answer. Never.
> Question. Did Mr Michan buy two gown pieces for Mrs Lewin?
> Answer. Mr Michan paid me for two gown pieces. Mrs Lewin had them afterwards.

Presumably this line of questioning was to establish some kind of improper relationship between Michan and Mrs Lewin. Johnson immediately sought to put the record straight:

> Question by the plaintiff (through Mr Johnson). Did you ever see anything in Mrs Lewin's conduct improper?
> Answer. Never.

Rachel must have later realised her answers may have been incriminating, because she tendered another statement through the Provost Marshal. Mr Smyth reported that Mrs Rachel Moore expressed herself sorry she had forgot in her evidence to inform the court that Mr Michan had been paid for the gown pieces by Mrs Lewin. This exchange not only shows that Mrs Lewin did not receive a dress from Michan free of charge (a bad sign), but it also incidentally reveals that Rachel Moore made a little money out of dressmaking. The court found in favour of Mrs Lewin and fined Thompson £30 for costs.

The Moore's reacquaintance with the Ravens only lasted about six months, for on 2 December, Raven and six of his officers sailed for England on the whaler *Britannia*. He was entrusted with dispatches for England, which, as Collins reports:

> from his earnest desire not to lose any time in delivering, he unfortunately lost. When the ship was within sight of the Isle of Wight, he got into a boat, which was captured by a small privateer, and was carried into France with his dispatches, not having had time to sink them. He was soon liberated himself, but was not able to obtain even the private letters that he had with him.[180]

As Raven sailed away, Thomas Moore's seafaring days were retreating as rapidly into the past, as his farming interests were expanding into the future. The 40 sheep he had in 1800 were gone by 1801, in favour of a few pigs (1800:6; 1801:5; 1802:4), and growing numbers of cattle (1800:8; 1802: 1 bull, 10 cows) and horses.[181] After buying his first horses perhaps in 1798 or 1799,[182] Moore owned four horses by 1800[183] and by 1802 (if not before) he was set up for breeding, owning 1 horse and 5 mares.[184] By 1804 he owned 10 of the colony's 404 horses (3 stallions and 7 mares), which presumably he kept on his Petersham/ Bulanaming property.[185] Over time, Moore gained a reputation for breeding horses of good quality. In an age before the motor car and, indeed, even before the railway, the horse was an important and valuable commodity. The list of the names of the various horse-owners

CHAPTER 3 ↓ *Building The Dockyard (2 October 1796 to 7 May 1803)* 163

in early NSW reads like a 'who's who' of the colony, evoking from one writer the comment that 'already we see the pattern that was to remain for the next century—the leaders in our political, commercial (and later our agricultural) life were those same people most prominent as breeders and owners'.[186] In this august company, we find Thomas Moore. (Figures 34 and 35).

One of Moore's duties in 1800 was at the Port Maskelyne gun battery. This was the largest of the four batteries, more than twice the size of the next largest. Moore was in charge of the battery, assisted by Mr Bloodsworth and Mr Brody, with the following number of men under their direction: Carpenters and Sawyers: 37; Lime and Masons: 13; Blacksmith: 10; Bricklayers: 20; a total of 80 men. The Battery itself consisted of eight 12 pounders, requiring eight men each (total: 64); two 6 pounders, requiring six men each (total: 12), and two men making wads and looking after the powder.[187]

This battery had been enlarged as part of the public works for 1800, according to the Report of Public Works: 'Built embrasures to the battery on Point Maskelyne (the west point), and raised a redoubt with eight embrasures on the east point, on which were mounted a part of the guns of H.M. Ship *Supply*. Two guns were likewise mounted on the high part of Garden Island'.[188] Presumably under Moore's direction, the now cashiered *Supply* had yielded her guns to the defences being erected against a potential invading enemy force. The war may have begun on the other side of the world, but the hostilities with the French could extend to wherever her ships might voyage. Sydney, too, had to be ready.

Despite all this work, however, when Governor King arrived he was appalled at its state:

> The battery on the west side of Sydney Cove being constructed with stones is now falling down and filling the embrasures, and must be immediately taken down to prevent its being totally useless in case it should be wanted, as it commands the whole approach of the harbour up to the settlement.[189]

In February 1800, Thomas and Rachel welcomed new neighbours. Robert Campbell from the Indian trading house, Campbell & Co,

164   A Portrait in his Actions. Thomas Moore of Liverpool (1762–1840)

had first come to Sydney in April 1798 seeking to set up a trading connection. The situation seemed eminently suitable, and so in February 1800 he arrived upon the *Hunter*, to set up his home and warehouse on land he had purchased earlier, right next door to the official residence of the Master Boat Builder.[190] (Figure 31).

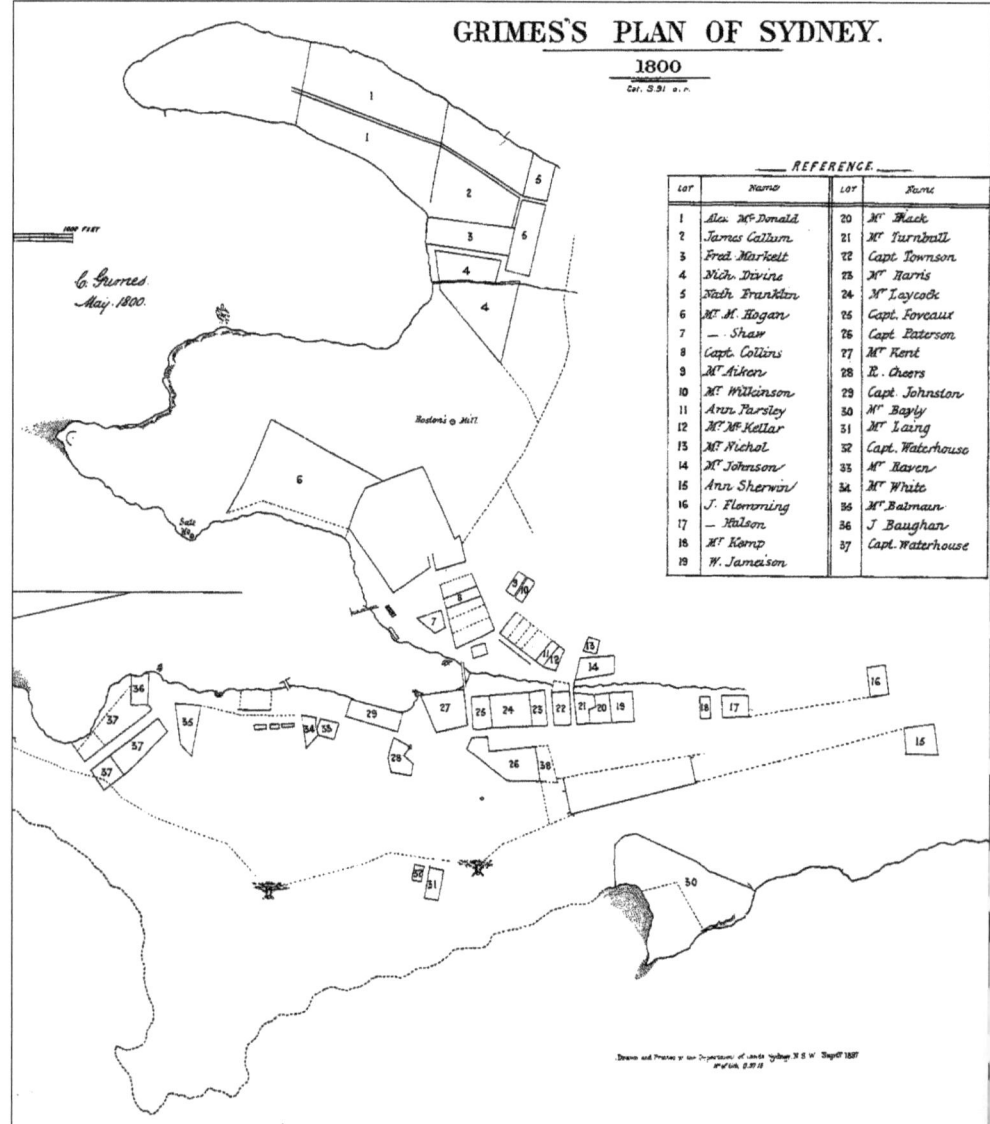

Figure 31. Grimes's Plan of Sydney (1800).

The arrival of Robert Campbell in Sydney and so his trading house, was a significant moment for the trading community. But it is also an indicator that a new situation had already emerged in Sydney trading. The Officer-Traders' monopoly of wholesale trade in the early 1790s had necessarily caused the rise of a number of significant middlemen, the dealers who acted for the officers to broker the goods to the retailers in the colony. These people rapidly made things more complex and 'the officers and their allies among the senior officials speedily became only the first big link in a chain connecting ship and customer'.[191] Simeon Lord, for example, began life in the colony as the assigned servant to Officer-Trader Captain Thomas Rowley, acted as his middle-man and so gained the leg up to become one of the most successful of the new breed of traders.[192]

The detailed records of the Commissariat Store under Hunter have not survived, but they have for Governor King's period (1800–1806). According to Hainsworth, they show that 'a cuckoo has taken over the nest and ousted the officers from their privileged position':[193]

> most Store receipts for grain and pork were received by 'dealers' of one kind or another, and […] only a small proportion of these receipts went to officers; whereas during at least the early 1790s it is reasonable to suppose that a majority of the receipts went to officers directly or indirectly.

Hainsworth suggests that the moment that the cuckoo took over can be almost pinpointed to the 11 January 1800. On that day, two ships arrived, the *Thynne*, under charter from the officers of the Corps, and the *Minerva* a transport also containing a speculative cargo.[194] With Hunter's permission, the officers conducted the subsequent trade of the goods from the *Thynne*—and it was the last ship they ever chartered. But in regard to the *Minerva*, eighteen men petitioned Hunter seeking permission to buy directly, and Hunter granted them this privilege —presumably aware of their rising prominence.

> The petitioners therefore were middlemen. They would be armed with Treasury bills obtained from the Store in exchange for grain paid to them for their retailed wares. Among them were emancipists Simeon Lord and Thomas Abbott, minor officials Nicholas Devine

and William Broughton, and the ex-missionary trader-preacher Rowland Hassall.[195]

The older monopoly had already lost some of its leading figures, and was about to lose some more. From 1800 onwards 'the commerce of New South Wales, in spite of its idiosyncracies, flowed steadily into more conventional channels'.[196] Receiving only 1/8th of the Treasury bills, the officers no longer monopolized the Store in this period.

> Moreover, the transfer of economic power from the officer group to the large diverse group of their local competitors must have been a gradual process which began much earlier than the year 1800. This is indicated by the emergence during the Hunter period of another group of entrepreneurs with sterling capital to invest, who were destined to transform the Sydney commercial scene: the emancipist traders.[197]

These traders who gained their success by being an adjunct to officer enterprise had already emerged by the time Robert Campbell arrived in 1800 to live next to Thomas Moore, who also took his place amongst this new breed.

As well as welcoming the Campbells into the neighbourhood, it was also a time for farewells in the Moore household, for in March 1800 Thomas and Rachel said their sad goodbyes to their beloved Andrew, six months short of his seventh birthday. Henry Waterhouse departed from the colony that month, on the *Reliance* in a very weakened state,[198] leaving his property in the hands of others—although he would later turn over his affairs to Thomas Moore.[199] His departure was the opportunity for Thomas and Rachel to entrust their boy into his care for the next stage of his life. Thomas Moore had doted on the young Andrew, who had now spent just over three years in Moore's home as his stepson. Since he had reached the age to prepare for schooling, Moore now sent him to England to gain the benefits of the good education he himself never had.

Because of their associated professions, Moore and Waterhouse had known each other for some years already, and when Rachel and Thomas moved into the newly built Master Builder's house at the end of the High Street late in 1799, they lived almost next to one of

CHAPTER 3 ⚓ *Building The Dockyard (2 October 1796 to 7 May 1803)*   167

Waterhouse's leases—the one he sold Robert Campbell in June 1799.[200] The two men were involved together in several official capacities and they became good friends—good enough for the Moores to entrust Andrew into his protection.[201] Waterhouse took the boy to England, where Andrew was placed under the care of his sister Elizabeth, who later became Mrs George Bass.[202] Despite John White having remarried in 1796, Andrew did not live with his father, but visited him in the holidays often enough to become regarded affectionately as 'brother' by John White's other children.[203]

After welcoming new neighbours one month, then farewelling Andrew the next, April was the month to welcome Philip Gidley King, who arrived in Port Jackson on the *Speedy* on 15th.[204] Since he was authorized to assume office only after Hunter could arrange passage home, the next few months were irritating to King. He did not enter into the Governorship until 28 September, and his relationship with Hunter, although quite cordial during his previous stint in the colony, now gradually decayed further and further.[205]

Perhaps inevitably, King could not restrain himself from instituting his ideas for the colony even before that time. With the need for serviceable ships still plainly apparent, within weeks of his arrival he initiated the purchase of the *Harbinger*, a brig from the Cape offered him by the master, Captain Black, who was 'compelled to offer her for sale'. Thomas Moore, 'Master Ship-Wright', and W. House, the first officer of the *Anne*, conducted the survey, finding her basically in good order, besides wanting a couple of new knees, some new leaden scuppers, and some caulking. Instead of the £1500 requested by Black, King offered £700, which was accepted, and Moore's dockyard team got to work on the repairs on the new vessel bought at such a bargain-basement price.[206]

Ever since his arrival, the sight of numerous neglected children in the colony distressed King. On 7 August 1800 he wrote to Rev. Richard Johnson and others to initiate a solution. When Lieut-Governor on Norfolk Island he established an orphan school, and he now wished to do the same thing in Sydney, in order to 'protect and instil proper notions in the minds of the younger part' of this number especially. To this end, he has purchased William Kent's house in town for 'the reception and education of part of the orphans, the number of whom, and of other real objects for such an institution, I am sorry to say, are 398 out of the 958 children accounted for at the general muster'. Johnson has some money and he, being about to leave for England, will give this to Marsden who will act as the Treasurer. The house will need some renovations to house more than 100 children, and 'plank for bedsteads is now sawing'. Richard Johnson, William Balmain, Samuel Marsden, John Harris, Mrs King and Mrs Paterson were requested to form a committee.[207]

In September the committee requested Thomas Moore, 'master carpenter', to give 'an estimate of the quantity of plank and scantling necessary for fifty bed cradles, to hold two children each [...] being 5 feet long, and 3 feet in the clear'.[208] Moore was actually the 'master boat builder', but his involvement here probably points to an extra duty he had acquired temporarily. The 'master carpenter' had been John Baughan, whose house was immediately next door to the block of ground at the end of High Street upon which the Master Boat Builder's official residence was constructed. However, Thomas and Rachel never knew Baughan as a close neighbour, because well before they moved in, on 25 September 1797 Baughan had died. The neighbour the Moores knew was Robert Campbell, who bought Baughan's lease when setting up his operations in Sydney. But presumably after Baughan died, Thomas Moore was the closest thing the colony had to a 'master carpenter', and so he temporarily filled the position. It is, however, also tempting to see this request as indicative of the committee's awareness that Moore would have an interest in the charitable objects of this new institution. Certainly this fits with his later concerns and involvements in causes for the public good.

It is difficult to know how much these extra little duties were distractions from Moore's major work at the dockyard, which kept rolling in. Under his supervision, since well before June the *Buffalo* had been refitting ready for Hunter's departure.[209] Hunter, too, had some preparations to do, and just before he left he wrote a series of reports. As well as noting that the Moores' house had been completed and that Hunter's dream, the 'naval yard', was also almost done,[210] the Governor's final reports show that other pressing duties had inhibited Moore's shipbuilding efforts:

CHAPTER 3 ↓ *Building The Dockyard (2 October 1796 to 7 May 1803)* 169

> The frame of a vessel on the stocks, the keel of which was laid in consequence of the condemnation of H.M. ship *Supply*: but from a scarcity of shipwrights, and the ruinous state in which all our floating craft were, and the constant repairs wanted by the Kings ships, have not been able to get her forward. She was designed to be about 150 or 160 tons, and fit for carrying a relief of military to Norfolk Island.[211]

The constant activity of the dockyard lies just below the surface of this report, as does the frustration of its Master Builder. The pressure of the urgent maintenance, not to mention building the yard itself, had kept Moore from completing his vessel with the leading-edge design. One of Hunter's lists also contains the annotations of the incoming Governor. From King's remarks added alongside Hunter's plans at this point, it is clear that the incoming Governor also got the message, for against the item he commented:

> This cannot be carried on for the want of shipwrights, iron, pitch, and tar, but would be a usefull vessel if we possessed the means of going on with it.

Despite the delay of this larger ship (the *Portland*), however, Hunter noted a smaller vessel was just about finished, and King too was enthusiastic:

> <u>Hunter</u>. A boat named *Cumberland*, on the stocks, nearly finished, about 27 tons burthen, intended to be schooner rigged, and to be armed for pursuing deserters, who were at the time her keel was laid in the practise of carrying away our boats.
>
> <u>King</u>. Will be finished without loss of time to accompany the *Lady Nelson* on survey when that vessel arrives or any other necessary service.

The urgent work keeping Moore's dockyard otherwise occupied is reflected in another of Hunter's September 1800 lists, 'Naval Establishment', which itemises the floating craft belonging to Government:[212] the colonial schooner *Francis* (44 tons), 'lately well repaired'; *Norfolk*, sloop (16); *Cumberland* schooner (28), 'Built at Port Jackson; ready to launch'; Three long boats, 'one of which built at Port Jackson'; A flat for unloading shipping and a lighter for same purpose, both built at Port Jackson, and both wanting repair; a brig (160 tons), rather optimistically (it seems) described with, 'built at P't Jackson', 'frame raised and nearly timbered'; a whale boat for the Governor's use, also built at Port Jackson; two pinnaces of HM Ship's *Reliance* and *Supply* left for the colony; several smaller boats for various uses, 'mostly, if not all, built at P't Jackson'; a large colonial pinnace, 'rebuilt'. Of these, the *Norfolk* was built at Norfolk Island in 1798; and the *Cumberland*, one long boat, the flat, the lighter, the brig, the whale boat, and most of the smaller boats were built at Port Jackson.

As Hunter wound up his affairs in September, he also reported that he had:

> Erected an elegant church at Parramatta one hundred feet in length and forty-four feet in width, with a room of twenty feet long, raised on stone pillars; intended for a vestry or council room. Prepared the foundation of a church at Sydney, but of larger dimensions.[213]

With St John's erected (Figure 32), King is eager to complete St Phillip's:

> Hunter: a church at Sydney; the foundation dug out and was to be built of stone until it became on a level with the base of the clock tower, then to have been completed with brick, for which and other uses the brick gangs at Sydney have been employed.
>
> King: Will be begun about as soon as possible, as the absolute necessity of that building is evident.[214]

No doubt with some joy that the two churches were progressing well, on 16 October, Chaplain Richard Johnson embarked to sail with Hunter on the *Buffalo* with Hunter's nephew William Kent at the helm,[215] leaving Samuel Marsden as the only official chaplain in the colony and officiating from Parramatta. Johnson would never return to New South Wales, although he kept an active interest in the colony and was involved in the process of recruiting Rev. William Cowper to be the third chaplain.[216] As Johnson left the colony, since he married the Moores and continued congenial relations with them, Boyce may well be correct to speculate that, 'from Mr. Moore's disposition we can think of him as taking a keen interest in the changes that came. There was most probably a warm-hearted farewell to Mr. Johnson'.[217]

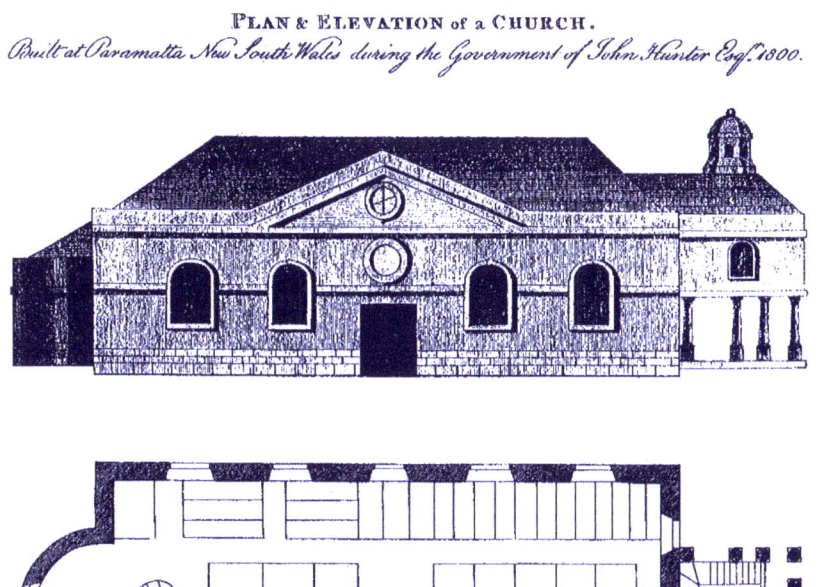

Figure 32: St John's Parramatta.

Governor Hunter left the colony on 17 October 1800, leaving the colony in King's hands.[218] He had embarked the *Buffalo* two weeks before, on Sunday 28 September, as reported by Collins:

> The governor's embarkation was attended with every mark of respect, attachment and regret. The road to the wharf, where the *Buffalo*'s boat was in waiting, was lined on each side with troops, and he was accompanied thither by the officers of the civil and military departments with a numerous concourse of the inhabitants; who manifested by their deportment the sense they entertained of the regard which he had ever paid to their interests, and the justice and humanity of his government.[219]

By this time, the Civil Officers included twenty-six men, nine women, and eight children,[220] and since this number included Thomas and

Rachel Moore, they would have been amongst the number lining the road to the wharf in appropriate farewell.

The Statement of Officers of the Civil Establishment, March 1801,[221] reflected the changeover of personnel in Sydney. Richard Johnson and James Williamson had gone back to England with Hunter's permission, Thomas Moore, 'Boat Builder', still remained. After beginning his life as an adventurer, once Moore took his place in New South Wales colonial society, he was here to stay. There were times that he toyed seriously with returning to England, even if only for a visit, but as the colony entered the nineteenth century Moore was at a productive and expansive phase of his life.

Perhaps a year after the Ravens had themselves returned to England, William Raven's wife died. By the end of the year the press reported that Captain William Raven of Hackney Terrace had married Miss Lucinda Wilson of the same place.[222] Hackney Terrace was one of the isolated instances of London's speculative building at the end of the eighteenth century,[223] and Lucinda, four years Raven's senior, was the daughter of Mr Thomas Wilson, Esquire. Wilson had been Chief Justice of Dominica from 1773 for about six or seven years, so presumably Raven knew Lucinda during the time they were both in the West Indies.[224] When it filtered back to New South Wales, Thomas and Rachel would have received both pieces of news with appropriate sadness and joy, the sea miles between them not hindering their friendship.

Moore's position at the dockyard brought him into contact with the various ship's captains whose vessels required his attention, which not only made him well-placed in regard to these key players in the colony's trading ventures, but also brought him new friendships and responsibilities. In August 1801, Captain Samuel Chace (or Chase), Commander of the *Harriet*, a prize of war taken in May 1797, appointed Moore as his 'true and lawful Attorney' to act in his name in all matters, just before he embarked on his next voyage.[225] Captain Chace needs to be distinguished from two other ship's captains operating in these waters at this time. Distinguishing him from Peter Chase is easy enough, but it is important to be alert to his namesake, Samuel Rodman Chace, who also had dealings with Thomas Moore.[226] Samuel

CHAPTER 3 ⚓ *Building The Dockyard (2 October 1796 to 7 May 1803)* 173

(not Rodman) Chace and Thomas Moore became closely associated over several years to come, joining in common cause as each sought to acquire his fortune. By granting the Power of Attorney, Chace joined the small band of ship's captains for whom Mr Moore acted as agent.

At this time the whaler, *Albion*, was also in Sydney, under the command of Eber Bunker—another ship's captain who formed a long-term friendship with Thomas Moore, his agent.[227] (Plate 43). The two men were roughly the same age and they both originally sailed with the Southern Whale Fishery—although this does not necessarily mean that they knew each other at that stage.[228] Bunker first landed in New South Wales on 28 August 1791, just short of a year before Thomas Moore's first visit. He came as master of the whaler, *William and Ann*, the oldest vessel of the Third Fleet, bringing convicts out in the hope of bringing whale oil home. Until 1825, when he took his last voyage in the *Alfred*, Bunker continued to sail ships in Australian waters[229]—including the *Pegasus*, part owned by Thomas Moore.

Adding further drama to colonial life, on Monday 14 September 1801, after being challenged by Lieut.-Colonel William Paterson to a duel and winning the toss for first to fire, Captain John Macarthur of the NSW Corps wounded his commanding officer in the right shoulder.[230] Governor King responded by placing him under arrest. One of the key members of the older Officer-Trader monopoly, Macarthur was already causing concern in the colony. Judge-Advocate Richard Atkins informed Governor King that his 'intrigues and transactions, so dangerous to the prosperity of an infant colony, were but too well known to your Excellency's predecessor, Governor Hunter, and will be remembered with the highest indignation as long as this colony exists'.[231] Atkins was concerned in particular with Macarthur's attempts to manipulate the court, which, he was pleased to report for the instance at hand, Macarthur showed that he did not have the power to do. But with continued practice, it will be surprising what Macarthur would be able to achieve a few years hence. Already unsettled by Macarthur and unsure of the chances of his fair trial in the colony, Governor King sent him home to England for a court martial. He left on the *Hunter* in November 1801 accompanied by two of his children, but he did not reach reach England until December 1802. Macarthur did not return to Sydney until June 1805, after avoiding censure or charge over the duel, resigning his commission from the Corps, and advocating a grand scheme for the development of the New South Wales wool industry, in which he, of course, would play a major role. Macarthur returned on the whaling ship *Argo*, which he now partly-owned, bringing his nephew Hannibal Macarthur and Walter Davidson to assist him with his new schemes. His military career now behind him, Macarthur set out to becoming a merchant and sheep-breeder. He had persuaded the British Government to grant him 5,000 acres in the Cowpastures, the best land in the colony, and Davidson was to have 2,000 acres, but Governor King was reluctant. He arranged for Macarthur and Davidson to occupy their grants provisionally, while he began to do battle with the British Government. When Bligh arrived, he did not confirm the grants either, and, not impressed with Macarthur's power and influence, the two men soon clashed. Because of his role in the 1808 insurrection, Macarthur left the colony in 1811 and did not return until 1817, and it took until 1822, after he had achieved some success in his wool breeding, for the land promised him in 1804 to be confirmed.[232]

Back in the colony since August, George Bass gave a dismissive report of the duel when he wrote to his new wife Elizabeth on 20 October:

> Tell Waterhouse that Capt McArthur will shortly sail for England in the *Porpoise* under Arrest. He is sent home to add or rather to restore peace to this country. He & Col. Paterson have been out together; the latter was wounded in the arm the first shot but is recovering fast. So much for the colonial news.[233]

Bass had married his 'dear Bess' on 8 October 1800 in a rushed ceremony in the midst of his preparations for a voyage in partnership with Charles Bishop bringing a speculative cargo for sale in New South Wales.[234] Elizabeth was Henry Waterhouse's sister, who, by the time of the wedding, had recently begun caring for Thomas and Rachel's son Andrew in her home, since his arrival in London with her brother. Bass's commercial venture could not be delayed and so, although very much in love, the couple parted on 9 January 1801, when a fair wind took Bass's *Venus* as part of a convoy from Spithead out into the Atlantic. To ease the pain of their separation, perhaps Elizabeth found pleasant distraction overseeing the early education of her newfound youthful charge.

Unfortunately, after the *Venus* sailed into Port Jackson on 29 August 1801, Bass found the Sydney market so glutted in this new day for trading, that his cargo of various wares was extremely difficult to move.[235] Three weeks after writing about Macarthur's duel, when he wrote again to Elizabeth to inform her of his own news, Bass revealed that Thomas Moore had become involved in his plans, even if behind the scenes. The Surgeon was still in Port Jackson, but was about to sail for the South Seas on a commission from Governor King to acquire Tahitian pork for the colony. King had already sent the *Porpoise* on one voyage for the same purpose, and then a second voyage along with the *Norfolk*. These two voyages were the only direct Government involvement in the Pork trade with Tahiti, but they represent the beginnings of what became an important avenue of trade for the early colony. Once it was established, between 1810–1830 about three shipments per year arrived in Sydney.[236] Even though Governor King had already sent the *Porpoise* and the *Norfolk* just before (Bass's *Venus* would arrive just after the *Norfolk*), he commissioned Bass to fetch some more. This effectively created competition with the Government's direct trade through those vessels, which drove the price of pork up.[237]

As he was about to depart, Bass bewailed the fact that the Bass-Bishop business venture had not gone well, but he hoped that this voyage will clear all their debts.

> we arrived in this part of the world upon the top of a general glut. Happy for us that we can find a gainful employment for our vessel and be waiting until the glut begins to take off.
>
> While we are gone for pork the most saleable part of our cargo will be left with Mr Moore the husband of little Andrew's mother.[238]

Sydney's market was flooded with goods. Just as he had done in 1796 for Raven and Leith when they had sailed away on the *Britannia*, now Thomas Moore agreed to act as Bass's agent, a dealer go-between, taking the products most likely to turn a profit at a more opportune time. The convoluted description Bass gave to Moore provides a relational connection for Bess with the only one in the family that she had met: 'Mr Moore the husband of little Andrew's mother'.

On 21 November 1801, George Bass left Sydney and two weeks later he reached Thomas Moore's old stamping-ground in Dusky Bay, New Zealand, for two weeks of timber-cutting to make the cases needed for the salt pork of Tahiti. His men also extracted some of the plank off the *Endeavour*, left there by Captain Bampton. As the new year opened, he wrote to Henry Waterhouse having arrived in Otaheite, informing him of the plans and progress of this new adventure.[239] The brig, *Harbinger*, bought by King and repaired by Moore, was in the islands as well, now renamed the *Norfolk* and also in quest of salt pork. Bass noticed how abundantly supplied with hogs the islands were, so he determined to set up his own curing works, which should give them two-fifths of what they require. The plan was for his partner, Charles Bishop, to remain to supervise this enterprise. Bass would himself sail on for the Sandwich Islands to fill the rest of the pork order, thus completing the whole venture in less time than originally budgeted for. Bass reported that he has made good friends with the Chief of the island, Pomare, although he is not impressed with his son, 'the most drunken profligate you ever knew'. The missionaries, 'poor creatures', are 'very civil and friendly in their little way'. He sends his greetings to the Waterhouses and to 'my wife Bess', jokingly assuring her that she has 'nought to fear' from the women of Tahiti.

Although occupying an increasingly important place amongst the traders and farmers of the colony, his duties as part of the Civil Establishment still called for his attention, such as on 31 December 1801, for example, when he acted as witness to the pay documents for HM *Lady Nelson*.[240] (Plate 41).

As Moore added George Bass to his 'agency' work, he continued to act for his previous clients. In March 1802, Captain Chace ran up a large account with Moore, payments made for boat hire, boat mending, to the watch maker, repairs to the Frying Glass, for apples, oranges and fish, as well as a bill to Simeon Lord. On the income side, Moore received money from John Palmer (1/9/1802) and Simeon Lord (24/2/1803). Moore also continued to manage William Raven's affairs,

CHAPTER 3 ↓ *Building The Dockyard (2 October 1796 to 7 May 1803)* 177

receiving money August 1802 from the Store, from Mr Laycock for Raven's farm, and from Watson through Captain Leith. The accounts show Moore dealing actively for Raven across the next few years, well into 1806.[241]

In the early months of 1802, Moore also revived an old client and gained a new. As already noted, in 1796 when Moore stayed behind in the colony he acted for Captain Raven and for fellow shipmate, John Leith. In February-March 1802, Moore opened up further accounts for Leith, who had by this stage gained the title of 'Captain'. At the same time, accounts were opened for a new client, Captain James Simter.

Having left London in June 1801, on 14 December John Leith brought the *Minorca*, James Simter the *Nile*,[242] and Captain William Williamson—the third Captain in their convoy—the *Canada* (1) into Port Jackson. Under charter, these three East India Company ships (owned by F. and T. Hurry, London) discharged both convicts and free settlers—many of whom were indigent poor—and by 6 February 1802 were cleared for China, eventually arriving in London on 11 February 1803.[243] Special instructions given to the Captains and the Surgeons ensured that when the three ships arrived, Governor King declared the convicts 'the healthiest and best conditioned that ever arrived here, being all fit for immediate labour'.[244]

Since Moore acted as the agent of his old shipmate once before, it was natural for Leith to retain him again—and also to recommend him to his colleague James Simter. The accounts show that while in Sydney Leith paid 10/6 to D.D. Mann for a lease on a house, which he then rented for three years for £30. Moore paid various bills for him, and, on the income side, sold a variety of goods (a cask of glass, bonnets and hats, whips, fancy muslin) and received other people's notes (those of Kenny, Palmer, and even one of his own). For Simter, Moore paid bills to Daniel McKay and Mr Meahy, and received quite a large amount from Simeon Lord (£70-8-1), suggesting Simter had supplied him with goods.[245]

The two men's accounts showed a small amount of action across the next couple of years, but neither of them apparently returned to the colony—even despite Leith's house. In addition to bringing

Thomas Moore a little commercial interest, the brief visit of these three ships represents a significant turning-point for the Bass Strait sealskin trade. This was really only just getting started, as Robert Campbell's brother John explained in October 1802:

> the encouragement we have given to a number of industrious seamen, settlers at Sidney, to embark in the Seal fishery at Bass's Straits and we have pleasure to say their first attempt has been pretty successful, for in about three months they sent to Sidney 3,000 prime furs, which we purchased immediately at 3/9 per skin and sent them to China last February on the Honourable Company's Extra Ship *Nile*.
>
> This trade is now in its infancy but promises fair to be a great branch in time, and will no doubt be of the greatest use to the colony, as well as lessen considerably the expense of the establishment to the Mother Country.[246]

Despite shipping 7,631 sealskins on the *Nile*, *Canada* and *Minorca*, Campbell and Co gained only 4,928 Spanish dollars. The China Market was proving less than ideal for the Sydney traders. However, at the same time as Canton slumped, news arrived of new processing techniques that were making Bass Strait sealskins so attractive in London that they were fetching 20 to 25 shillings each. This was sufficient incentive for the traders to turn their eyes towards London.[247]

On 10 April 1802 a register of arms was taken in the various districts around Sydney: Farm Cove, Petersham, Brickfield, Maskeline & Banks, and Bulanaming. In the latter, Mr Moore had one gun, Mr Smyth two, Mr Cropper one, Mr Palmer one, and Simeon Lord one, but no-one in this neighbourhood had any swords, pistols or bayonets. Whereas the 1801 Return showed Moore still having only 470 acres, the 1802 muster also rather mysteriously listed Moore as having a grant of 530 acres, 100 under cultivation. This indicates that, since the muster of the previous year he had acquired another sixty acres, which probably represents two farms of 30 acres as originally granted. In the muster of 25–30 July 1803, Thomas Moore had 502 acres under cultivation, whether sown with grain, pasture, or fallow, suggesting a further expansion of his holdings had taken place. As with the previous 470 acre grant in 1799, these acquisitions were not officially listed against his name until they were rolled into the next major grant he acquired on 1 October 1803: 700 acres in Bulanaming.[248]

Once he was home, Ex-Governor Hunter continued to advocate for New South Wales. On 22 March he wrote to Under-Secretary King. Now that England was planning to send out convict ships each spring and autumn, Hunter suggested some back-loads that might help reduce the costs of NSW.[249] Whereas others were advising Joseph Banks to introduce oak trees to New South Wales in order to 'in a certain number of years furnish the Colony & royal navy with any quantity of timber fit for any purposes',[250] Hunter was thinking in the opposite direction: he saw the naval yards at home supplied by the timbers of New South Wales. As the best option, given the present state of the colony, Hunter recommended 'the sending back such timber as may be thought fit for naval purposes, of which I think there are several kinds, viz., that called by us stringybark. It is something similar to the teak of India, and is, in general, sound'. His report proceeds to list the various timbers, with their qualities. This information may owe something to Daniel Paine's work in the New South Wales bush, for he did display an interest in timber if nothing else, but Hunter was well-aware of Thomas Moore's expertise in this area and there is no real doubt that this report reflects to a large degree the opinions of the man Hunter appointed to replace the Deptford-trained Paine. This is clear from the example he draws upon—Moore's innovative ship, the *Portland*, which his other duties had long kept him from finishing— even if Hunter appears to take credit for it:[251]

> The crooked limbs of most of the gum-trees, when sound, are very fit for ship timbers or ribs, and are uncommonly durable. The fact I proved by the raising the frame of a vessel of 160 tons, which for want of strength, I could not finish before I left the country, but she stood in frame, exposed to the weather, upwards of two years without the smallest appearance of any decay.

In the same report, and probably drawing upon Waterhouse's observations, Hunter speaks from the experience of Moore's repairs of the *Reliance*, after being battered into a very leaky state on the return from the Cape in 1797:[252]

> It was necessary to give her a very considerable repair, to do which the carpenter thought it necessary to put eight riders in of a side, from the gunwale down to the keelson, each in one piece, which was done, together with relaying the decks, repairing the top sides, and new waterways, from the wood of the country, and from trees fallen near where the ship lay.

Despite several voyages to Norfolk Island and a winter's passage around the Horn to St Helena and on to England, through many gales and much labour:

> Not one of the riders either shrunk, rent, or, when I left he ship in 1801, were in the least decayed. The ship is now lying at Sheerness (a receiving ship), where those riders may be seen, as well as the plank sheers, waterways, &c, which were put in her from the wood of that country.
>
> I must here remark that we had not any paint in the ship, or anything that could tend to preserve the wood in a warm and afterwards in a very cold climate. It is therefore in the same state as when cut down in the woods, and was not seasoned as ship timber in general is. It will be necessary to observe that there is so much resinous gum in the wood that it appears to be impervious to water, [...] I am therefore induced to think the wood of New South Wales more durable than oak or the teak.

Given the English Naval Yards' prejudice in favour of oak, and the high quality of the Indiamen built with teak,[253] this claim is truly remarkable. As a further illustration, he mentions a mizenmast and a bowsprit that were put into the *Buffalo*. The master, his nephew Kent, was so impressed with the bowsprit that he wouldn't let it be replaced by the English yard. The mizenmast made from Australian wood is now at Portsmouth yard for inspection.[254] Hunter then draws upon a memorandum on the timber of New South Wales, drawn up by Henry Waterhouse:[255]

> When this wood has been used for planking a ship, it has been found of so hard a nature that a scraper would hardly touch it, and a nail drove in, the carpenter of the *Reliance* said, they could not get out again. The bolts now in the riders of the *Reliance* will most probably confirm the assertion. [...] The carpenters, when in getting

CHAPTER 3 ⚓ *Building The Dockyard (2 October 1796 to 7 May 1803)* 181

> the timber for the repairs of the *Reliance*, stated that the timber necessary was in great abundance, but they were sometimes obliged to go for the crooked timbers that exactly suited their purpose some distance, but the ship was then lying alongside the rocks in the town of Sydney. Any quantity of strait or crooked timber was to be got close to the water's edge (I mean fit for naval purposes) through the whole harbour of Port Jackson, which is nearly seventeen miles in length, with almost numberless coves on each side, the parts cleared for cultivation being in general some distance inland. Rough timber may be fashioned where the tree is fallen, and in the heaviest gale of wind a small boat can go to any part of the harbour, it being in general considerably less than a quarter of a mile wide; consequently, water carriage is always certain.

Once again, the reports on timber turned in by Paine and Moore are just below the surface as Hunter waxes lyrical about their timber-gathering endeavours, which conform to the old-style methods of the Ship's Carpenter master craftsmen:

> If plank was necessary for the wales, or any other part of a ship, the pit could be made under the tree where fallen, and the plank cut out and shaded till seasoned. It is customary to do so in that country, the land being unoccupied, and for more than twelve miles a ship of 500 tons can be moored where most convenient for receiving spars, timber, or plank. Made masts could be finished in the woods, and be brought down in separate pieces to the water side. Anchor stocks, or yard-arm pieces could be furnished in the same way, and capstans, cross-trees, and billheads, with a certainty of their answering the purpose for which they were intended.[256]

In quality, the wood of NSW is hard enough for gun carriages, whose trucks and axles in other woods usually wear away quickly, and the resin-filled Australian timber also served to make drier magazines in which to store the gunpowder.

In July 1802, when Matthew Flinders was in Port Jackson about to sail northwards to map the coastline, he received a new boat built by Thomas Moore:[257]

> The boat which was built for us, was after the model of that whale boat in which Mr. Bass, coasted from Port Jackson to Western Port;

a distance not less than 400 miles, and returned safe. She was timbered with the largest kind of banksia, which is found to be more durable than mangrove, and planked with cedar. She is 28f. 7" over all, and will row eight oars when requisite, but is generally intended to use but six generally. She was built under the inspection of Mr. Thos. Moore, the master boat builder of the colony, and appears to be a fine boat. She was charged only £30 to the Navy Board, many of the materials having been furnished by government.

While his dockyard duties continued apace, Moore's other interests also expanded. About this time, horses were fetching good money. At the end of May, Captain Rowley sold a mare and filly for Henry Waterhouse to William Cox, who, after arriving on 11 January 1800 on the *Minerva*, had replaced John Macarthur as Paymaster for the Corps. Cox was quickly down to business in terms of trading, and this is reflected in Rowley's report to Waterhouse that, 'Cox has made a capital warehouse faceing your Kitching he as weather boarded it in a capital manner and a skilling at the End for a safe and to cure meat and many little things besides'. Rowley sold Waterhouse's two horses for 100 Guineas—and one of his own for £65. 'Horses is getting Plenty', he told his friend, 'and but few monied men to buy'.[258] At this stage, Rowley was planning to return to England at Christmas time, when he will bring Waterhouse's money with him, and he was pleased to report that he is posted to Parramatta, not Norfolk Island again.

Moore may have been one of the 'monied men' with enough to buy a horse or two, but he was, instead, looking to breed them himself, so that other people's money might come his way. At the muster of 1802, Thomas Moore is listed as having still only one grant, but now 100 acres out of the 470 are cleared, with 5 acres under wheat and maize. He now has eleven horned cattle, four hogs and one convict assigned to him—probably John Irvin—and six horses.[259] Almost all of his horses can be identified. The 1802 muster showed that he had acquired one stallion, which would have most likely been an Arab from India, and five mares, who can be identified with some probability from a list he kept of his mares' ages:[260] Old Bett, Young Bett, Dirma (born Nov 1798), Fanny (Nov 1799), and Dutches (Nov 1800) [possibly meaning 'Duchess'].[261]

CHAPTER 3 ⚓ *Building The Dockyard (2 October 1796 to 7 May 1803)* 183

When Moore sat as a member of the court on 6 July 1802 to try Luckyn Betts, and William Stow and others (those prosecuted by Betts), he was described as 'Master Boat-Builder and Planter'—so his farming activities had been noticed. Betts was charged with the murder of fourteen convicts during an attempted mutiny on board his ship, *Hercules* on 29 December 1801. He in turn charged Stow and others with mutiny. The other members of the court for the first case were William Paterson, John Palmer, Matthew Flinders, Robert Fowler, John Murray, Robert Campbell, Alexander Stirling, John Robinson, and Richard Atkins,[262] and for the second, Charles Grimes, Thomas Rowley 'planter', Owen Bunker, and William Tough replaced Flinders, Fowler, Stirling and Robinson.[263] It was a bit of a win for all parties, when Luckyn Betts was found guilty of manslaughter and fined £500, but subsequently pardoned by Governor King,[264] and Stow and the others were acquitted.

By September 1802, Moore's duties must have eased sufficiently for him to turn to shipbuilding once again, for he laid down the keel for a cutter, which would eventually be launched in January 1804 with the name *Integrity*.[265] When launched, she was judged to be a fine piece of workmanship. What received particular attention was the innovative design of a spacious cabin with a partition which could be extended to create a different configuration of cabin space.[266] Thomas Moore's leading-edge craftsmanship evidently continued to flourish.

In November 1802, George Bass arrived back in Sydney and in the new year he wrote to Henry Waterhouse, reporting that he was pleased that his pork voyage was his 'first successful speculation', trusting that this will be 'an earnest of our future'. Governor King had given him letters to introduce him to the Spanish posts of South America to purchase cattle for breeding in New South Wales, and he is also thinking of bringing some guanaco (a version of the llama) and pacos (alpaca) for the same purpose. After his trip to 'the Spanish coast', he proposes to go to Tahiti to recover the *Norfolk*—ex-*Harbinger* bought by King, repaired by Moore—which had been driven ashore there in a hurricane in November 1801. If he cannot find a Spanish governor willing to sell him cattle, he plans to go instead to the Sandwich Islands for pork, as in the previous successful voyage. Bass is confident of success, expecting 'to make a

1803

handsome thinking of it, and to be much expedited on my return to old England'—importing sealskins and oil on his return. He also intends to sail via Dusky Bay again, to extract some more iron from the *Endeavour*.[267] At the end of this letter he refers to others he has written to 'my beloved wife' and now sends compliments to the rest of the family.

Bass was very pleased with the performance of his brig, the *Venus*. Despite her heavy voyages she is still very strong and Bass is even contemplating selling her to the Spaniards, who 'cannot fail to admire so much beauty and strength'.[268] As he writes, the *Venus* is heaving down, and lies with her keel out to be re-coppered. Presumably this also tells us something of Thomas Moore's duties during the month of January. George Bass being in town, writing to his 'beloved wife' and her brother Henry, no doubt brought further memories for Thomas and Rachel about the young Andrew in her care, and perhaps a closer relationship between Bass and the Moores. It is interesting to wonder about the conversations between the two men, since, in time, Moore also launched speculative ventures of his own, similar to those Bass was presently engaged upon.

Bass's fertile brain was fired up by the commercial possibilities in the place at this time, and he made good use of his layover in Sydney to press his schemes further. On 30 January 1803, Bass wrote to Governor King with a proposal to decrease the necessity of sending out from England supplies of pork and beef for the convicts. This will become especially important in his view, since their numbers will be 'very considerably augmented' over the next few years, 'now that peace is established in Europe'.[269]

Bass is basking in the glow of the Treaty of Amiens, signed with the French on 25 March 1802. At last the war seemed to be over. Probably aware of previous experience in similar post-war periods in England, Bass realizes that the cessation of war will mean the demobbing of soldiers and sailors and a subsequent increase in crime and so of convicts, now to be sent to New South Wales. What Bass didn't know was that this was a short-lived peace, for hostilities began again a few months after his letter (18 May 1803). His prediction about greater numbers of convicts to the colony did indeed come true, but it would have to wait until after Trafalgar (1805) and Waterloo (1815).

His first voyage enabled pork to be sold from the Government Store at considerably lower cost than previously and Bass was hopeful that this would provide him sufficient credibility for King to support his next experiment. He requested a seven year lease granting him the exclusive rights of the South part of New Zealand, or that South of Dusky Bay at least, to supply salt fish once per week to the Government Store in Sydney. If the experiment turned out successfully, he would then want the lease renewed for twenty-one years.

On 3 February 1803, just before he sailed on his next voyage, Bass once again outlined his plans to Waterhouse.[270] He was going to Dusky Bay to strip Bampton's *Endeavour* and to visit the surrounding islands in search of seals and fish, with a view to the scheme he outlined to King. He now revealed that his scheme will have implications for Henry's sister:

> The fishery is not to be set in motion until after my return to old England, when I mean to seize upon my dear Bess, bring her out here, and make a *poissarde* of her, where she cannot fail to find plenty of use for her tongue.

No doubt Bass also shared these plans with the Moores causing them to wonder about the implications for young Andrew, so closely under Elizabeth's care. But the reality of this venture still lay some time in the future and, as Bass recognised, 'we have, I assure you, great plans in our heads; but, like the basket of eggs, all depends upon the success of the voyage I am now upon'.

The voyage will not be without its dangers. It will include visiting the coast of Chile, looking for provisions for the colony:

> And that they may not in that part of the world mistake me for a contrabandisto, I go provided with a very diplomatic looking certificate from the Governor here, stating the service upon which I am employed, requesting aid and protection in obtaining the food wanted. And God grant you may fully succeed, says your warm heart, in so benevolent an object; and thus also say I; Amen, says many others of my friends. […]
>
> Speak not of So[uth] America to any one out of your family, for there is treason in the very name!

In hindsight, these perhaps flippant suggestions of danger become poignant forebodings. In May, when Governor King reported Bass's plans to Lord Hobart, he also mentioned reports that had begun to arrive from the South American coast of ships being seized by the Spanish, simply 'to possess your Lordship of the hazard that any commercial enterprise on that coast is attended with'.[271] Indeed, this proved to be the final voyage for George Bass, who disappeared without trace after he left Port Jackson. Andrew would keep his surrogate mother, who would long grieve over her adventurous husband—missing in action just before she could join him at the other side of the world.

For some time afterwards, Thomas Moore apparently made inquiries in pursuit of George Bass. One of the last rumours about Bass was reported by Thomas Moore, in a letter written from Liverpool on 15 December 1817:

> I have just heard a report that Mr Bass is alive yet in South America. A captn. of a vessel belonging to this port, trading among the islands to the east, fell in with a whaler, and the captn. informed he had seen such a person, and described the person of Mr Bass. The captn. of a vessel out of this port knowing Mr Bass well, he is of a belief, the description that the master of the whaler gives of him, it's certainly Mr Bass—being a doctor too—which is still a stronger reason.[272]

In March 1803, the first issue of Sydney's first newspaper came hot off the press. As the *Sydney Gazette* hit the streets, Thomas Moore received a mention in passing, in the report that 'a labouring man, servant to Mr Thomas Moore, slipped off the side of a cask and broke his arm'.[273] This would not be the last time Moore's name bedecked the *Gazette* across the next thirty-seven years.

On 11 March 1803, HMS *Glatton* arrived in Port Jackson.[274] Just a few weeks later, Governor King directed her Lieutenant John Bowen to form a settlement on Van Diemen's Land, with him as commandant and superintendent, Jacob Mountgarret, surgeon of the *Glatton* as surgeon, and Mr Williams as storekeeper.[275] This was in view of 'it being expedient to establish His Majesty's right to Van Diemen's Land', for the French vessels *Géographe* and *Naturiliste* had been sniffing around in Bass Strait, and the Commandant did 'not avow having instructions to make any settlement' there.[276] In this period of peace under the Treaty

CHAPTER 3 ⚓ *Building The Dockyard (2 October 1796 to 7 May 1803)* 187

of Amiens, French ships could not be interfered with, but when Bowen sailed, he had some confidential instructions about what to do if any French vessels attempt to form an establishment on the island.[277]

When the *Buffalo* had sailed October 1800, at John Macarthur's request Governor King had sent home eight fleeces for Sir Joseph Banks' inspection. When the *Glatton* arrived, she brought the report of an English wool expert that was then published in the *Gazette*.[278] The wool from a Spanish sheep imported from the Cape was valued at 4s per pound and that of a ram bred from her, 5s. The expert was sure that if these two were preserved for their breed in the colony, 'they may make a good progress in their breed and wool'. Further samples were sent back to England for inspection with the *Glatton* when she eventually sailed for home. In the search for a staple for New South Wales, wool evidently was beginning to move in a promising direction.

In May 1803, the Southern Whale Fishery was having some success, with two ships filled with spermaceti oil ready to sail from Sydney:[279] Barnabas Gardner's *Venus*, which arrived 6 March with 1400 barrels of oil, and the *Greenwich*, Captain Law, which arrived 14 February. When these two ships arrived they brought news of other whalers working the coast of New Zealand at the time, including Eber Bunker's *Albion*, and Rhodes' *Alexander*.[280]

The news they brought of the *Harriet*, Samuel Chace, was rather confused. She had cleared Sydney in August 1802, and after whaling with the others off New Zealand, she was reported by the *Greenwich* to have sailed for England on 4 February full.[281] At this date she must have left the others, but she was not full and she had not gone to England. Thomas Moore received a letter from his friend Chace, written 'in sight of Lord Hows Island' on 29 April saying, 'it will be two or three months before I shall come to Sydney as I have got no more than six hundred Barrels of oil on board'.[282] He has been for refreshment at Norfolk Island, where he took on board 750 bushels of Indian corn. He wants Moore to purchase 20 or 30 bushels of wheat for him, to keep any letters from England, and he hopes Moore had obtained the cask from Mr Lord and the money for 45 gallons of wine at the expensive price of 5/6 per gallon—'a mistake of own acct'. Since he asks Moore, who as Chace's agent is conducting Chace's business on shore, to send a few lines by

Captain Gardner about news in Sydney and London, Gardner must have known he was still whaling and arranged for some rendezvous. Although Gardner's *Venus* was due to leave Sydney on 26 March, and then 6 May, by 15 May she still remained along with the *Greenwich* and HMS *Glatton*, 'ready to sail'.[283] Presumably, however, by the time Moore received Chace's letter of the 29 April, the *Venus* would have already left.

During 1803, Thomas Moore continued to work on his new vessel, with its innovative features. He also had the satisfaction of seeing another of his creations sail off with some notoriety. On 18 September 1803, the *Sydney Gazette* related the story of how the *Porpoise* and the *Cato*, the ship's on Matthew Flinders' cartographic voyage, were wrecked on a reef to the North East of Sandy Cape on 17 August 1802. It then reported that three vessels were expected to sail that same day. The *Rolla* will rescue the survivors and proceed to Canton where they would be placed upon Indiamen to England. Only the *Francis* will return to Sydney, presumably to report the outcome of the mission, for Matthew Flinders was intending to sail through Torres Strait and home to England on the *Cumberland*. This was the tiny schooner built in the colony and given a name in memory of the vessel seized by convicts in 1797. The *Sydney Gazette* was delighted:[284]

> This vessel is only 29 Tons burthen; but being built by Mr Moore under the direction of Governor HUNTER, at whose departure she was more than half finished, there is no doubt of her continuing as good a sea boat as experience has shewn her to be in very tempestuous weather off Norfolk Island and in Bass's Straits, and in every way equal to carry a sufficiency of Provisions and Water for Captain Flinders, the Officers, and nine men who are appointed to navigate the first Vessel built in this Colony to England—May her Voyage be safe and expeditious!

Despite the size of the vessel, Flinders managed to complete his investigation of the strait between New Holland and New Guinea, but was compelled to put in to Mauritius where he was imprisoned by the French. When he was released six and a half years later, Mr Moore's *Cumberland* remained, doing duty for Flinders' captors.

As was hinted at by the musters of 1802 and 1803, Thomas Moore had been gradually acquiring more land at Bulanaming. On 1 October

1803, he received a large grant of 700 acres in Bulanaming, which presumably consolidated some earlier farms.[285] The description on the grant itself reads:

> 700 acres in Bulanaming, bounded on the East by a swamp, on the South by the Cook's River, on the West by Hodgkinson & Hammerston farms, and on the North by Hammond, Griffin, Adams, Bolton, McKellar, and his present farms.[286]

Or for a more recent description for the contemporary reader:

> This extended his property southward to Cook's River and was approximately within the area of Marrickville bounded today by Stanmore Road to the North, Livingstone Road on the west, Princes Highway on the East and Cook's River on the South.[287]

While the *Glatton* was in Port Jackson, a group of men sought to hold a landmark meeting on board. As the convict knight, Sir Henry Browne Hayes reported it:

> Several of the officers of H.M. Ships *Glatton* and *Buffalo*, together with some respectable inhabitants of this place, wished to establish a Masonic lodge, and being in possession of a regular warrant, I was instructed to make a respectful application for that purpose. […]

Five days later, according to Hayes, he was called before the Judge-Advocate who read a paper 'to the following effect', that

> Instead of being president of a Freemason's lodge at Sydney, he will be put under a president at Castle Hill or Norfolk Island, to hard labour.[288]

Despite Governor King banning such an association (for fear of it being a vehicle of political foment, especially from the United Irishmen), a meeting did actually take place on 14 May 1803, now hailed as the foundation day of Australian freemasonry, and Sir H.B. Hayes was sentenced to hard labour in Van Diemen's Land for his role in calling it.[289] Thomas Moore had received a Masonic travelling certificate from the Friendship Lodge in London in 1790, but there is no evidence he took part in this meeting, and in fact it is highly unlikely that he did. He was a Civil Officer loyal to Governor King, who prohibited the association. And besides, by the time the meeting was held, he had already been alienated by Captain Colnett of the *Glatton*.

The freemason incident needs to be set against the rocky relationship that had emerged between King and Colnett during the *Glatton*'s visit to Sydney. Just five days before the illegal meeting and after a disagreeable exchange of letters between Captain and Governor, Thomas Moore found his own professional judgement called into question, when Colnett announced to King:[290]

> The carpenter [i.e. Thomas Wickey of the *Glatton*] has represented to me that a number of the logs received lately can be of no use in ship-building.

The gravity of this slur at this particular time in the history of New South Wales needs to be appreciated. For it came just two days after Governor King had appointed Thomas Moore to be the official 'Surveyor of Timber throughout the colony for naval purposes'.[291]

Timber 'for naval purposes' had been on the agenda for a long time prior to 1803, but this Government and General Order of 7 May 1803 came at a crucial moment in history. Thomas Moore's job at the dockyard in the little colony in Port Jackson was about to be strongly shaped by European affairs. From 1801 to 1804, 'the adequate supply of Naval timber was the [British Government's] paramount consideration' and in 1803–04, Britain's long-standing shortage of this necessity reached its greatest crisis ever, at precisely the moment Napoleon was poised to invade her.[292]

Despite the initial ban on shipbuilding in the colony, seeds were sown that eventually flowered into the King's Dockyard, especially under Hunter's encouragement.[293] Certainly the dockyard would serve local needs, but there was also a much larger agenda behind these plans, and the Naval Administration had a more global concern for this fledgling establishment and its Master. Even as John Hunter prepared to come to NSW, 'the Administration renewed its efforts to make the colony a supplier of naval materials, having Hunter seek out a person "to fill the office of boatbuilder &c at Port Jackson"'.[294]

Since the seventeenth century, England's need of 'naval materials', especially timber, had been a growing concern. In the mid-eighteenth century, home-grown English oak and crooked and compass (or great) timber especially was in short supply and, despite repeated warnings, the situation steadily grew worse.[295] It took a lot of timber to keep a wooden navy afloat, both for building new ships and repairing the existing fleet. To build a seventy-four gun ship of the line at the beginning of the 19th century, for example, required approximately 3,000 loads of timber and more was required for re-equipping and repair every two and one half years. A load was fifty cubic feet (1.5 cubic metres) and an average oak tree contained one load.[296] This demand for timber grew with the size of the ships, and by the 1840s the size of ships was reaching the safe limit for timber vessels.[297] In the earlier period of our interest, however, the timber shortage was not due to ships being too large.

The Navy had a strong prejudice in favour of English oak for their ships, but since the oak tree took about 100-120 years to reach the maturity needed to supply shipbuilding timber,[298] and the English had been engaged in a long period of sea-going warfare, supplies were dwindling. 'Crooked Timber' and 'compass timber'—the timber which grew in the right shapes and sizes for specialist pieces in the wooden vessels—was in drastically short supply.[299] By the end of the Seven Years War (1763), Britain had already become the master of the seas,[300] but if this mastery was to be retained, supplies of shipbuilding timber were absolutely essential. The American War of Independence (1775–1783), and then the outbreak of war with France (1793–) put timber supplies under further strain. The prejudice for English oak meant a corresponding prejudice against timber of other kinds and from elsewhere. Even when the Navy reluctantly moved towards utilising this other timber to a limited degree, there was a constant problem in securing supply—especially when the nation was at war. England may have been master of the seas, but the one who had control of the land was often the effective master of the trees![301] For these and other reasons, as the new colony was struggling to get on its feet at Port Jackson, the 'timber crisis' for the English Navy had already become acute.

Trafalgar (1805) and Waterloo (1815) were still to come, but when the Treaty of Amiens was signed on 25 March 1802 there was a brief, 14 month peace which many thought had come to stay.[302] John Jervis, *aka* Lord St Vincent, was apparently one of those people. After years of listening to others crying for reform, St Vincent took action. As soon as he was appointed First Lord of the Admiralty (March 1801), he set about reforming the dockyards and the timber contracting systems.[303] His reforms ultimately failed, because 'well-intentioned but untimely'.[304] In fact, Britain never succeeded in reforming the dockyards and the problems remained until the end of the era of wooden ships.

St Vincent's predecessor, Lord Middleton, managed to sustain the timber supplies despite the long war with France (1793–1802) by requiring stockpiles containing three years' supply.[305] When war resumed with France in May 1803, St Vincent's 'reforms' had run the supply of ship timber down to dangerously low levels.[306]

In 1803–1804 the crisis arrived with a vengeance, provoked by three problems: the problem of dry rot; the long-standing prejudice about where ship-building timber came from, and the politics associated with corruption and St Vincent's attempted reforms. Over many years, supply of naval timber had become the domain of the Timber Trust,[307] whose monopoly gave rise to a range of corrupt practices. By increasing prices, the Timber Trust precipitated 'one of the gravest crises in the history of the timber problem'.[308] To counter St Vincent's reforms, they cut off supply as Napoleon threatened England with invasion.

These reforms were one of the many disputes between the Navy Board and the Lords of the Admiralty. The Navy Board wished to retain supply through the Timber Trust, which would entail the acceptance of corrupt practices. St Vincent wished to break the monopoly and clean up the dockyards. In 1801 he structured the inspection of timber in the dockyards by appointing 'timber masters'.[309] This provoked bitter opposition from the Timber Trust, which attacked this new office throughout 1803–04. Believing the Peace of Amiens would last, St Vincent cancelled the Timber Trust contracts in favour of individual contractors, which resulted in a direct decrease in timber supplies and the alienation of the suppliers who controlled its replenishment.[310] When hostilities resumed in May 1803 the dockyards were almost completely empty, with less than one year's supplies in reserve.[311]

CHAPTER 3 ⚓ *Building The Dockyard (2 October 1796 to 7 May 1803)* 193

Even by February the contractors were seriously in arrears and early in 1804 the shortage was at its worst—especially of English oak and the crooked timber so crucial to wooden shipbuilding. When Lord Melville replaced St Vincent in 1805, the shortage had encouraged the development of new designs, such as the 'wall-sided' vessels and the use of iron-knees to diminish the need for crooked timber. Others were pinning their hopes on shipbuilding in India, close to the supply of teak.[312] As we have seen, Thomas Moore was himself an early innovator,[313] but it was another solution that probably had the biggest impact upon his role at the Sydney dockyard.

The timber shortage meant that the navy was at the centre of English politics from 1801 to 1806.[314] When St Vincent was appointed First Lord of the Admirality, he discovered the naval yards did not have the required three years' reserves of timber. At this stage the Navy Board expressed its intention to 'import such Timber from abroad as may be judged proper for Naval Purposes which, although perhaps not of so good a quality as Oak Timber of the growth of this Country, will be found useful in many instances'.[315] Consequently, large sums of public money were spent in the pursuit of timber supplies from the eastern Mediterranean and the Black Sea, and yet 'the Navy Board ultimately failed to tap this considerable source'.[316] Given that French and Spanish agents were also searching for supplies, this pursuit had to be done in some secrecy, and the changing politics of war-torn Europe meant that timber-supplying areas became blocked to the British, and that stockpiles of timber paid for with British money never saw service in a British ship.[317] Despite these set-backs, however, Britain's mastery of the waves enabled her quest for timber to encompass the globe, and with some success.[318] Napoleon could stop timber from Europe, but he could do nothing to stop the supply from the Americas, Asia, Africa, and the South Seas. During the Napoleonic decade (1805–1815), 'the Navy was supported by Britain's overseas possessions'.[319] The 7 May 1803 announcement of Moore's position as 'Surveyor' has to be seen as an antipodean response to this critical situation at home.

Before she sailed, the *Glatton* was filled with Timber collected by Thomas Moore and his team. After Mr Moore had served at the dockyard for just short of seven years and had established an excellent reputation for his work, the residents of Sydney were notified of an official new title he had acquired:

> His Excellency having appointed Mr. Thomas Moore, master boat-builder, to be surveyor of timber throughout the colony for naval purposes, neither him, nor any person employed under his direction, are to be hindered or molested in marking, cutting down, and removing such trees and timber as he may fix on.[320]

Hunter's vision had come into existence. By 7 May 1803, the ship's carpenter from Lesbury had built a naval yard on the western shore of Sydney Cove. In the light of the English crisis, his dockyard had suddenly assumed great significance for king and country, which, in turn, pressed more responsibility onto his own shoulders.

Thomas Moore stood ready to embrace the challenge.

4

TIMBER & TRADE

(7 MAY 1803 *to* 13 AUGUST 1806)

With the English timber crisis now pressing itself upon NSW, Thomas Moore's official duties took on an element of urgency. His Majesty's Ships began arriving to collect Moore's timber for scrutiny by the conservative Master Shipwrights of His Majesty's Navy. At the same time, Moore's farming interests were expanding and his growing herds of cattle and horses required more land. Since 1800 the grip of the Officer-Trader monopoly on wholesale goods had gone and a new class of traders was emerging in Sydney. Even if not a major trader himself, Thomas Moore was very much associated with this rising new breed.

As with the Officer-Traders, the civil officers had the advantage of being paid in real money, that is, sterling—which, in turn, was readily acceptable to the ship's captains bringing in the wholesale goods. Being supported by the Store also meant that much of Moore's annual salary could be saved for other purposes. As his farm grew in productivity, his sale of 'grain and swine's flesh' to the Government

Store also brought him Treasury bills, either directly or through the consolidation of store receipts.[1] This ready supply of sterling helped to set Moore up for investing in further commercial enterprise.

As Moore received his new job description, his yard was urgently repairing and refitting the *Porpoise* which had returned from Otaheite 'very weak in her frame, and her outside plank in many places rotten'.[2] She had to be ready for the homeward journey come September. The troubles with Colnett and his *Glatton* added extra urgency. From his arrival on 11 March he was difficult and the loss of an earlier order to get timber ready for transport meant that the demand came as a surprise.

Despite the new urgency, timber-gathering had always been part of the job and Moore's intimacy with New South Wales timber began long before the crisis. Not only is there a record of a gang sent out to cut 'crooked timber for the boat-builder' from 1798,[3] it stands to reason that from the time he took over from Paine, he would have continued to criss-cross the colony placing the 'broad arrow' upon trees reserved to the crown, according to Hunter's order. Even in the first year of Moore's regime, as the dockyard began to take shape, a steamer for seasoning plank was built, indicating that timbers were being brought to the yard for the preparation thought essential for shipbuilding.[4]

Hunter certainly had no doubts about Moore's understanding of timber, for in mid 1802 he confidently informed the Navy Board that 'a person properly qualified for the Selection of [timber] may be found at Port Jackson'.[5] When the May 1803 announcement came, it surely signalled not new duties, but that he had been officially appointed Surveyor on behalf of the Navy Board, as part of the answer to their present crisis.

The pressure on Moore arising from this work was apparent to a visitor to the colony during the peak years of the timber crisis (1803–1804). An unsigned and undated memorandum (thought to be written by Barrallier in 1804) noted that:

> An able assistant to the master shipwright is much wanted for the purpose of exploring the extensive forests, and selecting proper timber for constructing frames for ships of the line, and to point out the proper times and seasons for felling it; and occasionally to

CHAPTER 4 ♃ *Timber & Trade (7 May 1803 to 13 August 1806)* 197

examine the fine spars and timber said to abound on the island of New Zealand.[6]

The need for naval timber had been on the Australian agenda since the First Fleet. Indeed, consistent with the fact that the need for timber was advanced as one of the reasons for the settlement of New England and Canada,[7] some Australian historians have suggested that this need was also a primary reason for forming the new colony at Port Jackson.[8] Even if the penal nature of the early colony of New South Wales is sufficient evidence for why Prime Minister William Pitt sent the First Fleet, it is probably also true that—at least in some circles—'the region was valued for its capacity to provide flax and timber required by the Royal Navy for the rigging, sails and masts of its warships'.[9]

In 1798, Lord Hawkesbury had suggested drawing on reserves in Canada and other parts of the world in case the Baltic states started using the supply of timber to England as a political weapon, as subsequently happened in 1801–1806.[10] The experience of the Navy Board in Croatia and Southern Russia—and in more distant regions—had shown how difficult it was for the Navy Board 'to secure the supply of vital war materials in areas outside its control'.[11] On the other hand, the Cape of Good Hope, India, Canada, New Zealand and Australia were more accessible to sea transport, and to the protection of British seapower.[12] By 1802, timber from more remote lands was being discussed, and by 1804 it had started to roll in.

Until 1804 only four kinds of timber were used, but the crisis of 1803–04 meant that these old prejudices had to be broken down and soon dozens of kinds of timber were arriving from every continent, and some were even noted as the peer of English oak.[13] For some time, reports had been coming home with South Seas Captains about glorious forests of timber right down to the water's edge of sufficient quantity to solve Britain's timber problem forever. In the midst of this crisis, 'Admirals and Captains on every station, diplomats and consuls at every post were urged to co-operate in relieving the situation. Samples by the dozens were submitted'.[14]

New colonies also presented the opportunity of overcoming previous barriers to the timber supply. The Royal Navy was frustrated by the supply of timber by contractors, especially as their power had grown.[15] Reform was also somewhat hampered by the presence in Parliament of the Lords, since it was their forests which largely supplied oak to the contractors! New territories allowed for new contracting arrangements and for new practices, designed to yield the Government greater control.

Some of these 'new' practices were, in fact, a return to traditional ways. Shipwrights themselves were once involved in the fetching of timber. Although the development of the Timber Trust contracting system had led to the decline of this practice in England resulting in increased wastage, in foreign supply areas the Navy usually employed an expert to work with the timber agents, 'an inspector who understood the quality of timber necessary to the Navy'.[16] This shipwright assisted with the conversion of felled trees into the timber desired for shipbuilding.[17] When Raven boasted about Thomas Moore's New Zealand vessel, he mentioned cutting timber 'growing to the mould'. This refers to the various moulds traditionally used by shipwrights to select timber where it grew, before the trees were felled and converted on the spot.[18] South Seas conditions necessitated a return to traditional practices, giving shipwrights and ship's carpenters the satisfaction of more choice in the timber with which they would end up working.

Other traditional practices were not so acceptable. One controversial practice was the reservation of trees by the crown even on private land, such as in the system of *martelage* practiced in France.[19] In Tudor and early Stuart Britain, a system of 'purveyance of timber' theoretically enabled trees to be seized for the king, even if this did not often occur. In the decade before the civil war of 1642–1651, Parliament opposed this system and the king modified the policy. Under Cromwell's Protectorate (1653–1659) it was abolished altogether, having become associated with tyranny. At a later date, therefore, the English despised the French *martelage* as a sign of a despotic system and as being against the spirit of English freedoms. Given this history, it was a bold move when St Vincent attempted to reintroduce the system as part of his reforms. When Parliament refused him, it was probably not for any worthy political reasons, but more likely because it was the owners of the English timber who were the ones voting!

CHAPTER 4 ⚓ *Timber & Trade (7 May 1803 to 13 August 1806)*

Figure 33. Two examples of the 'broad arrow' marking the King's timber.

Despite the high-sounding philosophical principles forged across years of English history, however, the Parliament was not so strictly protective on the trees of Ireland or the colonies.[20] As British colonies sprang up, the practices resisted by the Lords to protect their own trees at home were permitted in lands far away. Those in the new world weren't too happy about this inconsistency, however, and the use of the broad arrow to reserve trees to the crown was one of the major grievances leading to the American Revolution.[21] This, in turn, led to the Navy turning to areas likely to remain under British control long-term, such as Canada.[22]

On this criterion, a penal colony like New South Wales must have been considered extremely controllable. For despite the trouble caused in the American experience, Australian naval timber was reserved to the crown from the very first leases. When James Ruse, Robert Webb, William Reid and Phillip Schäffer read the fine print, they found that their leases explicitly reserved such timber. The later lease from one of Moore's own holdings can be cited as an example: 'such timber as may be now growing or that may grow hereafter upon the said lands which may be deemed fit for Naval Purposes to be had reserved for the use of the Crown'.[23]

When Governor Hunter was sent to Australia, he was instructed to continue this reservation.[24] In 1795 he extended this to crown lands, forbidding indiscriminate felling and informing the colony that 'in order to preserve as much as possible such timber as may be of use either for building or for naval purposes, the King's mark will be forthwith put on all such timber',[25] and, as we have seen, this probably formed a large part of Daniel Paine's activity.

Of course, the reservation of timber was not simply theoretical. Some months before Moore first arrived in Australia, Governor Phillip sent a shipment of timber specimens home to be assessed for their suitability for naval purposes on the *Gorgon*, which sailed 18 Dec 1791.[26]

> Specimens of the timber of this country are put on board the *Gorgon* The natives so very frequently setting the country on fire, is I apprehend the reason we find so little timber that is sound. It must injure the very young trees which it does not destroy, and so very scarce is the sound timber, which is proper for masts, that there has been some trouble to get the *Supply* masted.[27]

By 1803, the potential of the NSW timber had once again come before the Navy Board and the pace of Moore's timber-gathering escalated to a more frantic level. The timber crisis provided a potential opportunity for a NSW staple of great potential value to the wider world, tied as it was to 'national security'. When he wrote to Government in 1802, the trading potential of NSW was clearly on John Hunter's mind. He even suggested a 'plan B':

> If the timber to be sent from New South Wales should not be approved in our dockyards, it would be found a convenient and valuable article for fuel or other purposes at the Cape, which lays so conveniently in the route homeward.[28]

Hunter was clearly applying gentle pressure to move towards a freer situation to trade, in the same letter mentioning the possibility of trading with the Cape and with India. As potential exports he mentions coal, bark (for tanning), flax, sheep, tobacco and indigo, in order 'to show that in due time much may be done to lessen the expenses of that settlement [i.e. Sydney]; but at the same time I conceive the timber and coals may be found the only articles by which a part of its expences may be immediately relieved'.[29]

Hunter's advice appears to have been heard well. The month after he wrote, the Board of Admiralty informed the Home Secretary of their decision to require HMS *Glatton* to fetch a backload of timber.[30] By May 1802,[31] Hunter informed the board that 'a person properly qualified for the Selection of [timber] may be found at Port Jackson' —namely, Moore—but they wished to provide him with an assistant.

The carpenter of the *Glatton* was 'not qualified for the Service being old and Infirm', so they suggested Thomas Weeks, present carpenter on *Dido* be appointed to the *Glatton* 'and employed upon this Service he being properly qualified to give the assistance required'. By June, drawings of the Frame Timbers had been submitted for a 98, 74, and 38 gun ship, 'for the purpose of providing the Timber at New South Wales',[32] and a letter is written to King (which he apparently did not receive), informing him that the plan to regularly convey convicts and to return home Timber has been approved, and directs him to 'take such steps as shall appear to you most advisable for preparing Timber of the description required, and in the manner recommended by the Navy Board (11 June 1802)'.[33]

Even before the announcement of his new official posting, Moore was busily engaged in loading the *Glatton* with timber. The *Gazette* noted in March 1803 that she was ready for loading.[34]

> Mr Moore has received the Governor's instructions to provide a quantity of the best timber that can be procured for ship-building. He has already been out to survey and make choice of the wood; and on Monday next a number of carpenters and labourers will begin the work. The trees are to be hewed according to the scale, and put on board His Majesty's ship *Glatton*, to be conveyed to England.—Red and other gums, string and iron bark, mahogany, and other hard woods will be selected in preference to any other.

March must have been the month for timber. With the *Glatton*'s arrival, Governor King was now well-primed about the needs back home, and he included specific instructions concerning timber as he outlined his plans for John Bowen, Lieutenant on the *Glatton*, about to form a settlement on the Derwent.

With the Peace of Amiens offering protection, French ships were in Australian waters with no fear of reprisal and so causing English concern about a potential French Settlement in the southern regions and Van Diemen's Land. In January 1803, King had commissioned Charles Grimes to survey a site for a settlement at Port Phillip Bay, and plans were already afoot in England to send David Collins with a party to settle there.[35] In the meantime, Governor King took some active steps to cover Van Diemen's Land by appointing (on 28 March) twenty-three year old Bowen. Given how the English timber crisis was already making an impact upon the colony, it is no surprise that Bowen received specific instructions to inform Governor King:

> whether the general timber in that country is fit for the purposes of being sent to England for the construction of King's ships, particularizing, as far as you are able, the different species, length of trunk, and diameter; also whether it grows mostly crooked or strait, and notice the facility of getting it on board ships.[36]

It is not difficult to hear the advice of the Governor's Master Boat Builder lying just beneath the surface of these instructions. As plans for this new settlement circulated and Thomas Moore's thoughts turned to its timber, had reports already come in from passing ship's captains about its potential and quality? Perhaps it was still too early for anyone to have penetrated the rugged bush far enough back from the coast to discover Tasmanian timbers such as the Huon and King Billy Pines, which would bring such delight to future shipbuilders at Hobart, Sarah Island, and beyond.

But before anyone started dreaming about the timber of the proposed settlement, the *Glatton* had to be loaded with the timber of New South Wales. In the process, Moore was making new discoveries:

> A species of wood which had not before been noticed, has recently been discovered about the Banks of the George's River. It bears a strong resemblance to the Lignum Vitae, used in sheaves and pins for Blocks. Mr Moore has received his Excellency's Instructions to examine it; when should it answer the above purposes, a quantity will be sent to England by His Majesty's ship *Glatton*.[37]

Within the week some of this new wood was added to the other shipbuilding timber laying ready at the dockyard for loading on the *Glatton*, which was mahogany and ironbark, 'hewed out agreeable to the scale dimensions'.[38] With the *Glatton* intending to sail on 24 April, loading began in earnest.[39] Although announcing on the 17th she was ready to sail,[40] by the 24th she remained in Sydney,[41] still loading and with a hint that her departure would be delayed even further: 'The quantity of ship timber received by the *Glatton*, on Friday amounted to 120 heavy pieces. She will continue to take in as long as she may remain here'.[42] On 15 May, the same *Gazette* which announced Thomas Moore's 7th May appointment as Surveyor of Timber, finally published a list of the timber that Moore had placed on the *Glatton*, and she sailed two days later.[43]

Writing to Lord Hobart, Governor King included Moore's own summary of the timber on the *Glatton*, signed with his new title: 'Master Builder and Actg. Purveyor of Timber':[44]

> NUMBER of Pieces of Timber (with the dimensions) for Ship building etc. Sent in His Majesty's Ship *Glatton*.
>
> 162 Pieces of Timber from 12 Feet length 12 Inches depth 12 Inches width to 29 Feet length 24 Inches depth 17 Inches width.
>
> 15" Lignum vitae from 6 1/2 feet to 18 feet.
>
> 6 Grind Stones.
>
> 2 Casks Iron Ore.
>
> 20 D°. Bark.

King's report to Sir Evan Nepean, Baronet Secretary to the Admiralty, included one from Thomas Moore, whom King's covering letter describes as 'a very Respectable Officer (who has served long in this Colony with reputation and Esteem)', on the colonial timbers.[45]

> Sir, From the Anxiety your Excellency has Shewn to procure as much Timber from this Country as can possibly be obtained for naval purposes, to send on Board HM Ship *Glatton*, and Conceiving it my Duty in Consequence of your Excellency's having Appointed me Purveyor of Timber, to afford you every Information in my Power; I now take the liberty to Acquaint you with the different kinds of Timber in this Country, and which appears to Me to be Most durable and Most Useful—The Timber that has been Shipped on Board the *Glatton* is of different Qualities, but such I trust will give Satisfaction When inspected into—the Reason that there has been such a small Number of long pieces put on Board arises from the lowness of the Raft-Port, which put me under the Necessity of Reducing them to such lengths as would go down her Hatchways—there may be had Timber of different Kinds in this Colony, such as the Iron Bark,

> the Stringy Bark, the Mahogany Blue Gum and Box—all, or any of which will answer for Line of Battle Ships, to the length of 60 or 70 feet in the Trunk—this in my Opinion, is far more durable than English Oak; and will answer for Beams for first Rates—Keels, Kelsons and Sternposts—as well as other occasions—and may be had in abundance—with quantities of Knees of different Sizes—and all such I flatter Myself will be found well calculated for Naval Purposes.—
>
> Some of the Short Timber put on Board the *Glatton* is not so good as I could wish—but owing to the Shortness of time—I was obliged to send it in the state it was in.
>
> The Timber of this Country when Green will not stand to be moulded—and when it is Necessary to bring it to a proper Scantling it should be cut down Six Months or More.[46]

Against the centuries old English prejudices, once again it is significant that Moore is prepared to say that the timber of his new home 'is far more durable than English Oak; and will answer for Beams for first Rates'.

The panic about loading the *Glatton* arose because an earlier letter of 11 June 1802 listing the timber requirements had gone astray. King promised better for the next ship. He also requested a salary increase for his new Surveyor of Timber as he did so:

> I am sorry I was not previously possessed of instructions respecting the timber, as I should have had sufficient to load that ship. We have got as much as possible during the *Glatton*'s short stay, and if it answers no better purpose it will serve as good samples of what we shall get and send by the first ship after the *Glatton*, as gangs of men shall be kept for that purpose alone. As all this timber is to be looked out and sized to particular dimensions according to the Navy Board plans, which will require much of the attention of one person of trust and confidence, I have fixed on the master boat-builder, who is every way equal to that business; and as he will have much to do in regulating the people's labor, &c, who are at that particular work, I beg to suggest the propriety and advantage of his having the extra allowance of 5s. a day for doing that duty, as long as obtaining timber from this country shall be considered an object, which I apprehend will

CHAPTER 4 ⚓ *Timber & Trade (7 May 1803 to 13 August 1806)* 205

> depend on its being found equal to the use it is intended for, as in that case any quantity can be sent from hence; and I have no doubt but the return of that article will greatly do away the expences of the colony, when the difference between sending convicts in transports is calculated and the expence of sending them in King's ships is so much lessened by the timber they will carry back, as it will be my duty to keep men preparing timber that there may be as little detention as possible when the ships arrive.[47]

Provisions were already being made to have vessels suited for the gathering of the timber in readiness for future ships, including the use of the hulk *Supply*. A survey conducted by Captain Colnett, William Kent, William Scott, Thomas Wickey, carpenter of HMS *Glatton*, John Coldwell, carpenter of HMS *Buffalo*, and Thomas Moore had recommended that she be cut down to the bends, to convert her bottom to 'the purpose of bringing Timber for Construction from the different parts of this Harbour to Sydney'.[48] King is confident that the value of the New South Wales timber will considerably reduce the expence of the colony in future, and requests a copy of the report on the timber sent by the *Glatton*.[49]

The fact that the original letter ordering the timber went astray was an initial cause of difficulty between Governor King and Captain Colnett, who outranked King and wished to hurry on home. His letter of 7 April announcing he would leave on 24th, effectively gave King just over two weeks more to load.[50] By return letter on the same day, however, King agrees with Colnett's proposal:

> Had I Received any Orders or Instructions of What was Wished by Government previous to Your Arrival I should most Certainly have Employed a Number of Men in preparing Timber to put on Board the *Glatton*, but as I only Received the Orders and Plans by that Ship, altho' not a moment is lost in procuring what Timber we are able, Yet it would require some months to Cut down and bring to this Place Sufficient Timber to load the *Glatton*. And as I observe by My Lords Commissioners of the Admiralty's Letter to Lord Pelham, that they Request the Convicts may be employed in preparing the Timber in the manner proposed by the Navy Board, previously to the Arrival of the *Glatton* that her detention may be

of as short a duration as possible. I agree with you that it will be more Conducive to the Interest of His Majesty's Service, for the Reasons you have Stated, that the *Glatton* should not wait for a full Cargo of Timber, which I shall do my utmost to procure by the Arrival of the next Ship. The Timber that is now fallen shall be prepared and brought down as fast as possible; I hope every thing will be Completed by the date you mention, at least, no exertion of mine shall be wanting.[51]

King's gracious reply in this instance did not prevent relations between the two men seriously breaking down. Amidst the interchange over an incident in which Thomas Whittle's son was mistreated whilst on board the *Glatton*, several other points of contention between the two emerged.[52]

It was in this context of controversy that the quality of Thomas Moore's work was impugned, two days after he was appointed to be the colony's 'Surveyor of Timber'. This was a brilliant way to insult the colony's Master Boat Builder himself and the Governor who appointed him! When King informed Colnett that no more timber would be put on board after 9 May, he also said that he had received no official notice that the *Glatton*'s carpenter has permission to collect timber in NSW.[53] Colnett questioned the quality of the timber placed on board, informing King that his carpenter had 'represented to [him] that a number of the logs received lately can be of no use in ship-building'.[54] King made his own inquiries of the carpenter and informed Colnett that 'he says the timber is all very fit for ship building, except the box, which does not run crooked; but it will do well for straight work, such as scarfing for keels, stern posts, &c'.[55] In return, Colnett sent King a letter from his carpenter, which he takes as denying 'whatever he said to you'.[56] King returned this letter written after their conversation, inscribed on the back with the testimony of 'two officers of veracity' contradicting what the carpenter now claims, along with a copy of his original letter for comparison.[57] At the same time, King wonders 'what motive [Colnett] had for casting such an indirect censure on myself and the officers of this colony as that contained in your letter on the 9th instant, therein quoting your carpenter's doubtful information'. Of course, as the colony's Purveyor of Timber, Thomas Moore was the

CHAPTER 4 ⚓ *Timber & Trade (7 May 1803 to 13 August 1806)* 207

'officer' brought into ill-repute by the offending comments.

To add insult to injury, the very next week, on 14 May, was the moment that Sir Henry Browne Hayes held his freemason's meeting, despite King refusing the request for such a meeting to be held with men from the *Glatton*, the *Buffalo* and citizens from the colony. For his troubles, the magistrates sentenced him to hard labour in the new settlement to be formed at Van Diemen's Land.[58]

After a delay long enough to fracture an already broken relationship between the two men, the *Glatton* sailed on 17 May.[59] Upon his arrival in England, Colnett wasted no time in complaining to Lord Hobart about the 'extraordinary insults and unofficer-like treatment' and 'frantick violence' he received from King.[60] If King's reputation was damaged by Colnett, that of the New South Wales timber was enhanced by the samples he brought home. The timber on the *Glatton* paved the way for the *Calcutta*'s cargo of timber which eventually received good report from the Navy's Master Shipwright at Woolwich:[61]

> the several kinds of Wood may be used for the Frames of Ships &c, as the greater part of it is compass, and as we have no doubt of its durability, we are of opinion the Importation of it may answer the intention of Government, particularly at this time when the present scarcity of Oak Timber of the growth of this Country, may render it necessary.

With the *Glatton* gone and Hayes sentenced, it was time for Governor King's thoughts to turn to the Derwent Settlement more actively and on Friday 10 June, he sent the *Lady Nelson* southwards. (Plate 41). The day before she sailed, Sydney welcomed back Matthew Flinders on the *Investigator*, badly in need of repairs. Flinders had sailed in July 1802, to map the coastline of New Holland, but he paid such close attention to detail, that he didn't get much more than the East Coast finished. One of his most significant achievements was finding a safe passage through Torres Strait, which promised a considerably shorter passage to India.[62] This would have been attractive news for the traders.

But what of the *Investigator*, was it seaworthy? Governor King ordered Actg. Lt. William Scott, Commander of the *Porpoise*, E.H.

Palmer, of the EIC ship *Bridgewater*, and Thomas Moore to conduct a survey, and they reported on 14 June.[63] Having found the vast majority of timbers examined to be unsound, they were 'unanimously of the opinion, that she is not worth repairing in any Country and that it is impossible in this Country to put her in a fit State for going to Sea'.[64] As for a replacement, the only private vessel that was in Port Jackson for sale was the *Rolla*, which was expensive, and HMAV *Porpoise* was a little small, but Flinders thought that it would suffice.

Even as Flinders' next mode of transport was being worked out, King still had his eye on the next load of timber. He was not going to be caught out again, and on the 12 June he made a public announcement about Moore's new priority.

> HIS EXCELLENCY has intrusted Mr Moore to keep a gang of men constantly employed in procuring such Timber as he may consider to be best adapted to Naval purposes. It will be deposited in the Dock Yard, and sent Home as opportunity may serve.[65]

At the end of the month he issued another general order on the subject, in which the NSW system of *martelage* is clear, for beginning from the 26 June the regulation applied to lands both public and private:[66]

> The great consumption of timber, and the requisition made by Government for as much as possible being reserved for the use of the Navy, the following regulations are to be observed by all and every of His Majesty's subjects resident or stationed in the territory, masters of ships, and all others:—
>
> Timber in this colony includes she and swamp oaks, red, blue, and black-butted gums, stringy and iron barks, mahogany, box, honeysuckle, cedar, lightwood, turpentine, &c, the property of all which, and every other kind of trees fit for timber, or likely to become so, lies in the proprietor of the land, either by grant or lease, excepting timber fit for naval or other public purposes, which those authorized by the Governor may mark, cut down, and remove in and from any situation, public or private.
>
> Any person cutting down, barking, damaging, or destroying any timber or trees fit, or likely to become fit, for ship-building, buildings, masts, or mechanical purposes, without the permission of the proprietor or of the Governor, if on any of the Crown lands,

will be answerable to the laws provided in that behalf, and according to the local situation of the inhabitants of this colony.

This regulation is not to preclude the inhabitants from getting such fuel from fallen woods as they can remove with wheelbarrows or carts drawn by one horse, excepting fuel requisite for Government uses. Masters and commanders of ships will be informed by the Naval Officer where they may procure fuel for their ships; and those who may obtain the Governor's or proprietor's permission to cut down and remove timber fit for the foregoing purposes, or for sale at any other port, are to pay a duty of three pounds sterling to the treasurer of the Orphan Fund for every thousand solid feet taken on board, of which they are to give notice to the measurer (John Thompson) as often as they receive it, and before it is hoisted into the ship, on pain of forfeiting five pounds sterling for each neglect on conviction before two magistrates.

With Flinders opting for the *Porpoise*, on 6 July 1803 King ordered John Aken, Master of the *Investigator*, Russel Mart, carpenter of the *Investigator*, and Thomas Moore 'Master Builder to the Territory' to conduct her survey. They reported on 9 July that she could be repaired to last a further two and a half years (as required by Flinders), but it wouldn't take less than twelve months to complete the work.[67] When King laid out the options for Flinders, he reported that Thomas Moore and Flinder's own carpenter Mart considered that the *Rolla* would require six months work to be made suitable. He also objected that the asking price was rather expensive, given her state. If Flinders did not wish to wait for the *Porpoise* to be repaired, he could have her for his passage home, and perform some of the duties of his original plan en route, namely, the mapping of Torres Strait. Flinders chose the last option, the crew of the *Porpoise* were discharged—many remaining in the colony—and Moore began fitting her for sea.[68]

The same day as the survey team were reporting (9 July), it became clear that the settlement at the Derwent was going to have to wait a little longer, for the *Lady Nelson* sailed back into Port Jackson. Forced by bad weather to return, she promptly ran aground on Bennelong Point causing some damage to add further to Mr Moore's work at the dockyard.[69]

In the midst of everything else going on this week, Thomas Moore also welcomed back one of the captains for whom he acted as agent. Captain Eber Bunker on the *Albion* sailed into Sydney Cove on 6 July, after whaling in the waters around New Zealand at the end of another venture begun from London in June 1802.[70] When he was last in the colony, thirty-nine and thinking about settling down, Bunker had purchased Surgeon Edward Laing's original grant from Thomas Fyshe Palmer in 1800.[71] (Figure23). He had not seen the property since he left for England on 26 August 1801, and, now that he had returned, he evidently went with his agent, Mr Moore, to inspect it. Unimpressed, the two men published a warning in response to what they had found:

> NOTICE IS HEREBY GIVEN, There being great quantities of TIMBER cut down and destroyed on my and Captain BUNKER's FARM adjoining to it, near Sydney, which would have been useful for Naval Purposes, It is therefore particularly requested, that no Person will cut down, unbark, or otherwisel [sic] damage any of the Trees, Posts, Paling, Shingles, &c on the said Premises, unless for the above Use, else they will be prosecuted to the utmost rigour of the Law provided against such Offenders. T. Moore[72]

Despite the special note in the leases and the Government mark on the trees, it was not easy to protect the timber from those with other plans. If Hunter's December 1795 order was in response to indiscriminate timber cutting on Crown land, newspaper advertisements suggest that the theft of timber from other people's grants was also quite common in the early days of the colony. And with Moore's new position, he presumably viewed the problem with newfound seriousness.

In his early visits to Sydney, Bunker never stayed terribly long. In the eight weeks he was there in July-August 1803, his thoughts turned again to settling down. He purchased 60 rods in the Town of Sydney, 'on the east side of the spring at the north end of Pitt's Row'. Originally leased to Thomas Hobby, the lot was purchased by Nicholas Bayly, who then sold it to Bunker.[73] Governor King issued the lease on 26 August, two days before Bunker departed. Thomas Moore now had another Bunker property to keep an eye on, and soon he would also oversee the construction of a beautiful stone house on the lot. Twelve months later, it would almost be completed in time for Bunker to see it before he returned to England to his family.[74]

CHAPTER 4 ⚓ *Timber & Trade (7 May 1803 to 13 August 1806)* 211

Moore had the *Porpoise* fit enough for Captain Flinders to sail on 10 August. Between 8 and 9 in the morning she was under weigh, and, leaving the whalers *Rolla* and *Albion*, and the snow, *L'Adele*, in the Cove, by noon she was clear of the heads. Governor King accompanied them as far as South Head and then returned in the *Lady Nelson*.[75] The *Gazette* reported that Flinders was bound for England, but first he would guide the *Bridgewater* and *Cato* through his newfound passage through Torres Strait into the Indian Ocean.

With his current commitment to timber, Governor King was disappointed that none could be stowed on the *Porpoise*, since the room was taken up with members of Flinders' crew as supernumeraries and all their provisions. Even by her departure he was ahead of the timber game, reporting on 7 August that he was ready for the next ship:[76]

> I have the honour to enclose a return of the timber now ready to be shipped on board the first ship that arrives for that purpose. A number of convicts, with timber carriages and boats, are kept employed cutting down and squaring timber to be sent to England when an opportunity offers.

But in the meantime, there was the counter-French move at the Derwent to organise. Since Bunker was in town, Governor King engaged the *Albion* to accompany the *Lady Nelson* to take Bowen and his party to found their settlement. Being larger, the *Albion* took the bulk of the passengers and freight. Bunker also gained King's permission to engage in whaling if the opportunity arose on the voyage down—as long as the convicts were secure during any whale-chase.[77] With Moore having finished her repairs, the *Lady Nelson* sailed on Sunday 28 August and the *Albion* followed on the Tuesday. They were at the Derwent by 13 September and what would become 'Hobart' was planted, and a week later Bunker turned around. He was seen off Sydney on 8 October before turning for the sealing grounds of New Zealand.[78]

One of the reasons for Bunker's 'sail past' at Sydney was to drop off a note to secure a little more land for his future. While running up the coast after leaving his passengers at the Derwent, Bunker wrote to Governor King thanking him in advance—that is, requesting!—a grant of 150 acres at the Hawkesbury, as he had only taken 50 at the Derwent.[79] There is no record of him ever receiving either grant. Instead, on 11 August 1804 Governor King granted Bunker 400 acres along the George's River in Banks Town from an allotment originally given to the artist John William Lewin—the land upon which Bunker later built his property Collingwood.[80] Years later the Bigge Commission was told that this land was given to him as a reward for transporting people to the first settlement at the Derwent.[81]

With Van Diemen's Land secure, by September King was awaiting the arrival of the *Calcutta*:[82]

> The *Calcutta* not being yet arrived I have every hope of having a complete cargo of ship timber ready to send by her, as a great quantity is now collecting, which requires the exertions of a great proportion of the convicts at public labor, altho' procuring it is now much facilitated by the construction of a proper vessel to transport it from different parts of the harbour to Sydney ready for being shipped.

Moore's teams had been busy, but the Governor still had bitter memories of his altercations with Colnett, which he recalled in a letter to Sir Joseph Banks.

> A great quantity of timber is now collected, ready for the *Calcutta*, which we are in hourly expectation of seeing. I hope to have a compleat load ready for her on her arrival; and I hope the captain will be better disposed towards us than Captain Colnett was.[83]

By the end of October the stockpile had grown 'of very fine timber for ship-building, to load the *Calcutta* or any other vessel when they may arrive'.[84]

The *Calcutta*, also part of the anti-French settlement strategy, had sailed from England on 24 April 1803 in company with the *Ocean*. Lieutenant-Governor Collins, on board the *Calcutta*, arrived at Port Phillip on 9 November, two days after the *Ocean*.[85] Deeming the site unsuitable, Collins sent word to King in Sydney by way of a volunteer (another Mr Collins—William) in a cutter, capable of being six-oared, who set off up the coast, but was later picked up by the *Ocean* and brought to Sydney on 24th.[86] HM Armed Tender *Lady Nelson* and a

CHAPTER 4 ⚓ *Timber & Trade (7 May 1803 to 13 August 1806)* 213

small schooner *Edwin* were dispatched immediately to take Collins and his party to the Derwent, and King also chartered the *Ocean* to return to assist in the task, and later also sent the *Francis*.[87] Captain Daniel Woodriff and his *Calcutta* could not do this duty, for he had urgent orders to pick up naval supplies at Port Jackson.[88]

Collins had a high regard for Woodriff, praising the 'propriety of [his superiors'] selection' of him for this mission. Being the son of a Deptford shipwright and carpenter's mate, and having a brother who was carpenter on HMS *Centaur*, Woodriff had a great deal of sympathy for the timber-gathering cause—even before factoring in his own career at sea from the age of six.[89] His diary for the brief time spent at Port Phillip pays close attention to the carpenters' not very successful attempts to gather ship's timber from both sides of the bay, and shows a more-than-casual interest in the types of timbers being sought.[90]

Whatever urgency about picking up the Port Jackson naval supplies Woodriff may have had when he sailed from England, on 13 December that urgency would have escalated. On 24 November, the day the *Ocean* arrived in Sydney, the American ship, *Paterson*, had also arrived, bringing news that filled the *Sydney Gazette* the following Sunday: Declaration of War.

Relations with the French during the Peace of Amiens had not been as cordial as they were supposed to be and, on 16 May, the Treaty was over and George III issued orders for 'General Reprisals' against French vessels. This was followed the next day by orders from the Admiralty 'to the Commanding Officers of all His Majesty's ships of war, authorizing them to CAPTURE, SINK, BURN, and DESTROY, the ships and vessels belonging to the Republic of France'.[91] When the *Ocean* sailed again for Port Phillip, it arrived on 13 December with copies of both proclamations. With hostilities resumed and the shortage of timber at its most critical, Woodriff knew his duty. The *Calcutta* arrived in Sydney on 26 December[92] and began taking take timber on board soon after. Having learned from the *Glatton* experience, this time Thomas Moore was ready, waiting next to his stockpile.

On 8 October and in England, Elizabeth Bass had written to her husband George—evidently still unaware of his disappearance at this stage—reporting the arrival of three ships from Pt Jackson, the

Glatton, Greenwich, and *Venus*.[93] Two weeks later she wrote again, alarmed at the sight of so many soldiers in London, 'there is great talk of an Invasion, how it will end God only knows'. Her brother Henry still has no ship, is improved in health and 'much disappointed at having no Letters from you or Governor King'. The same letter gives news about Thomas and Rachel's Andrew:

> Andrew White, the two Johnstones & Coniley Dined with us on Sunday they all look remarkably well, beg you will remember them to their parents and tell them they are very happy. Andrew was disappointed at not receiving a Letter from his Mother, he is much grown in perfect health & very Handsome it seems his Father has taken the care of him from us, but poor fellow were we not to see after him he would be totally neglected, as he has never inquired after him since the last Holodays, but he still considers this his home and will always find it so.[94]

Clearly unimpressed with John White's involvement with his son, Elizabeth and her family are filling the deficit—in fact, there seem to be a number of school-age waifs from colonial New South Wales! 'Coniley' is not easily identified, but quite probably the son of Andrew Connelly, the 1797 Hawkesbury settler. The 'two Johnstones' would be George Junior and his younger brother David, the sons of George Johnston of the Corps—promoted Major in 1800.[95] In 1820 when George junior died after falling from his horse, Andrew White remembered him as his 'old school fellow and early friend'.[96] Nelson concluded from this later note that both boys had done their schooling in Sydney,[97] but the letter from Elizabeth shows they were schooled in England. This no doubt explains for Yarwood, why George was 'surprisingly literate in spite of the colony's lack of educational facilities'.[98] Perhaps the news of soldiers in the streets of London fuelled Thomas and Rachel's fears about their young Andrew, now ten years old and learning his lessons well as England renewed the war with France. It is probably no surprise in this environment, that this young man was influenced towards a military career, as the need for a well-disciplined Army and Navy pressed upon him from all sides.

At the end of November, just six months after Bunker and Moore had noticed the timber theft from their Bulanaming properties,

Thomas Moore was obliged to take out another notice against the offenders:

> A caution having some time since appeared, against Cutting Timber or in anywise trespassing on the Farm and Premises situate in the District of Bulanaming, belonging to Mr THOMAS MOORE but that caution not being generally attended to as is required, Notice is hereby given, that Trespassers will be punished with every possible severity.[99]

Timber was now extremely important and, with the *Calcutta* eager to be filled, such depredations were against the colonial interests.

When Governor King announced Thomas Moore 'Surveyor of Timber throughout the colony for naval purposes' in May of 1803, he had immediately recommended him for a rise in salary.[100] The *Calcutta* had left England before this request would have arrived, but she nevertheless brought some bad news in this regard. Several people in the colony had been favoured with various salary increases, but Moore was not amongst them. He was disappointed.

As the new year arrived, Moore's disappointment was broken by the joy of seeing one of his own vessels launched to public acclaim. The speed with which the *Integrity* was built was as impressive as her design and launching was innovative. Captain Rushworth had replaced Captain Aicken on the *Francis*, when she sailed for Port Phillip on 4 December, for Aicken was slated for the *Integrity*. In announcing the prospect of its launch in the early days of 1804, the *Sydney Gazette* spoke about this vessel with some pride, perhaps reflecting that of her builder. The report also shows that it was not only in design that Moore innovated:

1804

> The Schooner *Integrity*, we are informed, will be launched either on the first day of the New Year, or on 'Twelfth Day'; her hull is now complete, and has undergone an experiment of being filled while on the stocks, in order to prevent her making any water after she may be launched. This vessel, built by Mr Moore, is allowed to be the first piece of workmanship that has hitherto been performed here; her cabin is spacious and commodious and by the introduction of a sliding and shifting partition, can be extended forward as far as the forecastle bulk-head; her keel

measures 46 feet, and she is 60 ft over-all; across the beam 16 feet 9 inches, and her computed tonnage 59 ¾ ths.[101]

John Harris was paid six cows, valued at £28 each, for superintending the construction of the *Integrity* and Thomas Moore was paid one—presumably as a bonus on top of the normal salary drawn for his dock-yard position.[102] Not too far into the future, Harris and Moore would join in a partnership for a trading speculation of their own. When she sailed on 4 February for her maiden voyage to Port Phillip and the Derwent, Governor King sailed with her to the heads. After being put on shore he brought back the report that 'it is acknowledged that both in salt sailing, working, and her appearance under way, this handsome vessel answers every expectation'.[103]

With his moment of glory passed, but his reputation enhanced, Thomas Moore came down to earth on 18 February to the more mundane duty of conducting a survey with Garnham Blaxcell of the Barrack Bedding and Furniture, and reported to the Governor.[104] The skills of surveying ships were apparently transferrable to other kinds of surveys too!

As the loading of the *Calcutta* neared completion, Governor King wrote a letter to send home, once again pleading the cause of his valuable and promising ship-builder.

> The master boat-builder, who has built two decked vessels and is beginning a third, exclusive of every other work incident to a person in his active situation, has made known to me his disappointment in not finding himself included in the advance. Could his pay be increased to 10s.a day I humbly conceive it would be securing the zeal and services of a very valuable man to this colony. He has selected and collected all the timber sent by the *Glatton* and *Calcutta*. I made an application by the former ship to the same purport as this, which I respectfully submit to your Lordship's consideration.[105]

As if to reinforce his request, when King outlined the duties of the various Civil Officers, Moore's position was described in glowing, but subtle, terms:[106]

> Boat Builder. Has built a very strong and useful cutter of 59 tons burthen [the *Integrity*]—value in materials and labour, £1022 7s 2d sterling—in fourteen months; repairing the Government Colonial vessels, building and repairing boats for Government use, selecting timber for England, and attending to the repair of such King's ships as are stationed or occasionally arrive here.

With the timber all but stowed on the *Calcutta*, Governor King signalled his intention to keep the supplies coming:

> I have the honour to enclose an invoice of the timber and plank put on board the *Calcutta*, being as much as that ship could take, which I hope will be found very useful in His Majesty's dockyards; and altho' it is not certain whether any King's ships may be sent here during the war, yet I shall keep a certain number of people collecting timber for the first conveyance to Europe.[107]

Perhaps even moving ahead one step further than his predecessor, King is not only concerned to supply dockyards at home, but he is keen to promote the shipbuilding potential of NSW. It seems he has big plans for the dockyard under Moore's direction, and the launch of the *Integrity* now becomes an additional showpiece for the authorities back home:

> In order to form some opinion in how short a time a vessel could be built, one of 59 tons [the cutter *Integrity*] burthen was laid down in September, 1802, and launch'd in January, 1804; and altho' there was much interruption in the work, yet the average was only four carpenters' labour for thirteen months, and one pair of sawyers twenty weeks exclusive of the labour in getting the timber. We have only two men that can be called ship carpenters, the rest being rough house carpenters and 'prentice boys. I have stated this circumstance to show the time it has taken with the people we have to build that vessel, which is extremely well put together and strong, and for her first voyage is gone to Basses Straits and the Derwent. If thirty shipwrights and caulkers could be collected at the different ports, and sent here with two good assistants from the King's yards, I make no doubt that a 38-gun frigate might be built in less than two years of the best materials; but it would be necessary to send iron and copper work, with cordage.[108]

While otherwise engaged with timber for the English cause, Thomas Moore's own property was still suffering through being the victim of malicious damage.[109]

> WHEREAS some evil-disposed Person or Persons have at sundry times committed divers Outrages upon the Farm, Yards, and Grounds of Mr THOMAS MOORE, lying and situate within the District of Bullanaming, by breaking down and destroying the Fences upon the said Farm, whereby much damage hath been sustained.
>
> All Persons therefore are hereby strictly Cautioned against repeating such Outrages, on pain of being rigorously prosecuted; and are likewise forbidden to Trespass upon the said Farm, by Cutting Timber or running Stock thereon, without the especial Permission of the aforesaid Proprietor being first had and obtained; and in order to bring to detection every Person who shall so offend herein, a Reward of
>
> TEN GUINEAS
> Will be paid by the said Mr. Thomas Moore to any Person who shall give true Information of, and prosecute to Conviction whomsoever may or shall offend herein.

The footnote to the advertisement further specifies the property in terms of Moore's rather impressive neighbours, all officers of the NSW Corps: 'N.B. The above farm is bounded by the Grounds of Major Johnstone and Captain Kemp of the New South Wales Corps; and those also of Thomas Rowley, Esq. and by Cook's River'. Captain Kemp must have been suffering the same affliction, for he ran a similar warning about his property (bounded by Johnston, White and Moore) at the end of the month.[110]

In the same paper, a second advertisement shows Mr Moore sought a new tenant for his house on High Street:

> TO BE LET
> For Twelve or Eighteen Months certain, And immediate Possession obtained, A DWELLING-HOUSE with all convenient Out-houses, and Kitchen detached, with excellent Garden containing some choice Fruit-trees; situate in the High Street of Sydney, nearly opposite the Hospital Wharf, known by the name of Mr MOORE's

CHAPTER 4 ⚓ *Timber & Trade (7 May 1803 to 13 August 1806)* 219

HOUSE; formerly occupied by Mr. William Tough, and recently by Messrs. Turnbull and Buvers. Of the superiority of the Situation for Trade and Commerce nothing needs be added, as the Premises are generally known.

This house now 'known as Mr Moore's house' was John White's property, where Thomas and Rachel had lived after they were first married before they moved to the newly constructed Master Boat Builder's house further down High Street on the Cove.[111] In a third advertisement in the same *Gazette*, Moore advertised the lease of Captain Bunker's 40 acres in Bulanaming—which would be the cleared portion of 'Laing's Farm'. Bunker was still on the voyage he commenced with his trip to the Derwent.

On the same day that the *Gazette* ran Moore's various advertisements, Sydney was disturbed by some military action. If it had been twelve months later, then Thomas Moore would have been involved as a Lieutenant of the Loyal Sydney Volunteers Association, but on 4 March 1804, he probably stayed at home. Nevertheless, that evening the 47 armed civilians who formed the Volunteers were summoned to join the 28 soldiers from the Corps, in response to a report that 233 convicts had started an uprising west of Parramatta. 140 marines and seamen were also landed from the *Calcutta* to stand ready. Under Major Johnston the Volunteers and troops set off from Sydney about 1am, and after marching and jogging ten hours through the night, they engaged and pursued the rebels. The operation lasted from about 11am to 4pm on Monday the 5th, with the convicts finally defeated at Rouse Hill in what became known as 'the battle of Vinegar Hill'.[112] (Plates 32, 33, 40). At a later date, Governor King was clear who were responsible for the uprising: 'Of the Irish convicts sent to this place there were some equal to any act of depravity. The greater part were sent from Ireland for murders during the rebellion [1798] and were the most active persons in the insurrection here in March 1804'.[113]

Despite standing ready, the men from the *Calcutta* saw no action that day. Governor King thanked them for their services nevertheless, and on 16 March 1804 the *Calcutta* sailed from Sydney.[114] With the shock of the uprising still fresh in the memory, on 2 April Thomas Rowley was appointed as Captain Commandant of the Loyal Sydney and Parramatta Volunteer Association—no doubt to strengthen the militia with his military training and experience.[115]

When the *Calcutta* departed NSW, it carried a special log of timber, a *Sydney Gazette* and a letter, all from Thomas Moore to his friend, naval captain Henry Waterhouse.[116] Reading between the lines of Waterhouse's reply, it was not the news of the recent battle that occupied the Master Boat Builder, but the welfare of Rachel's son Andrew—worried about his delicate constitution (which Waterhouse claimed to be denied by Andrew's constant good health!). Moore had also given a bad report of Waterhouse's farm.

Moore was having his own farm and animal troubles. At the beginning of March, it was the fences that were the subject of malicious damage. By the end of the month, the malice spread to Moore's animals.

> Whereas some designing and malicious Person at present unknown, did, during the last Week wickedly administer Poison to a valuable Yard Dog belonging to Mr THOMAS MOORE, which act could only have proceeded from a malevolence of disposition, as the Animal was never suffered to be at liberty during the day-time; Notice is hereby given, that if any Person whatever will give Information of the party by whom such potion was given to the Dog, he or they shall receive from the said Mr Thomas Moore the above Reward of Ten Guineas on prosecuting to Conviction.[117]

At the same time Moore was grieving his poisoned dog, he took on extra duties in regard to William Cox's estate. Cox's failure is one of the ironies of this period in the development of Sydney's commercial life. As Paymaster to the Corps in the heady days of the 1790s monopoly, John Macarthur gained a successful beginning to his commercial life. But beyond the tipping-point, his successor William Cox provides a strange contrast:

> The year 1800 ushered in a period of fierce competition, conducted by a numerous and diverse body of traders, and ironically the only major trader who was unable to stand the pace of this competitive period was Paymaster Cox of the New South Wales Corps, who defaulted sensationally in 1803.[118]

CHAPTER 4 ⚓ Timber & Trade (7 May 1803 to 13 August 1806) 221

William Cox arrived at exactly the transitional moment pinpointed by Hainsworth, on 11 January 1800 on the *Minerva*. On the same ship came 'General' Joseph Holt and three other Irish rebels at His Majesty's pleasure. Once Cox had taken over from John Macarthur as Paymaster, he began purchasing land, including the Brush Farm at Dundas, but by 1803 his borrowings had him facing a deficiency of £7,900 in his regimental accounts and he was suspended. Although £2,000 was secured, to pay the remainder 'his estate was assigned to trustees and sold for the benefit of his creditors, including the army agents'.[119]

In April 1803, advertisements began appearing in the newly published *Gazette*, as the trustees appointed to his estate, with Robert Campbell as treasurer, gradually began selling Cox's goods, farms and livestock—a process that lasted the rest of the year, and, indeed, long beyond.[120] An affadavit sworn by Cox that found its way into Mr Moore's papers provides a concrete example of the kind of losses sustained. In 1803, Rowley was acting as Henry Waterhouse's agent, as well as being a Trustee appointed by Cox's creditors. He proved a debt of £105 to Waterhouse and received a dividend of 15s in the pound (ie. £78-17-0), making the overall loss £26-5-0.[121]

Other examples of the losses come from four of the ship's captains for whom Thomas Moore acted as agent, each of whom lost money from Cox's failure: Samuel Chace, £4-16-6; William Raven, £15-0-0; James Simter, £5-16-0; and John Leith, £15-0-0 and £9-0-0. To Raven's account Moore appended the note: 'At the time of Mr Cox's failure I had £40 of Mr Cox's Bills in my hand belonging to Captn Raven and got paid £12-6 in the pound; and there is 45£ different [?] yet'.[122] Presumably this little collection indicates that, as per usual custom, Cox had used his Paymaster's Bills to pay for goods brought in by the ship's captains. The fact that Moore held the bills might mean that the ship's captains had then bought something from him using these bills as sterling, but, more probably it indicates that Moore was their agent or middle-man, keeping their goods for sale after they left the harbour—which explains why he kept accounts on their behalf. As indicative of this role, sometime in 1805, Moore received a 10% commission for collecting bills for Raven from Thomas and John Mather for £200.[123] Now with Cox's failure, all these men have lost money, and Mr Moore deducts the loss from their account. Evidently there was no hard feelings, for in 1827 when Cox was a magistrate as Windsor, Thomas Moore was still willing to loan him £1500 for three years at 10% per annum, despite his earlier dramatic failure.[124]

As friend or agent of several of Cox's creditors, Thomas Moore was not without some personal knowledge of Cox's loss well before the public meeting in March 1804, when he was appointed to the Trustees. Fellow Trustee Thomas Rowley had evidently not won everybody's favour in the previous year:

> A General Meeting of the Creditors of William Cox Esq. on 19 March requested the present Trustees continue the management of Mr Cox's affairs for six months longer, and elected Mr Thomas Moore as a Trustee in the room of Charles Grimes who had departed for Europe. At the same meeting, Mary Newton was 'so imprudent, rash, and indiscreet, as to utter some expressions highly injurious to, and tending to defame the character of Thomas Rowley', and Rowley began court proceedings against her, gained damages, which he then dismissed if she made a public apology, which she did.[125]

In July the three Trustees—Samuel Marsden, was the third—called for the settling of debts to Cox before 1 August, or action would be taken. Another meeting of the creditors and other interested parties was called for the 19 September, to table the exact state of Cox's affairs and deal with the termination of the present Trust Deed.[126] At this meeting, after hearing the state of affairs, Trustees Marsden, Rowley and Moore, had William Tough and James Williamson added to their number.[127] To add to the interplay between characters, Rowley was also the agent for William Tough, and Tough once rented Moore's High Street house.[128]

Thanks to the *Paterson*'s arrival in the previous November, the news of the breakdown of the Peace of Amiens was already well known in the colony when the whalers *Adonis* and *Alexander* brought Governor King the official letters announcing the events that took place a full year beforehand.[129] King is ordered to make the situation known widely, and to publish the need for ships to act as privateers to do damage to French vessels, along with the assurance that 'His Majesty will consider them as having a just Claim to the King's Share of all French Ships and Property, which they may make prize of'.

At the same time, Governor King received a copy of the instructions of HM George III for the Courts of Admiralty, dated 17 May 1803, which outlined the appropriate procedures to be followed in respect to the prizes that may be taken captive: 1. all witnesses are to be examined regarding the capture of the Prize by the 'Standing Interogatories' (copy enclosed); and 2. all papers from the ship must be received by the court with an oath that they are presented without fraud, addition or embezzlement.[130]

As the latest call for Privateering came to the colony, Thomas Moore was engaged with J. Houston, George Quested, James Wilson, and George Blakey in another survey of the *Investigator*. This time they found her bottom was basically sound, so that 'by cutting off her Upper Deck and topsides she may prove a serviceable Vessel for Four or Five Years or more after having the necessary repairs viz. Timber Heads, Stancheons, Bulwark and plank Sheers, Caulking'. The 'Master Carpenter' had advised King that, in this state she could be to then be used as a Brig for two or three years between Sydney and the settlements at Van Diemen's Land and Norfolk Island.[131] Moore had talked himself into another job for the latter months of 1804.

While Thomas's more public duties at the dockyard occupied much of his time, his own farming and business interests kept moving slowly forward in the background. In May, he was on the long list of those who had only paid their Quit-rent up to September 1802, and who were called to settle the difference.[132] A muster taken on 4 July 1804 showed Thomas Moore with 700 acres under Pasturage and 470 fallow—clearly the two grants in Bulanaming, from Petersham Hill to the Cook's River. On his total of 1,170 acres he kept 3 horses and 7 mares; 1 bull 13 cows 4 oxen; 6 hogs 7 sows. He was himself victualled from the stores, but Rachel was not. He had three servants, one victualled, two more were not.[133]

Having dispensed with his flock of forty sheep in 1801,[134] the future leanings of Moore's husbandry are already apparent. His 1 bull, 13 cows and 4 oxen, hint towards his future role as one of the largest suppliers of meat to the government stores. The three stallions are a strong indicator of Moore's intentions to breed horses, probably to expand his own mob for future sales.[135] Five of his seven mares can be, once again, identified from the 1812 list: Old Bett and Young Bett, as well as Dirma, Fanny and Dutches [?Duchess], who were just about ready to begin their breeding life—since the list shows they began to foal in their sixth year.[136] (Figure 37, cf. 34 and 35). As Binney notes, with ten horses, Moore was:

> one of the top half dozen horse owners in the colony [...]. The other major horse owners were all military officers or officials, apart from the emancipist Richard Fitzgerald who had a close working relationship with Captain John Macarthur. Undoubtedly, Thomas Moore used his seagoing knowledge and connections with ships' captains to build up his valuable livestock numbers.[137]

	STALLIONS	MARES	TOTAL
John Macarthur	12	14	26
John Palmer	10	11	21
Wm Kent	5	14	19
Mjr Johnston	4	11	15
Rich. Fitzgerald	2	10	12
Samuel Marsden	3	9	12
Thomas Moore	3	7	10
cf. The Crown	21	29	50
Governor	1	2	3
Lieut.-Gov.		1	1

Figure 34: Major private horse owners August 1804. There were a total of 404 horses in the colony.

CHAPTER 4 ⚓ *Timber & Trade (7 May 1803 to 13 August 1806)* 225

	STALLIONS	MARES	TOTAL
John Macarthur	14	17	31
John Palmer	12	19	31
Geo Johnston	5	12	17
John Harris	2	13	15
Samuel Marsden	4	10	14
Thomas Moore	4	9	13
cf. The Crown	20	16	36

Figure 35: Major private horse owners in August 1805. There were a total of 494 horses (205 M, 289 F) in the colony.

Alongside managing the dockyard and his burgeoning numbers of cattle and horses, Moore also continued to act as agent for a small number of ship's captains, such as Eber Bunker. After news had filtered back to Sydney in May of 1804 that Bunker's *Albion* was off Sandy Cape, the whaling Captain arrived back in Port Jackson on 4 July 1804 with 1400 barrels of sperm oil, giving notice that he would be proceeding to England by the end of the month. During his seven-week stay in Sydney, Bunker had the opportunity to see the new stone house being erected upon his Pitt's Row lease, which, unless he commenced the building himself after his arrival in July, had presumably begun under the supervision of Moore. In any case, as he left the colony this 'truly eligible and substantial STONE DWELLING HOUSE and PREMISES, Comprising all necessary Outhouses, Offices, and every convenience employed' was 'new nearly finished'.[138] The *Albion* was certainly ready to sail by 29 July, but she eventually got under weigh on 21 August with a freight of 13,000 Bass Strait sealskins for the Port of London, 10,000 of which were for Robert Campbell.[139] With the new techniques for tanning the skins, the London Market was now preferred to the more unpredictable market at Canton. Later news reported that Bunker was so 'impatient to get home to his family' that he left his escort and sailed without convoy from St Helena.[140] Perhaps Bunker was eager to tell them about the new house he had built for them in Sydney. On 2 September it was advertised for a twelve-month term from occupancy—perhaps an indication of how soon Bunker hoped to be back again. Applications from a 'genteel family' were to be made to Mr Thomas Moore—who was already busy paying the bills. (Figure 36).

1804						
Sept^r	6th	paid for 2,000 4d nails 0/3 Do to Brown for 2,000		1	3	4
"		Bricks @ 20/ and Carting inn		2	16	0
	7th	paid for 8 pair of Brass Ringes		1	0	0
	10	paid for 200 Bushels of lime		7	10	0
	15	paid for 6 lbs of Glue		0	12	0
	23	paid for 3 Gallons of paint oil and one keg of Red paint		1	16	10
Nov^r	7	paid Brown for 1500 Brick for the Necessary, and Carting in		2	2	0
1805						
March	27	paid Cox for Sundry Blacksmith work paid Taylor for painting		6	10	6
		& finding Black & White paint		5	0	0
August	5th	paid for 30 Bushels of lime at 1/6 p Bushel for Terrice		2	5	
Sept^r	30	paid Summerfull & Receipt		19	17	
		Paid for advertising the farm		00	2	6
Oct	14th	paid Roberts for Cart hire		17	2	0
	22	Bevan for Locks & Latches		5	17	6

Figure 36: Payments made by T. Moore on behalf of Eber Bunker, showing work done on Bunker's new house.

Thomas Moore's accounts show that William Roberts carted the stone; Mr Taylor did the painting; David Bevan supplied the locks, bolts and brass; Cox the blacksmith work; Hanks supplied the Jarrah; and Summerfell various sundries. On the income side of Bunker's account with Moore, many payments are listed as being 'to

CHAPTER 4 ⚓ *Timber & Trade (7 May 1803 to 13 August 1806)* 227

one watch', or 'parasol', suggesting that Bunker had left a supply of watches and parasols with Moore and this is what he used to pay the workers. Amongst these various payments in goods—so common for Sydney commercial transactions at this time—Nicholas Bayly paid £30 for one year's rent, thus identifying Bunker's first tenant.[141]

In August, when the 4 July muster was ready to be reported, Governor King gave a run-down of the various vessels built in the Colony—no doubt still pressing his ship-building agenda. He reported that the *Francis*, schooner, sent out in frame in 1792, is now 'much damaged, but will be useful for some time'; the *Cumberland*, Schooner, built here from 1798 to 1801, has gone to England with Flinders; the *Integrity*, Cutter, built here from 1802 to 1803, is in good condition; the *Resource*, Schooner, built from the *Porpoise* and *Cato*'s wrecks, 1803, is also in good condition, now employed between Sydney and the Coal Harbour; and a Punt built in 1803, in good condition, is employed in the harbour.[142] His list provides a brief summary of some of Mr Moore's work across the previous six years.

By his August report several months have passed since the Vinegar Hill uprising and King is pleased that there had been 'no appearance of the numerous Irish active respecting any of their wild plans'. He mentions certain characters who are watched, nevertheless, because they would:

> lose no secret means of stirring those deluded up to any act of atrocity. Among others, the persons I allude to are Maurice Margarot and Henry Brown Hayes. The first is well known in England and Scotland as a violent, unprincipled Republican. The other's character is also well known. In consequence of a systematic plan formed by Hayes some time ago of initiating Freemasons after I had forbid it, Hayes was detected presiding at a club, and would very soon have made every soldier and other person Freemasons had not the most decided means been taken to prevent it.

He is convinced the Scottish Martyr Margarot had been complicit in the March Irish Insurrection. His papers were seized and they 'contained many republic sentiments, and the grossest scurrility against my predecessor and myself and many others, as well as against the executive authority in England'. King had not sent him to

Coal River because of his infirmity. Margarot was evidently another source of discontented opinion being fed back to England about the Governor. King is unsure about the wisdom of sending more United Irishmen to the colony, unless the military presence was increased by ten companies.[143]

Thomas Moore's role at the dockyard seems to have never had a dull moment. On 16 October, the ship *Lady Barlow* was overset in a violent squall. Thomas Moore joined William Collins, late harbour master at the Derwent, and Mr Stewart, master of the *George* in attempting to raise the ship, an attempt 'which was afterwards so happily effected'.[144]

The week before Christmas, King was still pressing for an improvement in the colony's export potential. In a bold move applying antipodean support to the pressure being applied at home by those such as the Southern Whale Fishery (King was a friend of the Enderby's), he asked for permission to allow vessels to trade with China and England. King specified that this should only be for 'three vessels of not more than two hundred tons each and built within the limits of this territory and its dependencies'. Returning to what is by now a familiar theme, as an extra advantage King predicted this would give 'employment to so many artisans and their families, promote ship-building and raising sailors, which will give the increasing numerous youth in these settlements the means of acquiring trades to prevent them from pursuing the same paths their unfortunate parents have trod in'. He also saw political advantages, for the colonial vessels could engage in the risky trade of British goods in the Spanish and Portuguese colonies of the Americas.[145]

In the same letter he reflected upon the colonial timber most recently sent:

> Whether the ship timber sent from hence by the *Calcutta* may have determined the utility of that measure being persevered in I have not yet learned; but should it be considered an object the greatest quantity can be procured.[146]

In this pre-Christmas season, Thomas Moore found himself performing coronial duties on a friend. On Wednesday 19 December, Provost

Marshall Thomas Smyth—the man who witnessed his wedding to Rachel—suddenly died, and the Governor ordered an inquest, appointing Moore as the coroner. The inquiry assembled on the Thursday and Smyth was interred on the following Wednesday evening. Despite heavy rain, he was farewelled with an appropriate formal procession. According to the *Gazette*, 'he was universally respected for his humanity in acquitting himself of the duties of his office; the generosity and benevolence of his heart; the affability of his manners, and the placidity of his disposition'.[147]

ANDREW'S SCHOOLING

1805

Sometime early in 1805, the letter written by Henry Waterhouse on 20 October 1804, would probably have arrived with the Moores, answering their anxious questions about Andrew.[148] After thanking Moore for his letter and the special log of timber sent by the *Calcutta* and the seeds by *Venus*, whaler, and another log and a dove, Waterhouse assured Thomas and Rachel:

> Andrew has been constantly well, & far from what you suppose of a delicate Constitution, & I hope his improvement will meet yours & his Mothers approbation, he writes to you by this conveyance. he has been several times down with Mr White during the hollidays, who informs me he has always made him write to you.

By the end of the letter, Waterhouse fills the Moores in on news of some of the people known to them from NSW. The Naval news held hope of him seeing his friends again: 'Mr Thompson the Surgeon is trying to get out again. Captn. Hunter commands the *Venerable* a 74, & I hope soon to get a ship'. Rachel would be sad to hear that 'Balmain died about the time I wrote last', if only for the sake of her friend Margaret Dawson. They never married, but Balmain had taken Margaret back to England with him, as well as the three children born between 1797 and 1803, sailing with Bunker on the *Albion* on 26 August 1801, and provided for them in his will.[149] Waterhouse sadly notes that William Beckwith, a lieutenant in the NSW Corps,[150] had also died 'in a garret without a rag to cover him'. The Moores may have inquired about their former clergyman, Richard Johnson after news of his daughter's death reached NSW in about March 1804.[151] Milbah Maria, probably the first white person to bear an aboriginal name, was born in NSW on 3 March 1790. As another child in a rather small society, she may well have been one of Andrew's playmates in their early days, and her brother, Henry Martin born 19 July 1792 and so closer to Andrew's age, almost certainly was.[152] However, Waterhouse informs them 'I have not heard any thing of Mr Johnston the Clergyman since the death of his Daughter'.

Touching on farming news, Waterhouse alludes to his own Maria:

> sorry to hear so bad an account of my farm—as it is all I have to leave my little Girl who is very well—I have lost enough by Mr Cox—I know I need not say if you can assist Capt. Rowley in doing any thing to better my concerns in the Colony I shall feel very much oblig'd, & will thankfully repay any expences that if you can you will do it—

This was also the letter that has already been referred to in connection with Moore's purchase of the merino. Waterhouse was a fan of Australian timber after Thomas had used it to repair his *Reliance* and having sold some of the Merino sheep to Moore in 1797, Waterhouse now shared the good news that both these commodities may soon do some good for his friend:

> The spanish wool, & some of the woods of N.S. Wales, I believe will shortly be an object of attention to Government, from which I think you may profit, by keeping your wool & & c

As Thomas read this note his sheep were almost a distant memory, but the new interest in Australian timber had been running him off his feet for the last two years.

Waterhouse was glad for the newspapers from Australia, and informed Moore that he has sent some English ones to Captain Rowley, also intended for Moore's eyes. The papers will bring him up to date with changes for some of the officers of the NSW Corps.

> you will find Captn. McArthur has sold his Commission, & goes out as a settler, Capn. Townson has sold his Commission & is going out as a settler. Capn. Prentice is on half pay & means to return to New

CHAPTER 4 ⚓ *Timber & Trade (7 May 1803 to 13 August 1806)* 231

> South Wales indeed things are at such a pitch here that it is next to impossible to live here—I wish I was back again. I understand numbers of familys of from four to five hundred a year are making application to Government for encouragment to go to N.S. Wales & only wait some alteration in the mode of the Laws to embark.

The penal colony was apparently losing its terror as a place of transportation and exile, and, at least for some in the present fraught environment at home, it was a land of escape and opportunity. The situation with Napoleon's France was still tense.

> The Newspapers will give you an account of this country—I can only say we are in the same state we were a year ago expecting an invasion that England is a perfect garrison, well prepar'd to meet the Enemy—sanguine as the new Emperor seems to be, it is suppos'd he will attempt some blow, but that he has delay'd it too long.

It is difficult to imagine how this news would have affected Thomas and Rachel. On the one hand, England had been on the brink of invasion from France since before Thomas left Lesbury. But on the other, the present dark French cloud now also threatened their dear son, eleven and a half and four years away from home. As if reading their minds, just before he closed his letter with greetings to Rachel and to all his other friends in NSW, Waterhouse gave his solemn assurance:

> I hope to hear from you by ships coming to this Country, & be assur'd I shall not forget the promise I made you when I receiv'd him from you nor will my family should I be absent—in attending to the welfare of Andrew—

During 1804, Thomas Moore must have made arrangements for Andrew's formal schooling to begin—although where the earliest phase of his education took place remains a mystery.[153] But as the Moores were reading this latest letter from Henry Waterhouse, Andrew was already at his lessons. As was frequently the custom for children away from home for education, Andrew's handwriting copybook was later sent to his parents so that they could gain some insight into their pupil's progress. Two of Andrew's handwriting exercise books have survived, containing beautifully written lines—mostly moral maxims and a new one each day copied enough times to fill a page—from 23 January to 7 May 1805.[154] Those from his first two weeks, written from 23 January to 7 February, can provide a sample: 'Knavery is universally detested'; 'Beware of Hypocrites'; 'Mercy & compassion are man's best ingredients'; 'Divert melancholy'; 'Vanity indicates weak & narrow intellects'; 'Be given to Study'; 'How often is instruction lost by inattention'; 'Trust in perseverance'; 'Avoid speaking evil of any person'; 'Topymus was faithful'; 'Never pursue pleasure with too much avidity'; 'wisdom is desirable'; 'Foster every truly laudable desire'; 'Grieve not at trifles'.

While eleven and a half year old Andrew was being drilled in the beauties of good handwriting, high-level vocabulary, and good morals, his step-father received more responsibilities. On 2 March 1805, Thomas Moore, described as 'Gentleman', was commissioned as the Lieutenant of the Loyal Sydney Volunteer Association, Sydney, to replace his deceased friend Thomas Smyth.[155] (Plate 33). His superior officer was his friend and associate Captain Thomas Rowley, who had been appointed Captain and Commandant of the Loyal Sydney and Parramatta Volunteer Association, on 2 April 1804, in the wake of 'Vinegar Hill'.[156] At Parramatta, John Macarthur was Captain, and Walter Davidson, Lieutenant.[157]

The Volunteers were formed as part of a general concern over the potential for trouble amongst the Irish convicts, as King made plain some years later:

> When a spirit of turbulence was discovered among the Irish convicts, it was found necessary to embody two companies, called "the Loyal Sydney and Parramatta Associations"—the first composed of forty and the latter of thirty-seven officers and privates. The commissioned officers were officers of the civil department, and the privates selected from volunteer free housekeepers. They are victualled from the public stores and receive an annual suit of uniform clothing, which occasions an expence to the public of about £1,200 a year, in terms of their enrolment being as similar as possible to the Association in England. Events have fully justified the policy and necessity of these companies being continued.[158]

The use of the Volunteers to quell the insurrection of March 1804 not only justified their formation, but urged Major Johnston, in charge of the NSW Corps, to press upon the Governor his concern that the Corps was under-manned:

> In March 1804, when the colony was disturbed by insurrection, and when fifty men were sent against the rebels, there could not then have been found the like number out of that part of the Corps left at headquarters able to have undertaken a march up the country with that speed which the service would have required had it been the misfortune of the first party to meet with a defeat.[159]

In response, Governor King sent an urgent request to Earl Camden for consideration of the matters raised in Johnston's letter, especially given the deployment of a large number of his troops in the settlements at Van Diemen's Land.

Following the death of Thomas Smyth, his property in Bulanaming, which abutted Moore's farm, was taken over by the Commissary, John Palmer. The depredations in that area apparently continued, for in March Palmer placed the usual newspaper warning.[160]

The Statement of the Officers and Superintendents on the Civil Establishment, 30 April 1805, includes 'Thomas Moore Boat Builder',[161] still actively engaged at the Dock Yard. There were at this stage, however, a number of vacancies on the Civil Establishment. Richard Atkins was Deputy Judge Advocate, and John Palmer Commissary, with James Williamson and James Wilshire acting as his Deputies. Since the death of Thomas Smyth in December, Garnham Blaxcell was appointed temporarily to the post of Provost Marshall, and he was also covering William Neate Chapman, Secretary to the Governor, while he was in England. Chaplain Richard Johnson was also in England, Samuel Marsden doing his duties. William Balmain, Surgeon, is listed as being in England—evidently the news of his death had not reached official channels in NSW. Assistant Surgeon James Thompson also being in England, Thomas Jamison and Charles Throsby were keeping the medical establishment operating, with D'Arcy Wentworth assistant surgeon at Norfolk Island, James Mileham at Sydney, and John Savage at Parramatta. Augustus Alt was surveyor of Land, as was Charles Grimes, although on leave in England. George Evans had filled in for Grimes until discharged for fraud, and then it was Henry Williams.

The same statement expresses frustration at the inability to free Thomas Moore up for further shipbuilding.

> The constant work there has been for the few carpenters under the master-builder in repairing the *Buffalo*, cutting down and refitting the *Investigator*, and keeping the other Colonial vessels in repair, and building boats for this and the other settlements, has prevented any other vessel being begun for the use of the Crown, which will be commenced as soon as the indispensible work will admit of it.[162]

Part of the 'indispensible work' was conducting the regular surveys of ships, usually to ascertain what repairs were necessary to keep them seaworthy. At other times surveys had slightly different purposes. On 10 April 1805 Governor King directed Lieut. Symons of the *Lady Nelson*, Francis Gardner, Chief Mate of *Harrington*, and Thomas Moore to survey 'the *Estremina*, Armed Schooner, belonging to the King of Spain', providing an inventory of all her cargo and supplies, as well as a report of her general state of repair.[163] This survey was different, because the *Estramina* had been brought in as a Prize of War.

Now that English ships were commanded by their Sovereign to act as Privateers against France and her allies wherever their ships might be found, the Pacific had also become the Privateer's playground. As the only English colony in the Pacific, Sydney saw her share of vessels taken as Prizes. Unfortunately, however, since European news took a long time to reach the other side of the globe, seizing the ships of another country was not without its risks. What was legitimate under conditions of war, was, at other times, piracy. In 1805, Captain William Campbell of the *Harrington* found this out the hard way.

At the end of 1804, Campbell was sailing on the coast of South America holding Letters of Marque. On 26 September he took the Spanish Merchant brig, *St Francisco and St Paulo*, and on 2 October, the schooner *Estramina*, belonging to the king of Spain. The vessels were brought into Sydney by the *Integrity*, the cutter Moore had launched the previous January, 'after lying concealed in and about Kent's Group from the 2d of March last to the 17th of May, in charge of Mr Arnold Fisk, second Mate of the *Harrington*'. Despite the 'sinking state of the said Brig and the perishing State of her Cargo, joined to the Noisome stench of the vessel', William Campbell refused to apply for surveys of the *St Francisco and St Paulo*, and so Governor King assumed it as his duty 'to order surveys thereon by two officers' named, respectively, by the Governor and Campbell.[164]

Three weeks after the three men conducting the initial survey turned in their report on 11 April,[165] on 2 May 1805, Moore was instructed to go on board the *Harrington* to pump her out, since she had taken in water. Her master, William Campbell, had discharged his people and locked her up on the orders of the Governor.[166] Thomas Rowley explained the situation in a letter to his friend Henry Waterhouse written two weeks later, which was to be delivered by their mutual friend William Kent:[167]

> Here is nothing but rows here, Campbell, of the *Rebecca* when you was here [h]as been on the coast of Peru, and [h]as been acting as a pirate[.] he [h]as Brought in two prizes as he calls them, the Govr very properly as no war is kno[w]n of her[e] between the two Courts [h]as stop^d them and also [h]as dismantled the *Harrington* which Campbell commanded and himself cannot leave the Colony till advice is received from the British Court.
>
> Campbell has fell into the hands of Messrs Lord, Kable & Underwood and Micha[e]l Robinson as their writer, and they will ruin the fellow for a more accomplish^d set of scoundrels never linck together, and, more particular^y Lord,—the above concern is the cause of Kents going to England with dispatches[.] it is the opinion of the respectable Persons that Campbell will be to hung but the Low Gang things [thinks] not. I mean those I have mentioned.

As Rowley comments upon Campbell's situation, his letter incidentally shows one of the old Officer-Traders of the 1790s expressing his opinion about the new Emancipist-Traders of the 1800s. If the Officers were once regarded as the scoundrels of the colony, now they have another group to slander with this term. The extremely successful Simeon Lord is singled out by Rowley, but presumably not for his evident success in the new commercial environment he helped to create. And, in fact, since Lord gained his start in life from Rowley himself, perhaps the good Captain can also be congratulated for bringing in the new day.[168] Perhaps there is even an element of Australian affection in Rowley's description of this group of obvious scoundrels.

Campbell's fate was clearly the talk of the town, but it will not be the 'low gang' with whom he will emerge from this dark hole. To get out of his troubles, eventually Campbell will form an alliance with that old Officer-Trader himself, Mr John Macarthur—an alliance that will contribute to the colonial government being overturned.

At the time of his letter, Rowley was evidently looking after Waterhouse's various interests in the colony—a role that Thomas Moore would take over in due course. Waterhouse's farm on the Duck River, the *Vineyard*, had been sold on 7 March for £22.1.0, and his goods and chattels at the Brush farm were sold on 14 January for £5.16.01. His sheep, like Rowley's,[169] were doing well, and he had some fine cattle, some on the George's River. Rowley also reported that the effects of Cox's failure were still being felt, with merchant Robert Campbell having had a £5,000 Bill from him returned the previous month protested, 'which has prevented another dividend taken place for the present'. Rowley closed his letter with a greeting from his family, urging that 'Bet [=Elizabeth Selwyn] and the Children are all well and desires to be Remembered to you[.] Isabella is grown a fine Girl & tall^d as her mother'.[170]

On 25 May, Captain William Campbell assured the Governor that he was prepared to repair the vessels of which he had been dispossessed, 'and to return them if it appears war did not exist when they were captured', unless the Governor permitted him to resume command of the *Harrington* and to continue her voyage in order to recoup some of the heavy expenses he had incurred in the whole business. He appointed 'Mr Thomas Moore, Ship Builder' to act for him and his company, Messrs. Chace, Chinnery, McDouall, Ricketts and Co. of Madras.[171] Governor King appointed John Harris to act as agent for the king of Spain, and the two men were directed to sell the cargo at public auction.[172]

Moore had an additional difficulty in performing these duties, however, for just two days earlier, he had been injured in an accident:

> Last Thursday evening Mr. Moore, Master Builder, had the misfortune to be overturned in a chaise, and, we are extremely concerned to state, had his leg broke by the fall.[173]

CHAPTER 4 ⚓ *Timber & Trade (7 May 1803 to 13 August 1806)* 237

There were further consequences of the *Harrington*'s lust for prizes. In order to bring the two Spanish vessels back to Sydney, Campbell took on board a number of Otaheitans and Sandwich Islanders to man them. As a result of these newcomers to the colony, Governor King issued a Government and General Order, which not only reveals his desire to protect them, but also the abuses to which islanders were previously subjected in similar circumstances of dispossession:[174]

> It being intended by the persons who have hitherto been allowed to frequent the islands in Bass's Straits to send some of these credulous people to that place where their treatment and return are very suspicious and doubtful; and it being of the utmost consequence to the interest and safety of Europeans frequenting those seas, and more particularly the South Sea whalers, that these people should suffer no ill treatment, but, on the contrary, experience every kindness until they can return to their native country;—it is, therefore, hereby strictly forbid sending any Otaheitan, Sandwich Islander, or New Zealander from this settlement to any island or other part of this coast on any sealing or other voyage, or to any place to the eastward of Cape Horn.
>
> All masters of ships, foreign as well as English, are hereby forbid taking away any such Otaheitan, Sandwich Islander, or New Zealander from hence without the Governor's permission in writing, which will not be given unless with a certainty of the masters taking them to the islands they belong to.
>
> During their stay here, those whose service they are employed in are not to beat or ill use them; but if their employers, or those who brought them to this Colony, are not able to maintain and employ them, they are to report it to the Governor, who will take measures for their employment and maintenance until they can be sent home.
>
> And it is to be clearly understood that all such Otaheitans, &c, are protected in their properties, claims for wages, and the same redress as any of His Majesty's subjects.

No doubt Governor King's compassion for islanders away from home was aided by the memory of his two New Zealander friends, Tookee and Woodoo, who had travelled back home on the *Britannia* in

November 1793. At the end of 1805, Governor King would show great kindness to Tip-pa-he, a New Zealand Chief,[175] as well as using the opportunity to gather intelligence about the island, cannibalism, religious beliefs, polygamous practices, and the like.[176] The chief also befriended Rev. Samuel Marsden during his time in the colony—a friendship, which later became instrumental in the formation of Marsden's Christian mission to New Zealand. For his part, Thomas Moore, who also shared with King the memory of the *Britannia's* return of Tookee and Woodoo, because he worked so closely with incoming shipping would have come across many of these people. He probably had some of them working for him in the dockyard from time to time, such as the Otaheitian who took his name—a probable indicator that he had worked for Moore and been treated kindly by him.[177] At the end of 1813, when Samuel Marsden formed the 'New South Wales Philanthropic Society, for the Protection and Civilization of such of the Natives of the South Sea Islands who may arrive at Port Jackson', Thomas Moore was the person at Liverpool appointed to receive subscriptions.[178]

On 5 June Campbell wrote to the Governor again, requesting a resolution to the situation, for the *Eagle* was about to sail to Madras and he wished to send a report to his owners.[179] By the end of the month, King had directed Thomas Moore, with R. Best, Acting Carpenter of HMS *Buffalo*, Austin Forest, Master of the *Sydney*, and Philip Skelton, Master of the *Ferret*, a Southern Whaler, to conduct a survey of the repairs necessary to make the *St Francisco and St Paulo* seaworthy.[180] Campbell was not going to get out of Sydney quickly— the *Harrington*, and the two Spanish vessels had not moved by the end of September.[181] *Harrington* would be out of the water, in fact, until the arrival of Governor Bligh in August 1806, who brought orders for her release.[182] While detained, her owners, the House of Chace, Cheney, and Company in India, failed and so, by the time he eventually sailed her from Port Jackson on 28 January 1807, Campbell had found a new master.

Moore's timber-gathering continued throughout 1805, but the renewed war meant a consequent reduction in ships to take it home. In July, King wrote:

CHAPTER 4 ⚓ *Timber & Trade (7 May 1803 to 13 August 1806)* 239

> As a considerable quantity of timber for shipbuilding is lying at Sydney; and judging that no King's ship of sufficient burden will be sent for it until the present war is over; and as the *Sydney* must have necessarily ballasted with stone, the place of which the timber will supply, I have caused an agreement to be made for its being taken on board the *Sydney*, and delivered to the order of the principal Officers and Commissioners of His Majesty's Navy.[183]

The irregularity being alluded to here is that the *Sydney* was a Campbell & Co ship, not one of HM Navy. She arrived from Calcutta with a general cargo on 22 April, master Austin Forrest, but King chartered her to take his timber to England[184] and then loaded her throughout August and September. Moore's leg had evidently healed well enough to supervise loading the timber, although another man had a similar misfortune:[185]

> On Friday last a lascar belonging to the *Sydney* unfortunately had his leg broken in stowing the Government timber on board that vessel. He was immediately ordered to be received into the General Hospital, where every possible attention is paid to his recovery.[186]

With more experience and more time given to the task, the quality of the timber seemed to be improving.

> The whole of the ship timber procured by the convicts at public labour, under the inspection of Mr. Moore, consisting of 160 pieces, estimated to contain above 4,000 solid feet consigned to the Navy Board, has been shipped on board the *Sydney*. This is the best and most valuable collection of timber ever sent from the Colony, being for the major part well calculated for the most important uses in ship building.[187]

As the timber was loading, King wrote his report of the colony. Perhaps with his grand plans in view, he described Moore's position as 'Boatbuilder and Shipwright':

> Has the charge of the dock-yard and the artificers, laborers, & c, in that department. His employment is building and keeping in repair the Government Colonial vessels, boats, and small crafts. He has been much employed in selecting ship timber for England, and attending to the repairs of such King's ships as are stationed or occasionally arrive, and is a most useful and necessary officer.[188]

The following year, that old friend of New South Wales, Sir Joseph Banks, asked some questions about building ships in New South Wales, having heard of the colony's excellent timber—partly through the *Sydney*'s cargo, but also from her own Australian re-fit:

> Will it be necessary to enact anything relative to the registration of ships built in New South Wales, either by an act of Government there or on their arrival in England, if furnished with proper certificates, or do the present navigation laws attach upon His Majesty's territories there as soon as they are declared to be colonies? Timber costs nothing there, and ship timber of excellent quality is believed to exist on the coast, not far to the north of our settlements. Ships will in consequence be soon built there, notwithstanding the high price that labor must for some time continue to bear. If the masts sent Home and fixed in the *Sydney* prove good—and we are told that she herself has a   [blank in original]   mast standing in her cut in that country—the probability of ship-building becoming a trade there will be much increased.[189]

Moore's farming interests were expanding. According to the Return of August 1805, he had 1397 acres of pasturage and 3 acres of Orchard and Gardens, a total of 1400 acres. He now owned one bull, twenty cows and eleven oxen, six hogs and 10 sows. His mob of horses had also expanded to 4 horses and 9 mares. (Figure 37). He and Rachel were both victualled from the stores, as was one of his convicts, but two more he himself provides for.[190]

By the end of the year, Moore's land holdings expanded beyond Bulanaming. On 18 December 1805 he was granted 750 acres in the District of Banks Town, at a rent of 15 shillings per year. Several other grants already given to others were consolidated into Moore's grant: his old friend Thomas Smyth's 190 acres, Thomas Whittle's 90, and William Wilson's 100.[191] Presumably some of this land was therefore already cleared and ready for Moore's stock to be transferred.

In 1805 his horse-breeding endeavours were beginning to come to fruition. As his mares came into their productive season of life, there was something of a baby boom on the Moore properties. After Old Bett gave birth to Pegg in October 1804, a mare was born every couple of months for the next two years—a total of ten by Christmas 1806.[192] (Figure 37).

CHAPTER 4 ↓ *Timber & Trade (7 May 1803 to 13 August 1806)* 241

4	Jane	Daughter Fanny	Decr 25 1805
5	Pegg	do old Bett	Octr 1804
6	Nancy	Do of Dirma	Feb 13 1805
7	Juler	do of Fanny	Augt 18 do
8	Mary	do of young Bett	Sept 3rd 1805
9	Sloven	do of Dirma	Jany 7 1806
10	Venus	do of Dutches	Feb 16 do
11	Juno	do young Bett	August 9 do
12	Dido	do Jane	Novr 20 do
13	Naital	do Dirma	Decr 25 do

Figure 37: Thomas Moore's Mares born Oct 1804 to Dec 1806.

The same year Moore's holdings shifted towards the George's River, several of those who would be his neighbours and associates in that district in the future began to also head in that direction. In August and in Ireland, five men were embarked upon the *Tellicherry*, Michael Dwyer, John Mernagh, Hugh Byrne, Martin Burke and Arthur Develin, who would become associated in various ways with Thomas Moore. Their letter of introduction to Governor King, explained that they were men who:

> were engaged in treasonable practices here [Ireland], and who have requested to be allowed to banish themselves for life to New South Wales, to avoid being brought to trial; and as it has been deemed expedient to make such a compromise with them they are sent there. Not having been convicted they claimed the advantage of this distinction, the effect of which is not however to prevent their being subjected to all the laws and discipline of the settlement; and that any further indulgence is to be earned by their behaviour, of which there has been no reason to complain during the time of their confinement here.[193]

With any grand plans to increase the amount of ship building in his yard held over to the future, Moore had plenty of more mundane work to occupy his attention. At the end of October, he was part of the latest ship survey.

Captain Wilkinson of the *Commerce* having requested a Survey being taken of his vessel, Mr Moore, Master Builder, Captains Lucas, Sharpe, and Hingston were ordered on Survey, which occupied nearly the whole week; when they determined that the ship *Commerce* was past repair, and no longer sea-worthy.[194]

At the end of November, he was part of the team surveying the Spanish prize brought in by Campbell, the *Estramina*, in company with William House, Acting Master, and George Best, Acting Carpenter of the *Buffalo*, Edward Sharp, Master of the *Ceres* and Mr William Cousar, Shipwright.[195] Governor King explained that the *Integrity* had taken dispatches from him 'to the Government of Chili under a Flag of Truce respecting the capture of the King of Spain's Schooner *Estramina* and Merchant vessel *Saint Francisco and Saint Paulo* now detained in this Cove'. The *Estramina* had been hauled on shore and King was now keen to see what repairs are necessary so that she might be placed in public service until the *Integrity* returned from her mission. On 30 November the survey team provided a valuation of the vessel, which they set at £1700.[196]

While surveying Spanish vessels, Moore had his own interest in things European—of a completely different flavour. In 1806, Andrew was going to enter his senior school years and Thomas wanted to secure him an income to see him through. On 21 November 1805, Moore arranged for the boy to have authority to draw for his support from Mr Clementson, Moore's agent in London, 'the interest of three thousand six hundred pounds'.[197]

1806

There must have been some conversations between mother and step-father and his natural father at this important turning point in Andrew's life, for on 1 January 1806 John White signed over the High Street house in Sydney to his son.[198] Presumably across the fourteen years of this new lease, the rent would also be assigned to Andrew. However, it was not John White his natural father who paid for the education of this future military officer, but Thomas Moore.[199]

While his step-father's wealth was gradually accumulating in Sydney, Andrew was its beneficiary in London. In March 1806, Andrew Douglas White was enrolled at Charterhouse, being placed in Watkinson's House.[200] This was the school to which John Wesley, the founder of Methodism, was sent at the age of eleven. Despite being bullied by the older boys stealing his meat, this was 'by far the best institution of learning [Wesley] ever attended'.[201] Although the Moores were clearly sympathetic to Methodism as it emerged in New South Wales at a later date, it is impossible to tell whether these Methodist connections played a role in their choice of schooling for Andrew. It is possible that John White also had some influence in the choice, since his other son Richard Hammond White later attended the school, commencing in September 1809, the year after Andrew left. But given the relative dating, the influence could have been in the other direction—White having seen what Charterhouse did for Andrew. Either way, it was Thomas Moore who paid for Andrew's schooling, sending money through Isaac Clementson of London.[202]

Figure 38: Charterhouse School.

With his long-standing suspicion of the Irish and the Vinegar Hill uprising having occurred on his watch, Governor King was not pleased to find the political exiles on board the *Tellicherry* transport when she arrived on 18 February 1806:[203]

It is true that, since the late insurrection in March, 1804, there has been no seditious appearances of any consequence; and, from the attention bestowed in circumventing any designs of this nature, I hope any attempt to repeat their wild schemes will be fully prevented. Still, I cannot conceal from your Lordship that the arrival of the five United Irishmen, who appear to have been considerable leaders in the late rebellion in Ireland, without any conviction, added to the number of the disaffected of that class here already, will call forth the utmost attention of the officers of this colony.

Perhaps ironically, one week after King's complaint, he gave orders for another Irishman in the colony as a result of being implicated in the 1798 rebellion to be brought back to NSW. Rev. Samuel Marsden had requested permission to return to England for his health and to arrange some private concerns. In order to provide for his clerical duties King wrote to Piper on Norfolk Island, requesting that Rev. Henry Fulton be returned to Sydney by the first convenient opportunity.[204]

Once these men were landed and Governor King had time to collect his thoughts about what to do with them, he granted Michael Dwyer 100 acres of uncleared land along Cabramatta Creek, with his fellow United Irishmen alongside: Hugh 'Vesty' Byrne, John Mernagh, Arthur Devlin and Martin Burke.[205] Perhaps they would be no trouble if kept out of sight at what was the expanding edge of the colony.[206]

Figure 39: Charterhouse School. Dining Hall.

CHAPTER 4 ⚓ *Timber & Trade (7 May 1803 to 13 August 1806)* 245

After being in New South Wales five years, Governor King was not a well man physically, and he suffered under a great deal of pressure from those in the colony who objected to his policies, especially in regard to the importation of spirits. In May 1803 he had inquired about relief from the colony, and by the end of 1805 an answer had come. After learning 'by the arrival of a vessel from England, [...] that an officer was on his way out to relieve me in consequence of a request I had made to that purpose in May, 1803',[207] in March 1806 Governor King began finalising his reports. Despite pressure from other parts of his domain, King would have gained great satisfaction from summarising the previous year's productive work at the dockyard:[208]

> *Boat and Ship Builders.* Cutting off the upper works of the *Investigator* and fitting her for service; working on the repairs of His Majesty's vessels *Buffalo* and *Lady Nel[son]*, on the *Francis, Integrity*, and *Resource*, Colonial vessels; built four rowing and long boats for the use of this and other settlements, keeping the old boats and punt in repair; squaring 5,571 solid feet of ship timber, and much other incidental work.

King's report shows Thomas Moore victualled from the public stores because he is the Boat Builder, as well as being a Lieutenant in the Loyal Association[209]—not to mention his entitlement as a Civil Officer to 'the spirit ration under the third class'.[210] Such a salary arrangement ensured that Moore's sterling savings would be accumulating, which could then be poured into other business enterprises.

In mid-March the *Harrington* was the centre of attention again, when one of the soldiers guarding her stole six pounds of gunpowder out of her. She was still in mothballs, awaiting news from home about the legitimacy of Campbell's seizure of the two Spanish vessels, but the gunpowder was reported to have been taken from an unsecured room. Governor King ordered Captain A. Forrest, of the *Sydney*, Captain Thomas Cuzens, of the *Tellicherry*, and Thomas Moore to make a strict survey of the place from which it was stolen, to ascertain whether this part of the vessel was secured by locks. They reported signs of forced entry to the powder magazine and an attempt to make a hole into it from the hold, as well as finding that, not six pounds, but several casks of powder had gone, along with other items stolen from the Cabin.[211]

In April, the Rev. Henry Fulton arrived in the colony, recalled from Norfolk Island to replace Samuel Marsden while he went to England on a recruiting drive. Fulton found the colony reeling from major flooding along the Hawkesbury the previous month, and the loss of the greatest part of the wheat from the last harvest.[212] One of his first duties was to celebrate England's greatest maritime victory, for although the Battle of Trafalgar was fought and won on 21 October 1805, the news first reached NSW to be published on 13 April 1806.[213]

> Almighty God having blessed one of His Majesty's fleets (under the command of the much lamented and renowned Lord Nelson of the Nile, who with several distinguished officers and brave men were slain in the arms of Victory), the signal and decisive defeat of the French and Spanish combined fleet, greatly superior in number and force, His Excellency the Governor directs that Sunday next, the 20th instant, be observed as a day of general thanksgiving, for the mercy and goodness shewn to our Most Gracious Sovereign and his dominions.
>
> The Rev. Mr. Marsden will perform Divine service at Sydney, in the front of Government House, at 10 o'clock; the Rev. Mr Fulton at the church at Parramatta; Mr. Crook, missionary, at Castle Hill; and Mr Harris, missionary, at the Green Hills, Hawkesbury—at which places, all persons not prevented by sickness, or the necessary care of their dwellings, are expected to attend.

At Trafalgar England dealt a decisive blow to her enemies. This most recent conflict with the French went back to 1793, when revolutionary France declared war against England before overrunning Holland in 1795, and setting up the Batavian Republic—which then afforded England the opportunity to seize the Dutch colonial empire. Under Sir John Jervis the British easily defeated the Spanish at the Battle of St Vincent in 1797. As Napoleon was just coming into power, he realized that 'British seapower was his real enemy', and 'for several years he toyed with the idea of an invasion across the Channel [...], but in the end he knew that against the seapower of England he stood no chance'. In 1798, 'what was left of the once-great French Fleet' was defeated at the Battle of the Nile (Abukir Bay)—a battle which brought Horatio Nelson into prominence.

COLOUR PLATES ⚓ *A Portrait in his Actions. Thomas Moore of Liverpool (1762–1840)*

Plate 22. Port Jackson Painter, 7 March 1792.
Artist: T. Watling. Drawing 21. © National History Museum, London. No. 53639.
Government house is at the left, and in front on the shore is Mr Reid's boat shed, next to the Government wharf.
The hospital wharf can be seen on the western shore. The closest house up the hill is a depiction of John White's house.

Plate 23. A western view of Sydney Cove, ca 1798. Engraved: James Heath. Published Cadell & Davies, 1798.
National Library of Australia nla.pic-an7566580
The hospital wharf is across the water from the three chimneys on the closest shore. The middle chimney
points to John White's house up from the wharf where the Moores were living in 1798.

COLOUR PLATES ⚓ *A Portrait in his Actions. Thomas Moore of Liverpool (1762–1840)*

Plate 24: A direct south view of the town of Sydney taken from the brow of the hill leading to the flagstaff.
Artist: Edward Dayes based on T. Watling. Engraved: J. Heath.
Reproduced courtesy of the Australian National Maritime Museum. No. 00000874.
Government house to the far left with Reid's boathouse on the shore in front next to the Government wharf. High Street is dead centre and hospital wharf can be seen on this shore. John White's house is above the chimney of the building with the triangular roof on High St. The tree stump in the foreground would be close to the site of the future Master Builder's house.

COLOUR PLATES ⚓ *A Portrait in his Actions. Thomas Moore of Liverpool (1762–1840)*

Plate 25: Sydney - Capital New South Wales, ca.1800. Artist: Unknown.
State Library of NSW. a1528055.
Government House is the white house at the top of the street going up the picture to the right.
The second house is the chaplain's, with the orange trees planted by Richard Johnson in view.
The masts to the left give away the approximate location of the dockyard.

Plate 26: Nouvelle-Hollande: Nouvelle Galles du Sud, 1802. Artist: C A Lesueur.
Reproduced courtesy of the Australian National Maritime Museum. No 00004992.
Baudin's 1802 camp at Bennelong Point is in the foreground. His ship *Geographe* is careened on the
shore to the far left. Moore's Official residence is clear looking across the water between the large tent
and the first ship to its right. The dockyard stretches along the shore to the left of Moore's house.
At its far end the *Portland* can be seen on the stocks just above the water line.

COLOUR PLATES ⚓ *A Portrait in his Actions. Thomas Moore of Liverpool (1762–1840)*

Plate 27: A view of Sydney Cove, New South Wales, 1804. Artist: E. Daye. Published: F. Jukes, 1804. National Library of Australia nla.pic-an6016289
The *Portland* can be seen on the stocks, the southern end of the dockyard. Behind it is the open-sided timber-drying shed. Across High Street are the hospital buildings, and between their red roof and the drying shed the blue roof of John White's house can be seen.

COLOUR PLATES ⚓ *A Portrait in his Actions. Thomas Moore of Liverpool (1762–1840)*

Plate 28: Sydney Cove, 1808. Artist: J.W. Lewin. State Library of NSW. a1528463.
The dockyard can be seen running along the shore from the far left to behind the sails of the boat in centre. Moore's house is the first one after the sails. Then Robert Campbell's, then Campbell's warehouses and dock. The *Portland* is on the stocks in front of the building on the left.

COLOUR PLATES ⚓ *A Portrait in his Actions. Thomas Moore of Liverpool (1762–1840)*

Plate 29: Sydney Cove, 1808. J.W. Lewin. State Library of NSW. a928869.

A view down the East side of the cove towards Government House on the horizon at the far left, and a ship in the careening area on the shore, to the Government wharf on the right of the painting.

Colour Plates ⚓ *A Portrait in his Actions. Thomas Moore of Liverpool (1762–1840)*

Plate 30: View of the town and cove of Sydney, New South Wales, in Sepr. 1806 as seen from the east.
Artist: Emma Eburne (1819-1885). Published: Colnaghi & Puckle, 1840. National Library of Australia. nla.pic-an7890459.
The hospital wharf is in the centre, with the street running up to White's house. The house is enlarged from previously, and the trees of the orchard can be seen behind it.
The dockyard runs along the shore and Moore's house is framed by the right and centre masts of the ship.

COLOUR PLATES ⚓ *A Portrait in his Actions. Thomas Moore of Liverpool (1762–1840)*

Plate 31: New South Wales, view of Sydney from the east side of the cove. No. 2, ca. 1810. Artist: John H. Clark. Published: John Booth, 1810, National Library of Australia, nla.pic-an7890459.

Nelson went on to the bombardment of Copenhagen in 1801, and finally the climactic Battle of Trafalgar in 1805, in which he defeated the French and Spanish, regained unchallenged mastery of the seas, but lost his own life. The war continued on for another ten years, while England strangled the power of the continent with her blockading fleets and seized more of the colonies of Napoleon's unwilling allies, Spain and Holland.[214]

When the news reached Sydney, Thomas Moore was also involved in the Trafalgar celebrations. After Divine Service on 20 April 1806, three volleys were fired by the Loyal Sydney Association. At an appointed hour, a Royal Salute was also fired from the Dawes' Point Battery, 'in celebration of the glorious victory obtained over the combined fleets of the enemy on the 21st October last by the fleet under the command of the late Vice-Admiral Lord Nelson'.[215]

The celebrations had no doubt subsided by Wednesday 28 May 1806, when a Vice-Admiralty Court sat to hear the next stage of the drama surrounding the *Harrington* and the two Spanish prizes, *Estramina* and *St Francisco and St Paulo* (alias *Amiante*). The court heard that these two vessels were taken by the *Harrington* in September and October of 1804, but it was subsequently discovered that war with Spain had not commenced until 11 January 1805. The two ships were therefore treated as the property of the King of Spain, until the time that hostilities were known to have commenced. At this point, the boats of the *Buffalo* seized them, and John Shephard, that ship's purser, now appeared before the Court requesting that they be condemned, along with all the property belonging to them now found on board the *Harrington*, as lawful prizes to HMS *Buffalo*. John Harris, who had been appointed as the Agent for the rightful owners (the King of Spain and the Spanish Merchants), protested this claim. Thomas Moore, who had been appointed as Agent for the Master and Owners of the *Harrington* and William Campbell, the Master, did likewise. After a long deliberation, the Court declared that under the circumstances of their original seizure by the *Harrington*, they had been held in Trust by the British Government on behalf of the King of Spain, and so could not be declared lawful prizes now until a decision be obtained as to the legality or otherwise of their original seizure by the *Harrington*.[216]

While Thomas Moore was in court pleading on behalf of the *Harrington*, he was mourning the loss of his friend and colleague, Captain Thomas Rowley, who died at two in the morning the day before the Court sat, 'of a consumptive complaint long contracted'. He was the Captain Commandant of the Loyal Sydney Association and formerly a Captain in the NSW Corps, and one of the Officer-Traders of the 1790s. The *Sydney Gazette* spoke highly of Rowley: 'The philanthropy and many eminent virtues which adorned the character of that worthy Gentleman have too long been a subject of universal admiration to admit eulogium here: nor is it in the power of language to convey the slightest conception of the regret occasioned by the event to his family and numerous friends of the very first respectability in the Colony—in which sensation all classes of inhabitants participate'.[217]

The week was a full one for Mr Moore. After Rowley's death on Tuesday and the Vice-Admiralty Court on Wednesday, on Thursday 29th the Officers Civil and Military and their Wives, which therefore included Thomas and Rachel Moore, enjoyed 'an elegant entertainment' given by John Palmer at 'Wollamoola', in the presence of the Governor and Mrs King. The next day, the officers of the *Buffalo* provided a cold collation to the Governor and some of the Civil and Military Officers and their wives, sailing down Port Jackson from three to five, accompanied by the band of the NSW Corps in its own boat as far as Garden Island.[218]

After such pleasant distractions, Sunday the 1st June was the day to bury Thomas Rowley on his farm near Sydney in accordance with his wishes.[219] The Governor and all the Civil, Military and Naval Officers in the colony attended 'to pay the last duties of respect to an Officer whose long services lay claim to every honorable attention'.

> The New South Wales Corps, Sydney Loyal Association, and Marines and Seamen of His Majesty's ship *Buffalo* and *Lucy* private ship of war, marched off to join the procession at about half past ten; and at half past 12 the procession reached the place of internment, where the funeral service was performed by the Rev. Mr. MARSDEN; and when the bier was received into the vault martial honours were paid by a Company of the New South Wales Corps, firing three volleys over the grave. The general

sentiment that prevailed on the occasion was manifested in strong traits of sorrow which were conspicuous in every countenance.

In time to come, Thomas Moore would find himself closely associated —even entangled—with Rowley's family, although there was little hint of that future involvement when he died. Within the week, Rowley's post of Captain Commandant of the Sydney Loyal Association was given to Richard Atkins, the Judge-Advocate.[220]

While enduring the pressures and emotions of these various events, Thomas Moore had been quietly making a huge decision of his own. On 15 June, he suddenly announced that he was intending to leave the colony. He took out the usual advertisement in the *Gazette*, indicating that he was planning to be gone within the month.

> NOTICE. MR THOMAS MOORE intending shortly to depart for Europe, therefore takes an early occasion to require all Claims or Demands upon him to be presented for liquidation on or prior to the 16th day of July next ensuing; and at the same time to request that all persons indebted to him will liquidate their accounts respectively without delay, as his affairs require finally to be arranged within the period above named.[221]

If the advertisement had any success at all, it is not shown by any massive influx of payments into the accounts in Moore's Business Notebook. But why was he so urgent to leave? For sure, Thomas would have delighted to be able to see how his stepson was settling in to the next phase of his education, but that was probably not the reason for this projected visit. The most likely explanation is that news had been sent him that his mother was gravely ill. Despite having not seen his parents for so long, since at least 1802 he had been remitting them money through William Raven—a practice he would continue for his relatives at home across years to come.[222] Mary Moore had gone into decline about August 1805 and soon had to be carried in and out of bed. 'Spent to a shadow', she did not recover.[223] An epitaph composed for her burial day by Rev. Percival Stockdale, incumbent of St Mary's Lesbury, alluded to these last days as being times of suffering for her:

> Her frame, at length quite worn with years,
> an object for compassion's tears;

God save her from her woes release:
She lived industrious; died in peace.[224]

It would have taken some time before the family realised the moment had come to alert the distant Thomas, and even then several months would pass before the news reached New South Wales. On this reading of events, it is probable that Thomas heard about his mother late in May, and by the 15 June advertisement he had made up his mind to return home to see her for the last time.

However, despite the urgency with which he called for the liquidation of his debts, Thomas Moore never left the colony.[225] The reason once again appears to be simple. As Moore was making preparations to leave, he received a sad letter from his father, informing him that his 78 year old mother had died on 1 March and buried three days later.[226] Written on 20 March, Joseph's letter must have reached New South Wales in minimum time. 'With tears in [his] eyes', Joseph addresses his 'dutiful son and daughter', the two children far from home; Sally—who then forwarded it to her brother Thomas in New South Wales.[227] Mary died at 3 p.m., after Joseph had stepped out for a while, leaving her in the care of Mary Ann Dixon:

> She went away without either Frown or Struggle. I went up to the Church Clean it I spoke to her when I went out I asked her how she was I told her that whay I was going She Said I am very poorly My dear I was short time until Mary ann Sent for me She died instantly Mary Ann lithe [?] and distracted hung about my neck I Could not get her pacified for some time

Mr Stockdale was very good to him, and the funeral was a good send off: 'your brothers and sisters was all there She was buried very deacently we had the whole town several out of it intimate acquaintances'. Joseph concludes with Christian greetings, 'I Conclude may God bless you all this is all at present [?] from sorifull father Joseph Moore'.

Joseph is evidently concerned about money, even at this time of grief. He is glad that Thomas's brother William and sister Mary's husband, Thomas Trumble, paid the funeral expenses, and William is apparently going to write in regard to several other matters. These include some arrangements to be made with Captain Raven, which

CHAPTER 4 ⚓ *Timber & Trade (7 May 1803 to 13 August 1806)* 251

are clearly causing Joseph some consternation. Joseph requests Sally to see the sea captain (she, like Raven, lived in London), but suggests that, if she thinks it proper, she does not tell him about Mary's death, for fear that 'he will likely keep up a part of the money until we Can get a letter your brother'—presumably Thomas. Was Raven handing out an allowance from their distant son, with an accounting method that demanded it be halved when their two became one?

GOVERNOR BLIGH ARRIVES

In the first week of August, New South Wales received her new Governor, who took over the command from King on the 13th. William Bligh was already famous for his service in the Navy, serving alongside Lord Nelson in the recent glory days. He had also acquired some notoriety for his previous involvement with the mutiny on the Bounty (April 1789) and the mutiny on the Nore (May-June 1797)—although here he played an intercessory role with the sailors. This notoriety continued to dog him, especially as he had to face a mutiny of another kind in this penal settlement on the other side of the world.

After the *Lady Magdeline Sinclair* sailed through the heads on Tuesday 5 August 1806 with the *Porpoise*, King issued an order on the 7th that William Bligh was to be received with due honours the next day, after which King would retain government for one more week, before handing it over on the 13th and embarking on the *Buffalo* for his departure.[228] On Friday the 8th Thomas Moore did his duty, as the Sydney Loyal Volunteers Association joined the NSW Corps with colours flying to welcome the new Governor. The *Sinclair*, the *Porpoise* and the *Buffalo* each had their turn of firing fifteen guns; the *Porpoise* when Bligh went on board with his broad pennant. On arriving at the Government wharf, the land battery then fired its guns and several passing of the lines of the military men completed this rather explosive welcome to the colony. Subsequently the Military and Civil Officers were introduced by Governor King to their new Commander-in-Chief at Government House. This was Thomas Moore's first introduction to the man who will one day forbid him from leaving the colony.

After alienating the NSW Corps by his reforms regarding the sale of spirits and suffering under their enmity and that of others such as Captain Colnett of the *Glatton*, Maurice Margarot, Henry Browne Hayes, William Maum, and others not adverse to sending home bad reports,[229] King would have been pleased to receive Castlereagh's letter from Bligh's hand, expressing 'His Majesty's entire approbation of the conduct you have manifested in the important charge committed to you, and his satisfaction at the improvement which the colony has received under your superintendance'.[230] Remembering how difficult it was for him when he first arrived to have Hunter's extended delay in departure, King planned to hand over the Government to his successor immediately on his arrival and leave the colony altogether. Unfortunately, however, King was stricken with a severe attack of gout that confined him to his sickbed and delayed his departure by another six months.[231] He was not fit to sail until 10 February 1807, and the voyage was so troublesome that he did not reach England until November.[232]

The same day as Bligh arrived, Captain Bunker returned on the *Elizabeth*, one of Robert Campbell's ships, laden with a cargo of goods for sale. She also carried Bunker's wife Margrett and his family, Isabella, Henry, Mary Ann, Charlotte, James and the youngest, Charles Harris Bunker, who was born just before they left England but waited to be christened in St Phillip's Sydney. Thomas Moore had the Pitt's Row house ready for them to occupy.[233]

Amongst the despatches Bligh brought from Castlereagh was one permitting the *Harrington* to be liberated and King immediately ordered her release.[234] On 8 August, King directed a Survey to be taken of the *Harrington* after receiving a request from her master, William Campbell. Thomas Moore joined Lieut. John Oxley of the *Buffalo*, Henry Moor of the *Fortune*, and Alexander Ferguson of the *Lucy* on the survey team. They reported the next day. After being out of action for so long, she required a lot of work to make her seaworthy again, and it would be January 1807 before Campbell sailed her out of Port Jackson, eager to make up for lost time.[235]

As King closed off his reports the day before he handed over to Bligh, he gave an account of the colonial vessels: the *Buffalo* is 'fitting for sea'; *Lady Nelson* is fit for sea, but her crew is lent to the *Estramina*; the *Supply* cut down to lower deck, very useful in the harbour as a hulk;

CHAPTER 4 ⚓ *Timber & Trade (7 May 1803 to 13 August 1806)* 253

the *Integrity*, built here from 1802 to 1803, has 'Gone to Valparaiso with despatches under a flag of truce. Sailed 26th June, 1805'; the *Estramina*, 'former Spanish vessel', 'in very good condition, and coppered to light water mark. Purchased by auction to replace the *Integrity*, supposed to be lost or detained'; the *Resource*, Schooner, built from the *Porpoise* and *Cato*'s planks, 1803; a punt built here in 1803; and four coppered long boats and four rowing boats, also built here.[236] In his 'Present State of His Majesty's Settlements on the East Coast of New Holland, called New South Wales', King also reported upon Moore's duties:[237]

> *Boatbuilder and Shipwright*. Has the charge of the dock-yard and the artificers, laborers, &c, in that department. His employment is building and keeping in repair the Government Colonial vessels, boats, and small crafts. He has been much employed in selecting ship timber for England, and attending to the repairs of such King's ships as are stationed or occasionally arrive, and is a most useful and necessary officer.

The Master Boat Builder's work seemed to move out from that of the dockyard proper in ever expanding circles. So, for example, a comment from King to Bligh revealed that the convicts from the dockyard had always been sent to assist HM Ships' carpenters to repair their vessels if needed, during which time they were regarded as supernumaries on the ship's books for victuals. But this out-sourcing of convict labour then brought Moore additional responsibility, for it was done on the proviso of 'their work being subject to the occasional inspection of the master-builder to see that it is not diverted to private purposes'.[238] The week that Bligh arrived, Moore was engaged on work in a circle even more remote from the dockyard, for he had joined Mr. Richard Rouse on in an inspection of the public buildings and a listing of their necessary repairs.[239] First on the list was Moore's own house: 'The Master Builder's House wants plaistering, whitewashing, windows repairing, and a part of the foundation given away'. The second item he also knew well: 'The Dock-yard wants sheds for boats, and to work under for saw-pits; the blacksmith shop and storehouses and watchman's hut wants plaistering, whitewashing, new doors and shutters, rep'g tiles outside of staircase, also new posts and railing next the road'. The two men also referred to the new Church: 'the wall at one end down; and the tower; the roof only half up'; 'The Parsonage house wants new doors, window and fence, plastering, whitewashing, and tiling repaired'. At Parramatta, the church was proceeding well: 'The church covered in, but no pews or anything but a pulpit; tower not half built, walls broke, and will require rebuilding'.[240]

Governor Bligh soon had the opportunity to try out this 'useful and necessary officer' for himself. King had recommended to Bligh that the old hulk of the *Supply* that had been used within the harbour, was probably about ready to be broken up and should probably be surveyed with this end in view. The day before he officially took over, Bligh ordered Thomas Moore to conduct the survey, which he did, reporting the next day that 'she is in so Rotten and leaky a state that she is in danger of sinking at her Moorings; which will be a great Annoyance to the Harbour and a loss to Government'.[241]

The same day he reported on the *Supply*, Moore once again joined the troops and Officers Civil and Military, this time assembled to hear Governor Bligh's Commission read out and to witness him taking command of the colony. Bligh publicly announced Castlereagh's approbation of Governor King's service to the colony. All of King's regulations were to remain in place until further orders, and all his Officers likewise. William Gore was announced as Provost Marshall, Mr Fisk as Deputy Commissary, Lieutenant Putland the Governor's Aide-de-Camp, and Edmund Griffin his secretary.[242]

On Sunday 17, the *Gazette* printed an Address congratulating King on his departure, and another congratulating Bligh on his appointment to the colony,[243] with replies from both men dated 14 August. Both congratulatory Addresses were signed by Richard Atkins for the Civil Officers, George Johnston for the military, and John Macarthur for the free citizens of the colony.

On 18 August, Bligh found more for King's 'useful and necessary officer' to do, making the Master Boat Builder one of the first to be given orders under Bligh's new regime. This time the survey was of the stores on HMS *Porpoise*, and Moore was accompanied by J. Houstoun, J. Oxley, Wm Jackson all of the *Buffalo*, and J.H. Jackson of the *Sinclair*. Once again, the report came in the next day.[244]

Amongst his parting reflections, Governor King also noted that not more than 360 couples were married in the colony, 170 being united since 1800, adding the comment: 'It certainly would be desirable if marriage were more prevalent'.[245] This concern was shared by the early chaplains through into the Macquarie period at least. With Samuel Marsden's departure for England imminent, the responsibility for conducting marriages in the colony would rest firmly on the shoulders of Rev. Henry Fulton. Perhaps these extra kinds of responsibility provided Fulton additional motivation to write to his former Bishop in Ireland requesting his favourable intercession in order to secure him a proper commission as chaplain in NSW.[246]

On 22 September 1806, 135 Sydney Settlers signed yet another address to Governor Bligh—and it wouldn't be the last one. After congratulating him on his appointment, expressing confidence in his government, and requesting that he govern with an impartial hand, the signatories expressed their 'pleasing hope that, under your Excellency's auspices, agriculture will flourish, commerce increase, and we as British subjects enjoy our country's constitutional rights'—the latter a hint towards trial by jury. After outlining these positive agenda items, the memorialists then strongly disavowed knowledge of the former addresses to Bligh and King that had been printed in the *Gazette*, with John Macarthur's name at the foot. This, they declared, was an infringement on their liberty, and Macarthur was an unfit person to represent them, 'as we may chiefly attribute the rise in the price of mutton to his withholding the large flock of wethers he now has to make such a price as he may choose to demand'. With that off their chest, the memorialists finish with an assurance of the settlers' support of Bligh's administration. Bligh must have wondered what he had struck here. Certainly the address expressed tensions that already prevailed. No doubt it also flagged more tensions to come in the future.[247]

Tensions there were, and tensions there will be. But this was all part of an inevitable struggle as this penal colony sought to become a free society. This was a period which greatly contributed to the future shape of Sydney's commercial community.

> The odd, raffish, unorthodox trading community which grew in the unlikely environment of the Sydney penal settlement at the beginning of the nineteenth century founded Australian commerce,

industry and even banking. They helped to create a colony out of a prison by erecting a business community and a commercial structure suitable to a colony but increasingly unsuitable for a prison. Their experience, their ambitions, whether far-ranging or restricted, their readiness to leap in the dark and take the hazard, all played a part in shaping the economic environment for generations to come.[248]

If they had remained in England, these men may have never 'risen from provincial obscurity', but in Sydney 'they emerge as genuine historical characters. They do this not because they were colourful, nor because some became successful and affluent, but because of what they did'.[249]

Thomas Moore was one of these people rising from obscurity. The boy from Lesbury; Ship's Carpenter cum Adventurer cum Master Boat Builder cum shipwright; farmer and husbandman; minor trader and agent of ship's captains; Purveyor of Timber at a crucial moment in European history; Civil Officer, citizen; husband, step-father and friend. If this rising group of Sydney characters found their colour from what they did, Mr Moore was also beginning, with his actions, to paint a portrait for posterity.

5

SYDNEY IN TURMOIL: MOORE AMONGST THE REBELS

(13 AUGUST 1806 *to* 31 JULY 1808)

Several huge floods, with their devastating effects on the colony's supplies of grain, act as the interventions of Providence, strangely and strongly affecting the course of Thomas Moore's life. In 1810, the penchant for NSW rivers to rise in the heavy rains partly motivated Macquarie to found new towns to act as grain stores,[1] and this then catapulted Moore into prominence at Liverpool. Four years earlier, the record floods of March 1806, which decimated the colony's grain supplies, began the strange sequence of events that led to Sydney's famous 'Rum Rebellion', when Governor Bligh was cast out of office, not even eighteen months after his arrival. As it all began, Moore found himself assisting on the bench in a flood-provoked court case. As the events played out, he found himself increasingly tangled up amongst the rebels.

Hints at the fractured state of the colony came to the surface on 22 September 1806, in the two addresses presented to the new governor, William Bligh.[2] Hopes for impartial government, flourishing agriculture, increase in commerce and freedom of trade, and for English constitutional rights here in New South Wales, tell one story for those who hold the real power in a society, and another from those who don't. The 1790s trade monopoly had gone, and since 1800 the new traders were in the ascendancy, but how would that change the state of affairs for the free settlers of Sydney and those along the Hawkesbury? And what clashes would this bring? The settlers' vehement disavowal of John Macarthur's right to speak on their behalf testifies loudly that many were those who were looking for a new day of freedom in New South Wales. Their pledge of loyalty to Bligh expressed their hopes that he may well be the Governor who achieves this pleasant outcome.

The address from the Hawkesbury settlers had its own particular flavour reflecting the concerns and circumstances along the river. They arise from 'the deepest concern' over 'the greatest calamity' as the country is on the brink of famine following 'the great flood which it pleased Divine Providence to send in March last, the rise of the water being near ten feet perpendicular height greater than had been in this colony since it was first inhabited by Europeans'. (Figure 40). The floods compounded the difficulties caused by 'a mistaken policy in oppressing the merchants and inhabitants in general by sending from this port ships that arrived with merchandize, of necessaries and comforts, by not suffering them to land their goods for sale, although the colony was in the greatest want of the articles they brought'. Previous low grain prices had meant that 'the produce of the land would not pay the grower the expenses of cultivation, to the general ruin of the settler', and the practice of not paying for the crops in money or bills, meant that the settlers had no way of purchasing necessities. In other words, they disagreed with Governor King sending away some ships laden with spirits—the currency required to pay farm labourers.

After this preamble, they presented the Governor with a long list of requests: to restore freedom of trade; to permit commodities to be bought and sold at a fair open market; to prevent the monopoly and extortion previously practised; to protect merchant and trader and the rights of people in general; to let the laws of property take their due

CHAPTER 5 ⚓ Sydney in Turmoil (13 August 1806 to 31 July 1808)   259

course; to ensure justice is administered by the Courts; and to cause payment to be made in money or Government orders that will pass current in purchases without drawback or discount. In view of the dichotomy that has often been drawn between the 'farmer' and the 'trader', it is interesting to notice that this list of demands to protect trade came, not from the Sydney settlers, but from those on the Hawkesbury.[3] It is also significant to notice that the settlers of both groups were quite clearly disaffected with John Macarthur.

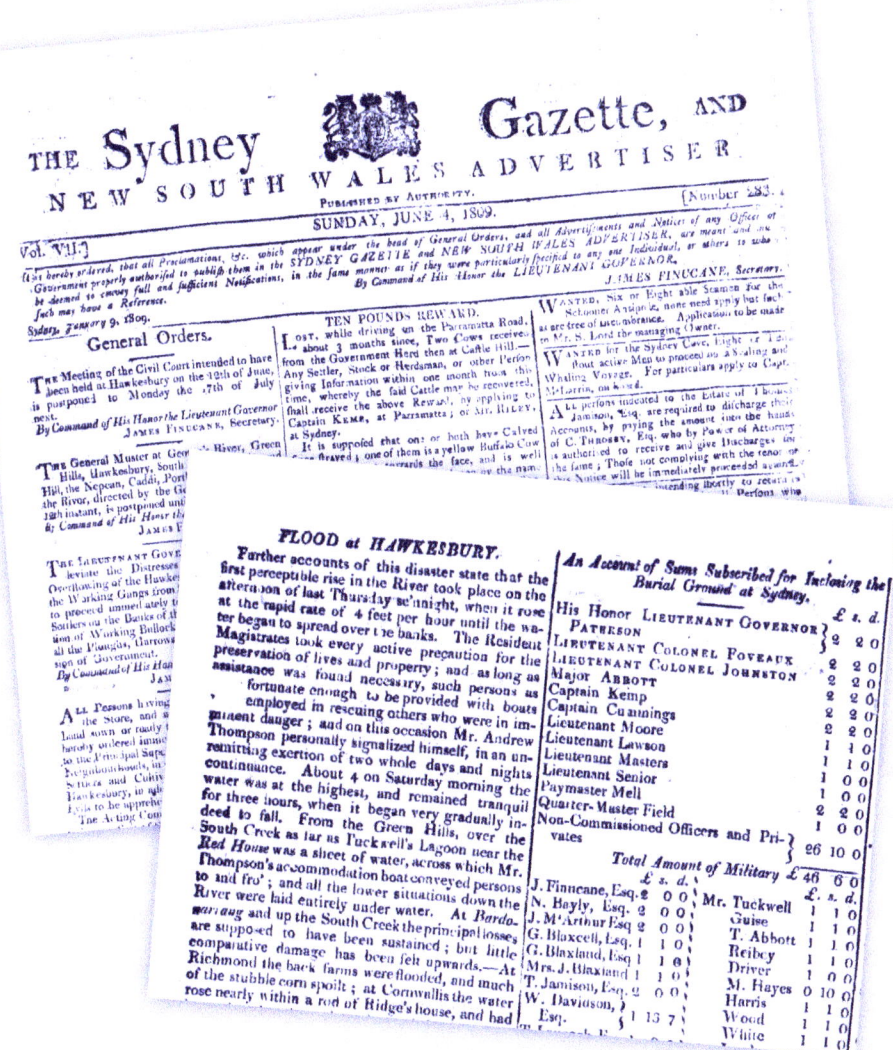

Figure 40: The Sydney Gazette on the floods of June 1809.

Despite this general disaffection towards him from the masses, John Macarthur still moved in the corridors of power and worked those connections against those who did not. On 15 October 1806, he provided the entertainment for a large party of Officers and their wives and both the old and the new Governors were in attendance, as well as the Lieutenant Governor, William Paterson.[4] A fortnight later he began proceedings against a man who was, in his opinion, at the opposite end of society—an emancipated convict who probably assisted in gathering signatures for the Hawkesbury address. Unfortunately (from Macarthur's perspective) New South Wales had been kind to Andrew Thompson, whose wide-ranging entrepreneurial schemes had made him wealthy and powerful—despite the station in life he occupied when he originally arrived in the colony. When Macarthur decided to sue him over a promissory note, it was a part of a chain of events leading relentlessly towards the overthrow of the legitimate government of the land.

Andrew Thompson was already 'the largest grain grower and the wealthiest settler in the colony'.[5] At least for those without ready access to sterling, through Paymaster's Bills or Treasury Notes, grain was the basis of the economy and served as a currency, and so this put Thompson in a strong economic position. After Bligh arrived and Thompson began managing Bligh's property along the Hawkesbury, it further strengthened his connections with colonial power. But in New South Wales, the grain supplies were dependent upon the weather, and—like many others—Thompson had suffered greatly from the floods earlier in the year.[6]

In March 1806, the heavens had opened and the rivers of the colony broke their banks. On the 1st and 2nd reports expressed relief that the violent rains had not caused as much damage as feared, although about 6,000 bushels of maize were lost in the low grounds, compounding the problems of an already bad wheat harvest. But by the 20th the flood was approaching a very dangerous height—almost to the high water mark of the disastrous flood of 2 March 1801, famous for the drowning of John Stogdell, one of Thomas Moore's original trading partners[7]—and the settlers were moving to higher ground. By Saturday the 22nd, the height of the water was horrifying and hundreds of people were in grave danger.[8]

Chief Constable Andrew Thompson sprang to the rescue. He launched his three boats and by the end of the day several hundred people owed their thanks to him for plucking them from trees, rooftops and high ground, or off rafts of straw floating in the flood. Thomas Biggers also rescued about 150 more. As the men worked their boats, stock and grain supplies kept floating past them, but with all energy invested in saving human lives, nothing could be done. More than two hundred stacks of wheat—covered in dogs, pigs and poultry seeking refuge—were swept along with the deluge, ever onwards towards the sea.[9]

By the end of October, the same floods that brought Thompson fame for his compassionate heroism, brought him into Judge-Advocate Atkins' court room to defend himself against John Macarthur. Atkins gave notice that the Court of Civil Jurisdiction would sit from Monday 27 October, which it did until adjourning on 24 November—not to reassemble until an emergency or further notice.[10] The rains of March had long gone and Sydney was beginning to swelter in the pre-summer heat.[11] Rev. Henry Fulton and Thomas Moore assisted Atkins on the bench, in a case that was about to also turn up the political temperature.

On the second day of sitting, John Macarthur brought a civil action against Thompson, which was the first in a sequence of five court cases which pushed him towards the overthrow of Governor Bligh on 26 January 1808.[12]

Macarthur held a note of hand for 99 bushels of storable wheat issued by Thompson to Thomas Rickerby, or bearer.[13] Such notes of hand were used as currency, and this note had come into Macarthur's possession when Rickerby purchased some of his sheep. Thompson had issued the note prior to the floods, when wheat was worth about 7s a bushel, and the note £34 10s. The loss of grain supplies in the March deluge had caused the price of wheat to skyrocket, and Macarthur now demanded payment at the present wheat price, making the note worth £341 10s. Thompson argued before Atkins, Fulton and Moore, that the Court had previously ordered other notes granted before the flood to be paid in money at their original value. He also argued that when his note had been used to purchase sheep from Macarthur, the purchase had established its wheat value to be 7s per bushel.

The case is significant for the development of contract law in Australia. 'Was the colony principally a place of trade in which contracts would be strictly enforced? Or was it more traditional, a place where what we now see as an older model of contract law was in place, one based on fairness?'[14] Atkins, Fulton and Moore decided in favour of Thompson, and so—perhaps more significantly—their decision went against John Macarthur.

This case spurred Bligh on in his much-needed reforms. On 1 November, while grain prices continued to soar, wheat and maize reaching £4 per bushel, and further actions were before the Court in regard to promissory notes, the Governor clarified the term 'currency', as being 'only applicable to money, not barter in goods'. So that 'the good faith of Individuals is not to be perverted', he announced that from January next 'all Checks and Promissory Notes issued shall by Public Proclamation be drawn payable in Sterling Money'.[15] As promised, this order was duly issued on 3 January 1807.[16]

Thomas Moore drew sterling money for his duties at the dockyard, which the end of year accounts showed to be £91.5.0 in 1806.[17] According to those accounts, the same sum was paid as an allowance to Mr White, late Surgeon of the colony—an intriguing state of affairs sine he had not been in the colony since 16 December 1794.[18] When White eventually retired in January 1820, he was paid exactly this amount as a half-pay pension,[19] which may suggest that he was also paid as a half-pay pension since the time he left NSW—despite him reviving his career in England. What happened to this money? Since it is on the colony's books, it must have been paid in New South Wales, but what then? Was it somehow sent back home to England? Or was this allowance paid to his ex-housekeeper and mother of his son, who was now Mrs Rachel Moore? Thomas Moore continued to look after White's interests in NSW for many years. Was this allowance paid towards the upkeep and maintenance of his holdings?

After being released on Bligh's arrival in August 1806 and her repairs being completed, the *Harrington* was at last cleared outwards

CHAPTER 5 ⚓ *Sydney in Turmoil (13 August 1806 to 31 July 1808)* 263

on 27 January 1807, in ballast and bound for China.[20] Governor Bligh had arrived with documents permitting her release from the detention in which King had placed her, and Captain William Campbell was keen to make up for lost trading time.[21] Whether this trip was strictly letter-of-the-law legal is another question. During the time of her detention, the vessel's owners, Chase, Cheney and Co, had failed, taken over by the Parrys. If Campbell had returned the vessel to Madras, he would have had to face his creditors. Instead, Campbell now sailed to the Fiji Islands for a cargo of sandalwood, and from thence to China, where he hoped to sell it for a handsome profit.

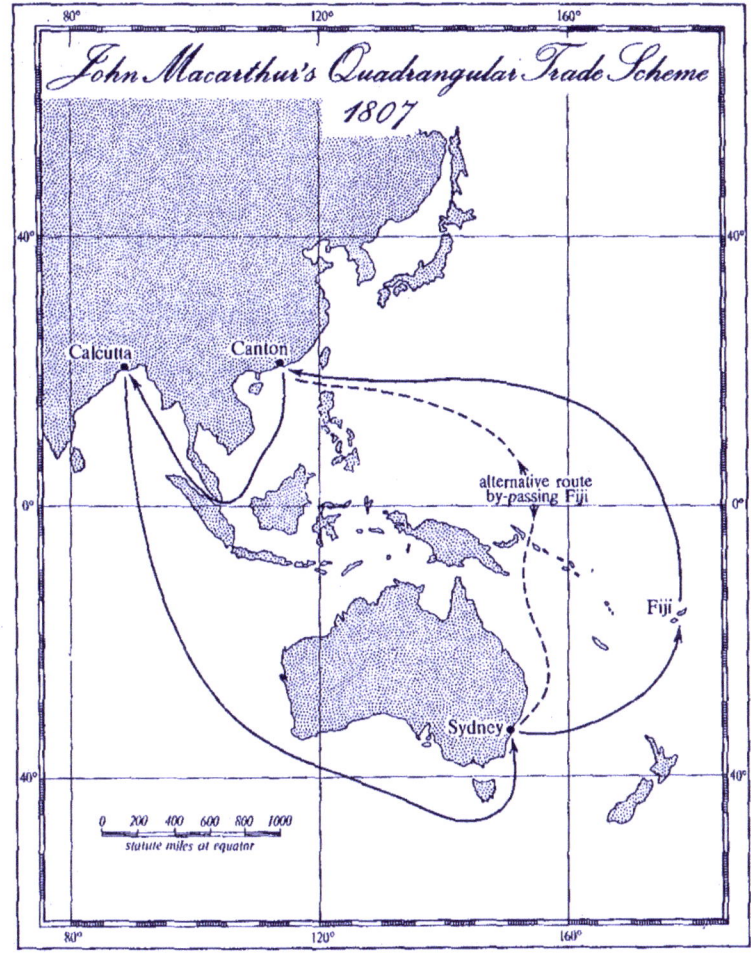

Figure 41: Map of Macarthur's trading Scheme.

The *Harrington*'s voyage was an experimental first in pursuit of a scheme arising from John Macarthur's entrepreneurial vision. (Figure 41). Conceived in December 1806, the scheme sought to open up trade between Sydney, Canton and Calcutta, where Macarthur's pastoral partner Walter Stevenson Davidson had a merchant relative. John Macarthur, Garnham Blaxcell, and Thomas Jamison made arrangements with the *Harrington* to pick up sandalwood from the Fiji Islands, which would then be sold in China by Davidson (travelling on board). Strictly speaking, Davidson had no right to trade in China, but this would be masked by the fact that the *Harrington* was registered as a 'country ship', giving it permission to trade in East India Company territory. With a pocket full of profits, Davidson was to proceed to Calcutta to establish a connection with a Calcutta house through his relative, and then, in company with the merchant house, buy a ship, and register it too as a 'country ship'. Having thus gained a ship capable of trading with the East India Company's permission, Davidson was to sail it back to Sydney. This vessel would then be laden with more cargo to be sold in Canton, where China goods would be bought for the Sydney market. The Calcutta merchant house would get a good percentage of the profits every step of the way, and the plan included China goods being taken to Calcutta on every second trip, and Calcutta goods then being sent to Sydney.

Despite what Hainsworth labels Macarthur's 'quasi-legal initiative', trading in China was not strictly permitted, for this was in breach of the shipping regulations protecting the East India Company. For some time in England, those with an interest in shipping in the South Seas, such as Enderby's Southern Fishery, had been challenging the regulations. As a result, the privileges accorded the East India Company were gradually disappearing, but they would not change completely until 1813. In other words, as the *Harrington* sailed in January 1807, Campbell, with Macarthur in the background, was deliberately planning to trade outside the law as it currently stood.

Unfortunately for Macarthur, Campbell's voyage did not prove the scheme a success. Two of Macarthur's vessels were supposed to meet the *Harrington* in Fiji to load his sandalwood, but they missed the rendezvous. Campbell therefore loaded his own sandalwood and

CHAPTER 5 ↓ *Sydney in Turmoil (13 August 1806 to 31 July 1808)* 265

Davidson sailed to China without Macarthur's trade-goods, where he spent what funds he did have on merchandise. Campbell invested what was now his own profit in China goods and turned the *Harrington* around for Sydney.[22]

Just after the *Harrington* sailed from Port Jackson, Governor Bligh pressed ahead further with his reforms. On 15 February he repeated an earlier order about illicit stills, and added a prohibition against bartering spirits for grain, other goods, or labour.[23] At every step, Bligh's reforms provoked intense opposition.[24] A week before he published these orders, Bligh wrote to the authorities at home.[25] His letter reveals the characteristic energy he had already applied to the problems of the colony, and also his awareness that not everyone was happy with his decisions. In his observations on the abuse of spirits as wages, or as the means of barter, he noted that:

> the barter of Spirits has its Advocates; but only those plead in its favor who are ignorant of its effects, or those very few who have imported a large quantity and gain immensely by it.

Since he had come to the colony with particular instructions in regard to the moral and religious education of the colony, he reported that this had become 'peculiarly the object of my attention', and that 'everything shall be done for the education of the children'. Given the role of the chaplains in achieving both aspects of this goal, he reported that 'all our Artificers [are] employed building the Church of Sydney, which I hope will be completed, or nearly so, in six Months'. His plans were then to complete the church at Parramatta. As these two buildings were being completed, a large building at the Hawkesbury was to be fitted out as a Church. Bligh noted that Marsden had been on his own, and that 'a Mr Fulton' had come from Norfolk Island to stand in for him, just before Bligh had arrived. Although sent out after the 1798 Irish uprising Fulton's 'character has been like a moral, good man, becoming his situation, and he has a wife and three children'. Bligh suggests that clergymen, who should all be married, will be needed at Parramatta, Hawkesbury, Port Dalrymple, and Norfolk Island—presumably assuming Marsden at Sydney. Bligh also suggested that 'four respectable men'—also married—should be sent as schoolteachers, to cope with the nearly four hundred children presently under tuition, and their successors. These suggestions evidently aimed to prepare his superiors to receive Marsden, who was just about to leave for England to recruit several more clergymen, as well as some 'lay settlers' to begin a mission to New Zealand. Marsden departed on 10 February 1807 aboard the *Buffalo*.[26]

The *Buffalo* also carried Philip Gidley King back home, his term as Governor of New South Wales now over:

> At 2 o'clock on Sunday afternoon [8th] His Excellency the late Governor and family finally embarked on board His Majesty's ship *Buffalo* for England, accompanied to the wharf by His Excellency, who expressed the most sensible regret at taking leave; His Honor the Lieutenant Governor and many Officers attended, also to share in the last duties of respect. At half past two the boat left the wharf, and was saluted by His Majesty's ship *Porpoise* as she passed; the following morning His Excellency's Dispatches were on board, and on Tuesday the ship sailed. Governor KING designing to touch at Norfolk Island on his way.[27]

Thomas Moore would have been amongst those 'many Officers' in showing the 'last duties of respect'. Under Governor King, with property and farming interests expanding and being well connected to ship's captains and the new breed of traders, Moore had begun to prosper.

His extra duties also continued to expand. On the day before the *Buffalo* sailed, the Deed of Trust governing William Cox's creditors and Estate expired and a new one was renewed. Cox also sailed for England in February to face charges for his failure—which, apparently, he never did.[28] Under the renewed Deed, Thomas Moore was once again chosen as a Trustee, along with Samuel Marsden and William Wilson. On the eve of sailing for England, Marsden joined Moore in announcing the new arrangements through the *Gazette*, as well as alerting the public that the Trustees had appointed ex-LMS missionary Rowland Hassall 'to collect the outstanding Debts of the Estate, by taking legal steps against those who do not immediately discharge the same'.[29]

Cox sailed without his family. From England the following March, he would send an affadavit to Moore that the late Captain Thomas Rowley proved a debt of £105 sterling as agent to Henry Waterhouse against Cox's Estate, and that Rowley had received a dividend of 15 shillings in the pound.[30] At the end of the month of his sailing, his wife and son added their signatures to a second address of loyalty to Bligh from 546 settlers along the Hawkesbury. The address arose in response to Bligh calling for a muster of arms along the Hawkesbury and an enrolment of those prepared to take them up against 'war and tumult', following another suspected revolt of Irish convicts, but it provide the opportunity for the settlers to express their thanks for Bligh's 'unwearied solicitude over the public welfare at all times […] over such extensive colonies, now rising again from late calamities unto happiness and opulence'.[31] Bligh's own farming concerns were based along the Hawkesbury, and his neighbours now expressed their satisfaction with the measures he was taking to relieve the lot of the smaller farmer.

Bligh's restrictions on the barter of spirits in mid-February,[32] however, caused his popularity to take a dive in other quarters. Although Fulton was still a recent arrival to the colony at this stage, he later recalled how obnoxious this regulation was perceived to be with Macarthur and others who had profited from the spirit trade:[33]

> The settlers were involved in debt, chiefly by their lust of spirituous liquors, and the great quantity of that noxious beverage which had been imported, as it was disposed of to them chiefly by barter. This practice, which had continued from the foundation of the colony, became very pernicious, for it destroyed the health and industry of the people; it cramped their exertions and dejected their spirits by keeping them in poverty, want, and misery. Some people got spirits by permission of former Governors, and in such quantities as those Governors chose, at from eight to ten shillings per gallon, and paid it away at two, three, or four pounds per gallon in barter to workmen, settlers, shopkeepers, butchers, &c. Sometimes they sold it privately by their agents, when scarce, at an enormous price. Therefore, Governor Bligh was determined to put a stop to it, and issued General Orders accordingly.

Fulton singled out Macarthur and his fellows for special attention:

> As John McArthur, formerly a captain in the New South Wales Corps; Thomas Jamison, Principal Surgeon; and other officers,

civil and military, either acquired considerable—some of them great—properties for such infant colony as this, or were enabled to live in a stile much superior to what they could have otherwise expected, by the means of bartering spirits, these General Orders were very disagreeable to them.[34]

Macarthur was already smarting from his loss before Atkins, Fulton and Moore, and had appealed that decision to the Governor. When the General Orders were issued prohibiting barter of spirits, according to Fulton, Macarthur said to him that

> the licensed retailers of spirits […] would have all the money in the colony, and that the soldiers would not suffer it. He said such measures would not be tolerated were there fifty men of spirit in the colony.[35]

While Macarthur was preparing to appeal the Thompson case, the Master Boat Builder had the delight of seeing some of his farming efforts come to maturity. At the end of March, he advertised two of his horses for sale, to be auctioned by David Bevan.

> Two very fine Horses, the property of Mr Thomas Moore, three years and a half old, newly broke in, free from vice, will answer as a pair for a chaise. The purchaser may have three months credit on approved security.[36]

Horses were highly valued in New South Wales at this time. In August 1806, somebody wrote some observations on the stock in NSW. Since these were discovered in the Alnwick Castle library, they were probably sent to the Duke of Northumberland. Since the Duke was his patron, it is likely that the author of the paper was Major George Johnston, who probably sent it home with Governor King on the *Buffalo*.[37] His observations on the horses of the colony are instructive. At the time he wrote there were 552 horses in NSW, originally brought from the Cape or from India, except for Major Johnston's stallion, a gift from the Duke, and William Kent's mare brought on the *Buffalo* in 1802. The colony-bred horses have proved 'far superior to the original stock', with the Cape breed better adapted than the Indian. In view of the immense benefit of the horse to the colony, both in agriculture and general convenience, the real question is whether the colonists will ever think of breeding more than simply what is required by the settlement (that is, as a commercial export). At present their price is high, with a horse fetching between £100 and 150 for a common mare. The price may well drop as more horses are bred, but the present high value encourages the breeding of good horses and great numbers.

Thomas Moore had evidently seen the value of a good horse for many years as he had been accumulating his breeding stock. With his mares coming into breeding age and the 'baby boom' happening on his properties, it was time for him to begin turning a profit. (Figure 37). When his neighbour, merchant Robert Campbell, purchased Moore's two horses at Bevan's auction, he took full advantage of the 3 months credit and paid him on 30 June, £230 for the pair.[38] This one sale brought Moore the equivalent of almost three years' salary as the Master Boat Builder. As three and a half year olds, the two he put up for sale in March 1807 were born in October 1803. From Moore's 1812 List of Mares,[39] we learn that as Moore was selling the two fine horses, he still had fourteen other mares in his possession. In this particularly fertile season, the breeding spell hit a high in 1806, with 6 new mares born before Moore's sale in March 1807: Sloven (of Dirma, 7/1), Venus (of Dutches, 16/2), Juno (of young Bett, 9/8), Dido (of Jane, 20/11), Naital (of Dirma, 25/12), and Eliza (of old Bett, Jan 1807). Since all these mares are still on his list in 1812, the two horses sold were extra, and there may have been more. Moore's horse breeding was beginning to become a profitable venture.

Not only were his farming interests starting to turn lucrative, but he was sufficiently established to expand his business interests further. One of the most prominent of Sydney's traders at this time was the emancipist Simeon Lord. On 28 May 1807, an agreement was made between John Harris and Simeon Lord, which involved a set of Bills of Exchange from Lord drawn upon his London agents, Plummer, Barham and Plummer.[40] Although the details of the agreement made on that day remain obscure, subsequent events show that this money was part of an investment in a speculative venture in which Thomas Moore also became involved. By the end of the year, the three men had purchased a ship by the name of the *Pegasus*.

In August 1807, the *Sydney Gazette* suspended publication due to shortage of paper on which to print. It did not resume until the issue of 15 May 1808, meaning that one of the most turbulent times in Australia's history went without any public news coverage.[41] By the time the *Gazette* went silent, the colony's trouble was already half-brewed.

Still peeved over losing his suit against Thompson, in July 1807 Macarthur appealed the decision to the Governor. In his own later version of events, Macarthur described his appeal being dismissed without him ever uttering a word.[42] Bligh heard only Thompson's evidence and dismissed the case. Some have detected a hint of favouritism here, since Bligh favoured farmers like Thompson over traders, and because Thompson managed Bligh's Hawkesbury estate.[43] According to Evatt, however, Bligh had good legal grounds for the dismissal of the appeal, even if his argument was based more in equity and morality, rather than being strictly a legal argument.[44] Although frequently in the Governor's company before the appeal, after it Macarthur broke off relations with Bligh altogether.

One of the reasons for Macarthur's disappointment arose from the fact that even before the appeal, the *Gazette* published an article which appeared to justify Bligh's decision in the Thompson case. In fairly strong terms, it referred to those who demand 'the specific terms of the contract [...] without any consideration of the excessive loss which must evidently fall upon an unfortunate debtor', asking, 'How conscience can reconcile the requisition'. The article therefore praised Bligh's Orders of 1 November 1806 and Proclamation of 3 January 1807, requiring notes to be paid now in money. It is in the interests of 'every well meaning man' to pay heed to these regulations, recognising they are designed 'to abolish the chicanery to which the inaccuracy of these instruments gave rise. Grain was once considered as a legal tender for a debt contracted, and was therefore one species of colonial currency'. It was clearly dangerous, however, for someone to bind themselves to a certain amount of a commodity for which 'unforeseen events may give even a ten fold value, and Shylock still insists upon his bond'.[45]

The *Gazette* didn't stop at one article. One week later, it contained a brief statement, specifically about wheat notes, and set up an argument in terms of a mathematical problem concerning three parties A, B, and C.[46] It proclaimed it 'an insult to common justice' for the present holder of the note (A), written by another (B), and payable on a third person (C), to demand a greater consideration on the note than they themselves received at the time they gained it. That is, if the note was used by B to pay for goods from A at the value of 8s a bushel, how is it right for A to retain the note until the price of wheat increases fivefold in order to demand a higher value from C? By what principle of equity can this possibly be done?

The parallels with Macarthur's case justify the offence that he felt at the statements made in these two articles, especially since he suspected the articles flagged that his appeal may be a foregone conclusion. Under the pseudonym 'an occultist', Macarthur replied to the *Gazette* article, to put the alternative case.[47] If the price of wheat fell, would the drawer of the note (C) be justified in demanding the difference in value from either A or B? If not (as he assumes the answer to be), then 'it appears that the literal tenor of every engagement ought to be fulfilled, and that specific contracts must be sacred and binding'. He added a 'P.S.' which took issue with the 'name-calling' found in the first *Gazette* article. The publisher then added his reply.

According to Atkinson, this case helped the gap between the townsfolk and Macarthur to close. 'The argument about Thompson's promissory note helped to prove that, under the current regime, Macarthur had much in common with other managers of capital'.[48] Thus, despite the earlier congratulatory addresses, one year into his Governorship, Bligh had become alienated from some very influential people.

A second court action that apparently moved Macarthur towards the 'Rum Rebellion' occurred in the same month as Macarthur's appeal against the Thompson matter. In July 1807, D'Arcy Wentworth, Assistant Surgeon at Parramatta, faced a court martial before George Johnston and Richard Atkins, for disobeying Captain Abbott's orders to admit two convicts into the hospital. Wentworth used his defence to publicly draw Bligh's name into the dispute, and apparently deliberately so, with no objection from the prosecutor (Abbott). Macarthur was in the background and, according to Evatt, the trial has the appearance of a collusive proceeding. Wentworth was found guilty and sentenced to a public reprimand, which Bligh duly administered. He was ordered back to work, but on 25 July, Bligh suspended him, until His Majesty's pleasure was known. Bligh had asked Atkins to investigate Wentworth's use of prisoners assigned to the hospital to work his own farm, and, that found, the suspension was duly and quite legally applied. Bligh's actions towards Wentworth, however, were later paraded as an example of Bligh's tyranny. The kind of tyranny that justified his removal from power.[49]

Having already fallen foul of Macarthur, in August 1807 the Governor received a letter from merchants Lord, Kable and Underwood, which he deemed to be 'couched in improper terms'. In response, he ordered their imprisonment for one calendar month.[50] By October Lieutenant Minchin, expecting soon to be dismissed from his post as Engineer, wrote to P.G. King 'from this unhappy place'. Turning the March 1806 floods into metaphor, he claimed that:

> a deluge worse than that of the Hawkesbury has since swept off every path to that industry and happiness which you had long endeavoured to nurture. You will here, my dear sir, say we always grumbled; and you will say so with justice; but we grumbled then without probably being able to describe the reason, and we feel now so severely oppressed that our disease is but too visible for one mistaking where the pain lays. I can only say, as an individual, I was happy under your government and I am now unhappy; and, if a military officer might be allowed to use the words "tyranny" and "oppression", I would tell you that until now I never experienced their weight.[51]

As Minchin wrote, Macarthur was preparing for another court case —the third action of the five that moved Macarthur closer to overthrowing Bligh. On 24 October he brought a suit against Robert Campbell, junior, the nephew of Thomas and Rachel Moore's next-door neighbour in the Rocks, Naval Officer Robert Campbell.[52] Abbott and Macarthur had imported two stills, despite them now being illegal equipment in New South Wales. Campbell (senior) permitted them to be offloaded to the Government stores, only so they could then be re-exported. Ex-Naval Officer John Harris, without any authority then permitted Macarthur to take the two boilers from the store, purportedly to remove medicines that had been packed inside. Bligh had ordered the boilers returned and Campbell junior, acting on instructions from his uncle (and originating from the Governor), had taken them from Macarthur. Macarthur objected that because the younger Campbell had no written warrant and gave no written receipt, this was an unlawful seizure of his property—even though these facts are 'entirely devoid of any legal significance'. All the relevant facts were proved in court. Macarthur's speech was 'an illogical and inflammatory speech' and, from a legal standpoint, simply 'rhetorical nonsense'. For some reason, however, Judge-Advocate Atkins, who had the deciding vote, 'was deceived or intimidated by Macarthur's invective', out of 'weakness' or 'his ignorance of the law', and decided in his favour. Despite its 'absence of legal backing', Macarthur's speech has great importance in the lead-up to the 1808 rebellion. In his rhetoric, he seized the higher ground. Because British law protects British subjects, this ought to prevent 'his property [being] wrested from him' for no other reason than 'that it was the Governor's order'. According to Evatt, his speech shows not only 'his determination to secure Bligh's humiliation', but also (because of its 'successful' outcome) that 'his skilful advocacy in court can be used, not only to persuade Atkins, but to inflame all the inhabitants against Bligh. The struggle between Macarthur and Bligh thus becomes more intense'.

Surgeon and ex-Naval Officer Harris, one of the witnesses in the case, wrote to King the day after Macarthur's victory—perhaps with new boldness? He claimed that under Bligh 'anything that bears the name of King is sufficient to dam the person that uses it'. Harris is openly contemptuous of the new Governor, who had dismissed him as Naval Officer and magistrate in May 1807:[53] 'But this I know: I don't care a dam for him, his name, or interest. He is at best a tyrannical villain'. He complained of Bligh's strictures on the supply of spirits; his depletion of the Government herds; his trial of the United Irishmen 'O'Dwyer, Burn, Burke, and Merney'; the unprecedented number of people executed under his reign; the imprisonment of Lord, Kable and Underwood; his displays of 'temper', such as when he abused some soldiers in church when he thought they had laughed at him, or when he abused some prisoners working in his garden; and some of his actions in regard to the military, by which he had fallen out with George Johnston. Harris names Campbell, Palmer, Lutterell, Gore, Devine, and Crossley as 'the Governor's friends' and 'consequently your enemies'.[54] To his credit, Ex.-Governor King urged those in England to exercise great caution in dealing with complaints about Bligh originating from Sydney, suggesting that they may have arisen from personal disappointments and antipathies.[55]

At about the same time Harris was dashing off his poison to King, Governor Bligh penned his progress report to his superiors, revealing that further tensions were bubbling away in the background. Arthur Phillip had left a memorandum suggesting that no part of the town of Sydney should be leased away, for it should always be considered the property of the Government. In June 1801, however, Governor King had permitted leases granted for five years. After his arrival Bligh discovered that in January 1806 on the eve of his departure, King had renewed some leases for fourteen years, and they included land that was 'wanted for Government purposes'. Macarthur and Lucas had leases on land belonging to the church; Blaxcell a portion of the Government Lumber-yard; Johnston a garden area next to the gaol, which could have been useful for the prisoners.[56]

In the same October letter that John Harris poured out his contempt of Bligh to ex-Governor King, he also expressed his great frustration at more Spanish prizes arriving in Sydney Cove. In April 1807, HM Frigate, *Marquis Cornwallis* had arrived in Sydney from Madras,[57] under the command of Captain Charles James Johnston, 'couzen to the Major'—'the finest frigate I ever beheld'.[58] After she sailed on 7 June for the coast of Peru, she began taking prizes of war and gaining great riches—she had taken a total of fifteen by the time she sent three in to Sydney.

It turned out that the first of the HMS *Cornwallis* prizes to reach Sydney was actually the third taken —the first two (the *Rosslla* and *Atlantic*) never arrived. Apparently writing on 1 October, Harris reported that a signal was made that morning when the strange ship came in view, and he soon found himself with a responsibility that he found distasteful:

> The vessels were consigned to me and [the] Governor's secretary. [...] This ship is laden with spirits, rice, and sugar—all in great demand. [...] The ship that is now coming in is called the *Pegasus*. Dam the prizes. I want to have nothing to do with them under such a Governor. I had enough of the last. [...][59]

The prize that had created a bitter taste in the Surgeon's mouth was the *Santa Anna*. On 28 December 1806 it was sold at auction under Governor Bligh's promise that the purchaser would be permitted to send her to China or India to procure goods. After spirited bidding it was sold to Simeon Lord for £3,200, which was 'a very high price for a ship condemned as a prize; but it was really the permit to go to China which was at auction'. Isaac Nichols, who did the bidding for Lord, later revealed that he had instructions to go no higher than £2,000, but then Surgeon Harris, one of the prize agents, announced that the sale included the privilege to go to China. Robert Campbell, who suggested this idea to Bligh in the first place, bid up to £3,000, but was then outbid by Lord's money. At that point, according to Hainsworth:

> doubtless angry that Campbell's bid had failed (for it had probably been expected that nobody would bid higher), and finding the purchasers had to spend weeks repairing the *Santa Anna*, [the Governor] seized on this as a pretext of withdrawing the privilege and granting it to Campbell's newly built brig *Perserverance*.[60]

Despite his reluctance about prizes, Harris would soon have a great deal more to do with this particular prize than he may have imagined.

The *Pegasus* entered Port Jackson on 12 November 1807, under the charge of Captain Thomas Graham as prize master.[61] She was laden with 163 bags of sugar, 195 bags of rice, 2 coils of cordage, 12 hides, 301 jars and 5 casks of spirits (4,970 gallons). She paid £2.0.6 entry fees, 16.19.0 wharfage, and 325.10.0 duties, a total of £344.9.6 (£18.19.6 to the Orphan Fund; £325.10.0 to the Jail Fund).[62] This was the largest payment made by any of the ships entering in the last six months of the year.

Unfortunately, because the *Sydney Gazette* was not being printed in this period, there is no newspaper to record what happened to the

Pegasus next. Following usual procedure, she would have been condemned as a prize and both she and her goods sold. When the *Gazette* recommenced publication on 15 May 1808, it reported at that stage that the owner of the *Pegasus* was Thomas Moore, also noting that he had bought her from the person to whom she was initially sold.

As for the identity of this first owner, Simeon Lord would be a good guess, even if only because he had bought all other prizes to date.[63] But there is more to the story. The documents relating to the *Pegasus* have actually survived amongst Moore's personal papers, and these show that Lord never gave up his interest in the ship. The *Pegasus* was a three-way venture between Lord, Harris, and Thomas Moore. Moore was the ship's husband, or the 'husband-owner', which meant that he looked after the running of the ship, the paying of the crew, and such-like. Moore had definitely become involved with her by 17 April, since by then was already paying her bills.[64]

Buying into a commercial venture such as a ship indicates that Moore must have become fairly well established by now.[65] Drawing a Government salary (£91.5.0 p.a.), while being fed off the stores as one of the civil officers certainly must have given him a good start, even before his trading and farming concerns. In September Thomas Moore apparently purchased William Raven's High Street lease next door to White's, thus expanding the potential of this centrally located piece of property that would be associated with his name for over a century. By 31 October 1807, Thomas Moore had a total of 1920 acres, 1703 ½ under pasture, 200 fallow, 3 ½ orchard, ½ an acre of potatoes, 1 acre of oats, 6 of wheat and 5 ½ of maize. He had one stallion and five mares; 2 bulls, 33 cows, and 20 oxen; 1 hog, 7 sows; 12 bushels of wheat in hand and 100 of maize; he and Rachel were victualled, as was one convict, and he had four more not victualled from the stores.[66] By year's end his house had not been repaired, although the dockyard had been, and the new church was almost finished and awaiting its first parson.[67]

When Samuel Marsden arrived in England, he quickly set to the task of finding some additional clergymen and schoolmasters. On 21 November 1807, he wrote to Under-Secretary Cooke,[68] painting a picture of the deplorable state of morality in NSW, which held out little hope for the rising generation unless some intervention occurred. 'Part of this work, it is evident, falls as an incumbent duty on His Majesty's Government at Home, part on the Governors and magistracy in the colony, and a great part on the clergy and schoolmasters who may be appointed to this important employment'. He then takes the liberty to outline the number of clergymen and schoolteachers he feels are required, taking care to stress that the qualities required of them are very different to what is required in England. 'Next to health, personal piety and an earnest desire to communicate Christian knowledge is necessary; and if he does not possess these he may as well stay at home, for no real good can be effected by him'. When Spencer Perceval wrote in support of similar requests from Bligh, he stated that on the clergymen and schoolteachers 'the future hopes of the colony must depend; and no reasonable expence which may be carefully applied to obtain and secure them ought to be spared'.[69] As the end of the year reports in NSW noted the church was almost finished, Lord Castlereagh was writing from England to assure Bligh that something was being done—and urgently:

> Mr Marsden has represented the religious state of the colony and laid it also before the Archbishop of Canterbury; and I hope means will be found to induce a sufficient number of clergymen to proceed to New South Wales by the next ship, or when Mr Marsden returns.[70]

At the same time in England, ex-Governor King was still trumpeting Thomas Moore's praise of the NSW timber, and the story of his long-unfinished ship on the stocks in the dockyard was still doing the rounds, as 'a farther proof of the goodness' of the NSW timber. 'For want of shipwrights', it was left in frame when Hunter returned home. Composed of the various woods of NSW, 'the frame was up seven years, exposed to all weathers, and when taken down to put into smaller vessels the whole was perfectly sound and good, nor could the treenails be drove out'.[71] (Plates 26, 27, 28).

December 1807 brought the next legal altercation that moved Macarthur closer to the rebellion. At the end of June, while he was preparing for his appeal in the Thompson matter, Macarthur's schooner *Parramatta* had cleared Sydney for the South Seas. On 28 June, the Judge-Advocate placed a public notice in the *Sydney Gazette* declaring that John Hoare, a convict serving a life sentence, had escaped the Government gaol gang and probably fled the colony on the *Parramatta*.[72] Later, evidence that came to hand from Tahiti confirmed this report and also revealed that Hoare had been treated as well as any passenger by Captain Glenn, and then transhipped at Tahiti for an American vessel to make good his further escape.[73]

When Glenn brought the vessel back into Sydney in December, her bond was forfeited for taking a convict out of the colony. As a consequence, on the 7th Macarthur wrote to Glenn telling him that he had abandoned the vessel. On the 14th Glenn and his crew went on shore, contrary to regulations, claiming Macarthur's action as their justification, as they had not been fed since. Bligh ordered an investigation, Richard Atkins summoned Macarthur to Sydney to explain the situation, and Macarthur replied defiantly. Atkins therefore issued a warrant, but when Francis Oakes attempted to serve it, Macarthur gave him a written and insulting letter for those who issued the warrant, and added some verbal insults to boot. Evatt notes that Macarthur's defiance of the warrant, 'was the starting point of an entirely new legal contest which turned out to be of crucial significance'.[74]

On 16 December, Macarthur was arrested, charged with Sedition.[75] The charge was on three counts: 1) his illegal importation of a still; the removal of the still; and the action of complaint against Robert Campbell junior; not for a bona fide purpose but for the seditious purpose of assembling a crowd before which he could libel the Governor, which he had then proceeded to do; 2) with a similar seditious purpose, he wrote the letter abandoning the *Parramatta*, thus creating disorder by forcing the crew to break the law, and he then wrote a defamatory letter to the authorities, spoke seditious words to Oakes, and 3) actually documented them in writing, all with the purpose of inflaming opposition to the Governor.[76] On 17 December, Macarthur appeared before a Bench of Magistrates, including Richard Atkins, Major Johnston, Captain Abbott and Robert Campbell, the Naval Officer. Macarthur immediately objected to Campbell because of their history, but even with Campbell removed, the magistrates committed him to trial before a Criminal Court, although granting him bail.

Evatt argues that at this stage Macarthur was in danger, and if he

CHAPTER 5 ⚓ *Sydney in Turmoil (13 August 1806 to 31 July 1808)* 279

was to achieve his own safety and the overthrow of Bligh, he had to secure unity amongst the officers—not an easy task, given their track record before and after the rebellion! But in the next six weeks, not only did he achieve this, but he also 'so arranged affairs that he procured officers of the regiment to take the initiative against Bligh, and finally to arrest and supplant him'.[77]

He did this by utilising two manoeuvres. Firstly, even though he was on bail to appear before Richard Atkins, he presented a bill drawn by Atkins on 4 February 1793 for £29 6s, but calculated by Macarthur to now amount to £82 9s 5d. Atkins promised to pay, but suggested that, given Macarthur was committed for trial on 25 January, it was not a present object for discussion. On 29 December Macarthur wrote to Bligh, intimating that Atkins withholding his money was 'a sort of precursor of a more severe vengeance that he is meditating at this threatened trial'. Macarthur also added a thinly-veiled threat that if Bligh didn't give him a hearing before a 'disinterested tribunal', then he would have to send the matter to the Secretary of State for the Colonies.[78] And so, on Evatt's reading of the events, by 12 January 1808 Macarthur is 'endeavouring to convert a claim for debt against Atkins into a grand cause of complaint against the Governor', that is, he 'is engaged in the deliberate manufacture of a cause for grievance against both the Governor and Atkins'.[79] At about this time Macarthur took up residence in Sydney, and Captain Abbott took Kemp's place at Sydney. Bligh thought this latter move was an attempt to stack the magistracy at Sydney, but he thwarted this by not retaining Abbott's services as a magistrate after he moved.

1808

Already there were plans in England to recall Bligh. His wife Elizabeth wrote to Banks on 1 February 1808, noting that the same day the *Morning Herald* had announced his recall, and asking Banks has this been decided?[80] But by the time she asked the question in England, it would already be over for her husband in Australia.

On the first day of January 1808, Thomas Moore added his signature to that of some 830 persons to yet another Address from the settlers to Governor Bligh.[81] Andrew Thompson was very active in obtaining signatures. These 'free and principal proprietors of landed property' began by expressing their gratitude for 'the manifold, great, and essential blessings and benefits we freely continue to enjoy from your Excellency's arduous, just, determined, and salutary government over us, happily evinced by the present plenteous and flourishing state of this country, rapidly growing in population, opulence, and all improvements calculate by a wise and patriotic government to make a large colony of people happy and rich in all their internal resources'. The Address had two concerns to lay before their Governor, being assured that he would do anything in his power for the welfare of the colony. The signatories humbly solicited him, should he deem it not improper, 'to make representation to His Majesty in Council that he might be graciously pleased to allow such privilege of trade to their country vessels and themselves as other colonies have, and that the law might be administered by trial by jury of the people, as in England'. New South Wales may have begun as 'a small colony of prisoners planted on these shores', but it was now time for it to move towards the kind of freedoms enjoyed in the motherland: free trade and trial by jury.[82] Across the years to come, Thomas Moore would add his signature to more documents seeking trial by jury. Right at the present time, however, he was probably more interested in free trade.

But as Andrew Thompson and the others showed their support of the Governor, while seeking positive change within the system, Bligh's opponents were about to use the system to overturn it.

On Monday 25 January 1808, Judge-Advocate Atkins swore in six officers of the New South Wales Corps (Captain A.F. Kemp, and Lieutenants W. Moore, W. Minchin, J. Brabyn, T. Laycock and W. Lawson) as a Criminal Court to hear charges against their former colleague in the Corps, John Macarthur. Once the swearing in was done, Macarthur immediately protested against Atkins sitting as judge.[83] The reason for his protest of Atkins' old promissory note now becomes clear.

At this point, Macarthur's second manoeuvre to secure a united opposition occurred. It may look like a simple and unfortunate coincidence that on the 13 January, while Macarthur was in the midst of a trial for sedition, Surveyor Grimes chose to inform Macarthur that his leasehold near the Church was required, and that he needed to choose another.[84] But this was no coincidence. Since Grimes was a close associate of Macarthur, it may have been perfectly orchestrated in order 'to create a grievance against Bligh which would more closely affect the military officers and their associates, whose assistance would soon be necessary'.[85] Bligh had already begun to move on King's 'midnight leases', offering exchange leases for the ones he wanted for Government. Macarthur responded to Grimes' request by selecting a portion of the Government wharf reserve, which was unleasable and so it was refused him. Macarthur then refused to select any other grant, begging leave to retain the one next to the church, which King had already granted him. He then assembled a gang of men from the Corps and ordered them to fence the land around the disputed lease. The excitement which spread through the town at Macarthur's defiance of the Governor's order, was further inflamed when Bligh ordered the constables to pull down the fence posts. By involving the soldiers in this action, Macarthur both conspired and managed 'to create the united anti-Bligh front' shortly before his trial. This unity was displayed and celebrated at a mess dinner on 24 January, the evening before the trial. Macarthur did not attend, establishing a good alibi by walking in the most prominent part of the town. The rest of the Corps were there, however, including the six officers who had been nominated to sit with Atkins on the panel the next day, and Major George Johnston—the perfect setting for a military-led rebellion to be conspired.

As soon as the trial began come morning, Macarthur protested Atkins sitting as his Judge, listing six objections and citing legal authorities for each. Following his objections and authorities, Macarthur addressed the members of the Court in grandiose terms, in the hearing of, according to Atkins' later testimony, 'one thousand persons or more assembled in the Court'.[86]

> You have the eyes of an anxious public upon you, trembling for the safety of their *property*, their *liberty*, and their *lives*. To you has fallen the lot of deciding a point which perhaps involves the happiness or misery of millions yet unborn. I conjure you in the name of Almighty God, in whose presence you stand, to consider the *inestimable value* of the precious deposit with which you are now entrusted.

He concluded by expressing confidence in his former colleagues: 'it is to the officers of the New South Wales Corps that the administration of justice is committed; and who that is just has anything to fear?'

After hearing the protest, the six officers on the Court considered the grounds of his objection valid, and Atkins was therefore not sworn in. At 11.25 a.m. they wrote to Bligh requesting him to 'determine on the propriety of appointing another Judge-Advocate' and also praying the Governor's protection from Atkins, who they claimed to have grossly insulted and threatened them. At 12.30 Bligh replied that there is no Court without the Judge-Advocate, that he had a right to deal with someone who insulted him in that context, and there was no other course except for the Governor to direct that he take his seat and act according to his Letters Patent. The officers requested his reconsideration, not being able in all conscience to sit with Atkins as Judge-Advocate in view of the thirteen or fourteen years of enmity that existed between the two men. At 2:15 Bligh requested Atkins' papers, and the document read by Macarthur, but the officers did not feel able to give them to any person unless another Judge-Advocate was appointed for the trial. At 3:30 they wrote again to Bligh, enclosing a deposition from Macarthur stating that Atkins had issued a warrant for his arrest for exercising his lawful right to issue a challenge against him, and requesting the Governor's protection of Macarthur against Atkins. At 3:45 Bligh issued a demand that the officers put in writing whether they will send the papers already requested, and repeated his statement that there is no Court without the Judge-Advocate. At 4 p.m. Macarthur was remanded to his former bail and Provost-Marshal, William Gore, was acquainted with the facts. Gore then deposed before a bench of magistrates (Atkins, T. Arndell, R. Campbell and J. Palmer) that Macarthur was not in custody, and he therefore obtained an escape warrant. At 5 p.m. the six officers adjourned the case until 10 o'clock the following day, and at the same time Bligh received their reply saying that they were willing to send certified copies of the papers, but the originals they would only deliver to another Judge-Advocate appointed for the trial. At 5:30 Bligh wrote to Major George Johnston requesting him to see him without delay. To end the extraordinary events of 25 January, Bligh received Johnston's reply, informing the Governor that he could not come, because he was dangerously ill.[87]

At 10 a.m. the next day, when the six officers adjourned the court

CHAPTER 5 ↓ *Sydney in Turmoil (13 August 1806 to 31 July 1808)* 283

Macarthur did not appear. They therefore summoned his sureties, Garnham Blaxcell and Nicholas Bayly, who testified that Macarthur had been delivered by the court into their custody, but some constables had wrested him away holding Gore's warrant, and that this warrant was based upon false testimony (ie that Macarthur had broken bail). Bayly and Blaxcell also testified that Macarthur was in danger in the gaol, because of the particular constable then on duty, and they requested that the court restore Macarthur to their custody. Enclosing these depositions, along with a copy of Macarthur's address from the day before, the officers wrote to Bligh saying that their oath obliged them to proceed with the trial of Macarthur and therefore begging His Excellency to appoint an impartial person to act as Judge-Advocate. They also declared the magistrate's decision based on Gore's false testimony to be illegal and threatening to subvert the legal authority of the Court of Civil Jurisdiction, and requested the Governor to 'discontinue such magisterial proceedings, pregnant with the most serious consequences to the community at large', and to take measures to restore John Macarthur to his former bail, so that the court might proceed with his trial.[88] Bligh gave them no reply, and at 3 p.m. the court adjourned 'until His Excellency's pleasure is known'.

Atkins, for his part, wrote to Bligh explaining his version of the events of the day before. Macarthur had been charged with 'seditious practices against His Majesty, his Crown, and dignity', arrested and bailed to penalty of £1,000. Atkins had sworn the officers in, but as he was about to be sworn in Macarthur protested. Atkins told him he could not object, for there was no court without the Judge-Advocate, but Captain Kemp declared that he was no more than a juryman and could or should be objected to and requested Macarthur to continue. Atkins said he then heard 'a great torrent of threats and abusive language' read by Macarthur, particularly citing the grandiose words with which he addressed the officers in the ears of the thousand odd people in the court-room. Fearful of what might happen, Atkins tried to dismiss the court and clear the court-room, but Kemp and the others called them back in, declaring 'we are a Court', and granting Macarthur a protective detail from the soldiers. Atkins further charged that the six officers had dined with Macarthur the day before the trial—

although later at the Court-Martial of Major Johnston, Bligh denied that this was true. It was Macarthur's son who was present, not him. As a result of Atkins' letter, Bligh sent a circular letter to each of the six officers, obliging them to present themselves before him on the following day at 9 a.m., also summoning the magistrates to attend, and writing to Major Johnston to inform him of Atkins' charges against the officers.[89] Little did he realise what would have come to pass by then!

Major Johnston ordered the Gaol keeper to surrender Macarthur into the custody of Blaxcell and Bayly, which he did. Shortly thereafter a requisition was sent to Major Johnston. It spoke of 'the present alarming state of this colony, in which every man's property, liberty, and life is endangered'. It therefore requested Johnston to put Governor Bligh under arrest and to assume command of the colony. Johnston obliged, proclaiming martial law and requesting Bligh to relinquish his command.

Figure 42: In the first column of the second page of the Arrest requisition of 26 January 1808 Moore's signature is clear in ninth position.

CHAPTER 5 ↓ *Sydney in Turmoil (13 August 1806 to 31 July 1808)* 285

The first signatory immediately under the letter of request was Macarthur, followed by John Blaxland, James Mileham, Simeon Lord, and Gregory Blaxland. The document has survived and in its present form, there are more pages of signatures, amounting to about over one hundred people.[90] On the second page, in ninth position, the signature of Mr Thomas Moore is unmistakeable.[91] (Figure 42).

What is the significance of Moore's signature being on the requisition to Johnston to arrest the King's Governor? Does his signature implicate him in some way? Was Moore amongst the rebels? These questions are not easy to answer.

After Macarthur was released from the gaol, he went to the barracks, where a large group of soldiers and others had assembled. Evidence given at Johnston's 1811 Court Martial indicated that Moore was certainly at the barracks that night, but some hesitation about whether he signed the address on the spot. This came out when Macarthur was cross-examined by a member of the Court about which civil officers were present, and where, on the night of the arrest:[92]

Member:	Was there a Mr Moore on the establishment?
Macarthur:	Yes; he was at the barracks.
Member:	What is Moore?
Macarthur:	He is master builder.
Member:	Did he sign the address?
Macarthur:	I think he did.

In the context of this examination, Moore being 'at the barracks' means that he was there amongst the assembly after Macarthur was released from gaol, where the requisition was written and signed, but he was not amongst those who marched to Government house, and neither was he at Government House when the arrest took place.

According to Macarthur's evidence, however, Moore was one of those behind the arrest:[93]

Member:	Now when you come to those of the magistrates and civil officers who recommended the arrest, tell us what their names are.

> Macarthur: There was the principal surgeon, Mr Jamieson; the surveyor-general, Mr Grimes; the principal assistant surgeon, Mr D'Arcy Wentworth; Mr Mileham, another assistant surgeon; and Mr Moore, the master builder; including, I believe, the whole of the civil establishment of the colony, except Mr Palmer, Mr Williamson, Mr Atkins, and Mr Gore.

Clearly Moore was present at the barracks in his capacity as one of the Civil Officers. But what of his signature? And what of Macarthur's claim that he was amongst those recommending the arrest?

At Johnston's trial (1811), in reply to Johnston's question whether solicitation was used to induce people to sign the address, Macarthur claimed: 'Signed spontaneously; I never heard of any solicitation whatever'. When a member of the court asked him if he was the principle adviser to Johnston, he denied it, saying that the revolution had been urged upon Johnston before he was released from gaol. He also claimed that he could not recall when he heard that Johnston had written to the Governor, and he 'never saw the letter until after the Governor's arrest'—perhaps 'a week or two after it was sent'.[94] But, despite Macarthur's protestations, it gradually came out that many of those who signed the requisition did not do so 'spontaneously', and many of them did not even sign it until after the Governor had already been arrested.

There were other addresses also signed under compulsion—on both sides of the political fence.

On 8 March an address was given to Johnston from 210 officials and inhabitants,[95] confessing that 'some of us have unwarily signed an address to [Gov. Bligh, i.e. that of 1 January], praying his interest with the King-in-Council to obtain free trade and trial by jury'. Evidently not wanting the rebels to get the wrong idea, the signatories claimed that the complimentary portion of the address was what he *ought* to be, rather than what he *was*. They claimed they were ignorant of the devices of the framers of that address, who used the two issues to elicit compliments to Bligh from the inhabitants, and it is only recently that they have learned of the impropriety of his conduct and the 'dangerous precipice' upon which they stood.

In regard to that of 30 January from the Settlers to Johnston, Thomas Arndell complained that the rebels 'proceeded, by the terror of military execution, to extort from [Bligh's] friends something on which they might found more plausible charges to palliate the enormity of their wickedness. By this terror I was, through weakness, induced to sign a paper which my heart and better judgment abhorred'.[96] At Johnston's court martial, a copy of this address was put in, but only four of 280 names were deemed to be original (including Arndell's).[97]

Given the significance of what the document asked for, signatures on the arrest requisition were particularly important, for the rebels claimed that they acted on behalf of many in the colony. Many found themselves signing 'at the point of the bayonet'. The methods of gaining signatures were protested in an Address from the Settlers (mostly along the Hawkesbury) to Lieut.-Gov. Paterson, written on 18 April. It spoke out 'against the means adopted to obtain signatures to a paper carried round to sanction what was done on [26 January]—threatening individuals with imprisonment; to be sent out of the colony by the first ships, and that they would be marked men who refused to sign it'.[98] At the end of the year, Commissary Palmer singled out Isaac Nichols as being 'particularly active at the time of the deposing Your Excellency, and by Subtile (sic) Artifice procuring Signatures to the address handed about by the rebellious party'.[99]

At Johnston's court martial, evidence was produced that John Blaxland (second on the list) signed before the arrest, but Charles Grimes (tenth on the list) signed it afterwards. In examining Captain Abbott, the Court asked him to identify many of those on the requisition by name, including Moore:

Court: Thomas Moore, Who is he?

Abbott: A very respectable man; he is master builder, and now a Magistrate of Sydney.[100]

We should note that, on this counting, Moore was the fourteenth signature.

In April, as the settlers wrote to Paterson, Bligh wrote a similar account to his superiors at home (although his letter was not actually sent until later). Despite the arrest warrant including reference to 'the respectable inhabitants of Sydney':[101]

> the fact is, that when the troops marched from the barracks not more than six or seven names had been affixed to the paper which exhorted them to commit this crime; while the whole of those who subscribed their names afterwards declare they did it at the point of the bayonet, which declaration Wentworth made three days afterwards. Constables were sent to that part of the town called the Rocks, and the other parts, to drive people to subscribe their names to this paper to Major Johnston, after the act of rebellion was done; and emissaries were sent with papers through the interior of the colony for the same purpose.

If Wentworth, who is seventh on the second page of the document, signed three days after the event, then this strongly indicates that Thomas Moore, who is in ninth position (separated by T. Laycock) and also a resident of the Rocks, must have also signed on or after the third day. A later note from Bligh in the margin reports that Harris had since declared to Bligh's secretary, to Fulton and to Palmer, that not one name was affixed at the time of the arrest. In 1811 at the trial of Johnston, it came out that the majority of the signatures were obtained after the event. It seems clear that many of those who signed did so 'more to keep favour with the rebel Government than for any other reason'.[102]

Bligh's April letter provides a copy of the arrest requisition, which lists the signatories in two columns as follows:

J. Macarthur	T. Moore
J. Blaxland	T. Laycock
J. Mileham	J. Gowen
S. Lord	N. Devine
G. Blaxland	W. Baker
D. Wentworth	J. Wilshire
N. Bayly	

The first five in the first column follow the order exactly of those

CHAPTER 5 ⚓ *Sydney in Turmoil (13 August 1806 to 31 July 1808)* 289

who signed on page one of the document. The rest of the names, however, do not follow the order of the second page, which may indicate that Bligh has particularly singled these men out for some reason.[103] Why was Thomas Moore the top of this second column? Did Bligh have a particular grievance against him at this time?

Or to put the question the other way around, did Moore have any cause for grievance against Bligh? Was he one of those who signed reluctantly, or was he (as Macarthur claimed) behind the arrest, justifying Bligh singling him out as being, not only amongst the rebels, but a rebel himself?

Certainly some of those on the arrest requisition, besides Macarthur himself, were aggrieved at the Governor. According to Fulton, the recent arrivals John and Gregory Blaxland and Doctor Robert Townson were 'discontented by those who had been long in the colony, so that all their minds were in a state of preparation to be worked upon by any factious and discontented leader who had address enough to deceive them and manage them for his own ambitious purposes'. In Fulton's opinion, Macarthur and Bayly (who was ex-NSW Corps, probably dismissed by Governor King) provided exactly that kind of leadership.[104] At Johnston's trial, Anthony Fenn Kemp suggested that Eber Bunker (Moore's friend and colleague) had the same grievance as the Blaxlands. Having brought out his family to NSW, Bligh refused to recognise the Secretary of State's requests on his behalf.[105] But what about Thomas Moore: had Bligh upset him somehow?

According to the evidence at the court martial, one of the biggest causes for concern in Sydney was Bligh's action against King's 'midnight leases', and this formed 'a principal feature of the Defence of Col. Johnston'.[106] Atkins claimed it was the main reason for dissatisfaction with Bligh's governance. Some houses, which had been constructed in the Government domain behind Government House, were pulled down (but probably less than five). Bligh's evidence showed that two of the people concerned had happily taken an alternative grant, and another was negotiating in this direction, before being interrupted by the rebellion. But several witnesses testified to a generalised hysteria amongst the soldiers and other townsfolk that Bligh might move on their house next! It was also widely rumoured that Bligh prohibited several people building on their own leaseholds, but hard examples were in short supply amongst the evidence at the court martial, and the one everyone seemed to be talking about was that of John Macarthur—naturally enough, given the very public confrontation he had provoked.[107]

It is in this context that a potential grievance against Bligh arises for Thomas Moore. In Captain (by 1811, Major) Abbott's evidence, he claimed three people were prevented from building on their leasehold, namely, John Macarthur, Simeon Lord, and Thomas Moore:[108]

Court:	Can you name the leaseholders whom you state to have been forbidden to build on their own ground?
Abbott:	Yes.
Court:	Who?
Abbott:	Mr Moore, the builder, told me that Gov. Bligh had refused him.
Court:	Did he show you any order from Gov. Bligh?
Abbott:	No, he did not; it was in conversation.

It is difficult to know what might lie behind this statement from Abbott. If there was any truth to the rumour, Bligh's threat would not have been against the house in which Thomas and Rachel lived at the end of High Street. This was a Government house supplied Moore as Master Boat Builder, and so presumably if there were problems, then Bligh could simply act. Abbott's rumour would have to concern Moore's town lease, the house in which the Moores used to live on the corner of Market Square, but which, by 1808, they rented out to others. Originally John White's lease, it was handed over to his son Andrew on 1 January 1806, and for fourteen years—thus making it one of those 'midnight leases' that caused Bligh some upset.[109]

But Abbott's claim seems most suspect. The 'lease and house' issue was presented in evidence many times at the trial, but Abbott was the only person who mentioned Mr Moore's supposed troubles. When cross-examined, Abbott himself seemed to forget about Moore, for he never came back to Moore's lease and he seems to be clear that the alarm in the community was created by the altercation over Macarthur's lease. Nobody else, including the significant players Bligh, Johnston, John Blaxland, A.F. Kemp, or Macarthur mentioned Moore in connection with a lease, and, perhaps most significantly, the Surveyor General Charles Grimes—who was intimately involved in the house and lease issue—mentioned both Lord and Macarthur as being prevented from building on their lease, but then declared that there was no other case to his knowledge.[110] Whatever Abbott may have heard Moore saying, there does not appear to be a provable grievance against Bligh behind this rumour.

On 27 January 1808, Johnston issued a proclamation that 'the public peace being happily and, I trust in Almighty God, permanently established, I hereby proclaim the cessation of martial law'. It then continued the grandiose rhetoric that was strangely reminiscent of that heard at Macarthur's trial, declaring that

> In future no Man shall have just cause to complain of Violence, Injustice, or Oppression; No free Man shall be taken, imprisoned, or deprived of his House, Land, or Liberty, but by the Law; Justice shall be impartially administered, without regard to or respect of Persons; And every Man shall enjoy the Fruits of his Industry in Security.[111]

The same day the officers and settlers signed an address to Major Johnston for his 'manly and honorable interposition to rescue us from an order of things that threatened the destruction of all which men can hold dear'. At Johnston's court martial, when Thomas Moore was mentioned as one of the signatories, there was some doubt raised about the document. The Judge-Advocate noted that the document they had before them was a copy, the original being with Johnston, and Lieutenant Minchin could not verify whether it was the same as the original, which he had seen (but was uncertain as to whether he had signed).[112] Later generations can have no doubt, however, for the original has survived. The first signatures were those of the magistrates (including Minchin), and ninth on the second page we again find that of Mr Thomas Moore.[113] This is his second signature in support of the revolution. (Figure 43).

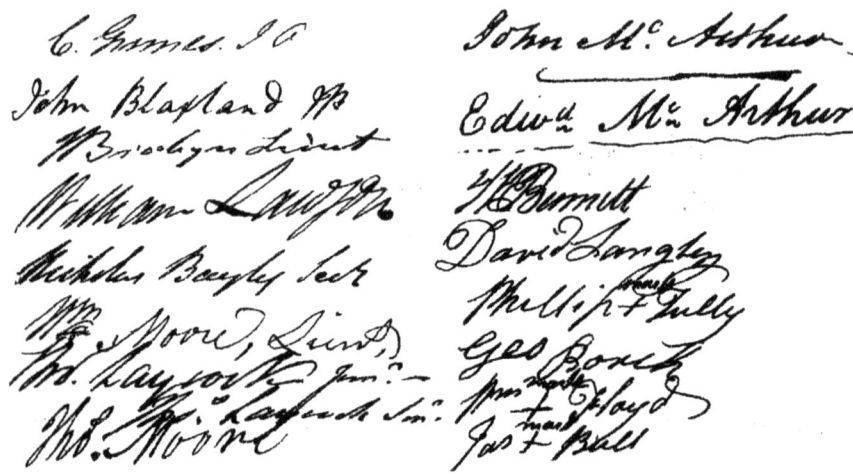

Figure 43: The congratulatory address 27 January 1808. Thomas Moore's signature is ninth on the list, three below that of Lieutenant William Moore.

On 30 January, an order informed the colony that the only official clergyman in the colony, Henry Fulton, had been suspended. Already transported once for being implicated in a rebellion, it is no surprise that he wanted nothing to do with this one. Because he supported Bligh, Fulton was dismissed by the rebels. By the same order, the Civil and Military Officers were ordered, and other inhabitants invited, to attend church.[114] So, on the following Sunday, as one of that number so ordered, Thomas Moore was amongst the throng summoned:

> To join in thanks to Almighty God for his merciful interposition in their favor, by relieving them, without bloodshed, from the awful situation in which they stood before the memorable 26th Instant.

There is no account of what went on at that service on 31 January. Later in the year, Bligh reported that its advertised purpose attracted the New South Wales Corps to the congregation, 'with their officers, in military order, under arms and colors flying. Major Johnston, McArthur, and all the junto, with their ladies, accompanied them'. When Bligh recounted the rebel's dismissal of Rev. Henry Fulton for his 'public and pointed disapprobation of their measures on the evening of the 26th January', he noted that John Macarthur introduced a prayer for Major Johnston into the Liturgy, wryly adding that he did so 'as ordinary'—that is, in Anglican parlance, 'as bishop'! Presumably Macarthur's liturgical addition received its first airing at this service, which would have been conducted by the ex-L.M.S. missionary from Tahiti, W.P. Crook, who was glad to be appointed by the rebels to perform divine service on Sundays and to baptise. Surveyor-General Charles Grimes, Captain Anthony Fenn Kemp, and Ensign Archibald Bell (the latter, a devout Anglican) were appointed to perform the ceremony of marriage.[115] After Macquarie arrived questions were raised about the legality of the marriages these men conducted, but it would not be until August when a regular Chaplain would resume duties. As the rebellion in the colony rolled on in these early days, Rev. William Cowper was blissfully unaware of the troubles in NSW, preparing to embark with his family upon the *Indispensable* to sail on 2 March.

Within a few days, Thomas Moore was at work for the new regime. By a Government and General Order, Moore, 'builder', joined the group to conduct an immediate survey of the stores and provisions in His Majesty's stores: Garnham Blaxcell, John Blaxland, Thomas Laycock, Captain Eber Bunker, and James Williamson. The dismissed Commissary Palmer was to attend and sign the final report. As the survey commenced, on 7 February the order was given that 'a moderate Supply of Spirits for [...] Domestic uses' could be now be purchased, and on the 8th that the ration of salt meat was to be reduced.[116] According to Bligh, even prior to 26 January the officers of the Corps had 'used every underhand means to smuggle' a cargo of spirits from the American ship, *Jenny*, but by June when he was writing, 48,710 gallons of wine and 12,650 gallons of spirits had already been imported, 'to the manifest injury of the colony'.[117]

Johnston explained to his superiors that the survey of the Store was to correct abuses:

> I was convinced from personal observation of the frauds and abuses practiced in the Commissary's Department, I ordered the papers in that office to be secured, and an immediate survey to be taken of every kind of store and every description of provisions remaining.

He hoped that by April the survey 'and a careful examination of the books' would enable him to transmit 'satisfactory information on every subject connected with that department'.[118]

On the other hand, Commissary Palmer reported that his keys had been taken on the night of the rebellion, and his books taken soon after. The survey took place a few days after his suspension, but it was months before the report was written and Palmer had not received a copy by 31 August. He also reported that 'immediately on their receiving the keys of the stores, and even before a survey took place, they began to issue articles from the store, and continued until the stores were nearly drained', citing some mill-stones taken by Macarthur, Blaxcell and Kable, and some arms, presumably for barter, placed upon the *Parramatta* bound for the South Seas.[119]

The first pressing business of the new regime was to finish the trial of John Macarthur. On 4 February, the Criminal Court sat to hear the charges that would have been brought against Macarthur by Atkins.[120] Unsurprisingly, Macarthur used the opportunity to deliver more grandiloquent speeches in his own favour and he was acquitted of all charges.

On Monday morning, 8 February, the bellman rang out notice that the inhabitants were to assemble in the new church at 8 p.m. The sound of Sydney's town crier, Mr Samuel Potter, working his way through the streets of Sydney, must have had a dramatic effect, for his role in calling the assembly is a detail repeated in later accounts of the events of that day.[121] A large amount of wine had been landed some days before, which meant that many of those who attended the evening meeting were well plied and the mob most disorderly. Thomas Moore's name does not appear on the list of the chief men of the 'disaffected party', later listed by Governor Bligh, although he may have been at the church.[122]

The meeting called for the appointment of a delegate to go to England to present the colonists' grievances under Bligh, and to pray redress. When someone suggested John Macarthur should do it, he was called for, immediately came, and began to give an account of recent events, in which he was clearly portrayed as the victim. Although Bligh's account of the extreme language he used may itself

CHAPTER 5 ⚓ *Sydney in Turmoil (13 August 1806 to 31 July 1808)* 295

be almost as colourful, it no doubt points to the high emotions of the evening: he had 'nearly fallen a victim to a band of bloody-minded and bloodthirsty butchers, villains who wanted to drink his blood'; the Bench of Magistrates were 'a parcel of assassins'; plans had been laid 'to overwhelm him in total ruin and destruction had it not been for the timely interposition of Divine Providence'.[123]

At the meeting Bayly, Blaxcell and Lord proposed that a sword should be given to Johnston for his role in removing Bligh. An address of thanks to the NSW Corps was requested, and another one particularly for John Macarthur 'as having been chiefly instrumental in bringing about the happy change which took place on that day'— which is an interesting reflection, given that he was purportedly a prisoner at the time. As Dando-Collins points out, this was, in fact, a masterstroke. Macarthur's enemies called this meeting as in instrument to get rid of Macarthur and to ensure that the English authorities were absolutely clear about the prime mover behind the events of the 26 January. Apparently congratulatory of Macarthur, this address let everybody know that he was responsible for the Bligh's overthrow. Funded by his 'friends' assembled that night, Macarthur was the one delegated by the colony to take that message back home to the authorities![124]

Even if others in the crowd didn't know what was really going on, Macarthur certainly did. By the end of the week he had 'scuppered the plan', by arranging for Johnston to appoint him a Magistrate and Secretary to the Colony, duly preventing him from travelling to England as the rebel delegate, and allowing him to nicely side-step the trap of his enemies.[125]

With John Macarthur manoeuvred into the driver's seat, it was time for the rebel purge to begin. On Wednesday, a Government and General Order summoned a Court of Civil Jurisdiction to assemble on the 15th instant, composed of Charles Grimes, Acting Judge-Advocate, Thomas Laycock, and Thomas Moore. By the end of the week, however, another Order announced that John Blaxland had replaced Moore on the Court—the master-builder having declined to serve in this capacity, pleading the pressure of his other duties.[126] Was it simply overwork that prevented Moore from joining this court? He had managed court duties before on top of his dockyard work, what was so pressing now? Perhaps him declining this duty arose more from principle, and as a sign that he wanted to remove himself a little from the centre of the rebel cause. The 'trial' of Macarthur had openly displayed what use could be made of the courts, and perhaps Moore didn't want to become entangled in further corrupt use of the colony's justice system. Or was he, in fact, simply over-pressed with duties at the office?

One of the additional duties thrust upon him at the dockyard by the revolution arose from the quest to find a suitable vessel in which Governor Bligh and his party could sail home to England. Come April, when Johnston wrote to explain all these events to Castlereagh, he stated:[127]

> I had no precedent to guide, and no choice but of difficulties. One of the Principal of these has been to determine how, and by what conveyance, Governor Bligh was to be sent to England.

Given that Bligh carried a Naval Commission as Commodore of His Majesty's ships in the colony, the simple question of his transport home was complicated, and the question apparently dominated the rebel regime for over twelve months. As decisions were made for a particular vessel, Thomas Moore was called in for advice on its refitting to suitably accommodate the Governor and his entourage.

As early in the rebellion as 1 February, despite being under lock and key at Government House, Commodore Bligh asserted his right to the *Porpoise*, requesting permission to sail home as soon as she arrived back in Port Jackson. At that stage, Major Johnston informed him that he was intending to send him home 'by a private ship and that every necessary accommodation shall be provided for you and your family'.[128]

The private vessel Johnston decided on was the Spanish prize that had been sent in by HMS *Cornwallis* in November, the *Pegasus*, if it proved in good condition on survey.[129] The owners represent an interesting band. Lord, Harris and Moore all signed the petition to Johnston to arrest Bligh. As one of those who sought to get rid of Macarthur to England at the meeting in the church on the night of 8

CHAPTER 5 ⚓ *Sydney in Turmoil (13 August 1806 to 31 July 1808)* 297

February, Lord was not a fan of Macarthur, but he was a rebel nevertheless. Harris was one of those Johnston took with him to England as a witness for the defence at his court martial—he also was a firm rebel. But Thomas Moore was apparently going soft on the rebellion, if ever his heart was really in it.

Johnston informed Bligh on 11 February of his decision offering to renovate the *Pegasus* cabin to Bligh's specifications.[130] Bligh replied the same day.[131] He would be sailing in winter, around Cape Horn and with a daughter (Mary Putland) who suffered severely from seasickness. Under these conditions, he suggested the names of several vessels he believed would soon be in the harbour. Apparently he did not need a survey to know that the *Pegasus* was not for him:[132]

> My objections to the *Pegasus*, under the impressions of the very long voyage I have to perform, are that I consider her too small and too weak for my safety and accommodation. If she was of a sufficient burthen I should then be under the necessity of objecting to her, as her iron fastenings are insecure; her bottom not sufficiently tight; her ironwork, from the great age of the ship, may be in a decayed state and not sufficient; her sheathing green wood, and that she will be dangerously leaky; that her pumps will not keep her free; that her rigging, from long wear in a hot climate, is become perished and will not support the masts in long and continued storms now to be met with; and that I do not consider her well found in either sails, anchors, or cables.

Johnston ordered the survey nevertheless, requesting James Symons, Commander of HMS *Porpoise*; Mr Roger Best, Carpenter, of the *Porpoise*; Mr O. Russell, Master of the *Brothers*; Mr Richard Smith, Master of the *Dart*; Mr Eber Bunker, late Master of the *Elizabeth*, to report particularly on the things Bligh had enumerated. Their report came in positively:[133]

> That the Ship's Hull, Timbers and Iron fastenings are good, that she makes no Water, her Bottom and Sheathing are good, Masts and Yards good and sufficient in number; her Lower Top Mast and running Rigging Sails, two Cables, one Hawser, and one Anchor, are in good State wanting the following Articles to proceed on so long a Voyage (vizt) Two Anchors, One 13 Cwt., the other between

2 and 5 Cwt. One 6 or 7 Inch Hawser, One Main Stay Sail, One Jib, One Fore Top Mast Stay Sail, One Mizen Course, and two Steps for the Fore and Main Masts.

And we are of Opinion that the Ship is in every respect (if furnished with the above Articles) capable of performing the voyage to England with the greatest Safety.

It is interesting to notice here that Thomas Moore was not part of the survey team, which is unusual, given he was the Master Boat Builder at the Dockyard, who has so regularly been part of surveys previously. This probably indicates that he was excluded by having a conflict of interest. In other words, even though his accounts show payments beginning 17 April, he already owned the *Pegasus* by 18 February.

If Moore wanted to detach himself from the rebel circles, it was not going to be an easy task. As part of the rebel reshuffle, in March Johnston removed the rebel-hated Richard Atkins from his position over the Loyal Sydney Volunteer Association, and appointed Thomas Moore as Captain Commandant in his place.[134] At the same time, the Association was praised for their offer to serve without receiving rations from the Government Stores.

Despite her positive survey, one month later the *Pegasus* was no longer an option for Bligh's voyage home. As Johnston explained to his superiors:

> When she had been favourably reported of, her owner, for some private reasons, considered it expedient to decline the bargain.[135]

To satisfy Bligh that he 'never entertained a thought of sending [him] Home in an insecure ship', Johnston sent the Governor a copy of the *Pegasus* survey, explaining that:

> a favourable report has been made; but, as circumstances have arisen which have induced her owners to decline freighting her to Government.[136]

Neither the Home Government nor Bligh are treated to an explanation of the 'private reasons' and 'circumstances' which made the owner/s decline the ship to Government. Whether it covertly had anything to do with Moore extracting himself from the rebel cause

CHAPTER 5 ⚓ *Sydney in Turmoil (13 August 1806 to 31 July 1808)* 299

remains a mystery. But, in a matter of weeks the overt reason was plain in the colony: the *Pegasus* was going sealing.

With winter approaching, Johnston was keen to embark Bligh as soon as possible. The other vessels Bligh had mentioned had not arrived and the only possibilities were the *Porpoise* or a smaller Southern Sealer, in which Macarthur had an interest, the *Dart*. Johnston offered to put Bligh on the *Porpoise* if he gave his word as an officer that, 'you will not attempt to assume any command, and that you will consider yourself in arrest until His Majesty's pleasure shall be signified on your late supercession'.[137] Bligh agreed to travel on the *Porpoise* under these conditions. At this point, Moore began to have more dealings with the Governor, not behind-the-scenes as the part-owner of the *Pegasus*, but face-to-face as the Master Builder of the Dockyard.

On 26 March, Lieutenant Symons, commanding the *Porpoise*, notified Johnston that he was ready to divide the cabins as required by Bligh, and he requested that he 'be furnished with carpenter and the materials to fit up Captain Bligh's cabin in the way he may wish'.[138] The next day, he requested 'the master carpenter may be sent on board HMS *Porpoise*, and I will point out the spaces that can be spared to erect the three cabins, and every assistance shall be given on my part to forward your wishes'. Johnston replied the same day:[139]

> I have ordered Mr Moore, the master carpenter, to attend you tomorrow morning at daylight, or at any other hour you may think proper to appoint, for the purpose of making the space that you propose to allot for the late Governor and his family, and for Lieut Minchin, on board His Majesty's Ship *Porpoise*.

At the same time Johnston expressed his regret that more room could not be spared. He wrote again on 29th, suggesting that Symons give Bligh the whole cabin. Symons replied, stating that he had already planned to give Bligh two-thirds of the cabin rather than half, and 'I have given such directions to the master-carpenter', but he could not go further without inconveniencing his men.[140] Bayly therefore informed Bligh the same day that 'W. Moore [sic!], the master carpenter, has had orders to attend you to receive your instructions for fitting up your accommodations on board His Majesty's ship *Porpoise* in any manner you may like', mentioning how much effort Johnston had expended in his attempt to secure the whole cabin.¹⁴¹

That same day Bligh requested Johnston to forward a letter to William Kent, who had just arrived in the *Lady Nelson*, giving him the Governor's warrant to take command of the *Porpoise*, being its legal first lieutenant. Johnston agreed to do so if Bligh did not take his order to Kent as a precedent for assuming command of the ship, and if he wrote to Kent pledging on his honor to this effect. Bligh refused to 'enter into any further conditions than I have already agreed to'. Taking this refusal as an indication that Bligh 'designed to take the Command of His Majesty's Ship the moment he put his foot on board her',¹⁴² thus breaking his arrest, Johnston began to make arrangements for him to be sent home on another vessel over which he could have no lawful authority, suggesting the *Dart*.¹⁴³

At this point in the negotiations, on 31 March the *Harrington* arrived, returning from China by way of Port Dalrymple, from whence she carried the convenient news that Johnston's superior Officer, Col. Paterson, was on his way. This allowed Johnston at this point to postpone Bligh's departure, leaving it to the Colonel 'to decide in what manner Governor Bligh shall be sent home'.¹⁴⁴

Colonel Paterson was the senior officer in the colony. Assuming him to be on his way from Port Dalrymple, a group of settlers chiefly from along the Hawkesbury, took the opportunity to send him an Address, dated 18 April, deploring the events of the rebellion and the fact that the colony had been placed in the hands of John Macarthur. Another Address to Johnston was probably written at the same time— it, too, strongly depreciative of Macarthur and calling for his removal from the Secretary's position.¹⁴⁵

Johnston responded on 26 April, by having a letter read to seventeen Officers assembled at headquarters, which he then also sent to all others in the colony, requesting anyone with allegations to make against Macarthur to come forward. Although appearing over Johnston's signature, this letter was later rumoured to have come from Macarthur himself.¹⁴⁶ As Captain of the Sydney Association, Thomas Moore was amongst those assembled to hear the praise of Macarthur's 'laborious duties' which he 'now discharges without reward or emolument', and to be called to pledge their words of honor to support Johnston in 'the annihilation of the party spirit that has unfortunately too much prevailed, almost ever since the day when you all urged me to assume the Government'. It is difficult not to hear the subtle, but nevertheless strong, threat contained in the last line. With their signatures on the various documents of the last two months, these officers could also be called to account for Johnston's action.

The same day the assembled Officers signed a response, being 'unanimously of opinion' that they cannot presume to call into question Johnston's consultation of anyone he may think proper. They assured him that 'they shall at all times feel much pleasure in obeying his orders, which is all they consider they have to do as officers serving under him'.[147] Only thirteen signed this reply—medical men J. Harris, T. Jamison and J. Mileham missing, as was Ensign A. Bell— but Thomas Moore was amongst them, once again, as Captain of the Loyal Association. This was the third time his signature appeared on a document pledging loyalty to the rebels. Was this heartfelt? Was it from a misguided sense of what was required from the Captain of the Loyal Association? Was it out of personal friendship with some of the rebels, perhaps with Johnston—whose sons were school chums with Andrew? Or, given all the rumours of strong-arm tactics, was there some compulsion brought to bear upon him?

As the rebel ranks were beginning to crumble, especially in regard to John Macarthur, Bligh gained some wisdom from hindsight. On 30 April, he wrote to Castlereagh outlining the chain of events, which he now viewed as inevitably leading to his overthrow: Abbott exchanging stations with Kemp; Macarthur committing himself by writing a contemptuous paper to Oakes, then coming to live at Sydney (and the previous troubles he had already stirred up); the previous seditious speech to the great crowd before a bench of magistrates to hear his case against Robert Campbell Jr over the two copper boilers. It all seemed so clear now to Bligh, who concluded: 'it will appear that this subversion of His Majesty's Government was effected in consequence of a settled plan of McArthur's, and not by a mere accident arising from the business of his trial'.[148] What could have motivated such a considered course of events that led inevitably towards the insurrection?

When William Campbell's *Harrington* sailed back into the harbour on March 31, completing the voyage she had commenced on 27 January 1807, it was as if perfectly timed to miss the rebellion.[149] According to Bligh's account, Campbell had exchanged his Fijian sandalwood in China, but since he could not clear China for Sydney (under the restrictions protecting the East India Company), he had sailed to Malacca, and from there, back to Sydney.[150] Reflecting upon the *Harrington*'s arrival date, Bligh later mused that:

> McArthur well knew, under these circumstances (particularly not having gone to her lawful owners), had the brig returned here while I had the power of acting, she would not have been permitted to land her cargo. One would almost pronounce as a certainty from this circumstance that McArthur had calculated the exact time when the Government would be subverted, for the additional purpose of bringing on illegal communications with the East Indies.

Rebel-dismissed chaplain Fulton evidently also shared this version of events, claiming that:

> McArthur has for some time past become a merchant, and knew that if he could get the chief command here he would be able to import goods from China without restraint, which Governor Bligh would not permit; and, though he must be conscious that such ill-gotten power must be of short duration, yet such is his avarice and ambition that they break through every prudential consideration.[151]

The timing of the *Harrington*'s arrival certainly seems suspicious in the scheme of things, and Bligh is probably right that Macarthur manipulated events with this imminent cargo in view. However, he probably misfired a little on the details by suggesting that Macarthur was afraid the Governor would turn the brig away.

As discussed above, although the *Harrington*'s voyage began with an arrangement between Macarthur and Campbell, this had all fallen apart when Macarthur's two vessels had missed the rendezvous. Because the China cargo was mostly his own—with only a small portion purchased by Davidson—Campbell was under no obligation to keep his arrangement with his former partners in the voyage,

Macarthur, Blaxcell and Jamison, which involved him selling the goods to them for a 75 per cent advance.

However, as the *Harrington* came through Sydney heads, Macarthur boarded her, reported Bligh's overthrow, and explained to Campbell the position he now wielded in the colony. Whatever his former intentions may have been, Campbell then sold his cargo according to the original arrangement. Years later he claimed that he had done this under compulsion, and this seems to be correct, for, as noted by Hainsworth, 'it is difficult otherwise to explain why he sold to them at all'.[152] Bligh claimed that he would have sent the goods away, but at the time this was because he viewed Macarthur and Campbell as 'close associates'. But they were, in fact, 'exploiter and victim'.[153]

Macarthur was probably concerned about another eventuality. When Chace, Chinnery and Co had failed, the Parrys of Madras became the *Harrington*'s new owners. Simeon Lord acted as the local agent for the Parrys, and so, once the goods were no longer Macarthur's, they would have been sold—quite legally—by Lord on commission. The emancipist Lord was not one of Macarthur's best friends, to say the least, especially since it was Lord who tried to get Macarthur out of the way on the fateful public meeting of 8 January 1808. But for someone as sure of his own importance as Macarthur was, and with his duel-prone personality, Lord's success must have been galling in the extreme. He was without doubt the most successful of the new traders who emerged under the accidental patronage of the older Officer-Trader monopoly; the cuckoo that took over the nest. To have Lord profit from what was supposed to be his trade, would have been unthinkable. To make matters worse for Macarthur, if Bligh was still Governor, he would have had no grounds for objection to this arrangement, for it was all strictly within the East India Company's usual way of operating to have an Indian registered 'country ship' trading through an agent for an Indian merchant concern. What was at risk here, from Macarthur's point of view, was not the loss of a cargo from Bligh turning it away, but through it being sold legitimately by a rival trader—and not just any rival trader, Simeon Lord. From this reasoning, Hainsworth concludes:

In view of this it is extremely likely that the impending return of the *Harrington* influenced Macarthur to accomplish the Governor's overthrow. Certainly Macarthur, Blaxcell and Jamison were three of the six most important leaders of the rebellion and all three had, in the *Harrington* investment, a strong interest in removing both Bligh and his Naval Officer, Robert Campbell.[154]

But, whatever the role of the *Harrington* in the timing of the revolution, the proceeds of Campbell's cargo certainly found their was into the pockets of Macarthur and his fellow rebel partners. By early May, Campbell had completed the discharge and the *Harrington* was lying just a little outside Sydney Cove, equipped and ready for sea. At this point, Thomas Moore again became even further tangled in amongst the rebels.

When the *Gazette* launched its return to publication, it announced that Moore had bought the *Pegasus*, and that she would be 'ready for sea in 18 or 20 days, and is designed for the seal trade'.[155] On the first page, Moore ran an advertisement concerning this new venture that must have reminded him of his own adventures in the early 1790s:

> Wanted, for the good ship *Pegasus*, bound on a Sealing Voyage, Six or Eight Seamen, and Twelve active Hands who understand the business of procuring Seals. Immediate application to made to Captain Bunker.[156]

The same day as the advertisement appeared, Moore paid his first seamen.[157] Bunker had left the *Elizabeth* in September 1807.[158] He had supported the rebels. According to later evidence at Johnston's court martial, he did so because he was grieved at Bligh ignoring promises made by the Secretary of State, in regard to Bunker bringing his family to New South Wales.[159] After the insurrection, Bunker joined Moore to survey the Commissariat stores. In March his wife Margrett died and by May it looks like Thomas Moore had coaxed him back to the sea, for on 15 May it was expected that in another 18 to 20 days, Bunker would take the *Pegasus* to sea in search of seals.

As Ship's-husband, Moore had been paying bills for the *Pegasus* in preparation for this voyage since 17 April.[160] The Carpenters had been at work prior to being paid on that date, presumably, and they continued to work through April and May. The Stover repaired the coppers and Mr

CHAPTER 5 ⚓ *Sydney in Turmoil (13 August 1806 to 31 July 1808)* 305

Lane was paid £1 to paint the stern. Mr McNanamé was paid a total of £75 19s 2d for supplying 9009 pounds of salt, ready for the salting down of the seal skins harvested on the voyage. From May 12 to 14, Moore acquired 2022 lbs of live pork, 858 lbs salted pork and 102 lbs of hog's lard. Further provisions were loaded, but paid for after the ship had sailed on 18 May, including more salt from Mr Wills (1708 lb) and salt pork from Mr Wilshire (4037 lbs), as well as £2 16s worth of corn and vegetables to supplement the pork provisions.

Thus in May, the *Pegasus* and the *Harrington*, two prizes of a European war that found their way to this colony on the other side of the world, were both preparing for sea; the *Harrington* riding the gentle harbour swell off Farm Cove.

From the early days of New South Wales, the authorities had been afraid that convicts might escape from the colony on pirated vessels. Even if the real reason for forbidding shipbuilding had more to do with protecting the rights of the East India Company, the prevention of convict escape was often the reason cited. The suspicion was, of course, well grounded. In a penal colony escapes were to be expected and they became a fairly frequent feature of New South Wales life. Lists of absconded convicts regularly appeared in the *Sydney Gazette*. In the early days, many took off into the bush in the misguided belief that China was close enough to justify such a bid for freedom. As would be expected in an island settlement completely dependent upon shipping, convicts regularly made their escape as stowaways, and sometimes they resorted to piratical seizure.[161] Following in this desperate tradition, on 16 May 1808, about forty convicts made their escape from New South Wales on board Campbell's *Harrington*.

If Bligh suspected a causal link between Macarthur's desire to land the *Harrington*'s cargo and the 26 January rebellion, others drew a line between the rebellion and the *Harrington*'s seizure, pointing to what one author has called the 'crime-wave' that hit Sydney following the rebellion.[162] Bligh himself appears to have made this link, naming this event as one of the 'extraordinary circumstances which have taken place under the present ruling power'.[163] George Caley, the naturalist and explorer sent to NSW as one of Sir Joseph Banks' 'gardners' and collectors,[164] was even more explicit. Describing to Banks the situation of the colony after the rebellion, Caley questioned recent events by creating an open letter to Major Johnston, which included a reference to the *Harrington*:

> The motley crowd which were encouraged, instead of being instantly suppressed, and the numbers you have let loose upon the public, would evidently open a source for the greatest evils; and from this I may attribute the numerous thefts and robberies which have of late been committed. Nothing can show a specimen of worse management than a number of convicts seizing a ship in the harbour, and escaping from the colony. It is a neglect of so foul a nature as not only to violate the law of nations, but to insult both justice and commerce.[165]

Certainly the event appears to have shocked everyone—even those involved with the rebels. In the week after the event, John Macarthur wrote to Captain Piper on Norfolk Island, 'You will be astonished at the capture of the *Harrington*, the particulars of which you will learn from Mr Barry [i.e. Alexander Berry], supercargo of the *City of Edinburgh*'.[166] By this stage the rebels were falling apart, and the loss of the *Harrington* was another blow to the 'deeply depressed' Macarthur.[167]

When the details were relayed to him, perhaps Piper would have heard a version of events flavoured by Macarthur's intimate connection with the vessel. From the other side of the conflict, Bligh's version is short and sweet:

> equipped and ready for sea (lying a little without the cove) [the *Harrington*] was taken possession of and her crew turned on shore by a prisoner called S—— (a determined man, who had frequently endeavoured to leave the colony in open boats, and in consequence was put to labor in the gaol gang, but after my confinement was liberated) and about forty other convicts, who carried her to sea on the 16th May and have not since been heard of.[168]

The seizure of the *Harrington* provided a dramatic story to help relaunch the *Sydney Gazette* after suspension of publication on 20 August 1807. The first issue of the new series was published the day before the *Harrington*'s seizure, but the next issue of 22 May ran the story: 'The Piratical Seizure of the Brig *Harrington*'.[169] Captain Campbell woke up to see Farm Cove empty where his brig used to be. On reporting the incident to Johnston at 8 a.m., investigation found that Robert Stewart and several other convicts had not turned up for work on their Government gang that morning. When it was also revealed that at daylight a vessel had been seen from South Head, 'no further doubt was to be entertained of her having been taken away by a body of desperadoes'. By 9 a.m. a small vessel, the *Halcyon* with a Sergeant and ten Privates from the Corps set out in hot pursuit, but unfortunately it was so calm they couldn't get out of the harbour until dark, and by that time the *Harrington* was long gone. After 3 p.m. her Chief Officer, Mr Fisk, and the crew arrived in two boats and the story of the piracy was told. The ship's company had been overpowered while asleep, and when the escape had been made, they were released at about seven that morning about 20 miles out to sea, and after 8 hours they had made it back to Sydney.

After the fruitless search on Monday, the next day the *Pegasus* was hired to go in pursuit. Because she was not yet fully rigged, all those in Government service and every hand that could be found worked solidly with 'wonderful energy' and in less than 24 hours, 'she was equipped, & furnished with water & provisions, several carriage guns, many stands of arms, sufficient ballast, and every thing else necessary for the expedition'. This would be a challenge for the *Pegasus*, for the *Harrington* was 'reputed to be the fastest vessel in the eastern seas'.[170] Suspecting the *Harrington* had made for the Bay of Islands and hopeful of her immediate capture,

> on Wednesday afternoon [the *Pegasus*] went out, having on board Captain Symonds, Captain Eber Bunker with his first and second officers, Captain Graham, and Captain Campbell. Mr Fisk, and part of the *Harrington*'s crew; the military detachment consisting of 20 privates, 2 corporals, and serjeants Johns and Bradley of His Majesty's New South Wales Corps.[171]

One week later, the *Gazette* gave its readers an update, still hopeful of an early resolution:

> We look forward with much anxiety for the return of the *Pegasus*, which will, it is ardently to be hoped, succeed in the object of her expedition without any resistance from the ill advised people whose temerity has been so unexampled.[172]

Here Thomas Moore's path once again crossed that of John Macarthur, only this time the Master Builder made some profit from the ex-Captain of the Corps—or at least from pursuing one of his vessels. It would not be without controversy for Thomas Moore, however. Because the *Pegasus* was purloined into Government service, not only was Moore paid at the end of the voyage, but he also received Government supplies to get her ready at its beginning. In the rush to fit her for sea, a long list of supplies were stowed on board, furnished by James Williamson, the Acting Commissary installed when the rebels replaced John Palmer. The receipt and two duplicates survive amongst Moore's papers, signed by Moore's partner John Harris. George Johnston also signed to certify that all was supplied by his order. No other contractual arrangement survives, which suggests that probably there was none.[173]

Despite all the fuss in the harbour, some were still reflecting upon the state of the rebellion. On the same day the *Pegasus* sailed after the *Harrington*, Chaplain Fulton wrote to Bligh, appalled at a paper apparently delivered to Bligh on 28 January.[174] He refuted every point. Bligh had not broken any laws, but stopped the iniquitous custom of bartering with spirits. He had not interfered with the courts, but ensured that no-one was above them. His actions had led the Officers of the Corps to take the colony into their own hands, 'that they might have enormous quantities of spirits for barter and import China goods at will to the great injury of the India Company'. But they had acted without forethought and 'now they would withdraw with eagerness from their present condition if they could with safety. They repent because they are embarrassed on every side'.

Even those within the rebel circle were noticing this withdrawal from the original plans. When Macarthur wrote to Captain Piper on Norfolk Island on 24 May[175] informing him of the capture of the *Harrington*, he bewailed the state of the rebel regime as they waited every day for the arrival of Joseph Foveaux. Some of Piper's 'old acquaintance' 'behaved most scurvily'. Abbott, amongst the worst; Minchin sent home with despatches; Grimes on the same errand, 'only for telling a few lies'; and Bayly, 'is become a violent oppositionist'. In fact, if Kemp, Lawson, and Draffin are exempted:

CHAPTER 5 ⚓ *Sydney in Turmoil (13 August 1806 to 31 July 1808)* 309

> there is not a man that affords Johnston the least support, and most of them oppose everything, although the whole called upon him to assume the government, and pledged their words of honor to support him. Pretty pledge, you will say. Harris has also been ordered to take a despatch Home, but he very conveniently fell sick.

And so, the rebels continued to fall apart.

While awaiting the return of his *Pegasus*, Moore had duties at the dockyard to keep him occupied. On Thursday 26 May, the *Porpoise* arrived from Port Dalrymple, and was soon placed in his care:[176]

> His majesty's Ship *Porpoise* was last week laid along-side the heaving down place, and will undergo a thorough repair.[177]

The heaving-down place was on the eastern side of Sydney Cove, opposite the dockyard. (Plate 29). Since the *Porpoise* was one of His Majesty's Ships, the refit would be done under the supervision of the Master Builder of the King's Dockyard—that's what a Naval Yard was for.[178]

Moore was also called in for official duties as Captain of the Loyal Association to celebrate the King's birthday on 4 June. After the NSW Corps fired three volleys, this:

> was repeated by the Sydney Loyal Association on their parade opposite the Dry Store, and followed by a royal salute from the battery at Dawe's point. At one o'clock His Majesty's ship *Porpoise* fired a royal salute; which was answered from several ships in the cove. His honor the Lieutenant Governor [George Johnston] received the compliments of the officers on the occasion, and in the evening gave a splendid entertainment to a large party.

The Harbour had several vessels at anchor at this time. On 3 July the *Gazette* listed as remaining with His Majesty's ship *Porpoise*, the *Cumberland* and *Sarah* whalers, the *Rose*, *Fox*, *Favorite*, *Eagle*, *Perseverance*, and the *Santa Anna*—the latter undergoing repair with Underwood.[179] In the next week, they were joined by the *Albion*, arriving in distress with another ship, the *Ben Cidadeo*, from Pulo [Palau] Penang, which was dismasted.[180] On 10 July the brig, *Commerce*, Captain Ceroni, arrived with 3,000 skins from 5 months in the sealing islands—a fairly pitiful yield. She brought news of the *Pegasus*. She had been at the Bay of Islands two days, when she saw a brig standing in, then suddenly hauling wind and sailing off to the east. Suspecting this was the *Harrington*, she sailed for the Feejees, in the hope of catching her prey there.[181]

However, despite the optimism expressed by the *Gazette* as the adventure commenced and by Ceroni's more recent report, the *Pegasus* arrived home on 22 July empty-handed.

> On Friday returned the *Pegasus*, after an unsuccessful cruise of nine weeks in search of the *Harrington*. She was last off Tongataboo, and returned by the way of New Caledonia; having for some weeks past felt severely a scarcity of provisions, as she took on board only a sufficiency for 6 weeks for 50 men, and the actual number were 58, including the military detachment.[182]

Within six weeks, Captain Campbell had taken the *Favorite*, firstly to the Feejees, and then to China—a voyage reminiscent of the Macarthur plan. He and his Chief Officer Fisk were joined by Mr Graham, the prize-master who had originally brought in the *Pegasus*.[183] Almost immediately after her return on 22 July, Moore began fitting up the *Pegasus* for her originally intended purpose, namely, a sealing voyage. His personal accounts with Campbell & Co for August show that he spent money on items clearly of use for the voyage, and six bags of rice probably to feed the crew during their

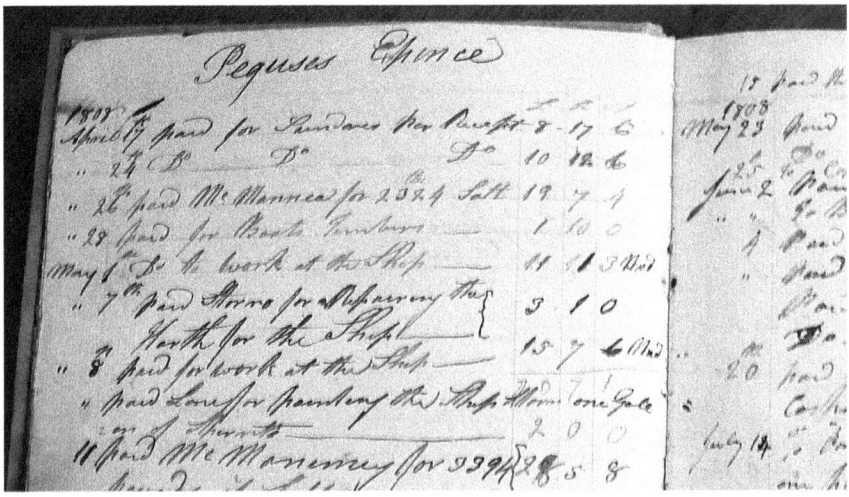

Figure 44: Pegasus Accounts.

time on shore (Figures 44 and 45). The *Pegasus* accounts show a fuller picture of the frenetic activity that went on in August to ready the vessel for her delayed sealing venture.[184] Carpenters John Richards and Patrick Carroll were set to work to build four boats, presumably to enable the sealers to get around on the islands where the gang would be landed. McDowal was paid 10s for the skylights and Chapman 8s for glazing them. All in all the refitting of the ship and the building of the boats required 4050 feet of timber, rope, iron work, log lines, pump leather, timbers, knees and gunwhales. Then there were the supplies to be loaded and paid for. The six dozen seal clubs were, of course, essential (£1.16), as were hogsheads and casks for packing the skins, and the rest of the equipment (tea kettle, knives and steels, frying pans, iron pots, axes and chisels, oars, a pump, a handsaw, caulking irons, mallet and adze, grindstones, boat nails, casks, puncheons, tin ware, glass, candles, etc), and the provisions (sugar, pepper, 'pork dead', live hogs, potatoes, tea, porter casks, fresh meat, 7 tons of wood [for the stove?]). Captain Brookes of the *Rose* supplied a wooden caboose (£3), and to get the ship out of the harbour, there was a ship's register, pilotage to Mr Watson (£3.10), and a gallon of spirits for the South Head soldiers.

Other accounts show the purchase of similar items of necessary equipment. In case the vessel came across any whales, she would be prepared with a whale line stowed, along with some lances and harpoons. For the sealskins, there were plenty of casks including some 'polar casks', and to keep the men alive, plenty of pork and mutton, and one sheep.[185]

The largest expense to Mr Moore, besides the bill to his partner Lord for 'sundries' (£498.9.9)[186] was the advance on wages to his Officers and Men, consisting of £346.19.0 ½—on top of already paying 8 crewmen £3 each for their nine weeks work, as well as paying two men two days wages (£1) due before the chase.[187] It was usual to issue such an advance on wages, and, in turn, the men kept an account with the ship's captain for provisions whilst at sea (tobacco, blankets, clothing, etc) which was then accounted for in the final settling of payments at the end of the voyage. Each person on the voyage would also receive a share of the profits, their 'lay'.

Despite its lack of success in terms of apprehension of the pirate-convicts on the *Harrington*, the first voyage of the *Pegasus* under his ownership was commercially successful for Thomas Moore. Against the expenditure for the forthcoming voyage, Moore was able to deduct the credit 'by the amount of freight of the ship in going after the *Harrington*', namely, £463.10.[188]

Mr Thos Moore Sydney				
Bot of Campbell & Co				
1808				
May	16	1 Jar of Paint Oil		£3.15.0
	20	1 Tub of Sugar Candy (Capt. Bunker) £9		
		1 Bag of Rice (— Do—)	2.10.-	11.10.0
June	14	1 Chest of Hysom		25.0.0
		1 Firkin of Butter		9.0.0
Augt	12	6 6 In Blocks	@6/-	1.16.0
		1 9 In Ditto		9.0
	18	6 Bags of Rice	30/	15.0.0
	20	1 Anchor wt 2.1.24	1/	13.16.0
		1 10 In Block		0.10.0
		1 Bag of Shot		1.8.0
	22	30t of Iron Hoops	9	1.2.6
		500 @24 nails		12.6
	24	2 Boat Hammers 7/- 3 / 4 nails @2/7—		
		22g Sheet lead 16/6		1.6.1
	25	2 Deep Sea Lines	16/	1.12.0
	26	1 Socket Chissell 3/- 1 Round File 3/-		6.0
Septr	12	30g Sheet Lead	@ 9	1.2.6
	14	500 20d Nails 10/		
		500 10d D° 6/8 1 Keg Brown paint		1.17.8
	21	120g Sheet lead	@9	4.10.0
	30	25 Galls Spirits—*Rose*		16.17.6
	"	25 D° D°– " (Captn Bunker)		16.17.6
				£128.8.3

Figure 45: Thomas Moore's Account with Campbell & Co rendered 30 September 1808.[189]

CHAPTER 5 ↭ *Sydney in Turmoil (13 August 1806 to 31 July 1808)* 313

By the end of the year, when exposing 'nefarious practices carried on' by the rebels, especially in regard to the mis-use of the Government Stores, ex-Commissary Palmer listed the provisions given to the *Pegasus* for expenses incurred in the *Harrington* pursuit amongst the other dodgy dealing:

> I believe your Excellency knew of a Ship called the *Pegasus* being sent after Captain Campbell's Brig *Harrington* and fitted out by Government. The Outfit, Stores &c were to be returned or charged —They were as well as Provisions given in Charge to Mr Symons, what Account he has rendered I know not, but this I can say, nothing of any consequence has been returned into Store— the deficiency amounts to about £870—exclusive of 6 weeks Provisions put on board for 71 Persons and 50 Gallons of Spirits.[190]

No doubt this 'intelligence' from Palmer contributed to Bligh's later antipathy to Thomas Moore, the known ship's-husband of the *Pegasus*. But now that the *Pegasus* accounts have come to light, it is clear that Palmer has misrepresented the facts, for the receipt (and duplicate) is extant amongst Moore's papers. Signed by Johnston on behalf of the government (at the time) and Harris on behalf of the owners on 18 May 1808 (the day of her sailing), it contains an exact listing of all supplies put on the *Pegasus*—including Palmer's '50 Gallons of Spirits'.[191] Although this list does not cost the supplies, Moore's own accounts for the *Pegasus* contain two items of relevance. As an expense, Moore listed 'Amount of articles received from HM Store, £245-7-3 ¼', and as already mentioned, as a credit he listed 'By amount of freight of the Ship in going after the Harringon, £463-10'.[192] These accounts suggest that an agreement had been struck that the Stores would be charged but then offset by 'freight', that is, they could then be used or sold by the *Pegasus*. Since the freight allowed was larger than the charge, this amounts to a payment of £116.3.8 ½ for the charter of Moore's vessel. It doesn't seem at all unreasonable to expect the government of the day—rebel or not—to pay for the charter of a private vessel, even if this came back to haunt Moore in the months to come.

The detailed 'accounts current' for each crew member of the *Pegasus* have also survived amongst Moore's personal papers. From one list it is clear that Moore not only gave the seamen an advance on their pay, but he also paid various accounts they had racked up while they were on shore (Figure 46).[193] The various creditors paid out by Moore on behalf of his crew consisted of Richard Podmore, Henry Kable, Catherine Johnston, Harry Yeats, Charles Busby, Edward Redman, an unnamed 'Hatter', George Grubb, Richard Calcutt, Harry Williams, Mrs Wills, Edward Edwards, Elizabeth Conday, William O'Neal, George Guy, Elizabeth Wood, Mary Peach, James Anderson, Bryan Egan, and Dennis McMary. On 19 August Moore put a list of detainers in to James Finucane on behalf of the crew, obligating himself to pay the same on demand.[194]

A regular feature on many of the men's accounts was 3 shillings paid for 'potter and fees', or for 'secretary fees'. Samuel Potter the town crier, presumably, called this man's name through the streets when it was time for his duties to recommence. This is clear from references in the accounts to Potter 'crying the ship', or 'crying the men' (he also 'cried' other things, such as 'crying the mare'—presumably when Moore had a horse for sale). Those not charged this fee were probably the ones able to be punctual under their own steam. The fee paid to the colonial secretary (who in 1809 was James Finucane, who took over from Macarthur in that role) is presumably some official fee required as a man left Sydney. Leaving required a public advertisement for claims upon the person to be presented, as well as the approval of the Governor, so perhaps the 3s was to cover these processes.

When compared to their wages earned for shipboard work, some of these bills settled by Moore were enormous (up to £41.11 for John Howe), putting these men severely into debt to Moore, even from the start of the voyage.[195]

With plenty of his own concerns to deal with, it is interesting to wonder about whether Moore also gave assistance or advice to other shipbuilders in the Cove. Certainly the convict labour of the dockyard was loaned to HM Ships to help the carpenters in repairs and refits and Moore evidently had a supervisory role over his men and some role towards the ships in Government service. But what about the private ships? Presumably he was the 'leading expert' on the spot capable and willing to give advice and guidance? Since he lived next door to

CHAPTER 5 ⚓ *Sydney in Turmoil (13 August 1806 to 31 July 1808)*

CREW OF THE PEGASUS	
Samuel Allen	Zackery Price
John White	Dennis O'Bryan
Benjamin Levett	Mark Monroe
Robert Current	John Clements
Lawrence Doyle	James Golvin
Peter Risden	Peter Jackson Day
Mr W. Wilson	Patrick Burne
David Christian	William Ramsden
John Harper	Thomas Dunn
Stephen Lawrence	John Howe
Abram Moseley	

Figure 46: The Crew of the Pegasus, taken from Moore's accounts.[196]

Robert Campbell, for example, how much advice was given 'over the back fence' in regard to Campbell's own ship building and repairing concerns? Perhaps especially in crisis situations, Moore would have lent whatever assistance possible—in the wake of an accident with the Brig, *Fox*, Captain Cockerill, for example. She had arrived on 21 March from the Cape of Good Hope, and remained in Port Jackson for some months.[197] Thomas Rushton was one of those who profited from her cargo and displayed some of the entrepreneurial spirit that was alive in Sydney in this decade. He announced that he had purchased her entire supply of hops and secured a continual supply of hops for the future, on the strength of which he had started a brewing business, which he was confident would be able to fulfil all orders.[198] From 12 June, lists of those joining her crew began to be published, signalling her imminent departure.[199] But on 20 July while sitting at anchor opposite Campbell's wharf, and so across the Cove from Thomas and Rachel's house, she was seen to be ablaze with flames. Campbell and Co suspected arson, and advertised a substantial reward of 500 Guineas for information leading to the culprit's apprehension.[200] After a month of repairs it was reported that the 'injury done by which is much less than was expected from the appearance and rapidity of the flames', but it would still be another month before the repairs were completed so she could sail.[201]

New South Wales was in the hands of three different men in the eighteen months of rebellion. Phase one started with George Johnston, although it soon became apparent that the real power was John Macarthur. Phase three was William Paterson, one of Macarthur's old Officer-Trader companions and one-time administrator of the colony (December 1794–September 1795). Paterson eventually handed over the reigns to legitimate government when Lachlan Macquarie arrived in December 1809. The bridge between Johnston and Paterson was Joseph Foveaux.

When he sailed from England Foveaux was destined for a return to Norfolk Island. When the *Sinclair* arrived in Sydney on 28 July, however, finding himself to be the ranking officer he took charge of the colony, and thereby commenced the second phase of the rebel regime.[202] He was not well when he first arrived, so remained on the ship. Bligh immediately sent a delegation on board, which included Rev. Henry Fulton. This was a tactical error, for Fulton had been a convict on Norfolk Island during Foveaux's time there (26 June 1800 to 9 September 1804). Confronted with an ex-convict as Bligh's delegate, Foveaux's opinion of Bligh soured as he found out the Governor had taken advice from such people.[203] He received only Bligh's letter, not the delegation itself and when he then went on to receive Major Johnston personally, Bligh was furious.

Foveaux was an old hand to New South Wales. In 1966 Fletcher stated that it was unknown whether he was one of the Officer-Traders of the monopoly in the 1790s,[204] but by 1972, Hainsworth's work on the Macarthur Papers leaves no doubt. Fletcher suspected something, noting that Paterson's absence from the colony left Foveaux in charge of the New South Wales Corps 'during a period when some of its officers were making their fortunes from trading and extending their landed properties' (August 1796 to November 1799), but Hainsworth went on to show that Foveaux was firmly amongst the traders from the beginning. (Figures 16, 22 and 47).

The kind of wealth acquired by the officers is difficult to estimate.

On their return to England some of them 'found war-time London distressingly expensive'—a comment confirmed by Waterhouse's reference to Lieutenant William Beckwith dying 'in a garret without a rag to cover him'.[205] Some certainly prospered, but 'the wealth they achieved would tend to be an Old Testament kind of wealth, flocks, herds and acres, but not a kind of wealth it was easy to transport from the colony'.[206]

In the early period, Foveaux amassed over 1,000 sheep with more than 2,000 acres to keep them on, making him the largest land and stock-holder in the colony.[207] When he left for Norfolk Island he sold 1,170 acres to Macarthur, and his sheep, for £2,000. According to Hainsworth, 'while this was a very substantial sum for an officer like Foveaux to amass during a few years' guard duty in a prison settlement, Macarthur must surely have had the best of the bargain'.[208] By this sale, Foveaux boosted his Paymaster's progress towards being one of the wool magnates of New South Wales in later years.

But even when grants of land are taken into account, did Foveaux grow his wealth at least partly through trading? In asking which officers took part in the early days, Hainsworth is confident that the senior officers would not have let Paymaster Macarthur monopolize the advantage.[209] 'The lion's share must have gone to the company commanders: Paterson, Johnston, Foveaux, Hill, Rowley, and to a lesser degree Nepean' with the junior officers having to be satisfied with a more modest share. In September 1793, William Raven received Paymaster's Bills totaling £320 made up of contributions from Johnston (£65), Macarthur (£35), McKellar and Piper (£20), and— each contributing £60—Paterson, Harris and Foveaux. In March 1794, Foveaux contributed £243-1-11 ½ towards the cargo of beef, pork and tea brought by Folger on the *William*. In August 1794, as William Raven departed for the Cape he received £3263 in Paymaster's Bills, including £250 from Foveaux and a further note for £45-9-7. In addition, amongst what appears to be 'holding funds' with Commissary Palmer, whereas the other officers each had a share of £38.8.10 of the *Britannia*'s cargo—Foveaux had two. There is no doubt at all of Foveaux' active, if not leading, part amongst the Officer-Traders:

Confused though the surviving records are, the broad picture is clear enough. The principal traders were Paterson, Johnston, Foveaux, Rowley, Macarthur, and to a lesser degree Harris. Apart from Harris, who was a surgeon, all these men had company funds passing through their hands. Another substantial investor was Laycock, who had risen from the ranks to Quartermaster, a position which has been notorious for providing the unscrupulous with a means to affluence even in modern times.[210]

Foveaux's period of government was not without its positive aspects, such as his general improvement of the state of the public buildings, which would be praised by Macquarie when he arrived.[211] On the other hand, his treatment of Bligh's supporters such as George Suttor, John Palmer and Robert Campbell was severe. In the case of Campbell, if it is true that Foveaux acted as a tool of officers who were 'jealous of Campbell's trading position' then Fletcher declares this to be 'a serious blemish on what was quite an enterprising administration'.[212]

Date	Paid to	For cargo from ship	Amount
Sept 1793	Raven	*Britannia*	£60
March 1794	Folger	*William*	£243-1-11
August 1794	Raven	*Britannia*	£250 £45-9-7 note

Figure 47: Joseph Foveaux's contributions to the early trading ventures of the NSW Corps.

When Joseph Foveaux disembarked on Friday 29th, Lieutenant Governor Johnston officially received him to the colony. Thomas Moore, as the Master Boat Builder, was also amongst 'the Officers, Civil, Military, and Naval' who accompanied Johnston in his welcome. Given the events of 26 January, it was not without some irony that as part of this official welcome of one of His Majesty's Military officers, as the batteries saluted, 'the New South Wales Corps, drawn up on the Parade, paid Military honours on the occasion'.[213] As the outranking officer, Foveaux assumed the command on the 31st.

CHAPTER 5 ↓ *Sydney in Turmoil (13 August 1806 to 31 July 1808)* 319

Bligh was already out of favour with Foveaux for sending Captain Short home to be court martialled after disagreements on Bligh's voyage out in 1806. He would also be aware of the difficulty of reinstating Bligh, given the views and recent actions of the Corps. Foveaux was apparently already convinced by the 'unanimous sentiment' he found amongst the principle inhabitants of the colony, of 'the absolute necessity of suspending Captain Bligh from the Government as the only means of preventing an insurrection'.[214] His real opinions were somewhat concealed when he issued a proclamation declaring that it was beyond his authority to judge between Governor Bligh and Major Johnston.[215]

> As the Government of this Colony has been upwards of six months out of the hands of William Bligh, Esquire; and as the circumstances attending his Suspension have been fully submitted to his Majesty's Ministers, who alone are competent to decide, LIEUTENANT GOVERNOR FOVEAUX conceives it to be beyond his authority to judge between Captain Bligh and the Officer whom he found in actual command of the Colony.
>
> In assuming the administration of the Government until His majesty's pleasure shall be known, Lieutenant Governor Foveaux is determined to adopt such measures as he deems to be most effectual for the preservation of the public tranquillity, and the security of public and private property; and to follow, in the discharge of the arduous duties imposed upon him, a system of the strictest oeconomy, and the most impartial justice between persons of every description.

The same proclamation announced the appointment of James Finucane as Secretary and, with that stroke of the pen, since this was (as Captain Abbott put it) 'in the room of McArthur',[216] Macarthur's powers were suddenly curtailed. His rebel days, and in fact his public life in the colony, had finally come to an end.

Although Foveaux had not released him from his captivity, Bligh did not give up hope that his arrival had brought the opportunity for restoration of order. Learning that Foveaux intended sending a vessel to Port Dalrymple to fetch the only officer in the colony that outranked him, Bligh wrote to Colonel Paterson, informing him of the rebellion and calling upon him 'to suppress this mutiny of the Corps under your command, that I may proceed in the government of the colony according to the powers delegated to me by our gracious Sovereign'.[217]

On the same day as he took command, Foveaux commissioned Thomas Moore to be Captain Commandant of the Loyal Sydney Volunteer Association, presumably confirming him in that position to which he was previously elevated by Johnston in March.[218] Why was this one of Foveaux's first duties? It is also interesting to note that within a month of his arrival, he restored the right of the Sydney and Parramatta Loyal Associations to be victualled from the public stores.[219] Was Foveaux looking to Moore and the Volunteers, for alternative military support due to some nervousness about the Corps, perhaps?

Or perhaps Foveaux had his eyes upon England's continued hostilities with France. Once again, the nation at war affected the colonies, even on the other side of the globe. The *Sydney Gazette* of 7 August 1808 published various orders presumably brought by Foveaux, which had been given in London in the previous November and December, relating to the need for HMS Ships to do their utmost to seize the ships of France, and her allies. All vessels trading to or from these countries or colonies and their cargoes when taken will be condemned as prizes for the captors.[220]

But Thomas Moore already had his prize, and the *Pegasus*, he hoped, was just about to make him a fortune!

6

SPECULATOR AND SETTLER

(31 JULY 1808 *to* 7 NOVEMBER 1810)

With the turmoil of the initial period of insurrection over, Sydney settled somewhat into the caretaker period of Joseph Foveaux. Paterson was yet to join him for the third and final phase of the rebel regime. In December 1809, Lachlan Macquarie would arrive to re-establish legitimate Government and begin to lay foundations that would move the penal colony of New South Wales further towards becoming a free society. Sharing a special friendship with Macquarie, Thomas Moore would find himself taking on many different roles to assist the building of that new society.

But in August 1808, Thomas Moore still had his own 'emancipation' to think of. His position as a civil officer, well-connected to the officer-traders of the old guard, and firmly amongst the emergent traders of the new, placed him in the unenviable position of being too close to the centre of the mutiny whichever way he looked at it. He had to disentangle himself and move on.

After the dramatic events of the previous year, anything that happened in 1809 must have appeared to be anticlimactic. But perhaps that was exactly what Thomas Moore was after. Now forty-six years old and having come so uncomfortably entangled in the insurrection, perhaps it is understandable that his thoughts were turning to retirement from public life—or at least from out of the fraught networks in Sydney Town.

Certainly his private interests had reached a level where they needed more attention. His growing numbers of cattle and horses required more space, if they were to be nurtured towards turning fruitful profits. Moore's good reputation and standing—with people on all sides of the political factions it seems—brought him extra responsibility on surveys, in the courtroom, as agent for various persons and trustee for various estates. In a colony without a legal tender, Moore's growing wealth and good reputation also brought him into the realm of being a banker before the banks. His employment allowed him to accumulate funds, including sterling, and as time went on 'Mr Moore's Bills' were recognised as solid payment. His position amongst the emergent traders gave him the opportunity for further financial growth and to play his part in laying the foundations of Sydney's commercial environment.

By virtue of the situation he had found himself in Thomas Moore had been uncomfortably and dangerously caught up in an insurrection against His Majesty's government. But by the same accident of historical circumstance, he had also been situated close to the centre of the networks of this emergent new society known as New South Wales. Being in the right place at the right time and among the right people ensured that Moore would continue to exert an influence on public life, even as he reaped the harvest from his own private concerns. Perhaps it was these kind of accidental circumstances that gave him such a firm view of God's providential care. At the end of his days, when thinking about the disposal of his substantial fortune towards the Church, he explained his motives quite simply: 'God gave it all to me, and I shall give it all back to Him'.[1] But God's gifts don't always come easily, and Moore still had some further uncharted waters to steer before he found himself on the peaceful banks of the George's River, listening to a legitimate Governor proclaiming the birth of a new town, and a whole new future for Thomas Moore.

On 21 August 1808 the *Gazette* announced that the *Pegasus* would sail shortly for the seal islands.[2] The following Friday (26th) the preparations were complete and she weighed anchor to sail for the fishery, the *King George* following her the next day.[3] Moore's duties weren't finished, however, and on September 30 he bought 25 Gallons of spirits from Campbell & Co for himself and another 25 for Bunker. (Figure 45). The spirits came from the *Rose*, and paying a total of £16 17s 6d for each parcel, the cost per gallon to Bunker and Moore was 13/6.

Owned by Campbell & Co, the *Rose* (Captain Brooks) arrived in Sydney on 15 April 1808 and after being repaired she departed again for England on 15 September.[4] Her cargo of spirits provoked Foveaux to express his annoyance at the spirits trade. Bligh had prohibited the importation of spirits into dependent settlements without first calling at Sydney to gain permission. Despite this regulation, however, on her journey from England the *Rose* put in at the Derwent and landed several thousand gallons of spirits, 'which have since been disposed of amongst the unfortunate settlers [evacuated] from Norfolk Island' who had sold their salted pork to the Government in order to be 'furnished with the means of indulging in dissipation and drunkenness for a few days, and deprived of the means of subsistence for years'.[5] With Johnston's permission, the *Rose* imported 526 gallons to Government, and 1706 ½ gallons to the Officers, Civil & Military and others.[6] Foveaux explained that the 'common circulating value' of the limited supply of spirits, because so short of the demand, usually fluctuates between two and three pounds per gallon. Three quarters of the quantity imported fall into the hands of 'persons in the employment of Government, or are obtained by the inhabitants of the town at an average price of about twelve shillings, and are again distributed by them at the advanced price amongst the settlers and labourers who live in the interior of the country'. Thus, at 13/6 per gallon, Campbell & Co had evidently given Moore and Bunker a wholesale price for the spirits. This may indicate that they were planning to retail it somewhere, or to use it for barter for goods for the ship, but perhaps it was more likely destined for the *Pegasus* crewmen as shipboard provisions.

The relatively settled state that descended on the colony with the arrival of Foveaux and his dismissal of John Macarthur enabled some reflection on the previous six months or so. While many worried about politics and trade in the tumultuous post-rebellion period, some were also concerned about the effect it had had on the spiritual life of the colony. Late in August, Rowland Hassall wrote to his old missionary society, that 'the present state of this colony is not pleasant to a reflecting mind'. He was not amongst those who signed Johnston's order of the 26 January, and he did not know 'ten respectable inhabitants in the whole colony that knew anything of the business until after it took place'. In fact, 'if the inhabitants was asked the question at this day how they approved of the measures that have taken place, there would not be one in twenty that would approve of them'. One of the serious effects of 'this revolution', is

> the silencing of a most valuable sound divine, the Rev. H. Fulton. The churches are so neglected that on Sunday last I went to the church to hear Bro. Crook, where there were not more than six persons besides myself and family. The Lord's Day is so abused that even the present chief constable carts his firewood out of roads close to the church doors during Divine service. The generality of the publick are in constant alarm, wishing and expecting some alteration in the government; and the industrious settlers, many of them, are so distressed through the events, that they have nothing to pay their creditors, so that numbers of them will be ruined.[7]

As one sign of favour to Governor Bligh, Foveaux removed the restrictions Johnston had placed on Bligh communicating with the *Porpoise*. Paterson later surmised this was from Foveaux's belief that Bligh would have learned from previous experience. However, it took only 'a short time [to prove] how erroneous had been his conclusion', and he reversed the decision.[8] With communication between himself and the *Porpoise* restored, Bligh began merrily issuing commands to her Captain, William Kent, to fly his broad pennant and the like, and refusing to agree to Foveaux's conditions of sailing, namely, that he does not command her, but travels under arrest—as Johnston had also insisted. Bligh seems to have gained new hope of being restored to government, writing to both Foveaux and Paterson that they take every

CHAPTER 6 ♎ *Speculator and Settler (31 July 1808 to 7 November 1810)* 325

step in this direction. But Foveaux quickly made it clear that this was just not going to happen and, as the *Estramina* sailed for Port Dalrymple with the Governor's letter to Paterson, it also carried one from Foveaux. Despite Bligh being 'extremely desirous' of reinstatement, he told Paterson, 'nothing can be more certain that his own destruction, as well as that of any person who might attempt to restore him, would be the inevitable result of such a step'.[9] By now Foveaux was satisfied that the suspension of Bligh was 'the only means of preventing an insurrection', and he was keen to get Bligh out of the colony as soon as possible. To help him formulate a plan 'to the disposal of Captain Bligh, should he not really mean to carry into effect the intention he has expressed of going to England in the *Porpoise*', he hoped that Paterson could return with the *Estramina* as soon as possible.

Despite his initial proclamation asserting he was unable to decide between Johnston and Bligh, in his letters Foveaux expressed himself quite strongly and clearly. On Johnston's actions, he was clear that if an investigation was ordered to take place in New South Wales 'which I think desirable, as the only measure that can ascertain the truth beyond the possibility of doubt, I will forfeit my existence if the verdict of an impartial tribunal will not completely justify the Measures which Major Johnston was call'd upon to adopt'. On Bligh's promises, he was equally clear that 'Captain Bligh has notified to me that he meant to proceed to England in the *Porpoise*, but I have every reason to be certain he entertains no such intention'.[10]

But the *Porpoise* would not be going anywhere fast. She had arrived back from Port Dalrymple at the end of May, damaged from striking ground. Since the first week of June she had been with Thomas Moore and by 3 August she was still under repair.[11] By mid-August according to the information Foveaux had received—presumably from Moore himself—it was still going to require some two months to fit her again for sea.[12]

With Bunker and the *Pegasus* safely despatched to Pegasus Island, around the edges of the *Porpoise* repairs, Moore could slowly work on his own domestic affairs. He had started building a house on the George's River, on the 750 acres at Banks Town granted in December 1805[13]—although it is not clear exactly when he began. It may have been as far back as February 1807, when he bought Iron and Nails. He also purchased 28 pounds of 4 inch spikes in November 1807—which must have been strange bedfellows in the shopping cart along with the two pairs of double milled pantaloons he bought for Rachel.[14] A jar of paint oil followed in May, but there is little other evidence of potential building activity until September 1808, when he purchased sheets of lead, quantities of nails, and a keg of brown paint (Figure 45), perhaps indicating the house was ready for roofing and prettying up. November must have afforded him opportunity for further activity on the house, for he bought more nails and two more kegs of brown paint that month, but the only purchase he made in December was a ham—perhaps with his Christmas celebrations in view.[15] These signs of building activity indicate that the new home on the banks of the peaceful George's River—a home Thomas and Rachel aptly named Moore Bank—was almost completed by the end of the year. It also shows that Thomas Moore was preparing to move from the turmoil of Sydney. The more settled life of the farmer was calling, and the larger property at the expanding edge of the colony catered for his pioneering spirit as well as for his extensive farming interests. At Moore Bank he would also be well positioned, ready to become the leading citizen of Liverpool.[16]

On 26 October 1808, Thomas Moore was appointed to act as Coroner to inquire into the death of Elizabeth Ford, who had fallen into a faint and died that morning. At the hearing, Thomas Moore inquired whether she was addicted to Liquor, which apparently she was—as well as melancholy—but a witness declared her sober when she died. After hearing the depositions, Moore found that she 'came to her death through the visitation of God'.[17]

Having willingly performed such extra duties for some years, it appears that Moore was beginning to divest himself from them a little. Earlier that same month, Moore had acquired duties in regard to the Estate of James Aicken. Since Aicken was a sea Captain, serving at various times on the *Francis*, then Moore's *Integrity*, then the *Marcia* on the voyage to Wreck Reef to salvage and burn the wreck of the *Porpoise* and *Cato*, before turning to trading vessels such as the *King George*, he would have been well-known to Moore.[18] But despite such

CHAPTER 6 ⚓ *Speculator and Settler (31 July 1808 to 7 November 1810)* 327

a long-term acquaintance, Moore applied for release from this responsibility, which was granted by the Judge-Advocate's office on 26 Nov 1808:[19]

> WHEREAS Mr THOMAS MOORE, of Sydney, Ship Builder, has duly relinquished and annulled his Trust to the Estate and Effects of the late Mr JAMES AICKEN, deceased, the Will being incomplete, and being moved thereunto by other good causes and reasons, as appears by an instrument signed and sealed by him, and bearing date the 21st of October, 1808—To the Estate and Effects of the late Mr JAMES AICKEN, now know ye, that Letters of Administration have been duly granted to SUSANNAH BALLARD, who has entered into the necessary Bonds with Sureties, to faithfully execute the Trust.

What 'other good causes and reasons' occupied the 'Ship Builder' were left undefined by the advertisement, but perhaps the extra building activity along the George's River would be a good guess. Susannah took out her own advertisement in the *Gazette* to the same effect, immediately under Moore's.

Moore continued to administrate Surgeon John White's interests in New South Wales. In November Moore advertised White's farm on the Parramatta road as for lease.

> To be Let, on Lease for any Term up to 21 years, a truly valuably situate, and excellent Pasture Farm, in all respects adapted to the improvement of the Dairy, being within 4 miles of Sydney, and immediately contiguous to Major JOHNSTON's Estate on the Parramatta road—comprising nearly 130 acres 40 clear, and capable of producing very excellent crops—the same being the property of JOHN WHITE, Esq. formerly Principal Surgeon of this Territory.—The whole delightfully watered, and in every respect commanding the most serious attention.—For further information apply to Mr THOMAS MOORE.[20]

Moore also looked after John White's house in town, and since September 1807 probably owned Captain Raven's adjoining property. Both these properties would have fallen under Foveaux's approbation of certain properties in Sydney Town. Anticipating what took place under Macquarie, Foveaux suggested in September 1808 that:

grants should be made to those persons who have expended large sums of money in the erection of houses, a few of which in the town of Sydney would not, I assure you, disgrace the most fashionable Square in London, and have cost the proprietors several thousand pounds, altho' built upon leases of very limited extent, the renewal of which must totally depend upon the will of the future Governors.[21]

This was in the context of Foveaux complaining of Bligh interfering with people's property and leases. Others, too, had not forgotten the former Governor, or his overthrow. On 4 Nov 1808 a group of settlers, probably led by George Suttor, wrote a petition to Castlereagh, explaining the 'cause and effect of the change of government that took place in Jan'y last'. The group disavowed any knowledge of the rebellion, and claimed that not twenty of the inhabitants of the colony had been consulted before it took place. Since several ex-LMS missionaries are amongst the signatories, including Rowland Hassall, it is not surprising that the petition mentions as a consequence of the rebellion the silencing of the only clergyman in the colony. One of their further complaints was that the rebellion had led to decreased agriculture, due to the soldiers monopolising the convict labour.[22]

Given that feelings were still running high, it must have been a strange event indeed when, on the 25th of December, a Government and General Order appeared in the *Sydney Gazette* announcing the promotions of William Paterson, to Colonel; George Johnston, to Lieut-Colonel, and Edward Abbott, to Major.[23] The promotions were dated 7 May 1808, before the news of the insurrection had reached England, but when the Christmas Day *Gazette* announced this news, it must have seemed like the Government at home had rewarded those in New South Wales who had just overthrown it.

1809

What a year it had been.

WILLIAM PATERSON ARRIVES

On 1 January 1809, newly promoted Lieut.-Colonel William Paterson finally arrived in Sydney from Port Dalrymple, marking the commencement of the third phase of the rebel regime and pleading

CHAPTER 6 ⚓ *Speculator and Settler (31 July 1808 to 7 November 1810)* 329

illness for his long delay.²⁴ As the *Porpoise* sailed through the heads, Foveaux sent him a message that Bligh intended to give orders to its Commanding Officer to put Paterson under arrest and detain him on board as a prisoner. Understandably, Paterson took offence.

After Paterson arrived, he did not restrict Bligh's communications and the Governor therefore continued to issue orders and interfere in various ways, much to Paterson's frustration, especially over the use of the *Porpoise* for the evacuation of Norfolk Island, which Bligh was preventing by exerting his authority over Captain Porteus. Seeing that it was best to remove Bligh from the colony, Paterson made arrangements for him to proceed in the *Admiral Gambier*. Paterson gave orders to the Master Builder to fit out the *Admiral Gambier*, but Bligh then sent word that he would proceed to Europe in the *Porpoise*.²⁵

After agreeing to leave for Europe, Bligh embarked on 20 February and by 12 March had announced his intention to sail on the first fair wind. As Bligh was preparing to leave the colony he received a letter from James John Grant, which once again reflected upon the insurrection, and the standover tactics that had prevailed, as he bewailed the colony's loss of a meritorious Governor:²⁶

> by a rebellious set of soldiery, a set of tyrants and usurpers, who extorted from us our names to their lawless proceedings to justify their infamous attack on the person of your Excellency. They succeeded in their views, and obtained the signatures of hundreds from fear, dread, and terror, as their rage had no seeming bounds; […] our signatures were obtained from motives of fear for our lives and property, and, when we are relieved from the iron rod of tyranny and oppression now suspended over our heads, it will appear that the signatures of the major part of the people were extorted form them nearly three weeks subsequent to the arrest of your Excellency.

Paterson was suspicious that Bligh would break the agreement.²⁷ As it happened, his suspicions were well founded. Bligh was proud of himself for getting hold of the *Porpoise*, for it was all part of his formulated plan. When the *Porpoise* sailed on 17 March 1809, the deposed Governor left a sealed letter with Palmer to be handed to the officer sent from England for his 'succour', which outlined his plan:²⁸

> I have at last by finesse got possession of my ship, but I am sorry to say my officers are very improperly disposed. Their connexions with the rebels have made them like themselves in opinion. Stratagems upon stratagems are devised by the rebels to circumvent me, and take me out of my ship. Therefore, not having any confidence of support, I mean to remove for the present to the Derwent, where you will immediately send me intelligence of your arrival; and, until I return, which will be as speedily as possible, I have to require you will detain in safe custody all persons connected with the rebellion, and for your information I enclose a copy of my proclamation of this date.

Bligh attempted to disseminate his proclamation as widely as he could, given the constraints he was under. As well as leaving a copy with Palmer on shore, as Rev. H. Fulton explained to Mrs Bligh, he 'left in the form of Letters sealed up & directed to the Masters of Ships & loyal Civil Officers of this Colony a Proclamation',[29] and for a short time the *Porpoise* sat outside the heads for the purpose of distributing flyers to the in- and out-going vessels.

In the proclamation, he styled himself 'Captain General and Governor-in-Chief in and over His Majesty's Territory of New South Wales and its Dependencies, and Commodore commanding His majesty's Ships and Vessels employed in the South Pacific Ocean, &c &c &c'. In his own mind, Bligh was still the lawful authority in the colony and this proclamation was therefore an official act of his Government. Paterson, for his part, saw it as a violation of the 'solemn engagement' he had reached with Bligh.[30] On 19 March he published his own proclamation, which included a true copy of the agreement Bligh had signed to depart for Europe that he had now breached. Paterson forbade any ship or person to receive communications from the *Porpoise* or assist her in any way, on threat of being dealt with 'as abettors of Sedition, and Enemies to the Peace and Prosperity of the Colony'.[31]

Bligh proclaimed the NSW Corps to be 'in a state of mutiny and rebellion', and he prohibited masters of ships from 'taking any person or persons connected, or supposed to be connected, in the rebellion, out of the colony'. He then particularly singled out along with the officers of the Corps, John McArthur, Nicholas Bayly, Garnham

CHAPTER 6 ↓ *Speculator and Settler (31 July 1808 to 7 November 1810)* 331

Blaxcell, Richard Atkins, Gregory Blaxland, John Townson, Robert Townson, Robert Fitz, Thomas Jamieson, Thomas Hobby, Alexander Riley, D'Arcy Wentworth, James Mileham, Walter Stephenson Davidson, and—in second last position—Thomas Moore.[32]

Why had Moore gained such a prominent place amongst the rebels in Bligh's mind? Was Moore truly amongst the rebels? Some of his biographers have been content to notice his presence on this list, but to pass over what this might imply;[33] others, to see his presence as an indication of his complicity in the rebellion.

> That he took a prominent part is evident, as Bligh, from on board the man-of-war in which he had been placed and deported, issued a notice including him with a few others who must not be allowed to leave the colony. He hoped for their punishment. But, of course, his power was gone.[34]

Robinson, however, rightly notes that Moore stands in a 'somewhat ambiguous position in relation to Bligh'[35]—and to the insurrection itself. Harris complained to King that Bligh had conducted something of a purge of the various Government positions when he came, but Moore retained his under Bligh—like Governor King had done, Bligh found him to be 'a useful and necessary officer' almost as soon as he stepped ashore. And yet, as he was forced to leave the colony, Moore was one of the fifteen civilians on his hit list. Yes, Moore had signed the petition and two further rebel addresses. He had surveyed the stores, and yet declined to serve on the Court of Civil Judicature—did he have 'qualms about the whole procedure'? He had dealings with the Governor throughout the whole fiasco of what ship he should be sent home on and its refitting, and he was the one who repaired the *Porpoise*, the vessel eventually gaining that honour. Evidently Bligh continued to think Moore a 'useful officer' in this regard, for as one of his last acts before he left the colony was to give the naval brig *Lady Nelson* into Moore's charge, with directions to hand her over to Paterson should he require her for the use of the colony.[36] Robinson suggests two reasons for Bligh's indictment of Moore. Firstly, rather than any overt act committed by Moore, it must have been because of the position he held as a Civil Officer in the colony and, perhaps especially, as an officer in the Loyal Association, who had nevertheless been a party to the arrest. Perhaps Bligh regarded the Loyal Association also in 'as mutinous a position as the New South Wales Corps itself'. The second reason suggested by Robinson related to the *Pegasus*. This vessel was at one point offered as Bligh's transport home (he refused it), then it was withdrawn, and then it was sent after the *Harrington*, equipped by Government Stores under the shadow of Palmer's insinuation of being another example of a more general purloining of supplies by the rebels. 'No doubt some of Bligh's annoyance and apprehension over the whole incident rubbed off on to the new owner of *Pegasus*'.[37]

If the *Pegasus* had provoked Bligh's chagrin already, then his ire would have been brought to the surface just as the *Porpoise* was readying herself to leave. Bligh announced his intention to sail on 12 March, and, two days before he sailed on the 17th, Bunker brought the *Pegasus* back into the harbour on the 15th —perhaps one of the first vessels to receive one of Bligh's flyers containing his proclamation?

Although the exact movements of the *Pegasus* after she sailed from Sydney on 26 August 1808 are not known, the next datable piece of information is a receipt from 7 February for stores left with the sealing party on a small island off the Northwest coast of what is now called Stewart Island at the tip of the South Island of New Zealand. Their name for it was 'Pegasus Island'; but more recently it acquired the name 'Codfish Island'. Presumably they reached this location fairly quickly, perhaps by the end of September, and commenced sealing. By February, when sufficient seal-skins had been gathered for a cargo back to Sydney, presumably at that point Bunker landed the supplies and the receipt was issued.

When they sailed from Sydney their destination was a closely guarded secret. As the seals of the Bass Strait Islands had been heavily harvested, the numbers were in serious decline and the industry already falling off. Even by October 1807, Surgeon Luttrell could write that the seal trade

> is greatly on the decline, as the seals are all nearly destroy'd on the southern islands on this coast, or, from the constant molestation they have suffer'd, have abandoned the islands. To get a cargo of skins, new and more distant islands must be discover'd, and the

CHAPTER 6 ↓ *Speculator and Settler (31 July 1808 to 7 November 1810)* 333

consequent risk and expence must be so much increased that the amount of the cargoes will hardly pay the charges.[38]

But when Bunker sailed the *Pegasus* into Port Jackson on 15 March 1809, he had 12,600 seal skins on board and he arrived in a boom time for their importation. No less than 45,000 skins arrived in Sydney that same week. (Figures 48 and 49). Since London was paying 30s per skin on average at this time, the total value of the week's imports from the sealing islands promised £72,000 on delivery to London, and when the 20,000 skins already stowed in the *Santa Anna* was taken into account, this figure went up to £102,500.[39]

ARRIVED SYDNEY	SHIP	MASTER	NUMBER
11 March 1809	Governor Bligh	Grono	10,000
15 March 1809	Fox	Cox	13-14,000
15 March 1809	Pegasus	Bunker	12,600
	Santa Anna		20,000
22 March 1809	Antipode		4,000

Figure 48: Seal-skins taken in to Sydney, 1809.

Nov 1792–Sept 1793	Britannia	Raven	4,500
Nov 1803 to June 1804	Endeavour, Surprise, Governor King		28,282[40]
19 March 1806	Venus	S.R. Chace	5,000[41]
30 Dec 1806	Star		14,000 +[42]
10 July 1808	Commerce	Ceroni	3,000[43]

Figure 49: Seal-skins taken in to Sydney, other periods.

But this was a very temporary boom. The extraordinary number of skins coming into Sydney in March 1809 was due to one simple thing: the discovery of a new strait, filled with fresh victims for the sealers' slaughter. Just as Moore's sealing profits began to come in, so too were they about to take a turn for the worse.

Because Bunker's sealing party was left behind in this newly discovered sealing ground, their secret location was to be maintained. Stephen Lawrence remained, in charge of the others and with supplies meant to last five or six months, along with quantities of between five and six tons of salt and provisions for the procuring of more seal skins.[44] Captain Bunker left strict instructions for Lawrence. He was to take at least ten men 'for the purpose of killing all the Seals you possibly can. Take all the care possible to salt them well & keep them dry'. With a healthy dose of paranoia, they were to be careful not to show any smoke lest any vessel come close, and they were not to lend any salt or provisions to any other sealing gang that may happen to be left on the island—why assist the competition? At the end of the period, the gang will have the choice to return to Port Jackson, where they will be 'secure in Mr Moors hand', or to proceed to England to 'have the benefit of the Market Prices there'. When Bunker returned for them he would fly a flag at the fore top gallant head. As a footnote Bunker adds: 'PS 'Those who go on to England in the Ship to make their voyage it will be left to Mr Moor whether or no the Market price will be Paid but I don't doubt But Mr Moor will give you that Indulgence'.[45]

Moore's accounts for March and April show that when the *Pegasus* arrived in Sydney, the men were discharged and the skins unloaded—or at least, wharfage fees were paid for 8700 skins (where were the other 4900)?[46] The accounts for each of the 25 crew have survived among Moore's papers.[47] They had already received an advance on wages at the commencement of the voyage, as was the usual practice. Various items were sold them on the voyage by Bunker, and now on discharge the accounts were to be settled and, in addition, they were to receive their lay. Several of the pay chits have written on the top 'the Nett proceeds of the Pegasus voyage, £2591-12', calculated on 8626 Seal Skins (£2587.16) and 76 pups @ 1s (£3.16), and each man would get his share of that, according to his agreed lay. This would be paid only at the end of the voyage and so those who were paid a share in April 1809, were those who were not going to take the next leg of the journey. (Figure 50).

CHAPTER 6 ⚓ *Speculator and Settler (31 July 1808 to 7 November 1810)* 335

CREWMAN	AMOUNT OWED AT START £.S.D	AMOUNT OWED TO SHIP AT END £.S.D	AMOUNT PAID BY SHIP £.S.D	BALANCE £.S.D
Lawrence Doyle	7.1.0	14.14.6	Not stated	Owe 14.14.6
John Clements	28.5.2	33.4.8	25.18.4 (1/100th)	Owe 7.6.4
David Christian	22.3.0	34.13.0	Not stated	Owe 34.13.0
John White	5.0.0	12.8.6	Not stated	Owe 12.8.6
Robert Currant	23.12.11 ½	33.2.5 ½	Not stated	Owe 33.2.5 ½
Abram Moseley	20.8.6	32.8	Not stated	Owe 32.8
John Howe	40.4.0	48.0.0	Not stated	Owe 48.0.0
Thos Dunn	10.6.0	19.14.6	Not stated	Owe 19.14.6
Stephen Lawrence	24.7.3 ½	33.1.9 ½	Paid the Advance	Owe 8.19.6
Daniel O'Brien	5.3.0	12.1.0	Not stated	Owe 12.1.0
Mark Munrow	10.13.11	20.0.11	25.18.4 (1/100th)	Owed 4.2.5
Benjamin Levett	7.3.0	10.12.6	Not stated	Owe 10.12.6
John Warney	0.0.0	6.15.0	Not stated	Owe 6.15.0
W. Wilson	30.0.0	45.6.8	64.15.9 (1/40th)	Owed 33.9.5 ½
John Harper	8.7.10	18.2.10	25.18.4 (1/100th)	Owed 7.5.6
John Carney	0.0.0	5.5.6	22.10.8 (1/115th)	Owed 17.5.2
James Allen	5.0.0	14.5.6	22.10.8 (1/115th)	Owed 6.17.2, or 15.13.6
Peter Risden	5.0.0	13.10.6	22.10.8 (1/115th)	Owed 9.0.2
Zachariah Price	5.0.0	14.13.0	23.11.1 (1/110)	Owed 8.13.1
Thomas Jackson	4.0.0	13.10.6	22.10.8 (1/110)	Owed 12.0.2
James Galvin	5.0.0	9.19.0	23.11.1 (1/110)	Owed 10.2.0
Patrick Byrne	11.4.0	19.14.0	25.18.4 (1/100)	Owed 6.4.4
Wm Ramsey	14.0.0	23.6.0	25.18.4 (1/100)	Owed 23.6.0

Figure 50: Payments of Pegasus crewmembers, April 1809.[48]

In a colony without its own specie and when payment was so often in goods, it makes sense that this should have been a 'zero sum' game in terms of the exchange of goods. Their advance on wages made it convenient for them to receive the kind of goods they required while they were at sea: Mr Wilson bought a fowling piece and another crewman a knife, but more standard items were trousers, stockings, waistcoats, jackets, mittens, caps, the occasional shoes and drawers, plenty of tobacco, some bundles of cigars, and everyone seemed to have multiple banyans. The latter items were loose fitting jackets from India. They may have been associated with the sailors' leisure. During the Vice Admiralty Court proceedings in relation to the Mutiny on the *Barwell*, it came out that one of the soldiers involved, William Hallam, had complained of the disparity between the sailor's provisions and their own, saying that the soldiers 'would have no banyan days—that they had hard duty'.[49] The ubiquitous presence of the banyan amongst the sailors of the *Pegasus* is a sign that someone on the supply side was a trader who had 'offloaded' some product onto Bunker, who then offloaded it to the crew. The supplier was probably not Mr Moore, for there is no evidence of such sales in his accounts, but one of the other owners, Simeon Lord, would certainly be a good candidate for the wholesaler behind Bunker's nice little earner. Unfortunately for many, the ship-board barter system meant that they started the voyage in debt and finished even further behind!

While sailing in Foveaux Strait, the *Pegasus* had 'struck upon a rock but received very little damage, and the *Governor Bligh* met a like accident, though with no material damage'.[50] On her return to Sydney, *Pegasus* was in good hands with her ship's-husband also being the colony's skilful Master Boat Builder. Moore would be keen to check the damage for himself and make some repairs. The ship was hove down, which cost Moore £1-1s in rum. Several labourers were employed for a number of days to fit the ship, and a sail maker engaged to ply his craft.[51] All kinds of equipment and provisions, both salt and fresh, were also stowed for the next voyage.

The return to Sydney also enabled a change in Captain, which took place on 8 April. This probably came about because the next leg of the journey would end up in England and Bunker's family was now

CHAPTER 6 ↭ *Speculator and Settler (31 July 1808 to 7 November 1810)* 337

based in New South Wales. Soon after his return, Bunker put his roots down even further in New South Wales, when he received a further 500 acres on 20 April 1809 alongside the George's River in the 'District of Cabramatta'.[52] The family still lived in the Pitt's Row house built for them under Thomas Moore's direction. On 2 June, Isabella Bunker married Lieutenant Thomas Laycock, the son of his namesake father famous for helping suppress the 1804 uprising. Thomas junior also had his own moment of glory when, in 1806, he was the first to walk from Port Dalrymple to Hobart and back again. He was a member of the court assembled to try John Macarthur and which played such an instrumental role in the lead-up to the 1808 rebellion. He supported Johnston against Bligh, and became the only casualty of the 'Rum Rebellion' when he fell through a manhole during the search of Government House. As a reward, Foveaux granted him 500 acres in Cabramatta, so Isabella married someone who already had some land-wealth.[53] However, Bunker did not leave the *Pegasus* to sit at home or to start farming his new land, but he was soon on his way to Calcutta to pick up another ship filled with wheat to sell to a colony low on grain supplies due to the 1809 Hawkesbury floods.[54] When Bunker left the ship on 8 April, Moore's old client Captain Samuel Chace took over the command of the *Pegasus*.

Since the original adventure of the *Britannia* at Dusky Bay, one of the profit-making beauties of the sealing voyage, as opposed to whaling, was that a gang of men could be left on an island to kill as many seals as they could, while the ship itself went off on other enterprises thus earning profits beyond the sale of the skins. At the end of March, Thomas Moore and his partners managed to score such an opportunity, when the *Pegasus* received a commission from the Government. As ship's-husband, Thomas Moore wrote to Colonel Paterson:[55]

> As you have directed that the Ship *Pegasus* should be taken up in the Service of Government to proceed to His Majesty's Settlement at the River Derwent with Stores and Provisions, I have to request you will be pleased to order a Survey to be held on the said Ship in order to ascertain whether she is capable of performing that Service and also of proceeding from thence to England, touching

at such Islands or Places as may be necessary for her to do to procure Seal Skins for the London Market so that I may be able to effect an Insurance from the report of Survey.

James Finucane replied on Paterson's behalf:

> Mr Finucane compliments Mr Moore, begs to acquaint him that the Lt Govr does not require any survey to be held on the *Pegasus*, as he is satisfied of her being fit for the Service on which Gov^t has occasion to employ her.
>
> A Survey for any other purpose is a matter with which the public Service is intirely unconcerned, & with which therefore the Lt Govr declines interfering.

Such a curt reply indicates quite clearly that Thomas Moore received no special indulgence from Paterson's rebel regime in this instance! Although the Governor refused to give Moore a free survey for insurance purposes, there were nevertheless certain business advantages in having the contract. Moore was paid £600 for the Charter Party, and he, in turn, drew out £620.19.6 worth of goods from the stores: clothing, rope, red paint, fish hooks, shot and gunpowder, and balls and flints, as well as pitch, oakum, nails, and salt provisions (pork and beef).[56] Mr Moore paid the £16.3.6 difference, but added a note that he neglected to charge it against the ship. In other words, the way this was going to work was the *Pegasus* was paid in freight and would make her money in what she charged at the other end.

On 9 April, the day after Chace took over from Bunker, Moore advertised for new crew:

> Wanted immediately six seamen for the ship *Pegasus* about to proceed to the River Derwent, and from thence on a Sealing Voyage; after which to England. Application to be made on board to Captain Chase.[57]

The acceptance of the Government contract caused a bit of a set-back in Moore's sealing venture. On Bunker's return from Pegasus Island, the crew unloaded the skins they had brought with them. The master discharged the Chief Mate, Mr Mason, and his permission possibly also covered Thomas Jackson and Zachariah Price. Jackson, in any

CHAPTER 6 ⚓ *Speculator and Settler (31 July 1808 to 7 November 1810)* 339

case, did not leave the ship until he did so with several others after the expiration of twenty-two days (John Clements, John Harpole, Peter Rosser, William Ramsden, and James Allen). Moore had ended up in arbitration with these men over their absence from the ship, which then required Samuel Rodman Chace (NB not the same person as the Chace who was now Captain of the *Pegasus*) to act as umpire between the two arbitrators (Messrs Stewart and Yates). Chace decided in favour of the men, who had either been dismissed by the commander, or had left after twenty-two days, and so were not in breach of their articles. Furthermore, because Moore had taken the Government contract, the route of the voyage and the commander of the vessel had changed and, even if the *Pegasus* had taken them back to the sealing gang, time would be lost, and so Sydney was effectively the port of discharge and Moore was liable to pay them their dues. The issue was not the men's absence without permission, but Moore's inability to provide them a ship upon which they could continue their service, and so, once the cargo was discharged, it was reasonable for them to leave. Moore was therefore ordered to pay the men their lay (share). The men for their part were directed, according to their agreement, to sell their skins to the owner (Moore) for six shillings, the current Sydney price, and they were also to bear the costs of arbitration and umpirage.[58]

The next day, 15 April, Captain Samuel Chace (not the umpire, Samuel Rodman Chace) wrote to his friend, Thomas Moore, 'Master of the King's Yard, Sydney'. Moore had been Chace's agent since 1801, and the ship's captain now reported that he had acquired one grant and two leases of land at the Derwent, leaving the leases with Captain William Collins, a naval officer who had come as a free settler on the *Ocean* to Port Phillip. He was the Mr Collins who took despatches to Sydney in the six-oared cutter, who subsequently joined the party who founded the original settlement at the Derwent in 1803. After holding several Government posts, such as harbour master and Naval Officer, he had turned to a variety of commercial pursuits by the time Chace availed of his services.[59] Having alerted Moore to the location of these leases, Chace asked him 'if any unforeseen axident should unfortunately happen to me on my Voyage you will do me the particular favour to inquire into my Affairs at the Derwent'.[60]

On 27th April, Thomas Moore, 'Master of the Dockyard at Sydney' and 'managing owner' on behalf of 'the owners' signed a memorandum of agreement with Chace. One of the witnesses was Eber Bunker, who also signed that his agreement with Moore came to an end on 8 April, the date Chace's began.[61] The owners of the *Pegasus*, with a burthen of 206 tons, agreed to provide all necessary supplies and provisions for a twelve month voyage, along with fishing gear and salt necessary for the procuring of seal skins, as well as to pay all the seamen their lays or wages according to their articles. Chace is firstly to take the Government cargo to the Derwent, being granted one twelfth of the freight money. Once the cargo is discharged, he is to proceed to the South Seas to acquire a cargo of seal skins. He is to call at 'a certain island near New Zealand' to take on board whatever skins the party of men left there have procured, and, again, Chace is entitled to one twelfth. The agreement didn't say what he should do with the men. Once this cargo is stowed, he is to proceed on a sealing voyage in the South Seas to wherever, according to his best judgement, he will find the most skins, and then to proceed to London. There he is to discharge the skins at the Customs House, and deliver the vessel to Thomas Moore's Agents, who will settle with Chace on Moore's behalf.

Bligh made himself scarce after Paterson's proclamation of 19 March and he arrived at the Derwent on 30 March 1809. Lieut.-Gov. Collins later observed that he was obviously firmly of the belief that he was 'Governor in Chief, and still possessed of the power and authority of that office'.[62] At first Collins received him with hospitality on shore. This changed, however, when the *Aeolus* arrived bringing the *Sydney Gazette* containing Paterson's proclamation against Bligh, which was read publicly by Rev Robert Knopwood in church and Collins gave an order to enforce it. Collins wrote to Bligh that he could have nothing further to do with Bligh, and from then on Bligh had trouble gaining supplies—or even water.[63] Bligh returned to the *Porpoise* and 'began to exercise his authority afloat, ordering the boats of the colony, when passing up or down the river in the daytime on the public service, to come within hail of his ship, upon pain of being fired into if they did not comply'.

On 2 May the Government supplies were shipped on board the

CHAPTER 6 ⚓ *Speculator and Settler (31 July 1808 to 7 November 1810)* 341

Pegasus. For the use of the settlement itself, 1551 bushels of wheat; 39 tierces of beef; 63 tierces of pork; and 612 iron hoops. Provisions for the Guard and prisoners sent on the passage: 3 tierces and 1 barrel of beef; 3 tierces and 1 barrel of pork; 2551 lbs of biscuit; 473 pints of pease; 20 canvas bags; 26 iron hoops on the casks; and sixty pairs of leg irons.[64] The next evening, Wednesday 3 May, Chace wrote to Moore:

> Dear Sir,
>
> I expect to sail in the morning at day light. I hope I shall get the bill of laden for the Government cargo as I give Mr Fitz the one that I had. As you have been always so Obliging to me I shall not charge you with my part or lay of Government freight. I say this to you to give you a hint. I do not think it right to allow any of my part to any of the rest of the owners. Therefore I think it right for you to charge them with the same and put this in the fire and there is an end to that part &c &c. Youl write to me by the *King George* and direct to the case of Wm. Colins, Esqr. And wishing you and Mrs Moore's health and happiness and forever remain your Affectionate friend, Sam Chace.
>
> P.S. Please give my compliments to Mr Fitz. I shall not forgit his goodness and kind respect to me. Likewise my best respect to Mrs Mary Harris and paid her good [grace?] for me and wish her a quick recovery and A long life.

Here Chace makes a sly suggestion as to how Mr Moore can profit from Chace's refusal of the freight, without passing on that profit to Moore's two partners, Harris and Lord. There is no evidence Moore took him up on the offer. The *Pegasus* sailed 'for His Majesty's settlement at Hobart Town, with provisions and upwards of 50 male prisoners, who are to be distributed among the Settlers removed from Norfolk Island thither'.[65] For the next two weeks, while Moore continued to pay the bills,[66] she sailed southwards to arrive at the Derwent on 19 May.[67]

Having dispatched his vessel on her speculative voyage with pay-dirt on the horizon, as the seal-skins were sold in the English market, Moore turned to deal with the petty problems of living in a penal colony. At the end of May he ran an advertisement about dockyard pilfering:

> Whereas an anonymous Letter has been dropped stating that a quantity of Junk had been stolen from the Dock-yard, I do hereby offer a Reward of Fifty Pounds Sterling to any person who will come forward and substantiate the assertion; or the like Reward to any person who will discover the writer of that Letter. Thos. Moore.[68]

On 28 May Samuel Terry advertised in regard to a lost 'Dark-brown Mare, rising 4 years old, with long tail, small star on the forehead, and a little white on the futlock of the off hind leg', last seen with an iron-grey filly foal, grazing with the other horses on Mr Moore's farm about a fortnight beforehand. With such a valuable animal now missing, Terry's offered reward of two pounds seems rather less than an attractive inducement.[69]

It wasn't just horses that strayed onto Moore's farm. On Wednesday morning 24 May, 'the lifeless body of John Driver, who had been many years a stockman in the neighbourhood of Sydney, was found hanging on a tree upon Mr Moore's farm, on the Parramatta road'. An inquiry was immediately ordered and the Coroner and jury turned in the verdict that the seventy year old had taken his own life. The *Gazette* commented that 'by a penurious mode of living was supposed to have saved a little money, which he never carried about with him; but the causes which had so powerfully operated on his mind as to provoke the horrible determination no one can form the least conception of. The body was interred on Friday near the place where the act was committed, and a stake driven through it'.[70]

At the end of May in New South Wales, the rain poured down and the rivers rose to similar levels to the record floods of 1806—even provoking comparison with the level of the water in 1801 which took John Stogdell's life.[71] The flooding of the Hawkesbury on 28 May was absolutely devastating, causing serious damage to the grain supplies of the colony.[72] The flooding even made international news, for the Scottish *Caledonian Mercury* picked up the *Sydney Gazette* report about the effect of the rain on the George's River:

> the banks of the George's river were unfortunately inundated at the same time; and a great quantity of stock and other property lost. In Major Johnston's stock-yard 490 sheep were drowned; Mr McCallum lost 300, and several houses were left in ruins.[73]

COLOUR PLATES ⚓ *A Portrait in his Actions. Thomas Moore of Liverpool (1762–1840)*

Plate 32: Convict uprising at Castle Hill, 1804. Artist: Unknown. National Library of Australia. nla.pic-an5577479.
Major Johnston is on the horse in the foreground, and to the left, Quartermaster Thomas Laycock strikes convict leader Phillip Cunningham on the head with his sword. The figure in clergyman's garb at the rear saying 'Lay down your arms my deluded country men' is catholic priest Father James Dixon. The figure on the horse in the blue uniform is Trooper Andlesark. The man uttering the words, 'liberty or death', to Major Johnston is a second depiction of Cunningham (so Stanley, *Remote Garrison*, 23). In the trees to the left, two corpses already hang on the gibbet—a depiction of what would happen after the battle. One is labelled [William] Johnston, the other [Samuel] Humes.

COLOUR PLATES ⚓ *A Portrait in his Actions. Thomas Moore of Liverpool (1762–1840)*

Plate 33: Loyal Volunteer Uniform (right), compared to that of the NSW Corps (left).

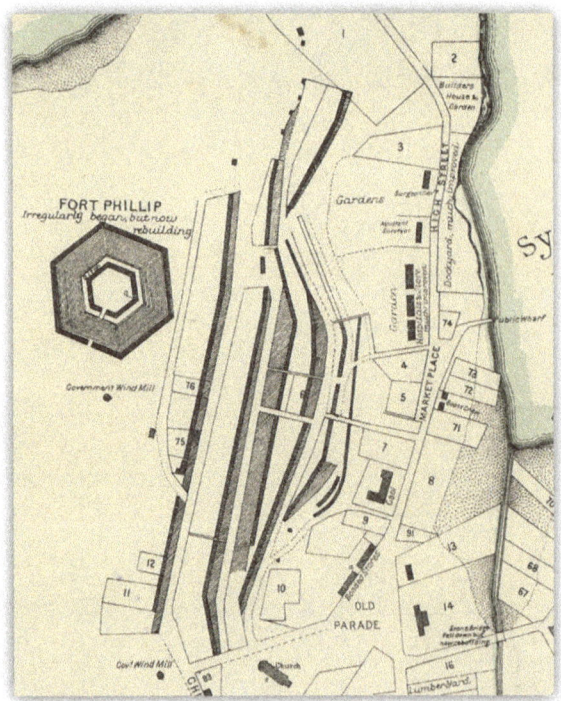

Plate 34: Detail of the Western Shore of Sydney Cove. Plan of the Town of Sydney in New South Wales, 1807.
Cartographer: James Meehan. National Library of Australia MAP F 105B
1,2: Robert Campbell. 3: William Balmain. 4: John White. 5: William Raven. 7: Henry Kable. 8. Maj. George Johnston.
72: Thomas Jameson. 73. Isaac Nichols. 74: Daniel McKay.

COLOUR PLATES ⚓ *A Portrait in his Actions. Thomas Moore of Liverpool (1762–1840)*

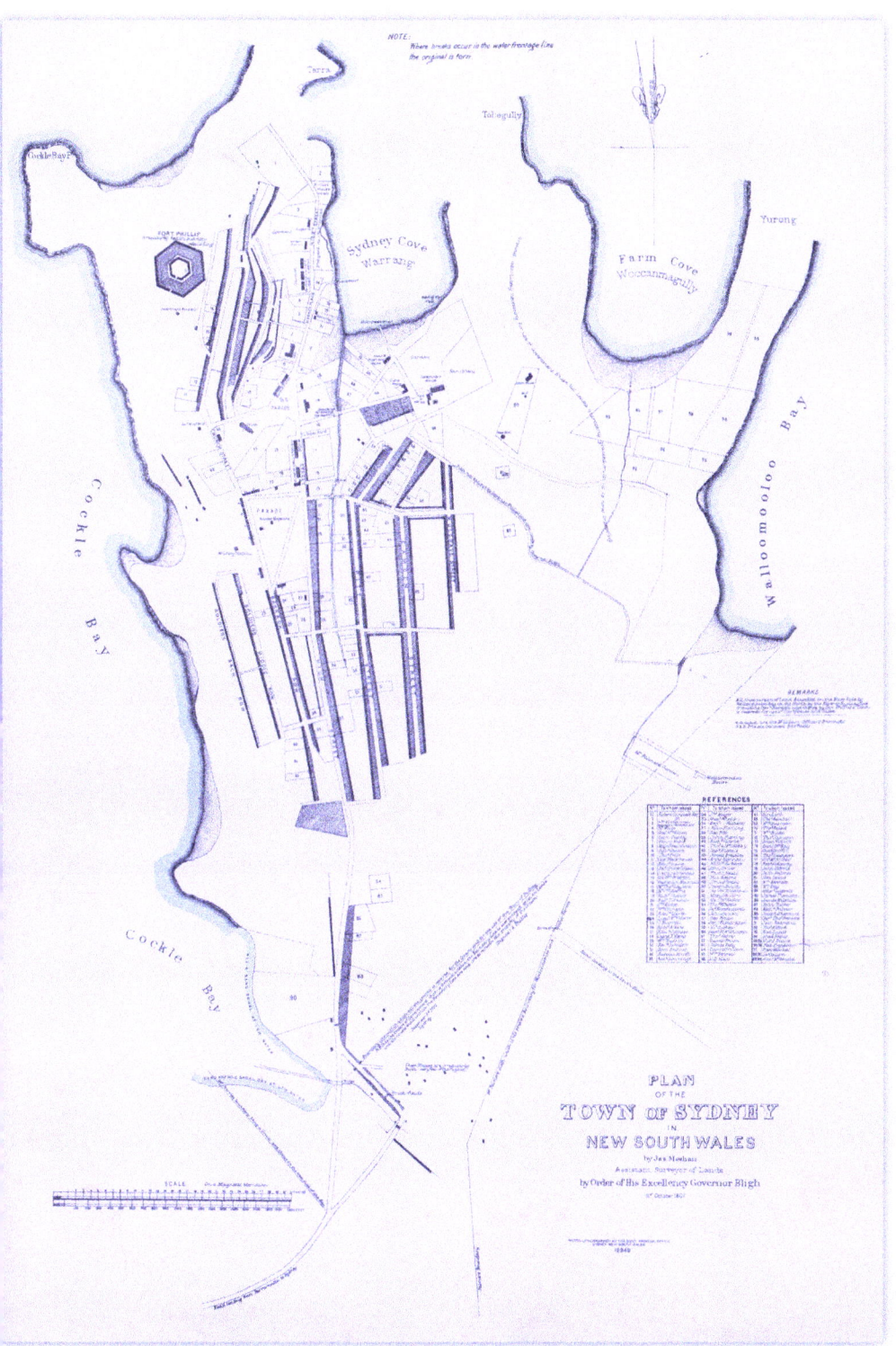

Plate 35: Plan of the town of Sydney in New South Wales, 1807. Cartographer: James Meehan. National Library of Australia MAP F 105B

COLOUR PLATES ⚓ *A Portrait in his Actions. Thomas Moore of Liverpool (1762–1840)*

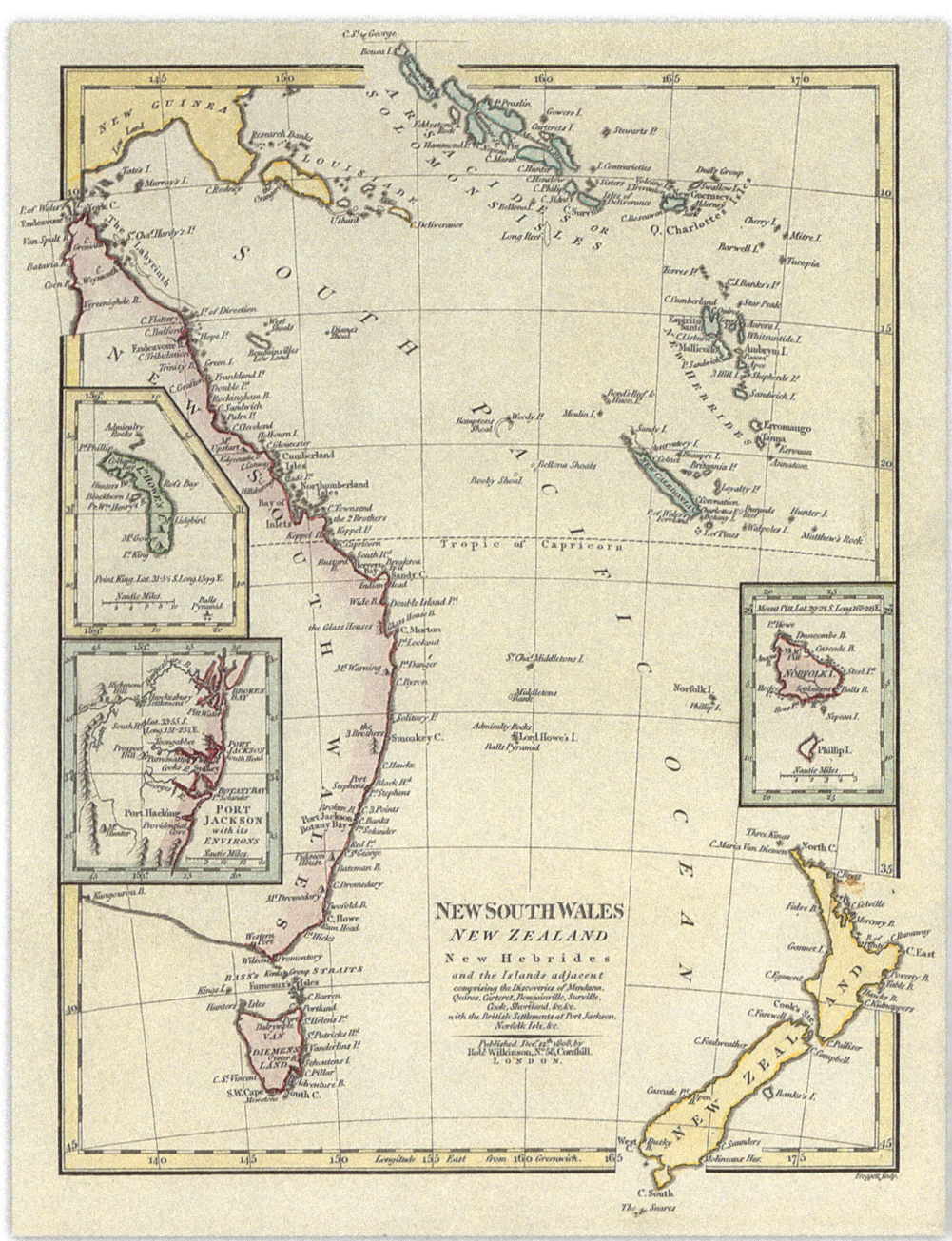

Plate 36: New South Wales, New Zealand, New Hebrides (1808). Robert Wilkinson, d. ca. 1825.
National Library of Australia. MAP T 1363

COLOUR PLATES ⚓ *A Portrait in his Actions. Thomas Moore of Liverpool (1762–1840)*

Plate 37: Simeon Lord, ca 1830. Artist: Unknown.
State Library of NSW. a128827.

Plate 38: John Harris
State Library of NSW. a2652001.

Plate 39: John Macarthur, 1800. Artist: Unknown. Copy of original made by Government Printer, 1898.
State Library of NSW. d1_12606.

Plate 40: Lt-Col George Johnston, ca. 1810. Artist: R. Dighton.
State Library of NSW. a1528248.

COLOUR PLATES ⚓ *A Portrait in his Actions. Thomas Moore of Liverpool (1762–1840)*

Plate 41: The "Lady Nelson" – Brig. Painting: ca. 1820's. Artist: Unknown. Based on engraving by S.I. Neele, published 1803.
State Library of NSW. a128461.
The ship is on the Thames.

Plate 42: George Bass. Artist: Unknown.
From miniature in the possession of Mr Pownall.
Copy of original made by Government Printing Office.
State Library of NSW. d1_12288.

Plate 43: Captain Eber Bunker, ca. 1810
State Library of NSW. a128664.

COLOUR PLATES ⚓ *A Portrait in his Actions. Thomas Moore of Liverpool (1762–1840)*

Plate 44: View of George's River, Residence of George Johnston, 1819. Artist: Joseph Lycett. State Library of NSW. a1120007.

Plate 45: Moore Bank, 1819. Artist: Joseph Lycett. State Library of NSW. a1120006.
The Moore's house is to the left, George's River on the right looking upstream to Liverpool.
Some of the features of the township are depicted in prospect—St Luke's never had a spire.

COLOUR PLATES ⚓ *A Portrait in his Actions. Thomas Moore of Liverpool (1762–1840)*

Plate 46: Moore Bank Site—riverside level. (2006) Photo: Geoff Bolt

Plate 47: Thomas Moore Park. Site of Moore Bank homestead (2006). Photo: Geoff Bolt

CHAPTER 6 ⚓ *Speculator and Settler (31 July 1808 to 7 November 1810)* 343

Another local report on the flooding in that district, incidentally reveals that Thomas Moore's house was completed:[74]

> At George's River the water was higher by 10 or 12 feet than it had been in the memorable flood of March 1806. At half past 6 on Friday morning 2 June it was at the highest, being then about 34 feet above the ordinary level of the river. Its ravages are distinguishable at the height of more than 30 feet, many situations that were before solid being now perfectly excavasated [sic]. The whole space extending from the bottom of the Horse-shoe Pond to the house of Mr Moore was totally under water, and had the resemblance of an extensive lake. The new house of Mr Knight is so much injured at the foundation as to render it necessary to be taken down and rebuilt. The lower part of the house was covered early in the evening of Thursday, and Mrs Knight and family were obliged to take refuge in a loft, from whence during the night they had the mortification to perceive the water rapidly gaining upon this last retreat, and in one hour rising 33 inches. The house of Emmerson the site of which was about 7 or 8 feet lower than Mr Knight's, was removed from its standing, and left in ruins. Much of the ground newly cropped was laid waste, and some stock supposed to be lost.

Whereas some homes were far too close to the river, situated on the high southern bank, the newly built 'Moore Bank' had survived its first baptism. (Plates 44–46).

Despite Moore Bank being ready for occupation, Moore was still very much involved in the life of Sydney Town. He still commanded the Loyal Sydney Volunteers Association, for example, and in June he received a new Lieutenant to assist him, Mr William Gaudry.[75]

It took the *Pegasus* fifteen days from Port Jackson to the Derwent, but Chace waited until mid-June before he wrote an update to Moore, whom he addressed as the 'Master of the King's Yard, Sydney'.[76] 'Have the pleasure to say that the *Pegasus* proves strong and tight and we have delivered the Government cargo in excel[l]ent order we are now fi[t]ting the ship and expect to sail from here in about eight or ten days'. Chace wasn't impressed with the convicts they had transported, however, some of whom had filed through their leg irons on the passage and plundered the goods in the hold. Thankfully the guard was praiseworthy in their duties. He has found the prices of supplies and provisions at the Derwent extremely high, but he has had to buy a cable and anchor and some sails. Captain Keith—who, while not reported by Chace, was on a schooner probably named the *Adventure*[77] —had arrived with only 3,000 skins, saying that there are gangs of sealers on every island about the coast.

Chace wrote again later the same day, sorry that they were now obliged to stay longer at the Derwent, having discovered the need for a new head for the main mast and new topmast rigging fore and aft, as well as other pieces of rigging and equipment.[78] Captain Keith's report had discouraged Chace a little. With gangs on all the islands he fears that they will not do as well as Bunker had predicted, and next season will be worse if more sealers arrive from England. He has on board nineteen people, still no second mate. He is unsure of how many from the island will join him, but they must be supported for they have not got twelve months provisions by calculation for twenty men. He suggests that Moore sends some more provisions over to the island, and that will be the rendezvous. As an afterthought as he ended the letter, he added a 'P.S.' that Moore better calculate for 30 men, 'I suppose your 10 men on the island will not let me take the skins without I take them home with me'.

On the 18th June he wrote again, sure that they would be leaving in three or four days, and now convinced that they will have plenty of salt provisions for the twenty-eight men, unless they leave some on the island. One of Chace's plans must have been to find the Cornwallis Island, but he strongly doubts that it exists. Captain Keith and others have had another look, but to no avail. Nevertheless, Chace will also have a look for it.[79]

When the *Estramina* came to the Derwent on 21 June, Bligh—still fighting the old battle—heard news that 'strong Measures were resorted to against the loyalists, and the most artful means used to win over every Person from holding any opinion in their favor, by granting to them Land, Leases, Cattle, and other indulgencies'.[80] In particular, 'they have been lavish in their Gifts and Indulgences to some of the worst characters, particularly to the Irish Rebels, Dwyer,

CHAPTER 6 ↕ *Speculator and Settler (31 July 1808 to 7 November 1810)*   345

Holt, and other principle ones; and the Romish Priest [James Harold?] is now wildly following his functions, which were before kept within proper bounds'.[81] Perhaps prompted by the sight of the *Pegasus* once again, now with him in the Derwent, Bligh also singles out Thomas Moore for some special attention:

> In order to secure payment to their new-created Officers (for their services)—Provost-Marshals, Secretaries, Judge-Advocates, Commandants, and Extra Superintendents—they have given them Cattle, Articles of Investment, Stores, and Copper Coin; and in this way they have paid Four hundred and ninety-six pounds, beside Provisions, to Thomas Moore, Boat Builder, for sending his Ship after the *Harrington*, which the Convicts ran away with in May last year, through the most unwarrantable neglect.[82]

This reveals the heart of Bligh's grievance with Moore. As he left Port Jackson, the *Pegasus* had just anchored in the Cove. This reminded him of the *Harrington* incident, fuelled further by Palmer's letter (4 Nov 1808) linking it with the purloining of stores.[83] Despite his previous regard for Moore's useful service at the dockyard, and with HM Ships, such as *Porpoise* and *Lady Nelson*, he had therefore placed Moore upon the list of those prohibited to leave the colony. Having been isolated at the Derwent, there is no reason to think that he would have heard anything to change his mind, and so by June, still simmering, he reveals his problem with Moore was the *Pegasus*.

As already noted previously, if this is what Bligh had against Moore, it was based upon misinformation. Firstly, Palmer had grossly exaggerated the figure, claiming that the 'deficiency amounts to about £870—exclusive of 6 weeks Provisions put on board for 71 Persons and 50 Gallons of Spirits'.[84] Secondly, Bligh's accounting with the figure £496, besides Provisions, is more realistic, but still not the whole story. Moore's own account books show that he loaded £245.7.3 ½ worth of HM Stores, was paid £463.10 in freight, and so was apparently paid the difference for the charter of the *Pegasus*, namely, £116.3.8 ½.[85]

On the 25 June, Chace wrote again to inform Moore that they would sail the following day, if granted a favourable wind. He is quite disappointed with the *Pegasus* venture, having spent a month discharging the cargo and refitting her for sea. 'My Dear Sir I am sorry to my very heart that I even took her and nothing but a good voyage I fear will make me Amends for I have been at a heavy expence already'. Two men were found stowed away, probably convicts.

On the eve of sailing, William Wilson also wrote to Moore, to pass on news and, because Moore acted as his agent, to check that 'a trifle' had been discharged with William O'Neale. When the arbitration took place between voyages, Wilson was the second mate, but by 2 May he had become Chief Mate, and when the *Pegasus* sailed she did so without a replacement for him as second mate.[86] Wilson's account of the voyage thus far, mentions that arrived at Hobart Town, the point of discharge, on 24 May, 'with our cargo of audacious thieves and Robbers'. He sounds a little more buoyant than Chace, being content that the ship has been made 'as substantial as Circumstances will admit'. They were ready for sea on the 25th, but a gale blew in from the southeast, but he hopes they will sail the next day. He reports the presence of Governor Bligh in the Derwent, hoping that they will 'be able to get out after passing a Ceremony of showing Gov[r] B[ligh] a list of our Provisions which he demands to see but the result cannot be Comprehended till it is over'.[87]

While Bligh was stopping the passing ships in the Derwent, another rumour altogether circulated in Sydney about his whereabouts. On 2 July the *Gazette* reported some news gained from a private communication 'on the accuracy of which there is every reason to rely' that Brigadier General Nightingall had been appointed to the Government of the colony, that the 73rd Regiment were about to embark to relieve the New South Wales Corps whose commanding officer was to be Lieutenant Governor, and that 'the arrival of Commodore Bligh in England was hourly expected'.[88] It is impossible to say how many Sydney-siders chose to trust this purportedly reliable report, for, as time would tell, its information proved accurate only in regard to the 73rd Regiment. Nightingall had, indeed, been appointed but due to subsequent illness he was forced to resign the position—at which point Francis Grose offered his services.[89] But the expectation of Bligh peacefully arriving in England was, of course, simply a fairy story. He was in the Derwent, where he had 'lately availed himself of his situation below the town, in Storm Bay Passage, and seized part of a supply of provisions which was coming here, and sent by Lieutenant-Governor Paterson for the use of this settlement'.[90] This was the last time his name was mentioned in the *Gazette* until January 1810, when Lachlan Macquarie arrived as his successor.

After the *Pegasus* got past the Bligh blockade, she arrived at Pegasus (now Codfish) Island on 16 July, and found the sealing-party in good health, with 2380 skins and another 1100 on some islands to the south. When Chace wrote to Moore on 2 August, he was planning to leave eight men on Pegasus Island and another six on the islands to the south, as it was pupping season, while he cruised adjacent islands. He hoped to get a good harvest of skins in time to sail home in December. He was planning to leave as many men as he could spare on the islands when he sailed, so he suggested that Moore should send more provisions. His dilemma was, however, that all those left by Bunker now wished to sail home to England when it came time for him to go.[91]

With this letter, Chace sent home Stephen Lawrence's accounts, kept from February, when Bunker had left them on Pegasus Island through to the time Chace took the cargo on 8 July. Since Bunker's share went through until 8 April, Chace sent a report back to Moore so that he could settle accounts with Bunker. By 20 February, the men had taken 323 seal skins, and by 8 April, 756. In July, Chace stowed a total of 3469 skins, his share therefore being 2713.[92] As Chace put it, this was very 'much short of our 20 Thousand here according to Capt Bunker's report of his Expectation'.[93]

As the usual story tells it, while in these uncharted waters, one William Stewart, purportedly the first Officer on the *Pegasus* rectified the deficiency. The *Pegasus* circumnavigated the large Island off the coast of the Southern tip of New Zealand, and named it after Stewart, who was furiously charting—'the reason for which has never been satisfactorily explained'.[94] The chart he made was later published in the *Oriental Navigator* in 1816. Captain Chace also gave his name to an island (now Pearl Island), and crewmen William Wilson and William Noble gained Noble Island and Wilson's Inlet, whereas Mr Mason, who was on her former voyage, accounts for Mason's Bay and

Mason's Head on the west coast of Stewart Island.[95]

McNab has already observed that, apart from the article in the *Oriental Navigator*, it is difficult to trace William W. Stewart and his connection to these islands or to the *Pegasus*. He was not recorded as being on board either the *Pegasus* or the *Governor Bligh* when they met in Foveaux Strait when the discovery was first noted.[96] It is interesting to observe that the discovery of the *Pegasus* documents amongst Moore's papers intensifies the mystery, for there is no William W. Stewart listed amongst her crew at any time—and especially not immediately before she sailed from Sydney on 26 August 1808.

There is even dispute about the identity of this William Stewart. William Stewart, the sealing master, came to Sydney originally in June 1801 from Calcutta on the *Harrington*, perhaps as an ex-prizemaster of a privateer. He used £1,500 in his possession to purchase a partnership with John Palmer in the Bass Strait sealing trade and between 1801 and 1805 his name frequently turns up in the sealing records, usually as a commander of the *George* or the *Edwin*, both of which were, like the *Harrington*, owned by Chace & Co. In 1805 he joined Campbell & Co, and led their sealing crews at Antipodes Island until, as the story goes, he turned up as first officer on the *Pegasus*, charting in New Zealand waters.[97]

This identification does not seem to be a correct. Besides the fact that he does not appear in the *Pegasus* accounts, in June 1809 William Stewart made the usual announcement of being about to leave the colony for claims to be made against him, and the vessel concerned was the *Antipode*.[98] This vessel had been in Foveaux Strait in mid-February when she spoke the *Pegasus*, when Captain Bunker was in charge of the voyage, arriving in Sydney on 22 March with only 4,000 skins.[99] The *Antipode* was originally built by John Blaxland from frames sent out on the *Brothers* and launched on 27 August 1807, and some strange changes of plans in 1809 may indicate that it came into the hands of Simeon Lord.[100] On 16 June an advertisement announced she was sailing for India, taking J.C. Burton and Eber Bunker with her.[101] But by 23 July Simeon Lord was advertising for 'ten or twelve able Seamen and Sealers' for her, but she didn't sail until July 1810, and in February 1810, William Stewart again announced his departure

CHAPTER 6 ↕ *Speculator and Settler (31 July 1808 to 7 November 1810)*   349

on her and requested claims be made against him.[102] In other words, this all sounds like this William Stewart remained in Sydney when the *Pegasus* sailed.

Given these various strands of evidence, Hodgkinson is probably correct in arguing that the William Stewart doing the charting was 'not the William Stewart the sealing master, who had been a business associate of John Palmer the Commissary, but a recent arrival in Sydney. He was a good cartographer'.[103] It appears to be incorrect, however, to identify Stewart (whoever he was) as the first officer on the *Pegasus*.

Stewart does appear, however, in another document in Moore's archive. Along with Mr Yates (most likely Henry), a Mr Stewart was one of the two arbitrators between Thomas Moore and the *Pegasus* officers and crew after their return to Sydney in March 1809: 'Messrs Stewart and Yates, Arbitrators, named and chosen, mutually, as well on the part and behalf of Mr Thomas Moore of Sydney, owner of the Ship *Pegasus* of the one part And the officers, Seamen and Assistants of the said Ship of the other part'.[104] Because these two men failed to reach an agreement, they were the ones to call in Samuel Rodman Chace to act as umpire. Nothing can be proved, but if this was the William Stewart the cartographer, perhaps this is when he heard of the new straits and islands being opened up by the sealers, and decided to hitch a ride on the *Pegasus* to do his mapping.

After circumnavigating Stewart Island, Chace took the ship further up the East Coast of the South Island. It was this voyage that caused Banks Peninsula to also acquire the name, 'Cook's Mistake'. Captain Cook missed the land joining to the coast and therefore named the Peninsula 'Banks Island'. The *Pegasus* discovered the mistake and gave her name to the bay to the north of it.[105] Next (again, according to the *Oriental Navigator*) she sailed to the Chatham Islands, where Stewart charted what was left uncompleted by Broughton. The voyage of the *Pegasus* is thereafter clothed in mystery until she turned up at Gravesend from Rio on 18 August 1810.[106]

MOORE RETIRES FROM THE DOCKYARD

The second half of 1809 brought a change in direction for Thomas Moore. As the third phase of the rebel administration was drawing to a close, the third phase of Thomas Moore's life was beginning to dawn. His early days spent in Lesbury and as an adventurer at sea gave way to the opportunity to build the Naval Yard as Sydney's first productive Master Boat Builder, Surveyor of Timber, and a whole lot more added on. Now he had build a new home on the George's River and the time had come to enter the third and final phase of his life. The time had come, in God's Providence, to bring him to Liverpool.

The *Indispensable* arrived on 18 August 1809 bringing the new chaplain to New South Wales. Rev. William Cowper disembarked on the 19th and, after making his acquaintance with Col. Paterson, was in the pulpit of St Phillip's on the 20th, preaching the first sermon of a ministry to Sydney which would last almost forty years.[107] Cowper and Moore would be involved in common causes in the years to come, and it is probable that Moore was amongst the Civil Officers who attended church with the Governor, sitting under Cowper's ministry.

News arriving in August closed another chapter of the *Pegasus* story. The *Lady Barlow* first brought news that the *Harrington* had been recaptured. The frigate *Phoenix* had fallen in with her in Indian waters on the way to Manilla. The convict ringleader, Robert Bruce Keith Stuart and others were removed, but many other convicts remained on the vessel. Unfortunately, the ship 'went on shore on the coast of Luconia' and her convict crew escaped.[108] During the next week the *Gazette* attained a copy of a Calcutta Newspaper dated 6 April, which enabled a further update:

> Robert Bruce Keith Stuart, a convict from New South Wales, was brought on shore from the *Phaeton* frigate, and lodged in jail, by an order from Government. It appears that this young man had been convicted of an offence in England, for which he was to New South Wales, from whence, in concert with several other convicts, he carried off in May last [i.e. 1808] the brig *Harrington*, and made the best of his way for Manilla. On the passage hither, when off the Coast of Leuconia, the *Dedaignense* frigate fell in with the brig *Harrington*, and sent a party of seamen on board to take possession,

and transhipping the party above named, to the frigate, brought him to Prince of Wales Island, where he was transferred to the *Phaeton*, on which frigate he has been brought on to this Port.[109]

Amongst those captured with Stewart was one Terence Flynn (alias Peter Hay, alias John Manchester),[110] who had once worked closely under Thomas Moore's supervision, as a young boy after arriving on a 14 year sentence in November 1800.

> Shortly after his arrival he was placed in the Dock Yard, to learn the art of boat building, under the humane presumption that with the advantages of a profession he might be enabled to obtain an honest livelihood, and that the youthful mind might by habits of industry be gradually alienated from those propensities with which he had at so early a period been assailed; but notwithstanding every effort to reclaim this hardy boy, his vices strengthened as his age matured, and clemency and severity at length were equally lost upon him.[111]

Flynn and Thomas Dawson, another convict involved in the *Harrington* piracy were later shipped back to the colony on board Bunker's *Venus*. When she arrived at the Derwent, however, they both escaped and on 17 February 1810, Flynn shot Dawson in the head, causing him to die about two weeks later. Flynn was tried in Sydney at the Court of Criminal Jurisdiction held 28–30 May 1810, found guilty of murder and sent back to Hobart to be executed and subsequently dissected.[112] Before sentencing him, the Judge Advocate admonished him 'to turn his thoughts seriously aside from the objects of this life and to endeavour by an earnest repentance to evince a solicitude for his welfare in a World which is eternal'. Given Moore's earlier involvement with his reform through learning a productive trade, this must have been a sad closure to the story of the *Harrington*.

Cowper, his wife and four children arrived in the midst of a food shortage. The May floods on the Hawkesbury diminished the grain supplies, and provisions in the colony were rather tight.[113] As one measure to resolve the problem, at the end of August, Paterson decreased the amount of people victualled from the public stores, and in the process he therefore dismissed the provisions, along with the drill and duties, of the Parramatta and Sydney Loyal Associations, until further notice.[114] Thomas Moore might be short on food, but at least this diminished his responsibilities and duties somewhat. Presumably with extra time on his hands as well, William Gaudry, Moore's Lieutenant in the Loyal Sydney Volunteers, married 'Miss Kable, eldest daughter of Mr Henry Kable, Merchant'.[115] The Bride was given away by Captain John Bader, of the brig, *Active*, and Rev. William Cowper performed the ceremony—the first of hundreds of marriages he conducted across the years to come. Perhaps Thomas and Rachel were present at the ceremony.

Some months earlier, on 14 July, Paterson granted Thomas Moore 79 ½ rods of land in High Street, at a rent of 2/6 per rod per year,[116] probably the properties of John White and Raven combined—Moore having bought Raven's house when it was auctioned in September 1807. The site, with a slight downsizing, was confirmed to Moore in a crown grant on 25 August 1812. In the 1820s and 1830s Moore let the buildings to Francis Mitchell, to run his lucrative ship's chandler business, and in 1839 Moore deeded it to Bishop Broughton to provide an endowment for the building of a Cathedral.[117]

No	Date	Acres	Location	Name
1642	1 Nov 1809	200	Holsworthy	'Clarke Farm'
1643	1 Nov 1809	160	Holsworthy	'Hudson Farm'
1644	1 Nov 1809	160	Holsworthy	'Turner Farm'
1645	1 Nov 1809	160	Holsworthy	'Turnbull Farm'
1646	1 Nov 1809	160	Holsworthy	'Nathaniel Farm'
1647	1 Nov 1809	160	Holsworthy	'Boits Farm'
Total:		1,000		

Figure 51: Thomas Moore's Land Grants 1 November 1809.[118]

This was not the only land granted to Thomas Moore under Paterson's regime. On 6 September he received 300 acres in the district of Banks Town, and on 1 November he received an additional 1,000 acres at Holsworthy.[119] (Figure 51). As long ago as January 1798, Hunter had reported that 'a few of the marine settlers are fixed upon the banks of a river which empties itself into Botany Bay, where the land promises well'.[120] Moore had explored the promising George's River district himself in Hunter's time, in the frenetic timber-gathering days of 1803. He received his first grant there in 1805, and now, with Moore Bank complete and tested by the floods, he extended his holdings southward along the river in the Holsworthy district.

From the point of view of public reputation and later suspicions, this was not a good time to receive land. Paterson was renowned for handing out land as favours to committed rebels or inducements for would-be sympathisers. According to Chaplain Henry Fulton,

> the present rebel rulers have been as busy as possible ever since the revolution in giving to their creatures & friends, tracts of land from 30 Acres to 4,000 each, according to the state condition or expectations of the persons thus oblig'd, & in giving pardons conditional & absolute, that they might qualify persons for such gifts, because bondmen cannot possess legally any property, so that the number of pardons & grants is immense. Every spot almost is given away, & the Herds of Government Cattle thinned by gifts of the same kind.[121]

Well aware of this problem, on 4 January 1810 when Macquarie issued his first proclamation after his arrival,[122] it nullified all grants of land given during the rebel regime. On 9 January 1810, Moore duly handed back 1300 acres of land along the George's River and the 79 ½ rods on High Street.[123] However, despite the fact that he had Paterson grants which he then surrendered, this should not be taken as an indicator of Moore's rebel sympathies, nor that he rendered rebel service.

During 1809, Moore's farm had already turned him a small profit, supplying Government with grain and animal food for which he received £127.6.6.[124] Moore's was amongst the other expenses listed in a letter from Paterson to Castlereagh, requesting Treasury Bills to liquidate them. At the same time, Paterson wrote a second letter informing Castlereagh that since his last on 14 October 'no event of any importance has taken place in this Colony'. He then proceeded to tell of the retirement of Charles Throsby from his position as Assistant Surgeon and Thomas Moore, from that of Master Boat Builder.

William Evans replaced Throsby and Charles Griffin took over from Moore at the dockyard. Both men had requested permission to retire, Throsby on account of his health. Both wished to become settlers. Of Moore, Paterson noted that 'from his having faithfully served in that capacity for upwards of 13 years, I have judged him a proper object of the indulgences given to Settlers of the most reputable class'.[125] If Moore's November 1809 grants were a reward for anything, it was not for his complicity in the rebel cause since January 1808, but for dedicated service to the colony since October 1796. In Thomas's own mind, as he explained to Macquarie in his January 1810 memorial, he received land as one of the normal indulgences granted to a free settler.[126]

As the month of October opened, Acting Commissary Robert Fitz became concerned about the state of the *Estramina*'s sails.[127] At 11am on the 4th, Thomas Moore joined Henry Best, Master of the *Indispensable*—who had brought Rev. Cowper and his family to Sydney—and W. Simmons, Master of the *Mary* at the Government Stores to conduct 'a strict and careful Survey on the sails so complained of and the Cause thereof'.[128] This survey may have been one of the last duties performed by Moore as Master of the King's Dockyard. The *Gazette* of 15 October announced that his resignation had been accepted:

> The Lieutenant Governor has been pleased to appoint Mr Charles Griffin to be Master Boat Builder, in His Majesty's Naval Yard, in the Room of Thomas Moore, Esq. who has requested Permission to resign.[129]

The description of the Yard that Moore had built from nothing speaks eloquently of what he had achieved across the last thirteen years of service. When he began he simply had John Hunter's grand idea of its possibilities and a muddy strip of shoreline. When he resigned, it was from 'His Majesty's Naval Yard'.

In the same issue, an advertisement may indicate that Moore was divesting himself of some of his property:

> To be sold by Private Contract, a capital Long Boat 27 feet over-all, and might be converted into a Hawkesbury Boat at a small expence;—Her masts and sails are complete, and she is of very fine

CHAPTER 6 ⚓ *Speculator and Settler (31 July 1808 to 7 November 1810)*   355

> appearance—To be viewed at the Hospital Wharf, and particulars known of Mr. Moore, in High Street.[130]

Thomas and Rachel were preparing to move from Sydney to their new home Moore Bank, on the expanding edge of the colony. As well as selling a boat that may have been a little large for the George's River, he also had to tidy up after his speculative sealing venture. Chace would take the skins being procured at the moment directly to London, but that left the skins Bunker had brought back to Sydney in March.

On 14 August, four days before parson Cowper had arrived on the *Indispensable* with 61 female convicts, the ship *Boyd*, Captain Thompson, had arrived from Cork, landing 137 of their male counterparts.[131] When she left in November for New Zealand, with the intention of gaining a cargo of spars and ship-timber, she had already picked up a cargo consisting of oil, and also of seal-skins belonging to Simeon Lord. According to the certificate of the shipping agents, 'two thousand two hundred and thirty fine salted fur skins' to be delivered to Messrs. John and William Jacobs, merchants, who would pay for the freight at twelve pounds sterling per ton.[132]

What doesn't appear in the official record, however, is that a second and far larger cargo of seal-skins was also placed upon the *Boyd*, belonging to the *Pegasus* consortium: John Harris, Simeon Lord and Thomas Moore. The record of this shipment is scribbled on the inside of the front cover of Moore's oldest Business Notebook, with an annotation which must have something to do with how the three-way split was to be calculated:[133]

Memd^n

> of Measurement of Seal Skins Shipped on Bord the Ship *Boyd* Captn Thompson Number 8679—
> and the distribution [?] is   15.6
>   12 –
>   4–6

Earlier in the year, the London Market was paying an average of 30s per skin, and so, at those prices, the *Pegasus* cargo promised a £13,018 sale.[134] Whatever Moore's share, he was about to make some big money from his first major speculation. With common business sense,

Moore insured his portion of the cargo as did Harris, but unfortunately Simeon Lord's credit was stretched to breaking point in London and he had trouble insuring his portion.[135] With that safety net Moore could rest easy, but as the *Boyd* sailed for New Zealand and then London there is no way he could have seen the future. For neither the *Boyd* nor the *Pegasus* skins ever made it to the London market.

Despite his dreams about a wealthy retirement in the peace and quiet of the George's River District, and despite his resignation from the Dockyard, Moore's public duties in Sydney continued. On 4 November, he sat as Coroner to inquire into the death of Thomas Jones, a Government Stock keeper, whose body had been found floating in Lane Cove. He was last seen preparing to wade across a stretch of water which 'is very deep and sometimes dangerous', and the verdict was unanimously brought down that he had accidentally drowned.[136]

No doubt taking the opportunity afforded by their own impending move, and in view of the need to rent their Town house, Thomas Moore undertook some renovations on their house during November 1809. He paid Evans £20 to build a verandah, with shingles and lattice work, and Martin Short to modify the 'small room' at the end of the house, and added two new doors—the entire job needing new brickwork to the tune of 40,000 bricks and costing £698.6.11.[137]

As the year drew to a close, on Wednesday 27 December, Thomas Laycock senior died, 'at his house in Pitt's Row, after a long and painful illness' and 'in his 54th year'.[138] Laycock was a little older than Thomas Moore, but they had both been in the colony for roughly the same time (Laycock arrived 1791; Moore first came 1792), and they would certainly have known each other reasonably well. In 1804 Laycock distinguished himself by leading the military detachment with George Johnston which put down the convict uprising at Castle Hill. After his wife Hannah left for England about 1805, however, he was criticised for indecent behaviour and mutinous language and in 1808 he was dismissed by the War Office from being Quartermaster, but not entirely disgraced. In October 1809, his sons William and Thomas told Paterson that he had become mentally deranged and could no longer manage his affairs. Paterson appointed his two sons, his son-in-law Nicholas Bayly, William Broughton, and D'Arcy

CHAPTER 6 ☙ *Speculator and Settler (31 July 1808 to 7 November 1810)* 357

Wentworth as his Trustees. No doubt this mental derangement was the story behind his reported 'long and painful illness'. When Laycock died, Thomas Moore joined Wentworth as a Trustee of his Estate, although with such a long list of trustees already operating in the last months of Laycock's life, it is difficult to know why. Perhaps Moore became involved by virtue of Isabella Bunker having married Thomas Laycock junior, and the fact that he was already Eber Bunker's friend and agent.[139]

> All persons having any claim on the Estate of the late Thos. Laycock, Esq. deceased, are desired to present the same to D. Wentworth, Esq. or Thos. Moore, Esq. in order that it may be settled within one Month from this date; and all Persons who stand indebted to the Estate of the late Thos. Laycock, Esq., are ordered to pay the same to D. Wentworth or Thos. Moore, Esqrs. Within the above period: December 30, 1809.[140]

Ironically, as the colony farewelled an old soldier whose family was so well connected to the beginning of the New South Wales rebellion, another soldier arrived to bring it to an end. On 29 December, after an eight month voyage, HMS *Dromedary* and *Hindostan* sailed into Port Jackson, and the *Gazette* quite simply announced that a new day had dawned—even if they switched the ships around and had to apologise in the next issue:

> In the *Hindostan* [it was the *Dromedary*] have arrived His Excellency Governor McQuarie and Lady; and Ellis Bent Esq Judge Advocate, and Lady; and in the *Dromedary* [it was the *Hindostan*] Lieutenant Governor O'Connell, Lieutenant Colonel for the Regiment [i.e. the 73rd].[141]

Mr John Thomas Campbell also sailed with the Governor, arriving to fill the role of Secretary to the Governor. The Governor's party disembarked at 10 a.m. on 30 December. The 102nd Regiment formed a line from the Government wharf to Government house and as the Macquaries left the ship a salute was fired from the ships and answered by the Dawes' Point battery. Lieutenant-Governor Paterson met Governor and Elizabeth Macquarie at the landing, with Colonel Foveaux, and all the Principal Officers, which presumably also included Thomas Moore amongst the Civil Officers. This party then moved up to Government House.

In the forenoon of Monday 1 January 1810, the 73rd Regiment disembarked and at noon they joined the 102nd on opposite sides of the parade ground, and the Governor and suite arrived in the centre to a general salute from the troops. The Judge-Advocate then read out the Macquarie's commission, proclaiming him His Majesty's Captain General and Governor in Chief of the Territory of New South Wales and its Dependencies, and then the Lieutenant-Governor's and his own commissions. The troops fired three volleys and Governor Macquarie then addressed them 'in a short and very animated speech, which was answered with three cheers', bands playing, 21 gun salute, and responses from HM ships. At the end of the festivities the 73rd marched out to their camp at Grose Farm, and that night there was an illumination in the town and on the ships in the Cove. The *Gazette* was pleased to reproduce Macquarie's speech, which expressed the hope that he might find at all times 'the cordial Support of those Gentlemen, Civil and Military, placed at the Heads of the several Public Departments of Government'. He was also sanguine in his hopes 'that all those Dissentions and Jealousies which have unfortunately existed in this Colony for some time past, will now terminate for ever, and give way to a more becoming Spirit of Conciliation, Harmony, and Unanimity, among all Classes and Description of the Inhabitants of it'. To do so, the upper ranks of society must hold out a good example to the lower.

Macquarie took this opportunity to 'strongly recommend to all Classes of the Community a strict Observance of all Religious Duties, and a constant and regular Attendance at Divine Worship on Sundays, and other Holidays set apart for that purpose'. He then added a special word to the magistrates about checking vice and immorality; a word about the proper treatment of 'the natives'; and finally a statement that he is here to be a friend and protector to this rising colony so well respected in His Majesty's eyes.[142]

On 4 January, Macquarie issued his first proclamation.[143] It expressed 'His Majesty's high displeasure at the arrest and removal of William Bligh'; that all appointments afterwards were illegal and invalid and so those persons are now displaced and those who held

CHAPTER 6 ⌘ *Speculator and Settler (31 July 1808 to 7 November 1810)* 359

the place before the rebellion were reinstated; that all grants of land and stock and leases (especially those made to the Officers of the 102nd) are null and void; and Trials and Investigations having taken place are invalid in law. Certain concessions were made, so, for example, application could be made for grants to be validated if they were not coloured by illegality, except in the case of grants made to the Officers of the 102nd after Bligh was overthrown.

Having absorbed the proclamation, on 9 January 1810, Thomas Moore presented a 'memorial and humble petition' to the new Governor.[144]

> That Memorialist held the Appointment of Master Builder to this Colony for upwards of thirteen years and was in the habit of doing other Duties not immediately attached to that Office, but which were calculated for the Public Service and to promote the Interests of the Colony.
>
> That Memorialist of Late years had accumulated a valuable Stock of Horned Cattle and Horses, and finding it necessary to devote his Time and Attention to the Care and Security of a Concern of increasing Magnitude and Importance, was induced about three months since to resign his Situation, intending to become a Settler and flattered with the Hope of enjoying the same Advantages and Indulgences usually granted to respectable Settlers, and [damaged edge: ?passed] when their long Services to the Country Carried them a Recommendation to Favor and Prospe[rity?]
>
> That Memorialist, with these [damaged edge: considerations asked?]
>
> Lieut-Governor Paterson for a Grant of Land, and that Gentleman was pleased to give Memorialist 1230 acres—Memorialist moreover purchased two grants, one of 80 and the other of 50 Acres, for each of which Memorialist paid £40—and this Purchase he was induced to make from the Consideration fo the Land being in the Center of that granted to him by Lt Gov Paterson, and to remove any Cause of Complaint of Memorialist's stock trespassing on the lands of others.
>
> Your Excellency's Petitioner begs leave to submit these Circumstances to your gracious Consideration, and humbly prays your Excellency to confirm the Grant of 1,230 acres, and to satisfy the Transfer or Conveyance of the 130 acres so purchased by Memorialist.

Moore's land may have looked suspicious at first glance, but under a steady gaze it was not. On Macquarie's arrival, Palmer handed Bligh's letter of 12 March, which contained the Proclamation with the list of Bligh's prohibited persons—including that of Thomas Moore.[145] If there was any irregularity in Moore receiving land from the rebels for rebel favours and the like, then this would be the moment of discovery. Instead, Moore's grants were confirmed and Macquarie became one of Moore's close friends.

In these early days Macquarie would have been trying to get everybody's measure. He had Moore on Bligh's 'hit list', kindly forwarded by Palmer, but he made his own inquiries too. The day after Moore handed back his land, Foveaux informed the new Governor that in regard to the *Lady Nelson*

> on the departure of His Majesty's Ship *Porpoise* in March last, Commodore Bligh ordered her to be dismantled and laid up in Ordinary in the King's yard. The Commodore gave her in charge to Mr Thomas Moor_, the Master builder, with Directions to hand her over to Colonel Paterson should he require her for the service of the Colony. Colonel Paterson applied for her immediately after the *Porpoise* had sailed from hence, manned her with hired seamen, and she has since continued in the employment of Government for the use of these settlements.[146]

Bligh evidently had no cause at that late stage for mistrusting Moore in his role at the dockyard and within the month, Macquarie would also be availing himself of the services of Governor King's 'most useful and necessary officer'.

Just when the colony appeared to be moving on from its rebel period, on Wednesday 17 January Governor Bligh sailed back through the heads. The *Porpoise* was saluted by HM ships and the Dawes' Point battery as she arrived in Sydney Cove. The next day Bligh and his daughter Mary Putland disembarked at 11 a.m., to be welcomed by full honours. They were met by Lieut.-Gov. Maurice O'Connell, who may have been rather struck by Mary's presence at that moment. Mary had come to New South Wales as the wife of Lieutenant John Putland, R.N., Bligh's Aide-de-Camp.[147] When the rebels took over the colony on 26 January 1808, Bligh was still dealing with the grief of his beloved daughter after the death of her husband on the 4th. Now, after two years mourning her Naval husband, she was met by the forty-two year old Military man, now Lieutenant-Governor, at the end of Government wharf. Love at first sight is probably impossible to detect at such a distance in time, but certainly something happened fairly soon, for when her father left the colony in May, Mary remained behind as Mrs Maurice O'Connell.[148]

O'Connell escorted Bligh and his daughter to Government House where they were received and entertained by Lachlan and Elizabeth Macquarie and a large company of officers, with the Macquaries showing 'every possible mark of attention and respect'. In the afternoon Bligh was taken to inspect the 73rd Regiment at its camp, and after arriving back at 3 p.m., Macquarie then visited the *Porpoise*. No doubt Bligh's memories were mixed ones as he returned to Government House, the scene of his deposition, now occupied by his official replacement. His settling back into Sydney was only for a few months before he returned to England in May.

Back at the end of January, the news reached Sydney that the price of seal-skins in London had plummeted and they were now fetching only 3s to 8s per skin.[149] Jefferson's Embargo Act of 1807 had severely curtailed the demand for English hats,[150] and the consequences were now ricocheting from America to England to the Sydney suppliers. As a consequence, Simeon Lord withdrew from the London market, commencing a long drawn-out battle with his brokers Plummer and Co. As the news of the crash arrived, Moore's heart would have sunk as the potential profits from his shipment in the *Boyd* disappeared before his eyes on the eve of his retirement to the George's River. And there was still more bad news to come.

Despite his resignation from the Dockyard in October, Moore's retirement evidently took a while to take effect. Governor Macquarie soon had Mr Moore doing the kind of things he had always done. So, for example, on 20 February, under orders of the Governor, Thomas Moore joined Nathaniel Lucas—someone who he would work with again at Liverpool—Thomas Legg, and John O'Herne, all resident at Sydney, on a survey of the house of William Moore of the 102nd Regiment, to 'make an estimate of the value of said House and Out

Houses or Offices thereunto belonging, and as soon as possible afterwards to send a regular signed Report thereon to His Excellency'.[151] When Lieutenant, William Moore was a major player in the rebellion and had already gone to England for George Johnston's court martial when his promotion to Captain was announced in December 1809— another of the rebels apparently rewarded for their insurrection![152] While he was gone, and with the rest of the 102nd about to be sent home, Macquarie was taking a look at his property.

At the end of February Macquarie again called upon Thomas Moore services. On 27th, he requested him—still addressed as 'Master Boat Builder'—to join Joshua Dodds, Master of the Brig *Experiment*, and J. Earl, Master of the Ship *Marian*, to proceed onto the *Estramina* to check the Inventory of her sails, anchors, cables and stores supplied the Governor by her Commander, John Apsey.[153] The Survey team found the inventory correct, and so John Palmer was directed to get these things landed and into the Government Stores.[154]

About the same time as the *Estramina* survey, Thomas and Rachel were dealing with a minor domestic crisis. One of their assigned servants, Mary Redman, absented herself from the Moore's service, necessitating the usual public notice that 'all persons are cautioned against harbouring or encouraging the said Absentee, on pain of prosecution according to law'.[155]

The same paper ran an advertisement which shows that Moore had vacated his Bulanaming property, which was now in the hands of Mr George Guest, and apparently still suffering under unwanted trespass:

> The public are hereby cautioned against trespassing either by Stock or otherwise, in any manner whatever on the farms of Mr. Thomas Moore, called or known by the name of Dowlas's Farm, and Boyle's Meadow, situate in the District of Bulanaming, as the said Farms are now my own Property. I do therefore publicly prohibit all persons grazing stock or cutting any timber thereon, on pain of the most rigid Prosecution.[156]

Presumably, therefore, by March 1810 Moore had moved his cattle and horses to his George's River property in preparation for the time when he and Rachel would join them there.

Further official duties called on Thomas's services in the following week, on 8 March, when he served as a juryman in the Coronial inquiry into the death of William Piper, a child of about three years of age, who on the previous day had been taken lifeless out of the water, accidental death by drowning.[157] But then on Saturday March 10 the *Gazette* announced that an even greater tragedy had taken place some months earlier.

The Boyd Massacre

Samuel Rodman Chace on the *King George* had arrived the day before, bringing news he gained from the Bay of Islands eighteen days before that. The *Ann*, Captain Gwynn, had prevented Chace from entering the Bay of Islands, having received from the *Albion*, Captain Skelton,

> the melancholy information of the *Boyd*'s capture by the New Zealanders under Tip-pa-hee, and the massacre of every one on board except a boy, two women, and a child; at a place called Whangaroa.[158]

The mention of the name of Tip-pa-hee in connection with this event added further shock to the Sydney readers. This was the young maori chief who came to Sydney in 1805 and had been shown great kindness by Marsden, Governor King and others, and who returned to New Zealand in February 1806.[159] Now he was reported as the leading figure in an act that became more chilling as further news filtered back to Sydney.

After taking on her cargo, the *Boyd* had left Port Jackson in November 1809, sailing for England via the Bay of Islands.[160] Captain William Swain of the ship *Cumberland* wrote on 6 Jan 1810. Having heard 'frequent reports of a ship being taken by the natives [...] and that the ship's crew were killed and eaten', he had investigated and found the *Boyd*'s remains, confirming the rumours to be true. Alexander Berry, supercargo of the *City of Edinburgh*, who had been on the confirmatory mission and rescued the survivors, wrote the same day. Both men named Tippahee as responsible for the massacre—a claim Marsden, after his own investigations in New Zealand, later denied.[161]

Marsden arrived back from his trip to England on the *Ann* on 27 February, just before the news of the *Boyd* broke in Sydney.[162] He brought with him a new chaplain for New South Wales, Rev. Robert Cartwright, and two settlers, John King and William Hall, who were intended to form the beginnings of his mission to New Zealand. Almost a decade later, Marsden recalled his great distress at hearing the news of the *Boyd*, for the potential set-back to the mission:

> On my arrival at Port Jackson, in February, 1810, I found all the [LMS] missionaries, with the exception of two, had left the Society Islands and returned to New South Wales, and that the ship *Boyd* and crew had been cut off at New Zealand. These were very painful circumstances, and created such difficulties as I was apprehensive it would not be in my power to overcome, as all hope of introducing the arts of civilization and the Christian religion amongst the different islands was now nearly extinguished.[163]

On 12 March, Macquarie wrote to inform the authorities in England of the *Boyd*, enclosing a statement given by Samuel Rodman Chace on the same day, which gave a version of events which, once again, implicated Tippahee in the massacre, although Chace admitted that he was only reporting the views of others, which he had heard in some haste and anxiety.[164] In April, a group of whalers sent news that, believing him to be the perpetrator, they had invaded Tippahee's island on 26 March and engaged his tribe in battle. They reported that they had found the *Boyd*'s longboat and some papers, which they sent back to Port Jackson.[165] A few days later William Leith, of the *Speke*, confirmed that the whalers had 'attacked and wounded Tip-pa-hee, destroyed his houses and property, and killed about 60 of his people'.[166] He also added his opinion that 'the masters of the different ships have to thank themselves for all the evils they have brought on by their injustice and ill-treatment of the natives'. If this is the same Wiliam Leith who was Thomas Moore's companion on the *Britannia* and who led the Dusky Bay sealing party in 1792–1793, then this man speaks as someone from that group with the longest experience of New Zealand, well aware of the atrocities since committed by European sea-farers in these waters.

Later in the year, on 1 September, the *Sydney Gazette* published a second statement from Samuel Rodman Chace concerning the *Boyd* massacre.[167] Since his report in March, Chace had learned more about this event from an Otaheitian. On its voyage outwards from Sydney, the *Boyd* had taken some New Zealanders who were displeased with their on-board treatment. Upon reaching home, they plotted revenge with their tribe and this resulted in the massacre. Despite all previous reports, Chace's source had now revealed that the perpetrators were not from Tippahee's tribe—now, courtesy of the whalers, 60-odd fewer in number—but they were from amongst his enemies. Tippahee had arrived at the scene the morning after the massacre and had attempted to rescue some survivors, but to no avail. The *Gazette* concluded strongly that 'from the foregoing details it appears that neither Tippahee nor his son Mytye had any share in the barbarous acts committed by those sanguinary miscreants; but that the old chief had, on the contrary, endeavoured to preserve the lives of several of the crew'. Apparently overlooking Chace's clear report concerning the prior mistreatment of the New Zealanders while on board the *Boyd*, the article nevertheless concluded with a caution to future adventurers against 'surprise and treachery' from 'the uncivilised islanders'.

Evangelicals in England and NSW were well aware of the horrifying behaviour of Europeans towards the indigenous populations wherever they had gone with their colonies. William Wilberforce, the great anti-slavery advocate spoke for them all when he said, 'Alas, in how many instances does our national conduct in foreign countries call aloud for the vengeance of Heaven!'.[168] In due course (December 1813) the chaplains of New South Wales gathered together a group of others into a small 'society', in an effort to stop the kind of abuses that had led to the massacre of the *Boyd*. Perhaps, like William Leith, the Dusky Bay experience still ran deep in Thomas Moore, for he was one of those who joined in common cause with the chaplains on behalf of the natives of the South Seas.[169]

Evidently Thomas Moore didn't hold any grudge against the New Zealanders for the massive financial loss he sustained when half of his sealing speculation went up in the *Boyd*'s smoke. His insurance would have provided some comfort—that is until he learned that one of the companies Harris had insured with went bankrupt and only paid 20s in the pound dividend. But still, he did receive some compensation for his loss. But his lack of grudge appears to run deeper than being somewhat financially compensated. Later in life he added his weight to the first of many 'societies' formed in New South Wales, the Benevolent Society, but in May 1813 when this was formed its name reflected a wider interest: 'New South Wales Society for Promoting Christian Knowledge and Benevolence in These Territories and in the Neighbouring Islands'. By December of that year, a second society formed with a much clearer focus and this society gained his immediate support: 'New South Wales Philanthropic Society for the Protection and Civilization of such of the Natives of the South Seas who may arrive at Port Jackson'.[170] Once Liverpool was founded, the town's needs for Christian ministry were served by Samuel Marsden, and so it is perhaps unsurprising that a over the next decades Liverpool developed a very prominent missionary interest. Amongst those circles, Moore became known as a great supporter of missionary work amongst the New Zealanders. Mr Moore held no grudge against the Maori. On the contrary, his portrait includes an active promotion of the welfare of those who once robbed him of a small fortune.

Official duties may have given Moore some distraction from his own failing speculative venture. On 6 April Moore served on the jury of a coronial inquiry into the death of Henry Giddes, a seaman from the *Porpoise*, who accidentally drowned by falling off the hospital wharf when thoroughly intoxicated. Garnham Blaxcell, was the foreman, and as fellow jurymen Moore was joined by William Elliston, Nicholas Divine, D. Langley, J. Gordon, Robert Campbell, jr, R. Watson, R. Jenkins, John Apsey, T. Collen, and R. Jones.[171]

In April there was a hectic round of farewells. Governor Bligh started the ball rolling on Tuesday 14th, when he hosted a farewell dinner for himself

> to a select party of Fashionables; which was succeeded by a ball and supper, conducted in an unusual style of elegance. Present, His Excellency and Lady, Lieutenant Governor O'Connell, R. Campbell, Esq. and Lady, J. Palmer, Esq. W. Gore, Esq. and Lady, C. Hook, Esq. and Lady, G. Palmer, Esq. and Lady, and many others of the first respectability.[172]

Presumably Moore was not on this guest list, which, apart from the Macquaries and O'Connell, reads like a 'who's who' of Bligh supporters

CHAPTER 6 ⚓ *Speculator and Settler (31 July 1808 to 7 November 1810)* 367

during the rebel regime. Thomas and Rachel had a greater chance of being invited to the 'splendid farewell Fete' on the Thursday immediately following, at which their neighbour and friend Robert Campbell played host to:

> a large party; of whose number were His Excellency and Lady, Commodore Bligh and daughter, Mrs. Putland; Captains Pasco and Pritchett, with many other principal Officers and their Ladies.[173]

At 11 a.m. on Tuesday, 1 May Colonel William Paterson embarked HMS *Dromedary*, walking from his residence to the Government wharf through a guard of honour formed by the 73rd Regiment, with the band playing 'God Save the King', accompanied by Lieut.-Gov. O'Connell and, at the wharf, farewelled by 'a numerous company of Officers Civil and Military, amongst whom presumably Thomas Moore took his place.[174]

> On taking water, a salute of 13 guns was fired from the Battery, and reiterated cheers were given by the spectators, on and about the Wharf, which were re-echoed from each vessel as the pinnance passed. When a-breast of the Public Landing Wharf the like salutes were given by a numerous body of Inhabitants who were there assembled; and ten crowded boats followed the COLONEL'S pinnance in succession, cheering all the way, as a public demonstration of respect towards an Officer who had for many years been the second in Command in the Colony and whose urbanity of manners, joined to a true benevolence of disposition, had endeared him to all classes of the Inhabitants.

Then on Thursday, Lieut.-Gov. O'Connell gave 'a splendid dinner' to 'a select party', including the Macquaries and, Governor Bligh, and Mrs Putland, with many other officers Civil, Military and Naval and their ladies, in preparation for Bligh leaving on the *Hindostan*, which was already flying his flag.[175] This dinner could well be regarded as a pre-nuptial celebration for O'Connell and Mary Putland, for on Saturday 12th, they were married by Rev. Samuel Marsden at Government House.[176]

With her marriage to a significant member of New South Wales Society, and a total of 3,000 acres granted to her and a further 2500 as a pre-wedding gift to her husband, Mary was now well established to remain in New South Wales. Her headstrong nature served her well to maintain the rage at her father's deposition over years to come. By 1813 Macquarie was recommending the removal of his deputy, reporting that Mrs O'Connell

> naturally enough, has imbibed strong feelings of resentment and hatred against all those Persons and their Families, who were in the least inimical to her Father's Government [...] tho' Lieutenant Colonel O'Connell is naturally a very well disposed Man, he allows himself to be a good deal influenced by his Wife's strong rooted Prejudices against the old Inhabitants of this country who took any active part against Governor Bligh.[177]

The O'Connells left Sydney for Ceylon with the main body of the 73rd Regiment in April 1814, but in December 1838 they returned when O'Connell, ranked Major-General and knighted, was appointed commander of the forces in New South Wales. In those closing years of Thomas Moore's life, he apparently had pleasant dealings with the O'Connells. A letter from July 1840 expresses their thankfulness for his generosity towards a new school teacher by the name of Emily [?Watkins?], to whom he had given money for clothes, and their eagerness for him to call upon them.[178] Had Mary's memory faded by that stage, or had she forgiven her father's enemies? Or did she know that, despite being on the 1809 'hit-list', Thomas Moore was not so much involved in, as enveloped by, the 1808 rebellion against her father?

In May, Moore was apparently winding up his involvement with the Sydney Association. On 9 May he handed in '37 Muskets, 38 poc[k]etries and belts, and 38 Side Belts with Bayonets, being the arms & accoutrements of the Sydney Association'.[179] (Plate 33). One month later, he signed a Return as Captain (4 June), which listed the strength of the Sydney Association: 1 Captain, 1 Lieutenant, 4 Sergeants, 3 Corporals, 1 Drummer, 1 Fife, and 32 privates.[180] Perhaps this Return was Moore's last act for the Association, signing off on his company. For Thomas and Rachel's move to Moore Bank was coming soon after.

In the Government and General Orders of 17 May, in which His Excellency announced that Simeon Lord and D'Arcy Wentworth were appointed justices of the peace and magistrates for the town of Sydney, he was also 'pleased to appoint Thomas Moore, Esq., to be justice of the peace and magistrate in the district of George's River, in the same county of Cumberland. Those gentlemen are accordingly to be respected and obeyed as magistrates from this date'.[181]

Presumably Moore was still in Sydney when Governor Macquarie requested him, along with Nathaniel Lucas and Thomas Storer, to proceed to Rose Bay the following day (1/6) to survey 'the Government Salt Pans at Rose Bay, and make an Estimate of their value, in order to their being disposed of'. In addition, they were to survey 'the small house on Windmill Hill with the Garden attached to it belonging to Mr Lord for the few remaining years of the Lease', for Macquarie was planning to purchase it for Government purposes.[182] The survey team, with Lewis Jones as an extra inclusion, valued the Rose Bay salt pan at £220.16.6, a price communicated to G. Marakby.[183] The same four-man survey, as requested, valued the Lord property on Windmill Hill at £161.13.4, and Macquarie wrote to Lord to offer to purchase the property for this price. However, because the valuation fell well below what Lord had originally estimated the value to be, and also below the original cost, to sweeten the deal Macquarie informed Lord that he 'had no objection to make your Payment of one half of the Purchase money in Spirits at twenty shillings per gallon'—presumably a price that will ensure Lord makes a little profit in the on-selling.[184]

Perhaps too, Moore was still in Sydney when on 11 June, with Gregory Blaxland he witnessed the document in which James Harris made over to D'Arcy Wentworth, Andrew Thompson and Simeon Lord, as Trustees and Commissioners of roads within the territory, some property at Freeman's Reach, Hawkesbury: 50 acres known as 'Contentment Cottage', and 1.25 acres of a farm at Green Hills, known as Sergeant Baker's Farm, and a farm of 50 acres at the Northern Boundary together with five mares and nine cows as security for my duty fulfilling my part of the undertaking specified in the annexe'— which has not survived.[185]

But perhaps it is an indicator that the Moores had moved to Moore Bank—or were about to immediately—when, in the middle of June, he called a public meeting of residents in that jurisdiction now entrusted him, with education on the agenda:[186]

> Notice is hereby given, that the Settlers of George's River are requested to attend at the house of T. Moore, Esq., on Monday the 2nd of July,

1810, for the purpose of building a School-house for that district.

Thus, as Moore's first official duty as resident magistrate of the George's River district, he turned to the education of the 'rising generation' by organising the building of a school. By September he was well-installed and ready to receive money, not only for schools, but also for bridges in the District:

> To the inhabitants of the District of George's River—Mr Thomas Moore begs leave to inform the Inhabitants of the above District, that he is ready to receive all Sums that may be voluntarily subscribed for the erecting of a Public School-house within the said District, and Five Bridges also upon the George's River Road, the necessity of which is very obvious. The names of the Subscribers, with Sums annexed, will be published in the *Gazette*, as well also a full account of the appropriation of all Sums received.

Even before the site for a township had been chosen, Moore was moving on education and transport. If there is some doubt about the exact week in June in which Moore Bank welcomed Thomas and Rachel into its peacefulness, it was certainly by the 28th of the month, when Governor Macquarie addressed a letter to Thomas at that location. He had only just moved, but Macquarie couldn't do without his services. The Governor requested that he come to Sydney on Monday 2 July, to take a further survey on the *Estramina* and submit a report.[187] While he was in town, Macquarie also requested that he organise with Thomas Boulton and Lewis Jones to meet on the 3rd, to survey and value two houses near the Burial Ground belonging to John Perkins.[188]

But from this time onwards, the George's River was Thomas Moore's home territory, and he was there amongst the pioneers as the District began to be developed. Perhaps as the first of many such Government circulars that would come across the next thirty years, in the middle of July Moore received news of the imminent arrival of a vessel full of female convicts. Macquarie wrote a circular to Andrew Thompson at Windsor, Lieut. Durie at Parramatta, and Thomas Moore at George's River, desirous that they 'dispose of' these women 'in the Speediest and best manner possible for their own Comfort and with

CHAPTER 6 ↓ *Speculator and Settler (31 July 1808 to 7 November 1810)* 371

a strict Regard to Moral Decency'. He requests these men to inform the settlers in their district of these circumstances, and that Macquarie intends to indent 'these females in due proportion among such of the Settlers as may be disposed to require their assistance in the necessary Business of a Country Life'. They are to form and transmit a list of who 'wish to provide this kind of aid, and the number that each is desirous of obtaining'. In the process, they were also to ascertain the desire for male convicts, because Macquarie is pretty sure a transport full of male prisoners was also likely to appear very soon.[189]

Another circular from the Governor in August requested the three magistrates to post the orders of 18th in prominent positions in their district, seeking 'to restrain the improper wandering of disorderly persons through the Country', a problem about which they must be 'sufficiently aware of' to warrant no further explanation.[190]

> In order as much as possible to prevent Prisoners and all other Persons of idle and profligate Characters from imposing themselves on the Public as Free men, as well as with a view to prevent such Persons from injuring the peaceable and industrious Inhabitants by strolling idly about the Country, and committing Depredations upon them [...]
>
> In future no Person whatever (excepting the Officers Civil and Military, Gentlemen and Settlers, or Tradesmen who came out free from England), shall be permitted to Travel or Pass from one Settlement to another in this Colony without being furnished with a regular written Pass Port from a Magistrate, or his master if an indented Servant, if Free by Servitude or Emancipation to produce a Certificate, and if permitted to be off the stores to work on his own account to produce his Ticket of Leave.

A consequence of this regulation was, of course, that the Magistrates and Constables received the extra duty of enforcing it, by taking into custody any person who could not produce the right paperwork, and to send them to Sydney for Government Public Works.

Macquarie must have known that Moore was visiting Sydney when this circular was addressed to him. The next day (25 August) he was summoned to join Nathaniel Lucas and Thomas Legge to make a survey and report on the premises near the Burial Ground where

Gregory Blaxland slaughtered his cattle. They were also to submit separately an Estimate of the expense of taking these premises down and re-erecting them near the place it was intended to erect a Market Wharf at Cockle Bay.[191]

On the morning of 7 September the *Canada* appeared off the heads, but could not get in until later that evening. Mrs Laycock, widow of Thomas senior, and her two daughters, was on board, returning to the colony, as well as eleven missionaries of the London Missionary Society.[192] Macquarie had already warned his magistrates about her 121 female convicts, but now that they had arrived, he wrote again instructing them to make this news known in their Districts. The distribution would take place on the 15th, and those not disposed of will be sent to Parramatta on 17th.[193]

On 20 September, Macquarie wrote again to Durie, Moore and Thompson, as well as to the three Chaplains Samuel Marsden at Parramatta, William Cowper at Sydney and Robert Cartwright on the Hawkesbury, transmitting his General and Government Order of the 15th, which announced the establishment of the Chaplains, and which also prescribed the form in which Returns of Births and Deaths were to be made. Where there was no Chaplain, the magistrate was to do this duty, paying particular care in it, given its 'evident importance'.[194] Since there was no Chaplain in the George's River District, this then became the duty of Thomas Moore.

By October 1810, Macquarie the builder decided to form a few more streets and lanes in the town of Sydney, looking to divide the town into more regular districts. Moore's Sydney house played a prominent role in some of the descriptions of the new lanes, as High Street now became George:[195]

> Essex-Lane: Extending from George-street, on the north side of Mr Moore's Lease, in a westerly direction into Harrington-street, and thence indirectly into Cambridge-street, and terminating in Cumberland-street.
>
> Suffolk-lane. Leading from George-street, on the north side of Mr Moore's Wall, in a westerly direction indirectly into Harrington-street, and thence on the north side of the new Watch-house in Cambridge-street, to Cumberland-street.

THE DEATH OF ANDREW THOMPSON

Andrew Thompson's exertions and immersions during the 1809 floods had left him in poor health. When Macquarie arrived he was restored to favour and appointed as magistrate at Green Hills (Windsor), the first emancipist magistrate. With fellow emancipist Simeon Lord, he was also trustee of the new toll road between Parramatta and the Hawkesbury, which caused trouble for the third trustee, Samuel Marsden, whose refusal to serve with emancipists struck 'the first blow in the fight against Macquarie's emancipist policy'.[196]

When Thompson died at his home on 22 October 1810, still a bachelor, he was hailed as the Governor's 'worthy and highly esteemed good friend'. He demonstrated this fact from his side, by leaving a quarter of his real and personal estate to Macquarie, a share of about £5000. Captain Henry Antill and Thomas Moore were appointed as his executors.

> ANDREW THOMPSON, Esq. late of Hawkesbury in this Territory, deceased, having by his last Will and Testament appointed us, the undersigned, to be the Executors, a Probate of his said last Will and Testament hath been duly obtained: this is therefore to require that all Persons having Claims on the Estate and Effects of the said Andrew Thompson, Esq. will present the same to Mr John Howe at the Hawkesbury, or Captain Antill at Sydney, on or before the 1st day of December next; and that all those who may be indebted to the said Estate will liquidate their Accounts respectively within the term above specified; in failure whereof legal measures must necessarily be resorted to, which it is jointly the wish of the Executors to avoid. H.C. Antill & Thos.Moore, Executors.

By mid-December, Moore and Antill had sorted out Thompson's affairs sufficiently to announce some of the first arrangements on behalf his Estate. By their order and on site at Windsor on the 27th of the month, Mr Gaudry—previously Thomas Moore's Lieutenant in the Loyal Association and now an auctioneer in Sydney—would sell Thompson's household and farm goods, including his boats, carts, his draught horse and some pigs.[197] Perhaps it is not without irony—given the famous 1806 court case between Thompson and John Macarthur—that the executors specifically stated that, although credit would be given on approved security for sums greater than ten pounds, the 25% deposit to be paid on the day had to be 'in Cash, Government, or other approved Sterling Money'. On the same day as the sale, Thompson's valuable house was also going to be let by auction for two years, as well as his West-hill Farm on South Creek, his farms at Agnes and Wardle Banks, Killarney Farm on the banks of the Bardo-narang, his Brewery at Windsor, the Toll-bridge across South Creek that he operated, two acres in Windsor, and his Salt-works, dwelling and other buildings on Scotland Island in Pitt-water.[198]

THE FOUNDING OF LIVERPOOL

But before Thompson's big sale day came, a new future would also open up for Thomas Moore. Just two weeks after Thompson died, at 6 p.m. on Tuesday 6 November, Governor Macquarie set out from Sydney on the first leg of his Tour of Inspection to the Interior of the Colony.[199] Macquarie rode and Elizabeth was in the carriage the 16 miles to Parramatta, where they were to stay the night. The rest of the party consisted of Captains Antill and Cleveland, Dr Redfern, Ensign John Maclaine, and Acting Surveyor Meehan. They set out the next morning at 6 a.m. on horseback for the George's River, arriving on the bank opposite Mr Moore's house at 8 a.m. The horses were sent ahead to a ford three miles up river, while the humans in the party crossed the river by boat to find that Rachel had breakfast already prepared for them. When well fed:

> Between 10 and 12 OClock, we all set out in a Boat, Dr. Redfern having previously joined, and accompanied by Mr. Moore, to view and survey the Ground intended for the new Township, which lies about a mile higher up the River above Mr. Moore's on the Left Bank of it.—We landed near Mr. Laycock's House, and having surveyed the Ground and found it in every respect eligible and fit for the purpose, I determined to erect a Township on it, and named it <u>Liverpool</u> in honor of the Earl of that Title—now the Secretary of State for the Colonies.—The Acting Surveyor Mr. Meehan was at the same [time] directed to mark out the Ground for the Town, with a Square in the Center thereof, for the purpose of having a Church hereafter erected within it.—

CHAPTER 6 ⚓ *Speculator and Settler (31 July 1808 to 7 November 1810)* 375

They walked over the location, imagining the new town and chatting over their various dreams. Returning to the boat they went up river for about two miles more, before turning around when their passage was blocked by fallen trees. After moving swiftly downstream again to Moore Bank, Mrs Macquarie stayed with Rachel while the men set off about 2 p.m. on horseback along the right-hand bank of the river to inspect the farms further down, in the direction of Botany Bay. Macquarie was impressed with some of the farms, which were 'well cultivated and had promising Fields of Wheat', ending the day about 7 or 8 miles downstream at Dr McCallum's farm, occupied by a man called Wells. Turning around at that point, Thomas Moore then led the party in a short-cut across country to arrive at Moore Bank at 4.30 p.m. Rachel's culinary skills had been at work all afternoon, and the Governor was delighted that 'Mrs. Moore had an excellent Dinner prepared for us'.

The heavy November rains pelted down all that night and on into the next day. Moore Bank was warm and dry so the party stayed in doors all morning, enjoying each other's company. The weather cleared a little about 2 p.m. so the Governor, Moore, Redfern, Antill and Meehan saddled the horses, crossed the ford upstream about 3 miles, aiming to view the farms in the Minto district west of the George's River. Passing through the farms of Mr Guise, Dr Throsby, they inspected Mr Meehan's own farm; then Mr Lewin's, the painter; then Mr Brookes, Dr Townson's, and finally to the farm called St Andrews, owned by Andrew Thompson from the Hawkesbury. Macquarie enjoyed taking a little time to examine 'this excellent Farm belonging to our late worthy Friend, which we found in excellent order and in a most improving flourishing state'. Thompson's farm and that of Dr Townson he felt to have the finest soil and pasturage he had yet seen in the colony.

Being gratified by fields of 'promising wheat' and numerous flocks of sheep and herds of horned cattle, Macquarie followed Moore's lead taking the direct route from St Andrews back to Moore Bank by 6 p.m. for another excellent meal from Rachel's kitchen.

Setting out at 6 a.m. Friday, the plan was a quick ride to see the remaining farms in the Banks Town District along the George's River towards Botany Bay before breakfast. After inspecting the southernmost farm, they turned across country to head home. Macquarie noted that 'good honest Mr Moore had never before explored that part of the country', and Surveyor Meehan had been sent early that morning to lay out the ground at Liverpool, so with no knowledgeable guide, the party found themselves lost and wandering in a 'boundless forest for upwards of three hours without knowing where we were'. Stumbling upon the river, they made it home to Moore Bank at about 10.30 a.m., with Elizabeth and Rachel waiting impatiently for their return. Rachel's cooking soothed any anxious feelings, for 'breakfast was ready for us and we soon got over all our fatigues'.

After a little rest for themselves and the horses Macquarie and Moore set out to view the remaining farms in the Minto district and to once again inspect the site of 'the intended Town of Liverpool'. Elizabeth and Antill planned to meet her husband at Dwyer's Farm later that afternoon, before they returned to Parramatta, and so the Governor took his leave of 'our kind Hostess Mrs Moore'. About 1 p.m. Thomas and he crossed the river in the boat to pick up their horses on the opposite bank.

> We proceeded first to Liverpool, where having marked out the Square for the Church &c. &c. I continued my Tour to the adjoining Farms belonging to Holt, Burn, Develin &c. &c. and ended it at Dwyer's, where I found Mrs. M. and Capt. Antill waiting for us.— Here we took leave of our worthy Guide & conductor Mr. Moore, who returned home, and we pursued our way to Parramatta, where we arrived at ½ past 5 O'Clock in the Evening.

On 15 December 1810, after Governor Macquarie had completed 'his late extensive tour of inspection through the various districts of this colony', he published a General and Government Order which praised the efforts at agriculture and husbandry he had observed, even if the state of the dwellings for both humans and animals left a bit to be desired, and people's clothing—both of which he hoped would improve by his next annual inspection. Then—and as another example of how the floods of NSW were instruments in the hand of Providence to shape the course of Thomas Moore's life—in view of 'the frequent inundations of the rivers Hawkesbury and Nepean' and

CHAPTER 6 ↲ *Speculator and Settler (31 July 1808 to 7 November 1810)* 377

their 'calamitous effects with regard the crops growing in their vicinity, and of consequence of most serious injury to the necessary subsistence of the colony', Macquarie announced his decision 'to erect certain townships on the most contiguous and eligible high grounds in the several districts subjected to those inundations for the purpose of rendering every possible accommodation and security to the settlers whose farms are exposed to the floods'. He noted that he had already selected the most eligible situations, and marked out some commons where the townships are to be established. The plan was to provide each settler 'an allotment of ground for a dwelling-house, offices, garden, corn-yard and stock-yard proportioned to the extent of the farm he holds within the influence of the floods'. These allotments will not be able to be sold or alienated, but always considered 'as forming an inseparable part of the said farms'. Macquarie announced that he had marked out five separate townships: Windsor, Richmond, Pitt Town, Wilberforce, Castlereagh.

As well as these towns along the Hawkesbury and Nepean, Macquarie 'having extended his views also to the situation of the settlers on George's River, has deemed it expedient to mark out the situation for a township on the west side (or left bank) of that river, in the district of Minto, to which he has given the name Liverpool'.[200] He is glowing in his prospects for this district, and already Thomas Moore is given a prominent role:

> The situation of this town is admirably calculated for trade and navigation, begin immediately on the bank of the river where the depth of water is sufficient to float vessels of very considerable burthen. At this town it is intended very soon to erect a church, a school-house, a gaol, a guard-house, &c. Leases of commodious and adequate allotments for houses and gardens will be given to suit free mechanics and tradesmen as may feel disposed to form a permanent residence there, on their giving regular and due security for their building comfortable and substantial houses, conformably to a plan that will be then them on application to Thomas Moore, Esq're, the Chief Magistrate in that district. Good tradesmen and mechanics settling at Liverpool will have the liberty of a large and contiguous common for grazing cattle, which is assigned for the benefit of the townships, and those persons who have not milch

cows will be supplied with one cow to each such person from the Government herds for payment on advantageous conditions. All applications on these heads are to be made to Thomas Moore, Esq're, who will explain the terms on which allotments may be obtained.

The same order also spoke of a new district having been selected, in which small grants of land would henceforth be made. It was situated between the Bunbury Curran Creek and the George's River, and would be known as Airds.

When he was a young boy at Lesbury, Thomas Moore lived on a river that led to the sea and, beyond it, to an expanding world filled with adventure, discovery, and perhaps a fortune to be made in worlds yet unknown.

When he was a man of forty-eight having just arrived at Moore Bank, Thomas Moore lived on a river deliberately away from the sea. His adventures were behind him. He had begun to acquire wealth. He had built a home away from the turmoil and factions of the Town recovering from its rebellion. His home had already been open for the new Governor as he explored the George's River district, dreaming his dreams for the future.

Macquarie was a Governor with big dreams for building. New South Wales was still a penal colony, but its future was going to be different. It was time to build places, to build people, to build a free society.

Thomas's devoted wife Rachel symbolised something of that new future. She had a colourful background; a convict past but through serving her time she had gained her freedom. She was an emancipist. She was an emancipist who was now married to one of the leading men of the colony, wealthy, respected, and valuable. This *Lady Juliana* woman opened her new home to the Governor and entertained the Governor's wife Elizabeth, forging the beginnings of a friendship that would last for the duration of the Macquarie's time in New South Wales. The ex-convict entertains the couple with the highest position in the Colony. The meals being eaten in Rachel's dining room spoke loudly of the new society that was on its way to New South Wales.

CHAPTER 6 ⚓ *Speculator and Settler (31 July 1808 to 7 November 1810)* 379

It was time for Thomas Moore to cross to the other side of the river. There was a town to build, a town filled with great hopes, as the colony expanded further to the South West. There would be a school, symbolizing the rising generation of Australians. There would be a court-house, symbolizing a just future; and there would be a church. The church would be situated on the town square—symbolizing the centrality of the Christian message to this new community. The young man from Lesbury knew about rural life centred around the parish church. Here was a model for the middle-aged man at Moore Bank with a new rural town to bring to completion.

A vast array of actions already splashed colour on the canvas of Moore's life. But there was still more to come. His portrait was not yet fully painted.

And so, at precisely this turning-point in New South Wales's history, feeling that his was under the good hand of God's Providence, Thomas Moore of Lesbury, came to Liverpool.

Endnotes

PAGE VII

1   Thomas Moore, *Memorandums & Occurrences*, Memorandum No 17, April 1822 (SDA: 0884 CH, Item 5).

INTRODUCTION

1   The portrait was commissioned specifically to hang in Moore College, where it still resides. For the story, see Bolt, 'Portrait'. Pollon, *Book of Sydney Suburbs*, 177, mistakenly published a portrait of the English poet. The picture of Moore that has often been utilised is that found in Loane, *Centenary History*, facing p.16. According to Bishop Donald Robinson (personal conversation with the author) this was an image created artificially by Rev. Frank Cash through manipulating a photograph of the Griffith Portrait to re-create what Moore might have looked like when he was younger.
2   The site of Moore's house is now commemorated as 'Thomas Moore Park' in Whelan Avenue, Chipping Norton. (Plates 46 and 47).
3   Boyce, *Thomas Moore*. In his autobiography, Boyce deals with his time as a student at Moore College in just two pages; Boyce, *Fourscore Years and Seven*, 15–16.
4   Boyce, *Thomas Moore*, 1.
5   Loane, 'Moore, Thomas (1762–1840)'; cf. *Centenary History*, Ch. 1; Bernard, 'Moore, 12', (1987); Dickey, 'Moore, Thomas' (1994).
6   [Aust.Enc.^{2}], 'Moore, Thomas (1762–1840)'; [Aust.Enc.^{3}], 'Moore, Thomas (1762–1840)'.
7   Robinson, 'Thomas Moore and the Early Life of Sydney' (1970); 'Thomas Moore of Moore Bank 1762–1840: The Father of Liverpool, Benefactor of Mankind' (1975).
8   Russell, *Thomas Moore and the King's Dockyard 1796–1816*. On the dockyard, see also Bolt, 'The King's Dockyard'.
9   Robinson, 'Thomas Moore & Early Life', 167 (3) n.11.
10 Robinson, 'Thomas Moore & Early Life', 187 (25) n.127.
11 It is also worth noting another lost source in regard to Moore's Liverpool period. Arthur Lukyn Williams had been the third Principal of Moore College from 1878 to 1884, while it was situated in Liverpool; Loane, *Centenary History*, Ch. 4. In an article published in the May 1937 issue of the Moore College student magazine, *Societas*, Williams reported that he used to speak with the old people of the town who still remembered Mr Moore, to gain information about the College's founder. Because Moore, after a long life as one of Liverpool's chief citizens, died in 1840, by Williams' time he was still part of living memory. Indeed, this living memory survived into the twentieth century, for F.B. Boyce, writing in 1914, knew that 'one aged and highly respected resident of the town still lives who was a scholar [at Liverpool school], and has a kindly recollection of [Moore] often coming to the school and showing a warm concern in its doings'; Boyce, *Thomas Moore*, 9. Williams claimed to have recorded the reminiscences he collected in an exercise book, which he eventually deposited in the Bishop's Registry. Unfortunately, despite my searching in the Sydney Diocesan Archives (the successor to the Bishop's Registry), the Mitchell Library, Moore College, and the Royal Australian Historical Society Archives, this potentially important source of information has not yet turned up. Donald Robinson

suggested to me (personal conversation, 1st December 2006) that the reminiscences in the *Societas* article may have come by way of T.C. Hammond, who was farewelled on his way to take up the Principal's position at Moore College, by a meeting in Cambridge chaired by Williams (see Loane, *Centenary History*, 140).
12   Boyce, *Thomas Moore*, 1.
13   [Aust.Enc.²], 'Moore, Thomas (1762–1840)', 145; Loane, 'Moore, Thomas (1762–1840)', 254–255; Bernard, 'Moore, 12' and 'Moore Theological College'; Dickey, 'Moore, Thomas', 265–266.
14   [Aust.Enc.²], 'Moore, Thomas (1762–1840)', 145. This was corrected in the third edition.
15   Robinson, 'Thomas Moore & Early Life', 167 (3) n.11, 187 (25) n.123. See Broughton to Watson, 29 Nov 1838; Broughton to Coleridge, 27 Dec 1841 (Moore: Broughton Papers).
16   These lectures grew in number across 2006 and were subsequently published, along with some additional essays, in *Thomas Moore of Liverpool (1762–1840)*.
17   I have documented the course of my discoveries in 'A Overdue Birth Announcement'.
18   Fletcher, 'Christianity and Free Society in New South Wales 1788–1840', 94. The study on convicts to which he refers is Grocott, *Convicts, Clergymen and Churches*.
19   Thomas Moore, *Memorandums & Occurrences*, Memorandum No 17, April 1822 (SDA: 0884 CH, Item 5).
20   Aikin, *Memoirs Of The Court Of Queen Elizabeth*. Apparently there is no evidence the proclamation was ever put into effect.

CHAPTER 1

1   *T. Moore's Account book, 1828-1840* (SDA: 0885CH, Item 6): entries for 13/11/1838: 'My Dear Wife departed this life at Quarter past Seven oClock in the Morning, and I hope and trust that the Almity God has sent her Gardin Angle to Conduct her passed therunto to his Heavenly Kingdom where I hope to meet her again to praise the Lord to part no more forever Amen'; and for 5 and 26/11/1839 (Clutter's bill).
2   *T. Moore's Account book, 1828-1840* (SDA: 0885CH, Item 6): entries for 18/10/1838 (Rachel's fall); 13/11/1838 (Rachel's death); 16/11/1838 (Rachel's burial); 26/11/1838 (opening vault); 28/11/1838 (changing will); 29/11 and 1/12/1838 (Hosking's bill).
3   *T. Moore's Account book, 1828-1840* (SDA: 0885CH, Item 6): entry for 16/11/1839 (opening the vault).
4   For the five towns: Government and General Order, 15 Dec 1810 (Col.Sec. 6038, SZ758, p.135; *HRNSW* 7.468–471); *SG* 15 & 22/12/1810. Once the marked-out burial grounds were consecrated by Principle Chaplain Marsden, Macquarie ordered that the previous practice of burying the deceased on farms should cease and all should be given a decent burial in the consecrated grounds. It was therefore necessary for the townships to raise subscriptions to enclose these grounds, and the Governor pledged £10 towards this work in each town; *SG* 18/5/1811. By July, Moore had been paid the Government money for the work; *SG* 20/7/1811. He supervised raising subscriptions in the George's River District for the school-house, bridges, and the burial grounds, and after announcing the completion of the work on the burial ground (*SG* 22/2/1812), he called for further subscriptions, the initial funds having proved inadequate (*SG* 29/2/1812).
5   Joseph Moor to his children, 20 Mar 1806 (SDA: 0853CH, Item 11, doc. 1b); William Moore to Thomas Moore, 2 July 1839 (SDA: 0853CH, Item 8, doc. 9); William Moor to Thomas Moore, 24 Dec 1839 (SDA: 0851CH, Item 6, doc. 35; cf. the copy resent on 28/1/1840: SDA: 0853CH, Item 8, doc. 10). I have published this correspondence in Bolt, 'The Family Correspondence of Thomas Moore'.

ENDNOTES

6   Hickes, *History*, 20.
7   Joseph is registered as a 'barn-man' in his son Joseph's christening entry, 8 Sept 1765, Lesbury, St Mary's Register; Bolam, *Registers*, 32; 'husbandman' Lesbury, St Mary's, burial Register (NBL RO: M246): 1812, 'Joseph Moore, of Lesbury, Husbandman d. 6th of Jany 1812, bur. 8th of Jany 1812, Aged 88 years'.
8   Baptisms: 'Joseph the son of Joseph Moor Xtned', Holy Island (Lindisfarne), St Mary the Virgin, Register (NBL RO: M677); 'Mary, daughter of Thomas Hudson of Melfield was baptised, January ye 28th 1727', Chillingham, St Peter's, Register (NBL RO: M251). Marriage: '1751: Joseph Moor in the Parish of Lesbury and Mary Hutson of Chillingham, December 8th', Chillingham, St Peter's, Register (NBL RO: M251).
9   His death notice: 'At his residence, Liverpool, on Thursday the 24th instant, in the 79th year of his age, Thomas Moore, Esq. Mr. Moore was one of our oldest colonists, and much esteemed for his piety and charity'; *Sydney (Morning) Herald* 28/12/1840 and *SG* 29/12/1840. His funeral announcement appeared in the two papers on the same day as the event, Tuesday 29th December 1840. See also Thomas Moore's Headstone, Pioneer Park, Liverpool, NSW.
10 Baptismal Register, St Mary's, Lesbury, 18 June 1762: 'Thomas, Son of Joseph & Mary Moore of Lesbury, Baptized'; Bolam, *Registers*, 30; IGI: P001291/ 0962712IT6/ 6905518.
11 Whellan, *History, Topography, and Directory of Northumberland* (1855).
12 Parson & White, *History*, 2.396. In 1855, Whellan, *History, Topography, and Directory of Northumberland*, adds the township of Bilton.
13 Parson & White, *History*, 2.396.
14 Hickes, *History*, 9, 31–32.
15 Hickes, *History*, 12; cf. 5.
16 Hickes, *History*, 15–17; quotation from p.15. In Alnwick this was originally known as 'the Four and Twenty', although by the 17th century this body only dealt with church affairs, a new civil body having emerged; p.33–34.
17 Hickes, *History*, 37.
18 Hickes, *History*, 37.
19 Hickes, *History*, 38.
20 Hickes, *History*, 11, 19, 22.
21 Hickes, *History*, 34–35, 47. See also note 16 above.
22 [Aust.Enc.^{2}], 'Moore, Thomas', 145, claimed he was born in Ireland, although this was corrected in the third edition. Other surveys placed his origins in England. Robinson, 'Thomas Moore & Early Life', 167 (3) n.11, added greater precision, when, working from hints in Bishop Broughton's correspondence, he rightly guessed that Moore originated in the northeast.
23 This was also aided by David Moor's family tree.
24 Joseph Moor to children, 20 March 1806 (SDA: 0853CH, Item 11, doc. 1b).
25 William Moor to Thomas Moore, 2 July 1839 (SDA: 0853CH, Item 8, doc. 9); William Moor to Thomas Moore, 24 Dec 1839 (SDA: 0851CH, Item 6, doc. 35); cf. the copy resent on 28/1/1840, arrived just one week after the original (SDA: 0853CH, Item 8, doc. 10); W. Moore to Bishop Broughton, 7 July 1842 (SDA: 0851CH, Item 7, docs. 1 & 2).
26 Courtesy of David Moor, a copy of the relevant sections of his family tree is in my possession.
27 Sally's own family can be traced a little further, thanks to a journal written by her son Nathaniel, extant amongst Moore's papers in the Sydney Diocesan Archives; see N. Clark, *Journal* (SDA: 0885CH, item 5).

28 Joseph Moor to children, 20 March 1806 (SDA: 0853CH, Item 11, doc. 1b). There are Trumbles from Alnmouth in the St Mary's Lesbury Register.
29 Warkworth, St Lawrence, Register (NBL RO: EP 66/2): 11/5/1755, Maria filia Josephi Moor de Low Buston.
30 Warkworth, St Lawrence, Register (NBL RO: EP 66/2): 25/9/1757, Henricus filius Josephi Moor de Low Buston
31 Bolam, *Registers*, 128: Buried: 28th June 1772, 'HENRY, s JOSEPH MOORE, Lesbury'.
32 Eglingham, St Maurice (NBL RO: EP 156), p.83: 1848: 'Elizabeth Scott, Abode: Gallo-law, bur.: June 20th, Aged: 88; by W.H. Norris, off. Min.'. Registration of Death: 1848, No. 402: died: Seventeenth June 1848 Gallowlaw; Elizabeth Scott; 88 years; widow of Walter Scott, Shepherd; cause: old age, not certified; informant: John Churnside, Occupier Gallowlaw; registered nineteenth June 1848'. In brother William's letter of July 1842, he says she is 83 years old; W. Moore to Bishop Broughton, 7 July 1842 (SDA: 0851CH: Item 7, docs. 1 & 2). If these ages are given precisely, the two would be reconciled with a birthday between 17 June (exclusive) and 7 July 1759.
33 Warkworth, St Lawrence, Register (NBL RO: EP 66/2): 2/12/1759: Elisabetha filia Josephi Moor de Low Buston; IGI: P001111, 1677—1812 / 0814228 IT 5 / 6905510.
34 Bolam, *Registers*, 44: 30 Dec 1792, 'THOMAS, *natural* s. WALTER SCOTT, Alnham and ELIZ. Moore of this P.'. Alnham is 13 miles west of Alnwick.
35 Lesbury, St Mary's, Register, Marriages 1794: 'WALTER SCOTT of the P. of Eglingham and ELIZABETH MOORE of this P. Wit.: James Scott and Joseph Moore Married by banns. J. Richardson, Curate'. The Banns were read on 13, 20, 27th April. Cf. Bolam, *Registers*, 92. From the 1841 census return, her grandsons were named James and Walter, then Joseph: presumably after Maternal grandfather, father, then paternal grandfather. This may indicate that the witnesses at the wedding were the two fathers.
36 William Moor to Thomas Moore, 24 Dec 1839 and 28 Jan 1840 (SDA: 0851CH, Item 6, doc. 35; and Item 8, doc. 10).
37 1841 Census: Beanley (NA-UK: HO 107/829/8).
38 Bolam, *Registers*, 32: 'JOSEPH, s. JOSEPH and MARY MOOR, barn-man, Lesbury'.
39 Baptism: Bolam, *Registers*, 43: 27th June 1790, 'HENRY, s. JOSEPH and ISABELLA MOORE of the P. of South Shields'. Marriage: http://genuki.cs.ncl.ac.uk/Transcriptions/DUR/SSH1780.html: Rounce-Bell Transcription of St Hilda's South Shields.
40 'Brother Joseph died about 30 years since[;] he left a son sho died of the Cholera about five years since'; William Moor to Thomas Moore, 24 Dec 1839 & 28 Jan 1840 (SDA: 0851CH, Item 6, doc. 35; and Item 8, doc. 10).
41 Bolam, *Registers*, 34: 'WILLIAM, s. JOSEPH MOOR, Lesbury'. In William's letter in July 1842, he puts his age as 73 years; W. Moore to Bishop Broughton, 7 July 1842 (SDA: 0851CH, Item 7, docs. 1 & 2).
42 For William, jnr., see William Moor to Thomas Moore, 24 Dec 1839 & 28 Jan 1840 (SDA: 0851CH, Item 6, doc. 35; and Item 8, doc. 10). The same letter reveals that William had a daughter buried 'in South Church yard'. A headstone still stands in the St Andrew's Auckland yard, three stones from the main gate, in memory of the three of them. This reveals that: a) William died 23/12/1847, age 78; b) his daughter, Ann Walker, died 16/8/1832, aged 34, and so was born 1798; c) William jnr, died 28/5/1847, aged 40, so was born about 1807; William Moore, Headstone, St Andrew's Auckland (South Church).
43 Joseph Moor to children, 20 March 1806 (SDA: 0853CH, Item 11, doc. 1b); Rev. P. Stockdale to S. Moore, 18 Mar 1806 (SDA: 0853, Item 11, doc. 1a).
44 Lesbury, St Mary's, Register (NBL RO: M246), 1786. There is no indication that Joseph and Nathanael were twins, as is frequently the case in that circumstance.

ENDNOTES 385

45 Lesbury, St Mary's, Burial Register (NBL RO: 246), 1787.
46 'Your nephew, Mr N. Clarke, having called on me, to inform me of his intention of shortly proceeding to New South Wales as a settler, and having requested a letter to you from me, I willingly comply with his request, as it gives me an opportunity of conveying to you in this manner, my best regards and good wishes for the Health, welfare, and happiness of yourself and Mrs Moore', Gov. L. Macquarie to T. Moore, 1 June 1824 (SDA: 0853CH, item 4, doc. 12).
47 N. Clark, Journal (SDA: 0885CH, Item 5), 77: Illness prevented him from going to the Moore's the day after he arrived in Sydney (arrived: 20 June 1825), but after three or four days' rest he made the journey.
48 *SG* 7 November 1825: 'Died, suddenly, at his lodgings in Pitt Street, on Thursday evening last, Nathaniel Clark, Esq. nephew to Thomas Moore, Esq. of Liverpool. Mr. Clark, who had been for some time in a bad state of health, an abscess having formed on his liver, was on the above evening seized with a violent fit of coughing, and in the exertion unfortunately burst an artery, and almost instantaneously expired from suffocation, occasioned by the overflow of blood'.
49 For the day and month: N. Clark, Journal (SDA: 0885CH, Item 5), 15; the year is calculated backwards from his age (40) at death in November 1825.
50 Thomas Moore's Business Notebook, Rear (SDA: 0884CH, Item 1), p. 49: 'Received a letter this 22nd day of August 1821—dated January 17 1820 per favor of Mr Galhossy [?] Surgeon, of her being no more but not noting the day of her Death'. The year before, he had had a foreboding of this event, of sufficient moment for him to make a journal entry: '1819, June 29th: I Dreamed I thought my Sister Sarah was dead'.
51 Sally's family tree will be found in *A Portrait in his Actions. Part 2: Liverpool to Legacy*.
52 David Moor's tree lists: William (b. 1714), Eleanor (b.1716), Ralph (b.1718), George (b.1719), Jean (b. 1720), Ann (b. 1721), Frances (b. 1725), Rachel (b. & d. 1727), Rachel (b. 1728), James (b. 1734), Grace (b. abt. 1737).
53 Joseph acted as a witness at the wedding. David Moor's tree has made the same supposition, but lists no offspring of the union. Joseph Ferrow is above James Moor on the 1762 Lesbury Militia list, which may speak of a family connection. See also IGI: M001291, 1689 - 1812 /0962712 IT 6 /6905519.
54 For schoolmaster: Lesbury militia list, 1762; Baptism record for his sons Robert (5/4/1763), Henry (18/2/1765) and Joseph (25/12/1778), and in his own burial record (8/6/1794); see Lesbury, St Mary's, Registers; Bolam, *Registers*, 30, 31, 38, 139. For being the brother: Joseph is a witness at James and Margaret's wedding on 4/7/1762; Lesbury, St Mary's Register; Bolam, *Registers*, 81. David Moor's Tree has made the same supposition.
55 Bolam, *Registers*, 81: '4th July 1762, James Moor and Margaret Linton, both of this P. Wit. Wm. Lough and Joseph Moore'.
56 Bolam, *Registers*, 139: bur. '8th June 1794 'JAMES MOORE, sexton and schoolmaster, Lesbury, aged 60 years'. For Margaret's death: Bolam, *Registers*, 150: 6 April 1809: 'Margt. (died April 4th), widow of the late James Moore, Lesbury, aged 74 years'; Downer & Henslee Family History.
57 Bolam, *Registers*, 30: '5th April 1763 ROBERT, s. JAMES and MARGARET MOORE, schoolmaster, Lesbury'; Bolam, *Registers*, 31: '18th February 1765, HENRY, s. JAMES and MARGARET MOORE, schoolmaster, Lesbury'.
58 Bolam, *Registers*, 33: c. '6th October 1767, ELIZABETH, d. JAMES and MARGARET Moor, Lesbury' (NB: Lesbury is not in original). Bolam, *Registers*, 135: bur. '2nd June 1786, ELISABETH, d JAMES MOORE, Lesbury'.

59 Bolam, *Registers*, 34: c. '24th June 1770, JAMES, s. JAMES MOORE, Lesbury'. Bolam, *Registers*, 139: bur.: '22nd September 1793, JAMES, s JAMES MOORE, sexton, Lesbury, aged 23 years'.
60 Bolam, *Registers*, 36: c. '26th June 1774, JOHN, s. JAS. MOORE, Lesbury and MARGARET h.w.'.
61 Bolam, *Registers*, 38: c. '25th December 1778, JOSEPH, s. JAMES MOORE, Lesbury, schoolmaster and MARGARET h.w.'. His descendants have been traced a little further, by David Moor, and by Downer and Henslee Family History—although with differences. In the 1841 Census his family were listed at Lesbury: Joseph (60) Agricultural labourer; Thomas (20) Blacksmith; Elizabeth (20), Margaret (15), William (10). 1841 Census, Lesbury (NA-UK: HO 107/819/22).
62 'Joseph the son of Joseph Moor Xtned', Holy Island (Lindisfarne), St Mary the Virgin, Register (NBL RO: M677); see also David Moor's family tree.
63 Hickes, *History*, 9–10, 23–24.
64 Tristram, 'Religious History' (Website).
65 'Alnwick Quaker Meeting' (Website).
66 Hickes, *History*, 44, and *passim*.
67 Hickes, *History*, 39.
68 Hickes, *History*, 29; Lesbury PCC, *St Mary's Parish Church Lesbury*, 7.
69 Hickes, *History*, 39, 64.
70 *The Evangelical Repository*, 172.
71 Coleman, *Two Thousand Confessors*, 237. For details of the Northumberland Ministers ejected or silenced for nonconformity, see Calamy, *The Nonconformist Memorial*, 3.52ff., who deals with: Allenton, Mr. Strong; Alnwick (curacy), Gilbert Rule, M. D.; Ancroft (curacy), Mr. John Foreside; Bedlington (vicarage), Mr. John Darton; Benton Magna (vicarage), Mr. Alexander White; Berwick upon Tweed (vicarage), Luke Ogle and Nicholas Wressel, M. A.; Bolam (vicarage), Mr. Robert Leaver; Bothal (rectory, £200), Mr. John Thompson; Chatton (vicarage), Mr. James Duncanson; Chollerton (vicarage), Mr. Taylor; Cornhill, Mr. Henry Erskine, father of Ebenezer Erskine; Earsdon (rectory), Mr. William Henderson: Randal mentions Henderson as an intruder, ejected from Earsdon curacy and Elsdon rectory in 1662; Edlingham (vicarage), Mr. John Murray; Eglingham (vicarage), Mr. John Pringle; Ellingham (vicarage), Mr. Patrick Bromfield; Felton (vicarage), Mr. John Seaton; Hartborn (vicarage, salary £130), Ralph Ward, M. A.; Haughton, Mr. John Hume; Houghton, Long (vicarage), Mr. Samuel Lane; Kirkharle (vicarage), Mr. Robert Blunt; Mitford, Mr. Benlows; Norham (vicarage), Mr. Edward Ord: Randal says, "Edward Ogle, an intruder." ; Ovingham (vicarage), Mr. Thomas Trurant; Ponteland (vicarage), Mr. Humphrey Bell; Stannerton, Mr. John Owens; Stannington (vicarage), Mr. Haddon: Randal has it George Howden, M.A. 24th September, 1661; Tweedmouth and Spittle chapels, Mr. William Merse; Tynemouth (vicarage), Mr. Alexander Gourdon; Whalton (rectory), Mr. Ralph Wickliffe; Warkworth (salary £100), Mr. Archibald Moor; Whittingham (rectory), Abraham Hume, M. A.; Wooler (vicarage, salary £100), John Lomax, M. A.
72 Calamy, *The Nonconformist Memorial*, 52–55 (Rule); 75 (Lane); 82 (Moor).
73 Hickes, *History*, 64–65.
74 Although during the eighteenth century, several families on Holy Island became Presbyterian; Tristram, 'Religious History'.
75 Calamy, *The Nonconformist Memorial*, 67.
76 Parson & White, *History, Directory, and Gazetteer*, lxxii.
77 http://www.unitariansocieties.org.uk/historical/hsrecords.html (9/7/2010). It is also the only Northumberland Chapel listed amongst these records, admittedly incomplete.

78 See Bolt, 'Thomas Moore's Bookshelf' for a listing and analysis.
79 In Bolt, 'Thomas Moore's Bookshelf', 198, I list four of his authors in this category. One book was also possibly Swedenbourgian (p. 141), and there were others on the shelf that were associated with enlightenment thought and radical politics—although those in the latter category probably belonged to his stepson, Captain Andrew Douglas White. For completion's sake, it should also be noted that Moore probably possessed the work by Bowles, which had an anti-Unitarian bent (pp.155–156).
80 See Turner, *The Lives Of Eminent Unitarians*, 2.214–238.
81 Bolt, 'Thomas Moore's Bookshelf', 158–159.
82 Turner, *The Lives of Eminent Unitarians*, 27–28, says 'about nine', but the *Dictionary of National Biography* puts his birth date as 1742.
83 For this paragraph, see Turner, *The Lives of Eminent Unitarians*, 27–28, 29, 31, 41; Mott, *A Short History of Unitarianism*, 38–40.
84 Balleine, *History of the Evangelical Party*, 82. Overton, *Evangelical Revival*, also doesn't deal with anybody north of Yorkshire.
85 In the latter category we might include Governor John Hunter, Justice Barron Field, J.J. Moore and perhaps his brother-in-law Deputy Judge-Advocate John Wylde, merchants Edward Riley, Robert Campbell and Richard Jones, and Major H.C. Antill; see Fletcher, 'Christianity and Free Society', 96–97.
86 Hickes, *History*, 55.
87 J. Wesley to Mayor of Newcastle, 12 July 1743; in Everett, *The Wall's End Miner*, 217–218.
88 Hickes, *History*, 43.
89 Lesbury, St Mary's, burial Register (NBL RO: M246): 1806, 'Mary Moore, wife of Joseph Moore, Sexton of Lesbury, d. March 2nd, bur. March 4th, Aged 78 years'.
90 Mackenzie, *An Historical, Topographical, and Descriptive View*, 205.
91 Nichols, 'Rev. Percival Stockdale (1814)'. E.g. Stockdale was absent from the parish from 1788–1790, visiting Tangiers and the Mediterranean. He was probably also absent when J. Richardson signed the registers (see some of the records cited above).
92 Nichols, 'Rev. Percival Stockdale (1814)'. A note, coincidentally in the Lesbury Burial Register on the same page as Joseph Moore's burial, reads: 'The Revd Percival Stockdale of Lesbury died 14th and was buried the 21st of Sep^r [1811] at Cornhill aged 74 years'; Lesbury St Mary's, Burial Register, page beginning 1812; Lesbury PCC, *St Mary's Parish Church Lesbury*, 9.
93 See Hickes, *History*, Ch. 4; Lesbury PCC, *St Mary's Parish Church*.
94 Hickes, *History*, 26.
95 Hickes, *History*, 27–28.
96 For St Luke's, see Bolt, 'A Man, A Church, A College'.
97 See Bolt, 'Moore and the Merino'.
98 The fact that Rachel was illiterate is suggested by her inability to read the 'confession' submitted to the court during her original trial at the Old Bailey, to which she had only made her mark. Rachel signed her name at her wedding, but not with a polished hand. Thomas noted in his business account book when he paid for Rachel's lessons: '1829, July 10: Paid Mrs White for Rachell schooling for one Quarter up to the first of July 1824, £10'; '1829, Sept 29: Paid for Rachell Schooling by Bradley, £10', *T. Moore's Account book, 1828-1840* (SDA: 0885CH, Item 6).
99 Bishop Broughton's latin oration at the opening of St James' Lyndhurst, pre-Christmas 1846, translated by George Fairfowl Macarthur and George Gregory; Quoted from Robinson, 'Thomas Moore. Early Life', 165 (1). Broughton's comments may lie behind

Loane, 'Moore, Thomas (1762–1840)': 'He had little education, but was endowed with robust common sense and developed a character of great stability'.
100   MacLeod, 'Shipwrights', 288–289.
101   Parson & White, *History*, 396.
102   See below, chapter 2.
103   For Raven's comment: King to Dundas, 19 Nov 1793, Enclosure: Raven to King, 2 Nov 1793 (*HRNSW* 2.95); For traditional practice: Albion, *Forests*, 100, 80-81.
104   W. Raven to Lieut.-Gov. King, 2 Nov 1793 (*HRNSW* 2.94–96; *HRNZ* 1.177–179).
105   Robinson, 'Thomas Moore & Early Life', 170 (6).
106   In 1664 the Navy Board ordered apprentices to be 16 years old at entry, and to serve for 7 years (a term which was not reduced to 6 years until 1890). The age on entry was lowered to 15 in 1765, and 14 in 1769. MacLeod, 'Shipwrights', 285–286.
107   MacLeod, 'Shipwrights', 286–287.
108   MacLeod, 'Shipwrights', 287. In 1788 this practice was changed to require two-thirds to his master and one-third to his parents.
109   This was the standard pay from 1660 until 1788, and nominally until 1809; Richardson, 'Wages of Shipwrights', 265. It has been confirmed by the following sample (courtesy: Ann Coats): NA-UK: ADM 42/564 Deptford Extra Ordinary 1774 and 1775. Shipwrights; ADM 42/1290 and 1291 Portsmouth Dockyard Extra Pay Book January-December 1774 and 1775. Shipwrights; ADM 42/1292 Portsmouth Dockyard Extra Pay Book January-March 1776. Shipwrights; ADM 42/885 and 886 Plymouth Dockyard Extra Pay Book January–Dec 1774 and 1775. Shipwrights; ADM 42/887 Plymouth Extra Ordinary 1777. Shipwrights. If shipwrights worked a six day week, this annual (313 days) wage amounts to £32.12s.1d. As Master Boat Builder at the King's Dockyard in Sydney, Moore earned £91.5s p.a.
110   Hickes, *History*, 5.
111   See especially, Rowland, *The Alemouth or Corn Road*.
112   Hickes, *History*, 50: 'There is little doubt that the first and most important event to occur in this new century and which contributed the most to local history was when the River Aln changed its course and its outlet into the sea'.
113   Mackenzie, *An Historical, Topographical, and Descriptive View*; followed by Parson & White, *History*, 396–397. Hickes, *History*, 42: 'This was a large ship for the time'.
114   These vessels are mentioned on the Alnmouth website, *www.alnmouth.org.uk*, but I have been unable to confirm the source behind the statement.
115   For Sunderland: Smith & Holden, *Where Ships are Born*, 10; for South Shields: Flagg, *Notes on the History of Shipbuilding in South Shields*.
116   Baptism: Bolam, *Registers*, 43: 27th June 1790, 'HENRY, s. JOSEPH and ISABELLA MOORE of the P. of South Shields'. Marriage: http://genuki.cs.ncl.ac.uk/Transcriptions/DUR/SSH1780.html: Rounce-Bell Transcription of St Hilda's South Shields.
117   That is, Wallis's and Forster's on Shadwell Street, the Winship-Broderick's and the Broderick's on Wapping Street, and Wallis's Middle-Dock. For details, see what follows.
118   Flagg, *Notes on the History of Shipbuilding in South Shields*, 3–8.
119   Flagg, *Notes on the History of Shipbuilding in South Shields*, 29–32.
120   Flagg, *Notes on the History of Shipbuilding in South Shields*, 57, 67–68.
121   Flagg, *Notes on the History of Shipbuilding in South Shields*, 75–76, 134.
122   Flagg, *Notes on the History of Shipbuilding in South Shields*, 85–87.
123   Flagg, *Notes on the History of Shipbuilding in South Shields*, 99–100. Like Joseph Moore, the Temples were parishioners of St Hilda's, South Shields; see pp.122–123.
124   *Lloyds Register of British and Foreign Vessels*, 1790, 1791, 1792.

125 Smith & Holden, *Where Ships are Born*, 10.
126 Cited in Smith & Holden, *Where Ships are Born*, 1.
127 Smith & Holden, *Where Ships are Born*, 2, 22. These establishments were those associated with the following families/persons: Goodchilds (pp.7–8), Burns (p. 8), Collins (p. 8), Henry Rudd (p. 9), Reay (p. 9), Thomas Havelock (p. 9), Tiffin (p. 9), Nicholsons (p. 96), Pile (p. 18).
128 Smith & Holden, *Where Ships are Born*, 10, citing the House of Commons Report of 1806. http://www.thisisthenortheast.co.uk/the_north_east/history/shipbuilding generalises this number by saying 'by 1790 Sunderland was building around nineteen ships per year'. Smith & Holden give the actual figures from the House of Commons Report in 1806 as: 1790: 19; 1791: 6; 1804: 51. Average tonnage built 144, 202, 163 respectively; and largest tonnage: 312, 356, 349.
129 For further history of shipbuilding in Sunderland, especially in the nineteenth century, see the following exchange: Ville, 'Rise to Pre-Eminence'; Clarke, 'Comments on Simon Ville'; Ville, 'Sunderland Shipbuilding: Pre-Eminence Restated'; Craig, 'A Note on Shipbuilding'; Ville, 'Craig on Sunderland Shipbuilding'.
130 See Bolt, 'Thomas Moore S/Purveyor of Timber', 62–65.
131 Cook, 'Men of Lincoln', 123. *Robinson Crusoe* went into four editions by the end of the century.
132 Cook, 'Men of Lincoln', 118–120, quotation p.120.
133 Ingleton, 'General Introduction', 4.
134 Ingleton, 'General Introduction', 5.
135 *HRNZ* 1.36–41. Ingleton, 'General Introduction', 4–5.
136 For this paragraph, Dallas, 'Enderby, Samuel (1756–1829)'.
137 Dunbabin, 'William Raven', 297. Francis Grose described Raven to Governor Phillip as part owner; F. Grose to Gov. Phillip, 4 Oct 1792 (*HRNZ* 1.148).
138 This system gives rise to two sets of documents: Militia Muster Rolls or Enrolment Lists, containing the names of the 'drawn men', or their substitutes; and the Militia Ballot Lists, containing the names of all the men liable to the ballot.
139 Lesbury Militia Lists http://communities.northumberland.gov.uk/008835FS.htm and http://communities.northumberland.gov.uk/008836FS.htm (3/7/2010).
140 NA-UK: WO 13/1645: 1780-97, 1st Northumberland Militia.
141 See Forster Charlton Certificate of the reduction of the tenth or Newcastle volunteers last year, Alnwick 16 May 1783 (NA-UK: WO 13/1645: 1780-97, 1st Northumberland Militia).
142 Mackenzie, 'Historical events: 1783–1825'.
143 Mackenzie, 'Historical events: 1783–1825'.
144 *Lloyds Register of British and Foreign Vessels*, 1790, 1791, 1792.
145 There are three Clarks listed with the SWF in 1789: 'T. Clark' who left London on 15 August on the *Liberty*, the same day as Raven left on *Jackal*, and S. Smith on the *Lucas*—were the three ships working together?; Charles Clark, *Trelawney*, out of Yarmouth on 25 July 1789; and a William Clark, who had departed from Yarmouth November 6, 1789, on the *Sparrow* (250 tons). *Diary or Woodfall's Register*, 18 Aug 1790. The Enderby's were also well-connected with Clark's in London, including Richard Clark, an alderman from 1776 to 1798, including Lord Mayor of London 1784–1785, and London's Chamberlain, 1798–1831; see http://www.danbyrnes.com.au/blackheath/ships2.htm (14/12/2008).
146 Thomas Moore, Certificate of Membership in Freemason's Lodge, 6 July 1790 (SDA: 0851CH: Item 2, doc. 1).

147 Diane Clements to Peter G. Bolt, 6 & 10 Aug 2007.
148 *Lloyds Register of British and Foreign Vessels*, volume for 1790. Warng's name is crossed through with Young's inserted under it.
149 *Lloyds Register of British and Foreign Vessels*, volume for 1791.
150 Murray, *Journal*. Since the Lloyds Register is published on 1 July, providing details for the year to 30 June, the mistake is hard to explain. Perhaps the original plan was to sail to New South Wales via Antigua? There is not a hint of this in Murray's *Journal*, however.
151 *Lloyds Register of British and Foreign Vessels*, volume for 1792. Three pieces of evidence establish Moore as being on the *Britannia*. 1. On a protest sworn in 27 July 1792 he signed as ship's carpenter; Cobley, *Sydney Cove* 1791–92, 284–285. 2. His EIC commission (Chapter 2, n 198). 3. Daniel Paine's reference to him as Second Mate of the *Britannia* (Chapter 2, n 221).
152 Paine, *Journal*, 23. For much of the following paragraph see Parsons, 'Raven, William (1756–1814).
153 Daily Mirror, 'Human Seafarer', 71.
154 Parsons, 'Raven, William (1756–1814)', drawing upon Masters' Qualifications, 1748–1805 (NA-UK: Adm 106/2938).
155 Parsons, 'Raven, William (1756–1814)', drawing upon Masters' Qualifications, 1748–1805 (NA-UK: ADM 106/2938).
156 Collins, *Account*, 2.149.
157 His rank in the Navy still commanded respect, however. Cf. Murray, *Journal*, [068], who comments that the *Boddingtons* gave preference to the *Britannia* in June 1793, because she 'was commanded by an officer of H.M. Navy'.
158 Lord Sydney to the Lords Commissioners of the Treasury, 18 Aug 1786 (*HRNZ* 1.49). Ingleton, 'General Introduction', 5–6.
159 http://www.merchantnetworks.com.au/periods/1775after/swf1.htm (7/5/2008).
160 *Times* 23/7/1789, p.4: 'To be peremptorily sold (if not dispensed by Private contract), at the New York Coffee House in Sweetings Alley, Cornhill on Tuesday the 28th Instant, at Five o'clock in the afternoon, THE FOLLOWING GOODS, viz. About 16,000 SEAL SKINS, in Pickle, and in high preservation; 1,933 dried CAT SKINS. The seal skins are the remaining part of the cargo of the *Jackall*, William Raven, commander and lays at the Orchard House, Blackwall'.
161 'August 15, *Jackall*, William Raven, 196 tons', *Diary or Woodfall's Register*, 18 Aug 1790. Thomas Melville and E[bor] Bunker were on the same list—two other ship captains who later came to NSW. Bunker later sailed Moore's ship the *Pegasus*, and became one of Moore's friends and neighbours at Liverpool.
162 *Public Advertiser*, 6/5/1786.
163 *World*, 7/5/1790.
164 These discussions eventually issued in *Southern Whale Fishery Act* (1798).
165 Frost, *Arthur Phillip*, 148; Ingleton, 'General Introduction', 6; http://www.foundingdocs.gov.au/resources/transcripts/nsw2_doc_1787.pdf (30/6/2010).
166 Frost, *Arthur Phillip*, 153–154; Ingleton, 'General Introduction', 7.
167 Rachel Turner, Theft: Simple Grand Larceny, 12 Dec 1787; http://www.oldbaileyonline.org/browse.jsp?ref=t17871212-13 (30/6/2010). Rienits, 'Biographical Introduction', 21, puts her sentence date in March 1788. For a summary of her trial, see Cobley, *Lady Juliana, Crimes of the Lady Juliana*, 86.
168 Cobley, *Lady Juliana*, 23. Cobley notes that he could not establish the ages of all the convicts (p.23). The youngest age he recorded was that of Mary Wade, age 11 (p.87);

the next youngest was Margaret Williams, age 13 (p.91); and then at age 14, Ann Bryant, Elizabeth Carter, Alice Fidoe, Jane Forbes, Mary Read, and Jane Whiting (Mary Wade's accomplice) (pp.34, 35, 48, 49, 75, 90). For an account of the *Lady Juliana*'s voyage, see Rees, *Floating Brothel*.
169 Collins, *Account*, 1.200.
170 R. Johnson to S. Thornton, July 1790; (Mackaness, *Some Letters*, 1.9; Murray, *Australian Christian Life*, 11).
171 Murray, *Australian Christian Life*, 11.
172 Macintosh, *Richard Johnson. First to Preach*, 9. A rumour circulated that Johnson handed out bounty from a public collection made in England, but this was contradicted by the Governor, and the prisoners were made aware of the fact that this came at the Chaplain's discretion; Collins, *Account*, 1.98.
173 Collins, *Account*, 1.98–99. Robinson, 'Thomas Moore—Early Life', 174 (10); [Gov. P.G. King], Present State of His Majesty's Settlements, 12 Aug 1806 (*HRNSW* 6.150).
174 Chisholm, 'Editor's Introduction', 9, 11.
175 Chisholm, 'Editor's Introduction', 12.
176 Chisholm, 'Editor's Introduction', 11.
177 Chisholm, 'Editor's Introduction', 11; Rienits, 'Biographical Introduction', 16, 28.
178 Rienits, 'Biographical Introduction', 19.
179 Rienits, 'Biographical Introduction', 19–20.
180 Rienits, 'Biographical Introduction', 20; *Public Advertiser* 31/12/1790.
181 Rienits, 'Biographical Introduction', 20–21.
182 Collins, *Account*, 1.93.
183 Rienits, 'Biographical Introduction', 21.
184 Rienits, 'Biographical Introduction', 21.
185 Rienits, 'Biographical Introduction', 22.
186 Rienits, 'Biographical Introduction', 23.
187 Collins, *Account*, 1.132, 139. Rienits, 'Biographical Introduction', 24.
188 Rienits, 'Biographical Introduction', 24.
189 Collins, *Account*, 1.155. Rienits, 'Biographical Introduction', 24.
190 Gov. Phillip to H. Dundas, 19 Mar 1792 (*HRNSW* 1.2.596); Rienits, 'Biographical Introduction', 24.
191 Collins, *Account*, 1.170, 172, 175–177; Rienits, 'Biographical Introduction', 25.
192 *Lloyds List*, 24/1/1792; *Public Advertiser*, 25/1/1792, which on 30/1/1792 also adds 'wind WSW'.
193 Dunbabin, 'William Raven', 297.
194 Collins, *Account*, 1.187.
195 The following summary of the voyage refers to dates in Murray's *Journal*.
196 Dunbabin, 'William Raven', 297. Loane, 'Moore, Thomas (1762–1840)', gives the date of the arrival October, 1791—a confusion with Melville's *Britannia* which has often been made. See Collins, *Account* 1.567 n.10.
197 Collins, *Account*, 2.149.
198 Collins, *Account*, 1.190–191.
199 Lieut.-Gov. Grose to H. Dundas, 3 Sept 1793 (*HRA* 1.1.447).
200 Collins, *Account*, 1.188.
201 Murray, *Journal*, [033].
202 Loane, 'Moore, Thomas (1762–1840)', suggests Moore may have met Rachel on his first visit.

203 Rienits, 'Biographical Introduction', 25, that is, Thomas Arndell and John Irving, and John Harris and Edward Laing, the surgeon and surgeon's mate from the NSW Corps.
204 Frost, *Arthur Phillip*, 217–218.
205 J. White to Sir A.S. Hamond, 11 Dec 1792 (*HRNSW* 1.2.675); Rienits, 'Biographical Introduction', 25.

CHAPTER 2

1 Murray, *Journal*, [032]. Collins, *Account*, 1.190 gives the date of discharge as 17th.
2 Dunbabin, 'William Raven', 297.
3 Murray, *Journal*, [032]. Collins, *Account*, 1.198 has her quitting the cove on the last day of September, and returning on 3 October to refit for the Cape.
4 F. Grose to unknown correspondent, 2 April 1792 (Mitchell: MLMSS 6825).
5 Hainsworth, *Sydney Traders*, 21–22.
6 Hainsworth, *Sydney Traders*, 22 and 225.
7 Hainsworth, *Sydney Traders*, 16.
8 See Hainsworth, *Sydney Traders*, 22.
9 Hainsworth, *Sydney Traders*, 16.
10 Hainsworth, *Sydney Traders*, 26.
11 Hainsworth, *Sydney Traders*, 26–27.
12 Hainsworth, *Sydney Traders*, 25.
13 This cannot be proven since the Commissariat's records have not survived, but it can be safely assumed; see Hainsworth, *Sydney Traders*, 25, 27.
14 Collins, *Account*, 1.202.
15 Murray, *Journal*, [032].
16 Gov. Phillip to H. Dundas, 4 Oct 1792; Gov. Phillip to Maj. Grose, 4 Oct 1792 [encl.] (*HRNZ* 1.147–149).
17 Hainsworth, *Sydney Traders*, 23. For arrival and departure dates, Collins, *Account*, 1.145, 152.
18 Collins, *Account*, 1.198.
19 Hainsworth, *Sydney Traders*, 225.
20 F. Grose to Gov. Phillip, 4 Oct 1792 (*HRNZ* 1.148).
21 From Hainsworth, *Sydney Traders*, 27.
22 Hainsworth, *Sydney Traders*, 24.
23 Hainsworth, *Sydney Traders*, 24–25. Beyer sent the *Thynne* laden with goods for the officers—9,106 gallons of rum, with sugar, tea, coffee, pepper and textiles; Officers to Hunter, 13 Jan 1800 (*HRNSW* 4.19). Hainsworth (p.42): 'The *Thynne* was not the first of a series of vessels chartered by the officers: there is no evidence that they were ever to charter another'.
24 Collins, *Account*, 1.198–199.
25 Collins, *Account*, 1.201–202; Clark, *A History of Australia*, 1.136.
26 Murray, *Journal*, [032]. Cf. W. Raven to Lieut.-Gov. King, 2 Nov 1793 (*HRNSW* 2.94–96). For the despatches: Collins, *Account*, 1.202, who gives the date of sailing as the 24th.
27 This makes Raven's *Britannia* 'the first ship to take sperm whales on the Australian coast', not Melville's *Britannia*, which came out with the Third Fleet, as mistakenly claimed by Dallas, 'Enderby, Samuel (1756–1829)'. The mis-identification of these two vessels is frequently encountered in the literature.
28 Murray, *Journal*; cf. Dunbabin, 'William Raven', 297–298.

ENDNOTES 393

29 Murray, *Journal*, [036].
30 Murray, *Journal*, [036].
31 After he left the *Britannia* to join Bampton's *Endeavour*, Murray made comments on the New Zealand timbers, explicitly drawing upon Moore's expert opinion: 'The timber which grows here, would answer very well for plank, for the Ship Builder, Joiner, or Cabinet Maker. This is the opinion of our Carpenter in the *Britannia*, he being as well acquainted with its properties as any man of his profession; and the Joiner preferred it to the wood of Port Jackson or the Brazil Wood. But I think it would be a task of some trouble, to get a Cargo of spars, sufficiently long for the masts of ships'; Murray, *Journal*, [153].
32 Murray, *Journal*, [037].
33 J.M. Matra, 'Proposal for Establishing a Settlement', 23 Aug 1783 (*HRNZ* 1.38).
34 Lieut.-Gov. Grose to H. Dundas, 3 Sept 1793 (*HRA* 1.1.447): 'belonging to Mr Barbe'; F. Grose to Gov. Phillip, 4 Oct 1792 (*HRNZ* 1.148), notes that Raven 'is also an owner'.
35 Begg, *Dusky Bay*, 69.
36 Murray, *Journal*, [050].
37 Malaspina's Narrative, February 1793 (*HRNZ* 1.162–165).
38 Lieut.-Gov. Grose to H. Dundas, 19 April 1793 (*HRNZ* 1.161).
39 Collins, *Account*, 1.246–247.
40 Murray, *Journal*, [067].
41 Collins, *Account*, 1.246.
42 Murray, *Journal*, [069].
43 Murray, *Journal*, [070].
44 Murray, *Journal*, [070–071].
45 Murray, *Journal*, [071].
46 Hainsworth, *Sydney Traders*, 31. The picture painted by the pioneer historians was that of 'a long struggle fought between, on one side, devoted and public spirited Governors, bent on founding a stable colony of time-expired convicts and free settlers, and on the other, a clique of self-interested officer-official traders and pastoralists, bent only on satisfying their own avarice'. The writings of Brian Fitzpatrick, H.V. Evatt and A.O.G. Shann propagate this view, but, according to Hainsworth, 'their stance is too restricted. As a result their vision, though often compelling and always interesting, is distorted' (p.1).
47 Hainsworth, *Sydney Traders*, 31.
48 Gov. Hunter to Under-Secretary King, 14 Nov 1796 (*HRNSW* 3.178); Hunter to Portland, 12 Nov 1796 (*HRNSW* 3.169). Hainsworth, *Sydney Traders*, 31.
49 Collins, *Account*, 1.251.
50 Hainsworth, *Sydney Traders*, 32.
51 Fletcher, 'Development of Small Scale Farming'.
52 Collins, *Account*, 1.257.
53 Lieut.-Gov. Grose to H. Dundas, 3 Sept 1793 (*HRA* 1.1.447). Collins, *Account*, 1.252.
54 Murray, *Journal*, [068].
55 Lieut.-Gov. Grose to H. Dundas, 3 Sept 1793 (*HRA* 1.1.446–447).
56 Collins, *Account*, 1.257.
57 The request for stores and the Charter are found as enclosures to Lieut.-Gov. Grose to H. Dundas, 3 Sept 1793 (*HRA* 1.1.448–451). Collins, *Account*, 1.258.
58 Hainsworth, *Sydney Traders*, 28, 225.
59 Collins, *Account*, 1.258.
60 Rev. R. Johnson to H. Dundas, 3 Sept 1793 (*HRA* 1.1.451–452); Lieut.-Gov. Grose to H.

Dundas, 4 Sept 1793 (*HRA* 1.1.451). Collins, *Account*, 1.258–259, provides a more sympathetic version of Johnson's work and request.
61 Grose to Dundas, 30 May 1793. [Encl.] Return of Lands Granted 31/12/1792 to 1/4/1793. (*HRA* 1.1.438); Rienits, 'Biographical Introduction', 27.
62 Rienits, 'Biographical Introduction', 28, referring to LTO: Land Grants Register 1, vol. 1, f. 189. Ryan, *Land Grants*, 219 No 13. On 1 January 1806, White transferred this lease to his son Andrew; p.252.
63 J. White to Sir A.S. Hamond, 11 Dec 1792 (*HRNSW* 1.2.675); Rienits, 'Biographical Introduction', 25.
64 He was christened by Richard Johnson on 30th; St Philip's Register (SAG 90), 30 September 1793. The Register also records his birth date.
65 W. Raven to Lieut.-Gov. King, 2 Nov 1793 (*HRNSW* 2.94–96), says they left Port Jackson on the 8th.
66 Murray, *Journal*, [076].
67 Murray, *Journal*, [076].
68 Murray, *Journal*, [146, 152].
69 Murray, *Journal*, [076].
70 Murray, *Journal*, [076].
71 Murray, *Journal*, [078].
72 Collins, *Account*, 1.270.
73 Collins, *Account*, 1.270.
74 Collins, *Account*, 1.270–271.
75 Collins, *Account*, 1.271.
76 Lieut.-Gov. King to H. Dundas, 19 Nov 1793 (*HRNZ* 1.169 and note); Begg, *Dusky Bay*, 222.
77 For this paragraph, see Collins, *Account*, 1.290, 237, 426–429.
78 W. Raven to Lieut.-Gov. King, 2 Nov 1793 (*HRNSW* 2.94–96).
79 See Bolt, 'Thomas Moore: S/Purveyor of Timber' for a more concentrated look at the timber issue and Chapter 3 and 4 below.
80 Lieut.-Gov. King to H. Dundas, 19 Nov 1793 (*HRNZ* 1.170).
81 Parsons, 'Jamison, Thomas (1753?–1811)'. In October 1799 he returned to Port Jackson until September 1800, and then after a period of leave he arrived back in Sydney in June 1802 to replace William Balmain as Surgeon-General, leaving the colony in June 1809 to act as a witness for George Johnston at his court-martial, subsequently signing over his land holdings in NSW to his son Sir John Jamison, who arrived in 1814 to take them up. Like Moore, Jamison was granted land at the Georges River (in 1807), and he also found himself on Governor Bligh's list of persons prohibited to leave the colony after the January 26, 1808 rebellion.
82 T. Jamison to a friend at Lincoln, *Saunder's News-Letter* 15 July 1794 (*HRNZ* 1.182–185).
83 Lieut.-Gov. King to H. Dundas, 19 Nov 1793 (*HRNZ* 1.170–173).
84 See Lieut.-Gov. Grose to Lieut.-Gov. King, 25 Feb 1794 (*HRNZ* 1.187–189); Lieut.-Gov. King to H. Dundas, 10 Mar 1794 (*HRNZ* 1.189–192); Lieut.-Gov. King to Lieut.-Gov. Grose, 19 Mar 1794 (*HRNZ* 1.193–194); Duke of Portland to Gov. Hunter, 10 June 1795 (*HRA* 1.1.496; *HRNZ* 1.199–202).
85 Collins, *Account*, 1.290. Cf. Lieut.-Gov. King to H. Dundas, 19 Nov 1793 (*HRNZ* 1.169).
86 Murray, *Journal*, [080–082].
87 Murray, *Journal*, [083, 086].
88 Murray, *Journal*, [097].

89	Ke, 'Piracy, Seaborne Trade, and Rivalries', 221, 224.
90	Ke, 'Piracy, Seaborne Trade, and Rivalries', 221–222.
91	Ke, 'Piracy, Seaborne Trade, and Rivalries', 222–223.
92	Ke, 'Piracy, Seaborne Trade, and Rivalries', 223–224.
93	Ke, 'Piracy, Seaborne Trade, and Rivalries', 224–225.
94	Ke, 'Piracy, Seaborne Trade, and Rivalries', 225–228.
95	Ke, 'Piracy, Seaborne Trade, and Rivalries', 228–229.
96	Ke, 'Piracy, Seaborne Trade, and Rivalries', 230. In 1819 Raffles set up Singapore; and in 1839 'White Rajah' James Brooke gained Sarawak, increasing the British presence.
97	Hanes & Sanello, *Opium Wars*, 20. A century later England's consumption of tea amounted to twelve million pounds per year imported from China.
98	Hanes & Sanello, *Opium Wars*, 20. During this period Britain paid £26 million in silver, and sold only £9 million in goods to China.
99	Hanes & Sanello, *Opium Wars*, 20–21.
100	Hanes & Sanello, *Opium Wars*, 14–19.
101	Hanes & Sanello, *Opium Wars*, 21–22.
102	Murray, *Journal*, [099]. For the location of St John's Island and Point Romania, see Newbold, *Political and Statistical Account*, 1.266, 287. (Figure 21; Plate 19)
103	Ke, 'Piracy, Seaborne Trade, and Rivalries', 225.
104	Ke, 'Piracy, Seaborne Trade, and Rivalries', 230.
105	Ke, 'Piracy, Seaborne Trade, and Rivalries', 230. At the beginning of the nineteenth century the British East India Company also supported them as privateers against its Dutch counterpart, the VOC, but they were too powerful to be controlled, and in 1824 the Europeans by treaty joined forces against the common threat of local piracy.
106	Warren, *Iranun and Balangingi*, 186.
107	Ke, 'Piracy, Seaborne Trade, and Rivalries', 230.
108	Warren, *Iranun and Balangingi*, 102–104, 5. Some of the worst crises for the villages of the Philippines occurred in the 1780s and 1790s, but the Iranun suffered a series of defeats between 1796 and 1818 (pp.113–114).
109	Warren, *Iranun and Balangingi*, 2; for explanation of term, see 168, 261, 521.
110	Warren, *Iranun and Balangingi*, 3–5.
111	Warren, *Iranun and Balangingi*, 3.
112	Warren, *Iranun and Balangingi*, 18.
113	Murray, *Journal*, [099].
114	Murray, *Journal*, [102].
115	Mignet, *History of the French Revolution*, 233.
116	Murray, *Journal*, [102].
117	Dundas to F. Grose, 15 Feb 1794 (*HRA* 1.1.465, cf. p. 476).
118	Ke, 'Piracy, Seaborne Trade, and Rivalries', 228.
119	Murray, *Journal*, [102].
120	*Lloyds List*, 27/6/1794: 'The *Britannia*, Raven, of London, was well off Batavia on the 16th February last'.
121	W. Raven to Lieut.-Gov. Grose, 1 June 1794 (*HRA* 1.1.480).
122	Captain Bampton to Lieut.-Gov. Paterson, 1 June 1795 (*HRNZ* 1.198–199).
123	Cook arrived in Batavia on 10 October 1770, malaria and dysentery destroyed the good health record of the ship thus far. Several of the crew died before they left; several more on the way to the Cape. The dead included Lieutenant Hicks, the *Endeavour*'s astronomer (Green), master (Molyneux), and surgeon (Monkhouse); see Kemp, 'Cook,

James (1728–79)', 199.
124 Collins, *Account*, 1.312.
125 Collins, *Account*, 1.312. Parsons, 'Nepean, Evan (1752–1822)', 281.
126 Murray, *Journal*, [103]. I have punctuated the sentence to make better sense. Murray has already mentioned there were 30 hands [099], so here it seems he is saying that 11 were sick, leaving only 19 to make up the duty watches.
127 'The *Britannia*, Raven, from Batavia, and the *Speedy*, Melville, arrived early in June, All Well'; *Lloyds Evening Post*, 25/2/1795; *London Packet or New Lloyds Evening Post*, 25/2/1792; *St James's Chronicle or the British Evening Post*, 26/2/1795; *Star* 28/2/1795.
128 Collins, *Account*, 1.311, who provides a list of the supplies (beef, pork, sugar, rice) and prices, and notes the total expense was £9,759 11s 10d (pp. 311–312).
129 The officers had a stake in Bampton's voyage, giving him £490 in Paymaster's bills from April 6–13, 1793. Hainsworth, *Sydney Traders*, 225.
130 Collins, *Account*, 1.312.
131 Murray, *Journal*, [111].
132 Murray, *Journal*, [111].
133 Hainsworth, *Sydney Traders*, 28–29.
134 Hainsworth, *Sydney Traders*, 28–29. He notes that Palmer's Account is an oddity on the list, but suggestive of him also being involved in the trading. It included moneys due to Paterson, Johnston, Foveaux, Rowley, Bain, Lucas, Laycock and Harris.
135 Hainsworth, *Sydney Traders*, 30.
136 Collins, *Account*, 1.312.
137 For what follows, see Fletcher, 'Grose, Francis (1758?–1814)'; and Fletcher, 'Development of Small Scale Farming', 1–4.
138 Fletcher, 'Grose, Francis (1758?–1814)'.
139 Although none of the Scottish Martyrs had heard Johnson before, T.F. Palmer said that they would have liked to have heard his sermon the first Sunday after Hunter arrived: 'He exposed the last Government, their extortion, their despotism, their debauchery and ruin of the colony, driving it almost to famine by the sale of liquors at 1,200 per cent profit. He congratulated the colony at the abolition of a military government, and the restoration of a civil one, and of the laws'; T.F. Palmer to Rev. T. Lindsey, 15 Sept 1795 (*HRNSW* 2.881). Rev. R. Johnson to Gov. Hunter, 5 July 1798; Surgeon Arndell to Gov. Hunter, 25 July 1798; Rev. S. Marsden to Gov. Hunter, 11 Aug 1798 (*HRNSW* 3.432–437; 437–439; 439–442).
140 Fletcher, 'Grose, Francis (1758?–1814)'.
141 Return of Lands Granted (*HRA* 1.1.472–473). The land was granted 8 January 1794 for King; 20 February 1794 for Abell, Jeffries and Hughes; 1 April 1794 for Alford and Young; 3 October 1794 for Laing; and 11 November for Wood. See also Return of Land Grants since Last Return by Kitty (*HRNSW* 3.212) and Ryan, *Land Grants*, 18 (No 137, King), 26 (No 194, Laing), 29 (No 226, Wood). I have not been able to further identify Thomas Wood. Another Grant is listed for Robert King, 25 acres in Bulanaming, and another 20 for his wife Catherine, 14 Mar 1795; Ryan, *Land Grants*, 48 (No 405, and 406). What is the relationship between John and Robert? On Hunter's 1796 map the only King listed with land in Bulanaming is Robert (*HRNSW* 3, after title pages).
142 St Philip's Sydney, Register: 'Novr 30th Andrew Douglass White, son of John White & Rachel Turner, born Sepr 23d 1793', St Philip's Sydney, Register (SAG 90).
143 Dundas to F. Grose, 15 Feb 1794 (*HRA* 1.1.465 cf. 476), received 10 Dec 1794 saying there is now no reason why White 'may not have leave of absence by the first convenient

ENDNOTES 397

opportunity'; Rienits, 'Biographical Introduction', 27–28.
144 Rienits, 'Biographical Introduction', 27. St Philip's Sydney, Register: 'Novr 30th Andrew Douglass White, son of John White & Rachel Turner, born Sepr 23d 1793'.
145 *Lloyds List*, 3/3/1795: 'The *Britannia*, Raven, arrived at the Cape of Good Hope from Port Jackson'. Robinson was tentative in assuming Moore's presence on the various voyages of the *Britannia* after the one which picked him up from Dusky Bay; Robinson 'Thomas Moore—Early Life', 172 (8) n.29. However, since (as we will see below nn 198, 221) he was granted an EIC commission as a privateer in 1795; and since Daniel Paine speaks of him still in connection with the ship in 1796; there is no reason to think he had left the ship prior to his appointment to the dockyard in September 1796.
146 Murray, *Journal*, [127].
147 Murray, *Journal*, [128].
148 Murray, *Journal*, [128, 136].
149 Murray, *Journal*, [136].
150 Murray, *Journal*, [139]. Collins, *Account*, 1.343. Paterson to Dundas, 21 Mar 1795 (*HRA* 1.1.490).
151 W. Paterson to H. Dundas, 15 June 1795, Encl. No 7 (*HRA* 1.1.508). Government: 4 stallions and 8 mares; Private: 4 stallions, 33 mares.
152 Richard Johnson to Jonathan Stonard, 27 Nov 1795 (Mackaness, No 23, II.12. See also No 25, II.16).
153 Lieut.-Gov. Paterson to H. Dundas, 21 Mar 1795 (*HRA* 1.1.490; *HRNZ* 1.195–198). Collins, *Account*, 1.335.
154 Lieut.-Gov. Paterson to H. Dundas, 21 Mar 1795 (*HRA* 1.1.491; *HRNZ* 1.195–198). The editor of *HRNZ* identifies the mahogany with *Eucalyptus resinifera* and the cedar with *Cedrela Australia*, which he adds is 'pretty well exterminated' now along the Hawkesbury.
155 Collins, *Account*, 1.344–345.
156 Collins, *Account*, 1.349. W. Paterson to H. Dundas, 15 June 1795 (*HRA* 1.1.498), plus enclosures No 2: Charter of the *Britannia* (pp.503–505), and No 3: Paterson's Orders to W. Raven.
157 Collins, *Account*, 1.384. The mistake probably arises because there was also a John Leith in the colony. His name appears in Thomas Moore's account books.
158 Begg, *Dusky Bay*, 80.
159 Murray, *Journal*, [146].
160 Murray, *Journal*, [153].
161 Collins, *Account*, 1.384: 'The *Fancy* and *Providence* arrived safe at Norfolk Island, whence they sailed for China on the 31st day of January last [1796]'. For the *Endeavour* story, see also: Lieut.-Gov. King to Duke of Portland, 19 Jan 1796; Captain Bampton to Lieut.-Gov. King, 19 Jan 1796 (*HRNZ* 1.203–204, 204–205).
162 Murray, *Journal*, [158].
163 Collins, *Account*, 1.350.
164 Lieut.-Gov. Paterson to H. Dundas, 21 Mar 1795 (*HRNZ* 1.195–198); Collins, *Account*, 1.334.
165 See Turner, *The Lives Of Eminent Unitarians*, 2.214–238.
166 Chisholm, 'Editor's Introduction', 14.
167 Chisholm, 'Editor's Introduction', 15–16.
168 Rienits, 'Biographical Introduction', 28.
169 Rienits, 'Biographical Introduction', 28–29, referring to Andrew's Will. Probate Office: Will 1571 (1).

170 Robinson, 'Thomas Moore & Early Life', 174 (10).
171 See Henry Waterhouse to Thomas Moore, 20 Oct 1804 (Moore: Waterhouse Papers): 'Andrew has been constantly well, ... he has been several times down with Mr White during the hollidays [sic]'; and especially: 'be assur'd I shall not forget the promise I made you when I receiv'd him from you nor will my family should I be absent—in attending to the welfare of Andrew'. cf. Nelson, 'John White', 167–168.
172 Watling, Letters, 20, 18; Rienits, 'Biographical Introduction', 26–27.
173 Nelson, 'John White', 160 and n.34.
174 Under-Sec. King to Gov. Hunter, 30 Oct 1795 (HRA 1.1.548)
175 Robinson, 'Thomas Moore & Early Life', 175 (11).
176 D. Byrne, 'The Blackheath Connection', http://www.danbyrnes.com.au/blackheath/thebc41.htm. Byrne has no idea who these two women are, commenting in n.165: 'I have not followed up these convicts'. Guessing that she was owned by Bennett, Byrne notes that the Indispensable did not go whaling, but continued to Canton to fulfil a charter for the East India Co.
177 Robinson, 'Thomas Moore & Early Life', 175 (11).
178 The Britannia was in Sydney five times: between 26 July and 22nd October, 1792; 26 June and 6 September, 1793 (although Moore was not with her); 1 June and 31 August, 1794; 3 March and 17 June, 1795; and 11 May to 29 September, 1796.
179 Cobley, Sydney Cove 1791–1792, 288. Richard Bowen, John White, and Thomas Laycock conducted the survey of the Britannia on 2 August 1792. They were ordered by Arthur Phillip to take 'a Strict and Careful Survey on the Cases and Bales complained of which were Landed from the Britannia Store Ship'. They found the 385 yards of cloth, 'wet rotten and totally decayed'; 132 hats 'wet mildewed and eat by Rats'; 3,720 yards of Oznaburghs, 'wet rotten and totally decayed'; 19 rugs, 'damaged by wet and partly rotten'. They concluded 'all which appears to us to have been Occasioned by wet Received on Board the Ship on her passage out'.
180 This lease was confirmed by Hunter in 1799. Lands Granted since 1 Aug 1796 [Encl.], Gov. Hunter to Portland, 6 February 1800 (HNRSW 4.47). The 1800 Grimes' (HRNSW 5, prior to index) and 1807 Meehan's map (Plates 34 and 35) show the two properties next to each other at the top of the Market Square. Ryan, Land Grants, 222 No 28. This lease was put up for auction in August 1807 (SG 23 & 30/8/1807), and was presumably bought by Thomas Moore. Robinson, 'Thomas Moore—Early Life', 177 (13).
181 Robinson, 'Thomas Moore & Early Life', 175 (11).
182 So Boyce, Thomas Moore, 3; cf. Loane, 'Moore, Thomas (1762–1840)', 254.
183 Government and General Order, 17 May 1797 (HRNSW 3.208): 'His Majesty has been pleased to appoint by Commission, Wm. Balmain, Esq., to be the principal surgeon to this colony and its dependencies, in the room of John White, Esq., who has Resigned. Jno. Hunter.'
184 Robinson, 'Thomas Moore & Early Life', 175 (11).
185 Collins, Account, 1.350–351.
186 Here Collins adds a note (p.397*): 'The Loyalty Islands are situated between New Caledonia and the New Hebrides, and extend from about 21 degrees 30 minutes to 20 degrees 50 minutes S and from the longitude of 168 degrees to 167 degrees E. Mr. Raven supposed them to be a large group of islands, which, being pressed for time, he could not stop to survey. All that he had opportunity to determine was, the longitude and latitude of some of the head-lands. Many fires were seen on them in the night; the whole appeared to be full of wood, and in some places in high cultivation. These islands,

ENDNOTES 399

certainly a discovery belonging to Mr. Raven, may be thought worthy of being explored at some future day, and become an object of consequence to the settlement in New South Wales'.
187 Collins, *Account*, 1.396–397.
188 Collins, *Account*, 1.397.
189 Collins, *Account*, 1.396.
190 At the trial, the date of sailing was given as the 9 May [1795], but this must be from faulty memory. Note also that Chilton was supposed to have escaped after five years in the colony, but this probably means something like, 'in the fifth year after his October 1791 conviction'.
191 Old Bailey, 'Trial of John Chilton (30/10/1805)' (T18051030–46).
192 Collins, *Account*, 2.39.
193 Collins, *Account*, 1.396.
194 For this paragraph, see Bassett, 'The Surrender of Dutch Malacca, 1795'; quotation, p.358.
195 The British gained a firmer foothold in South East Asia in the nineteenth century. In 1819 Raffles set up Singapore; and in 1839 'White Rajah' James Brooke gained Sarawak; Ke, 'Piracy, Seaborne Trade, and Rivalries', 230.
196 'The *Britannia*, Raven, from Botany Bay, is arrived at Calcutta', *Daily Advertiser* 15/4/1796 (from an extract from a letter of 20th February); *Oracle and Public Advertiser*, 15/4/1796; 'Arrival, *Britannia*, Raven, from Botany Bay', *Evening Mail*, 13/4/1796; *Lloyds Evening Post*, 13/4/1796.
197 Collins, *Account*, 1.378.
198 Thomas Moore, 2nd Lieutenant Commission for East India Company, 18 Dec 1795. A copy of this Commission came into my possession through Donald Robinson, but I have been unable to ascertain the Archive from whence it originated. Against Robinson's query (see n. 145), this commission provides evidence that Moore was on the *Britannia* at this time.
199 Collins, *Account*, 1.395.
200 See Bengal Military Department to Gov. Hunter, 11 Jan 1796 (*HRA* 1.1.584–585).
201 Collins, *Account*, 1.396.
202 Collins, *Account*, 1.395.
203 Collins, *Account*, 1.396.
204 Collins, *Account*, 1.395.
205 Collins, *Account*, 1.359; for George Bass, p.365.
206 Collins, *Account*, 1.396. Gov. Hunter to Portland, 15 Aug 1796 (*HRA* 1.1.583).
207 M. Johnson to H. Fricker, 21 Dec 1795 (ML: MLMSS 6722).
208 Collins, *Account*, 1.405–406. Cf. W. Paterson to H. Dundas, 15 June 1795 (*HRA* 1.1.498).
209 Gov. Hunter to Portland, 20 Aug 1796 (*HRA* 1.1.590).
210 Gov. Hunter to Portland, 27 Aug 1796 (*HRA* 1.1.643).
211 Collins, *Account*, 1.410–411.
212 Collins, *Account*, 1.412–413.
213 Collins, *Account*, 1.413–414.
214 Collins, *Account*, 1.417, 445–448. *Lloyds List*, 30/6/1797: 'Liverpool, arrived from Botany Bay, *Britannia*, Raven'.
215 *Lloyds Evening Post* 21/7/1797 (from a letter from Gravesend, July 23: 'passed by [Gravesend] … the *Britannia*, Raven, from Botany Bay'; *Lloyds List*, 25/7/1797: 'Gravesend, arrived *Britannia*, Raven, Botany Bay'.

216 The accounts referred to in what follows can be found in Thomas Moore's Business Notebook (rear) (SDA: 0884 CH, Item 1), 3 (Stogdell 1796, & Leith), 4 (Raven), 6 (Stogdell 1798, & Hanks). Hanks' account is not dated but on the same page as Stogdele's 1798 account.
217 Hainsworth, *Sydney Traders,* 177.
218 Collins, *Account* 1.246.
219 Rienits, 'Biographical Introduction', 29. See above n.176 for Shelton's account dated 17 October 1795, the copy already complete by that date.
220 Under-Sec. King to Surg. White 10 Aug 1796 (*HRNSW* 3.63); Balmain's Commission was issued on 16 August 1796 (*HRNSW* 3.70); Rienits, 'Biographical Introduction', 29. Portland to J. Hunter, 11 Aug 1796 (*HRA* 1.1.582).
221 Government and General Order, 13 September 1796 (ML Col.Sec. 6037, ML Safe 1/18b; *HRA* 1.1.698; *HRNSW* 3.115); Collins, *Account*, 1.410. His predecessor at the Dockyard, Daniel Paine, provides the information that Moore was the second mate at the time of the appointment to the dockyard, the position originally held by William Leith; *Journal of Daniel Paine 1794–1796*, 22nd August 1796, p.31. This is further evidence he was on board (see nn 145, 198).
222 Collins, *Account*, 1.412–413.

CHAPTER 3

1 Geo III to Phillip 25/4/1787, PRO CO 201/1: f.40. See Paine, *Journal*, 67, App.1. Cf. Russell, *Thomas Moore*, 3.
2 Phillip to Dundas, 19 Mar 1792 (*HRA* 1.1.337).
3 Knight & Frost, 'Introduction', xviii.
4 Hunter to Under-Secretary King, 1 May 1794 (*HRNSW* 2.214).
5 Estensen, *George Bass*, 36–37; *Matthew Flinders*, 44–45; Dark, 'Bennelong (1764?–1813)'.
6 Knight & Frost, 'Introduction', xix.
7 Knight & Frost, 'Introduction', xvii.
8 Instead, it was almost certainly Thomas Moore who properly deserves the honour of being 'the pioneer of shipbuilding in Australia'; so Russell, *Thomas Moore*, 3.
9 Russell, *Thomas Moore*, 7.
10 Knight & Frost, 'Introduction', xxi.
11 Hunter to Portland, 25 Oct 1795, Encl.: Return of Civil Establishment (*HRA* 1.1.537–538). Hunter to Portland, Despatch 20, per *Britannia*, Encl.: Return of the Civil Establishment, 20th Sept 1796 (*HRA* 1.1.665). Hunter to Portland, 12 Nov 1796, Order dated 13 Sept 1796 (*HRA* 1.1.698).
12 Hunter to Portland, 12 Nov 1796, Order dated 18 July 1796 (*HRA* 1.1.696).
13 Hunter to Portland, 21 Dec 1795 (*HRA* 1.1.549).
14 Paine, *Journal*, 22.
15 Collins, *Account*, 1.381.
16 Hunter to Portland, 30/4/1796 (*HRA* 1.1.568). Knight & Frost, 'Introduction', xx–xxi nn. 32, 33.
17 Paine, *Journal*, 22, entry for 18 February 1796. For the Scottish Martyrs, see the articles by Earnshaw, 'Gerrald, Joseph (1760–1796)'; 'Muir, Thomas (1765–1799)'; 'Palmer, Thomas Fyshe (1747–1802)'; 'Skirving, William (—1796)'; and Roe, 'Margarot, Maurice (1745–1815)'. Bladen collects documents relating to these men in *HRNSW* 2, Appendix F.

ENDNOTES 401

18 Collins, *Account*, 1.390, gives his date of death as 16 March, but Daniel Paine's *Journal*, 22, has the 14th. Paine notes that Gerrald's 'Days appeared to have been shortened by his strong propensity to Drinking and which the general manners in the Colony too much favoured'. Although both Paine and Collins (p.363) acknowledge that his health was not good when he arrived. Collins ascribes his death to 'a consumption which accompanied him from England', and Skirving's to dysentery (p.390). According to Paine, Skirving had spent much time on his farm and was 'much respected'.
19 W. Skirving to Rev. J. Joyce, December 1794 (*HRNSW* 2.872).
20 T.F. Palmer to Rev. T. Lindsey, 15 Sept 1795 (*HRNSW* 2.881).
21 T. Muir to a friend in London, 13 Dec 1794 (*HRNSW* 2.869), reprinted from the *Morning Chronicle* 29/7/1795.
22 Collins, *Account*, 1.382.
23 This is the translation given by Scott, 'Scottish Martyr's Farms', 163, from *Histoire de la Tyrannie du Gouvernement Anglais exercée envers le célèbre Thomas Muir, Ecossais*.
24 Watson, 'Some Notes'.
25 Scott, 'Scottish Martyrs' Farms', 164, 166: Lightfoot's farm was not two miles away and, since it was visible from Sydney Cove, there would be no reason for Muir to give the mileage; neither was it suitable for seclusion or cultivation; records show that it was cancelled and given to Robert Ryan by Hunter, who had purchased it from Lightfoot; and there were no farms contiguous to Lightfoot's farm. For the dismissal of Muir's association with Hunter's Hill, see also Sherry, 'Thomas Muir and the Naming of Hunter's Hill'.
26 Scott, 'Scottish Martyrs' Farms', 166, refers to Old Register No 4 (Registrar–General's Department, Deeds Branch). Ryan, *Land Grants*, has no record of this transaction, although listing Laing's grant as 100 acres in Bulanaming, granted 3 Oct 1794 (p.25, No 194). The letter is T.F. Palmer to Rev. T. Lindsey, 15 Sept 1795 (*HRNSW* 2.881).
27 Scott, 'Scottish Martyrs' Farms', 166.
28 Scott, 'Scottish Martyrs' Farms', 167. Note he lists Thomas Wood as an ex–convict.
29 Scott, 'Scottish Martyrs' Farms', 167. As his sentence was nearly completed, Palmer sold his own farm to Eber Bunker on 17 March 1800 for £90.
30 Estensen, *George Bass*, 36–37.
31 Estensen, *George Bass*, 64. Surgeon John White and George Bass also associated with the Scottish Martyrs, bringing Thomas Moore's family into these circles.
32 Estensen, *George Bass*, 64. Palmer left the colony in January 1801. In July 1805, Margarot was sent to Norfolk Island, Van Diemen's Land, and then Newcastle.
33 Estensen, *Matthew Flinders*, 53, 55, drawing upon Flinders, *Narrative*, 1, and Paine, *Journal*, 1. In time, Thomas Moore also built a boat for Flinders (p.212)—or two, if we count the *Cumberland*.
34 Paine, *Journal*, 38–39.
35 His interest in a sawmill may place him at the leading edge of technology, certainly for someone trained in a conservative British Naval yard. Although they had been operating in Europe before the 17th century, and America since 1623, Britain was extremely conservative, introducing sawmills only in the late 18th century. Even by 1860, half the timber in the dockyards was still converted by hand. Albion, *Forests*, 70, 102, 103, 147, 233, 269.
36 Paine, *Journal*, 23.
37 Paine, *Journal*, 23.
38 See Paine, *Journal*, 22ff. This explanation is overlooked by Robinson, 'Thomas Moore —Early Life', 172 (8), in his remark that 'no reason for Paine's supersession is given in

the records'. As I have also done, Robinson nevertheless implies that Paine was part of that group of persons with which Hunter was disaffected (pp. 172–3).
39 NSW Archives, 2/8286, pp. 7–8; Paine, *Journal*, 24.
40 Knight & Frost, 'Introduction', xx.
41 Hunter to Portland, 12 Nov 1796, Order dated 8 Dec 1795 (*HRA* 1.1.683 = Paine, *Journal*, 68, App. 1, doc. 1).
42 E.g. Albion, *Forests*, 111, and see index. Stamping a serial number was part of the English contract checking system, and so presumably would be unnecessary in Australia; see p. 72.
43 Hunter to Under Secretary King, 20 Aug 1796 (*HRA* 1.1.587–88). For the suggestion that the building of the ship in Dusky Bay was good for Moore's career, see Robinson, 'Thomas Moore—Early Life', 169 (5): 'The Dusky Bay episode was more than a passing adventure for Moore. It may well have had a decisive effect on his future in connection with his becoming a member of the civil establishment of New South Wales'; p. 170 (6): 'It can hardly be a coincidence that within three years of the Dusky Bay enterprise, Moore had been appointed Master Boat Builder to the colony of New South Wales'; see also p.173 (9).
44 For this paragraph, Knight, '"Carpenter" Master Shipwrights', 411.
45 Knight, '"Carpenter" Master Shipwrights', 422.
46 See Knight, 'Sandwich, Middleton & Dockyard Appointments'; and Knight, ' "Carpenter" Master Shipwrights'.
47 Knight, 'Sandwich, Middleton & Dockyard Appointments', 179.
48 Knight, 'Sandwich, Middleton & Dockyard Appointments', 183.
49 When the *Sirius* was wrecked on Norfolk Island, Hunter returned to England in the Dutch snow *Waaksamheyd*, reaching Portsmouth in April 1792, after a voyage of thirteen months; Auchmuty, 'Hunter, John (1737–1821)'.
50 Earnshaw, 'Palmer, Thomas Fyshe (1747–1802)'. George Bass also had an Encyclopaedia amongst his books in 1799. The *Encyclopaedia Britannica* was first published in 1768–1771, but there were others; Roe, 'New Light on George Bass', 267. Palmer provides an example of how convicts could prosper in the colony. Presumably from trading, he acquired enough capital to purchase two vessels which were both wrecked. He then joined a syndicate of ex-convicts, who bought the former Spanish prize *El Plumier*, by which Palmer left the colony in January 1801 on 'a disastrous voyage which ended at Guam two years later'; Hainsworth, *Sydney Traders*, 41, 164–165.
51 Ozanam also published *Dictionnaire Mathématique* (1691), which devoted some space to sea terms; Anderson, 'Early Books', 61.
52 See Bolt, 'Thomas Moore's Bookshelf'. Numbers in brackets on the table refer to the listing of the book in Moore's catalogue. My essay follows the same classification, providing a little information about each of the books.
53 In 1635 a Newcastle bookseller, William London, published 'a Catalogue of the most Vendible Books in England', in which Divinity was the largest category, but it also contained thirteen works on Nautical science. These books are listed and discussed by Taylor, 'The Seaman's Bookshelf'. Moore has none on his bookshelf.
54 See Anderson, 'Eighteenth–century Books'.
55 George Bass had at least eleven volumes of voyages on his two lists of books; see Roe, 'New Light on George Bass', 267–272.
56 Anderson, 'Early Books', 56.
57 Anderson, 'Eighteenth–Century Books', 221–222. The other classic was Chapman, *Architectura Navalis Mercatoria* (1768).
58 Anderson, 'Eighteenth–Century Books', 220.

59 Anderson, 'Eighteenth–Century Books', 224.
60 Anderson, 'Eighteenth–Century Books', 224. George Bass also had a copy of this volume on his second booklist (Cash–book of *Venus*); Roe, 'New Light on George Bass', 271.
61 See Knight, 'Sandwich, Middleton & Dockyard Appointments'.
62 Bass, on the other hand, had 2 volumes of 'Papers on Naval Architecture' on his second booklist (Cash–book of *Venus*); Roe, 'New Light on George Bass', 271.
63 See above, p. 109.
64 Nelson, 'John White', 164–165.
65 Nelson, 'John White', 166.
66 Nelson, 'John White', 166. When Rienits wrote his 'Biographical Introduction', 30, he did not know Elizabeth's surname. Andrew Douglas White's will, as well as some letters amongst Moore's personal papers from White's family after Andrew died allow a fuller picture to emerge. Clara Bernal to T. Moore, [undated, 1838] (SDA: 0851 CH, Item 6, doc 24); Anne Losack to Thomas & Rachel Moore, 11 Aug 1838 (SDA: 0853 CH, Item 11, doc 10). Not knowing of White's second marriage, Rienits confused Elizabeth Losack with White's second wife, Elizabeth Hope (married 22/4/1829), when he stated: 'She had a fortune of £7000, owned a house in Seymour Place, London, and held on lease No. 13 Bedford Square, Brighton'. Nelson has now shown that Elizabeth (Losack) died in 1825, and White married Elizabeth Hope in 1829.
67 After testimonials from W. Buchan and S. de Leon, the University of St Andrews conferred upon him the degree of Doctor of Medicine on 10 March 1797; Nelson, 'John White', 166.
68 Rienits, 'Biographical Introduction', 30–31: 'Richard entered the Navy in 1813, obtained his lieutenancy in 1825, and died, probably unmarried, in 1859. Clara became the second wife of Ralph Bernal, M.P., a man of considerable wealth with large properties in the West Indies, and by him had five sons, of whom two died in infancy, and a daughter. Augusta married Lieutenant (later Lieutenant–General) Henry Sandham, of the Royal Engineers, by whom she had five sons and two daughters'.
69 See St Philip's Register, p.52, No 250, 11 January 1797 (SAG 90). NSW Registry of BDM: 380 Vol. 3A and 240 Vol. 4). [Aust. Enc^2], 'Moore, Thomas', 145, mistakenly gives the year as 1796.
70 Robinson, 'Thomas Moore—Early Life', 176 (12).
71 Murray, *Journal*, [141].
72 Ryan, *Land Grants*, 220 (No 18).
73 Ryan, *Land Grants*, 119 (No 839).
74 As some of the evidence for this affection, we could list the following: Moore named his Bulanaming farm, Douglas's Farm, in honour of his step son; he paid for his schooling, and possibly his military commissioning (see Robinson, 'Postscript'); he speaks fondly of Andrew when he visits Sydney for six months in 1823; some of Andrew's early handwriting books are still amongst Thomas's papers in the Sydney Diocesan Archives (SDA 0884CH, Items 2 and 3 [1805])—kept by an affectionate step–father.
75 Collins, *Account*, 1.410–411.
76 See further Bolt, 'Moore and the Merino'.
77 Hainsworth, *Sydney Traders*, 1–17.
78 When Governor Phillip reported home in July, there were 26 sheep still alive. Phillip to Sydney, 9 July 1788, Encl. 1: An Account of Livestock, 1 May 1788 (*HRA* 1.1.52) shows: 1 stallion, 3 mares, 3 colts, 2 bulls, 5 cows, 29 sheep, 19 goats, 49 hogs, 25 pigs, 5 rabbits, 18 turkeys, 29 geese, 35 ducks, 122 fowls, 87 chickens. A note is appended saying that

since that Return 3 of the sheep have died, and the cows and bulls lost. To put this in proportion, 1030 people were landed and Phillip reports that 966 of these were victualled (HRA 1.1.51 and 727).

79 Morrison, *Aldine Centennial History*, 1.268: 'Australia attaches more importance to her pastoral, agricultural, mineral, and commercial interests than to any other. She is one of the leading pastoral countries of the world. [...] She is the first among the nations in the production of wool, and America comes second'. At the time this was written, the comparative value of wool per annum was: Aust: £20,000,000; USA: £14,500,000.

80 The debate runs from the nineteenth century through to the 1960s. Ker, 'Wool Industry', Part 1, 29: 'The fact that these sheep arrived is of great importance, it is relatively valueless to quibble over who was responsible for bringing them'. Cf. Part 2, 50–51, where she speaks of 'the much–debated first imports' and cites the *Sydney Gazette* of 26 August 1826 saying the issue is 'a matter of little moment', and 'to cavil on that point is [...] absurd'—a view similar to her own. Others thought the dispute over historical facts far from insignificant. The *Sydney Gazette* of 25 July 1828 published a letter from 'A Constant Reader' addressed to the editor of London's *Morning Herald*, which attempted to set the record straight by a brief exchange of letters between Sir Joseph Banks and Henry Waterhouse dating to 1806.

81 It seems reasonably clear that the person behind the claim that John Macarthur was responsible for introducing the merino was John Macarthur himself. Evidence of John Macarthur to J.T. Bigge, cited from Clark, *Select Documents*, 1.267: 'In the year 1796 (I believe) the two sloops of war on this station were sent to the Cape of Good Hope, and as their Commanders were friends of mine, I requested them to enquire if there were any wool–bearing sheep at the Cape. At the period of their arrival at the Settlement there was a flock of Merino sheep for sale, from which about twenty were purchased'. Enclosure in letter addressed to Elizabeth 19/8/1816: Copy of letter to Lord Bathurst (undated), 'Your Lordship is without doubt informed of the extent and nature of my establishment in N.S. Wales: [...] I allude, My Lord to the introduction into that distant Colony of a breed of Merino Sheep, specimens of the Wool of which I once had the honour to submit to your Lordship's notice. The approbation your Lordship was pleased to express upon that occasion excite hopes that any additional evidence may not be unacceptable of the progressive advancement ...'; Onslow, *The Macarthurs of Camden*, 268–269.

It is clear, however, that Macarthur knew who was really responsible, for he wrote to Henry Waterhouse on 4 March 1804, of 'the improvement of the Wool, produced by the Spanish Breed of Sheep that you introduced into that Colony, [...]'. Onslow, *The Macarthurs of Camden*, 83–84.

Once the rumour got started, however, it seemed to stick, probably because of Macarthur's subsequent importance for the wool industry. So, for example, in 1828, the London papers the *Morning Herald* and the *Quarterly Review* spoke of Macarthur having introduced the merino; see the letter by A Constant Reader in the *SG* 25 July 1828.

82 Samuel Marsden arrived in NSW as a Chaplain in December 1794, receiving a grant of 100 acres in the district known as Hunter's Hill, that is, the area north of the Parramatta River through to the Hawkesbury. By 1802 he had received 201 acres in grants and another 239 by purchase and had cleared 200 acres, and by 1805 his holdings totalled 1730 acres. In 1802 he owned 480 sheep, and by 1805 this figure had grown to over 1000'. Loane, *Hewn From The Rock*, 11; who draws upon B.M. Smith, *Quench Not the Spirit*, 29–30. After 1815 Marsden took up land around Bathurst. In 1827 he had received 3631 acres by grant, 1600 by purchase. He kept accumulating more land, and by his

ENDNOTES

death his total holdings were over 10000 acres. Even as late as 1902 the *Yorkshire Daily Observer*, and *Dalgety's Review*, claimed that Marsden held the honour of introducing the merino to Australia. The Appendix to Hassall, *In Old Australia*: The Origin of the Australian Wool Trade, a reprint from *Dalgety's Review* March 1902, cites the Yorkshire Daily Observer: 'There are various claimants for the honour of being the first to introduce the merino sheep into Australia, but that honour appears to belong to a countryman of our own in the person of the Rev. Samuel Marsden'; Hassall, *In Old Australia*, 199.

83   Gov. King to Sir Joseph Banks, 14 Aug 1804 (*HRNSW* 5.450); Gov. King to Lord Hobart, 14 Aug 1804 (*HRNSW* 5.427).
84   See Ker, 'Wool Industry'.
85   Ker, 'Wool Industry', Part 1, 28, 36, 37–38.
86   Ker, 'Wool Industry', Part 2, 31–34.
87   'Marsden must be linked with John Macarthur as the founder of sheep breeding and wool growing in this country', Loane, *Hewn From The Rock*, 12.
88   Ker, 'Wool Industry', Part 1, 18.
89   According to Ker, 'Wool Industry', Part 2, 50, this was part of the criticism made of Macarthur amongst his contemporaries, even though they were prepared to discount such things in the light of his positive contribution to the colony.
90   The British took their agriculture with them as they expanded into other lands. Some, such as Samuel Marsden, had theological reasons for doing so, believing that agricultural pursuits were part of the 'civilization' that made the natives of the new mission fields receptive to hearing the Christian gospel. Admitting that: 'I may be too fond of the Garden, the Field, and the Fleece. These would be the first objects of my attention were I placed amongst a savage nation'. Marsden sought to introduce the New Zealanders to agriculture on the belief that this 'will add greatly to their civilization and comfort, and prepare the way for greater blessings to be communicated to them, even the blessings of Christianity'. In keeping with these principles, Marsden built a house for his New Zealanders at his 'Newlands' property at Parramatta, where, alongside general and religious education, he taught them how to farm; Hassall, *In Old Australia*, 161, 168. For Marsden's missionary strategy, especially as it was manifested in New Zealand, see Falloon, *To Plough or to Preach?*. It is worth noting that the priority Marsden gave to civilization was not the only, or even the predominant, view of Christian mission, even at the time.
91   According to Ker, 'Wool Industry', Part 1, 31, a symptom of seeking to replicate English small farming practices in New South Wales.
92   Sir J. Banks to Fawkener, Sept 1803 (*HRNSW* 5.224–225).
93   Banks to H. Waterhouse, 8 July 1806 (*HRNSW* 6.109); Captain H. Waterhouse to Sir J. Banks, 16 July 1806 (ML: Series 23:43 [online]; *HRNSW* 6.110–112); Both documents were reprinted in *SG* 25/7/1828.
94   1828 *Gazette* version has 'or 4 guineas'.
95   1828 *Gazette* version has 'on my arrival'.
96   H. Waterhouse to W. Waterhouse, 20 Aug 1797 (*HRNSW* 3.287); cf. Lieut. Kent to Sec. Nepean, 16 May 1797 (*HRNSW* 3.286), from the Cape: 'after having taken on board the cattle, &c'.
97   H. Waterhouse to W. Waterhouse, 20 Aug 1797 (*HRNSW* 3.287).
98   Because Moore looked after Waterhouse's NSW affairs from 1812 (Henry Waterhouse to Thomas Moore, 24 April 1812), this letter, as well as that granting power of attorney and the deed to 'the Vineyard' are therefore now amongst the Waterhouse papers held in Moore College Library.

99 Ryan, *Land Grants*, 3, Nos 1–4 in the order given.
100 Indenture between Philip Schäffer and Henry Waterhouse, 17 Aug 1797 (Moore: Waterhouse Papers).
101 Land Grant to Henry Waterhouse, issued by Gov. Hunter 17 Oct 1797 (Moore: Waterhouse Papers), granting four and a half acres 'in the District of Parramatta and bounded on the West side by a Creek which is the Eastern boundary of the Farm known by the name of the Vineyard'. Ryan, *Land Grants*, 106 (No 744). He had already received 25 acres at Liberty Plains on 1 May 1797; Ryan, *Land Grants*, 84 (No 610).
102 Henry Waterhouse to Thomas Moore, 24 April 1812; William Waterhouse to Thomas Moore, 21 September 1812 (Moore: Waterhouse Papers). Henry died on 27 July 1812.
103 Captain H. Waterhouse to Sir J. Banks, 16 July 1806 (ML: Series 23:43 [online]; *HRNSW* 6.110–112); reprinted in *SG* 25/7/1828.
104 Captain Waterhouse to Sir J. Banks, 16 July 1806 (ML: Series 23:43 [online]; *HRNSW* 6.110–112); *Gazette* version: 'I supplied Capt. Kent, Capt. McArthur, Mr Marsden, Mr Laycock, Mr Williamson, Capt. Rowley, Mr Moore, Mr Grimes, and in fact any person who wished to have them'. What Waterhouse says here about Macarthur is difficult to reconcile with Macarthur's claim to have asked him to purchase sheep from the Cape before embarking on the voyage (see note 81 above). If Macarthur had commissioned the purchase of the sheep, then why would Waterhouse be reluctant to give them to him on arrival?
105 The identity of this Mr Moore is left open by both the Mitchell Library Card Index, and the Index to the *SG* (for the latter: *SG* 25/7/1828, 3c: A Mr Moore purchased Merino sheep from Capt. Waterhouse in 1797 when he brought them from the Cape).
106 The mistake is made by the index in *HRNSW* 6.864, and Ker, 'Wool Industry', Part 1, 29 n.11. The military William Moore enlisted in the NSW Corps on 7 March 1795, arrived as an Ensign, but was later promoted to the rank of Lieutenant. Return of Officers of the New South Wales Corps, 31 Dec 1801 (*HRNSW* 4.650). William Moore was on Norfolk Island from 1796 to 1801, which would make it difficult for him to be amongst those who purchased sheep in 1797. These two men are quite regularly mistaken in both primary and secondary sources.
107 When publishing Waterhouse's letter amongst the Banks Papers, the State Library website identified this Moore as the colony's first solicitor William Henry Moore (http://www.sl.nsw.gov.au/banks/series_23/23_43.htm). W.H. Moore was 'one of the solicitors sent out by the British government on a salary of three hundred pounds per annum to practise under the charter of justice', arriving on the *Broxbornebury* with Jeffrey Hart Bent and the assistant chaplain Rev. Benjamin Vale (Clark, *History* 1.306) —three characters who would each become rather infamous in the colony. See also McKay, 'Moore, William Henry (1788?–1854)'.
108 Henry Waterhouse to Thomas Moore, 20 Oct 1804 (Moore: Waterhouse Papers).
109 He was appointed by Government and General Order, 7 May 1803 (Col.Sec. 6037 SZ 991, p.17; *HRNSW* 5.107). See below.
110 Gov. King to Sir Joseph Banks Sept 1803 (*HRNSW* 5.229).
111 This suggestion was made by Robinson, 'Postscript': '[Waterhouse] introduced the first merino sheep into N.S.W. from the Cape of Good Hope in 1797, and supplied lambs to Macarthur and Marsden, with well-known consequences. Did he also sell lambs to Moore? In October 1804 he wrote to Moore: "The Spanish wool ... I believe will shortly be an object of attention to the Government, from which I think you may profit, by keeping your wool etc".'

112 In the 1801 muster, Thomas Moore, Master Boat Builder is listed as having received one land grant, given by Hunter in October 1799, of 470 acres, with only 5 acres cleared, and none sown with wheat and maize. At this time he had one horse and five hogs. One convict had been assigned him. HRNSW 4.648. Ryan, *Land Grants*, 119 (No 836).
113 The 1801 muster lists the following persons having sheep: Governor King (8) [NB: with no land of his own]; Judge–Advocate Atkins (134); Commissary John Palmer (650); Chaplain Samuel Marsden (340); Storekeeper Rowland Hassall (5); Magistrate Thomas Arndell (50); Chief Constable George Barrington (25); Superintendents Richard Fitzgerald (95) and Nicholas Divine (5).
114 Moore kept a list of his mares with their ages, 1798–1812. His two oldest were born in 1798 and 1799, but the list shows that he had had another two called 'Old Bett' and 'Young Bett'. This evidence may suggest he began gathering horses in 1798 or 1799, perhaps earlier, but certainly prior to the date of the first official grant; Ages of Mares, 1798–1812 Thomas Moore's Business Notebook (SDA: 0884CH, Item 1).
115 Grose largely ignored his instructions regarding the granting of land; cf. Lieut–Gov. Grose to H. Dundas, 29 April 1794 (*HRA* 1.1.469 n.251, cf. p.441 n.237). His summary of land grants does not agree with the tabular statement he transmitted: 3 x 110 ac, instead of 2; 5 x 100 ac instead of 6; 35 x 30 ac, instead of 34. Robinson, 'Thomas Moore & Early Life', 180 (16), speculates that Thomas Moore could have received an allotment as early as 1794. Robinson argues that the note about Hunter consolidating previous grants 'presumably means that Moore had acquired some sort of title to land even before the arrival of Hunter in 1795, that is while he, Moore, was still on *Britannia*. He was, as we remember, on shore for a time during 1794 when Grose was acting governor and again from March to June 1795 in Paterson's administration. His name does not appear among the Bulanaming allotments on Grimes' 'Plan of the Settlements in New South Wales' of 1796 (*HRNSW* 3.frontespiece), and neither does Smyth's, but he may have had some sort of holding nevertheless'. The practice of occupying land well before receiving it as a grant goes back as far as the very first land grants (e.g. Phillip Schäffer and James Ruse), and a version of this practice no doubt continued in later periods.
116 Ryan, *Land Grants*, 49, No 416: 1 June 1795, Raven received 100 acres in the Eastern Farms by purchase from Charles Peat.
117 Hunter to Portland, 6/2/1800 (*HRNSW* 4.45).
118 Gov. P.G. King to Sir J. Banks, 9 May 1803 (*HRNSW* 5.135).
119 In 1800 he had a flock of 40 sheep, but by the following year, they were all gone; Baxter, *Musters & Lists. 1801–1802*, List 2 (1800), items AB010–012, compared with List 7 (1802), item AG478. Moore still has no sheep on the Return of 14 Aug 1804 (*HRNSW* 5.432–433).
120 H. Waterhouse to W. Waterhouse, 20 Aug 1797 (*HRNSW* 3.287).
121 Government and General Order, 28 Oct 1797 (*HRNSW* 3.305–306).
122 Hunter to Portland, 12 Nov 1796, Order dated 18 July 1796 (*HRA* 1.1.696).
123 Gov. Hunter to Sec. Nepean, 19 Nov 1797 (*HRA* 1.2.112).
124 T. Moore, W. Stevenson, J. Coldwell, R. Scott, Survey of Reliance. Enclosure to Gov. Hunter to Sec. Nepean, 19 Nov 1797 (*HRA* 1.2.113).
125 Cf. Deuteronomy 24:5, 'If a man has recently married, he must not be sent to war or have any other duty laid on him. For one year he is to be free to stay at home and bring happiness to the wife he has married'.
126 Return of Labour at Sydney, &c (*HRNSW* 3.337, 338). One of them was Joe Smith, whom Matthew Flinders called 'my blade' and sought his emancipation; a request refused by the Governor; M. Flinders to G. Bass, 15 Feb 1800 (ML: MLMSS 7046).

127 J. Hunter to Portland, Encl.: Work perform'd since October 1796, 10 June 1797 (*HRNSW* 3.221).
128 Return of Labour at Sydney, &c (*HRNSW* 3.337).
129 Gov. Hunter to Under Secretary King, 14 Nov 1796 (*HRA* 1.1.705).
130 Government and General Order 28 Oct 1797 (*HRNSW* 3.305–30; Gov. Hunter to Portland, 10 Jan 1798 (*HRNZ* 1.218).
131 Return of Labour at Sydney, &c (*HRNSW* 3.337).
132 Perhaps because of their distance from the conservatism of the Naval Yards at home, the colonial shipbuilders could try their hand at innovation. The same would be true of David Hoy's attempt to lead the world in ship–design through the ships built by convicts at Sarah Island on the West coast of Van Diemen's Land from his arrival in 1827. Brand, *Sarah Island*.
133 Gov. Hunter to Under–Sec. King, 25 Sept, 1800, Encl. No 2: Return of Public Buildings erected since 1796 (*HRNSW* 4.153).
134 Return of Livestock, and, Return of Land in Cultivation, 31 December 1797 (*HRNSW* 3.341).
135 Minute of the Board of Trade, 26 December 1797 (*HRNSW* 3.335; *HRNZ* 1.216–217).
136 Gov. Hunter to Portland, 10 Jan 1798 (*HRNZ* 1.219).
137 Gov. Hunter to Portland, 1 Mar 1798 (*HRNSW* 3.363).
138 Robinson, 'Thomas Moore—Early Life', 179 (15). There is a whale boat listed among the items constructed in the dockyard in 1797; see Return of Labour 1797 (*HRNSW* 3.337; cf. 4.157).
139 Agreement between Officers and Others, 18 June 1798 (*HRNSW* 3.405—406).
140 Government and General Order, 25 June 1798 (*HRNSW* 3.408).
141 Hainsworth, *Sydney Traders*, 40–41: 'In future the officers who remained in New South Wales (either in the services or as civilians) tended to concentrate on pastoral farming, especially highly profitable cattle raising'.
142 Vice–Admiralty Court, 20 Aug 1798 (*HRNSW* 3.453ff.).
143 Macintosh, *Richard Johnson*, 87.
144 Gov. Hunter to Under–Sec. King, 25 Sept 1800, Encl. No 2: Return of Public Buildings erected since 1796 (*HRNSW* 4.153).
145 Statement of Work during 1798 (*HRNSW* 3.521).
146 For what follows see Hunter to Portland 10 Jan 1798 (*HRNSW* 3.345), and Collins, *Account*, 2.35, 42, 225 (for long quotation). Collins himself appears to be quoting from Hunter, see Gov. Hunter to Under–Sec. King, 25 Sept 1800, Encl. No 3: Return of Public Buildings Proposed to be Erected by Gov'r Hunter (*HRNSW* 4.156).
147 Statement of Work during 1798 (*HRNSW* 3.521).
148 Statement of Work during 1798 (*HRNSW* 3.522).
149 Collins, *Account*, 1.448.
150 Portland to Gov. Hunter, 26 Feb 1799 (*HRA* 1.2.338).
151 Portland to Gov. Hunter, 21 Dec 1798 (*HRNSW* 3.519).
152 Lieut.–Gov. P.G. King to Sir Joseph Banks, 13 February 1799 (*HRNZ* 1.219–220).
153 Sir J. Banks to Dr W. Roxburgh, 7 Jan 1799 (*HRNSW* 3.527).
154 Trial of Isaac Nichols, 21 Feb 1799 (*HRA* 1.2.285).
155 Trial of Isaac Nichols, 21 Feb 1799 (*HRNSW* 3.608; *HRA* 1.2.304–305).
156 *SG* 4/3/1804.
157 Gov. Hunter to Judge–Advocate Dore, 3 April 1799 (*HRNSW* 3.609; *HRA* 1.2.306).
158 Hainsworth, *Sydney Traders*, 36. I am sure Mary will forgive Hainsworth for placing her

ENDNOTES 409

amongs the 'men'.
159 Hainsworth, *Sydney Traders*, 40 and n.17, referring to Supreme Court Papers Bundle 18 Item 30 NSW Archives 1112.
160 McMartin, 'Nichols, Isaac (1770–1819)'.
161 H. Waterhouse to Gov. Hunter, and, Observations by Captain Waterhouse, 22 May 1799 (*HRNSW* 3.622–627; *HRA* 1.2.324–330).
162 Observations by Captain Waterhouse, 22 May 1799 (*HRNSW* 3.627).
163 Lieut. Flinders to Gov. Hunter, 30 April 1799 (*HRA* 1.2.330–334).
164 Observations of Matthew Flinders on the Trial of Isaac Nichols, 30 April 1799 (*HRA* 1.2.333).
165 Trial of Isaac Nichols, 21 Feb 1799 (*HRA* 1.2. 286, cf. 331, 337).
166 Trial of Isaac Nichols, 21 Feb 1799 (*HRA* 1.2.287).
167 William Kent's observations on the Trial of Isaac Nichols, 30 April 1799 (*HRA* 1.2.337).
168 Robinson, 'Thomas Moore—Early Life', 177–178 (13–14). He also notes how closely associated Moore and the Campbells became. Robert Campbell Junior became one of the Executors of Moore's will and, after Moore died in 1840, a trustee of his estate.
169 Smyth's 470 acre grant eventually came to the Bishop of Australia as a bequest for a church in Bulanaming from Robert Campbell, who had gained the property as a result of an agreement with John Palmer, dated 30 and 31 December 1808; Indenture between Robert Campbell and Bishop of Australia, 7 Dec 1837 (SDA: Registrar's Office–Correspondence, 1994/18/3). It was described in this document as butting on the Northwest to the grants of Thomas Moore and John Fincham.
170 Lands Granted since 1 Aug 1796 [Encl.], Gov. Hunter to Portland, 6 February 1800 (*HNRSW* 4.37–48; *HRA* 1.2.461). Ryan, *Land Grants*, 119 (No 836); 145 acres of the grant came from 30 acre parcels granted previously to Thomas Hughes (20/2/1794, p.19, No 19), Thomas Alford (1/4/1794, p.23, No 178), James Young (1/4/1794, p.23, No 179) and Thomas Wood (11/11/1794, p.29, No 226), and a 25 acre parcel (the soldier's amount) previously issued to Robert King (14/3/1795, p.48, No 405).
171 [Aust. Enc.²], 'London Missionary Society', 361. Gunson, 'Henry, William (1770–1859)'.
172 Gunson, 'Henry, William (1770–1859)': 'Another party of *Duff* missionaries arrived in February 1800. John Buchanan (b.1765), James Cooper (1768–1846), and William Shelley, arrived in the *Betsy* from Tonga, and Seth Kelso (b.1748) and James Wilkinson (b.1769) arrived with John Harris in the *Anna Josepha*'.
173 Lands Granted since 1 Aug 1796 [Encl.], Gov. Hunter to Portland, 6 February 1800 (*HNRSW* 4.44, 46, 47).
174 Collins, *Account* 2.149.
175 Lands Granted since 1 Aug 1796 [Encl.], Gov. Hunter to Portland, 6 February 1800 (*HNRSW* 4.47). Ryan, *Land Grants*, 125, No 872; 234, No 85, both on 12 Nov 1799.
176 See *Monthly Magazine and British Register*, Volume 11, Issue 1, June 1, 1801, p. 450, under 'Marriages and Deaths in and around London': 'Died, Mrs Raven, wife of Captain W. Raven, of Hackney Terrace'.
177 Mander–Jones, 'Lewin, John William (1770–1819)'.
178 John Lewin's father, William, was also a member of the Linnean Society, so there may have been some connection with John White; Mander–Jones, 'Lewin, John William (1770–1819)'.
179 John William Lewin v. George Thompson [1799] NSWKR 8, Dore J.A., 4 and 30 November 1799, 3 February 1800; Court of Civil Jurisdiction Proceedings, 1788–1814, State Records N.S.W 2/8150 (http://www.law.mq.edu.au/scnsw/html/Lewin%20v%20Thompson,%201799.

htm). See also Court of Civil Jurisdiction Proceedings, 1788–1814, State Records N.S.W., 2/8147, p. 257; Kercher, *Debt, Seduction and Other Disasters*, 74, 82, 99–100, 120.
180 Collins, *Account*, 2.195 n.
181 Baxter, *Musters & Lists. 1801–1802*, List 2 (1800), Items AB010–012: List 9, Items AJ 088–92; List 5, Item BE 021; List 7 (1802), Item AG478.
182 *Thomas Moore's Business Notebook* (SDA: 0884CH, Item 1), lists the age of his mares from 1798–1812.
183 In Baxter, *Musters & Lists. 1801–1802*, List 2 (1800), items AB 010–012, his Bulanaming property, 470 acres of which came from his own grant, 30 from John Jeffries, and 30 from Robert Abell. Incidentally, when they were still convicts, Jeffries and Abel were both engaged to unload *The Lady Juliana*, upon which Rachel arrived, and by the end of the week were each flogged with 200 lashes for somehow purloining sugar between the ship and the shore inventory-taking; see Rees, *The Floating Brothel*, 200–201, 209.
184 Baxter, *Musters & Lists. 1801–1802*, List 7 (1802), item AG 478.
185 Return of Acres sown (*HRNSW* 5.432–433). In April of the same year, Robert Campbell imported the Colony's second pure Arab stallion and sold it to Governor King who then bartered it to the Government.
186 Barrie, *The Australian Bloodhorse*, 12.
187 Appointments for manning the various batteries, 1800 (Col.Sec. 6041, 4/719, p.53).
188 Gov. Hunter to Under-Sec. King, 25 Sept 1800, Encl. No 2: Return of Public Buildings erected since 1796 (*HRNSW* 4.152).
189 Gov. Hunter to Under-Sec. King, 25 Sept 1800, Encl. No 3: Return of Public Buildings Proposed to be Erected by Gov'r Hunter, with remarks by Gov. King (*HRNSW* 4.156).
190 Steven, 'Campbell, Robert (1769–1846)'.
191 Hainsworth, *Sydney Traders*, 34.
192 Hainsworth, *Sydney Traders*, 39.
193 Hainsworth, *Sydney Traders*, 35.
194 List of Vessels Entering Port Jackson 3 Nov 1799 to 13 May 1800 (*HRNSW* 4.164).
195 Hainsworth, *Sydney Traders*, 42.
196 Hainsworth, *Sydney Traders*, 42–43 and n.26. Clephan, Nepean, Hill, Edward Abbott, and others had already gone home. Paterson was in England 1796–1799 and probably did not trade after his return. Macarthur went home 1801, and was a civilian after 1803. Rowley resigned his commission in 1802. Foveaux was on Norfolk Island until 1804 and in England until 1808. Balmain went home in 1801 and died there 1803. Piper, a minor member of the ring, was on Norfolk Island in the King-Bligh period, co-operating with Simeon Lord.
197 Hainsworth, *Sydney Traders*, 35.
198 [*Aust. Enc²*], 'Waterhouse, Henry', 9.213–4. Gov. Hunter to Capt. Waterhouse, 12 Feb 1800 (*HRNSW* 4.53).
199 On 24 April 1812 Henry wrote to Moore, granting him power of attorney over his affairs in conjunction with Colonel Davey, and requesting that they both 'justly dispose' of his property in New South Wales. Henry Waterhouse to Thomas Moore, 24 April 1812. In a matter of months, however, Henry died (on 27 July 1812), and his father gave Moore the sole power of attorney; William Waterhouse to Thomas Moore, 21 September 1812 (Moore: Waterhouse Papers).
200 Macquarie to Castlereagh, 30 April 1810 (*HRA* 1.7.269, 809 n.90). Campbell bought John Baughan's lease, and Henry Waterhouse's which adjoined it. Waterhouse probably lived in his other property up at the top of the hill from the hospital. (Plates 34, 35).

ENDNOTES 411

201 For example, Henry Waterhouse and Thomas Moore joined Matthew Flinders on the Vice–Admiralty Court held 20 August 1798 in regard to the mutiny on the *Barwell* (*HRNSW* 3.453ff.). They were also both involved in the trial of Isaac Nichols, and Waterhouse gave some of his sheep to Moore in 1797.
202 Robinson, 'Postscript'. The Waterhouse family are amongst those who kept Thomas and Rachel informed about Andrew's progress and welfare over many years: William also passes on news of Andrew in W. Waterhouse to T. Moore, 9/6/1813, 18/12/1813, 28/7/1814 (SDA: 0852 CH, Item 7, docs. 4, 5, 6, and 7); 16/8/1816 (SDA: 0851 CH, Item 4, doc. 8) and 9/12/1819 (SDA: 0852 CH, Item 7, doc. 7). For other informants see: Isaac Clementson to Thomas Moore 21 Jan 1807 (SDA: 0853 CH, Item 11, doc.2); J. Harris to T. Moore, 31 May 1811 (SDA: 0854 CH, Item 1, doc. 17); ex–Gov. L. Macquarie to T. Moore, 20 December 1819 and 1 June 1824 (SDA: 0853 CH, Item 4, docs. 4 and 12).
203 When Rienits, 'Biographical Introduction', 31, stated 'White's natural son, Andrew Douglas, was apparently accepted into the household', he was wrong in his timing, but ultimately correct. Clara Bernal's heartfelt letter to Thomas and Rachel on hearing (through the newspaper!) of Andrew's death is a particularly poignant example of his half-siblings' affection for him; Clara Bernal to T. Moore, [undated, 1838] (SDA: 0851 CH, Item 6, doc 24). See also Anne Losack to Thomas & Rachel Moore, 11 Aug 1838 (SDA: 0853 CH, Item 11, doc 10).
204 Gov. Hunter to Portland, 20 April 1800 (*HRNSW* 4.73).
205 Shaw, 'King, Philip Gidley (1758–1808)'.
206 Gov. P.G. King to Portland, 1 May 1801, and Encl. No 1: Report of Survey of Brig *Harbinger* (*HRA* 1.3.88–89), 'she will supply the place of another King's ship for the present at a hundredth part less expence to the Crown'.
207 Lieut.–Gov. P.G. King to Rev. R. Johnson & others, 7 Aug 1800 (*HRA* 1.2.534–536; *HRNSW* 4.136).
208 Proceedings of Committee for Orphan Institute, 15 Sept 1800 (*HRA* 1.2.537; *HRNSW* 4.138).
209 Lieut.–Gov. King to Under–Sec. King, 27 June 1800 (*HRNSW* 4.110).
210 Gov. Hunter to Under–Sec. King, 25 Sept 1800, Encl. No 2: Return of Public Buildings erected since 1796 (*HRNSW* 4.153): 'Built a commodious stone house near the naval yard for the master boat-builder'; 'Paled in a naval yard on the west side of the cove, and erected a joiner's and a blacksmith's shop; sheds for vessels repairing, and for the workmen; a steamer, a store–house, a warder's lodge, and an apartment for the clerk'.
211 Gov. Hunter to Under–Sec. King, 25 Sept 1800, Encl. No 3: Return of Public Buildings Proposed to be Erected by Gov'r Hunter (*HRNSW* 4.156).
212 Gov. Hunter to Under–Sec. King, 25 Sept 1800, 'Encl. No 5: Naval Establishment', (*HRNSW* 4.157).
213 Gov. Hunter to Under–Sec. King, 25 Sept 1800, Encl. No 2: Return of Public Buildings erected since 1796 (*HRNSW* 4.151–154).
214 Gov. Hunter to Under–Sec. King, 25 Sept 1800, Encl. No 3: Return of Public Buildings Proposed to be Erected by Gov'r Hunter (*HRNSW* 4.155).
215 Acting Gov. King to Portland, 10 Mar 1801, Encl. 13: Statement of Officers of the Civil Establishment, March 1801 (*HRA* 1.3.53). Macintosh, *Richard Johnson*, 92.
216 Bolt, 'The Case of the Disappearing Chaplain'.
217 Boyce, *Thomas Moore*, 4.
218 Gov. King to Portland, 10 Mar 1801 (*HRNSW* 4.315). Collins, *Account*, 2.218, gives 21 October, probably the date of sailing.

219 Collins, *Account*, 2.218.
220 Clark, *A History of Australia* 1.151.
221 Acting Gov. King to Portland, 10 Mar 1801, Statement of Officers of the Civil Establishment, March 1801 (*HRA* 1.3.53). On the Statement of Officers on the Civil Establishment, 30 June 1801 (*HRA* 1.3.153), the return mistakenly names William Moore as Boat Builder—which is not the last time Thomas would be confused with this officer of the NSW Corps at this time stationed at Parramatta, whether in contemporary or later documents; Return of NSW Corps, 21 Aug 1801 (*HRNSW* 4.495). See also Statement of Officers, 21 May 1802 (*HRA* 1.3.494).
222 *The Gentleman's Magazine*, Vol. 90 Supp, 1801, p.1205: under 'marriages of notable persons', 24 Nov 1801; *Jackson's Oxford Journal*, 5 Dec 1801.
223 [British History], 'Hackney'.
224 So http://myweb.tiscali.co.uk/redgravehistory/wilson/twbiogr.htm (21/5/2010).
225 S. Chace to T. Moore, Letter of Attorney, 17 Aug 1801 (SDA: 0853 CH, Item 15, doc.1); Shipping Return, 1 July to 31 Dec 1801 (*HRNSW* 4.647). The *Harriet* sailed on 20 August.
226 See Druett, 'Samuel Rodman Chace'.
227 The *Albion* sailed on 26 August; Shipping Return, 1 July to 31 Dec 1801 (*HRNSW* 4.647).
228 Bunker was born 7 March 1761 into a puritan family community in Plymouth, Massachusetts. He moved to the Thames, probably after the American Revolution, and took his first command in June 1788 on the *Spencer*; Hodgkinson, *Eber Bunker*, 4–5. An 'E. Bunker' appears on the list of ships in the Southern Whale Fishery in *Diary or Woodfall's Register*, 18 Aug 1790.
229 Hodgkinson, *Eber Bunker*, 42–43.
230 Captain McKellar's Account, 15 Sept 1801 (*HRNSW* 4.560–561).
231 Judge–Advocate R. Atkins to Gov. P.G. King, 29 Sept 1801 (*HRNSW* 4.583).
232 Steven, 'Macarthur, John (1767–1834)'.
233 Geo. Bass to Elizabeth Bass, 20 Oct 1801 (Mitchell—Waterhouse Papers: ZML MSS 6544 [Safe 1/187] CY 3970), [screen 406].
234 Estensen, *George Bass*, 132–133.
235 Estensen, *George Bass*, 141–142. Hainsworth, *Sydney Traders*, 49, 158, 186.
236 For the development of the trade, see Hainsworth, *Sydney Traders*, 157–164.
237 Hainsworth, *Sydney Traders*, 158.
238 Geo. Bass to Elizabeth Bass, 12 Nov 1801 (Mitchell—Waterhouse Papers: ZML MSS 6544 [Safe 1/187] CY 3970), [screen 419].
239 G. Bass to H. Waterhouse, 30 Jan 1802 (*HRNZ* 1.225).
240 Pay List for HM *Lady Nelson*, 1/7–31/12/1801 (ML: King Papers, vol. 1, p.30, A1976).
241 Thomas Moore's Business Notebook (Rear) (SDA: 0884 CH, Item 1), 15, 16.
242 The shipping returns printed in *HRNSW* 4 mistake Simter's name, twice giving 'Sunter' and once 'Hunter' (pp. 646, 759, 794). The *HRA* 1.3 also mistakes his name as 'Sunter' (pp. 93, 94, 379, 452, 501, 639). Their logs are both preserved: for *Minorca*, 30 March 1801 to 28 Feb 1803, to Port Jackson and Whampoa; for *Nile*, James Simter, 30 March 1801 to 5 March 1803, to Port Jackson and Canton; see [East India Company], *List of Marine Records*, 83.
243 List of Ships cleared Outwards 1 Jan 1802 to 21 May; List of Ships cleared Outwards 1 Jan 1802 to 30 June (*HRNSW* 4.759, 794); *SG* 25/12/1803. *Canada*, *Nile* and *Minorca*, brought out settlers, about forty families of whom were so poor the agent for transports was instructed to provide clothing worth £5 on average per family. Under-Sec. King to Transport Commissioner, 16 April 1801 (*HRNSW* 4.346). List of

Ships entered Inwards 1 Oct to 31 Dec 1801 (*HRNSW* 4.646); Gov. King to Portland, 1 Mar 1802 (*HRNSW* 4.714), who gives the 15th—probably the date of disembarkation.

244 Transport Commissioners to Masters of the Convict Ships, Minorca, Canada, and Nile; and to the Surgeons, 8 June 1801; Convict Ships, 10 June 1801 (*HRNSW* 4.389, 390, 399ff.). Gov. King to Under-Sec. King, 2 Feb 1802 (*HRNSW* 4.691).

245 Thomas Moore, Business Notebook (Rear) (SDA: 0884 CH, Item 1), 15, 22, 23, 34. Leith evidently has a house in Sydney, for these accounts show £30 paid for three years rent, entered for 26 June 1802. In 1804 Moore paid the 5s quit rent for two years, suggesting that Leith bought the house while in Sydney early 1802.

246 J. Campbell to Bengal Authorities, 20 Oct 1802 (EI Co Papers, Home Public Series, Consult. 70, 4 Nov 1802); cited from Steven, *Merchant Campbell*, 108–109.

247 Steven, *Merchant Campbell*, 116–117.

248 Return of Land and Stock of Officers, 1801 (*HRNSW* 4.648). July 1800, *1800–02 Muster and Lists: NSW and Norfolk Island*. Register of Arms, 10 April 1802 (Col.Sec. 6041, 4/1719, p.85). Baxter, *Musters and Lists. 1801–1802*, List 7 (1802), Item AG478. Agricultural Returns, 25–30 July 1803 (*HRA* 1.4.314). Moore has the same amount on the list of 11 Feb 1804 (*HRA* 1.4.498). Ryan, *Land Grants*, 163: No 1145, 1 Oct 1803, Thomas Moore Granted 700 acres in the district of Bulanaming. Rent: £1 per year commencing after five years.

249 Ex–Gov. Hunter to Under–Sec. King, 22 Mar 1802 (*HRNSW* 4.728–733; *HRNZ* 1.227). See Paine, *Journal*, 77–78, App. 2, docs. 1–3. Ex–Gov. Hunter to Under–Sec. King, 22 Mar 1802 (*HRNSW* 4.728–733; *HRNZ* 1.227).

250 Thomas Clark to Sir Joseph Banks, 25 June 1802 (SLNSW: Series 23.14).

251 Ex–Gov. Hunter to Under Sec. King, 22 Mar 1802, *HRNSW* 4.729. Cf. Russell, *Thomas Moore*, 9, 25, 27.

252 Ex–Gov. Hunter to Under–Sec. King, 22 Mar 1802 (*HRNSW* 4.730–731).

253 For shipbuilding in India, see Wadia, *The Bombay Dockyard*.

254 Ex–Gov. Hunter to Under–Sec. King, 22 Mar 1802 (*HRNSW* 4.731).

255 Waterhouse, 'Memorandum on the Timber of New South Wales', ca. March, 1802, = Paine, *Journal*, 78–81, App.2, doc. 4; cf. Ex–Gov. Hunter to Under Sec. King, 22 Mar 1802 (*HRNSW* 4.731).

256 Ex–Gov. Hunter to Under–Sec. King, 22 Mar 1802 (*HRNSW* 4.731–732).

257 Matthew Flinders—*Journal on HMS 'Investigator'*, vol. 1, 1801–1802, p.517.

258 T. Rowley to H. Waterhouse, 2 June 1802 (SDA: 0851 CH, Item 4, doc. 1).

259 List of Civil and Military Officers holding Land, 1802 (*HRA* 1.3.613). According to Cowan, 'Early History', it is likely that he was the same man as the John Erwin who died aged 46 at Parramatta in 1826, because, if not, there is no other registered death up till 1849 that could be him. http://www-personal.usyd.edu.au/~rcowan/genealogy/irvine_name.html (25/9/07).

260 Baxter, *Musters & Lists. 1801–1802*, List 7 (1802), item AG 478.

261 Age of Mares, 1798–1812. Thomas Moore's Business Notebook (SDA: 0884 CH, Item 1). Presumably Young Bett is no longer with him in 1812, for she does not appear on the list and her birthday is therefore not listed. Her name, however, suggests she was born from 'Old Bett', which I presume to have been his first mare.

262 The Trial of Captain Betts (*HRA* 1.3.536); The Trial of William Stow & Others (*HRA* 1.3.550–551).

263 The Trial of William Stow & others, 14 July 1802 (*HRA* 1.3.550–551).

264 Remission of the Sentence on Captain Betts, 9 Aug 1802 (*HRA* 1.3.549–550).
265 King to Hobart, 1 Mar 1804 (*HRNSW* 5.338; *HRA* 1.4.540).
266 *SG* 11/12/1803.
267 G. Bass to H. Waterhouse, 5 Jan 1803 (*HRNSW* 5.1–3; *HRNZ* 1.240–242).
268 G. Bass to H. Waterhouse, 5 Jan 1803 (*HRNSW* 5.1–3; *HRNZ* 1.240–242).
269 G. Bass to Gov. P.G. King, 30 Jan 1803 (*HRA* 1.4.156–157; *HRNZ* 1.242–244; this letter is not in *HRNSW*).
270 G. Bass to H. Waterhouse, 2 Feb 1803 (*HRNSW* 5.14–15); for King's certificate, 3 Feb 1803 (*HRNSW* 5.15–16; *HRA* 1.4.154–156). For Governor King's report on Bass's venture, see King to Hobart, 9 May 1803 (*HRA* 1.4.147).
271 Gov. King to Hobart, 9 May 1803 (*HRA* 1.4.148).
272 Thomas Moore to [?], 15 Dec 1817 (*HRNSW* 3.313). At the time of publication of *HRNSW*, the letter was said to be in the PRO in London. I have been unable to locate it in the National Archives at Kew, the replacement for the PRO.
273 *SG* 5/3/1803.
274 *SG* 12/3/1803.
275 Government and General Order 29 Mar 1803 (*HRNSW* 5.80); Gov. P.G. King to Sir J. Banks, 9 May 1803 (*HRNSW* 5.134–135); Bowen's instructions: Gov. King to Hobart, 9 May 1803 [Encl. No 3] (*HRA* 1.4.152–153).
276 Gov. P.G. King to Sir J. Banks, 9 May 1803 (*HRNSW* 5.135); Gov. P.G. King to Hobart, 9 May 1803 (*HRA* 1.4.144; *HRNZ* 1.246), for quotation. The latter letter also relishes the loss of a French schooner among the Cape Barren Islands, 'which may stop any more adventurers from that quarter'.
277 Gov. King to Hobart, 9 May 1803 [Encl. No 3] (*HRA* 1.4.153–154).
278 'Specimens of Wool Grown in NSW', *SG* 26/3/1803 (*HRNSW* 5.80–81); cf. Gov. King to Sir J. Banks, 9 May 1803 (*HRNSW* 5.135).
279 Gov. P.G. King to Hobart, 9 May 1803 (*HRA* 1.4.145; *HRNZ* 1.246).
280 *SG* 5 and 12/3/1803.
281 *SG* 5/3/1803.
282 S. Chace to T. Moore, 29 April 1803 (SDA: 0853 CH, Item 15, doc. 2).
283 *SG* 8 and 15/5/1803.
284 *SG* 18/9/1803. See above p 154.
285 Ryan, *Land Grants*, 163: No 1145, 1 Oct 1803, Thomas Moore Granted 700 acres in the district of Bulanaming. Rent: £1 per year commencing after five years.
286 Gov. King, Land Grant to Thomas Moore, 1 October 1803, 700 acres in Bulanaming (ML: R. Wardell papers, MS A 5330, item 7). It also adds: 'This Grant is a consolidation of the several grants given by Lieut. Gov. Grose to John Jeffries and Robert Abell and by Governor Hunter to the present grantee which he had acquired; ... etc.'
287 Robinson, 'Thomas Moore—Early Life', 181 (17) and 183 (19).
288 *SG* 11/12/1803.
289 Calculation of the Value of Government Stock Alienated to Individuals, 1806 (ML: King Papers, vol. 9, pp.161 a–b).
290 H.B. Hayes to Lord Hobart, 6 May 1803 (*HRNSW* 5.106).
291 Lynravn, 'Hayes, Sir Henry Browne (1762–1832)'.
292 Captain Colnett to Gov. King, 9 May 1803 (*HRNSW* 5.109)
293 Government and General Order, 7 May 1803 (*HRA* 1.4, 340 and *HRNSW* V.107; = Col.Sec. 6037 SZ 991, p.17). Also published in *SG* 15/5/1803. Surveyor and Purveyor are both used for this position in the sources although the two can be distinguished; as

ENDNOTES 415

in Albion, *Forests*, 212 — but without explanation. I suspect that the term 'purveyor' is the older term, and that it had overtones of the system of pre-emption of timber (see below, Chapter 4), whereas 'surveyor' was more neutral. If so, it is interesting to notice that, despite the official announcement using 'Surveyor', when Thomas Moore referred to himself, he used the term 'Purveyor'; see King to Hobart, 9 May 1803, Enclosure 11, 9 May 1803 (*HRA* 1.4, 105): 'Actg. Purveyor'; and King to Nepean, 9 May 1803, Enclosure: Moore to King 13 May 1803 (*HRA* 1.4, 265): 'having appointed me Purveyor of Timber'.

294 Albion, *Forests*, 54, 95, 321 (quotation), 427.
295 For the story of the Dockyard, see Russell, *Thomas Moore*; Bolt, 'King's Dockyard'. Hunter writes of the urgent need of repairs to the boats of the settlement soon after his arrival; Hunter to Portland, 21/12/1795 (*HRA* 1.1.549).
296 Knight & Frost, 'Introduction', xiii.
297 Albion, *Forests*, 96. The warnings came through books (in 1766, 1787), and a series of 17 official reports between 1783–1793; pp. 135, 430, 453, 439.
298 Crimmins, 'Search', 86 n.9. Cf. Albion, *Forests*, 20, 45.
299 'By the 1840s ships were reaching the ultimate size that could safely be built in timber, and there was already an embarrassing shortage of good shipbuilding timber in Western Europe', Kemp, 'Shipbuilding', 789–797.
300 Albion, *Forests*, 95.
301 Paine, *Journal*, 73, App. 2. For a fuller account of the entire problem, see Albion, *Forests*, who deals with crooked timber on pp. 5–9, 19, 21, 80–120 (esp. 99, 112, 114, 116), 225–6, 393–4, 400, 406. See also Russell, *Thomas Moore*, 9–11.
302 Canby, *History*, 66.
303 A number of factors were involved. See Crimmins, 'Search', 114–115: 'In the contest between naval and military power, Napoleon's victorious armies in the Adriatic between 1806 and 1809 put it out of the power of the Royal Navy to control the essential timber on which British naval pre-eminence rested ultimately and for which it had paid large sums. The vulnerability of seapower thus stands revealed: dependent on supplies outside its control, though, in theory and popular belief, after Trafalgar "commanding the sea", yet only one year later unable to gain access to the commodity which would enable it to continue to exert that command. Nevertheless, in a wider context this military menace was almost incidental. The real problem was the lack of financial and commercial facilities, the logistic difficulties, the problems of handling bulk cargoes, and the inadequate amounts of the right sort of shipping capacity. In wartime these handicaps could not be overcome'.
304 Canby, *History*, 72.
305 Albion, *Forests*, 317–318.
306 Albion, *Forests*, 317.
307 Albion, *Forests*, 46. Incidentally, Middleton was a prominent Anglican layman, associated with Samuel Marsden through the London Missionary Society; Yarwood, *Marsden—Survivor*, 86.
308 Crimmins, 'Search', 83; referring to Albion, *Forests*, 46.
309 For this paragraph, see Albion, *Forests*, Ch. 8, and 47, 55ff., 59.
310 Albion, *Forests*, 58. Timber costs: 1793–1802: £20 to £21 per ton; 1803: £34.10; 1805: £36 — the maximum price ever.
311 Albion, *Forests*, 74, 245, 319–324.
312 Albion, *Forests*, 46, 245, 317–24.
313 Albion, *Forests*, 46, 319.
314 For this paragraph, Albion, *Forests*, 321, 323, 365, 379–81, 393. For the history of

shipbuilding in Bombay, see Wadia, *The Bombay Dockyard*.
315   This is not surprising, him being from the merchant marine. Advances in design were found in the East India Company, the Merchant Marine, and foreign navies, long before the Royal Navy adopted them; see Albion, *Forests*, 80.
316   Paine, *Journal*, 73.
317   Paine, *Journal*, App.2, 74 = PRO, ADM 106/2229:222–4; 30 Mar 1802.
318   Crimmins, 'Search', 84–85. Crimmins' essay explains the reasons for this failure.
319   Crimmins, 'Search', 87.
320   Crimmins, 'Search', 84. See Albion, *Forests*, Chapter 9.
321   Albion, *Forests*, 346; cf. 304, 365; 400–401.
322   Government and General Order, 7 May 1803 (*HRA* 1.4, 340 and *HRNSW* 5.107; = Col.Sec. 6037 SZ 991, p.17). Also published in *SG* 15/5/1803.

CHAPTER 4

1   P.G. King reports a bill for £103.0.0 drawn on the Treasury for Mr Thomas Moore, June 30 1803, in a group listed as paid for 'Grain and Swine's Flesh' between 1 April and 30 June; Gov. King to Hobart, 1 Mar 1804, Encl. 4: Account of Bills, 1801–1803 (*HRA* 1.4.474); Gov. King to Hobart, 1 Mar 1804 [#2]: Encl. No 1: Treasury in Account Current with John Palmer, 31 Dec 1803 (*HRA* 1.4.521); Encl. No 2: List of Bills drawn on Treasury by J. Palmer (*HRA* 1.4.522, cf. 529).
2   Gov. P.G. King to Hobart, 9 May 1803 (*HRA* 1.4.143; *HRNZ* 1.246).
3   Cited from Russell, *Thomas Moore*, 10.
4   Hunter Return of Labour, 1797 (*HRNSW* 3.337; = Paine, *Journal*, 68, App. 1, doc. 3). The seasoning shed—used for planks and deals which, unlike masts which were kept in ponds, had to be kept out of the weather (Albion, *Forests*, 63)—is probably that seen to the right of the vessel on the stocks in Edward Dayes', 'View of Sydney Cove—1804' (Plate 27).
5   Navy Board to Sec. of Board of Admiralty, 26 May 1802 (PRO, ADM 106/2229, p.388; = Paine, *Journal*, 83–84, App.2, doc. 8).
6   Memorandum concerning New South Wales, [1804?] (*HRNSW* 7.249; *HRNZ* 1.291).
7   Albion, *Forests*, x, xi.
8   Frost, *Convicts and Empire*, summarised in Hughes, *Fatal Shore*, Ch. 2; Cf. Russell, *Thomas Moore*, 3.
9   Fletcher, 'Sydney Town', 7. The many observations made on timber by early arrivals shows how much this need was on the agenda; e.g. Pickersgill on Cook's voyage 5 May 1770 (*HRNSW* 1.1.215); on Norfolk Island (1.2.126, 187, 429); on NSW by Phillip (1.127–8), Ross (1.172–3), an officer (1.222), on the Nepean (1.306, 710), etc.
10   Albion, *Forests*, 180–181.
11   Crimmins, 'Search', 112.
12   Crimmins, 'Search', 113. Crimmins does not mention Australia, but the argument holds just as well.
13   Albion, *Forests*, 15–16, 30–33, 399.
14   Albion, *Forests*, 33, 361, 364.
15   Crimmins, 'Search', 85.
16   Crimmins, 'Search', 109.
17   See Crimmins, 'Search', 94, cf. 105.
18   Albion, *Forests*, 100, 80–81. W. Raven to Lieut.–Gov. King, 2 Nov 1793 (*HRNSW* 2.94–96).

ENDNOTES 417

19 Russia had a similar system.
20 For this paragraph, see Albion, *Forests*, 60–63, 322.
21 'In an area hitherto untapped for naval stores the customary contract could hardly apply and the Board employed agents, first to look for timber, hemp and other articles, and then to negotiate suitable terms', Crimmins, 'Search', 85. Parliament had denied *martelage* in England, yet an Act of 1729 virtually imposed it on English colonies. Originally American leases did not have reservation of timber to the crown, but the 1729 Act corrected this, causing affront to the colonists. See Albion, *Forests*, 230, 232, 250, 254–5, Ch. 6.
22 Albion, *Forests*, 290.
23 See lease James Redman/ Mary Marlborough/ T. Moore, and the Schäffer lease on 'the Vineyard', one of first in NSW (Moore: Moore Papers); as well as the lease governing Moore's 470 acres in the Bulanaming district (Hunter, Land Grant to Thomas Moore, 5 Oct 1799 [ML: R. Wardell papers, MS A 5330, item 6]). Governor King later judged that the phrase 'that may grow hereafter' was preventing people from planting 'exotic' trees, such as the oak, to the detriment of future generations. He therefore modified the wording of the lease to make an exception of exotic trees planted by the lease–holder, which could be reserved for their own use, or, should they choose not to use the timber, with the Government taking first offer at a fair valuation. See Government and General Order printed in *SG* 7/7/1805; and Gov. King to Earl Camden, 20 July 1805 (*HRNSW* 5.659).
24 Governor Hunter's Instructions, 23 June 1794, item 10 (*HRA* 1.1.523–524).
25 Hunter to Portland, 12 Nov 1796, Order dated 8 Dec 1795 (*HRA* 1.1.683).
26 Phillip to Dundas, 19 Mar 1792 (*HRA* 1.1.337). Whilst Administrator, Captain Paterson also permitted the *Experiment* to take a cargo of timber to India, but this was mahogany and cedar, clearly sent in the hope of future trade, not in the interests of the naval timber crisis. Paterson to Dundas, 21 Mar 1795 (*HRA* 1.1.491): 'I have permitted the master of the *Experiment* to take with him a cargo of mahogany and cedar of this country, in the hope that if it should prove valuable in India it may be of advantage to his Majesty's interest in any future intercourse with that country which may be directed by Government'. Given the previous shipment on the *Gorgon*, Russell, *Thomas Moore*, 14, is not strictly correct in citing that of the *Glatton* as 'the first shipment', unless he meant the first *under Thomas Moore's supervision*.
27 Phillip to Sec. Stephens, 16 Nov 1791 (*HRA* 1.1.304); Cf. Phillip to Nepean, 18 Nov 1791 (*HRA* 1.1.308). Once the samples had arrived in July, they were then tested for their qualities. Sec. Stephens to Gov. Phillip 21 July 1792; Received by Lieut.–Gov. Grose 16 Jan 1793 (*HRA* 1.1.368): 'The specimens of the timber of New South Wales which you sent in the *Gorgon* have been received, and trials will be made of their qualities'.
28 Ex-Gov. Hunter to Under Sec. King, 22 Mar 1802 (*HRNSW* 4.729).
29 Ex-Gov. Hunter to Under Sec. King, 22 Mar 1802 (*HRNSW* 4.730).
30 Board of Admiralty to Home Secretary, 4 April 1802 (PRO CO 201/23: ff.171–2; = Paine, *Journal*, 83, App. 2, doc. 7). After speaking of having ordered the *Glatton* to be prepared to convey Convicts to NSW, the letter then proceeds: 'As it is highly expedient from the Scarcity of Timber in this County that every opportunity should be taken for procuring Timber for His Majesty's Dockyards, and as we have reason to believe that Supplies to any extent may without difficulty by [sic] obtained from New South Wales, it is our intention that the Ships to be employed in conveying the Convicts thither should bring home as much Timber as they can conveniently contain,' adding that they have therefore enclosed instructions to the Governor 'by the first Opportunity to employ the Convicts under his direction in preparing the Timber in the manner proposed to the Navy Board previously to

the arrival of the *Glatton*, that her Detention there may be of as short duration as possible'.
31 Navy Board to Secretary of the Board of Admiralty, 26 May 1802 (PRO ADM 106/2229, p.388; = Paine, *Journal*, 83–84, App. 2, doc. 8).
32 Navy Board to Under Sec. of State, 11 June 1802 (PRO CO 201/23: f.305; = Paine, *Journal*, 84, App.2, doc. 9).
33 Secretary of War to Governor King, 29 Aug 1802 (PRO CO 202/6: ff.54; = Paine, *Journal*, 84, App. 2, doc. 10).
34 *SG* 19/3/1803.
35 *SG* 27/11/1803. Collins was appointed in January and received his instructions on 7 February; Lord Hobart to Admiralty 15 Jan 1803; Lord Hobart to Lieut-Gov Collins, 7 Feb 1803 (*HRNSW* 5.4, 16).
36 Gov. King to Lieut. Bowen, 28 March 1803 (*HRNSW* 5.76). King to Hobart, 9 May 1803, Encl. 3: Instructions to Lieut. Bowen 28 Mar 1803 (*HRA* 1.4.152). In 1805, Paterson reported the discovery of sassafras near Port Dalrymple, more fit for boats than others he had previously seen; Paterson to King, 21 Feb 1805 (*HRNSW* 5.555).
37 *SG* 26/3/1803.
38 *SG* 2/4/1803.
39 *SG* 10/4/1803.
40 *SG* 17/4/1803.
41 *SG* 24/4/1803.
42 *SG* 1/5/1803.
43 *SG* 15/5/1803; *SG* 22/5/1803: 'Sailed on Tuesday for England, His Majesty's Ship *Glatton*, with the *Greenwich* and *Venus* whalers'.
44 King to Hobart, 9 May 1803, Encl.11 (*HRA* 1.4.105). The full invoice listing types and dimensions of timber was sent to Nepean, see King to Nepean, 9 May 1803, Encl. 2 (*HRA* 1.4.253–258).
45 King also enclosed a request to the Commissioners of the Navy for payment for work done on, and for stores supplied to, the *Glatton*, the *Porpoise*, the *Buffalo*, and the *Lady Nelson*, and apprising the Commissioners of the delay at receiving orders, the timber samples placed on the *Glatton*, and his intention to make ready timber for the next vessel. He also requests a report on the timber sent by the *Glatton*. King to the Commissioners of the Navy, 9 May 1803 (*HRA* 1.4.269).
46 T. Moore to Gov. P.G. King, 13 May 1803, [Encl.] King to Nepean 9 May 1803 (*HRA* 1.4.265); (ML: King Papers A1980–2, pp.100–102).
47 Gov. King to Hobart, 9 May 1803 (*HRA* 1.4.145–146, cf. 106).
48 Gov. King to Hobart, 9 May 1803, Encl. 4: Survey of the Hulk Supply (*HRA* 1.4.154).
49 King to Hobart, 'Marine', 9 May 1803 (*HRA* 1.4.145–146).
50 King to Nepean, 9 May 1803, Encl. 1(a): Colnett to King, 7 April 1803 (*HRA* 1.4.252).
51 King to Nepean, 9 May 1803, Encl. 1(b): King to Colnett, 7 April 1803 (*HRA* 1.4.253).
52 King regarded himself as having been ill-treated by Captain Colnett as Governor; Gov. King to Nepean, 13 May 1803 (*HRA* 1.4.271–272). For the Whittle incident, see Encl. No 5 and 8 (*HRA* 1.4.273, 275). Other issues such as the amount of beef delivered to the ship, advice given or not given by Colnett to King, the supply or not of indents, whether or not Colnett has insulted King and the colony, whether or not King's Secretary had betrayed Colnett's confidences; disputes over purser's receipts, Colnett's failure to dine with King nor furnish an explanation for this action, Colnett refusing to take individual receipts for convicts landed, a deficiency of supplies landed; the stowage of plants for Sir Joseph Banks; the attribution of a lie to King's secretary Chapman; etc. King later attributes Colnett's

ENDNOTES 419

'unofficer-like conduct' to his own refusal to grant 100 acres at King's Island to Colnett; and to his refusal to grant 'a free pardon to a female convict for life, who had never left the *Glatton* or the captain's cabin'; King to Hobart, 20 Dec 1804 (*HRNSW* 5.525, note*), and King to Banks,—Dec 1804 (*HRNSW* 5.529). King's refusal to allow a meeting of freemasons from the colony may also be an additional factor in the friction (*HRNSW* 5.106, 150, 451).

53 King to Nepean, 9 May 1803, Encl. No 7 & 13: King to Colnett, 4 and 9 May 1803 (*HRA* 1.4.274, 278–279). Recall that the Navy Board had wanted Wickey to act as Moore's assistant, see above.
54 King to Nepean, 13 May 1803, Encl. 12: Colnett to King, 9 May 1803 (*HRA* 1.4.278).
55 King to Nepean, 13 May 1803, Encl. 15: King to Colnett, 10 May 1803 (*HRA* 1.4.281).
56 King to Nepean, 13 May 1803, Encl. 16: Colnett to King, 11 May 1803 (*HRA* 1.4.281).
57 King to Nepean, 13 May 1803, Encl. 17: King to Colnett, 11 May 1803 (*HRA* 1.2.281).
58 Government and General Order, 17 May 1803 (*HRNSW* 5.150).
59 *SG* 22/5/1803: 'Sailed on Tuesday for England, His Majesty's ship *Glatton*, with the *Greenwich* and *Venus* whalers'.
60 Captain Colnett to Lord Hobart, 7 Nov 1803 (*HRNSW* 5.253).
61 Master Shipwright, Woolwich Dockyard, to Navy Board, 9 March 1805 (PRO ADM 106/1791; = Paine, *Journal*, 94–95, App.2, doc. 22).
62 *SG* 12/6/1803.
63 Flinders had sent a previous survey: M. Flinders to Gov. King, 10 June 1803, Encl. No 1 & 2: Survey of *Investigator* (*HRA* 1.4.370–373).
64 Survey of H.M. Sloop *Investigator*, 14 June 1803 (*HRA* 1.4.374–375). The *Investigator*'s bottom did, in fact, get home to England, causing King to hope that 'no carping cur will cast any censure on [Flinders]' as a result; Gov. King to Sir J. Banks, 21 July 1805 (*HRNSW* 5.671).
65 *SG* 12/6/1803.
66 Government and General Order, 21 June 1803 (*HRNSW* 5.156–157). *SG* 26/6/1803.
67 King to Nepean, 7 Aug 1803, Encl. No 6 & 7: Survey of HMS *Porpoise* (*HRA* 1.4.378–379).
68 For this paragraph: King to Nepean, 7 Aug 1803: Encl. No 4 (16 June), 6 (6 & 9 July), 7 (10 July), 8 (11 July), & 13 (19 July) (*HRA* 1.4.376–382).
69 *SG* 17/7/1803: 'The Lady Nelson was hauled on shore at the Dock-yard to repair a part of the Fore-foot which had been carried away in coming round Bennelong's Point'.
70 *SG* 10/7/1803. She arrived on Wednesday 6 July. News had arrived earlier that the *Albion* and *Venus* were expecting to be in Port Jackson to refit by June; *SG* 5/3/1803.
71 Scott, 'Scottish Martyrs' Farms', 167. Palmer sold his own farm to Eber Bunker on 17 March 1800 for £90. Hodgkinson, *Eber Bunker*, 7, 12.
72 *SG* 17/7 & 20/11/1803; see also 4/3/1804.
73 Ryan, *Land Grants*, 237 (No 101, Hobby), 239 (No 115, Bunker: Gov. King's lease, 26 Aug 1803, for 14 years); cf. 260 (No 258, Bunker: same lease renewed for 14 years by Paterson, 20 June 1809).
74 *SG* 2/9/1804.
75 *SG* 14/8/1803.
76 King to Nepean, 7 Aug 1803 (*HRA* 1.4.368–369, 370).
77 Hodgkinson, *Eber Bunker*, 9.
78 *SG* 4/9 and 9/10/1803.
79 E. Bunker to Gov. King, 5 Oct 1803 (*HRNSW* 5.231).
80 Hodgkinson, *Eber Bunker*, 11. Ryan, *Land Grants*, 169 (No 1194, Lewin), 170 (No 1199, Bunker). On 11 August Lewin received 100 acres in Parramatta; p.176 (No 1252). He

didn't make much of the farm, being too pre-occupied with his journeyings in pursuit of his art; Mander-Jones, 'Lewin, John William (1770–1819)'.
81 J.T. Bigge Report 2250 (Mitchell: BT Box 5); Hodgkinson, *Eber Bunker*, 12.
82 King to Hobart, 17 Sept 1803 (*HRNSW* 5.221). Prior to leaving England, her Captain had requested the equipment needed 'to procure and load timber', including some 'timber measures', presumably for the procurement of crooked timber; see Captn. Woodriff to Nepean, 22 Nov 1802 (*HRNSW* 4.910).
83 King to Sir Joseph Banks, Sept 1803 (*HRNSW* 5.229).
84 King to Hobart, 31 Oct 1803 (*HRNSW* 5.247).
85 Lieut.-Gov. Collins to Gov. King, 5 Nov 1803 (*HRNSW* 5.247).
86 *SG* 27/11/1803. D. Woodriff, *Journal of HMS Calcutta*, entries for 6 and 7 November (*HRNSW* 5.236).
87 D. Woodriff, *Journal of HMS Calcutta*, entries for 13 & 15 Dec (*HRNSW* 5.239). *SG* 27/11/1803.
88 Collins to King, 5 Nov 1803 (*HRNSW* 5.247).
89 Tilghman, 'Woodriff, Daniel (1756–1842)'.
90 D. Woodriff, *Journal of HMS Calcutta*, 9 Oct to 15 Dec 1803 (*HRNSW* 5.232–239).
91 *SG* 27/11/1803.
92 Gov. King to Lieut.-Gov. Collins, 30 Dec 1803; Shipping Return 30 June—31 Dec (*HRNSW* 5.281, 288, cf. 317 n.).
93 Elizabeth Bass to George Bass, 8 Oct 1803 (Mitchell—Waterhouse Papers: ZML MSS 6544 [Safe 1/187] CY 3970).
94 Elizabeth Bass to George Bass, 19 Oct 1803 (Mitchell—Waterhouse Papers: ZML MSS 6544 [Safe 1/187] CY 3970), [screen 467].
95 Yarwood, 'Johnston, George (1764–1823)'; 'Johnston, George (1790–1820)'. Ryan, *Land Grants*, 102: No 707, Andrew Connelly and two others, 1 May 1797, 75 acres on the banks of the Hawkesbury, Mulgrave Place. This is the only Connelly (any spelling) on the Colonial Secretary's index whose dates make him a likely candidate (Col.Sec. Fiche 3267; 9/2731 p.86). George Junior was still away in 1808, when Robert Townson complained about Major Johnston granting land to his eldest son who 'was not at this time in the colony; he is only a lad of about 17 years of age'; Dr Townson to Castlereagh, 5 Sept 1808 (*HRNSW* 6.739).
96 Andrew Douglas White to Mrs Elizabeth Bass, 7 Aug 1820: 'I have also received a letter from Mr Moore dated Feb 7th last [1820] … Mr Moore mentions in his letter to me the death of my old school fellow and early friend George Johnston, he died in consequence of [?] severe fall from his horse and was buried the day Mr Moore's letter was written'. Quoted from Nelson, 'John White', 196 n.68.
97 Nelson, 'John White', 167.
98 Yarwood, 'Johnston, George (1790–1820)'.
99 *SG* 20/11/1803.
100 Gov. King to Hobart, 9 May 1803 (*HRA* 1.4.145–146).
101 *SG* 11/12/1803. For Aicken's appointment see *SG* 4/12/1803.
102 Calculation of the Value of Government Stock Alienated to Individuals, 1806 (ML: King Papers, vol. 9, pp.161 a–b).
103 *SG* 5/2/1804.
104 Government and General Order, 18 Feb 1804 (Col. Sec. 6037 SZ 992 p.11).
105 King to Hobart, 1 Mar 1804 (*HRNSW* 5.340). For the recommendation of a pay rise see Gov. King to Hobart, 9 May 1803 (*HRA* 1.4.145–146).
106 King to Hobart, 1 Mar 1804 (*HRA* 1.4.540).

ENDNOTES   421

107 King to Hobart, 1 Mar 1804 (*HRNSW* 5.337–338). The second extract is also found in Paine, *Journal*, App. 1, doc. 10.
108 King to Hobart, 1 Mar 1804 (*HRNSW* 5.338).
109 *SG* 4/3/1804.
110 *SG* 25/3/1804.
111 Loane is mistaken in the claim that Moore 'lived on a grant which he had been given beside the Tank Stream, on what became the southern side of Bridge Street in Sydney. This was a three-acre orchard and the centre of his business activities'; Loane, 'Moore, Thomas', 254–255.
112 See Yarwood, *Marsden—Survivor*, 95–97.
113 Gov. King's rough notes, 2 Jan 1806 (*HRNSW* 6.9).
114 For the Governor's vote of thanks for the *Calcutta*'s services, see *SG* 11/3/1804. For the departure, *SG* 18/3/1804; Shipping Return, 31 Dec 1804 (*HRNSW* 5.534).
115 Government and General Order 2 April 1804 (*HRNSW* 5.365).
116 Henry Waterhouse to Thomas Moore, 20th Oct 1804 (Moore: Waterhouse Papers).
117 *SG* 25/3/1804.
118 Hainsworth, *Sydney Traders*, 2.
119 Hickson, 'Cox, William (1764–1837)'.
120 *SG* 10 & 24/4, 1, 8 & 22/5, 26/6, 3/7, 7 & 21/8/1803; 31/3, 7 & 14/4/1805.
121 Affadavit from William Cox re Waterhouse's debt to him, 9 March 1808 (0851 CH, Item 4, doc. 3).
122 Thomas Moore's Business Notebook (Rear) (SDA: 0884 CH, Item 1), 10 (Chace), 14 (Simter), 16 (Raven), 22 (Leith), 34 (Simter and Leith again).
123 Captn Wm Raven a/c to T. Moore, 17/2/1819 (SDA: 0853 CH, Item 15, doc. 10). For the debt, see Thomas Moore's Business Notebook (Rear) (SDA: 0884 CH, Item 1), 16, '2 May 1805, By account of Bills on Mrs Mathers, £200'.
124 T. Moore (0884 CH, Item 6 [Rear], [p.22] 25; (SDA: 0884 CH, Item 1 [Rear], 67–68). Cox paid his first repayment in January 1828, £150.
125 *SG* 8/7/1804.
126 *SG* 2/9/1804.
127 *SG* 23/9/1804.
128 *SG* 8/7/1804: 'All persons indebted to Captain Rowley, as Agent to Mr Wm Tough, are hereby required to adjust their Accounts on or before the 31st proximo, as a final arrangement is about to take place'.
129 Hobart to King, 16 May 1803 (*HRA* 1.4.284). A circular letter, per whalers *Adonis* and *Alexander*; acknowledged by Governor King, 15 May 1804.
130 Hobart to King, 17 May 1803, Encl.: Instructions for Courts of Admiralty (*HRA* 1.4.299). Acknowledged by King 15/5/1804.
131 King to Nepean, 14 May 1804, and Encl. No 2 (*HRA* 1.4.633, 634–635).
132 *SG* 5/5/1804.
133 Government and General Order, 4 July 1804 (*HRNSW* 5.392). It was reported in August: King to Hobart, 14 Aug 1804, Encl No 3: Return of Land (*HRNSW* 5.432–433).
134 In 1800 he had a flock of 40 sheep, but by the following year, they were all gone; Baxter, *Musters & Lists. 1801–1802*, List 2 (1800), items AB010–012, compared with List 7 (1802), item AG478.
135 Moore never advertised the services of his stallions in the *Gazette* as others did, although he may have provided the services by private arrangement.
136 Thomas Moore's Business Notebook (SDA: 0884CH, Item 1).

137 Binney, *Horsemen of the First Frontier*, 93.
138 *SG* 2/9/1804.
139 *SG* 20/5, 8 & 29/7, 26/8/1804. Hodgkinson, *Eber Bunker*, 11; Hainsworth, *Sydney Traders*, 150.
140 *SG* 3/10/1805. Hodgkinson, *Eber Bunker*, 12–13.
141 Thomas Moore's Business Notebook (Rear) (SDA: 0884 CH, Item 1), 26, cf. 29.
142 Statement of HM Ships and Colonial Vessels, 4 Aug 1804 (*HRNSW* 5.436).
143 King to Sullivan, 21 Aug 1804 (*HRNSW* 5.451).
144 *SG* 28/10/1804.
145 King to Hobart, 20 Dec 1804 (*HRNSW* 5.526).
146 King to Hobart, 20 Dec 1804 (*HRNSW* 5.527). King added the note: 'A quantity is now collecting for the next opportunity'.
147 *SG* 23/12/1804.
148 Henry Waterhouse to Thomas Moore, 20 Oct 1804 (Moore: Waterhouse Papers).
149 Fletcher, 'Balmain, William (1762–1803)'; Hodkingson, *Eber Bunker*, 7.
150 New South Wales Corps, Officers Muster Roll 25 Dec 1792 to 24 June 1793 (*HRNSW* 2.49).
151 Presumably the news was fairly recent when Samuel Marsden wrote: 'I am truly sorry to hear of the death of Mrs. Goff & also of poor Milbah Johnson—both Mr. and Mrs. Johnson would be greatly afflicted', S. Marsden to Miss Mary Stokes, 13 Mar 1804; Mackaness, *Some Private Correspondence*, #13.
152 Macintosh, *Richard Johnson*, 46–47.
153 He did not commence at Charterhouse until the following year, in March 1806. Charterhouse Register 1769–1872, p.401.
154 Andrew Douglas White's handwriting books 1 & 2 (SDA: 0884 CH, Items 2 & 3).
155 Thomas Moore, Commission as Lieutenant, Loyal Sydney Volunteer Association, 2 March 1805 (SDA: 0851 CH, Item 2, doc. 2). If he had previous militia experience as a young man, this would not be 'his first experience in the militia'; *pace* Robinson, 'Thomas Moore—Early Life', 185 (21).
156 Government and General Order 2 April 1804 (*HRNSW* 5.365).
157 Return of Land, August 1805 (*HRNSW* 5.684–685).
158 [P.G. King], Present State of His Majesty's Settlements in NSW, 12 Aug 1806 (*HRNSW* 6.143).
159 B.–Maj. Johnston to Gov. King, 24 April 1805 (*HRNSW* 5.593).
160 *SG* 31/3/05. Smyth's 470 acre grant eventually came to the Bishop of Australia as a bequest for a church in Bulanaming from Robert Campbell, who had gained the property as a result of an agreement with John Palmer, dated 30 and 31 December 1808; Indenture between Robert Campbell and Bishop of Australia, 7 Dec 1837 (SDA: Registrar's Office–Correspondence, 1994/18/3). It was described in this document as butting on the Northwest to the grants of Thomas Moore and John Fincham, the latter receiving 30 acres on 12 Nov 1799; Ryan, *Land Grants*, 125 (No 877).
161 Statement of Officers on the Civil Establishment, 30 April 1805 (*HRNSW* 5.611).
162 Gov. King to Earl Camden, 30 April 1805 (*HRNSW* 5.610).
163 P.G. King to Lieut. Symons, T. Moore & F. Gardner, 10 April 1805 (ML: King Papers, vol. 8, 281; A 1980–2).
164 P.G. King to J. Harris & T. Moore, 26 May 1805 (Col.Sec. 6020, 4/1093.1, pp.132–134); *SG* 26/5/1805.
165 Lieut. Symons, T. Moore & F. Gardner to P.G. King, 11 April 1805 (ML: King Papers,

vol. 8, 282–288; A 1980–2).
166 P.G. King to T. Moore, 2 May 1805 (Col.Sec. 6020 4/10931, p.119).
167 T. Rowley to H. Waterhouse, 16 May 1805 (SDA: 0851 CH, Item 4, doc. 2).
168 Lord was Rowley's assigned servant which helped him gain a footing in Sydney trading circles.
169 Rowley had purchased two of the Spanish Rams that Waterhouse brought back from the Cape, and in August 1805 he had a total of 519 sheep; Gov. King to Earl Camden, 10 Oct 1805, Encl. No 4: T. Rowley to Gov. King, 9 August 1805 (*HRNSW* 5.703).
170 T. Rowley to H. Waterhouse, 16 May 1805 (SDA: 0851 CH, Item 4, doc. 2).
171 W. Campbell to P.G. King, 25 May 1805 (Col.Sec. 6020, 4/1093.1, p.132); *SG* 26/5/1805.
172 P.G. King to J. Harris & T. Moore, 26 May 1805 (Col.Sec. 6020, 4/1093.1, pp.132–134); *SG* 26/5/1805.
173 *SG* 26/5/1805.
174 Government and General Order, 26 May 1805 (*HRNZ* 1.257–258); *SG* 26/5/1805.
175 Gov. King to Under–Sec. Cooke, 31 Dec 1805 (*HRNZ* 1.258–259).
176 Gov. King's rough notes, 2 Jan 1806 (*HRNSW* 6.6–7).
177 *SG* 22/2/1807, he travelled by the *Star* to Tahiti, along with his friend, who also had a namesake in the colony: 'Simon Lord and Thomas Moore, Otaheitans'. Cf. the aboriginal Tom Rowley who travelled on the *Britannia* in 1795.
178 *SG* 22/1/1814. For the formation of this Society, see Bolt, *William Cowper*, 118–121.
179 W. Campbell to P.G. King, 5 June 1805 (Col.Sec. 6020, 4/1093.1, p.134).
180 P.G. King to T. Moore, R. Best, A. Forest, P. Skelton, 28 June 1805 (ML: King Papers, vol. 8, p.266; A 1980–2).
181 *SG* 22/9/1805.
182 'This was a well–known vessel, which I found here on my arrival in the colony, for she had been detained by Governor King for piratically taking two Spanish vessels on the coast of Peru. I brought out orders for her release and she was given up accordingly, and sailed on the 28th January, 1807'. Gov. Bligh to Castlereagh, 30 June 1808 (*HRNSW* 6.671; *HRA* 1.6.535).
183 Gov. King to Earl Camden, 20 July 1805 (*HRNSW* 5.659).
184 Return of Ships entered Inwards, 31 Mar 1805 to 31 Dec; Return of Ships cleared Outwards, 31 Mar 1805 to 31 Dec (*HRNSW* 5.745, 746). The *Sydney* left on 5 October, initially for the Derwent and Norfolk Island; *SG* 6/10/1805.
185 *SG* 22/9/1805.
186 *SG* 22/9/1805.
187 *SG* 22/9/1805.
188 [King, by handwriting], Present State of His Majesty's Settlements on the East Coast of New Holland, called New South Wales, 12 Aug 1806 (*HRNSW* 6.139). According to Russell, *Thomas Moore*, 15, Moore was appointed master shipwright in 1801.
189 [Joseph Banks, by handwriting], Some Observations on a Bill admitting the Produce of New South Wales to entry at the Customs–house of the United Kingdom, 7 July 1806 (*HRNSW* 6.108).
190 Return of Land, August 1805 (*HRNSW* 5.686–687). This is evidently where Loane, 'Moore, Thomas', 254–255, found evidence for Moore's 3 acre orchard, but I have not been able to confirm its location on the southern side of Bridge Street by the Tank Stream. Richard Johnson had ground there, and he kept an orchard. It would be an interesting connection if this was Johnson's orchard, and Moore took it over after Johnson left.

191 Ryan, *Land Grants*, 182 (No 1309, Moore); 115 (No 811, Smyth); 139 (No 964, Wilson).
192 Thomas Moore's Business Notebook (front) (SDA: 0884 CH, Item 1), 1.
193 A. Marsden to Gov. King, 17 Aug 1805 (*HRNSW* 5.683). John Fitzpatrick and Lawrence Fenlon also embarked under similar conditions.
194 *SG* 27/10/1805.
195 P.G. King to T. Moore, W. House, G. Best, E. Sharp, & W. Cousar, 20 Nov 1805 (ML: King Papers vol.8, pp. 277 and 279; A 1980–2). This was probably the William Cosar (Cossar) who was Master Builder at the Dockyard from 1812–1821; see *SG* 22/2/1812 and Russell, *Thomas Moore*, 27.
196 T. Moore, W. House, G. Best, E. Sharp, & W. Cousar to P.G. King, 30 Nov 1805 (ML: King Papers vol.8, pp. 278 and 280; A 1980–2).
197 T. Moore, Account of the Late Captn White, August 1840 (SDA: 0853 CH, Item 11, doc. 14). More noted that Andrew continued to draw on this interest for about thirty years.
198 Ryan, *Land Grants*, 219 (No 13), 252 (No 204).
199 Isaac Clementson to Thomas Moore, copy of 21/1/07, sent with 11/3/1807 (SDA: 0853 CH, Item 11, doc. 2). The accounts for the 10 September 1806 are on the reverse, which include payments for Master White's schooling, a payment to Captain Waterhouse, and petty disbursements, and salary.
200 Charterhouse Register 1769–1872, p.401, 'WHITE, Andrew Douglass'. John White's son Richard Hammond, also attended Charterhouse, and also in Watkinsons, commencing September 1809, the year after Andrew left.
201 Daniels, *Illustrated History of Methodism*, 75. Cf. Telford, *Popular History of Methodism*, 16: 'Charterhouse made the future Evangelist of England a sound scholar, and thus contributed largely to his influence'.
202 Attendance: *Charterhouse Register* 1769–1872, p.401; Moore's payment of fees: Isaac Clementson to Thomas Moore, 21 Feb 1807 (SDA: 0853 CH, Item 11, doc. 2).
203 Gov. King to Earl Camden, 22 Feb 1806 (*HRNSW* 6.21). For arrival date: Shipping Return, Inwards 1 Jan to 12 Aug 1806 (*HRNSW* 6.125).
204 Gov. King to Capt. Piper, 27 Feb 1806 (*HRNSW* 6.21).
205 Ryan, *Land Grants*, 201–202 (No 1466, Dwyer; No 1467, Devlin; No 1468, Byrne; No 1469, Mernagh; No 1470, Burke).
206 O'Donnell, 'Dwyer, Michael (1772?–1825)'.
207 Gov. King's rough notes, 2 Jan 1806 (*HRNSW* 6.8).
208 Gov. King to Earl Camden, 15 Mar 1806, Encl. No 2: Public Labour from 1 January to 31 December 1805 (*HRNSW* 5.43).
209 Gov. King to Earl Camden, 15 Mar 1806, Encl. No 3: General Statement of Inhabitants (*HRNSW* 5.44–45).
210 Spirit Ration under third class, ?1806–1808 (Col.Sec. 6041, 4/1721, pp.63–64).
211 G. Johnston to P.G. King, 18 Mar 1806; P.G. King to A. Forrest, T. Cuzens, & T. Moore, 21 Mar 1806; A. Forrest, T. Cuzens, & T. Moore to P.G. King, 22 Mar 1806 (Col.Sec. 6020, 4/1093.1, p.142–147).
212 H. Fulton to Capt. Piper, 27 May 1806 (*HRNSW* 6.81); Government and General Order, 13 April 1806 (*HRNSW* 6.69); H. Fulton to [Castlereagh], 20 July 1808 (*HRNSW* 6.696).
213 *SG* 13/4/1806.
214 For this paragraph, Canby, *History of Ships and Seafaring*, 72.
215 Government and General Order, 15 April 1806 (*HRNSW* 6.70).
216 *SG* 1/6/1806.

ENDNOTES 425

217 *SG* 1/6/1806.
218 *SG* 1/6/1806.
219 *SG* 8/6/1806.
220 Government and General Order, 8 June 1806 (*HRNSW* 6.91).
221 *SG* 15 and 22/6/1806.
222 The first record is 2 August [?1802], £20. On 25 November 1803 £10 was remitted to 'J. Moore Senr', costing £3 postage; with a further postage charge of £2-1 on 3 December, perhaps for letters. Raven remitted £10 for Moore to his father 23 Sept 1806, and the same amount to 'Mr Scott' on 9 July 1807, plus postage of letters (£5). This could be his sister Elizabeth's husband, Walter. Captn Wm Raven a/c to T. Moore, 17/2/1819 (SDA: 0853 CH, Item 15, doc. 10).
223 According to Joseph, she died 'after a sickness of 7 months'; Joseph Moore to his children, 20 Mar 1806 (SDA: 0853 CH, Item 11, doc. 1b).
224 Rev. Percival Stockdale to Sally [Clark], 18 Mar 1806 (SDA: 0853 CH, Item 11, doc. 1a).
225 This is evident from the many activities in which he is involved across the next months (see below).
226 Lesbury, St Mary's Burial Register, 4 Mar 1806 (Nbl RO: M246): 'Mary Moore, wife of Joseph Moore, Sexton of Lesbury, died March 2^d, buried March 4th, aged 78 years'. Despite the note to the 2nd, Joseph's letter says it was the 1st.
227 Joseph Moore to his children, 20 Mar 1806 (SDA: 0853 CH, Item 11, doc. 1b). It is attached to another letter to Sally from the Rev. Percival Stockdale, enclosing his epitaph for Mary. Rev. Percival Stockdale to Sally [Clark], 18 Mar 1806 (SDA: 0853 CH, Item 11, doc. 1a).
228 *SG* 10/8/1806; Ex.–Gov. King to Sec. Marsden, 6 Sept 1806 (*HRNSW* 6.185).
229 Shaw, 'King, Philip Gidley (1758–1808)'.
230 Castlereagh to Gov. King, 20 Nov 1805 (*HRNSW* 5.735).
231 King & King, *Philip Gidley King*, 142.
232 Shaw, 'King, Philip Gidley (1758–1808)'.
233 *SG* 10/8/1806. Hodgkinson, *Eber Bunker*, 14–15.
234 Ex. Gov. King to W. Windham, 6 Sept 1806 (*HRNSW* 6.185).
235 P.G. King to J. Oxley, T. Moore, H. Moore & A. Ferguson, 8 Aug 1806; J. Oxley, T. Moore, H. Moore & A. Ferguson Report of *Harrington* Survey, 9 Aug 1806 (Col.Sec. 6020, 4/1093.1, pp.156–157).
236 Statement of Colonial Vessels, 12 Aug 1806 (*HRNSW* 6.127).
237 [P.G. King], Present State of His Majesty's Settlements in NSW, 12 Aug 1806 (*HRNSW* 6.139).
238 Ex.–Gov. King to Gov. Bligh, 20 Aug 1806 (*HRNSW* 6.170).
239 T. Moore & R. Rouse, Public Works and Buildings, 13 Aug 1806 (*HRNSW* 6.163–164).
240 Boyce, *Thomas Moore*, 6, takes these references to show that 'at that time Moore's care for the well-being and general interests of the church'. This may be so, but not necessarily. This was simply a public survey, and the construction of these two early churches were under the direction of the Government.
241 Gov. King to Gov. Bligh, 12 Aug 1806; T. Moore to Gov. Bligh, 13 Aug 1806; Gov. Bligh to Sec. Marsden, 5 Nov 1806 (*HRA* 1.6.33–34).
242 *SG* 17/8/1806; Government and General Order, 15 Aug 1806 (*HRNSW* 6.167–168). Note that the *HRNSW* dates this order the 15th, and implies that the commission was read that day. King's prior announcement, and the *Gazette*, however, indicate it was on the 13th.

243 Address to Governor Bligh, 14 Aug 1806 (*HRNSW* 6.165–166).
244 Gov. Bligh to J. Houstoun, J. Oxley, Wm Jackson, J.H. Jackson & T. Moore, 18 Aug 1806; J. Houstoun, J. Oxley, Wm Jackson, J.H. Jackson & T. Moore to Gov. Bligh, 19 Aug 1806 (*HRA* 1.6.22–23.
245 [P.G. King], Present State of His Majesty's Settlements in NSW, 12 Aug 1806 (*HRNSW* 6.151).
246 Bp. of Derry to Archbp. Of Canterbury, 5 Aug 1807, Encl.: H. Fulton to Bp. of Derry, 1 Sept 1806 (*HRNSW* 6.276–277). In response, on June 30, 1808, Castlereagh wrote to Bligh to consider Fulton favourably, apparently with a complete lack of awareness that both Bligh and Fulton had been deposed; Castlereagh to Gov. Bligh, 30 June 1808 (*HRA* 1.6.584).
247 Free Settlers' Address to Governor Bligh, 22 Sept 1806 (*HRNSW* 6.188–189).
248 Hainsworth, *Sydney Traders*, 4–5.
249 Hainsworth, *Sydney Traders*, 5.

CHAPTER 5

1 Government and General Order, 15 Dec 1810 (Col.Sec. 6038, SZ758, p.135; *HRNSW* 7.468–471); *SG* 15/12/1810 and the 22nd.
2 Sydney Settlers' Address to Gov. Bligh, 22 Sept 1806; Hawkesbury Settlers' Address, 1806 (*HRNSW* 6.188–189, 190–192). The Hawkesbury address is undated, but likely to have been written at the same time as that from Sydney.
3 Hainsworth, *Sydney Traders*, 1–4, points out that the pioneers of the writing of Australian history drew a dichotomy between public-spirited Governors fighting on behalf of emancipist and free settlers pursuing agriculture, and a small group of Officer-Traders. This dichotomy was perpetuated by other writers, including a version in Evatt, *Rum Rebellion*, which has Bligh supporting the farmer against the trader. Fletcher's work on the Hawkesbury settlers and Hainsworth's on the Sydney Traders urges caution in too strictly drawing such a dichotomy. Fletcher, 'The Development of Small Scale Farming'.
4 *SG* 19/10/1806.
5 Byrnes, 'Thompson, Andrew (1773?–1810)'.
6 During the proceedings of his suit against Thompson, Macarthur tried to prove that Thompson had not lost as much actual grain as others had. Thompson showed that he had lost a great deal from debts in wheat that could now not be paid.
7 John Stogdell's drowning haunted Sydney for over fifty years. That the 1801 floods brought about his death became a benchmark for the severity of later Hawkesbury inundations, such as those of 1809 and 1811. His drowning found its place amongst the colony's 'memorable events' in an almanac of 1828, which was once again referred to in 1855 (*SG* 28/5/1809, 30/3/1811; *SMH* 13/4/1855 and *Maitland Mercury* 18/4/1855).
8 *SG* 16, 23 & 30/3/1806.
9 *SG* 30/3/1806.
10 *SG* 26/10 & 23/11/1806.
11 On 27 & 28 November the 'inclement heat' was 'highly injurious to vegetation', the temperature at 7 a.m. being 82° F, rising to 91° by 3 p.m.; *SG* 30/11/1806 (Supp. p.2).
12 His cases were heard 28, 30 Oct and 4 Nov 1806; 3 April 1807; Court of Criminal Judicature NSWSA 2/8148, pp.906–923, 959. See Evatt, *Rum Rebellion*, Chs. 18–22.
13 Macarthur v. Thompson [1806] NSWKR 3.

ENDNOTES 427

14 Macquarie Law notes on this case. Opinion is divided over who the 'villain' might be in the incident. Ellis, *John Macarthur*, 294–295, is strongly slanted against Thompson, following the version of events put forward by Macarthur in his later 'mock trial'. Evatt, *Rum Rebellion*, 106–109, argues that the law is not only on Thompson's side, but it also justifies Bligh's subsequent dismissal of Macarthur's appeal.
15 *SG* 2, 9 & 16/11/1806. Bread was becoming a scarce commodity, and bad weather preventing boats from coming down to Sydney further added to the supply of foodstuffs.
16 *SG* 4/1/1807.
17 Expenditure, 1 Jan to 31 Dec 1806 (*HRNSW* 6.233). In 1840 Moore wrote a note that he earned £90-5-0 salary from 1797 to 1808, omitting the extra pound; Thomas Moore, Account of the Late Captn White, August 1840 (SDA: 0853 CH, Item 11, doc 14).
18 This has dropped a little from 1800–1801, where the estimate allowed White was £112.0.0; Portland to Gov. King, June 1801. Encl.: Estimate of Charge for Civil Establishment of NSW from 10 Oct 1800 to 10 Oct 1801 (*HRNSW* 4.426).
19 Rienits, 'White, John (1756?–1832)'.
20 Shipping Return, 1 Jan to 30 June 1807 (*HRNSW* 6.272).
21 For an account from those suspicious of Campbell, due to his association with Macarthur, see those of Bligh and his supporter Henry Fulton; Gov. Bligh to Castlereagh, 30 June 1808 (*HRNSW* 6.671–672; *HRA* 1.6.535); H. Fulton to [Castlereagh], 20 July 1808 (*HRNSW* 6.696–697). For an account from one in sympathy with Macarthur's 'broad if frustrated' entrepreneurial vision; see Hainsworth, *Sydney Traders*, 67–70, whose lead is followed below.
22 The above follows Hainsworth, *Sydney Traders*, 67–69, who draws upon Macarthur and Blaxcell's instructions to Davidson, dated 12 Jan 1807, a copy of which is found in Appeals Court Papers, Campbell v. Macarthur 1822, NSW Archives X37, 4–7. For Hainsworth's edited transcript, see *Builders*, 35–37.
23 *SG* 15/2/1807.
24 Shaw, 'Bligh, William (1754–1817)'.
25 Bligh to Windham, 7 Feb 1807 (*HRNSW* 6, 250–251; *HRA* 1.6.124–125).
26 Marsden arrived in Portsmouth on 8 November. *The Morning Chronicle* 11/11/1807, published a report from Portsmouth, Nov. 9: 'The *Buffalo* storeship, Lieut. Bligh, arrived here yesterday from New South Wales'.
27 *SG* 15/2/1807.
28 Hickson, 'Cox, William (1764–1837)'.
29 Marsden sailed on 10 February and the advertisement was dated 7th; *SG* 15/2/1807.
30 Affadavit from W. Cox re his debt to Waterhouse, 9 Mar 1808 (SDA: 0851 CH, Item 4, doc. 3).
31 Second Address from Hawkesbury Settlers, 25 Feb 1807; cf. Government and General Order, 22 Feb 1807 (*HRNSW* 6.257, 255).
32 Government and General Order, 14 Feb 1807 (*HRNSW* 6.253). *SG* 15/2/1807.
33 H. Fulton to [Castlereagh], 20 July 1808 (*HRNSW* 6.696).
34 H. Fulton to [Castlereagh], 20 July 1808 (*HRNSW* 6.696).
35 H. Fulton to [Castlereagh], 20 July 1808 (*HRNSW* 6.697).
36 *SG* 22/3/1807.
37 Manuscripts in the Alnwick Castle Library: Observations on Live Stock (*HRNSW* 6.177–182): Horned cattle (pp.177–179); Sheep (pp.179–181); Horses (pp.181–182).
38 T. Moore's Account with Campbell & Co, 1806–1808 (SDA: 0851 CH, Item 6, doc. 3).
39 T. Moore's Business Notebook, front section (SDA: 0884CH, Item 1), p.1.

40 For the date of the agreement see the Appeal proceedings from Lord, 21 Aug 1811 (Col.Sec. 6042, 4/1724, p.49).
41 SG 15/5/1808. See 'Note on the production of this volume', in the *Facsimile Reproduction of Volumes Six and Seven*.
42 The Trial of John Macarthur, 2 Feb 1808 (*HRNSW* 6.485).
43 Atkinson, *Europeans*, 1.283.
44 Evatt, *Rum Rebellion*, 108–109.
45 SG 5/7/1807. Cf. The Trial of John Macarthur, 2 Feb 1808 (*HRNSW* 6.486).
46 SG 12/7/1807.
47 SG 26/7/1807.
48 Atkinson, *Europeans*, 1.287.
49 For this paragraph, see Evatt, *Rum Rebellion*, 110–120. The propensity to use convicts assigned to public service for private purposes also lies behind the need for Moore, as the Master Boat Builder of the colony, to supervise convict labour for the dockyards assigned to help on repairs of HM Ships, to 'see that it is not diverted to private purposes'; see Ex.–Gov. King to Gov. Bligh, 20 Aug 1806 (*HRNSW* 6.170).
50 Lord & Co to Gov. Bligh, 10 Aug 1807 (*HRNSW* 6.277–278); SG 16/8/1807.
51 Lieut. Minchin to Ex.-Gov. King, 20 Oct 1807 (*HRNSW* 6.331).
52 For the summary that follows, and the quotations, see Evatt, *Rum Rebellion*, 121–125. After Moore's death, Robert Campbell Junior became one of the first three Trustees of his Estate.
53 Fletcher, 'Harris, John (1754–1838)'.
54 Surgeon Harris to Ex.-Gov. King, 25 Oct 1807 (*HRNSW* 6.337). Governor Bligh had arrested Dwyer and several of his friends in February on charges of sedition, but they were acquitted. Bligh, however, was convinced that the Irishmen were guilty; see Gov. Bligh to W. Windham, 31 Oct 1807 (*HRNSW* 6.363; *HRA* 1.6.159). He also mentions that two of the men received corporal punishment and the whole gang were divided up between Norfolk Island, Derwent, Port Dalrymple, and Sydney. Cf. O'Donnell, 'Dwyer, Michael (1772?–1825)'.
55 Ex.-Gov. King to Cooke, 18 June 1808 (*HRNSW* 6.655).
56 Gov. Bligh to W. Windham, 31 Oct 1807 (*HRNSW* 6.359; *HRA* 1.6.155–156).
57 SG 19/4/1807; SG 7/6/1807.
58 Surgeon Harris to Ex.-Gov. King, 25 October 1807 (*HRNSW* 6.348), although his 'my dear Mrs King' indicates this section was apparently to the Governor's wife. See also Gov. Bligh to W. Windham, 31 Oct 1807 (*HRNSW* 6.363; *HRA* 1.6.159).
59 *HRNSW* Editor notes it arrived on 1 October 1807, or, as the *NSW Almanac 1808* put it, on '31st September'. Since the first part of Harris's letter was written on the same day as the ship was sighted, but dated 25th October, he must have taken a few weeks to complete it. The Shipping Return gives a different arrival date: '12 Nov, *Pegasus*, Master Thomas Graham, Prize to HMS *Cornwallis*, owned by Capt. Johnston, from the Coast of Peru, filled with general merchandise' (*HRNSW* 6.404; *HRA* 1.6.618). Although Cumpston, *Shipping Arrivals*, 62, gives both alternatives, the dating of the Harris letter proves that the return was wrong, or perhaps it provides the date of completing the discharge?
60 For this account of the *Santa Anna*, including the quotation, Hainsworth, *Sydney Traders*, 171.
61 Shipping Return (Inwards), 1 July to 31 Dec 1807 (*HRNSW* 6.404; *HRA* 1.6.618).
62 Abstract of Duties and Fees, 2 May to 31 Dec 1807 (*HRA* 1.6.620).
63 See the list in Hainsworth, *Sydney Traders*, 125: *Hunter* ex-*Bethlehem* (1799); *Anna Josepha*

(1800); *Santa Anna* (1806).
64   Account No 1 of *Pegasus*, 17 April 1808 to 10 October 1808 (SDA: 0852CH, Item 6, doc. 3).
65   Cf. Hainsworth, *Sydney Traders*, 40, who takes Lord's purchase of prize ships *Hunter* in 1799, and *Anna Josepha* in 1800 to demonstrate he was 'sufficiently established'. Raven's house was advertised for auction in *SG* 23 & 30/8/1807.
66   Gov. Bligh to W. Windham, 31 Oct 1807, Encl. No 1: Return of Land Sown &c (*HRNSW* 6.408–409; *HRA* 1.6.163, 165). Note the list confuses his horses, itemising 5 stallions and 1 mare, instead of vice versa —as his own List of Ages of Mares demonstrates.
67   Gov. Bligh to W. Windham, 31 Oct 1807, Encl. No 2: Statement of Government Buildings (*HRA* 1.6.163, 165, 169).
68   S. Marsden to Under-Sec. Cooke, 21 Nov 1807 (*HRNSW* 6.380–382).
69   S. Perceval to [unknown], 27 Dec 1807 (*HRNSW* 6.393). After becoming Prime Minister in October 1809, in 1812 Perceval became the only British Prime Minister to be assassinated.
70   Castlereagh to Gov. Bligh, 31 Dec 1807 (*HRNSW* 6.399–400).
71   P.G. King on Australian Timbers, Dec 1807 (*HRNSW* 6.397–398; *HRNZ* 1.286–287). Moore is in the background when King says, 'if the experience of those who have worked those woods can be relied on, from their making choice of it to build their vessels, it ought to be equally considered with the rest […]'.
72   *SG* 28/6/1807. Hoare had been indented to Captain Ralph Wilson, but had escaped in January purportedly to the Hawkesbury to fraudulently recover debts owing to Wilson; *SG* 18/1/1807; cf. *SG* 19/7/1807, where he had taken a note written in 1805 by Sarah Broadhurst to Wilson for £20.
73   Evatt, *Rum Rebellion*, 126–129.
74   Evatt, *Rum Rebellion*, 129; for the sequence of events, see pp. 126–128. For Bligh's account: Gov. Bligh to Castlereagh, 30 April 1808 (*HRNSW* 6.610–611). According to Bligh, the paper to Oakes read: 'I never will submit to the horrid tyranny that is attempted until I am forced; that I consider it with scorn and contempt, as I do the persons who have directed it to be executed'.
75   For what follows, see Evatt, *Rum Rebellion*, 137–139.
76   Evatt's legal argument considers that Macarthur would be found guilty in a court of law on the second and third counts, although on the first count only if the intention could be proven.
77   Evatt, *Rum Rebellion*, 142.
78   J. Macarthur to Gov. Bligh, 1 Jan 1808 (*HRNSW* 6.411–412); Judge-Adv. Atkins to J. Macarthur, 10 Jan 1808 (*HRNSW* 6.412).
79   Evatt, *Rum Rebellion*, 145.
80   Mrs Bligh to Sir J. Banks, 1 Feb 1808 (*HRNSW* 6.461).
81   Address of Settlers to Gov. Bligh, 1 Jan 1808 (*HRNSW* 6.410–411, which puts the number of signatories at 833; *HRA* 1.6, 542, which puts the number at 830). See also Andrew Thompson to Gov. Bligh, 1 Jan 1808 (*HRNSW* 6.410).
82   Boyce, *Thomas Moore*, 6, describes it as 'a very temperate and respectful letter to the Governor, asking that shipping here might have the same privileges as those in England, and that trial by jury might be instituted. Both requests appear most reasonable. Trial by jury! Does not the nature and spirit of the Englishman here show itself?'.
83   Trial of John Macarthur, 25 Jan 1808 (*HRNSW* 6.422; *HRA* 1.6.543).
84   Surveyor-Gen. Grimes to J. Macarthur, 13 Jan 1808 (*HRNSW* 6.413).
85   Evatt, *Rum Rebellion*, 146. What follows summarises his discussion, pp.146–151.

86 Judge-Adv. Atkins to Gov. Bligh, 26 Jan 1808 (*HRNSW* 6.432); *A Charge of Mutiny*, No. XVII, pp. 440–444.
87 Trial of John Macarthur, 25 Jan 1808 (*HRNSW* 6.422–427).
88 Trial of John Macarthur, 25 Jan 1808 (*HRNSW* 6.428–429).
89 Gov. Bligh to Each Member of Court, 26 Jan 1808; Gov. Bligh to Major Johnston, 26 Jan 1808 (*HRNSW* 6.433).
90 At Johnston's trial the Judge-Advocate put the number at one hundred and fifty; *A Charge of Mutiny*, 354.
91 Major Johnston to Keeper of His Majesty's Gaol; J. Macarthur & others to Major Johnston; Proclamation; Major Johnston to Gov. Bligh, all dated 26 Jan 1808 (*HRNSW* 6.433–434).
92 *A Charge of Mutiny*, 209.
93 *A Charge of Mutiny*, 210.
94 *A Charge of Mutiny*, 208, 210.
95 Address to Major Johnston, 8 Mar 1808 (*HRNSW* 6.534–535).
96 T. Arndell to Gov. Bligh, 6 Mar 1808 (*HRNSW* 6.533).
97 Address of Settlers to Major Johnston, 30 Jan 1808 (*HRNSW* 6.458–459).
98 Settlers to Lieut.-Gov. Paterson, 18 April 1808 (*HRNSW* 6.596).
99 Commissary Palmer to Gov. Bligh, 4 Nov 1808 (*HRA* 1.6.688).
100 Governor Macquarie appointed Moore as Magistrate of the George's River district in 1810.
101 Gov. Bligh to Castlereagh, 30 April 1808 (*HRNSW* 6.620; *HRA* 1.6.432).
102 Hawkey, *Bligh's Other Mutiny*, 105.
103 Their proper order on page two by column and number in column is: N. Bayly (1,2), T. Moore (1,9), T. Laycock (1,8), J. Gowen (5,4), N. Devine (2,14), W. Baker (either 2,13, or 1,15), J. Wilshire (5,3).
104 H. Fulton to [Castlereagh], 20 July 1808 (*HRNSW* 6.696).
105 *A Charge of Mutiny*, 217, 229. On 8 February meeting, Bunker subscribed £20 to send Macarthur to England; Subscriptions, 8 Feb 1808 (*HRNSW* 6.515).
106 As noted by Bligh in his summing up speech; *A Charge of Mutiny*, 393.
107 For hysteria over losing houses (*A Charge of Mutiny*, pp. 175 [Atkins], 351 [Abbott], 375 [Cox]); Gore testified there were less than 6 houses removed (p.98), Atkins 4 or 5 (p.169); Bligh's 'happy customers' were Meurant and Austin, and D.D. Mann was in negotiations (p.393); alongside Macarthur's conspicuous case, Bligh listed those forbidden to build as Lord, Nathaniel Lucas, McCoy, Sergt-Major Whittle and John Redman, explaining or denying each case as he did (p.394); Johnston doesn't mention Moore when asked about the issue (pp.56–60); neither does Kemp, who knows of only Macarthur's case (p.278), nor John Blaxland, who knows of only one, Perkins (p.295); Macarthur mentions only Blaxcell as sure knowledge to him (p.198), and that Whittle's house was threatened with destruction but still stood (according to A.F. Kemp, he made the lease over to Johnston for protection; p.228), but that no-one else was dispossessed except Macarthur himself (p.208).
108 *A Charge of Mutiny*, 362.
109 Ryan, *Land Grants*, 252 (No 204).
110 *A Charge of Mutiny*, 270–271.
111 Proclamation, 27 Jan 1808 (*HRNSW* 6.453; *HRA* 1.6.240–241).
112 *A Charge of Mutiny*, 269–270.
113 For the address, see *HRNSW* 6 following p.434 and for a 'true copy' Col.Sec. 6041, 4/1721, pp.336–337. Boyce, *Thomas Moore*, 7, mentions Moore signing this address, but Loane, 'Moore, Thomas', does not.

ENDNOTES 431

114 Government and General Order, 30 Jan 1808 (*HRA* 1.6.272).
115 Gov. Bligh to Castlereagh, 30 June 1808 (*HRNSW* 6.666).
116 Government and General Order, 31 Jan and 8 Feb 1808 (*HRNSW* 6.460; *HRA* 1.6.272, 272).
117 Gov. Bligh to Castlereagh, 30 June 1808 (*HRNSW* 6.671; *HRA* 1.6.534).
118 The Trial of John Macarthur, 4 Feb 1808 (*HRA* 1.6.323–324); Gov. Bligh to Castlereagh, 30 April 1808 (*HRNSW* 6.624).
119 Maj. Johnston to Castlereagh, 12 April 1808 (*HRNSW* 6.590).
120 Commissary Palmer to Gov. Bligh, 31 Aug 1808 (*HRNSW* 6.722).
121 Capt. Abbott to Ex-Gov. King, 13 Feb 1808 (*HRNSW* 6.832–833); Gov. Bligh to Castlereagh, 30 April 1808 and 30 June 1808 (*HRNSW* 6.625, 667). Henry James Washington to Sir Joseph Banks, 21 Sept 1808, published in the *National Register* 2/10/1808. Copy enclosed with E. McArthur to Sir Joseph Banks, 10 Oct 1808, along with McArthur's reply of 7 Oct 1808. Banks Papers. CY 3007/ 869–874. Online: http://www2.sl.nsw.gov.au/banks/series_43/43_05.cfm.
122 Gov. Bligh to Castlereagh, 30 June 1808 (*HRNSW* 6.667): Minchin, Lawson, Wentworth, E. Macarthur, G. Blaxland, Wm Moore, J. Harris, T. Jamison, R. Townson, I. Nichols, H. Kable. 'Besides these', he also lists: N. Bayly, G. Blaxcell, S. Lord. John Macarthur was not, at first, present, but sent for when the question of a delegate to England was raised.
123 Gov. Bligh to Castlereagh, 30 June 1808 (*HRNSW* 6.667).
124 Dando-Collins, *Captain Bligh's Other Mutiny*, 104–106.
125 Dando-Collins, *Captain Bligh's Other Mutiny*, 107.
126 Government and General Orders, 10, 12, 17 Feb 1808 (*HRNSW* 6.515, 521; *HRA* 1.6.273, 274).
127 Maj. Johnston to Castlereagh, 11 April 1808 (*HRA* 1.6.216).
128 Gov. Bligh to Major Johnston; N. Bayly to Gov. Bligh, 1 Feb, 1808 (*HRNSW* 6.460).
129 Johnston to Castlereagh, 11 April 1808 (*HRNSW* 6.583; *HRA* 1.6.216); See also *Charge of Mutiny* App. XIV, p.427. At Johnston's trial, Bligh insinuated that Macarthur was the real author of this despatch (*Proceedings*, 389, 391).
130 Nicholas Bayly to Governor Bligh, 11 Feb 1808 (*HRNSW* 6.516; *HRA* 1.6.247).
131 Governor Bligh to Major Johnston, 11 Feb 1808 (*HRNSW* 6.517–518; *HRA* 1.6.247–248).
132 Governor Bligh to Major Johnston, 11 Feb 1808 (*HRNSW* 6.517–518; *HRA* 1.6.247–248).
133 G. Johnston, Order & Report of Survey of the *Pegasus*, 18 Feb 1808 (*HRA* 1.6.250–251).
134 Government and General Order, 3 Mar 1808 (*HRNSW* 7.532; *HRA* 1.6.275); Loane, 'Moore, Thomas', 255, says 'a captain', but he was not one amongst many, but held the senior rank in Sydney. No commission from this time can be found amongst Moore's papers, although that presented him in July by Foveaux has survived; See T. Moore, Commission as Captain and Commandant, 31 July 1808 (SDA: 0851CH, Item 2, doc. 3). His old position of Lieutenant was filled on 17 June 1809 by William Gaudry; *SG* 18/6/1809: 'The LIEUTENANT GOVERNOR has been pleased to appoint Mr William Gaudry to be Lieutenant in the Loyal Sydney Volunteer Association, commanded by Captain Moore'.
135 Johnston to Castlereagh, 11 April 1808 (*HRNSW* 6.583; *HRA* 1.6.217); See also *Charge of Mutiny* App. XIV, p.427. (=Macarthur, see n.129 above).
136 Nicholas Bayly to Governor Bligh, 19 Mar 1808 (*HRNSW* 6.540).
137 Cf. Johnston to Castlereagh, 11 April 1808 (*HRNSW* 6.583; *HRA* 1.6.217); See also *Charge of Mutiny* App. XIV, p.427. (=Macarthur, see n.129 above).
138 Lieut. Symons to Maj. Johnston, 26 Mar 1808 (*HRNSW* 6.549–550).

139 Maj. Johnston to Lieut. Symons, 27 Mar 1808 (*HRNSW* 6.550–551).
140 Maj. Johnston to Lieut. Symons; Lieut. Symons to Maj. Johnston, 29 Mar 1808 (*HRNSW* 6.565).
141 N. Bayly to Gov. Bligh, 29 Mar 1808 (*HRNSW* 6.566).
142 Maj. Johnston to Castlereagh, 11 April 1808 (*HRA* 1.6.216).
143 Gov. Bligh to Maj. Johnston, 29 Mar 1808; N. Bayly to Gov Bligh, 30 Mar 1808; Gov. Bligh to Maj. Johnston, 30 Mar 1808; N. Bayly to Gov. Bligh, 30 and 31 Mar 1808 (*HRNSW* 6.565–566; 566–567).
144 Maj. Johnston to Castlereagh, 11 April 1808 (*HRA* 1.6.216). The *Harrington* arrived on 31 March; Return of Vessels (inward) during 1808 (*HRNSW* 6.818).
145 Settlers to Lieut.-Gov. Paterson, 18 April 1808 (*HRNSW* 6.596); Settlers to Maj. Paterson, [undated] (*HRNSW* 6.597), which calls Macarthur, 'the last man we would depute to represent us in any case whatever', 'the scourge of the colony by fomenting quarrels between His Majesty's officers, servants, and subjects, [whose] monopoly and extortion have been highly injurious to the inhabitants of every description'.
146 Maj. Johnston to Officers, 26 April 1808 (*HRNSW* 6.600–601; *HRA* 1.6.518). For the suggestion it came from Macarthur's pen, see G. Caley's 'Open Letter to George Johnston', G. Caley to Sir J. Banks, 7 July 1808 (*HRNSW* 6.689).
147 Officers to Maj. Johnston, 26 April 1808 (*HRNSW* 6.601–602; *HRA* 1.6.519–520).
148 Gov. Bligh to Castlereagh, 30 April 1808 (*HRNSW* 6.621; *HRA* 1.6.433).
149 Return of Vessels (inward) during 1808 (*HRNSW* 6.818); *SG* 22/5/1808.
150 Gov. Bligh to Castlereagh, 30 June 1808 (*HRNSW* 6.671–672; *HRA* 1.6.535). Bligh dates her arrival in Sydney to 31 March, which is also recorded on Return of Vessels (Inwards) during 1808, 30 Dec 1808 (*HRNSW* 6.818), although this Return also records the duplicate date of the 3rd, which is probably a mistake (no Captain is recorded for this entry either). Both times she is recorded as laden with Merchandise from China.
151 H. Fulton to [Castlereagh], 20 July 1808 (*HRNSW* 6.696–697).
152 Hainsworth, *Sydney Traders*, 69–70.
153 Hainsworth, *Sydney Traders*, 70 n.21. For Bligh's comment: Gov. Bligh to Castlereagh, 30 June 1808 (*HRNSW* 6.671; *HRA* 1.6.535).
154 Hainsworth, *Sydney Traders*, 70.
155 Account No 1 of *Pegasus*, 17 April 1808 to 10 October 1808 (SDA: 0852CH, Item 6, doc. 3), shows that Moore was paying the bills from 17 April 1808. *SG* 15/5/1808.
156 *SG* 15/5/1808.
157 T. Moore, Account No 1, of Pegasus, 17/4/1808 to 10/10/1808 (SDA: 0852 CH, Item 6, doc. 3).
158 For this paragraph, see Cumpston, 'Bunker, Eber (1761–1836)' and Hodgkinson, *Eber Bunker*.
159 *A Charge of Mutiny*, 217, 229.
160 T. Moore, Account No 1, of Pegasus, 17/4/1808 to 10/10/1808 (SDA: 0852 CH, Item 6, doc. 3).
161 The seizure of the *Harrington* was compared to that of the *Norfolk* and the *Venus*; *SG* 29/5/1808. For the latter, stolen from Port Dalrymple on 16 June 1806, see Public Notice, 18 June 1806 (*HRNSW* 6.98–99); The convicts seizing the *Marcia* were condemned, then pardoned by Johnston; Abbott to Ex.-Gov. King, 13 Feb 1808 (*HRNSW* 6.833).
162 Dando-Collins, *Captain Bligh's Other Mutiny*, 135. The thin thread of historical fact behind this charge consists in the man who led the seizure proving to be one gaoled by Bligh, but released by the rebels.

163 Bligh to Castlereagh, 30 June 1808 (*HRNSW* 6.671).
164 Else-Mitchell, 'Caley, George (1770–1829)'.
165 G. Caley to Sir J. Banks, 7 July 1808 (*HRNSW* 6.689).
166 J. Macarthur to J. Piper, 24 May 1808 (*HRNSW* 6.643–644).
167 Dando-Collins, *Captain Bligh's Other Mutiny*, 141–142.
168 Gov. Bligh to Castlereagh, 30 June 1808 (*HRNSW* 6.671; *HRA* 1.6.535).
169 *SG* 22/5/1808.
170 Hainsworth, *Sydney Traders*, 230.
171 *SG* 22/5/1808. Cf. Cumpston, *Shipping Arrivals*, 62: 18 May Captn Symonds, in pursuit of *Harrington*; p.63–64: *Pegasus* 18th May, Capt Symonds, Capt Eber Bunker with his first and second officers, Capt Graham, Capt Campbell, Mr Fisk and part of *Harrington*'s crew, Detachment NSW Corps. Several carriage guns. Total personnel 58. In pursuit of *Harrington* — Bay of Islands.
172 *SG* 29/5/1808.
173 Receipt for stores supplied the Pegasus on Gov't service, 18 May 1808 (SDA: 0854 CH, Item 1, doc. 2). Duplicate of same Receipt (SDA: 0854 CH, Item 1, doc. 3), and that amongst the correspondence in regard to Lord's litigation (SDA: 0852 CH, Item 6, doc. 1).
174 H. Fulton to Gov. W. Bligh, 18 May 1808 (*HRNSW* 6.639–641).
175 J. Macarthur to Capt. Piper, 24 May 1808 (*HRNSW* 6.643–644).
176 *SG* 29/5/1808.
177 *SG* 5/6/1808.
178 Dando-Collins, *Captain Bligh's Other Mutiny*, 153, speculates in the wrong direction mentioning the private yards of Isaac Nichols and Robert Campbell.
179 SG 3/7/1808; Hainsworth, *Sydney Traders*, 119.
180 SG 10 & 17/7/1808.
181 *SG* 17/7/1808.
182 SG 24/7/1808.
183 SG 11/9/1808.
184 T. Moore, Account No 1 of *Pegasus*, 17 April 1808 to 10 October 1808 (SDA: 0852 CH, Item 6, doc. 3).
185 T. Moore, Account of Provisions for Pegasus, May to August 1808 (SDA: 0854 CH, Item 1, doc. 4).
186 See also S. Lord's invoice to the owners of the Pegasus, 19/4/1808 to 21/8/1808 (SDA: 0852 CH, Item 6, doc. 2). He supplied Dammar [an Indian gum, used as varnish], Furm [I presume another kind of caulking compound], Tar, Pitch, rope, some planes, black varnish, sugar, 615 bushels of salt and ten casks. There was also an additional account from Lord on this latter document, not accounted for in Moore's Account No 1.
187 *Pegasus* Accounts, April to August 1808, T. Moore Expense Book, (SDA: 0885 CH, Item 1), p.4: 'July 28, 1808: Paid the men 8 in number 3£ Each to being out 9 weeks after the *Harrington*, £24.0.0'; see also Account No 1 of *Pegasus*, 17 April 1808 to 10 October 1808 (SDA: 0852 CH, Item 6, doc. 3), pp.1, 3, 5.
188 T. Moore, Account No 1 of *Pegasus*, 17 April 1808 to 10 October 1808 (SDA: 0852 CH, Item 6, doc. 3).
189 T. Moore's Account with Campbell & Co, 1806–1808 (SDA: 0851 CH, Item 6, doc. 3, sheet 4).
190 Commissary Palmer to Gov. Bligh, 4 Nov 1808 (*HRA* 1.6.689).
191 Receipt for stores & provisions supplied Pegasus on Government Service 18/5/1808 (SDA: 0852 CH, Item 6, doc 1).

192 Account No 1 of Pegasus 17/4/1808 -10/10/1808 (SDA: 0852 CH, Item 6, Doc 3).
193 Accounts Current of crew of Pegasus to various merchants, n.d. [ca. 19 Aug 1808] (SDA: 0854 CH, Item 1, doc. 1). Dating by comparison with T. Moore to J. Finucane, List of Detainers given in on behalf of the Pegasus Crew, 19 Aug 1808 (SDA: 0854 CH, Item 1, doc. 5).
194 T. Moore to J. Finucane, List of Detainers given in on behalf of the Pegasus Crew, 19 Aug 1808 (SDA: 0854 CH, Item 1, doc. 5).
195 Accounts Current of crew of Pegasus to various merchants, n.d. [ca. 19 Aug 1808] (SDA: 0854 CH, Item 1, doc. 1).
196 Accounts Current of crew of Pegasus to various merchants, n.d. [ca. 19 Aug 1808] (SDA: 0854 CH, Item 1, doc. 1); T. Moore to J. Finucane, List of Detainers given in on behalf of the Pegasus Crew, 19 Aug 1808 (SDA: 0854 CH, Item 1, doc. 5).
197 *SG* 22/5/1808.
198 *SG* 19/6/1808. The advertisement is repeated in subsequent issues.
199 *SG* 12, 19, 26/6, 3, 10/7/1808.
200 *SG* 24/7/1808.
201 *SG* 21/8/1808. She sailed on 30 September, *SG* 2/10/1808.
202 Gov. Bligh to Castlereagh, 31 Aug 1808 (*HRNSW* 6.709–712), and enclosed correspondence between Bligh and Foveaux (pp.712–721). Abbott put the date at 29th, but this was probably the date of his disembarkation, since Foveaux was ill when he first arrived; Capt. Abbott to Ex-Gov. King, 4 Sept 1808 (*HRNSW* 6.834–835).
203 Lieut-Col. Foveaux to Castlereagh, 4 Sept 1808 (*HRNSW* 6.728–735). This theme is repeated in Lieut-Col. J. Foveaux to Col. Paterson, 16 Aug 1808 (*HRNSW* 6.736).
204 Fletcher, 'Foveaux, Joseph (1767–1846)'.
205 Henry Waterhouse to Thomas Moore, 20 Oct 1804 (Moore: Waterhouse Papers). Despite being a junior officer, Beckwith was still amongst the traders; Hainsworth, *Sydney Traders*, 22, 27, 29.
206 Hainsworth, *Sydney Traders*, 32.
207 The figures differ for Foveaux's land and sheep holdings. Fletcher, 'Foveaux, Joseph (1767–1846)', gives him 1027 sheep on 2020 acres; Hainsworth, *Sydney Traders*, 32, 228, gives him 1350 sheep on 1170 acres. Comparison with Ryan, *Land Grants*, 118 (No 834), 132 (No 919), 135 (No 940), shows that Hainsworth only refers to the land at Toongabbie Fletcher sold to Macarthur on 5 December 1801. According to Ryan, 16 (no 120), 17 (no 122), 21 (No 162), 25 (No 187), 110 (No 174), he had a further 430 acres, bringing the total to 2200 acres. He also had a block of ground along the water supply in Sydney (p. 220, No 15).
208 Hainsworth, *Sydney Traders*, 32.
209 For what follows, Hainsworth, *Sydney Traders*, 27–29.
210 Hainsworth, *Sydney Traders*, 29.
211 Hainsworth, *Sydney Traders*, 207: 'Lieut.-Col. Foveaux accomplished more in the provision of badly needed public building s than had his two predecessors combined. Foveaux built a new military barracks at Sydney and a granary at Parramatta, and began an extensive range of stone warehouses on the shore of Sydney Cove, displaying an initiative and energy that was admired by Macquarie'.
212 Fletcher, 'Foveaux, Joseph (1767–1846)'.
213 *SG* 31/7/1808.
214 Lieut.-Col. Foveaux to Col. Paterson, 16 Aug 1808 (*HRNSW* 6.736).
215 J. Foveaux, Proclamation, 31 July 1808 (*HRNSW* 6.701); *SG* 31/7/1808. Henry Fulton

ENDNOTES 435

spoke contemptuously of him, 'pretending that he cannot decide between Captain Bligh (as he calls him) and the officer whom he found in command'; H. Fulton to [Castlereagh], 20 July 1808 (HRNSW 6.698). See also Gov. Bligh to Castlereagh, 31 Aug 1808 (HRNSW 6.711). For Foveaux's own account, see Lieut-Col. Foveaux to Castlereagh, 4 Sept 1808 (HRNSW 6.728–735).
216 Capt. Abbott to Ex-Gov. King, 4 Sept 1808 (HRNSW 6.835).
217 Gov. Bligh to Col. Paterson, 8 Aug 1808 (HRNSW 6.701).
218 T. Moore, Commission as Captain Commandant, Loyal Sydney Volunteer Association, 31 July 1808 (SDA: 0851 CH, Item 2, doc. 3).
219 Government and General Order, 22 Sept 1808 (HRNSW 6.761).
220 SG 7/8/1808.

CHAPTER 6

1 Williams, 'Moore College'.
2 SG 21/8/1808.
3 Return of Vessels (Outward) during 1808 (HRNSW 6.819); SG 28/8/1808: 'On Friday sailed the *Pegasus*, and yesterday the *King George*, for the fishery'.
4 Return of Vessels Entered Inwards & Return of Vessels Cleared Outwards during 1808 (HRNSW 6.818–819). The extra reference to the clearance of the *Rose* on 31 August, 'Captain Brecks', is evidently a garbled mistake. Foveaux had entered into controversy with Richard Brookes over whether or not the *Rose* had a licence from the EIC and a clearance from London's custom house to bring the spirits, and this controversy ran for a few days from 31/8 to 3/9 (HRNSW 6.742–747).
5 Lieut.-Col. Foveaux to [Under-Sec. Chapman], 10 Sept 1808 (HRNSW 6.753).
6 Return of Spiritous Liquors imported by Permission of Maj. Johnston, 27 Jan to 31 July 1808 (HRNSW 6.742).
7 R. Hassall to London Missionary Society, 26 Aug 1808 (HRNSW 6.708).
8 Lieut-Gov. Paterson to Castlereagh, 12 Mar 1809 (HRNSW 7.69).
9 Lieut-Col. J. Foveaux to Col. Paterson, 16 Aug 1808 (HRNSW 6.736).
10 Lieut-Col. J. Foveaux to ———, 10 Sept 1808 (HRA 1.6.662).
11 SG 5/6/1808: 'His Majesty's ship *Porpoise* was last week laid along-side the heaving down place, and will undergo a thorough repair'; Gov. Bligh to Castlereagh, 31 Aug 1808 (HRNSW 6.711).
12 Lieut-Col. J. Foveaux to Col. Paterson, 16 Aug 1808 (HRNSW 6.736).
13 Ryan, *Land Grants*, 182 (No 1309).
14 T. Moore's Account with Campbell & Co, Aug–Nov 1807 (SDA: 0885 CH, Item 2).
15 T. Moore's Account with Campbell & Co, 1806–1808 (SDA: 0851 CH, Item 6, doc. 3, sheets 4 and 6).
16 Loane, 'Moore, Thomas', 255: 'In 1809 Moore gave up his post as master boatbuilder and withdrew from Sydney. He had received a large grant in the George's River district known as Moorebank, and the site which he chose for his home was to make him the first citizen of Liverpool'.
17 T. Moore, Coroner's Report into the Death of Elizabeth Ford, 26 Oct 1808 (Col.Sec. 6021, 4/1819, p.217).
18 *Francis*: SG 10 & 24/7/1803; *Integrity*: SG 4/12/1803; *Marcia*: SG 8/7/1804. In 1805 he sailed for England on the *Harriet*, SG 12/5/1805. It subsequently was revealed that,

contrary to Governor King's orders, he had then transhipped to the American vessel *Criterion*, picked up a cargo of sandalwood in the Feejees, and sold it at Canton, in clear breach of the Orders securing the EIC rights; Proclamation, 12 July 1806 (*HRNSW* 6.109–110). He had become a trader. By 1 March 1807 he was master of the Kable & Co's *King George* sailing for the Feejees once again; Return of Ships cleared outwards, 1 Jan to 30 Jun 1807 (*HRNSW* 6.272).

19   *SG* 27/11/1808.
20   *SG* 27/11/1808. John White was granted by Phillip 2 acres 'between the church land and the ground used as a brickfield, without the town of Sydney' on 8 Dec 1792; and by Grose 100 acres at Petersham Hill on 28 May 1793 and another 30 on 3 December 1794. He took out his town lease on 15 May 1794; Ryan, *Land Grants*, 218 (No 2); 14 (no 101), 39 (No 328); 219 (no 13).
21   Lieut-Col. J. Foveaux to ———, 10 Sept 1808 (*HRA* 1.6.663). When Macquarie was confronted by the same issue, he acted in this direction, then sought approval for his action; see Macquarie to Castlereagh, 30 April 1810 (*HRA* 1.7.269), in regard to Robert Campbell and Simeon Lord, 'opulent and respectable merchants, having already built very spacious and elegant Houses and Warehouses'. Macquarie took it on himself to promise 'to convert their Leases into permanent Grants'.
22   Settlers' Petition to Viscount Castlereagh, 4 Nov 1808 (*HRNSW* 6.802–804). Ex-LMS missionaries amongst the signatories were: William Shelley, John Youl, Rowland Hassall, and Francis Oakes.
23   *SG* 25/12/1808; Government and General Order, 25 Dec 1808 (*HRNSW* 6.817).
24   Col. Paterson to Castlereagh, 12 Mar 1809 (*HRNSW* 7.67).
25   Lieut-Gov. Paterson to Castlereagh, 12 Mar 1809 (*HRNSW* 7.72).
26   J.J. Grant to Gov. Bligh, 11 Mar 1809 (*HRNSW* 7.65).
27   Lieut-Gov. Paterson to Castlereagh, 12 Mar 1809 (*HRNSW* 7.72).
28   Gov. Bligh to ———, 12 Mar 1809 (*HRNSW* 7.67).
29   H. Fulton to Mrs Bligh, 1809, SLNSW, Banks Papers, online collection: http://www.sl.nsw.gov.au/banks/series_42/42_07.cfm, CY 811. Fulton then repeats the words of the proclamation exactly.
30   Lieut-Gov. Paterson to Castlereagh, 26 Mar 1809 (*HRA* 1.7.72).
31   *SG* 19/3/1809.
32   Proclamation, 12 Mar 1809 (*HRNSW* 7.66; *HRA* 1.7.73; Appendix XXVII, *A Charge of Mutiny*, 457–458). For having published the proclamation after Bligh's departure, Palmer and Hook were fined and imprisoned by a Court of Criminal Judicature.
33   Loane, 'Moore, Thomas', 255: 'his name was listed amongst those whom Bligh forbade any shipmaster to assist to leave the colony'.
34   Boyce, *Thomas Moore*, 7.
35   For what follows, cf. Robinson, 'Thomas Moore—Early Life', 186–187 (22–23).
36   Col. Foveaux to Gov. Macquarie, 10 Jan 1810 (*HRNSW* 7.268).
37   Robinson, 'Thomas Moore—Early Life', 187 (23).
38   Surgeon Luttrell to Under-Sec. Sullivan, 8 Oct 1807 (*HRNSW* 6.292; *HRNZ* 1.282).
39   McNab, *Murihiku*, 157.
40   Steven, *Merchant Campbell*, 109.
41   Shipping Return, Inwards 1 Jan to 12 Aug 1806 (*HRNSW* 6.125).
42   *SG* 4/1/1807.
43   *SG* 17/7/1808.
44   Receipt from Stephen Lawrence for stores from Pegasus, 7 Feb 1809 (SDA: 0854 CH,

Item 1, doc. 6).
45 Eber Bunker's instructions to Sealing Party left on Pegasus Island, 7 Feb 1809 (SDA: 0854 CH, Item 1, doc. 7).
46 Pegasus Account and Outfit, 21/3/1809 to 26/5/1809 (SDA: 0852 CH, Item 6, doc. 13); and Duplicate (0852 CH, Item 6, doc. 9).
47 Chits for payments of 25 crewmen of the Pegasus, April 1809 (SDA: 0853 CH, Item 10, docs. 3–25) and Account for cash/slops advanced for crew of Pegasus [n.d. =April 1809] (SDA: 0854 CH, Item 1, doc. 13).
48 From Chits for payments of 25 crewmen of the Pegasus, April 1809 (SDA: 0853 CH, Item 10, docs. 3–25) and Account for cash/slops advanced for crew of Pegasus [n.d. =April 1809] (SDA: 0854 CH, Item 1, doc. 13).
49 Proceedings of the Mutiny on the *Barwell*, 21 Aug 1798 (*HRNSW* 3.457).
50 *SG* 12/3/1809.
51 Pegasus Account and outfit, 21/3/1809 to 26/5/1809 (SDA: 0852 CH, Item 6, doc. 13); and Duplicate (0852 CH, Item 6, doc. 9).
52 Ryan, *Land Grants*, 197 (No 1431) – the site is not given. Although the previous grant was in Castlereagh, the following grant was in Banks Town. When the deed was reissued by Macquarie after his arrival, the location is clear; Hodgkinson, *Eber Bunker*, 21–22.
53 Stancombe, 'Laycock, Thomas (1786?–1823)'.
54 Hodgkinson, *Eber Bunker*, 23.
55 T. Moore to Lieut-Gov. Paterson; and J. Finucane to T. Moore, 30 Mar 1809 (Col.Sec. 6041, 4/1722, pp.70–73; and 6001, SZ 757, p.41b).
56 Account with Government for Pegasus, 30/3/1809 to 25/4/1809 (SDA: 0852 CH, Item 6, doc. 6).
57 *SG* 9/4/1809.
58 Declaration of Samuel Rodman Chace's arbitration between Thomas Moore and members of the Pegasus Crew, 14 April 1809 (SDA: 084 CH, Item 1, doc. 9).
59 Pretyman, 'Collins, William (1760?–1819)'.
60 S. Chace to T. Moore, 15 April 1809 (SDA: 0853 CH, Item 15, doc. 6; leases: docs. 3, 4, 5).
61 Memorandum of Agreement between T. Moore & other Owners of Pegasus and Capt Samuel Chace, 27 April 1809 (SDA: 0854 CH, Item 1, doc. 10).
62 Lieut.-Gov. Collins to Castlereagh, 31 May 1809 (*HRNSW* 7.157).
63 Gov. Bligh to Castlereagh, 8 July 1809, from the Derwent (*HRNSW* 7.189; *HRA* 1.7.162); 'Clericus' [probably H. Fulton], Newspaper Extracts, 31 Aug 1809 (*HRNSW* 7.207).
64 Memo of provisions shipped by R. Fitz on Pegasus, 2 May 1809 (SDA: 0852 CH, Item 6, doc. 7).
65 *SG* 7/5/1809.
66 Pegasus Account and Outfit, 21/3/1809 to 26/5/1809 (SDA: 0852 CH, Item 6, doc. 3) and Duplicate (0852 CH, Item 6, doc. 9).
67 Gov. Bligh to Castlereagh, 10 June 1809 (*HRNSW* 7.180). McNab, *Murihiku*, 159.
68 *SG* 21 & 28/5/1809.
69 *SG* 28/5/1809.
70 *SG* 28/5/1809. Presumably this is not the same John Driver, the convict husband of Elizabeth Driver, a free woman. This pair of dealers operated out of Pitt's Row. At this time they were being sued for a debt of about £8000, and sometime around this time John died, for Elizabeth his widow was also acting as his administratrix in 1810. If it was the same John Driver, the debt and court case may provide something of a motive for his death. It is probably a different person, however, for the *Gazette* regularly advertised the

sale of goods from John Driver's Pitt's Row premises, and it seems unlikely that, if this were him, he would only be called a stockman.

71　SG 28/5/1809.
72　SG 4/6/1809; Col. Paterson to Castlereagh, 9 July 1809 (*HRNSW* 7.191–192).
73　SG 4/8/1809; reprinted in *Caledonian Mercury* 15/10/1810.
74　SG 4/6/1809. Although Ryan, *Land Grants*, does not list a grant for Emmerson in this district (but see the grant on Norfolk Island, 8/4/1797; p.71, No 545), Isaac Knight was granted 100 acres in the district of Banks Town on 30 April 1804; p.167 (No 1171).
75　SG 18/6/1809: 'The Lieutenant Governor has been pleased to appoint Mr William Gaudry to be Lieutenant in the Loyal Sydney Volunteer Association, commanded by Captain Moore. June 17, 1809'.
76　S. Chace to T. Moore, 15 June 1809 letter 1 (SDA: 0854 CH, Item 1, doc. 11).
77　McNab, *Murihiku*, 157. The *Pegasus* had fallen in with this English vessel in Foveaux Strait previously (*SG* 12/3/1809), when it had had little success. It arrived back at Gravesend on 15 September 1810.
78　S. Chace to T. Moore, 15 June 1809 letter 2 (SDA: 0854 CH, Item 1, doc. 12). The letter included the accounts for stores bought at the Derwent (SDA: 0853 CH, Item 6, docs. 11 & 12).
79　S. Chace to T. Moore, 18 [June] 1809 (SDA: 0852 CH, Item 7, doc. 1).
80　Gov. Bligh to Castlereagh, 8 July 1809, from the Derwent (*HRNSW* 7.189; *HRA* 1.7.162).
81　Gov. Bligh to Castlereagh, 8 July 1809, from the Derwent (*HRNSW* 7.190; *HRA* 1.7.163). Father James Harold took over in 1808 from Father James Dixon in his private clerical duties; see Perkins, 'Harold, James (1744–1830)'; and Parsons, 'Dixon, James (1758–1840)'.
82　Gov. Bligh to Castlereagh, 8 July 1809, from the Derwent (*HRNSW* 7.191; *HRA* 1.7.163–164).
83　Commissary Palmer to Gov. Bligh, 4 Nov 1808 (*HRA* 1.6.689).
84　Commissary Palmer to Gov. Bligh, 4 Nov 1808 (*HRA* 1.6.689).
85　T. Moore, Account No 1 of *Pegasus*, 17 April 1808 to 10 October 1808 (SDA: 0852 CH, Item 6, doc. 3). See also Account of deficiencies of stores put on Pegasus, Charged to Thomas Moore, [n.d.] (SDA: 0852 CH, Item 6, doc. 4).
86　Declaration of Samuel Rodman Chace's arbitration between Thomas Moore and members of the Pegasus Crew, 14 April 1809 (SDA: 0884 CH, Item 1, doc. 9); Thomas Moore's Business Notebook (rear), p.10, account dated 2/5/1809 (SDA: 0884 CH, Item 1 [rear]) he is called 'Chief Mate of the Pegasus'; for no second mate, see S. Chace to T. Moore, 15 June 1809 letter 2 (SDA: 0854 CH, Item 1, doc. 12).
87　W. Wilson to T. Moore, 27 June 1809 (SDA: 0854 CH, Item 1, doc. 15).
88　SG 2/7/1809. It also told that the NSW Corps were to become the 103rd on arrival home and 'in future the Military Service of the Colony was to be performed by a Regiment of the line, to be relieved every 4 or 5 years'.
89　Brig.-Gen. Nightingall to [unknown], 10 Mar 1809; Maj.-Gen. Grose to Under-Sec. Cooke, 16 April 1809 (*HRNSW* 7.64, 99).
90　Lieut.-Gov. Collins to Castlereagh, 20 July 1809 (*HRNSW* 7.195). This letter also shows that the news of Nightingall's appointment to replace Bligh had reached the Derwent by 20 July.
91　S. Chace to T. Moore, 2 Aug 1809 (SDA: 0854 CH, Item 1, doc. 16).
92　S. Chace to T. Moore, memorandum of sealskins procured by party on Pegasus Island 6/2 to 8/7 (SDA: 0854 CH, Item 1, doc. 8). The account specifically says it runs through to 8 July, but the itemised listing of skins seems to run up to the 8 May. The sequence of dates runs February, March, April, and then, on the next page, the edge of the document

ENDNOTES 439

is damaged, removing the month and it seems to be a continuation, on into May. However, since the *Pegasus* was in Hobart on 19 May, the July date must be correct.
93   S. Chace to T. Moore, 2 Aug 1809 (SDA: 0854 CH, Item 1, doc. 16).
94   Foster, 'Stewart, Captain William W. (1776–1851)'.
95   McNab, *Murihiku*, 160.
96   *SG* 12/3/1809.
97   For this paragraph, Foster, 'Stewart, Captain William W. (1776–1851)'.
98   *SG* 18/6/1809.
99   *SG* 12/3/1809; *SG* 26/3/1809.
100 For construction, *SG* 14/6/1807; for launch, *SG* 30/8/1807. Hainsworth, *Sydney Traders*, 237, confirms that Lord bought Blaxland's share (the other partner was Messrs. Hulletts), but gives no details.
101 SG 18/6/1809 also 25/6/1809.
102 SG 17/2/1810.
103 Hodgkinson, *Eber Bunker*, 22.
104 Declaration of Samuel Rodman Chace's arbitration between Thomas Moore and members of the Pegasus crew, 14/4/1809 (0854 CH, Item 1, doc. 9).
105 McNab, *Murihiku*, 160–161, referring to the article in the *Oriental Navigator*, 91. Chace's discovery of this peninsula was also noted by D'Urville, *Voyage de L'Astrolabe*, 1.22.
106 McNab, *Murihiku*, 161, drawing upon *Lloyd's List*, 21 August 1810.
107 For Cowper's story, see Bolt, *William Cowper*.
108 *SG* 20/8/1809.
109 *SG* 27/8/1809.
110 *SG* 2/6/1810.
111 *SG* 23/6/1810.
112 *SG* 2 & 23/6/1810.
113 Col. Paterson to Castlereagh, 9 July 1809 (HRNSW 7.191–192).
114 Government and General Order, 26 Aug 1809 (HRNSW 7.206; Col.Sec. 6037, SZ 993, 135).
115 SG 10/9/1809.
116 Ryan, *Land Grants*, 262, No 271. An affixed note shows that the lease was destroyed 5 September, 1825, by F. Goulburn.
117 Robinson, 'Thomas Moore—Early Life', 177 (13). Raven's house for sale: *SG* 23 & 30/8/1807. It was amongst the grants surrendered on 9 January 1810 under Macquarie's orders, but 68 ¾ rods were awarded back to him on 25 Aug 1812 (HRA 1.7.304, 654). See also *The Saint Andrew's Cathedral Property Investment Ordinance of 1906*.
118 Ryan, *Land Grants*, 213, No 1568: 6 Sep 1809, Thomas Moore. 'Granted 300 acres in the district of Bankstown. Rent: 6 shillings per year commencing after 5 years'; 1 November grants, p.292. For both see also List of Grants of Land surrendered, 30 April 1810 (HRA 1.7.304).
119 Hunter to Portland, 10 Jan 1798 (HRNSW 3.347). Hunter's chart, enclosed at this point in HRNSW 3, shows eight properties marked in this location.
120 Ryan, *Land Grants*, 292.
121 H. Fulton to Mrs Bligh, 1809, SLNSW, Banks Papers, online collection: http://www.sl.nsw.gov.au/banks/series_42/42_07.cfm, CY 819.
122 *SG* 7/1/1810.
123 List of Grants of Land surrendered, 30 April 1810 (HRA 1.7.304).
124 W. Paterson to Castlereagh, 6 November 1809, [letter 2] (Col.Sec. 6001, SZ 757,

125 W. Paterson to Castlereagh, 6 November 1809, [letter 1] (Col.Sec. 6001, SZ 757, pp.78a–79a; *HRA* 1.7.177).

126 T. Moore, Petition to Gov. L. Macquarie, 9 Jan 1810 (Col.Sec. Fiche 3007, 4/1822 no. 230).

127 This was just one month before Fitz was dismissed by Paterson (7 November) on suspicion of maladversion of the Stores; a charge on which he was later vindicated after his books were sent to England; Parsons, 'Fitz, Robert (1768?–1834)'.

128 J. Finucane to T. Moore, H. Best, and J. Symmonds, 3 Oct 1809; and Report (Col.Sec. 6041, 4/1722, pp.94–94b). The third signature on the Report reads W. Simmons. Presumably Finucane mistook the Master of the *Mary* for John Symons of the *Lady Nelson*.

129 Government & General Order, 11 Oct 1809 (Col.Sec. 6037, SZ 993, pp.172–173; *HRNSW* 7.216); *SG* 15/10/1809.

130 *SG* 15/10/1809. This assumes the boat mentioned was his own, on the slim grounds that it is not to be viewed at the Dockyard, and Moore is to be inquired of at his home (High St) rather than his place of work.

131 Col. Paterson to Castlereagh, 14 Oct 1809 (*HRNSW* 7.219). The *Boyd* left England on 4 Sept 1808; Return of Vessels sailed from England to NSW in 1808 (*HRNSW* 6.819).

132 Certificate of Shipping Agents, 11 Oct 1809; Macquarie to Castlereagh, 12 Mar 1810 (*HRNSW* 7.261, 312).

133 Thomas Moore's Business Notebook (SDA: 0884 CH Item 1), inside front cover. That the cargo was loaded is confirmed by a letter in regard to 'Insuring the Skins sent home in the *Boyd*' with Jacobs and Jacobs; J. Harris to T. Moore, 18 May 1810 (SDA: 0854CH, Item 1, doc. 17).

134 After the skins were lost (see below), Samuel Chace expressed his sorrow on Moore's account, for 'had the skins kept up the price as was in London when you speccullated the Cargo would come to a good Acc^t but the great fall of skins …'; Capt S. Chace to T. Moore, 11/1/1814 (SDA: 0851 CH, Item 3, doc. 8).

135 When Harris wrote in May 1810 the insurance (for £10,000) seemed unsettled, but his letter twelve months later (written in the midst of Johnston's court martial) shows that he had secured insurance for Harris and Moore's part of the *Boyd* cargo for £1736 and for their share of the *Pegasus* for £1150, but Jacobs refused to insure Lord; J. Harris to T. Moore, 18/5/1810 (SDA: 0854CH, Item 1, doc. 17); J. Harris to T. Moore, 31/5/1811 (SDA: 0854 CH, Item 1, doc. 18).

Lord's immediate problem was a bill he drew upon Kable and Underwood for £3200 for the *Santa Anna* that was protested and which Harris sent back to Thomas Moore to sort out in New South Wales. Lord's wider problem was that he was in debt to his chief brokers and agents the Plummers (Hainsworth, *Sydney Traders*, 79), who threatened to seize the *Pegasus* on arrival to cover Lord's debt, and perhaps to others too— for Jacobs told Harris there were upwards of £20,000 of Lord's Bills in England without means of payment; J. Harris to T. Moore, 18/5/1810 (SDA: 0854CH, Item 1, doc. 17). Hainsworth, *Sydney Traders*, 85, notes that Lord's running account with Plummers from 1804 to 1810—including that of Lord, Kable and Underwood— 'amounted to £102,120, and included bills he drew on Plummers for more than £60,000, a sum equivalent to nearly three-quarters the total of [Governor] King's whole Treasury bill expenditure over a comparable period of time'. Plummers were themselves in trouble because of the decline in prices after 1808; Hainsworth, *Sydney Traders*, 153.

136 Coronial Inquiry into the death of Thomas Jones, 4 Nov 1809 (Col.Sec. 6021, 4/1819,

ENDNOTES 441

pp.355–356).
137 T. Moore Expense Book, Rear p.1 (SDA: 0885 CH, Item 1).
138 *SG* 31/12/1809.
139 [ADB], 'Laycock, Thomas (1756?–1809)'; Stancombe, 'Laycock, Thomas (1786?–1823)'.
140 *SG* 31/12/1809 & 7/1/1810. His goods were auctioned on 4/1/1810.
141 *SG* 31/12/1809; corrections in 7/1/1810.
142 *SG* 7/1/1810.
143 *SG* 7/1/1810.
144 T. Moore, Petition to Gov. L. Macquarie, 9 Jan 1810 (Col.Sec. Fiche 3007, 4/1822 no. 230).
145 Gov. Bligh to ———, 12 Mar 1809 (*HRNSW* 7.67).
146 J. Foveaux to Gov. L. Macquarie, 10 Jan 1810 (Col.Sec. 6042, 9/2736, p.14; *HRNSW* 7.268–269).
147 *SG* 17/8/1806.
148 [ADB], 'O'Connell, Sir Maurice Charles Philip (1768–1848)'.
149 *SG* 21/1/1810; McNab, *Murihiku*, 165.
150 Hainsworth, *Sydney Traders*, 97.
151 J.T. Campbell, Circular to T. Moore, N. Lucas, T. Legg & J. O'Herne, 19 Feb 1810 (Col.Sec. 6002, 4/3490A, p.27; 6002, 4.3490B, p.87).
152 Government and General Order, 29 Dec 1809; Bligh to Manners Sutton, 16 Nov 1810 (*HRNSW* 7.248, 459).
153 J.T. Campbell to T. Moore, J. Dodd & J. Earle, 27 Feb 1810 (Col.Sec. 6002, 4/3490B, p.118).
154 J.T. Campbell to J. Palmer, 2 Mar 1810 (Col.Sec. 6002, 4/3490B, p.116).
155 *SG* 3/3/1810.
156 *SG* 3/3/1810.
157 Inquest into death of William Piper, 8 Mar 1810 (Col.Sec. 6021, 4/1819, pp.531–533).
158 *SG* 10/3/1810.
159 P.G. King, Rough Notes: New Zealand Natives, undated [?1806] (*HRNSW* 6.2–8). Cf. Parsons, 'Bruce, George (1778?–1819)'. George Bruce returned to New Zealand with Tip-pa-hee and married his daughter.
160 For an account, see Mackaness, 'The Massacre of the Boyd'.
161 Swaine to Macquarie, 6 Jan 1810 (*HRNZ* 1.293–295); A. Berry to Macquarie, 6 Jan 1810 (*HRNZ* 1.295–296). Mackaness, 'The Massacre of the Boyd', 295, thinks Marsden's evidence cannot be regarded as reliable, since it was gathered some years after the event. See Yarwood, *Samuel Marsden. Survivor*, 127–129.
162 *SG* 3/3/1810.
163 S. Marsden to Commissioner Bigge, 28 Dec 1819 (Bigge's Appendix, vol. 130; *HRNZ* 1.450).
164 Gov. Macquarie to Castlereagh, 12 Mar 1810 (*HRNZ* 1.296–98); S.R. Chace, Loss of the Ship Boyd, 12 Mar 1810 (*HRNZ* 1.298–299).
165 Whalers to Gov. Macquarie, 10 April 1810 (*HRNZ* 1.299–300). J.L. Nicholas, who visited New Zealand with Samuel Marsden in 1814, described the whaler's invasion of the island as 'an indiscriminate slaughter of the guiltless inhabitants, sparing neither age nor sex' (*Narrative of a Voyage to New Zealand*, 1.229, quoted *HRNZ* 1.300).
166 W. Leith to Messrs. Lord, Williams, and Thompson, 15 April 1810 (*HRNZ* 1.301–304).
167 *SG* 1/9/1810; reprinted in *HRNSW* 7.406–408 and *HRNZ* 1.306–309.
168 William Wilberforce to W. Hey, [undated]; from Wilberforce, *The Life of William Wilberforce*, 3.401.

169 See Bolt, *William Cowper*, 118–121.
170 *SG* 22/1/1814.
171 Inquiry into the death of Henry Giddes, 6 April 1810 (Col.Sec. 6021, 4/1819, pp.219–220).
172 *SG* 14/4/1810.
173 *SG* 14/4/1810.
174 *SG* 5/5/1810. Paterson died on 20 June as the ship rounded Cape Horn; *SG* 22/12/1810.
175 *SG* 5/5/1810.
176 *SG* 12/5/1810.
177 Cited from [ADB], 'O'Connell, Sir Maurice Charles Philip (1768–1848)'.
178 Eliza Watkins to Thomas Moore [undated, but postmarked Sydney 30/7/1840] (SDA: 0853CH, Item 11, doc. 13).
179 J. Gowen, Receipt for Stores, 9 May 1810 (*Col.Sec.* 6042, 4/1725, pp.11–13, 15).
180 Sydney Association Return, 4 June 1810 (Col.Sec. 6042, 4/1725, p.11–12). This is now found in the Colonial Secretary's papers with a list of names of the members of this association, not compiled by Moore himself (since the compiler makes the regular confusion between him and William): Wm [sic] Moore, Captain; Wm Gaudry, Lieutenant; John Griffiths, Seg^t Maj.; Richard Harding, Serj.; Obadiah Ikin, do; Richard Smith, do; Richard Palmer, Corporal; John Mullett, do; James Salmon, do; Benjamin Miles, Drummer; Morris Conroy, Fifer; and the privates: James Anslip, George Atkinson, Gilbert Baker, John Burgess, Charles Beazley, Robert Lack, William Forster, John Lane, John Haynes, Thomas Sutters, Charles Evans, Richard Holding, William Goodwin, John Templeton, Samuel Hockley, John Jones, Thomas Jones, Frederick Meredith, Joseph Larkin, Joseph Morley, Peter Hinney, Thomas Mansfield, James Bell, George Pashley, George Phillips, Thomas Rose, Thomas Salmon, John Shea, John Smith, William Holniss, Daniel Reed, William Tonks.
181 Government and General Order, 17 May 1810 (Col.Sec.6038 SZ 758, p.40; *HRNSW* 7.381); *SG* 19/5/1810.
182 J.T. Campbell to T. Moore, N. Lucas & T. Storer, 31 May 1810 (Col.Sec. 6002, 4/3490C, p.73).
183 J.T. Campbell to G. Marakby [?], 5 June 1810 (Col.Sec. 6002, 4.3490C, pp.75–76).
184 The following day Campbell clarified that this would be 100 Gallons of Spirits rated at 20s per Gallon, and the remainder in Casks; J.T. Campbell to S. Lord, 6 June 1810.; J.T. Campbell to S. Lord, 7 June 1810 (Col.Sec. 6002, 4/3490C, pp.79–80).
185 J. Harris Agreement with Trustees & Commissioners of Roads, 11 June 1810 (Col.Sec. 6042, 4/1725, pp.16–17).
186 *SG* 16/6/1810.
187 J.T. Campbell to T. Moore, 28 June 1810 (Col.Sec. 6002, 4/3490C, p.105).
188 J.T. Campbell to T. Moore, 2 July 1810 (Col.Sec. 6002, 4/3490C, p.109).
189 J.T. Campbell, Circular to A. Thompson, Lieut. Durie, and T. Moore, 19 July 1810 (Col.Sec. 6002, 4/3490C, pp.129–130). Lieut. Durie, Commander of the 73rd Regiment at Parramatta, was appointed JP and magistrate by the Government and General Order of 16 June 1810, *SG* 16/6/1810.
190 J.T. Campbell Circular to A. Thompson, Lieut. Durie, and T. Moore, 24 August 1810 (Col.Sec. 6002, 4/3490C, pp.163–164).
191 J.T. Campbell to T. Moore, 25 Aug 1810 (Col.Sec. 6002, 4/3490C, p.165).
192 *SG* 8/9/1810.
193 J.T. Campbell to T.Moore, A. Thompson, and Lieut Durie, 10 Sept 1810 (Col.Sec. 6002,

4/3490C, p.168).
194 J.T. Campbell to S. Marsden, W. Cowper, R. Cartwright, Lieut. Durie, T. Moore, and A. Thompson (Col.Sec. 6002, 4/3490C, p.176).
195 *SG* 27/10/1810.
196 Byrnes, 'Thompson, Andrew (1773?–1810)'.
197 *SG* 15 & 22/12/1810.
198 *SG* 15/12/1810.
199 For what follows, Macquarie, *Journal*, Nov 6–8, 1810.
200 Government and General Order, 15 Dec 1810 (Col.Sec. 6038, SZ758, p.135; *HRNSW* 7.470; *HRA* 1.7.397–401); *SG* 15/12/1810 and the 22nd.

Bibliography

1. Primary Sources – Thomas Moore

Mitchell Library
Colonial Secretary Papers
Wardell Papers

Moore College Library:
Broughton Papers
Moore Papers
Waterhouse Papers

Sydney Diocesan Archives (SDA):
After he died, Thomas Moore's papers were deposited in the Bishop's Registry, which was later subsumed by the Sydney Diocesan Archives. In the notes I have cited them by archive–assigned number (CH), and the item and document number assigned by me. The full description refers to the deposit:

The Trustees of the Estate of the Late Mr Thomas Moore, Esq.

Unknown Archive
Thomas Moore, 2nd Lieutenant Commission for East India Company, 18 Dec 1795. Copy in possession of author.

2. Primary Sources – Other

Addresses and Sermons
Broughton, W.G. ~ Latin Oration at the opening of St James' Lyndhurst, pre–Christmas 1846, translated by George Fairfowl Macarthur and George Gregory

Anglican Diocese of Sydney
Saint Andrew's Cathedral Property Investment Ordinance of 1906.

Books, Registers & Reports
Ashe, Thomas ~ *The Liberal Critic, or Memoirs of Henry Percy. Conveying a Correct Estimate of the Manners and Principles of the Present Times* (1812), 3 Vols.

Bladen, F.M. (ed.) ~ *Historical Records of New South Wales* (Sydney: 1892–1901; reprinted: Mona Vale, NSW: Lansdown Slattery, 1978–1979).

Charterhouse ~ *Charterhouse Register 1769–1872* (R.L. Arrowsmith, ed.; Phillimore & Co, 1974).

Collins, D. ~ *An Account of the English Colony in New South Wales, from its first settlement in January 1788 to August 1801* (London: vol. 1: 1798; vol. 2: 1802, ²1804). Also online at several locations, e.g. http://freeread.com.au/ebooks/e00010.html.

Cumpston, J.S. ~ *Shipping Arrivals and Departures, Sydney.* 1: 1788–1825 (Canberra: Roebuck Society, 1977 [1963–64]).

East India Co. ~ *List of Marine Records of the Late East India Company and of Subsequent Date preserved in the Record Department of the India Office, London* (1896). http://www.archive.org/stream/cu31924023223757 (18/10/2010).

Flinders, M. ~ *Narrative of his Voyage in the Schooner Francis, 1798, Preceded and Followed by Notes on Flinders, Bass, the Wreck of the Sydney Cove &c* (G. Rawson, ed.; Golden Cockerel Press, 1946).

Lloyds ~ *Lloyds Register of British and Foreign Vessels* 1790, 1791, 1792.

McNab, R. (ed.) ~ *Historical Records of New Zealand* (2 vols.; Wellington: John Mackay, Government Printer, 1908–1914; repr. 1973, 2010).

Ryan, R.J. (ed.) ~ *Land Grants 1788–1809. A Record of Registered Grants and Leases in New South Wales, Van Diemen's Land, and Norfolk Island* (Sydney: Australian Documentary Library, 1974).

Watson, F. (ed.) ~ *Historical Records of Australia* (F. Watson, ed.; Sydney: Library Committee of the Commonwealth Parliament, 1914–1925).

Census Documents, Australia: Musters
Baxter, C.J. (ed.) ~ *Musters & Lists of New South Wales and Norfolk Island 1801, 1802* (Sydney: ABGR & SAG, 1988).

Baxter, C.J. (ed.) ~ *Musters of New South Wales and Norfolk Island 1805–06* (Sydney: ABGR & SAG, 1989).

Census Documents, Britain
1841 Census: Beanley (HO 107/829/8).

1841 Census: Lesbury (HO 107/819/22).

Correspondence and Conversations:
Clements, Diane, to Peter G. Bolt, 6 & 10 Aug 2007.

Moor, David, to Peter Bolt, 9 August 2006, per email.

Robinson, Donald, personal conversation with Peter Bolt, 1st March 2006.

Directories, Gazetteers, &c
Mackenzie, E. ~ *An Historical, Topographical, and Descriptive View of the Country of the County of Northumberland* (Newcastle–upon–Tyne: Mackenzie & Dent, 1825). Google Books.

Parson, W.M., & W.M. White, *History, Directory and Gazetteer of the Counties of Durham and Northumberland and the Towns and Counties of Newcastle–upon–Tyne and Berwick–on–Tweed* (2 vols; Leeds: Mercury, 1828), vol. 2. Google Books.

Whellan, W. ~ *History, Topography, and Directory of Northumberland* (London: Whittaker, 1855). Google Books.

Genealogical Records
Downer & Henslee Family History, http://www.familytresearch.com/getperson.php?personID=1317&tree=2 (12/08/08, no longer accessible). Copy of relevant section held by Peter Bolt.

Moor Family Tree, in possession of David Moor, St Alban's, UK. Copies of relevant sections are held by Peter Bolt.

International Genealogical Index, see www.family.org

NSW Registry of BDM: 380 Vol. 3A and 240 Vol. 4.

UK Registration of Death:
1839, Northumberland North Second, No 112: Walter Scott.

1848, No. 402: Elizabeth Scott.

Government Acts, Reports & Court Records
[Bartrum] ~ *A Charge of Mutiny. The Court Martial of Lieutenant Colonel George Johnston for deposing Governor William Bligh in the Rebellion of 26 January 1808* (Mr Bartrum, shorthand notes; Canberra: National Library of Australia, 1988 [1811]).

Bigge Report ~ *Report of the Commissioner of Inquiry into the state of the colony of New South Wales* (3 vols.; Adelaide: Libraries Board of South Australia, 1966).

Bigge Report, Appendix, Mitchell Library

John William Lewin v. George Thompson [1799] NSWKR 8, Dore J.A., 4 and 30 November 1799, 3 February 1800; Court of Civil Jurisdiction Proceedings, 1788–1814, State Records N.S.W 2/8150 http://www.law.mq.edu.au/scnsw/html/Lewin%20v%20Thompson,%201799.htm.

Macarthur v Thompson [1806] NSWKR 3, Court of Civil Jurisdiction, Atkins R.A. 27 October – 4 November 1806. Court of Civil Jurisdiction Proceedings, 1788–1814, SRNSW 2/8149. http://www.law.mq.edu.au/scnsw/html/McArthur%20v%20Thompson,%201806.htm (19/8/2010).

Militia Act, 1757 (30 George II 25)

Militia Act, 1758 (31 George II 26),

Southern Whale Fishery Act (1798) (London: George Eyre & Andrew Strahan, 1798). NLA: 2361738.

Journals and Memoirs
Clark, Nathaniel ~ Journal. Sydney Diocesan Archives: Trustees of the Estate of the Late Thomas Moore Esq., 0885 CH, Item 5.

Flinders, Matthew ~ Matthew Flinders – Journal on HMS 'Investigator', vol. 1, 1801–1802. http://acms.sl.nsw.gov.au/album/albumView.aspx?acmsID=412367&itemID=823222 (3/8/2010).

Macquarie, Lachlan ~ *Lachlan Macquarie Governor of New South Wales. Journal of his Tours in New South Wales and Van Diemen's Land, 1810–1822* (Sydney: Library of Australian History and Library Council, NSW, 1979 [1956]). Macquarie, Lachlan. *Memoranda & Related Papers*. 22 December 1808-14 July 1823 (ML: A772.29f.; Microfilm CY301 Frame #36). Online: http://www.library.mq.edu.au/digital//lema/

Murray, Robert ~ *Journal of a Voyage to Port Jackson, New So Wales in the Years 1792, 1793, 1794 & 1795 in the Ship Britannia Mr W. Raven Comm^r. by R^t Murray* [SLNSW =PMB 215]. Extracts are also published in Begg, *Dusky Bay*. When page numbers are given, they refer to the PMB film and are given in square brackets.

Nicholas, John L. ~ *Narrative of a Voyage to New Zealand Performed in the years 1814 and 1815 in Company with the Rev Samuel Marsden* (London: James Black and Son, 1817).

Paine, Daniel ~ *The Journal of Daniel Paine, 1794–1797: together with documents illustrating the beginning of government boat–building and timber–gathering in New South Wales, 1795–1805* (R.J.B. Knight & A. Frost, eds.; Sydney: Library of Australian History in association with the National Maritime Museum, Greenwich, England, 1983).

White, John ~ *Journal of a Voyage to New South Wales* (R. Rienits, ed.; Sydney: Angus & Robertson, 1962 [Original: 1790]).

Letters

Letters found in Sydney Diocesan Archives and Moore College are not listed separately.

Bass, G. & E. ~ Mitchell: Waterhouse Family Papers, 1782–1819. ZML MSS 6544 [Safe 1/187] CY 3970.

Flinders, Matthew ~ M. Flinders to G. Bass, 15 Feb 1800 (ML: MLMSS 7046, safe 1/222). http://acms.sl.nsw.gov.au/album/albumView.aspx?acmsID=412971&itemID=846750 (26/7/2010).

Grose, Maj. Francis ~ Francis Grose to an unknown correspondent, 2 April 1792 (Mitchell: MLMSS 6825). http://acms.sl.nsw.gov.au/album/albumView.aspx?acmsID=402786&itemID=823442 (2/7/2010).

Johnson, Mary ~ M. Johnson to H. Fricker, 21 Dec 1795 (ML: MLMSS 6722). http://acms.sl.nsw.gov.au/item/itemDetailPaged.aspx?itemID=402336 (19/7/2010).

Johnson, Rev. Richard ~ G. Mackaness, *Some Letters of Richard Johnson, Chaplain to New South Wales* (Sydney: D.S. Ford, 1954), Parts 1 & 2.

Johnson, R. to S. Thornton, July 1790 (Murray, *Australian Christian Life*, 11).

Marsden, S. ~ G. Mackaness, *Some Private Correspondence of the Rev. Samuel Marsden and Family 1794–1824* (Australian Historical Monographs; Sydney: Mackaness, 1942; Dubbo: Review, 1976).

Waterhouse, H. ~ H. Waterhouse to Sir J. Banks, 16 July 1806 (SLNSW: Series 23:43). http://www2.sl.nsw.gov.au/banks/series_23/23_43.cfm (3/8/2010).

Watling, Thomas ~ Letters from an exile at Botany-Bay to his aunt in Dumfries: giving a particular account of the settlement of New South Wales, with the customs and manners of the inhabitants. (Mitchell: CY1158). Online: http://library.sl.nsw.gov.au/

Wesley, J. ~ J. Wesley to Mayor of Newcastle, 12 July 1743; in Everett, *The Wall's End Miner*, 217–218.

Manuscripts, Catalogues & Archival Material

Mitchell Library

Colonial Secretaries Papers, Microfiche

Hassall Correspondence

King Papers

Macarthur Papers

Macquarie, Lachlan, Diary

Macquarie, Lachlan, Memoranda

Wardell Papers

Waterhouse Papers

Wentworth Papers

Moore College Library

Broughton Papers

Moore Papers

Waterhouse Papers

National Archives (UK)

Admiralty Papers (Courtesy: Ann Coats)

> ADM 42/564 Deptford Extra Ordinary 1774. Shipwrights.
>
> ADM 42/564 Deptford Extra Ordinary 1775. Shipwrights.
>
> ADM 42/885 Plymouth Dockyard Extra Pay Book January–Dec 1774. Shipwrights.
>
> ADM 42/886 Plymouth Dockyard Extra Pay Book January–Dec 1775. Shipwrights.
>
> ADM 42/887 Plymouth Extra Ordinary 1777. Shipwrights.
>
> ADM 42/1290 Portsmouth Dockyard Extra Pay Book January–December 1774. Shipwrights.
>
> ADM 42/1291 Portsmouth Dockyard Extra Pay Book January–December 1775. Shipwrights.
>
> ADM 42/1292 Portsmouth Dockyard Extra Pay Book January–March 1776. Shipwrights.

Admiralty Papers (cited from V. Parsons)
Adm 106/2938 Masters' Qualifications 1748–1805

War Office Papers
WO 13/ 1645: War Office and predecessors: Militia and Volunteers Muster Books and Pay Lists 1778–1878; 1780–97, 1st Northumberland Militia.

Sydney Diocesan Archives
Registrar's Office– Correspondence, 1994/18/3.
Trustees of the Estate of the Late Thomas Moore Esq.

Maps & Charts
See also List of Plates and List of Figures.

C. Grimes, Plan of Sydney, 1800 (*HRNSW* 5, prior to index).

J. Meehan, Plan of the Town of Sydney, 31 Oct 1807 (*HRNSW* 6. between pp.366–367). (Plates 34& 35).

Newspapers, Magazines, and Press Clippings
Caledonian Mercury
Dalgety's Review
Diary or Woodfall's Register
Evangelical Repository (Google Books)
Evening Mail
Gentleman's Magazine
Jackson's Oxford Journal,
Monthly Magazine and British Register
Quarterly Review
Lloyds Evening Post,
Lloyds List
London Morning Herald
London Packet or New Lloyds Evening Post,
Maitland Mercury
Oracle and Public Advertiser
Public Advertiser
Saunder's News-Letter
Societas
St James's Chronicle or the British Evening Post, Daily Advertiser
Sydney Gazette
Sydney [Morning] Herald
Yorkshire Daily Observer

Parish Registers
Chillingham, St Peter's Church. Northumberland Record Office: M251.

Eglingham, St Maurice. Northumberland Record Office: EP 156.

Holy Island (Lindisfarne), St Mary the Virgin. Northumberland Record Office: M677.

Lesbury (Nbl), St Mary's, Baptismal Register. Northumberland Record Office: M246.

Lesbury, St Mary's, Burial Register. Northumberland Record Office: M246.

Lesbury, St Mary's. Bolam, J. (transc.) & Peacock, R. (ed.), *Registers of Lesbury, privately printed for the Durham and Northumberland Parish Register Society in 1907* (Durham: Durham and Northumberland parish register society, 1907). This contains baptisms from 1690–1812; marriages from 1689–1812 and burials from 1690–1812.

Sydney, St Philip's, Register. St Philip's Church, York St; SAG 90; and Mitchell Library.

Warkworth, St Lawrence, Register, Northumberland Record Office: EP 66/2.

Portraiture
See also List of Plates.

Cash, F. ~ 'Portrait of Thomas Moore', printed in Loane, *Centenary History*, facing p.16. Original once hung at Moore College, since stolen. (Plate 2).

Dayes, Edward, ~ 'View of Sydney Cove – 1804' (Plate 27).

Griffith(s), W. ~ 'Portrait of the Late Thomas Moore Esq.', now housed at Moore College, Sydney. (Plates 1 & 3, Cover).

Proceedings of the Old Bailey:
Rachel Turner, Theft: Simple Grand Larceny, 12 Dec 1787; http://www.oldbaileyonline.org/browse.jsp?ref=t17871212-13 (30/6/2010).

Trial of John Chilton (30/10/1805), THE PROCEEDINGS OF THE OLD BAILEY REF: T18051030–46; From http://www.oldbailey online.org/browse.jsp?ref=t18051030–46 (19/7/2010).

Realia
Moore, Rachel, memorial, St Luke's, Liverpool, NSW (Plate 4).

Moore, Rachel, tombstone, Pioneer Park, Liverpool, NSW (Plate 5).

Moore, Thomas, tombstone, Pioneer Park, Liverpool, NSW (Plate 5).

Moore, William, William jnr., & Ann Walker, Headstone, St Andrew's Auckland (South Church), Co. Durham, England.

White, Andrew, tombstone, Pioneer Park, Liverpool, NSW (Plate 5).

3. Secondary Sources – Thomas Moore

[Aust.Enc.²], ~ 'Moore, Thomas (1762–1840)', *The Australian Encyclopaedia* (Sydney: Angus and Robertson, ²1958 [1926–1927]), 7.145.

[Aust.Enc.³], ~ 'Moore, Thomas (1762–1840)', *The Australian Encyclopaedia* (Sydney: Groler Society, ³1977), 4.226.

Begg, A.C. & N.C. ~ 'Appendix D', *Dusky Bay* (Christchurch: Whitcombe & Tombs, 1968 [1966]), 222–223.

Bernard, J.R.L. (gen.ed.), ~ 'Moore, 12' and 'Moore Theological College', *The Penguin Macquarie Dictionary of People and Places. A Handy Guide to Who & Where* (Ringwood, Vic.; Penguin [Australia], 1987).

Bolt, P.G. ~ *Thomas Moore of Liverpool: One of Our Oldest Colonists. Essays & Addresses to Celebrate 150 Years of Moore College* (Camperdown, NSW: Bolt Publishing Services, 2007). Chapters referred to:

~ Ch.3: 'An Overdue Birth Announcement: In Quest of the Long-Lost Family of Thomas Moore', pp.29–42. An earlier version was delivered to the Anglican Historical Society on 2 September 2006 and published in *Journal of the Anglican Historical Society, Sydney Diocese* 51.2 (December 2006), 35–45.

~ Ch. 4: 'Moore and the Merino', pp. 43–59. An earlier version was delivered as a library lecture at the Moore College Library Open Day, 1st July 2006.

~ Ch. 5: 'Thomas Moore: S/Purveyor of Timber', pp.61–103.

~ Ch. 6: 'A Man, A Church, A College: Thomas Moore and St Luke's Liverpool', pp.105–114. An earlier version was preached at St Luke's, Liverpool, on 5th March 2006, as the first public event in the Sesquicentenary Celebrations of Moore College.

~ Ch. 7: 'Thomas Moore's Bookshelf', pp.115–210.

~ Ch. 9: 'Portrait of The Late Thomas Moore, Esq.', pp. 233–247.

Bolt, P.G. ~ 'The Family Correspondence of Thomas Moore, Esq., of Liverpool', P.G. Bolt & M.D. Thompson (eds.), *Donald Robinson Selected Works: Appreciation* (Camperdown, NSW: Australian Church Record & Moore College, 2008), 279–302.

Boyce, F.B. ~ *Thomas Moore. An Early Australian Worthy* (London: Rowell & Sons, 1914).

Dickey, B. ~ 'Moore, Thomas', *Australian Dictionary of Evangelical Biography* (Sydney: Evangelical History Association, 1994), 265–266.

Hammond, T.C. ~ 'Thomas Moore', *Societas* (1940–41), 5–6.

Loane, M.L. ~ 'Moore, Thomas (1762–1840)', *Australian Dictionary of Biography* (Melbourne: Melbourne University Press, 1967), 2.254.

Robinson, D. ~ 'Thomas Moore and the Early Life of Sydney', *JRAHS* 56.1 (1970), 165–192. Soon to be reprinted in *Donald Robinson: Select Works. 3: Biblical and Historical Studies* (P.G. Bolt & M.D. Thompson, eds.; Camperdown: Australian Church Record & Moore College, [forthcoming]).

Robinson, D. ~ 'Postscript', to 'Thomas Moore and the Early Life of Sydney'. Moore College Library. Soon to be reprinted in *Donald Robinson: Select Works. 3: Biblical and Historical Studies* (P.G. Bolt & M.D. Thompson, eds.; Camperdown: Australian Church Record & Moore College, [forthcoming]).

Robinson, D. ~ 'Thomas Moore of Moore Bank 1762–1840: The Father of Liverpool, Benefactor of Mankind', in P.G. Bolt & M.D. Thompson (eds.), *Donald Robinson: Select Works. 3: Biblical and Historical Studies* (Camperdown: Australian Church Record & Moore College, [forthcoming]). Originally delivered as the Ward Havard lecture for City of Liverpool and District Historical Society, 2nd August 1975.

Russell, E. ~ *Thomas Moore and the King's Dockyard 1796–1816* (Somersby, NSW: Old Sydney Town, 1975).

Williams, A.L. ~ 'Moore College', 1878–1884', *Societas* (May, 1937), 17–18.

4. Secondary Sources – Other

[ADB] ~ 'Laycock, Thomas (1756?–1809)', *Australian Dictionary of Biography* (Melbourne: Melbourne University Press, 1967), 2.97.

[ADB] ~ 'O'Connell, Sir Maurice Charles Philip (1768–1848)', *Australian Dictionary of Biography* (Melbourne: Melbourne University Press, 1967), 2.294–296.

Aikin, L. ~ *Memoirs Of The Court Of Queen Elizabeth* (London: Longman, Hurst, Rees, Orme, & Brown, 1818). Google Books.

Albion, R.G. ~ *Forests and Sea Power: The Timber Problem of the Royal Navy 1652–1862* (Cambridge, Mass.: Harvard University Press, 1926).

Anderson, R.C. ~ 'Early Books on Shipbuilding and Rigging', *Mariner's Mirror* 10 (1924), 53–64.

Anderson, R.C. ~ 'Eighteenth–Century Books on Shipbuilding, Rigging and Seamanship', *Mariner's Mirror* 33.4 (1947), 218–225.

Atkinson, A. ~ *The Europeans in Australia. A History.* Vol. 1: *The Beginning* (3 vols.; Oxford: Oxford University Press, 1997).

Auchmuty, J.J. ~ 'Hunter, John (1737–1821)', *Australian Dictionary of Biography* (Melbourne: Melbourne University Press, 1966), 1.566–572.

[Aust.Enc.^{2}] ~ 'Waterhouse, Henry', *Australian Encyclopaedia* (Sydney: Angus & Robertson, ^{2}1958 [1926–27]), 9.213–214.

[Aust. Enc.^{2}], ~ 'London Missionary Society', *Australian Encyclopaedia* (Sydney: Angus and Robertson, ^{2}1958 [1926–1927]), 5.360–361.

Balleine, G.R. ~ *A History of the Evangelical Party in the Church of England* (London: Longmans, Green & Co, 1908). www.archive.org.

Barrie, D.M. ~ *The Australian Bloodhorse* (Sydney: Angus & Robertson, 1956).

Bassett, D.K. ~ 'The Surrender of Dutch Malacca, 1795', *Bijdragen tot de Taal–, Land– en Volkenkunde* 117.3 (1961), 344–358. http://www.kitlv-journals.nl/index.php/btlv/article/viewFile/2415/3176 (14/7/2010).

Begg, A.C. & N.C. ~ *Dusky Bay* (Christchurch: Whitcombe & Tombs, 1968 [1966]).

Binney, K. ~ *Horsemen of the First Frontier (1788–1900) and the Serpent's Legacy* (Sydney: Volcanic, 2005),

Bolt, P.G. ~ *William Cowper (1778–1858): The Indispensable Parson. The Life & Influence of Australia's First Parish Clergyman* (Studies in Australian Colonial History 2; Camperdown, NSW: Bolt Publishing Services, 2009).

Bolt, P.G. ~ 'The King's Dockyard', The Dictionary of Sydney (2009). http://www.dictionary ofsydney.org/entry/kings_dockyard.

Bolt, P.G. ~ 'The Case of the Disappearing Chaplain: Rev. Richard Johnson's "Missing Years"', *Journal of the Royal Australian Historical Society* 95.2 (Nov 2009), 176–195.

Boyce, F.B. ~ *Fourscore Years and Seven: the Memoirs of Archdeacon Boyce, for over Sixty Years a Clergyman of the Church of England in New South Wales* (Sydney: Angus & Robertson, 1934).

Brand, I. ~ *Sarah Island* (Launceston: Regal Publications, 1984).

[British History], ~ 'Hackney: Building after c.1800', *A History of the County of Middlesex: Volume 10: Hackney* (1995), pp. 14–18. URL: http://www.british-history.ac.uk/report.aspx? compid=22695 Date accessed: 21 May 2010.

Byrnes, J. V. ~ 'Thompson, Andrew (1773?–1810)', *Australian Dictionary of Biography* (Melbourne: Melbourne University Press, 1967), 2.519–521.

Calamy, E. ~ *The Nonconformist Memorial; being an account of the Lives, Sufferings, and Printed Works of the Two Thousand Ministers Ejected by the Church of England chiefly by the Act of Uniformity, Aug. 24 1662* (3 Vols.; S. Parker, abridgr.; London: Button & Son, ^{2}1803). Google Books.

Canby, C. ~ *A History of Ships and Seafaring* (The New Illustrated Library of Science and Invention; London: Leisure Arts Limited, n.d. [1963]).

Chisholm, A.H. ~ 'Editor's Introduction', to John White, *Journal of a Voyage to New South Wales* (A.H. Chisholm, ed.; Sydney: Angus & Robertson, 1962 [Original: 1790]), 9–16.

Clark, C.M.H. ~ *A History of Australia* I. *From the Earliest Days to the Age of Macquarie* (Melbourne: Melbourne University Press, 1962, repr. 1985).

Clarke, J. ~ 'Comments on Simon Ville, "Rise to Pre-Eminence: The Development and Growth of the Sunderland Shipbuilding Industry, 1800–1850"', *IJMH* 2.2 (1990), 183–194.

Cobley, J. ~ *Sydney Cove 1791–1792* (Sydney: Angus & Robertson, 1965).

Cobley, J. ~ *The Crimes of the Lady Juliana. Convicts —1790* (Sydney: Library of Australian History, 1989).

Coleman, T. ~ *The Two Thousand Confessors of Sixteen Sixty Two* (London: John Snow, 1861 [new edition]). Google Books.

Cook, A.M. ~ 'Men of Lincoln Who Sailed with Cook', *JRAHS* 35 (1950), 116–130.

Cowan, R. ~ 'Early history of the Irvine name in NSW & Van Diemen's Land', http://www-personal.usyd.edu.au/~rcowan/genealogy/irvine_name.html (11/10/2010).

Craig, R. ~ 'A Note on Shipbuilding in the Port of Sunderland', *IJMH* 3.2 (1991), 109–119.

Crimmin, P.K. ~ '"A Great Object With Us to Procure This Timber …". The Royal Navy's Search for Ship Timber in the Eastern Mediterranean and Southern Russia, 1803–1815', *IJMH* 4.2 (1992), 83–115.

Cumpston, J.S. ~ 'Bunker, Eber (1761–1836)', *Australian Dictionary of Biography* (Melbourne: Melbourne University Press, 1966), 1.178.

Daily Mirror ~ 'Humane Seafarer Helped Pull Colony Out of Harsh Era', *Daily Mirror* (22/10/1982), 71.

Dallas, K.M. ~ 'Enderby, Samuel (1756–1829)', *Australian Dictionary of Biography* (Melbourne: Melbourne University Press, 1966), 1.357.

Dando–Collins, S. ~ *Captain Bligh's Other Mutiny* (Sydney: Random House, 2007).

Daniels, W.H. ~ *The Illustrated History of Methodism in Great Britain and America from the Days of the Wesleys to the Present Time* (Sydney & Melbourne: James & Coffey, 1882).

Dark, E. ~ 'Bennelong (1764?–1813)', *Australian Dictionary of Biography* (Melbourne: Melbourne University Press, 1966), 1.84–85.

Druett, J. ~ 'Of Ships and Seals and Savage Coasts: Samuel Rodman Chace in the Southern Ocean, 1798–1821', *Journal of New Zealand Studies* ns 2–3 (2003–2004), 129–148.

Dunbabin, T. ~ 'William Raven, R.N. and his Britannia, 1792–95', *Mariner's Mirror* 46.4 (1960), 297–303.

D'Urville, J.D. ~ *Voyage de L'Astrolabe* (4 vols.; Paris, 1830–1835).

Earnshaw, J. ~ 'Gerrald, Joseph (1760–1796)', *Australian Dictionary of Biography* (Melbourne: Melbourne University Press, 1966), 1.438–439.

Earnshaw, J. ~ 'Muir, Thomas (1765–1799)', *Australian Dictionary of Biography* (Melbourne: Melbourne University Press, 1967), 2.266–267.

Earnshaw, J. ~ 'Palmer, Thomas Fyshe (1747–1802)', *Australian Dictionary of Biography* (Melbourne: Melbourne University Press, 1967), 2.312–313.

Earnshaw, J. ~ 'Skirving, William (–1796)', *Australian Dictionary of Biography* (Melbourne: Melbourne University Press, 1967), 2.449–450.

Ellis, M.H. ~ *John Macarthur* (Sydney: Angus & Robertson, ²1973 [1967]).

Else–Mitchell, R. ~ 'Caley, George (1770–1829)', *Australian Dictionary of Biography* (Melbourne: Melbourne University Press, 1966), 1.194–195.

Estensen, M. ~ *The Life of Matthew Flinders* (Sydney: Allen & Unwin, 2002).

Estensen, M. ~ *The Life of George Bass. Surgeon and Sailor of the Enlightenment* (Sydney: Allen & Unwin, 2005).

Evatt, H.V. ~ *Rum Rebellion: A Study Of The Overthrow Of Governor Bligh By John Macarthur And The New South Wales Corps; Including The John Murtagh Macrossan Memorial Lectures Delivered At The University Of Queensland, June 1937* (Sydney : Angus & Robertson, ⁵1944 [1937]).

Everett, J. ~ *The Wall's End Miner; or a Brief Memoir of the Life of William Crister* (Manchester: Thomas Johnson, ³1850).

Falloon, M. ~ *To Plough or to Preach? Mission Strategies in New Zealand During the 1820s* (London: Latimer, 2010).

Flagg, A.C. ~ *Notes on the History of Shipbuilding in South Shields 1746–1946* (South Shields: South Tyneside Borough Council Library Service, 1979).

Fletcher, B.H. ~ 'The Development of Small Scale Farming in New South Wales under Governor Hunter', *JRAHS* 50.1 (1964), 1–31.

Fletcher, B.H. ~ 'Balmain, William (1762–1803)', *Australian Dictionary of Biography* (Melbourne: Melbourne University Press, 1966), 1.51–52.

Fletcher, B.H. ~ 'Foveaux, Joseph (1767–1846)', *Australian Dictionary of Biography* (Melbourne: Melbourne University Press, 1966), 1.407–409.

Fletcher, B.H. ~ 'Grose, Francis (1758?–1814)', *Australian Dictionary of Biography*

(Melbourne: Melbourne University Press, 1966), 1.488–489.

Fletcher, B.H. ~ 'Harris, John (1754–1838)', *Australian Dictionary of Biography* (Melbourne: Melbourne University Press, 1966), 1.519–520.

Fletcher, B.H. ~ 'Christianity and Free Society in New South Wales 1788–1840', *JRAHS* 86.2 (2000), 93–113.

Fletcher, B.H. ~ 'Sydney Town: The First Twenty Years', in A.M. Blanch (ed.), *The Parish of St Philip Church Hill, Sydney. Three Bicentennial Lectures* (Sydney: Churchwardens of St Philip's, 2002), 7–22.

Foster, J. ~ 'Stewart, Captain William W. (1776–1851)', *An Encyclopaedia of New Zealand* (A. H. McLintock, ed.; originally published in 1966. *Te Ara – the Encyclopedia of New Zealand*, updated 22–Apr–09). http://202–160–117–179.colo.onesquared.net/en/1966/stewart–captain–william–w/1 (4/10/2010).

Frost, A. ~ *Convicts and Empire: A Naval Question* (Melbourne: Oxford University Press, 1980).

Frost, A. ~ *Arthur Phillip 1738–1814. His Voyaging* (Melbourne: Oxford University Press, 1987).

Grocott, A.M. ~ *Convicts, Clergymen And Churches: Attitudes Of Convicts And Ex–Convicts Towards The Churches And Clergy In New South Wales From 1788 To 1851* (Sydney: University of Sydney Press, 1980).

Gunson, N. ~ 'Henry, William (1770–1859)', *Australian Dictionary of Biography* (Melbourne: Melbourne University Press, 1966), 1.251–253

Hainsworth, D.R. (ed.) ~ *Builders and Adventurers: The Traders and the Emergence of the Colony 1788–1821* (Melbourne: Cassell, 1969).

Hainsworth, D.R. ~ *The Sydney Traders: Simeon Lord And His Contemporaries, 1788–1821* (Melbourne: Melbourne University Press, ²1981 [Cassell: 1972]).

Hanes, W.T., III & F. Sanello, ~ *Opium Wars. The Addiction of One Empire and the Corruption of Another* (Naperville, Ill.: Sourcebooks, 2002). Google Books.

Hassall, J.S. ~ *In Old Australia, Records and Reminiscences from 1794* (North Sydney, N.S.W.: Library of Australian History, 1981 [1902]).

Hawkey, A. ~ *Bligh's Other Mutiny* (London: Angus and Robertson, 1975).

Hickes, J.C. ~ *The History and Development of Lesbury and Alnmouth* (Alnwick: Gazette, n.d.).

Hickson, E. ~ 'Cox, William (1764–1837)', *Australian Dictionary of Biography* (Melbourne: Melbourne University Press, 1966), 1.258–259.

Hodgkinson, R. ~ *Eber Bunker Of Liverpool: The Father Of Australian Whaling* (Roebuck Society Publication No 15; Canberra: Roebuck, 1975).

Hughes, R. ~ *The Fatal Shore. A History of the Transportation of Convicts to Australia, 1787–1868* (London: Collins Harvill, 1987).

Ingleton, G.C. ~ 'General Introduction', to John White, *Journal of a Voyage to New South Wales* (A.H. Chisholm, ed.; Sydney: Angus & Robertson, 1962 [Original: 1790]), 1–8. Also published as *Sydney's First Four Years* (Sydney: Angus and Robertson, & Royal Australian Historical Society, 1961).

Ke, Xu ~ 'Piracy, Seaborne Trade and the Rivalries of Foreign Sea Powers in East and Southeast Asia, 1511 to 1839: A Chinese Perspective', in G.G. Ong–Webb (ed.), *Piracy, Maritime Terrorism and Securing the Malacca Straits* (Singapore: ISEAS, 2006), 221–240.

Kemp, P. ~ *The Oxford Companion to Ships and the Sea* (Oxford: Oxford University Press, 1988).

Kemp, P. ~ 'Cook, James (1728–79)', *The Oxford Companion to Ships and the Sea* (Oxford: Oxford University Press, 1988), 199–203.

Ker, J. ~ 'The Wool Industry in New South Wales 1803–1830', Parts 1 & 2: *Bull. Of Business Archives Council* 1.8 (1961), 28–49, and *Business Archives & History* 2.1 (1962), 18–54.

Kercher, B. ~ *Debt, Seduction and Other Disasters: The Birth of Civil Law in New South Wales* (Leichhardt: Federation, 1996).

King, J. & J. King, ~ *Philip Gidley King. A Biography of the Third Governor of New South Wales* (North Ryde, NSW: Methuen, 1981).

Knight, C. ~ '"Carpenter" Master Shipwrights', *Mariner's Mirror* 18 (1932), 411–422.

Knight, R.J.B. ~ 'Sandwich, Middleton & Dockyard Appointments', *Mariner's Mirror* 57 (1971), 175–192.

Knight, R.J.B.& A. Frost, ~ 'Introduction', *The Journal of Daniel Paine, 1794–1797: together with documents illustrating the beginning of* government boat–building and timber–gathering in New South Wales, 1795–1805 (Sydney: Library of Australian History in association with the National Maritime Museum, Greenwich, England, 1983), i–xxix.

Lesbury PCC ~ *St Mary's Parish Church, Lesbury* (Alnwick: Lesbury PCC, 1991).

Loane, M.L. ~ *A Centenary History of Moore Theological College* (Sydney: Angus & Robertson, 1955).

Loane, M.L. ~ *Hewn From the Rock. Origins & Traditions of the Church in Sydney* (The Moorhouse Lectures 1976; Sydney: AIO, 1976).

Lynravn, N. S. ~ 'Hayes, Sir Henry Browne (1762–1832)', *Australian Dictionary of Biography* (Melbourne: Melbourne University Press, 1966), 1.526–527.

Macintosh, N.K. ~ *Richard Johnson. Chaplain to the Colony of New South Wales. His Life and Times 1755–1827* (Sydney: Library of Australian History, 1978).

Macintosh, N.K. ~ *The Reverend Richard Johnson. First to Preach the Gospel in Parramatta Town* (Sydney: Pilgrim International, 2000 [1975]).

McKay, R.J. ~ 'Moore, William Henry (1788?–1854)', *Australian Dictionary of Biography* (Melbourne: Melbourne University Press, 1967), 2.255–257.

Mackaness, G. ~ 'The Massacre of the Boyd', *JRAHS* 50.4 (1964), 293–297.

Mackenzie, E. ~ 'Historical events: 1783 –1825', *Historical Account of Newcastle–upon–Tyne: Including the Borough of Gateshead* (1827), pp. 66–88. URL: http://www.british-history.ac.uk/report.aspx?compid=43321 Date accessed: 03 July 2010.

MacLeod, N. ~ 'The Shipwrights of the Royal Dockyards', *Mariner's Mirror* 11.2 (1925), 274–291.

MacLeod, N. ~ 'The Shipwright Officers of the Royal Dockyards', *Mariner's Mirror* 11.3 (1925), 355–369.

McMartin, A. ~ 'Nichols, Isaac (1770–1819)', *Australian Dictionary of Biography* (Melbourne: Melbourne University Press, 1967), 2.283.

Mcnab, R. ~ *Murihiku : A History Of The South Island Of New Zealand And The Islands Adjacent And Lying To The South, From 1642 To 1835* (Wellington, N.Z.: Whitcombe & Tombs, 1909). Online: www.nzetc.org/tm/scholarly

Mander–Jones, P. ~ 'Lewin, John William (1770–1819)', *Australian Dictionary of Biography* (Melbourne: Melbourne University Press, 1967), 2.111–112.

Mignet, F.–A.–M.–A. ~ *A History of the French Revolution, from 1789 to 1814* (BiblioBazaar, 2008 [Original: 1824]). Google Books.

Morrison, W.F. ~ *The Aldine Centennial History of New South Wales, Illustrated* (2 vols.; Sydney: Aldine, 1888).

Mott, F.B. ~ *A Short History of Unitarianism since the Reformation* (Unitarian Sunday School Society, 1893; reprinted General Books, 2009). Bibliobazaar/ Google Books.

Murray, I.H. ~ *Australian Christian Life From 1788. An Introduction And An Anthology* (Edinburgh: Banner of Truth Trust, 1988).

Nelson, E.C. ~ 'John White A.M., M.D., F.L.S. (c. 1756–1832), Surgeon–General Of New South Wales: A New Biography Of The Messenger Of The Echidna And Waratah', *Archives of Natural History* 25 (1998), 149–211.

Newbold, T.J. ~ *Political and Statistical Account of the British Settlements in the Straits of Malacca, viz Pinang, Malacca and Singapore* (2 vols; London: John Murray, 1839). Google Books.

Nichols, J. ~ 'Rev. Percival Stockdale (1814)', in *Literary Anecdotes of the XVIII Century (1812–15)* 8:18–30. http://198.82.142.160/spenser/BiographyRecord.php?action=GET&bioid=36371 (7/10/07).

O'Donnell, R. ~ 'Dwyer, Michael (1772?–1825)', *Australian Dictionary of Biography* (Melbourne: Melbourne University Press, 2005), Supplementary Volume, 110.

Onslow, S.M. (ed.), ~ *The Macarthurs of Camden* (Sydney: Rigby, 1973 [1st published 1914]).

Overton, J.H. ~ *The Evangelical Revival in the Eighteenth Century* (London: Longmans, Green & Co, 1886). www.archive.org.

Parsons, V. ~ 'Bruce, George (1778?–1819)', *Australian Dictionary of Biography* (Melbourne: Melbourne University Press, 1966), 1.170–171.

Parsons, V. ~ 'Dixon, James (1758–1840)', *Australian Dictionary of Biography* (Melbourne: Melbourne University Press, 1966), 1.309.

Parsons, V. ~ 'Fitz, Robert (1768?–1834)', *Australian Dictionary of Biography* (Melbourne: Melbourne University Press, 1966), 1.380–381.

Parsons, V. ~ 'Jamison, Thomas (1753?–1811)', *Australian Dictionary of Biography* (Melbourne: Melbourne University Press, 1967), 2.12–13.

Parsons, V. ~ 'Nepean, Evan (1752–1822) and Nicholas (1757–1823)', *Australian Dictionary of Biography* (Melbourne: Melbourne University Press, 1967), 2.281.

Parsons, V. ~ 'Raven, William (1756–1814)', *Australian Dictionary of Biography* (Melbourne: Melbourne University Press, 1967), 2.364–365.

Perkins, H. ~ 'Harold, James (1744–1830)', *Australian Dictionary of Biography* (Melbourne: Melbourne University Press, 1966), 1.512–513.

Pollon, F.& G. Healy, ~ *The Book of Sydney Suburbs* (Sydney: Angus & Robertson, 1988).

Pretyman, E.R., ~ 'Collins, William (1760?–1819)', *Australian Dictionary of Biography* (Melbourne: Melbourne University Press, 1966), 1.240.

Rees, S. ~ *The Floating Brothel* (Sydney: Hatchette, 2001, reprint 2006).

Richardson, H.E. ~ 'Wages of Shipwrights in H.M. Dockyards 1496–1788', *Mariner's Mirror* 33 (1947), 265–274.

Rienits, R. ~ 'Biographical Introduction', to John White, *Journal of a Voyage to New South Wales* (A.H. Chisholm, ed.; Sydney: Angus & Robertson, 1962 [Original: 1790]), 17–34.

Rienits, R. ~ 'White, John (1756?–1832)', *Australian Dictionary of Biography* (Melbourne: Melbourne University Press, 1967), 2.594–595.

Roe, M. ~ 'Margarot, Maurice (1745–1815)', *Australian Dictionary of Biography* (Melbourne: Melbourne University Press, 1967), 2.206–207.

Roe, M. ~ 'New Light on George Bass, Entrepreneur and Intellectual', *JRAHS* 72.5 (1987), 251–273.

Rowland, T.H. ~ *The Alemouth or Corn Road: Alnwick–Alnmouth: Hexham, Wall, Chollerton, Rothbury* (Morpeth, Northumberland: T.H. Rowland, 1982).

Scott, J. ~ 'The Scottish Martyrs' Farms', *JRAHS* 46.3 (1960), 161–168

Shaw, A. G. L. ~ 'Bligh, William (1754–1817)', *Australian Dictionary of Biography* (Melbourne: Melbourne University Press, 1966), 1.118–122.

Shaw, A. G. L. ~ 'King, Philip Gidley (1758–1808)', *Australian Dictionary of Biography* (Melbourne: Melbourne University Press, 1967), 2.55–61.

Sherry, B. ~ 'Thomas Muir and the Naming of Hunter's Hill', 19 Nov 2009, *The Hunter's Hill Trust*. http://huntershilltrust.org.au/2009/11/thomas–muir–and–the–naming–of–hunter's–hill/ (10 Oct 2010).

Smith, B.M. (ed.) ~ *Quench Not the Spirit. Merino Heritage* (Melbourne: Hawthorn Press, 1972).

Smith, J.W. & T.S. Holden, ~ *Where Ships are Born. Sunderland 1346–1946. A History of Shipbuilding on the River Wear* (Sunderland: Thomas Reed & Co, 1946).

Stancombe, G.H. ~ 'Laycock, Thomas (1786?–1823)', *Australian Dictionary of Biography* (Melbourne: Melbourne University Press, 1967), 2.97–98.

Stanley, P. ~ *The Remote Garrison. The British Army in Australia 1788–1870* (Kenthurst, NSW: Kangaroo Press, 1986).

Steven, M. ~ *Merchant Campbell 1769–1846. A Study in Colonial Trade* (Melbourne: Oxford University Press, 1965).

Steven, M. ~ 'Campbell, Robert (1769–1846)', *Australian Dictionary of Biography* (Melbourne: Melbourne University Press, 1966), 1.202–206.

Steven, M. ~ 'Macarthur, John (1767–1834)', *Australian Dictionary of Biography* (Melbourne: Melbourne University Press, 1967), 2.153–159.

Taylor, E.G.R. ~ 'The Seaman's Bookshelf on the Eve of the Restoration', *Mariner's Mirror* 18.4 (1932), 403–410.

Telford, J. ~ *The Popular History of Methodism* (London: C.H. Kelly, ³1899).

Tilghman, D. C. ~ 'Woodriff, Daniel (1756–1842)', *Australian Dictionary of Biography* (Melbourne: Melbourne University Press, 1967), 2.621–622.

Turner, William ~ *The Lives Of Eminent Unitarians: With A Notice Of Dissenting Academies* (London: Unitarian Association, 1843), 2.214–238. Google Books.

[unknown] ~ *Histoire de la Tyrannie du Gouvernement Anglais exercée envers le célèbre Thomas Muir, Ecossais* (Paris: Chez Prudhomme, 1798).

Vickers, J. A. (ed.) ~ *A Dictionary of Methodism in Britain and Ireland* (Peterborough, UK: Epworth, 2000).

BIBLIOGRAPHY 455

Ville, S. ~ 'Rise to Pre–Eminence: The Development and Growth of the Sunderland Shipbuilding Industry, 1800–1850', *IJMH* 1.1 (1989), 65–86.

Ville, S. ~ 'Sunderland Shipbuilding: Pre–Eminence Restated', *IJMH* 2.2 (1990), 195–211;

Ville, S. ~ 'Craig on Sunderland Shipbuilding: A Comment', *IJMH* 4.1 (1992), 155–158.

Wadia, R.A. ~ *The Bombay Dockyard and the Wadia MasterBuilders* (Bombay: R.A. Wadia, ²1957 [1955]).

Warren, J.F. ~ *Iranun and Balangingi: Globalization, Maritime Raiding and the Birth of Ethnicity* (Honolulu: University of Hawaii Press, 2002). Google Books.

Watson, J.H. ~ 'Notes on Some Suburbs of Sydney', *JRAHS* 13, Part 1 (1927), 25-27.

Wedd, M. ~ *Australian Military Uniforms 1800–1982* (Kenthurst, NSW: Kangaroo Press, 1982).

Wilberforce, R.I. & S. ~ *The Life of William Wilberforce* (5 Vols.; London: John Murray, 1838).

Williams, A.L. ~ 'Moore College, 1878–1884', *Societas* (May, 1937), 17–18.

Yarwood, A.T. ~ *Samuel Marsden. The Great Survivor* (Carlton, Vic.: Melbourne University Press, 1977, 1996).

Yarwood, A.T. ~ 'Johnston, George (1764–1823)', *Australian Dictionary of Biography* (Melbourne: Melbourne University Press, 1967), 2.20–22.

Yarwood, A.T. ~ 'Johnston, George (1790–1820)', *Australian Dictionary of Biography* (Melbourne: Melbourne University Press, 1967), 2.22

5. Websites

Alnmouth ~ www.alnmouth.org.uk

Alnwick Quaker Meeting ~ http://www.alnwickquakers.org.uk/alnhistory.htm

Archive.org ~ http://www.archive.org

British History Online ~ http://www.british–history.ac.uk/

Byrne, Dan
    Blackheath Connection
        http://www.danbyrnes.com.au/blackheath/ thebc41.htm
        http://www.danbyrnes.com.au/blackheath/ ships2.htm

    Merchant Networks
        http://www.merchantnetworks.com.au/periods/1775after/swf1.htm

Cowan Genealogy ~ http://www–personal.usyd.edu.au/~rcowan/genealogy/

Dictionary of Sydney ~ http://www.dictionaryofsydney.org

Downer & Henslee Family History,
    http://www.familytresearch.com/getperson.php?personID=I317&tree=2 (12/08/08, no longer accessible).

Encyclopaedia of New Zealand ~ http://202–160–117–179.colo.onesquared.net/en/1966

Founding Documents~ http://www.foundingdocs.gov.au/resources/transcripts/

Google Books ~ http://books.google.com.au

Hunter's Hill Trust ~ http://huntershilltrust.org.au

International Geneaological Index (IGI) ~ www.family.org

KITLV Journals ~ http://www.kitlv–journals.nl/index.php/btlv/article/viewFile/2415/3176

Lindisfarne ~ http://www.lindisfarne.org.uk

Literary Anecdotes ~ http://198.82.142.160/spenser/BiographyRecord.php?action=GET&bioid=36371

Macquarie University
    Lachlan & Elizabeth Macquarie Archive
        http://www.library.mq.edu.au/digital//lema/

    Macquarie Law
        http://www.law.mq.edu.au/scnsw/html/Lewin%20v%20Thompson,%201799.htm

New Zealand Electronic Texts ~ www.nzetc.org/tm/scholarly

Northeast ~ http://www.thisisthenortheast.co.uk/the_north_east/history/shipbuilding

Northumberland Communities:
  http://communities.northumberland.gov.uk/008835FS.htm
  http://communities.northumberland.gov.uk/008836FS.htm

Old Bailey Online
  Rachel Turner ~ http://www.oldbaileyonline.org/browse.jsp?ref=t17871212-13.
  John Chilton ~ http://www.oldbaileyonline.org/browse.jsp?ref=t18051030-46.

Redgrave History ~ http://myweb.tiscali.co.uk/redgravehistory/wilson/twbiogr.htm

Rounce-Bell Transcription of St Hilda's South Shields,
  http://genuki.cs.ncl.ac.uk/Transcriptions/DUR/SSH1780.html

State Library of NSW
  Banks Series
    http://www.sl.nsw.gov.au/banks/series_23/23_43.htm
    http://www2.sl.nsw.gov.au/banks/series_43/43_05.cfm
    http://www.sl.nsw.gov.au/banks/series_42/42_07.cfm
  Flinders' Journal
    http://acms.sl.nsw.gov.au/album/albumView.aspx?acmsID=412367&itemID=823222

Unitarian Societies ~ http://www.unitariansocieties.org.uk/historical/hsrecords.html

Indexes

Thomas Moore

& Aboriginal People
83, 112, 238, 364–366.

Agent

~ his agents
243, 340, 355.

~ for others
120, 121, 173, 175, 176, 177, 187, 210, 219, 221, 222, 225, 248, 253, 256, 322, 327, 339, 346, 357.

~ for John White
56, 109, 264, 327, 352.

~ see also George Bass, Eber Bunker, Samuel Chace, John Leith, James Simter, William Raven, John Stogdell, William Wilson.

Apprenticeship
32, 34, 35–40, 41, 43, 44, 45, 132, 133, 135.

Arrival in Australia
8, 55.

Banking, Finance & Business
10, 11, 166, 195, 196, 221, 222, 245, 262, 322, 342, 353.

Benefactor of Church of England
11, 13.

Benefactor of Moore College
7, 9, 11, 106, 379 n1.

Benefactor of St Andrew's Cathedral
352, 437 n117.

Benevolent Society
366

Books
29, 120, 121, 134, 135, 136, 232, 345.

& Christianity
Chapter 1; 7, 10, 11, 13, 24, 230, 243, 322, 350, 374, 376, 377.

Civil Officer
63, 73, 98, 124, 151, 153, 171, 189, 195, 216, 245, 251, 254, 256, 276, 285, 286, 321, 330, 331, 350, 358.

Coroner
229, 326, 342, 356, 363, 366.

Dealer
120, 121, 152, 165, 175.

Education
34–40, 152, 166, 386 n99.

Education, interest in
34–40, 166, 168, 214, 232, 243, 369, 370, 382 n2.

Emancipist sympathy
109, 157, 166, 236, 271, 373.

~ see also Rachel Moore.

Family
9, 15, 19–25, 29, 32, 43, 45, 46, 117, 176, 214, 250, 251.

~ see also other Moore relatives.

~ Clark; Bass; White on Index of Names.

Farming
10, 18, 34, 56, 99, 127, 138, 143, 144, 162, 176, 178, 182, 189, 195, 210, 215, 218, 220, 223, 241, 256, 266, 268, 269, 276, 326, 342, 352, 353, 362.

Freemasonry
45, 115, 189, 190, 207, 227.

Houses
~ built at Dusky Bay
70, 78, 82, 104.

~ John White's
109, 156, 157, 159, 218, 219, 222, 291, 328, 356, 372.

~ Master Builder's
150, 154, 158, 159, 161, 166, 168, 254, 276, 291, 315, 327.

~ William Raven's
276, 327, 328, 352.

~ Moore Bank
1, 8, 14, 325, 326, 343, 352, 355, 368, 369, 370, 374, 375, 376, 379 n2.

~ Liverpool
7, 15.

Humane Treatment of animals
220.

Husbandry
~ cattle
10, 34, 145, 162, 182, 195, 225, 322, 359, 362.

~ horses
10, 34, 102, 144, 145, 151, 162–163, 182, 195, 223–224, 225, 241, 268, 269, 322, 342, 359, 362, 375, 376, 405 n114.

~ sheep
142–145, 151, 162, 223, 230.

~ pigs
151, 162, 182, 223, 240, 276.

Intellectual history
see education, books, apprenticeship.

Land & Property
10, 11, 98, 99, 100, 127, 144, 159, 178, 179, 182, 189, 195, 210, 223, 241, 325, 328, 352, 353, 354, 359, 360, 378.

Liverpool School
369, 370, 377, 380 n4.

Loyal Sydney Association
42, 219, 232, 245, 247, 248, 249, 251, 298, 301, 309, 320, 332, 343, 351–352, 373.

Magistrate
7, 11, 13, 153, 257, 261, 285–287, 368, 369, 370, 371, 372, 377.

Marriage
109, 136–137, 148, 150, 159, 229, 385 n98.

Master Boat Builder
8, 10, 36, 80, 122, 123, 127, 131, 132, 136, 143, 149, 150, 154, 159, 164, 166, 167, 168, 169, 181, 182, 183, 190, 194, 195, 196, 202, 203, 204, 206, 209, 216, 219, 220, 223, 234, 236, 242, 253, 254, 256, 268, 269, 285, 286, 287, 290, 295, 298, 299, 308, 309, 318, 329, 336, 339, 340, 343, 350, 353, 354, 359, 360, 362.

Missionary interest
19, 25, 366.

~ & LMS missionaries
160, 266.

Portrait
7, 11.

& *Pegasus*
173, 269, 275–276, 296–299, 304–313, 315, 320, 323, 325, 332–341, 343, 345–350, 355, 356.

Philanthropic Society
238, 366.

Reputation
35, 45, 80, 83, 131, 133, 201, 239, 253, 254, 331, 360, 376.

& Rum Rebellion
Chapter 5; 10, 285, 289, 297, 298, 301, 304, 321, 331, 332, 360, 368.

Sealing
See Pegasus.

Ship Builder

~ *Providence*
35, 78, 79, 103, 104, 149, 150, 395 n161.

~ *Portland (Elizabeth Henrietta)*
133–134, 154, 169, 179, 215, 277.

~ *Cumberland*
154, 169, 170, 188, 227, 309.

~ *Integrity*
183, 215, 216, 217, 227, 234, 242, 245, 253, 326.

Ship's Carpenter
34, 35, 39, 40, 41, 44, 46, 54, 55, 59, 68, 69, 70, 73, 79, 80, 82, 83, 84, 91, 103, 104, 109, 118, 131, 132, 133, 135, 136, 138, 181, 194, 198, 201, 206, 223, 234, 256, 299, 304, 314, 388 n151.

Ship's Husband
173, 276, 304–305, 336, 337.

Speculation
See Pegasus.

& St Luke's Liverpool
4, 13, 15, 33, 378.

& Surveys
146, 167, 169, 205, 208, 209, 216, 223, 234, 235, 236, 241, 242, 245, 252, 254, 293, 294, 296, 298, 304, 322, 331, 354, 361, 362, 369, 370, 371.

Timber S/Purveyor
143, 190, 193, 194, 196, 203, 204, 206, 215, 256, 350.

Trader
96, 98, 120, 152, 166, 176, 195, 256, 259, 266, 321, 322.

Trial by Jury
255, 280, 286, 427 n82.

Trustee
221, 222, 236, 266, 322, 357.

Will
7, 13.

OTHER FAMILY MEMBERS (see family tree at Figure 4):

Ann Moore (Walker)
~ niece
19, 22, 384 n42.

Elizabeth Moore (Scott)
19, 20, 21, 23, 24, 28, 43.

Henry Moore
~ brother
19, 20, 24.

James & Margaret Moore & Family
23–24.

Joseph Moore
~ father
15, 19, 20, 21, 22, 23, 28, 34, 43, 45, 250, 251.

Joseph Moore
~ brother
21, 22, 32, 38.

Mary Moore (Hutson)
~ mother
15, 19, 20, 22, 23, 28, 32, 249, 250, 251.

Mary Moore (Trumble)
~ sister
19, 20, 23, 250.

Sarah (Sally) Moore (Clark)
~ sister
19, 20, 22, 23, 45, 250, 251, 383 n27.

William Moore
~ brother
19, 20, 21, 250.

Rachel Moore
13, 14, 19, 24, 34, 48, 50, 51, 52, 53, 56, 76, 99, 106, 107, 108, 109, 112, 121, 136, 137, 138, 150, 154, 156, 158, 159, 160, 161, 162, 163, 166, 168, 172, 174, 184, 214, 219, 220, 223, 229, 231, 240, 248, 262, 272, 276, 290, 315, 326, 341, 352, 355, 362, 367, 368, 370, 374, 375, 376, 380 n2, 385 n98, 388 n167, 389 n202, 394 n142, 395 n144, 401 n66, 408 n183, 409 n202.

Andrew Douglas White
20, 24, 100, 106, 107, 108, 109, 138, 150, 166, 167, 174, 175, 176, 184, 185, 186, 214, 220, 229–230, 232, 243, 290, 301, 385 n79, 392 n62, 394 n142, 395 n144, 395 n169, 396 n171, 401 n66, 401 n74, 409 n202, 409 n203, 418 n96, 420 n154, 422 n197, 422 n200.

~ See Surgeon John White, Losack on Name Index.

Index of Names

Abaroo
51.

Abell, Robert
99, 396 n141, 410 n183, 414 n286.

Abbott, Capt. Edward
157, 165, 271, 272, 278, 279, 287, 290, 291, 301, 308, 319, 328, 410 n196, 430 n107, 434 n202.

Aicken/Aken, Capt. James
209, 215, 326, 327, 420.

Allen, James or Samuel
(*Pegasus* Crew) 315, 335, 339.

Alt, Augustus
105, 153, 233.

Amiens, Treaty/Peace of
184, 187, 191, 192, 201, 213, 222.

Annandale Farm (G. Johnston)
75.

Anslip, James Pte. LSVA
442 n180.

Arndell, Thomas
99, 105, 153, 282, 287, 392 n203.

Atkins, Richard
105, 153, 183, 233, 249, 254, 261, 262, 268, 271, 272, 273, 278, 279, 280, 281, 282, 283, 284, 286, 289, 294, 298, 331, 407 n113.

Atkinson, George Pte. LSVA
442 n180.

Bain, Rev. James
84, 106, 396 n134.

Banks, Sir Joseph
40, 41, 139, 155, 179, 187, 212, 240, 305.

Baker, Gilbert Pte. LSVA
442 n180.

Baker, William
105, 288, 369, 430 n103.

Ballard, Susannah
327.

Balmain, Surg. William
51, 105, 107, 108, 121, 122, 137, 154, 158, 159, 168, 229, 233, 394 n81, 398 n183, 400 n220, 410 n196. See Margaret Dawson.

Barrington, George
122, 407 n113.

Bass, George
29, 107, 117, 124, 127, 152, 174, 176, 183, 184, 186, 401 n31, 402 n50, 402 n55, 403 nn60 & 62.

Bayly, Nicholas
156, 210, 227, 283, 284, 288, 289, 295, 299, 308, 330, 356, 430 n103, 431 n122.

Beazley, Charles Pte. LSVA
442 n180.

Beckwith
(ex-NSW Corps) 62,66, 229, 317, 434 n205.

Bell, Ensign Archibald
293, 301.

Bell, James Pte. LSVA
442 n180.

Bell, Matthew
43.

Bell, Naval Surgeon
96.

Bennelong
51, 124.

Bennelong Point
209, 419 n69.

Bent, Ellis
357.

Bent, Jeffrey Hart
406 n.107.

Berry, Alexander
306, 363.

Best, George
238, 242, 424 n195.

Best, Capt. Henry
354, 440 n128.

Best, Roger
238, 297, 423 n180.

Blakey, George
223.

INDEX OF NAMES   461

Bligh, Gov. William
  63, 174, 238, 251, 252, 253, 254, 255, 257,
  258, 260, 261, 262, 263, 265, 267, 270, 271,
  272, 273, 274, 275, 277, 278, 279, 280, 281,
  282, 283, 284, 286, 287, 288, 289, 290, 291,
  292, 293, 294, 295, 296, 297, 298, 299, 300,
  301, 302, 303, 304, 305, 306, 308, 313, 316,
  318, 319, 323, 324, 325, 328, 329, 330, 331,
  332, 333, 336, 337, 340, 344, 345, 346, 347,
  348, 358, 359, 360, 361, 366, 367, 368, 394
  n81, 423 n182, 426 n3, 427 n14, 428 n54,
  429 n74, 430 n107, 432 n150, 433 n162, 434
  n202, 435 n215, 436 nn32 &33, 438 n90.

Blaxcell, Garnham
  216, 233, 264, 274, 283, 284, 293, 294, 295,
  303, 304, 331, 366, 427 n22, 430 n107, 431
  n122.

Blaxland John
  285, 287, 288, 289, 291, 293, 295, 348, 430
  n107.

Blaxland, Gregory
  285, 288, 289, 331, 369, 372, 431 n122.

Bonaparte, Napoleon
  190, 192, 193, 231, 246, 247, 415 n303.

Bond, Capt.
  64.

Bond, Ensign George
  153.

Botany Bay
  40, 41, 47, 53, 61, 69, 111, 112, 353, 375,
  376.

Braithwaite, Lieut. Robert
  140, 141, 142, 153.

Brooks, Capt. Richard
  311, 323, 375, 435 n4.

Broughton, William
  105, 157, 166, 349, 356.

Broughton, Bp. William Grant
  9, 19, 34, 352, 387 n99, 409, n 169, 422
  n160.

Bruce, George
  441 n159.

Bunker, Capt. Eber
  173, 183, 187, 210, 211, 212, 214, 219, 225,
  226, 227, 229, 252, 289, 293, 297, 304, 307,
  312, 323, 325, 332, 333, 334, 336, 337, 338,
  340, 344, 347, 348, 351, 355, 357, 390 n161,
  412 n228, 433 n171.

Bunker, Magrett
  252, 304.

Bunker, Isabella (Mrs T. Laycock)
  252, 337, 357.

Bunker Children: Isabella, Henry, ary Ann,
Charlotte, James, Charles Harris
  252.

Burgess, John Pte. LSVA
  442 n180.

Burke, Martin
  241. 244. 273.

Byrne, Hugh 'Vesty'
  241, 244, 273.

Byrne/ Burne, Patrick (*Pegasus* Crew)
  315, 335.

Bulanaming
  99, 100, 106, 125, 126, 127, 138, 159, 162,
  178, 179, 188, 189, 214, 215, 219, 223, 233,
  240, 362, 396 n141, 401 n26, 403 n74, 407
  n115, 409 n169, 410 n103, 413 n248, 414
  nn285 & 286, 422 n160, 417 n23.

Calcutta
  53, 65, 67, 74, 76, 86, 91, 92, 93, 110, 111,
  113, 116, 150, 239, 264, 337, 348, 350.

Caley, George
  155, 305, 306.

Campbell, Lieut. (EIC)
  115, 117.

Campbell, John (Robert's brother)
  178.

Campbell, John Thomas
  357, 442 n184.

Campbell, Robert
  44, 153, 158, 159, 163, 165, 166, 167, 168,
  178, 183, 221, 225, 236, 252, 269, 272, 274,
  275, 278, 282, 304, 315, 318, 366, 367, 387
  n85, 409 nn168 & 169, 410 nn185 & 200,
  422 n160, 433 n178, 436 n21.

Campbell, Robert jr.
  272, 273, 278, 301, 366, 409 n168, 428 n52.

Campbell, Capt. William
  234, 235, 236, 237, 238, 242, 245, 247, 252,
  263, 264, 265, 302, 303, 304, 305, 306, 307,
  310, 313, 427 n21, 433 n171.

Campbell & Co
  163, 178, 239, 310, 312, 315, 323, 348.

Campbelltown
10.

Canton/ China
41, 42, 46, 60, 69, 81, 86, 87, 88, 89, 110, 177, 178, 188, 225, 228, 263, 264, 265, 275, 300, 302, 305, 308, 310.

Carney, John
(*Pegasus* Crew)

Cartwright, Rev. Robert
31, 364, 372.

Castle Hill
189, 246, 356.,

Castlereagh, Lord
252, 254, 277, 296, 301, 328, 353.

Chace, Capt. Samuel
172, 173, 176, 187, 188, 221, 337, 338, 339, 340, 341, 343, 344, 345, 346, 347, 349, 355, 440 n134.

Chace, Capt. Samuel Rodman
172, 333, 339, 349, 363, 364, 365.

Chace, Chinnery & Co
236, 238, 263, 303, 348.

Champion, Alexander
42.

Christian, David (*Pegasus* Crew)
315, 335.

Churches (UK):
    Alnmouth
        33.
    St Peter's, Chillingham
        15, 28, 383 n8.
    St Mary le Bone, London
        137.
    St Mary the Virgin, Holy Island
        15.
    St Mary's Lesbury
        16, 18, 20, 21, 25, 26, 32, 33, 43, 250.
    St Lawrence, Warkworth
        20.

Churches (NSW):
    Church of England (Aust)
        7, 11, 13, 322.
    Hobart
        340.

Richard Johnson's Church
75, 153.

St John's, Parramatta
170, 171, 246, 254, 265.

St Luke's, Liverpool
4, 13, 15, 33, 374, 376, 377, 379.

St Phillip's/St Philip's, Sydney
100, 106, 153, 154, 170, 246, 252, 265, 273, 274, 275, 276, 277, 280, 281, 294, 296, 350.

Clements, John (*Pegasus* Crew)
315, 335, 339.

Clementson, Isaad
242, 243.

Collins, David
49, 50, 54, 71, 74, 80, 85, 93, 94, 98, 103, 105, 110, 111, 112, 115, 116, 117, 119, 12o, 122, 126, 154, 162, 171, 201, 212, 213, 295, 340.

Clephan
66, 119, 410 n186.

Collins, William
212, 228, 339, 341.

Coldwell, Capt. John
146, 205.

Colnett, Capt.
190, 196, 205, 206, 207, 212, 252.

Conroy, Morris, Fifer LSVA
442 n180.

Cook, Capt. James
40, 41, 68, 69, 70, 81, 92, 93, 349.

Cooke, Under-Sec.
276.

Cook's River
10, 99, 189, 218, 223.

Conday, Elizabeth
314.

Connelly, Andrew & son
214, 420 n95.

Cover, James Fleet
160. See London Missionary Society.

Cowper, William
31, 170, 293, 350, 351, 352, 354, 355, 372.

Cox, Capt. (*Fox*)
333.

INDEX OF NAMES 463

Cox, William
182, 220, 221, 222, 226, 230, 236, 266, 267, 421 n124.

~ family
266, 267.

Cox & Greenwoord
96.

Crook, William P.
246, 293, 324.

Currant, Robert (*Pegasus* Crew)
315, 335.

Dalrymple, Alexander
110.

Davidson, Walter Stephenson
174, 232, 164, 265, 302, 331.

Dawson, Margaret
108, 137, 138, 229.

Dawson, Thomas
351.

Day, Peter Jackson (*Pegasus* Crew)
315.

Derwent
201, 207, 209, 211, 212, 213, 216, 217, 219, 228, 323, 330, 337, 338, 339, 340, 341, 343, 344, 345, 346, 351, 423 n184, 428 n54, 438 n78, 438 n90.

Devlin, Arthur
241, 244.

Dixon, Fr. James
438 n81.

Dixon, Mary Ann
250.

Doyle, Lawrence
(*Pegasus* Crew) 315, 335.

Draffin
308.

Driver, John (x2?)
342, 437 n70.

Driver, Elizabeth
437 n70.

Dunn, Thomas (*Pegasus* Crew)
315, 335.

Dwyer, or O'Dwyer, Michael
241, 244, 273, 344, 376, 428 n54.

East India Company (EIC)
42, 53, 64, 87, 88, 89, 92, 93, 114, 117, 118, 123, 131, 151, 177, 208, 264, 302, 303, 305.

Brabyn
280.

Ellis, James
127, 134.

Ellison, Rev. Nathaniel
32.

Elliston, William
366.

Emmerson
343, 438 n74.

Evans, ?
356.

Evans, Charles Pte. LSVA
442 n180.

Evans, George,
233.

Evans, James
38.

Evans, William
354.

Farm Cove
178, 305, 306

Fenlon, Lawrence
424 n193.

Ferguson, Alexander
252.

Fielding, Rev. George
9.

Finucane, James
314, 319, 338, 434 n196, 440 n128.

Fitz, Robert
331, 341, 354, 440 n127.

Fitzgerald, Richard
224, 407 n113.

Fitzpatrick, John
424 n193.

Flinders, Matthew
40, 51, 124, 128, 153, 156, 158, 181, 183, 188, 207, 208, 209, 211, 227.

Flynn, Terence
351.

Ford, Elizabeth
314.

Forster, Rev. William
32.

Forster, William (Shipwright)
38, 39.

Forster, William Pte. LSVA
442 n180.

Foveaux, Joseph
66, 74, 96, 97, 308, 316, 317, 318, 319, 320, 321, 323, 324, 325, 327, 328, 329, 337, 357, 360, 396 n134, 410 n196, 411 n134, 434 nn202, 207 & 211, 435 n215, 436 n21.

Foveaux Strait
333, 336, 348, 438 n77.

Fox, George
25.

Freemasonry
45, 115, 189, 190, 207, 227.

Fulton, Rev. Henry
288, 289, 292, 302, 308, 316, 324, 330, 353.

Galvin, or Golvin, James (*Pegasus* Crew)
315, 335.

Gaudry, William
244, 246, 255, 261, 262, 265, 267, 268, 288, 343, 352, 373, 431 n134, 438 n75, 442 n180.

George II
42, 43.

George III
51, 88, 98, 124, 213, 223.

George Street
372.

George's River
7, 10, 11, 14, 202, 212, 236, 241, 322, 325, 326, 327, 337, 342, 343, 350, 353, 355, 356, 361, 368, 370, 372, 374, 375, 377, 378, 382 n5, 395 n81, 430 n100, 435 n16.

Gerrald, Joseph
125, 126, 401 n18. See Scottish Martyrs.

Gloucester, Mr (Caulker, *Britannia*)
93, 94.

Gloucester, Mrs
94.

Gloucester, Mary
94.

Goodwin, William Pte. LSVA
442 n180.

Gore, William
161, 254, 274, 282, 283, 286, 366, 430 n107.

Grant, James John
329.

Gregory, George
387 n99.

Griffin, Charles
354.

Griffin, Edmund
254.

Griffin, Michael
189.

Griffith, William
7, 11, 381 n1.

Griffiths, John, Segt Maj. LSVA
442 n180.

Grimes, Charles
105, 164, 183, 201, 222, 233, 280, 281, 286, 287, 291, 293, 295, 308, 406 n104.

Grose, (Sketch Artist)
33.

Grose, Francis
55, 60, 61, 64, 65, 66, 71, 73, 74, 75, 76, 82, 84, 85, 98, 99, 102, 106, 109, 144, 153, 346, 358, 389 n137, 407 n115, 414 n286, 436 n20.

Grubb, George
314.

Guise, Richard
375.

Guy, George
314.

Hall, William (NZ Settler)
364.

Hall & Co
47.

Hallam, William
153, 336.

Hamond, Andrew Snape
57, 75, 76.

Harding, Richard Serj.
LSVA 442 n180.

INDEX OF NAMES

Harper, or Harpole, John (*Pegasus* Crew)
315, 335, 339.

Harris, James
369.

Harris, Surg. John
45, 66, 74, 96, 97, 168, 216, 225, 236, 247, 269, 272, 273, 274, 275, 276, 288, 296, 297, 301, 308, 309, 313, 317, 318, 331, 341, 355, 356, 365, 392 n203, 396 n134, 431 n122, 440 n135.

Harris, John (Emancipist publican)
157.

Harris, John (LMS Missionary)
246, 409 n172.

Harris, Mary
341.

Hassall, Rowland
160, 166, 266, 324, 328, 407 n113, 436 n22.

Hawkesbury
73, 98, 120, 154, 197, 212, 214, 246, 258, 259, 260, 265, 267, 270, 272, 287, 300, 337, 342, 351, 354, 369, 372, 373, 375, 376, 377, 397 n154, 404 n82, 420 n95, 426 nn2, 3 & 7, 429 n72.

Hayes, Sir Henry Browne
189, 207, 227, 252.

Haynes, John Pte. LSVA
442 n180.

Hinney, Peter Pte. LSVA
442 n180.

Hobart (Lord)
186, 203, 207.

Hobart (Town)
202, 211, 337, 341, 346, 351, 439 n92.

Hobby, Thomas
210, 331.

Hockley, Samuel Pte. LSVA
442 n180.

Holding, Richard Pte. LSVA
442 n180.

Holniss, William Pte. LSVA
442 n180.

Holt, Joseph
221.

Hoskings, John
13.

Howe, John (*Pegasus* Crew)
314, 315, 335, 373 (?same man?).

Hunter, Gov. John
36, 73, 98, 102, 103, 105, 106, 109, 116, 117, 118, 119, 120, 121, 123, 124, 125, 129, 130, 131, 132, 133, 136, 137, 144, 145, 146, 148, 149, 150, 151, 152, 153, 154, 155, 156, 157, 158, 159, 160, 165, 166, 167, 168, 169, 170, 171, 172, 173, 179, 180, 181, 188, 190, 194, 196, 199, 200, 210, 229, 252, 277, 352, 353, 354, 387 n85, 396 n139, 401 n25, 402 n38, 402 n49, 407 n112, 407 n115, 414 n286.

Hunter's Hill
401 n25, 404 n82, 415 n295.

Hunter's River
154.

Ikin, Obadiah Serj. LSVA
442 n180.

Ireland/Irish
9, 19, 24, 30, 102, 111, 155, 189, 199, 219, 221, 227, 228, 232, 241, 243, 244, 255, 265, 267, 273, 344, 428 n54.

Irish Rebels.
See Martin Burke, Hugh Byrne, Arthur Devlin, Michael Dwyer, Lawrence Fenlon, John Fitzpatrick, John Mernagh.

Jackson, J.H.
254.

Jackson, Thomas (*Pegasus* Crew)
335, 338.

Jackson, William
254.

Jacobs, John & William
355, 440 nn133 & 135.

Jamison, Sir John
394 n81.

Jamison, Thomas
84, 233, 264, 267, 286, 301, 303, 304, 331, 394 n81, 431 n122.

Jefferson, Thomas
361.

Johnson, Henry Martin
230.

Johnson, Mary (Burton)
51, 117, 161, 230, 422 n151.

Johnson, Milbah Marie
230, 422 n151.

Johnson, Rev. Richard
31, 49, 50, 51, 75, 98, 102, 105, 117, 122, 137, 153, 159, 161, 162, 167, 168, 170, 172, 230, 233, 391 n172, 393 n60, 394 n64, 396 n139, 422 n151, 423 n190.

Johnston, Catherine
314.

Johnston, Capt. Charles James
274, 428 n59.

Johnston, George
66, 74, 75, 96, 97, 122, 156, 159, 214, 218, 219, 224, 232, 233, 254, 268, 271, 274, 278, 281, 282, 284, 285, 286, 287, 288, 289, 290, 292, 293, 294, 295, 296, 297, 298, 299, 300, 301, 306, 307, 308, 309, 313, 316, 317, 318, 319, 320, 323, 324, 325, 327, 328, 337, 342, 362, 394 n81, 396 n134, 420 nn95 &96, 430 n107, 432 n161, 440 n135.

Johnston, George Jr.
214, 420 nn95 & 96.

Johnston's Creek
126.

Jones, John Pte. LSVA
442 n180.

Jones, Lewis
369, 370.

Jones, Thomas Pte. LSVA
442 n180.

Jones, Thomas
356.

Jones, Richard
366, 387 n85.

Kable, Henry
157, 294, 314, 352, 431 n122. See Lord, Kable & Underwood.

Kable, Miss (Mrs Gaudry)
352.

Kemp, A.F.
218, 279, 280, 283, 289, 291, 293, 301, 308, 430 n107.

Kent, Capt. William
117, 140, 141, 142, 153, 156, 158, 160, 167, 170, 180, 205, 224, 235, 268, 300, 324, 406 n104.

Kent, Naval Surgeon
96.

Kent's Group
234.

King, of Spain
247, 234, 236, 242, 247.

King, John or Robert
127, 396 n141, 409 n170.

King, John (NZ Settler)
364.

King, Gov. Phillip Gidley
35, 50, 81, 82, 83, 84, 85, 94, 119, 133, 139, 140, 141, 142, 144, 155, 156, 157, 165, 167, 169, 170, 171, 173, 174, 175, 176, 177, 183, 184, 185, 186, 187, 189, 190, 201, 202, 203, 204, 205, 206, 207, 208, 209, 210, 211, 212, 213, 214, 215, 216, 217, 220, 222, 223, 227, 228, 232, 233, 234, 235, 236, 237, 238, 239, 241, 242, 243, 244, 245, 248, 252, 252, 253, 254, 255, 258, 263, 266, 268, 272, 273, 274, 277, 281, 289, 331, 360, 363, 407 n113, 410 n185, 417 n23, 418 nn45 & 52, 423 n182, 436 n118, 440 n135.

King, Mrs Anna Josepha
168, 248, 428 n58.

King, Under-Secretary
108, 174.

King's Dockyard
Chapter 3. 8, 10, 131ff., 133, 147, 309, 339, 343, 354, 360, 388 n109.

Kissing Point
51.

Knight, Isaac & Mrs
343, 438 n74.

Knopwood, Rev Robert
340.

Lack, Robert Pte. LSVA
442 n180.

Laing, Edward
62, 66, 97, 99, 106, 126, 127, 210, 219, 392 n203, 396 n141, 401 n26.

Lane, John Pte. LSVA
442 n180.

Lane Cove
356.

Larkin, Joseph Pte. LSVA
442 n180.

Lawrence, Stephen
(*Pegasus* Crew) 315, 334, 335, 347.

Lawson, William
280, 308, 431 n122.

Laycock, Hannah
356, 372.

Laycock, Isabella (nee Bunker)
252, 337, 357.

Laycock, Lieut. Thomas
62, 96, 97, 105, 177, 318, 356, 357, 396 n134, 398 n179, 406 n104.

Laycock, Lieut. Thomas (jr.)
280, 288, 293, 295, 337, 356, 357, 374.

Laycock, William
356.

Laycock daughters
372.

Legg, Thomas
361, 371.

Leith, Capt. John
103, 120, 121, 175, 177, 221, 397 n157, 413 n245.

Leith, William
70, 71, 76, 81, 82, 83, 103, 120, 364, 365, 400 n221.

Levett, Benjamin (*Pegasus* Crew)
315, 335.

Lewin, Anna Maria
161, 162.

Lewin, John William
161, 212, 375, 409 n178, 419 n80.

London
22, 30, 32, 42, 44, 45, 46, 47, 63, 96, 107, 108, 136, 172, 174, 177, 178, 188, 189, 210, 214, 225, 242, 243, 251, 269, 317, 320, 328, 333, 338, 340, 355, 356, 361.

London Missionary Society
160, 266, 328, 364, 372, 415 n307, 436 n22.

Lord Howe Island
187.

Lord, Kable & Underwood
235, 272, 274, 436 n18, 440 n135.

Lord, Simeon
120, 157, 165, 176, 177, 178, 187, 235, 269, 275, 276, 285, 288, 290, 291, 295, 296, 297, 303, 311, 336, 341, 348, 355, 356, 361, 368, 369, 373, 410 n196, 423 n168, 429 n65, 430 n107, 431 n122, 433 n173, 436 n21, 439 n100, 440 n135.

Losack (White), Elizabeth Priscilla
137, 403 n66.

Lucas, Capt.
242.

Lucas, Lieut. James Hunt
156, 396 n134.

Lucas, Nathaniel
274, 361, 369, 371, 430 n107.

Luncheon Cove, Dusky Bay
70, 78, 103, 104.

Luttrell, Surg.
274, 332.

Macarthur, Edward
431 n122.

Macarthur, Elizabeth
139.

Macarthur, George Fairfowl
387 n99.

Macarthur, Hannibal
174.

Macarthur, John
63, 66, 74, 96, 97, 139, 142, 173, 174, 175, 182, 187, 220, 221, 224, 225, 230, 232, 236, 254, 255, 258, 259, 260, 261, 262, 263, 264, 265, 267, 268, 270, 271, 272, 273, 274, 277, 278, 279, 280, 281, 282, 283, 284, 285, 286, 288, 289, 290, 291, 292, 293, 294, 295, 296, 297, 299, 300, 301, 302, 303, 304, 305, 306, 308, 310, 314, 316, 3117, 318, 319, 324, 330, 337, 373, 404 n81, 405 nn87 & 89, 406 nn104 & 111, 410 n196, 426 n6, 430 n107, 431 n129, 432 nn145 & 146, 434 n207.

Macartney, Lord George
88.

McCallum, Dr
342, 375.

Macdonald, Alexander
157.

Macquarie, Elizabeth
139, 357, 361, 366, 367, 374, 375, 376, 378.

Macquarie, Gov. Lachlan
1, 11, 14, 22, 45, 255, 257, 293, 316, 318, 321, 327, 347, 353, 354, 357, 358, 360, 361, 362, 364, 366, 367, 368, 369, 370, 371, 372, 373, 374, 375, 376, 377, 378.

McKellar, Neil
62, 66, 74, 156, 189, 317.

Mann, D.D.
177, 430 n107.

Manning, Capt. (*Pitt*)
61, 62.

Mansfield, Thomas Pte. LSVA
442 n180.

Margerot, Maurice
125, 126, 128, 129, 227, 228, 252, 401 n32. See Scottish Martyrs.

Marsden, Rev. Samuel
31, 99, 105, 139, 142, 168, 170, 222, 224, 225, 233, 238, 244, 246, 248, 255, 265, 266, 276, 277, 363, 364, 366, 367, 372, 373, 382 n4, 404 n82, 405 n87, 405 n90, 406 n104, 406 n111, 407 n113, 415 n307, 422 n151, 427 n26, 427 n29, 441 n161, 441 n165.

Mason, Mr (Chief Mate, *Pegasus*)
338, 347.

Mason's Head
348.

Mileham, James
233, 285, 286, 288, 301, 331.

Miles, Benjamin, Drummer LSVA
442 n180.

Meredith, Frederick Pte. LSVA
442 n180.

Mernagh, John
241, 244, 273.

Methodism
31, 32, 243.

~ 'methodist' as slur
75.

Minchin, W.
272, 280, 291, 299, 308, 431 n122.

Moore, William (NSW Corps)
143, 280, 292, 361, 362, 406 n106, 431 n122.

~ Mistaken for Thomas
143, 299, 412 n221, 442 n180.

Morley, Joseph Pte. LSVA
442 n180.

Moseley, Abram (*Pegasus* Crew)
315, 335.

Muir, Thomas
125, 126, 127, 128, 400 n17, 401 n25. See Scottish Martyrs.

Mullett, Mrs
158.

Mullett, John Corporal LSVA
442 n180.

Munrow or Monroe, Mark (*Pegasus* Crew)
315, 335.

Nanbaree (Andrew Snape Hamond Douglas White)
51.

Nepean, Nicholas
62, 66, 84, 94, 317, 410 n122.

Newton, Mary
222.

Nightingall, Brig.-Gen.
346.

Norfolk Island
52, 81, 84, 85, 94, 103, 119, 149, 151, 155, 156, 167, 169, 170, 180, 182, 187, 188, 189, 223, 233, 244, 246, 265, 266, 306, 308, 316, 317, 323, 329, 341, 397 n161, 401 n32, 402 n49, 406 n106, 410 n196, 416 n9, 423 n184, 428 n54, 438 n74.

Oakes, Francis
160, 278, 301, 429 n74, 436 n22. See London Missionary Society.

O'Connell, Maurice
357, 360, 361, 366, 367, 368. See Mary Putland.

O'Brien, Daniel or Dennis (*Pegasus* Crew)
315, 335.

O'Herne, John
61.

Paine, Daniel
36, 46, 117, 120, 122, 123, 124, 125, 127, 128, 129, 130, 131, 133, 145, 150, 179, 181, 196, 199.

Paine, Thomas
44.

Palmer, E.H. (EIC)
208.

Palmer, Commissary John
97, 105, 119, 120, 122, 176, 177, 178, 183, 224, 225, 233, 248, 274, 282, 286, 287, 288, 293, 294, 308, 313, 317, 318, 329, 330, 332, 345, 348, 349, 360, 362, 366, 396 n134, 407 n113, 409 n169, 419 n71, 422 n160, 436 n32.

Palmer, Richard Corporal LSVA
442 n180.

Palmer, Thomas Fyshe
29, 106, 125, 126, 127, 134, 210, 396 n139, 402 n50. See Scottish Martyrs.

Pashley, George Pte. LSVA
442 n180.

Paterson, Mrs
168.

Paterson, William
66, 74, 93, 96, 97, 102, 105, 109, 119, 129, 140, 141, 142, 144, 160, 173, 174, 183, 260, 287, 300, 316, 317, 318, 319, 321, 324, 325, 328, 329, 330, 331, 337, 338, 340, 347, 350, 351, 352, 353, 354, 355, 357, 359, 360, 367, 396 n134, 407 n115, 410 n196, 417 n26, 418 n36, 419 n73, 432 n145, 440 n127, 442 n174.

Peach, Mary
314.

Pegasus Crew
276, 310, 311, 313, 314, 315, 323, 334, 335, 336, 338, 347, 348, 349, 438 n86.

~ see individual listings.

Pegasus (Codfish) Island
325, 332, 338, 347, 438 n92.

Petersham Hill
10, 99, 159, 162, 178, 223, 436 n20.

Phillip, Gov. Arthur
48, 51, 52, 56, 57, 64, 65, 66, 67, 71, 74, 75, 76, 123, 124, 138, 141, 200, 274, 389 n137, 398 n179, 403 n78, 436 n20.

Phillips, Surg. (EIC)
115, 117.

Phillips, George Pte. LSVA
442 n180.

Piper, Capt. John
62, 66, 74, 97, 244, 306, 308, 317.

Pitt's Passage
111.

Pitt's Row/Street
210, 225, 252, 337, 356, 385 n48, 437 n70.

Pitt Town
377.

Pittwater
374.

Pitt, William
197.

Port Dalrymple
265, 300, 309, 319, 325, 328, 337, 418 n36, 428 n54, 432 n161.

Port Jackson
42, 53, 54, 59, 67, 71, 81, 82, 83, 93, 94, 96, 101, 104, 105, 110, 111, 119, 124, 128, 138, 140, 141, 142, 149, 160, 167, 169, 170, 175, 177, 181, 186, 189, 190, 191, 196, 197, 200, 208, 209, 225, 238, 248, 252, 265, 275, 296, 315, 333, 334, 343, 345, 357, 363, 364, 366.

Port Phillip
201, 212, 213, 215, 216, 339.

Porteus, Capt.
329.

Potter, Samuel
294, 314.

Prentice, Capt.
66, 230.

Price, Zachariah (*Pegasus* Crew)
335, 338.

Putland, Lieut. John
254, 360, 361.

Putland, Mary (Bligh)
297, 360, 367, 368. See O'Connell.

Quested, George
223.

Ramsey, or Ramsden, William (*Pegasus* Crew)
315, 335, 339.

Raven, Capt. William
35, 36, 42, 45, 46, 47, 53, 54, 55, 56, 59, 64, 65, 67, 69, 70 71, 73, 74, 75, 76, 80, 81, 82, 83, 84, 85, 89, 92, 93, 94, 95, 96, 97, 103, 104, 109, 110, 111, 112, 114, 115, 116, 118, 120, 121, 128, 129, 133, 138, 144, 155, 156, 157, 160, 161, 162, 172, 175, 176, 177, 198, 221, 249, 250, 251, 276, 317, 318, 327, 333, 352, 389 n137, 389 n145, 390 nn160 & 161, 392 n27, 393 n34, 396 nn 127 & 145, 398 n186, 399 nn196 & 215, 407 n116, 409 n176, 425 n222, 429 n65, 439 n117.

Redman, Mary
362.

Reed, Daniel Pte. LSVA
442 n180.

Regiment, 73rd
346, 357, 358, 361, 367, 368, 442 n189.

Regiment, 102nd (NSW Corps)
357, 358, 359, 361, 362.

Reiby, Mary
157.

Reid, William
123, 124, 130, 141, 148, 199.

Riley, Alexander
139, 331.

Riley, Edward
387 n85.

Risden, or Rosser, Peter (*Pegasus* Crew)
315, 335, 339.

Rose Bay
369.

Rose, Thomas Pte. LSVA
442 n180.

Rosser, Peter (*Pegasus* Crew)
339.

Rowley, Capt. Thomas
62, 66, 96, 97, 112, 142, 143, 165, 182, 183, 218, 219, 221, 222, 230, 232, 235, 236, 248, 249, 266, 267, 317, 318, 396 n134, 406 n104, 410 n196, 421 n128, 423 n168.

~ See Elizabeth Selwyn.

Rowley, Tom (Aboriginal Australian)
112, 423 n177.

Rowley, Isabella & other children
236, 249.

Salmon, James Corporal LSVA
442 n180.

Salmon, Thomas Pte. LSVA
442 n180.

Schäffer, Phillip
141, 199, 407 n115.

Scottish Martyrs
106, 125, 126, 127, 396 n139, 401 nn25 & 26. See Gerrald, Margarot, Muir, Palmer, Skirving.

Scott, Thomas Hobbes
9.

Selwyn, Elizabeth (de facto Rowley)
236.

Shea, John Pte. LSVA
442 n180.

Shipping

~ *Active*
352.

~ *Admiral Gambier*
329.

~ *Adonis*,
222.

~ *Aeolus*
341.

~ *Alexander*
187, 222.

~ *Alfred*
173.

~ *Albion* (Bunker)
173, 187, 210, 225, 229, 309, 419 n70.

~ *Albion* (Raven)
46.

~ *Albion* (Skelton)
363.

~ *Ann*
363.

~ *Anna Josepha*
409 n172, 428 n63, 429 n65.

~ *Anne*
167.

~ *Antipode*
333, 348.

INDEX OF NAMES 471

~ *Barwell*
153, 336, 411 n201.

~ *Ben Cidadeo*
309.

~ *Boyd*
355, 356, 361, 363, 364, 365, 440 nn 131 133 & 135.

~ *Bridgewater*
208, 211.

~ *Britannia* (Raven)
35, 39, 40, 42, 44, 45, 46, 53, 54, 55, 56, 59, 64, 65, 66, 67, 70, 71, 73, 74, 75, 76, 79, 80, 81, 84, 85, 87, 88, 89, 90, 91, 93, 94, 95, 96, 98, 99, 101, 102, 103, 104, 105, 106, 108, 109, 110, 111, 112, 113, 114, 115, 116, 117, 118, 119, 120, 122, 128, 129, 132, 133, 135, 138, 144, 155, 160, 175, 237, 238, 317, 333, 337, 364, 390 n151, 392 n127, 393 n31, 395 n120, 396 n127, 397 n145, 398 nn178 & 179, 399 nn196 198 214 & 215, 407 n115, 423 n177.

~ *Britannia* (Melville)
391 n196, 392 n27.

~ *Britannia*, Whaler
162.

~ *Britannia*, other
92, 121, 132.

~ *Buffalo*
47, 155, 160, 161, 168, 170, 171, 180, 187, 189, 205, 207, 234, 238, 242, 245, 247, 248, 251, 252, 254, 266, 268, 418 n45.

~ *Calcutta*
143, 207, 212, 213, 215, 216, 217, 219, 220, 228, 229.

~ *Canada* (1)
177, 178.

~ *Canada* (2)
372.

~ *Cato*
188, 211, 227, 253, 326.

~ *Commerce*
242, 309, 333.

~ *Dart*
297, 299, 300.

~ *Discovery* (Vancouver)
74.

~ *Dromedary*
357, 367.

~ *Duff*
160, 409 n172.

~ *Eagle*
238, 309.

~ *Edwin*
213, 348.

~ *Elizabeth*
252, 297, 304.

~ *Endeavour* (sealer)
333.

~ *Estramina*
234, 235, 242, 247, 252, 253, 325, 344, 354, 362, 370.

~ *Favorite*
309, 310.

~ First Fleet
48, 50, 51, 56, 61, 84, 107, 120, 123, 133, 139, 107.

~ *Fox*
309, 315, 333.

~ *George*
228, 348.

~ *Glatton*
186, 187, 188, 189, 190, 193, 196, 200, 201, 202, 203, 204, 205, 206, 207, 213, 214, 216, 252.

~ *Gorgon*
200, 417 nn26 & 27.

~ *Governor Bligh*
333.

~ *Governor King*
333.

~ *Harriet*
172, 187, 435 n18.

~ *Harrington*
234, 235, 236, 237, 238, 245, 247, 248, 252, 262, 264, 265, 300, 302, 303, 304, 305, 306, 307, 308, 310, 312, 313, 332, 345, 348, 350, 351, 372.

~ *Hindostan*
357, 367.

~ Hunter (ex-Bethlehem)
  164, 173, 429 nn63 & 65.
~ Indispensable (Wilkinson)
  94, 108.
~ Indispensable (Best)
  293, 350, 355.
~ King George
  323, 341, 363, 435 n3, 436 n18.
~ L'Adele
  211.
~ Lady Juliana
  48, 49, 50, 52, 378, 410 n183.
~ Lady Nelson
  169, 176, 207, 209, 211, 212, 239, 252, 300, 331, 345, 360, 418 n45, 419 n69, 440 n128.
~ Lucas
  389 n145.
~ Marcia
  326, 432 n161, 435 n18.
~ Mary
  440 n128.
~ Mary Ann
  53.
~ Minerva
  111, 155, 165, 182, 221.
~ Minorca
  177, 178, 412 n242.
~ Nile
  177, 178, 412 n242.
~ Ocean
  212, 213, 339.
~ Otter
  125, 128.
~ Paterson
  213, 222.
~ Pegasus
  173, 269, 275–276, 296–299, 304–313, 315, 320, 323, 325, 332–341, 343, 345–350, 355, 356.
~ Perseverance
  309.
~ Pitt
  61, 62, 73.

~ Porpoise
  155, 156, 174, 175, 188, 196, 207, 208, 209, 211, 227, 251, 253, 254, 266, 296, 297, 299, 300, 309, 324, 325, 326, 329, 330, 331, 332, 340, 345, 360, 361, 366, 418 n45, 435 n11.
~ Rolla
  188, 208, 209, 211.
~ Rose
  309, 311, 312, 323, 435 n4.
~ Santa Anna
  275, 309, 333, 428 nn60 & 63, 440 n135.
~ Second Fleet
  48, 49, 50, 52, 53.
~ Sinclair (Lady Magdeline)
  251, 254, 316.
~ Star
  333, 423 n177.
~ Surprise
  150, 333.
~ Third Fleet
  53, 57, 173, 392 n27.
~ Venus (Campbell & Co?)
  419 n70. MORE
~ Venus (Bass)
  175, 184.
~ Venus (Bunker)
  351.
~ Venus (S.R. Chace)
  333.
~ Venus (Gardner)
  187 188, 214, ?219.
~ William & Ann
  173.
~ William Pitt
  92.
Simter, Capt. James
  177, 221, 412 n242.
Skirving, William
  125, 126, 127, 401 n18. See Scottish Martyrs.
St George's Channel
  111.
St John's Island
  89, 395 n102.

Index of Names

Sarah Island
202, 408 n132.

Short, Martin
356.

Shortland, Capt. John
111, 153, 154.

Smith, George
39.

Smith, John Pte. LSVA
442 n180.

Smith, Richard Serj. LSVA
442 n180.

Smyth, Thomas
99, 120, 122, 137, 138, 159, 162, 178, 229, 232, 233, 240, 407 n115, 409 n169, 422 n160.

South Church, Coundon
22.

Southern Whale Fishery
42, 45, 47, 53, 66, 70, 151, 173, 187, 228, 264.

Spain
47, 87, 140, 234, 247. See King of Spain.

Stewart, Capt. (*George*)
228.

Stewart/ Stuart, Robert Bruce Keith
306, 307, 351, 350.

Stewart, William (sealing master)
348, 349.

Stewart, William W. (cartographer)
339, 347, 348, 349.

Stewart Island, NZ
332, 347, 348, 349.

Stirling, Alexander
183.

Stogdell, John
120, 121, 260, 342, 426 n7.

Storer, Thomas
369.

Sutters, Thomas Pte. LSVA
442 n180.

Suttor, George
318, 328.

Sydney Cove
54, 55, 56, 60, 71, 75, 76, 101, 102, 108, 118, 123, 126, 131, 133, 148, 150, 151, 158, 159, 163, 194, 210, 211, 219, 242, 274, 304, 309, 314, 315, 345, 358, 360, 392 n3, 401 n25, 411 n210, 434 n211.

Tahiti /Otaheite
160, 175, 176, 183, 196, 237, 278, 293, 423 n177.

Temasek (Singapore)
85, 86, 89, 90, 395 n96, 399 n195.

Templeton, John Pte. LSVA
442 n180.

Thompson, Andrew
157, 260, 261, 262, 268 270, 271, 277, 279, 280, 369, 370, 372, 373, 374, 375, 426 n6, 427 n14.

Thompson, Captain (*Boyd*)
355.

Thompson, George
161, 162.

Thompson, Surg. James
99, 105, 229, 233.

Thompson, John
209.

Throsby, Dr Charles
233, 353, 354, 375.

Tip-pa-Hee
238, 363, 364, 365, 441 n159.

Tonks, William Pte. LSVA
442 n180.

Townson, Capt. John
230, 331.

Townson, Dr Robert
230, 331, 375, 420 n95, 431 n122.

Warney, John (*Pegasus* Crew)
335.

Washington, George
128.

Waterhouse (Bass), Elizabeth
107, 167, 174, 175, 176, 185, 213, 214, 279.

Waterhouse, Capt. Henry
107, 117, 124, 138, 139, 140, 141, 143, 143, 144, 145, 153, 156, 157, 158, 159, 166, 167, 174, 176, 179, 180, 182, 183, 185, 220, 221, 229, 230, 231, 235, 236, 266, 317, 398 n171, 404 n80, 404 n81, 406 n111, 410 n199, 410 n200, 411 n201, 423 n169, 424 n199.

Waterhouse, Maria
230.

Waterhouse, William
140, 145.

[?Watkins], Emily
368.

Wentworth, D'Arcy
233, 271, 272, 286, 288, 331, 357, 368, 369, 431 n122.

Wesley, John
31, 242, 243.

White, Andrew Douglas
See Thomas Moore Index.

White, Andrew Snape Hamond Douglas (Nanbaree)
51.

White, Surg. John
14, 24, 29, 50, 51, 52, 53, 56, 57, 75, 76, 96, 99, 100, 106, 107, 108, 109, 112, 121, 122, 127, 136, 137, 150, 156, 157, 159, 167, 214, 218, 219, 243, 264, 278, 292, 329, 354, 403 nn66 &67, 409 n178, 411 n203, 427 n18, 436 n20.

~ See Losack, Nanbaree.

~ See also Andrew Douglas White & Rachel Moore on Thomas Moore Index.

White, John (*Pegasus* Crew)
317, 337.

White, Richard Hamond
137.

White, Clara Christiana (Bernal)
137, 403 n66, 411 n203.

White, Augusta Catherine Anne
137, 403 n66, 411 n203.

Wilberforce, William
365.

Wilberforce (Town)
377.

Williams, storekeeper at Derwent
186.

Williams, Harry
314.

Williams, Henry
233.

Williamson, James
105, 122, 142, 153, 172, 222, 233, 286, 293, 308, 406 n104.

Wilshire, James
233, 288, 305.

Wilson, James
223.

Wilson, Lucinda (Mrs Raven)
172.

Wilson, Thomas (Lucinda's father)
172

Wilson, Thomas (*Britannia* seaman)
82.

Wilson, William (*Pegasus* Crew)
315, 335, 336, 346, 347.

Wilson, William
240, 266.

Wood, Elizabeth
314.

Yates, Henry
339, 349.

Youl, John
436 n22. See London Missionary Society.

List of Plates

Block 1

Plate No.	Title/Acknowledgement
1	Portrait of the Late Mr Thomas Moore, Esq. 1840. William Griffith. Photo: Alice Bolt (2010).
2	Frank Cash 'Portrait'. Photographic manipulation of Griffith portrait. Loane, *Centenary History*, facing p.16
3	Portrait of Rachel Moore. Detail of Portrait of the Late Mr Thomas Moore, Esq. 1840, William Griffith. Photo: Alice Bolt (2010).
4	Memorial to Mrs Rachel Moore, St Luke's Liverpool. Photo: Peter Bolt (2006).
5	Headstones of Thomas & Rachel Moore, and Andrew Douglas White. Pioneer Park, Liverpool. Photo: Geoff Bolt (2006).
6	St Mary's Lesbury and the author. Photo: Peter Bolt (2009).
7	Alnmouth, across the river from South Photo: Peter Bolt (2009).
8	Captain Arthur Phillip, 1786. Artist: Francis Wheatley. State Library of NSW. a928087
9	Portrait of Captain Francis Grose, 1790–1799. Artist: John Kay. National Library of Australia. nla.pic-an9597965.
10	Colonel William Paterson, ca. 1800. Artist: William Owen. State Library of NSW. a928495
11	Vice-Admiral John Hunter, second Governor of NSW 1795-1800. Artist: William Mineard Bennett. State Library of NSW. a128403
12	Philip Gidley King, ca. 1800-1805. Artist: Unknown. State Library of NSW. a830002
13	Admiral William Bligh, 1805. Artist: H.A. Barker. State Library of NSW. a1528244
14	Revd. Richard Johnson, B.A., chaplain to the settlement in New South Wales. ca. 1787. Artist: Garnet Terry. National Library of Australia. nla.pic-an9594799.
15	Reverend Samuel Marsden, formerly Senior Chaplain of New South Wales and founder of the New Zealand mission. Artist: Unknown. Richard Jones' Album. State Library of NSW. a928171
16	Mr White, Harris and Laing with a party of Soldiers visiting Botany Bay. Artist: T. Watling. © National History Museum, London. No. 38080.
17	Portrait of an Aboriginal boy named Nanbree. Artist: T. Watling. © National History Museum, London. No. 12034.
18	View of the City of Batavia from the Anchorage in the Roades, the church bearing S.S.W. off shore 1 ½ miles, 1791. Artist: George Raper. Drawing No. 31. © National History Museum, London. No. 15131.
19	Straits of Malacca. Google Maps.
20	Kinkaid Map of Australia, 1790. Detail: Port Jackson. Published: Kinkaid, 1840. National Library of Australia. MAP T 800
21	Dusky Bay, Luncheon Cove. Google Maps.

Block 2

Plate No.	Title/Acknowledgement
22	Port Jackson Painter, 7 March 1792. Artist: T. Watling. Watling Drawing No 21. © National History Museum, London. No. 53639.

23	A western view of Sydney Cove, ca 1798. Engraved: James Heath. Published Cadell & Davies, 1798. National Library of Australia. nla.pic-an7566580
24	A direct south view of the town of Sydney taken from the brow of the hill leading to the flagstaff. Artist: Edward Dayes based on T. Watling. Engraved: J. Heath, 25 May 1798. Reproduced courtesy of the Australian National Maritime Museum. No. 00000874.
25	Sydney – Capital New South Wales, ca.1800. Artist: Unknown. State Library of NSW. a1528055.
26	Plate 26. Nouvelle-Hollande: Nouvelle Galles du Sud, 1802. Artist: C A Lesueur. 1807 Engraving. Reproduced courtesy of the Australian National Maritime Museum. No 00004992.
27	A view of Sydney Cove, New South Wales, 1804. Artist: E. Daye. Published: F. Jukes. National Library of Australia. nla.pic-an6016289.
28	Sydney Cove, 1808. Artist: J.W. Lewin. State Library of NSW. a1528463.
29	Sydney Cove, 1808. Artist: J.W. Lewin. State Library of NSW. a928869.
30	View of the town and cove of Sydney, New South Wales, in Sepr. 1806 as seen from the east. Artist: Emma Eburne (1819-1885). Published: Colnaghi & Puckle, 1840. National Library of Australia. nla.pic-an7890459.
31	New South Wales, view of Sydney from the east side of the cove. No. 2, 1804. Artist: John H. Clark. Published: John Booth, 1810. National Library of Australia. nla.pic-an6016104

Block 3

Plate No.	Title/Acknowledgement
32	Convict uprising at Castle Hill, 1804. Artist: Unknown. National Library of Australia. nla.pic-an5577479.
33	Loyal Sydney Volunteer Uniform. From Stanley, *The Remote Garrison*, 23; Wedd, *Australian Military Uniforms*.
34	Detail of the Western Shore of Sydney Cove. Plan of the Town of Sydney in New South Wales, 1807. Cartographer: James Meehan. National Library of Australia. MAP F 105B.
35	Plan of the town of Sydney in New South Wales, 1807. Cartographer: James Meehan. National Library of Australia. MAP F 105B.
36	New South Wales, New Zealand, New Hebrides (1808). Robert Wilkinson, d. ca. 1825. National Library of Australia. MAP T 1363 (Copy 1).
37	Simeon Lord, ca 1830. Artist: Unknown. State Library of NSW. a128827
38	John Harris. Artist: Unknown. State Library of NSW. a2652001
39	John Macarthur, 1800. Artist: Unknown. Copy of original made by Government Printer, 1898. State Library of NSW. Gov Printing Off 1 -12606 d1_12606
40	Lt-Col George Johnston, ca. 1810. Artist: R. Dighton. State Library of NSW. a1528248.
41	The "Lady Nelson" – Brig. Painting: ca. 1820's. Artist: Unknown. Based on engraving by S.I. Neele, published 1803. State Library of NSW. a128461
42	George Bass. Artist: Unknown. From miniature in the possession of Mr Pownall. Copy of original made by Government Printing Office. State Library of NSW. d1_12288.
43	Captain Eber Bunker, ca. 1810. Artist: Unknown. State Library of NSW. a128664
44	View of George's River. Residence of George Johnston, 1819. Artist: Joseph Lycett. State Library of NSW. a1120007
45	Moore Bank, 1819. Artist: Joseph Lycett. State Library of NSW. a1120006
46	Moore Bank Site, riverside level (2006). Photo: Geoff Bolt
47	Thomas Moore Park. Site of Moore Bank homestead (2006). Photo: Geoff Bolt

List of Figures

Figure	Page	Title/Acknowledgement
1	15	Liverpool Town plan showing Burial Grounds, Old and New.
2	16	Map of the North East of England (2010). Google Maps.
3	17	Lesbury district (2010). Google Maps.
4	19	Thomas Moore's Family Tree
5	27	Northumberland parishes with ministers evicted after 1662 Act of Uniformity. Based on a map from Genuki.com
6	29	Thomas Fyshe Palmer (1747–1802). Kay, John, 1742-1826. Edinburgh: Published as the Act directs by W. Skirving, [1793]. National Library of Australia. nla.pic.an9801104
7	33	St Mary's Lesbury. Artist: Beilby. From Hickes, *History*.
8	37	Map Alnmouth. From Hickes, *History*.
9	49	Ages of female convicts on Lady Juliana. Table assembled from information in Cobley, *Crimes of the Lady Juliana*.
10	50	R. Johnson's Estimates of mortality and morbidity on Second Fleet ships
11	50	John White's statement of mortality and morbidity on First Fleet ships.
12	54	Sailor's day symbols used by Murray in his journal and Moore in his business note books. From Begg & Begg, *Dusky Bay*.
13	61	Map of New Zealand showing Dusky Bay. From Begg & Begg, *Dusky Bay*.
14	62	Officers of the New South Wales Corps who paid Captain Manning, Pitt, in Paymaster's Bills, April 1792. Information from Hainsworth, *Sydney Traders*, 22.
15	63	Role of the Officers in Commercial Transactions in 1790s. Information from Hainsworth, *Sydney Traders*.
16	66	Estimated share of profits from Officer Trading. Information from Hainsworth, *Sydney Traders*, 27.
17	68	Dusky Bay, New Zealand. From Begg & Begg, *Dusky Bay*.
18	69	Crooked Timber. Trees of the right shape for ship's timbers had to be found. Canby, *History*, 70.
19	77	Anchor Island, Dusky Bay. From Begg & Begg, *Dusky Bay*.
20	78	Luncheon Cove, Anchor Island, Dusky Bay. From Begg & Begg, *Dusky Bay*.
21	89	Map showing St John's Island, Temasek (Singapore)
22	97	Officers' Payments to W. Raven, August 1794. Information from Hainsworth, *Sydney Traders*, 28–29.
23	100	The Northern Corner of Moore's Bulanaming Property in relation to earlier land grants. From Scott, 'Scottish Martyrs' Farms', 165.
24	105	Robert Murray's list of 'The establishment at New South Wales', August 1795 Robert Murray, *Journal*.
25	132	Carpenter Master Shipwrights in Foreign Yards from 1790 to 1810. From information in Knight, '"Carpenter" Master SHpwrights', 422. Thomas Moore is added.
26	134	Books of interest to the Seafarer on Thomas Moore's bookshelf. List of Books the Property of T. Moore Esq [?1840] (SDA: 0853 CH, Item 5).

27	141	Waterhouse Sheep available for distribution. Complied from figures given in H. Waterhouse to J. Banks, 16 July 1806 (*HRNSW* 6.110–112).
28	147	Midsection of 74 Gun Ship showing ship's timbers. From Albion, *Forests*, 9.
29	157	Detail from Meehan's 1807 Map of Sydney. National Library of Australia. MAP F 105B. (Plates 34 & 35).
30	158	Detail from Meehan's 1807 Map of Sydney. National Library of Australia. MAP F 105B. (Plates 34 & 35).
31	164	Grimes's Plan of Sydney, 1800. *HRNSW* 5, prior to index.
32	171	Plan & Elevation of St John's Parramatta. From Collins, *Account*, 2.223.
33	199	Two examples of the 'broad arrow' marking the King's timber. King's Mark Resource Conservation & Development Project, Inc http://ccrpa.org
34	224	Major private horse owners August 1804. Source: Barrie, *The Australian Bloodhorse*, 12. *HRNSW* 5.432–435.
35	225	Major private horse owners in August 1805. Source: *HRNSW* 5. 684–687.
36	226	Payments made by T. Moore on behalf of Eber Bunker, showing work done on Bunker's new house. Thomas Moore's Business Notebook (rear) (SDA: 0884 CH, Item 1), 26, cf. 29.
37	241	Thomas Moore's Mares born Oct 1804 to Dec 1806. Thomas Moore's Business Notebook (front) (SDA: 0884 CH, Item 1), 1.
38	243	Charterhouse School. From Daniels, *Illustrated History of Methodism*, 76.
39	244	Charterhouse School. Dining Hall. From Daniels, *Illustrated History of Methodism*, 77.
40	259	*The Sydney Gazette* on the floods of June 1809.
41	263	Map of Macarthur's trading Scheme. From Hainsworth, *Sydney Traders*, 68.
42	284	The second page of the Arrest requisition, 26 January 1808. *HRNSW* 6, after p. 434.
43	292	The congratulatory address 27 January 1808. *HRNSW* 6, after p. 454.
44	310	Pegasus Accounts
45	312	Thomas Moore's Account with Campbell & Co rendered 30 September 1808 T. Moore, Account no 1 of *Pegasus*, 17 April to 10 October 1808 (SDA: 0852 CH, Item 6, doc. 3).
46	315	The Crew of the Pegasus, taken from Moore's accounts. Accounts Current of crew of Pegasus to Various Merchants n.d. [ca 19 Aug 1808] (SDA: 0854 CH, Item 1, doc. 1)
47	318	Joseph Foveaux's contributions to the early trading ventures of the NSW Corps. Information from Hainsworth, *Sydney Traders*.
48	333	Seal-skins taken in to Sydney, 1809. Information derived from Hainsworth, *Sydney Traders*, and the *Sydney Gazette*
49	333	Seal-skins taken in to Sydney, other periods. Information derived from Hainsworth, *Sydney Traders*, and the *Sydney Gazette*
50	335	Payments of Pegasus crewmembers, April 1809. Chits for payment to Pegasus Crew, April 1809 (SDA: 0853 CH, Item 10, docs. 3–25); and Account for cash & slops advanced for crew of Pegasus [April 1809] (SDA 0854 CH, Item 1, doc. 13).
51	352	Thomas Moore's Land Grants 1 November 1809. Ryan, *Land Grants*, 213.

www.ingramcontent.com/pod-product-compliance
Lightning Source LLC
Chambersburg PA
CBHW062107290426
44110CB00023B/2744